# Mathematical Structures in Language

CSLI
Lecture Notes
No. 218

# Mathematical Structures
# in Language

Edward L. Keenan & Lawrence S. Moss

CSLI
PUBLICATIONS
Center for the Study of
Language and Information
Stanford, California

Copyright © 2016
CSLI Publications
Center for the Study of Language and Information
Leland Stanford Junior University
Printed in the United States
19 18 17 16     1 2 3 4 5

*Library of Congress Cataloging-in-Publication Data*

CIP Data Pending

ISBN-13: 978-1-57586-872-1 (cloth)
ISBN-13: 978-1-57586-847-9 (pbk.)
eISBN-13: 978-1-68400-021-0 (electronic)

∞ The acid-free paper used in this book meets the minimum requirements
of the American National Standard for Information Sciences—Permanence
of Paper for Printed Library Materials, ANSI Z39.48-1984.

CSLI was founded in 1983 by researchers from Stanford University, SRI
International, and Xerox PARC to further the research and development of
integrated theories of language, information, and computation. CSLI
headquarters and CSLI Publications are located on the campus of Stanford
University.

Visit our web site at
http://cslipublications.stanford.edu/
for comments on this and other titles, as well as for changes
and corrections by the author and publisher.

# Contents

# Preface

The purpose of this book is twofold. First, to present mathematical background to help the student of linguistics formulate generalizations concerning the structure of natural languages. This is a goal we share with Partee et al. (1990). Chapter 2 focuses on this background material, and Chapters 4, 7, 8 and 10 make modest additions. This material is used in many areas of mathematical inquiry and is well understood. But the linguistic material we are using these mathematical tools to understand is less well understood. In general a major step in coming to understand something new consists in formulating it in terms of concepts and notation that we already understand:

Understanding is translation from the unknown to the known

As the mathematical concepts and notation we introduce here are well known, formulating linguistic generalizations in terms of them helps us achieve understanding. This is our first answer to a question we are frequently asked: "Why study language mathematically?".

The second purpose of this book follows upon the first: once we have formulated some linguistic regularities mathematically we can study our formal models to derive further generalizations that were unsuspected, perhaps even unformulable, in the absence of a way to say them. The point bears repeating: Most of us look at sunflowers, conch shells and pine cones and see pretty swirls. T.A. Cook (1914) and D'Arcy Thompson (1942) looked and saw logarithmic curves and Fibonacci sequences – something precise, that they could seek explanations for. It is difficult to see regularities of nature if you don't know what to look for. The German adage below expresses this succinctly:

Man sieht was man weiss
*One sees what one knows*

We offer many instances of this in Chapters 9, 11, 12, 13 and one in Chapter 3. "Lexical NP (proper name) denotations are monotone increasing" is one simple generalization. That such denotations are a set of complete boolean generators for DP denotations is a much deeper one. And, we must acknowledge, the half-life of a new generalization is often short – once a generalization is formulated we want to check further cases, refine it and generalize it. This is part of the healthy feedback between theory formation and observation.

We invite you to critique our generalizations, and we welcome you to Linguistics.

**A Guide to Using this Book**  Chapter 1 introduces the reader to iterative processes in natural language, of which just a few, say relative clause formation and boolean compounding should be learned as representative. Chapter 1 also gives us our first example of alternate ways of describing linguistic structure. Chapter 2 is entirely math background. All other chapters presuppose this one. Chapter 3 introduces in the domain of phonology our first application of equivalence classes and of boolean closure. Chapters 4 and 5 illustrate some basic syntactic formalization, useful later in Chapter 13. Chapter 13 itself is the last chapter and is a bit advanced for a beginning text. It can be omitted on first reading.Chapters 6 and 7 introduce some mathematical work in formal language theory and are largely self contained. Chapters 8 through 12 are semantic, with later chapters building on the earlier ones. In Chapters 8 and 10 the logic summaries are self contained and can be skimmed on first reading. Chapters 11 and 12 have fewer exercises than the others and focus on generalizations we can make using our formal tools concerning the logico-semantic nature of natural language.

Several chapters have some small addenda supplementing material in the text. The pure beginner can skip these on first reading, except for the addendum **2.12 Some Initial Hints on Setting up Proofs** in Chapter 2.

**Words of Thanks**  We thank our many classes over the years for their reactions to this material. Special thanks to Thomas Graf, Bruce Hayes, Jeff Heinz, Anoop Mahajan, Uwe Moennich, Richard Oehrle, Kie Zuraw, and Daniel Wymark for comments on earlier versions of this manuscript. And we owe a big debt to Nicholas LaCasse and Jos Tellings both for the early and final LaTeX versions of the text and also for clarification and organizational remarks on the text itself. Lastly, Edward Keenan would like specifically to thank his wife Carol Archie for suffering through endless weekends of apparently endless effort. She still thinks we should call the book *Sex, Lies and Language*. And Larry Moss thanks Hans-Joerg Tiede for teaching a version of the material many years ago and for many discussions over the years about pedagogical issues in the presentation. He also thanks Madi Hirschland for her unfailing love and support, and for continuing to remind him that as beautiful as language and mathematics are, there are many other aspects of the world that need to be understood and changed.

# 1

# The Roots of Infinity

We begin our study with a fundamental query of modern Linguistics:

(1)   What enables speakers of natural language to produce and
understand novel expressions?

*Natural languages* are ones like English, Japanese, Swahili, ... which
human beings grow up speaking naturally as their normal means of
communication. There are about 7,000 such languages currently spoken in the world[1]. Natural languages contrast with *artificial languages*
consciously created for special purposes. These include *programming
languages* such as Lisp, C++ and Prolog and *mathematical languages*
such as Sentential Logic and Elementary Arithmetic studied in mathematical logic. The study of natural language syntax and semantics
has benefited much from the study of these much simpler and better
understood artificial languages.

The crucial phrase in (1) is *novel*. An ordinary speaker is *competent*
to produce and understand arbitrarily many expressions he or she has
never specifically heard before and so certainly has never explicitly
learned. This chapter is devoted to supporting this claim, introducing
some descriptive mathematical notions and notations as needed.

In the next chapter we initiate the study of the linguists' response
to the fundamental query: namely, that speakers have internalized a
*grammar* for their language. That grammar consists of a set of *lexical
items* – meaningful words and morphemes – and some *rules* which
allow us to combine lexical items to form arbitrarily many complex
expressions whose semantic interpretation is determined by that of the
expressions they are formed from. We produce, recognize and interpret

---

[1]This figure is "rough" for both empirical and conceptual reasons. For example,
how different may two speech varieties be and still count as dialects of the same
language as opposed to different languages?

novel expressions by using our internalized grammar to recognize how the expressions are constructed, and how expressions constructed in that way take their meaning as a function of the meanings of what they are constructed from – ultimately the lexical items they are built from. This last feature is known as *Compositionality*.

In designing grammars of this sort for natural languages we are pulled by several partially antagonistic forces: Empirical Adequacy (Completeness, Soundness, Interpretability) on the one hand, and Universality on the other. Regarding the former, for each natural language $L$ the grammar we design for $L$ must be *complete*: it generates *all* the expressions native speakers judge grammatical; it must be *sound*: it *only* generates expressions judged grammatical, and it must be *interpretable*: the lexical items and derived expressions must be semantically interpreted. Even in this chapter we see cases where different ways of constructing the same expression may lead to different ways of semantically interpreting it. Finally, linguists feel strongly that the structure of our languages reflects the structure of our minds, and in consequence, at some deep level, grammars of different languages should share many structural properties. Thus in designing a grammar for one language we are influenced by work that linguists do with other languages and we try to design our (partial) grammars so that they are similar (they cannot of course be identical, since English, Japanese, Swahili, ... are not identical).

## 1.1 The Roots of Infinity in Natural Language

Here we exhibit a variety of types of expression in English which support the conclusion that competent speakers of English can produce, recognize and understand unboundedly many expressions. What is meant by *unboundedly many* or *arbitrarily many*? In the present context we mean simply *infinitely many* in the mathematical sense. Consider for example the set $\mathbb{N}$ of natural numbers, that set whose members (elements) are the familiar 0, 1, 2, .... Clearly $\mathbb{N}$ has infinitely many members, as they "continue forever, without end". A less poetic way to say that is: a set $L$ is *infinite* if and only if for each natural number $k$, $L$ has more than $k$ members. By this informal but usable definition we can reason that $\mathbb{N}$ is infinite: no matter what number $k$ we pick, the numbers 0, 1,..., $k$ constitute more than $k$ elements of $\mathbb{N}$; in fact precisely $k + 1$ elements. So for any $k$, $\mathbb{N}$ has more than $k$ elements. This *proves* that $\mathbb{N}$ is an infinite set according to our definition of *infinite*.

**Jargon** In mathematical discourse *if and only if*, usually abbreviated *iff*, combines two sentences to form a third. *P iff Q* means that *P* and

$Q$ always have the same truth value: in an arbitrary situation $s$ they are both true in $s$ or both false in $s$. *iff* is often used in definitions, as there the term we are defining occurs in the sentence on the left of *iff* and the sentence we use to define that term occurs on the right, and the purpose of the definition is to say that whenever we use the word being defined, we may replace it by the definition which follows.

**When are sets the same?** In what follows we shall often be interested in defining sets—for example, sets of English expressions with various properties. So it will be important to know when two verbally different definitions define the *same* set. We say that sets $X$ and $Y$ are *the same* iff they have the same members[2]. For example, let $X$ be the set whose members are the numbers $1, 2, 3$, and $4$. And let $Y$ be the set whose members are the positive integers less than 5. Clearly $X$ and $Y$ have the same members and so are the same set. To say that $X$ and $Y$ are the same set we write $X = Y$ read as "$X$ equals $Y$". And to say that $X$ and $Y$ are *different* sets we write $X \neq Y$, read as "$X$ does not equal $Y$". Observe that $X \neq Y$ iff one of the sets $X, Y$ has a member the other doesn't have. Were this condition to fail then $X$ and $Y$ would have the same members and thus be the same set ($X = Y$).

**On sets and their sizes** The number of elements in a set $X$ is noted $|X|$ and is called the *cardinality* of $X$. We first consider finite sets. A set $X$ is *finite* iff for some natural number $k$, $X$ has exactly $k$ elements. That is, $|X| = k$. This definition is in practice useful and easy to apply. For example, the set whose elements are just the letters $a$, $b$, and $c$ is finite, as it has exactly three elements. This set is usually noted $\{a, b, c\}$, where we list the names of the elements separated by commas, with the whole list enclosed in curly brackets (not angled brackets, not round brackets or parentheses). To say that an object $x$ is a member (element) of a set $A$ we write $x \in A$, using a stylized Greek epsilon to denote the membership relation. For example, $3 \in \{1, 3, 5, 7\}$. To say that $x$ is not a member of $A$ we write $x \notin A$. For example, $2 \notin \{1, 3, 5, 7\}$.

One finite set of special interest is the *empty* set, also called the *null* set, and noted $\emptyset$. It is that set with no members. Note that there could not be two different empty sets, for then one would have to have a member that the other didn't, so it would have a member and thus not be empty.

We have already mentioned that the set $\mathbb{N}$ of natural numbers is infinite. Sometimes we refer to it with a *pseudolist* such as $\{0, 1, 2, \ldots\}$

---

[2]In fact this criterion for identity of sets is one of the axioms (the *Axiom of Extensionality*) of Set Theory. It reads: For all sets $A, B$ $A = B$ iff for all $x$, $x \in A$ iff $x \in B$.

where the three dots means simply that "the reader knows how to continue the list". This is a useful notation when in fact we know how to continue the list. But it does not count as a definition since there are many ways the initial explicitly given segment of the list, namely $0, 1, 2$, could be continued. Here we take it that in practice the reader has a working familiarity of the natural numbers. For example $2 \in \mathbb{N}$, but $\frac{1}{2} \notin \mathbb{N}$.

We demonstrate shortly that English has infinitely many expressions. To show this we consider three ways of showing that a set $A$ is infinite. The first we have already seen: show that for every natural number $k$, $A$ has more than $k$ elements. This is how we convinced ourselves (if we needed convincing) that the set $\mathbb{N}$ of natural numbers was infinite. A second way uses the very useful subset relation, defined as follows:

**Definition 1.1.** A set $A$ is a *subset* of a set $B$, noted $A \subseteq B$, iff every element of $A$ is also an element of $B$. More formally, $A \subseteq B$ iff for all objects $x$, if $x \in A$ then $x \in B$.

When $A \subseteq B$, it is possible that $A = B$, for then every element of $A$ is, trivially, an element of $B$. But it is also possible that $B$ has some element(s) not in $A$, in which case we say that $A$ is a *proper subset* of $B$, noted $A \subset B$. Note too, that if $A$ is not a subset of $B$, noted $A \not\subseteq B$, then there is some $x \in A$ which is not in $B$.

And we can now give our second "infinity test" as follows: a set $B$ is infinite if it has a subset $A$ which is infinite. The reasoning behind this plausible claim is as follows. If $A \subseteq B$ and $A$ is infinite then for each natural number $k$, $A$ has more than $k$ elements. But each of those elements are also in $B$, so for any $k$, $B$ has more than $k$ elements and is thus infinite.

A last, and the most useful infinity test, is to show that a set $B$ is infinite by showing that it has the *same cardinality* as a set (such as $\mathbb{N}$) which is already known to be infinite. The idea of sameness of cardinality is fundamental, and does not depend on any pretheoretical notion of natural number. We say that sets $A$ and $B$ have the same number of elements (the *same cardinality*) iff we can match the elements of one with the elements of the other in such a way that distinct elements of one are always matched with distinct elements of the other, and no elements in either set are left unmatched. The matching in (2) shows that $A = \{1, 2, 3\}$ and $B = \{a, b, c\}$ have the same number of elements. The matching illustrated is one to one with nothing left over:

(2)  $\underline{A}$                    $\underline{B}$

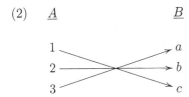

Other matchings, such as 1 with $b$, 2 with $c$ and 3 with $a$, would have worked just as well. A more interesting illustration is the matching given in (3), which shows that the set $EVEN$, whose elements are just 0, 2, 4, ..., is infinite. To give the matching explicitly we must say what even number an arbitrary natural number $n$ is matched with.

(3)      $\mathbb{N}$    0   1   2   $\cdots$   $n$   $\cdots$
              $\updownarrow$   $\updownarrow$   $\updownarrow$       $\updownarrow$
       $EVEN$   0   2   4   $\cdots$   $2n$   $\cdots$

So each natural number $n$ is matched with the even number $2n$. And distinct $n$'s get matched with distinct even numbers, since if $n$ is different from $m$, noted $n \neq m$, then $2n \neq 2m$. And clearly no element in either set is left unmatched. Thus $EVEN$ has the same size as $\mathbb{N}$ and so is infinite.

**Exercise 1.1.** This exercise is about infinite sets.

 a. Show by direct argument that $EVEN$ is infinite. (That is, show that for arbitrary $k$, $EVEN$ has more than $k$ elements).

 b. Let $ODD$ be the set whose elements are 1, 3, 5, ....

  a. Show directly that $ODD$ is infinite.

  b. Show by matching that $ODD$ is infinite.

We turn now to an inventory of types of expression in English whose formation shows that English has infinite subsets of expressions.

**Iterated Words** There are a few cases in which we can build an infinite set of expressions by starting with some fixed expression and forming later ones by repeating a word in the immediately previous one. $GP$ below is one such set; its expressions are matched with $\mathbb{N}$ showing that it is an infinite set.

(4)

| $\mathbb{N}$ | $GP$ |
|---|---|
| 0 | my grandparents |
| 1 | my great grandparents |
| 2 | my great great grandparents |
| ... | ... |
| $n$ | my (great)$^n$ grandparents |
| ... | ... |

In line $n$, (great)$^n$ on the right denotes the result of writing down the word *great* $n$ times in a row. Thus $great^1 = great$, $great^2 = great$ *great*, etc.

When $n = 0$ we haven't written anything at all: so *my (great)$^0$ grandparents* is simply *my grandparents*. We often leave spaces between words when writing sequences of words from a known language (such as English). We usually do not do this when concatenating random sequences of letters: $(aab)^3 = aabaabaab$.

One sees immediately from the matching in (4) that the set $GP$ is infinite. Hence the set of English expressions itself is infinite since it has an infinite subset. Moreover the expressions in $GP$ all have the same category, traditionally called *Noun Phrase* and abbreviated NP. So we can say that $PH(\text{NP})$, the set of phrases of category NP in English, is infinite.

Note too that each expression in $GP$ is meaningful in a reasonable way. Roughly, *my grandparents* denotes a set of four people, the (biological) parents of my parents. *my great grandparents* denotes the parents of my grandparents, an 8 element set; *my great great grandparents* denotes the parents of my great grandparents, a 16 element set, and in general the denotation of *my (great)$^{n+1}$ grandparents* denotes the parents of my (great)$^n$ grandparents. (For each $n \in \mathbb{N}$, how many (great)$^n$ grandparents do I have[3]?).

We turn in a moment to more structured cases of iteration which lead to infinite subsets of English. But first let us countenance one reasonable objection to our claim that *my (great)$^n$ grandparents* is always a grammatical expression of English. Surely normal speakers of English would find it hard to to interpret such expressions for large $n$, even say $n = 100$, so can we not find some largest $n$, say $n = 1,000,000$, beyond which *my (great)$^n$ grandparents* is ungrammatical English?

Our first response is a practical one. We want to state which sequences of English words are grammatical expressions of English. To this end we study sequences that are grammatical and ones that aren't

---

[3]This is a tricky question.

and try to find regularities which enable us to predict when a novel sequence is grammatical. If there were only 25 grammatical expressions in English, or even several hundred, we could just list them all and be done with it. The grammaticality of a test expression would be decided by checking whether it is in the list or not. But if there are billions in the list that is too many for a speaker to have learned by heart. So we still seek to know on what basis the speaker decides whether to say Yes or No to a test expression. In practice, then, characterizing membership in large finite sets draws on the same techniques used for infinite sets. In both cases we are looking for small descriptions of big sets.

Our task as linguists is similar to designing chess playing algorithms. Given some rules limiting repetitions of moves, the number of possible chess games is finite. Nonetheless we treat chess as a game in which possible sequences of moves are determined by rule, not just membership in some massive list.

The second response is that even for large $n$, speakers are reluctant to give a cut off point: $n = 7$?, $17$?, $10^{17}$ ? In fact we seem *competent* to judge that large numbers of repetitions of *great* are grammatical, and we can compute the denotation of the derived expression, though we might have to write it down and study it to do so. It is then like multiplying two ten digit numbers: too hard to do in our head but the calculation still follows the ordinary rules of multiplication. It seems reasonable then to say that English has some expressions which are too long or too complicated to be usable in practice (in *performance* as linguists say), but they are nonetheless built and interpreted according to the rules that work for simple expressions.

We might add to these responses the observation that treating certain sets as infinite is often a helpful simplifying assumption. It enables us to concentrate on the simple cases, already hard enough! We return now to the roots of infinity.

**Postnominal Possessives** Syntactically the mechanism by which we build the infinite set GP above is as trivial as one can imagine: arbitrary repetition of a single word, *great*. But English presents structurally less trivial ways of achieving similar semantic effects with the use of relation denoting nouns, such as *mother, sister, friend*, etc. Here is one such case, with the matching defined more succinctly than before:

(5)    For each natural number $n$, let $M(n)$ be the result of writing down the sequence *the mother of $n$* times followed by *the President*. That is, $M(n) = (the\ mother\ of)^n\ the\ President$.

Clearly $M$ matches distinct numbers $n$ and $n'$ with different English expressions since $M(n)$ and $M(n')$ differ with regard to how many times the word *mother* occurs: in $M(n)$ it occurs $n$ times, and $M(n')$ it occurs $n'$ times. Clearly then the set whose elements are $M(0)$, $M(1)$, ... is an infinite set of English NPs.

Moreover, what holds syntactically holds semantically: when $n \neq n'$, $M(n)$ *and* $M(n')$ denote different objects. Think of the people $M(n)$ arranged in a sequence $M(0)$, $M(1)$, $M(2)$, ... = *the President, the mother of the President, the mother of the mother of the President, ....* Now think of the sequence of denotations $y_0$, $y_1$, ..., they determine. *the President* denotes some individual $y_0$, and each later expression, *(the mother of)$^k$ the President*, denotes an individual $y_k$ who is the mother of the immediately preceding individual $y_{k-1}$. Since no one can be their own (biological) mother, grandmother, greatgrandmother, etc., all these individuals $y_i$ are different. So $y_n$, the denotation of *(the mother of)$^n$ the President*, is different from $y_{n'}$, the denotation of *(the mother of)$^{n'}$ the President*.

## Exercise 1.2.

a. Exhibit the matching in (5) using the format in (4).

b. Like *great* above, *very* can be repeated arbitrarily many times in expressions like *He is tall, He is very tall, He is very very tall,....* Define a matching using any of the formats so far presented which shows that the number of expressions built from *very* in this way is infinite.

Observe that the matching function $M$ introduced in (5) has in effect imposed some *structure* on the expressions it enumerates. For any $n > 0$, $M(n)$ is an expression which consists of two parts, (*constituents*), namely *the mother of*, written $n$ times, and *the President*. And the leftmost constituent itself consists of $n$ identical constituents, *the mother of*. We exhibit this structure for $M(1)$ and $M(2)$ below. (6c) is a *tree* representation of the constituent structure of $M(2)$.

(6)    a. $M(1)$: [the mother of][the President]

   b. $M(2)$: [(the mother of)(the mother of)][the President]

   c.

the mother of    the mother of    the President

Now $M(1)$ is not a constituent of $M(2)$. Therefore given Compositionality, the meaning of $M(1)$ is not part of the meaning of $M(2)$. This seems slightly surprising, as one feels that $M(2)$ denotes the mother of the individual denoted by $M(1)$. For example, if Martha is the mother of the President then $M(2)$ denotes the same as *the mother of Martha*. So let us exhibit a different, *recursive*, way of enumerating the expressions in (5) in which $M(1)$ is a constituent of $M(2)$.

(7)    For each $n \in \mathbb{N}$, $F(n)$ is a sequence of English words defined by:

      a. $F(0) = $ *the President,*

      b. For every $n \in \mathbb{N}$, $F(n+1) = $ *the mother of $F(n)$.*

(Note that $F$ succeeds in associating an expression with each number since any number $k$ is either 0 or the result of adding 1 to the previous number). Observe too that $M$ and $F$ associate the sequence of English words with same number (try some examples!). So, for each $n$, $F(n) = M(n)$. But $F$ and $M$ effect this association in different ways, ones which will be reflected in the semantic interpretation of the expressions. Compare $F(2)$ with $M(2)$. $F(2)$ has two constituents: *the mother of* and $F(1)$, the latter also having two constituents, *the mother of* and *the President*. (8) exhibits the constituent structure imposed by $F$ in $F(1)$ and $F(2)$. The gross constituent structure for $F(2)$ is given by the tree in (8c).

(8)    a. $F(1)$: [the mother of][the President]

      b. $F(2)$: [(the mother of)[(the mother of)(the President)]]

      c.

          the mother of

                    the mother of    the President

On the analysis imposed by $F$, $F(1)$ is a constituent of $F(2)$, and in general $F(n)$ is a constituent of $F(n+1)$. So $F(n)$ will be assigned a meaning in the interpretation of $F(n+1)$.

**Exercise 1.3.** Exhibit the constituent structure tree for $F(3)$ analogous to that given for $F(2)$ in (8c).

So these two analyses, $M$ and $F$, make different predictions about what the meaningful parts of the expressions are[4]. Our original sugges-

---

[4]In fact both analyses are amenable to a compositional semantic analysis, but the analyses differ and the $M$ one requires a richer semantic apparatus than the $F$ one.

tion for an $F$-type analysis was that the string $M(1)$ – a *string* is just a sequence of symbols (letters, words, ...) – was a meaningful part of $M(2)$. Notice that the fact that the string $M(1)$ occurs as a *substring* of $M(2)$ was not invoked as motivation for an $F$-type analysis. And this is right, as it happens often enough that a substring of an expression is, accidentally, an expression in its own right but not a constituent of the original. Consider (9):

(9)    The woman who admires John is easy to please.

Now (10a) is a substring of (9), and happens to be a sentence in its own right with the same logical meaning as (10b) and (10c).

(10)    a. John is easy to please.

b. To please John is easy.

c. It is easy to please John.

But any attempt to replace *John is easy to please* in (9) by the strings in (10b) or (10c) results in ungrammaticality (as indicated by the asterisk):

(11)    a. *The woman who admires to please John is easy.

b. *The woman who admires it is easy to please John.

The reason is that *John is easy to please* is not a constituent, a meaningful part, of (9).

The constituent structure trees for the $F$ analysis in (8) are *right branching* in the sense that as $n$ increases, the tree for $F(n)$ has more nodes going down the righthand side. Compare the trees in Figure 1.1.

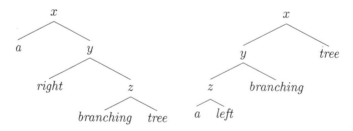

Figure 1.1: Two trees.

*Verb final* languages, such as Turkish, Japanese, and Kannada (Dravidian; India) are usually Subject+Object+Verb (SOV) and favor right branching structures: [John [poetry writes]]. By a very slight margin SOV is the most widespread order of Subject, Object and Verb across areas and genetic families (Baker, 2001, p. 128) puts this type at about 45% of the world's languages. Its mirror image, VOS, is clearly a minority word order type, accounting perhaps for 3% of world languages. It includes Tzotzil (Mayan, Mexico), Malagasy (Austronesian; Madagascar) and Fijian (Austronesian; Fiji). VOS languages prefer left branching structures: [[writes poetry] John]. The second most common word order type, SVO, like English, Swahili, Indonesian, accounts for about 42% of the world's languages, and VSO languages, such as Classical Arabic, Welsh, and Maori (Polynesian; New Zealand) account for perhaps 9%. The branching patterns in SVO and VSO languages are somewhat mixed, though on the whole they behave more like VOS languages than like SOV ones. See Dryer (2007, pp. 61–131) for excellent discussion of the complexities of the word order classification.

Finally we note that our examples of postnominal possessive NPs in (8) are atypically restricted both syntactically and semantically. It is unnatural for example to replace the Determiner *the* with others like *every, more than one, some, no, ...*. Expressions like *every mother of the President, more than one mother of the President* seem unnatural. This is likely due to our understanding that each individual has a unique (exactly one) biological mother. Replacing *mother* by less committal relation nouns such as *friend* eliminates this unnaturalness. Thus the expressions in (12) seem natural enough:

(12)  *the President, every friend of the President,*
      *every friend of every friend of the President, ....*

Now we can match the natural numbers with the elements of the pseudolist in (12) in a way fully analogous to that in (5). Each $n$ gets matched directly with $(every\ friend\ of)^n$ followed by *the President*.

**Exercise 1.4.** Exhibit a matching for (12) on which *every friend of the President* is a constituent of *every friend of every friend of the President*.

This has been our first instance of formalizing the same phenomena in two different ways ($M$ and $F$). In fact being able to change your formal conceptualization of a phenomenon under study is a major advantage of mastering elementary mathematical techniques. Formulating an issue in a new way often leads to new questions, new insights, new proofs, new knowledge. As a scientist what you can perceive and formulate and thus know, is limited by your physical instrumentation (microscopes, lab techniques, etc.) and your mental instrumentation (your mathematical concepts and methods). *Man sieht was man weiss* (*One sees what one knows*). Mathematical adaptability is also helpful in distinguishing what is fundamental from what is just notational convention. The idea here is that significant generalizations are ones that remain invariant under changes of descriptively comparable notation. Here the slogan is:

> If you can't say something two ways you can't say it.

Worth emphasizing here also is that mathematically we often find different procedures (algorithms) that compute the same value for the same input, but do so in different ways. Here is an example from high school algebra: compare the functions $f$ and $g$ below which map natural numbers to natural numbers:

(13)　　a. $f(n) = n^2 + 2n + 1$

　　　　b. $g(n) = (n+1)^2$

$g$ here seems to be a simple two step process: given $n$, add 1 to it and square the result. $f$ is more complicated: first square $n$, hold it in store and form another number by doubling $n$, then add those two numbers, and then add 1 to the result. But of course from high school algebra we know that for every $n$, $f(n) = g(n)$. That is, these two procedures always compute the same value for the same argument, but they do so in different ways. A cuter, more practical, example is given in the exercise below.

**Exercise 1.5.** Visitors to the States must often convert temperature measured on the Fahrenheit scale, on which water freezes at 32 degrees and boils at 212, to Celsius, on which water freezes at 0 degrees and boils at 100. A standard conversion algorithm $C$ takes a Fahrenheit number $n$, subtracts 32 and multiplies the result by 5/9. So for example $C(212) = (212 - 32) \times 5/9 = 180 \times 5/9 = 20 \times 5 = 100$ degrees Celsius, as desired. Here is a different algorithm, $C'$. It takes $n$ in Fahrenheit, adds (!) 40, multiplies by 5/9, and then subtracts 40. Show that for every natural number $n$, $C(n) = C'(n)$.

**Prenominal Possessors** are possessive NPs like those in (14a), enumerated by $G$ in (14b).

(14)　　a. the President's mother, the President's mother's mother, the President's mother's mother's mother, ...

　　　　b. $G(0) = $ *the President*, and for all $n \in \mathbb{N}$, $G(n+1) = G(n)$ *'s mother*.

So $G(2) = G(1)$'s mother $= G(0)$'s mother's mother $=$ the President's mother's mother. This latter NP seems harder to process and understand than its right branching paraphrase *the mother of the mother of the President*. Note that the natural tree structure for *the president's mother's mother* is left branching.

**Adjective stacking** is another right branching structure in English, easier to understand than iterated prenominal possessives but ultimately more limited in productivity. The easy to understand expressions in (15) suggest at first that we can *stack* as many adjectives in front of the noun as we like.

(15)  a. a big black shiny car

  b. an illegible early Russian medical text

But attempts to permute the adjectives often lead to less than felicitous expressions, sometimes gibberish, as in *a medical Russian early illegible text*. Now if we can't permute the adjectives, that suggests that adjectives come in classes with fixed positions in relation to the noun they modify, whence once we have filled that slot we can no longer add adjectives from that class, so the ability to add more is reduced. And this appears to be correct (Vendler, 1957). We can substitute other nationality adjectives for *Russian* in (15b), as in *an illegible early Egyptian medical text*, but we cannot add further nationality adjectives in front of *illegible*, *an Egyptian illegible early Russian medical text*. It is plausible then that there is some $n$ such that once we have stacked $n$ adjectives in front of a noun no further ones can be added. If so, the number of adjective-noun combinations is finite. In contrast, postnominal modification by relative clauses seems not subject to such constraints:

**Relative clauses** have been well studied in modern linguistics. They are illustrated by those portions of the following expressions beginning with *that*:

(16)  a. This is the house that Jack built.

  b. This is the malt that lay in the house that Jack built.

  c. This is the rat that ate the malt that lay in the house that Jack built.

  d. This is the cat that killed the rat that ate the malt that lay in the house that Jack built.

These examples of course are adapted from a child's poem, and suggest that relative clauses can iterate in English: for each natural number $n$ we can construct a relative clause with more than $n$ properly nested relative clauses, whence the number of such clauses is infinite, as is the number of NPs which contain them. One might (rightly) quibble about this quick argument from the above example, however, on the grounds that successively longer relative clauses obtained as we move down the list use words *not in the previous sentences*. So if the number of words in English were finite then perhaps the possibility of forming novel relative clauses would peter out at some point, albeit a very distant point, as even desk top dictionaries in English list between $100,000$ to $150,000$ words. But in fact this is not a worry, as we *can* repeat words and thus form infinitely many relative clauses from a small (finite) vocabulary:

(17)  Let

$$H(0) \quad = \quad every\ student,\ \text{and for all } n \in \mathbb{N},$$
$$H(n+1) \quad = \quad every\ student\ who\ knows\ \text{H(n)}.$$

Thus

$H(1) =$  *every student who knows H(0)*

$\quad\ =$  *every student who knows every student*

$H(2) =$  *every student who knows H(1)*

$\quad\ =$  *every student who knows every student who knows every st.*

And so on. Clearly $H$ enumerates an infinite set of NPs built from a four-word vocabulary: *every, student, who, knows*.

The relative clauses in these examples consist of a *relative pronoun*, *that* or *who*, followed by a sentence with an NP missing. In the cases that iterate in (16) it is always the *subject* that is missing. Thus in *the malt that lay in the house* ... *that*, which refers back to *malt*, is the subject of *lay in the house* ...; in *the rat that ate the malt* ..., *that* is the subject of *ate the malt*..., and in *the cat that killed the rat*..., *that* is the subject of *killed the rat* .... In the rightmost relative clause, *that Jack built*, *that*, which refers to *house*, is the *object* of the transitive verb *build*. Notice that the matching function $H$ in (17) provides a right branching structure for the NPs enumerated. This analysis, naively, follows the semantic interpretation of the expressions. Viz., in $H(n+1)$, $H(n)$ is a constituent, in fact an NP, the sort of expression we expect to have a meaning. But as we increase $n$, the intonationally marked groups are different, an intonation peak being put on each noun that is later modified by the relative clause, as indicated by square bracketing in (18) in which each right bracket ] signals a slight pause and the noun immediately to its left carries the intonation peak:

(18)  [This is the cat][that killed the rat][that ate the malt] ...

A matching function $H'$ that would reflect this bracketing in (18) would be: $H'(n) = every\ student\ (who\ knows\ every\ student)^n$.

Attempts to iterate object relatives rather than subject ones quickly lead to comprehension problems, even when they are right peripheral. (19a) is an English NP built from an object relative. It contains a proper noun *Sonia*. (19b) is formed by replacing *Sonia* with another NP built from an object relative. Most speakers do not really process (19b) on first pass, and a further replacement of *Sonia* by an object relative NP yielding (19c) is incomprehensible to everyone (though of course you can figure out what it means with pencil and paper).

(19)    a.  some student who Sonia interviewed.

        b.  some student who some teacher who Sonia knows
            interviewed.

        c.  some student who some teacher who every dean who Sonia
            dislikes knows interviewed

The comprehensibility difference between the iterated object relatives in (19) and iterated subject ones in (16) is quite striking. Linguists have suggested that the reason is that the iteration of object relatives leads to *center embedding*: we replace a $Y$ in a string with something that contains another $Y$ but also material to the left and to the right of that new $Y$, yielding $XYZ$. So the new $Y$ is center-embedded between $X$ and $Z$. One more iteration yields a string of the form $[X_1[X_2YZ_2]Z_1]$, and in general $n + 1$ iterations yields

$$[X_1 \ldots [X_n [X_{n+1} Y Z_{n+1}] Z_n] \ldots Z_1].$$

**Postnominal Prepositional Phrase (PP) modification** is illustrated by NPs of the form $[_{NP}$ Det N $[_{PP}$P NP$]]$, such as *a house near the port, two pictures on the wall, a doctor in the building*. Choosing the rightmost NP to be one of this form, [Det N [P NP]], we see the by now familiar right branching structure. Again a children's song provides an example of such iterated PPs:

(20)    a.  There's a hole in the bottom of the sea.

        b.  There's a log in the hole in the bottom of the sea.

        c.  There's a bump on the log in the hole in the bottom of the
            sea.

    d. There's a frog on the bump on the log in the hole in the bottom of the sea.

As with the relative clauses we must ask whether we can iterate such PPs without always invoking new vocabulary. We can, but our examples are cumbersome:

(21)    a. a park near [the building by the exit]

       b. a park near [the building near [the building by the exit]]

       c. a park (near the building)$^n$ by the exit

Note that one might argue that PP modification of nouns is not independent of relative clause modification on the grounds that the grammar rules of English will derive the PPs by *reducing* relative clauses: *a house near the port* $\Leftarrow$ *a house which is near the port*. Perhaps. If so, then we have just shown that such reduction is not blocked in contexts of multiple iteration.

**Sentence complements** concern the objects of verbs of thinking and saying such as *think, say, believe, know, acknowledge, explain, imagine, hope*, etc. They would be most linguists' first choice of an expression type which leads to infinitely many grammatical expressions, as shown in (22):

(22)  $SC(0) =$ he destroyed the house;
        $SC(n + 1) =$ he said that $SC(n)$.

*SC* enumerates in a right branching way *he said that he said that ... he destroyed the house.* Note too that such expressions *feed* relative clause formation: *the house which (he said that)$^n$ he destroyed*, yielding another infinite class of NPs.

**Sentential subjects** in their simplest form resemble sentence complements but function as the subject of a verb rather than as the objects. They determine center embeddings, and as with the earlier cases become virtually impossible to understand after one embedding:

(23)    a. That Sue quit surprised me.

       b. That that Sue quit surprised me is strange.

       c. That that that Sue quit surprised me is strange is false.

Even (23b) is sufficiently hard to understand that we perhaps should just consider it ungrammatical. However if the sentential subjects are replaced by sentence complements of nouns, such as *the claim that Sue left early*, the resulting Ss improve:

(24)  a. The claim that Sue quit surprised me.

  b. The belief that the claim that Sue quit surprised me is strange.

  c. The fact that the belief that the claim that Sue quit surprised me is strange is really outrageous.

Here (24b) can be given an intonation contour that makes it more or less intelligible. Another variant of (23) concerns cases in which the sentential subject has been *extraposed*, as in (25).

(25)  a. It surprised me that Sue quit.

  b. It is strange that it surprised me that Sue quit.

  c. It is false that it is strange that it surprised me that Sue quit.

These are right branching expressions and are considerably easier to comprehend than their center embedding paraphrases in (23).

**Caveat Lector**  On the basis of (23) and (19) we are tempted to conclude that center embedding in general is difficult to process. Don't! One robin doesn't make a spring and English is but one of about 7,000 languages in the world (Lewis, 2009). SOV languages present a variety of expression types which induce center embedding. These types include some that translate the right branching sentence complements in English. Consider for example sentence (26) from Nepali:

(26)  *Gītāle    Rāmlāī    Anjalīlāī    pakāuna    sahayog garna*
      Gita    Ram    Anjali    cook    help
      *sallāh garī.*
      advised.
      Gita advised Ram to help Anjali cook.

In these, *lāī* is a postposition carried by human names which are objects of transitive verbs, and *le* is a postposition associated with the past tense form. The forms *pakāuna* and *sahayog garna* are infinitives. As one can see from this example, the subjects are grouped together ahead of all of the verbs. The form is the center embedding pattern

$$NP_1 \ NP_2 \ NP_3 \ V_3 \ V_2 \ V_1,$$

with two proper center embeddings, rather than the (rough) form of its English translation:

$$NP_1 \ V_1 \ NP_2 \ V_2 \ NP_3 \ V_3.$$

(Again, the subjects and verbs, whether in the main clause or in embedded clauses, have special endings that need not concern us.)

Now, impressionistically, Nepali speakers seem to process Ss like (26) easily, arguing against rash conclusions concerning the difficulty of center embedding. More psycholinguistic work is needed.

Formally, though, the existence of unbounded center embedding would remove languages that have it from the class called *regular* those recognizable by finite state machines (the lowest class in the Chomsky hierarchy). See Chapter 7 or Hopcroft et al. (2001) for the relevant definitions and theorems.

**Exercise 1.6.**    a. Exhibit an enumeration of infinitely many Ss of the sort in (23) allowing repetition of verbs, as in *that he quit surprised me, that that he quit surprised me surprised me, . . .*

   b. Exhibit an enumeration of its extraposed variant, (25a), under the same repetition assumptions.

**Infinitival complements** come in a variety of flavors in English illustrated in (27–29). The infinitival complements in (27) and (28) are the untensed verbs preceded by *to*. Verbs like *help, make, let* and perception verbs like *watch, see, hear* take infinitival complements without the *to*.

(27)    a. Mary wanted to read the book.

   b. She wanted to try to begin to read the book.

(28)    a. She asked Bill to wash the car.

   b. She forced Joe to persuade Sue to ask Sam to wash the car.

(29)    a. She helped Bill wash the car.

   b. She let Bill watch Harry make Sam wash the car.

The b-sentences suggest that we can iterate infinitival phrases, though the intransitive types in (27) are hard to interpret. What does *He began to begin to begin to wash the car* mean? The transitive types in (28) and (29), where the verb which governs the infinitival complement takes an NP object, iterate more naturally: *She asked Bill to ask Sue to ask Sam to . . . to wash the car. She helped Bill help Harry help Sam . . . wash the car* or *She watched Bill watch Mary watch the children . . . play in the yard.* Repeating proper names here, however, can be unacceptable: *\*She asked Bill to ask Bill to wash the car.* But to show that this structure type leads to infinitely many expressions it suffices to choose a *quantified* NP object, as in (30).

(30)    a. She asked a student to ask a student to ... to wash the car.

      b. She helped a student help a student ... wash the car.

**Exercise 1.7.**

    a. Exhibit an enumeration of one of the sets in (30).

    b. Another way to avoid repeating NP objects of verbs like *ask* is to use a previously given enumeration of an infinite class of NPs. Exhibit an enumeration of *She asked every friend of the President to wash the car, She asked every friend of the President to ask every friend of every friend of the President to wash the car, ....*

**Embedded questions** are similar to sentence complements, but the complement of the main verb semantically refers to a question or its answer, not a statement of the sort that can be true or false. Compare (31a), a True/False type assertion, with (31b), which requests an identification of the *Agent* of the verb *steal*, and (31c), an instance of an embedded question, where in effect we are saying that John knows the answer to the question in (31b).

(31)    a. Some student stole the painting.

      b. Which student stole the painting?

      c. John knows which student stole the painting.

The question in (31b) differs from the assertion in (31a) by the choice of an interrogative Determiner *which* as opposed to *some*[5]. The embedded question following *knows* in (31c) uses the same interrogative Det. And of course we can always question the subject constituent of sentences like (31c), yielding Ss like (32a), which can in turn be further embedded, *ad infinitum.*

(32)    a. Who knew which student stole the painting?

      b. John figured out who knew which student stole the painting

      c. Which detective figured out who knew which student stole the painting?

      d. John knew which detective figured out who knew which student stole the painting

---

[5]This simple relation between declaratives and interrogatives only holds when we question the subject. In other types of constituent questions the interrogative expression is moved to the front of the clause and the subject is moved behind the auxiliary verb if there is one; if there isn't an appropriately tensed form of *do* is inserted. Compare: *John stole some painting* with *Which painting did John steal?*

In distinction to sentence complements, attempts to form relative clauses from embedded questions lead to expressions of dubious grammaticality (indicated by ?? below):

(33)  ?? the painting that John knew which detective figured out which student stole

**Exercise 1.8.** The function *EQ* exhibited below (note the notation) matches distinct numbers with distinct expressions, so the set of embedded questions it enumerates is infinite.

$$EQ \qquad n \mapsto \textit{Joe found out (who knew)}^n \textit{ who took the painting.}$$

Your task: Exhibit a recursive function *EQ'* which effects the same matching as *EQ* but does so in such a way as to determine a right branching constituent structure of the sort below:

*Joe found out [who knew [who knew [who took the painting]]].*

**Notation and a Concept** The matchings we have exhibited between $\mathbb{N} = \{0, 1, 2, \ldots\}$ and English expressions have all been *one-to-one*, meaning that they matched distinct numbers with distinct expressions. More generally, suppose that $f$ is a function from a set $A$ to a set $B$, noted $f : A \to B$. $A$ is called the *domain* of the function $f$, and $B$ is called its *codomain*. So $f$ associates each object $x \in A$ with a unique object $f(x) \in B$. $f(x)$ is called *the value* of the function $f$ at $x$. We also say that $f$ *maps* $x$ to $f(x)$. "Unique" here just means "exactly one"; that is, $f$ maps each $x \in A$ to some element of $B$, and $f$ does not map any $x$ to more than one element of $B$. Now, $f$ is said to be *one-to-one* (synonym: *injective*) just in case $f$ maps distinct $x, x' \in A$ to distinct elements $f(x), f(x') \in B$[6]. So a one-to-one function is one that preserves distinctness of arguments (the elements of $A$ being the *arguments* of the function $f$). A function which fails to be one-to-one fails to preserve distinctness of arguments, so it must map at least two distinct arguments to the same value.

We also introduce some notation that we use in many later chapters. Let $[A \to B]$ denote the set of functions from $A$ to $B$. (In the mathematical literature this set of functions is often noted $B^A$, but this notation is awkward to iterate).

**Exercise 1.9.** In the diagram below we exhibit in an obvious way a function $g$ from $A = \{a, b, c, d\}$ to $B = \{2, 4, 6\}$. The use of arrows tells

---

[6]A one-to-one function is actually "two-to-two."

us that the elements at the tail of the arrow constitute the domain of $g$, and those at the head lie in the codomain of $g$.

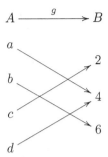

a. Is $g$ one-to-one? Justify your answer.

b. Do there exist any one-to-one functions from $A$ into $B$?

c. Exhibit by diagram two different one-to-one functions from $B$ into $A$.

Returning now to functions, we say that a set $A$ is less than or equal in size (cardinality) to a set $B$, written $A \preceq B$, iff there is a one-to-one map from $A$ into $B$. (We use *map* synonymously with *function*). This (standard) definition is reasonable: if we can copy the elements of $A$ into $B$, matching distinct elements of $A$ with distinct elements of $B$, then $B$ must be at least as large as $A$.

Observe that for any set $A$, $A \preceq A$. *Proof:* Let $id$ be that function from $A$ into $A$ given by: $id(\alpha) = \alpha$, for all $\alpha \in A$[7]. So trivially $id$ is injective (one-to-one).

**Exercise 1.10.**

a. Let $A$ and $B$ be sets with $A \subseteq B$. Show that $A \preceq B$.

b. Show that $EVEN \preceq \mathbb{N}$, where, $EVEN = \{0, 2, 4, \ldots\}$, and $\mathbb{N} = \{0, 1, 2, \ldots\}$.

c. Show that $\mathbb{N} \preceq EVEN$.

---

[7]$\alpha$ is the first "lower case" letter of the Greek alphabet, given in full at the end of this text. The reader should memorize this alphabet together with the names of the letters in English, as Greek letters are widely used in mathematical discourse.

Mathematically we define sets $A$ and $B$ to have the same size (cardinality), noted $A \approx B$, iff $A \preceq B$ and $B \preceq A$. A famous theorem of set theory (the Schröder-Bernstein Theorem, see Section 9.9) guarantees that this definition coincides with the informal one—matching with nothing left unmatched—given earlier. On this definition, then, $EVEN \approx \mathbb{N}$, that is, the set $\{0, 2, 4, \ldots\}$ of natural numbers that are even has the same size as the whole set $\mathbb{N}$ of natural numbers. Using the cardinality notation introduced earlier we see that $A \approx B$ iff $|A| = |B|$. So for example, $|EVEN| = |\mathbb{N}|$. Can you show that $\mathbb{N} \approx ODD$, the set $\{1, 3, 5, \ldots\}$ of natural numbers that are odd?

Here are two useful concepts defined in terms of $\preceq$. First, we say that a set $A$ is *strictly smaller* than a set $B$, noted $A \prec B$, iff $A$ is less than or equal in size to $B$ and $B$ is not less than or equal in size to $A$. That is, $A \prec B$ iff $A \preceq B$ and $B \npreceq A$. For example, $\{a, b\} \prec \{4, 5, 6\}$. An alternative way to say $A \prec B$ is $|A| < |B|$.

One might have expected that $|EVEN| < |\mathbb{N}|$. But that is not the case. The map sending each even number $k$ to itself is a one-to-one map from $EVEN$ into $\mathbb{N}$, so $EVEN \preceq \mathbb{N}$. And the map sending each natural number $n$ to $2n$ is one-to-one from $\mathbb{N}$ into $EVEN$, so $\mathbb{N} \preceq EVEN$, whence $|EVEN| = |\mathbb{N}|$

People sometimes find it "unintuitive" that $EVEN$ and $\mathbb{N}$ have the same cardinality, given that $EVEN$ is a very proper subset of $\mathbb{N}$. $\mathbb{N}$ after all contains infinitely many numbers not in $EVEN$, namely all the odd numbers (1, 3, 5, ... ). Here is an informal way to appreciate the truth of $EVEN \approx \mathbb{N}$. Consider that a primary purpose of $\mathbb{N}$ is to enable us to count any finite set. We do this by associating a distinct natural number with each of the objects we are counting, Usually the association goes in order, starting with 'one'. Then we point to the next object saying 'two', then the next saying 'three', etc. until we are done. $\mathbb{N}$ in fact is the "smallest" set that enables us to count any finite set in this way. But we could make do with just the set of even numbers. Then we would count 'two', 'four', 'six', etc. associating with each object from our finite set a distinct even number. So any set we can count with $\mathbb{N}$ we can count with $EVEN$, since they are equinumerous.

This relation between $EVEN$ and $\mathbb{N}$ provides a conceptually pleasing (and standard) way to define the notions *finite* and *infinite* without reference to numbers. Namely, an infinite set is one which has the same cardinality as some proper subset of itself. So a set $A$ is *infinite* iff there is a proper subset $B$ of $A$ such that $A \approx B$. And $A$ is *finite* iff $A$ is not infinite (so $A$ does not have the same size as any proper subset of itself). These definitions identify the same sets as we did earlier when we said that a set $A$ is infinite iff for every natural number $k$, $A$ has more than $k$ elements. And $A$ is finite iff for some natural number $k$, $A$ has exactly $k$ elements. But these earlier (and quite useful) definitions do rely on prior knowledge of the natural numbers. Our later ones above characterize *finite* and *infinite* just in terms of matchings—namely, in terms of one-to-one functions.

We return now to a final case of structure building operations in English.

## 1.2 Boolean Compounding

**Boolean compounding** differs from our other expression building operations which build expressions of a fixed category. The *boolean connectives* however are *polymorphic*, they combine with expressions of many different categories to form derived expressions in that same category. The boolean connectives in English are *(both) ... and, (either) ... or, neither ... nor ..., not* and some uses of *but*. Below we illustrate some examples of boolean compounds in different categories. We label the categories traditionally, insisting only that expressions within a group have the same category. We usually put the examples in the context of a larger expression, italicizing the compound we are illustrating.

(34) Boolean Compounds in English

a. Noun Phrases *Neither John nor any other student* came to the party. *Most of the students and most of the teachers* drink. *Not a creature* was stirring, *not even a mouse*.

b. Verb Phrases
She *neither sings nor dances*, He *works in New York and lives in New Jersey*, He *called us but didn't come over*.

c. Transitive Verb Phrases
John *both praised and criticized* each student, He *neither praised nor criticized* any student, He *either admires or believes to be a genius* every student he has ever taught.

d. Adjective Phrases
This is an *attractive but not very well built* house. He is *neither intelligent nor industrious*. She is a *very tall and very graceful* dancer.

e. Complementizer Phrases
He believes *neither that the Earth is flat nor that it is round*. He believes *that it is flat but not that it is heavy*. He showed *either that birds dream or that they don't*, I forget which.

f. Prepositional Phrases

That troll lives *over the hill but not under a bridge.* A strike must pass *above the batter's knees and below his chest.*

g. Prepositions

There is no passage *either around or through* that jungle. He lives *neither in nor near* New York City.

h. Determiners

*Most but not all* of the cats were inoculated. *At least two but not more than ten* students will pass. *Either hardly any or else almost all* of the students will pass that exam.

i. Sentences

*John came early and Fred stayed late. Either John will come early or Fred will stay late. Neither did any student attend the lecture nor did any student jeer the speaker.*

In terms of productivity, boolean compounds are perhaps comparable to iterating adjectives: we can do it often, but there appear to be restrictions on repeating words which would mean that the productivity of boolean compounding is bounded. There are a few cases in which repetition is allowed, with an intensifying meaning:

(35)  John laughed, and laughed, and laughed.

But even here it is largely unacceptable to replace *and* by *or* or *neither . . . nor . . .*: *John either laughed or laughed or laughed.* Equally other cases of pure repetition seem best classed as ungrammatical:

(36)  *Either every student or every student came to the party. *Fritz is neither clever nor clever. *He lives both in and in New York City.

On the other hand judicious selection of different words allows the formation of quite complex boolean compounds, especially since *and* and *or* combine with arbitrarily many (distinct) expressions, as per (37b):

(37)  a. either John and his uncle or else Bill and his uncle but not Frank and his uncle or Sam and his uncle

b. John, Sam, Frank, Harry and Ben but not Sue, Martha, Rosa, Felicia or Zelda

Note too that the polymorphism of the boolean connectives allows the formation of Ss for example with boolean compounds in many categories simultaneously:

(38)   Every student, every teacher and every dean drank and
       caroused in some nightclub or bar on or near the campus until
       late that night or very early the next morning

**Concluding Remarks**  We have exemplified a variety of highly productive ways of forming English expressions. This led to the conclusion that English has infinitely many expressions. Note though—an occasional point of confusion—each English expression itself is finite, that is, it is a finite sequence of words. Our claim is only that there are infinitely many of these finite objects. (Similarly there are infinitely many finite sets of natural numbers).

We also raised the general linguistic challenge of accounting for how speakers of English (or any natural language) produce, recognize and interpret large numbers of novel expressions. Our general answer was that speakers have learned a grammar and learned how to compositionally interpret the infinitely many expressions it generates. In the remainder of this book we concern ourselves with precisely how to define such grammars and how to interpret the expressions they generate. In the process we shall enrich the mathematical apparatus we have begun to introduce here. And as with many mathematics-oriented books, much of the learning takes place in doing the exercises. If you only read the text without working the exercises you will miss much.

> Learning mathematics is like learning to dance:
> You learn little just by watching others.

## 1.3   References

Center-embedding has been the subject of numerous papers in the linguistic and psychological literature. Some of the earliest references are Chomsky and Miller (1963), Miller and Isard (1964), and de Roeck et al. (1982).

Since 1990 the subject of center-embedding has again been taken up by researchers interested in processing models of human speech. Some references here are Church (1980), Abney and Johnson (1991), and Resnik (1992).

A paper presenting psycholinguistic evidence that increasing center embedding in SOV languages does increase processing complexity is Babyonyshev and Gibson (1999).

# 2

---

# Some Mathematical Background

This chapter and part of the next are solely concerned with basic mathematical notions and notation regarding sets, functions and relations. These notions and notation are very widely used throughout mathematics, not just in the mathematical study of language.

## 2.1 More about Sets

Consider the three element set $\{a, b, c\}$. Call this set $X$ for the moment. $X$ has several subsets. For example the one-element set $\{b\}$ is a subset of $X$. We call a one-element set a *unit set*. Recall that $\{b\} \subseteq X$. This is so because every element of $\{b\}$ – there is only one, $b$ – is an element of $X$. Similarly the other unit sets, $\{a\}$ and $\{c\}$, are both subsets of $X$. Equally there are three two-element subsets of $X$: $\{a, b\}$ is one, that is, $\{a, b\} \subseteq X$. What are the other two? And of course $X$ itself is a subset of $X$, since, trivially, every object in $X$ is in $X$. (Notice that we are *not* saying that $X$ is an *element* of itself, just a subset.) There is one further subset of $X$, the *empty set*, $\emptyset$. This set was introduced on page 3. Recall that $\emptyset$ has no members. Trivially $\emptyset$ is a subset of $X$ (indeed of any set). Otherwise there would be something in $\emptyset$ which isn't in $X$, and there isn't anything whatsoever in $\emptyset$.

The set of subsets of a set $X$ is called *the power set* of $X$ and noted $\mathcal{P}(X)$. In the case under discussion we have:

$$\mathcal{P}(\{a, b, c\}) \quad = \quad \{\emptyset, \{a\}, \{b\}, \{c\}, \{a, b\}, \{b, c\}, \{a, c\}, \{a, b, c\}\}.$$

On the right we have a single set with 8 elements; those elements are themselves all sets. Indeed, on the right we have just listed all of the subsets of our set $X$. Note that $\{a, b, c\}$ has 3 elements, and $\mathcal{P}(\{a, b, c\})$ has $2^3 = 2 \times 2 \times 2 = 8$ elements. So in this case, in fact in every case, $X \prec \mathcal{P}(X)$. Now let us arrange the 8 elements of $\mathcal{P}(\{a, b, c\})$ according to the subset relations that obtain among them, with the largest set,

$\{a, b, c\}$, at the top of our diagram (called a *Hasse diagram*) and the smallest one, $\emptyset$, at the bottom. See Figure 2.1.

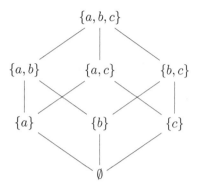

Figure 2.1: The Hasse diagram of $\mathcal{P}(\{a, b, c\})$

We have used the lines (*edges*) between set symbols here to indicate certain subset relations that obtain between the sets pictured in the diagram. Specifically, if you can move *up* from a set $A$ to a set $B$ along lines then $A \subseteq B$. Note that we have not for example drawn a line directly from $\{a\}$ to $\{a, b, c\}$. Our diagram allows us to infer that $\{a\} \subseteq \{a, b, c\}$, since it shows that $\{a\} \subseteq \{a, b\}$, and also $\{a, b\} \subseteq \{a, b, c\}$, and we know that subset is a *transitive* relation:

(1)    Transitivity of subset: For all sets $A$, $B$, and $C$: if $A \subseteq B$ and $B \subseteq C$, then $A \subseteq C$.

*Proof.* Let $A$, $B$, and $C$ be arbitrary sets. Assume that $A \subseteq B$ and $B \subseteq C$. We must show that $A \subseteq C$, that is, that an arbitrary element of $A$ is also an element of $C$. Let $x$ be an arbitrary element of $A$. Then $x$ lies in $B$, since our first assumption says that everything in $A$ is in $B$. But since $x$ lies in $B$, we infer it also lies in $C$, since our second assumption says that everything in $B$ is also in $C$. Thus given our assumptions, an arbitrary element of $A$ is an element of $C$. So $A \subseteq C$, as was to be shown.    □

There is one instance of the subset relation not depicted in Figure 2.1. Namely, we have not drawn a line from each set to itself to show that each set is a subset of itself. This is because we know that the subset relation is *reflexive*, that is, $Z \subseteq Z$, no matter what set $Z$ we pick (even $Z = \emptyset$), as we have already seen. So here we rely on our general knowledge about sets to interpret the Hasse diagram. For the record,

(2)  Reflexivity of subset: For all sets $A$, $A \subseteq A$.

(3)  Non-subset-hood: $A \not\subseteq B$ iff there is some $x \in A$ which is not in $B$.

**Exercise 2.1.** Exhibit the Hasse diagram for each of:

a. $\mathcal{P}(\{a, b\})$.

b. $\mathcal{P}(\{a\})$.

c. $\mathcal{P}(\{a, b, c, d\})$.

d. $\mathcal{P}(\{\emptyset\})$.

Hasse diagrams of power sets incorporate more structure than meets the eye. Specifically they are *closed* under *intersection*, *union*, and *relative complement*:

**Definition 2.1.** Given sets $A$ and $B$,

a. $A \cap B$ (read "A intersect B") is that set whose members are just the objects which are elements of both $A$ and of $B$. For example,

    i. $\{a, b\} \cap \{b, c\} = \{b\}$,

    ii. $\{a, b\} \cap \{a, b, c\} = \{a, b\}$,

    iii. $\{a, b\} \cap \{c\} = \emptyset$.

b. $A \cup B$ (read "$A$ union $B$") is that set whose members are just the objects which are members of $A$ or members of $B$ (and possibly both). For example,

    i. $\{a, b\} \cup \{b, c\} = \{a, b, c\}$,

    ii. $\{b\} \cup \{a, b\} = \{a, b\}$,

    iii. $\{c, b\} \cup \emptyset = \{c, b\}$.

c. $A - B$ (read "$A$ minus $B$") is the set whose members are those which are members of $A$ but not of $B$. Today people often write $A \backslash B$ for $A - B$. For example,

    i. $\{a, b, c\} - \{a, c\} = \{b\}$,

    ii. $\{a, c\} - \{a, b, c\} = \emptyset$,

    iii. $\{b, c\} - \emptyset = \{b, c\}$.

$A - B$ is also called *the complement of B relative to A*. Now to say that $\mathcal{P}(\{a, b, c\})$ is *closed under intersection*, $\cap$, is just to say that whenever $A$ and $B$ are elements of $\mathcal{P}(\{a, b, c\})$, then so is $A \cap B$. In fact, for all sets $X$, $\mathcal{P}(X)$ is closed under $\cap$.

To define a set it is sufficient to say what its members are. Formally, sufficiency is guaranteed by one of the axioms of the mathematical theory of sets, namely the Axiom of Extensionality (footnote 2, Ch. 1), which states for all sets $A, B$

$$A = B \text{ iff for all objects } x, \ x \in A \text{ iff } x \in B.$$

From this, it follows that if $A$ and $B$ are *different* sets, then one of them has a member that the other doesn't. Also, to prove that given sets $A$ and $B$ are the same (despite possibly having very different definitions), it suffices to show that each is a subset of the other. In fact, we have

(4)    For all sets $A$, $B$, $A = B$ iff $A \subseteq B$ and $B \subseteq A$.

This is called the *antisymmetry property of the inclusion relation* $\subseteq$. Notice that the *proper* subset relation, noted $\subset$, is transitive but not antisymmetric, where we define:

**Definition 2.2.** $A$ is a *proper* subset of $B$, noted $A \subset B$, iff $A \subseteq B$ and $A \neq B$.

By the antisymmetry of $\subseteq$, if $A \subset B$ then $B \not\subseteq A$. That is, there is a $x \in B$ such that $x \notin A$. So $A \subset B$ iff $A \subseteq B$ and for some $x$, $x \in B$ and $x \notin A$.

**Terminology**    A paraphrase of $A$ *is a subset of B* is $B$ *is a superset of A*, noted $B \supseteq A$. Similarly $A$ *is a proper subset of B* means the same as $B$ *is a proper superset of A*, noted $B \supset A$. [Warning: some math texts write $A \subset B$ to mean what we mean by $A \subseteq B$, and they express proper subset by writing $A \subsetneq B$].

**Exercise 2.2.** Let $K$ be any collection of sets. What does it mean to say that $K$ is closed under union? under relative complement? Is it true that for any set $X$, $\mathcal{P}(X)$ is closed under union and relative complement?

**Exercise 2.3.** Complete the following equations:

   a.  $EVEN \cap ODD = $ _____.

   b.  $EVEN \cup ODD = $ _____.

   c.  $\mathbb{N} - EVEN = $ _____.

   d.  $(\mathbb{N} - EVEN) \cap ODD = $ _____.

   e.  $(\mathbb{N} \cap EVEN) \cap ODD = $ _____.

   f.  $(\mathbb{N} \cap EVEN) \cap \{1, 3\} = $ _____.

   g.  $\{1, 2, 3\} \cap EVEN = $ _____.

   h.  $\{1, 2, 3, 4\} \cap ODD = $ _____.

   i.  $\{1, 2, 3\} \cap (EVEN \cup ODD) = $ _____.

   j.  $(\mathbb{N} \cap \emptyset) \cup \{0\} = $ _____.

   k.  $(ODD \cup ODD) \cap ODD = $ _____.

**Exercise 2.4.** Prove each of the statements below on the pattern used in (1). Each of these statements will be generalized later when we discuss the semantic interpretation of boolean categories (not yet defined).

   a.  For all sets $A$ and $B$, $A \cap B \subseteq A$ (and also $A \cap B \subseteq B$).

   b.  For all sets $A$ and $B$, $A \subseteq A \cup B$ (and also $B \subseteq A \cup B$).

**Exercise 2.5.** Some Boolean Truths of Set Theory

   a.  *Tests for subsethood.* Prove each of the three statements below for arbitrary sets $A, B$:

      i.  $A \subseteq B$ iff $A \cap B = A$ .

      ii.  $A \subseteq B$ iff $A - B = \emptyset$

      iii.  $A \subseteq B$ iff $A \cup B = B$

   b.  *Idempotent laws.* For all sets $A$:

      i.  $A \cap A = A$

      ii.  $A \cup A = A$

   c.  *Distributivity laws.* For all sets $A, B, C$:

    i. $A \cap (B \cup C) = (A \cap B) \cup (A \cap C)$

    ii. $A \cup (B \cap C) = (A \cup B) \cap (A \cup C)$

d. *de Morgan's laws.* Writing $\neg A$ for $E - A$, where $E$ is the domain of discourse, that is, $E$ is the set of objects under discussion, of which $A$ and $B$ are understood to be subsets:

    i. $\neg(A \cap B) = (\neg A \cup \neg B)$

    ii. $\neg(A \cup B) = (\neg A \cap \neg B)$

## 2.1.1 Cardinality

We will be concerned at several points with the notion of the *cardinality* of a set. The idea here is that the cardinality of a set is a number which measures how big the set is. This "idea" is practically the definition in the case of finite sets, but to deal with infinite cardinalities one has to do a lot more work. We will not need infinite cardinals in this book at many places, so we only give the definition in the finite case and the case of a *countably infinite set.*

**Definition 2.3.** Let $S$ be a finite set. If $S = \emptyset$, then the cardinality of $S$ is 0, and we write $|S| = 0$. If $S \neq \emptyset$ then let $k$ be the unique natural number such that $S \approx \{1, 2, \ldots, k\}$. Then the cardinality of $S$ is $k$, and we write $|S| = k$. And when $S$ is infinite, if $S \approx \mathbb{N}$, the set of natural numbers, then we say that $S$ is *countably infinite* (or *denumerable*), and write, standardly, $|S| = \aleph_0$ (read "aleph zero"). $\aleph$ is the first letter of the Hebrew alphabet. This cardinal is also noted $\omega_0$ (read "omega zero"), $\omega$ being the last letter in the Greek alphabet.

Here are some (largely familiar) examples of this notation: $|\emptyset| = 0$. For $a$ any object $|\{a\}| = 1$. Similarly $|\{a, a\}| = 1$. For $a$ and $b$ distinct objects, $|\{a, b\}| = 2$. And of course $|EVEN| = \aleph_0 = |\mathbb{N}|$. We should note that there are infinite sets that are larger than $\mathbb{N}$. We have already noted (and we prove shortly) that $X \prec \mathcal{P}(X)$, where $X$ is any set and recall that $\mathcal{P}(X)$ is the set whose members are the subsets of $X$. So as a special case $\mathbb{N} \prec \mathcal{P}(\mathbb{N})$. However larger sets than $\mathbb{N}$ do not arise naturally in linguistic study.

**Exercise 2.6.**

a. Say why $|\{5, 5, 5\}| = |\{5\}|$.

b. Is $|\{5, (3 + 2)\}| = 2$? If not say why not.

c. Prove that for all sets $A, B$, if $A \subseteq B$ then $|A| \leq |B|$.

d. Exhibit a counterexample to the claim that if $A \subset B$ then $|A| < |B|$.

e. As a corollary to part c. above say why $|A \cap B| \leq |A|$ and $|A| \leq |A \cup B|$ for $A, B$ any sets. (A *corollary* to a theorem $P$ is one that follows from $P$ in a fairly obvious way.)

f. Let the set *ODD* of odd natural numbers be given by the pseudolist $\{1, 3, 5, \ldots\}$. Show that $EVEN \approx ODD$.

## 2.1.2 Notation for Defining Sets

We have already seen how to define sets by *listing*: write down names of the elements of the set separated by commas and enclose the list in curly brackets. For example $\{0, 1\}$ is a 2 element set. But definition by listing is inherently limited. You can't write down an infinite list, and even when you know the set to be defined is finite, to define it by listing each element of the set must have a name in whatever language you are writing in. In mathematical discourse this condition often fails. To be sure, in the language of arithmetic the natural numbers have names, namely '0', '1', '2', etc. But in the language of Euclidean geometry the points on the plane don't have proper names. Moreover when the set is large defining it by listing is often impractical. The set of social security numbers of American citizens could be listed but writing down the list is a poor use of our time.

We have also seen productive means of defining new sets in terms of old ones—ones that are already defined. So if we know what sets $A$ and $B$ are then we can refer to $A \cap B$, $A - B$, $A \cup B$, and $\mathcal{P}(A)$.

A last and perhaps most widely used way of defining new sets in terms of old is called (unhelpfully) definition by *abstraction*. Here, given a set $A$, we may define a subset of $A$ by considering the set of those elements of $A$ which meet any condition of interest. For example, we might define the set of even natural numbers by saying:

$$EVEN =_{df} \{n \in \mathbb{N} \mid \text{for some } m \in \mathbb{N}, n = 2m\}.$$

(In giving definitions in this format some authors write a colon : where we have written a vertical line, |. Both notations are common). We read the right hand side of this definition as "the set of $n$ in $\mathbb{N}$ which are such that for some $m$ in $\mathbb{N}$, $n$ is 2 times $m$". The definition assumes that $\mathbb{N}$ is already defined (it also assumes that multiplication is defined). More generally if $A$ is any set and $\varphi$ any formula, $\{a \in A \mid \varphi\}$ is the set of elements $a$ in $A$ of which $\varphi$ is true. So note that, trivially, $\{a \in A \mid \varphi\}$

is always a subset of $A$. $\varphi$ can be any formula, even a contradictory one. For example, consider

$$\{n \in \mathbb{N} \mid n < 5 \text{ and } n > 5\}.$$

Clearly no $n \in \mathbb{N}$ satisfies the condition of being both less than 5 and greater than 5. Still, the displayed expression defines a set, namely the empty set, $\emptyset$.

Returning to the definition of *EVEN* above, an even more succinct way of stating the definition is given by:

$$EVEN =_{df} \{2n \mid n \in \mathbb{N}\}$$

Informally this commonly used format says: "Run through the numbers $n$ in $\mathbb{N}$, for each one form the number $2n$, and consider the collection of numbers so formed. That collection is the set of even (natural) numbers."

## 2.2 Sequences

We are representing expressions in English (and language in general) as sequences of words, and we shall represent languages as sets of these sequences. Here we present some basic mathematical notation concerning sequences, notation that we use throughout this book.

Think of a sequence as a way of choosing elements from a set. A sequence of such elements is different from a set in that we keep track of the order in which the elements are chosen. And we are allowed to choose the same element many times. The number of choices we make is called the length of the sequence. For linguistic purposes we need only consider finite sequences (ones whose length is a natural number).

In list notation we denote a sequence by writing down names of the elements (or *coordinates* as they are called) of the sequence, separating them by commas, as with the list notation for sets, and enclosing the list in angled or round brackets, but never curly ones. By convention the first coordinate of the sequence is written leftmost, then comes the second coordinate, etc. For example, $\langle 2, 5, 2 \rangle$ is that sequence of length three whose first coordinate is the number two, whose second is five, and whose third is two. Note that the sequence $\langle 2, 5, 2 \rangle$ has three coordinates whereas the set $\{2, 5, 2\}$ has just two members.

A sequence of length 4 is called a 4-tuple; one of length 5 a 5-tuple, and in general a sequence of length $n$ is called an $n$-tuple, though we usually say pair or ordered pair for sequences of length 2 and (ordered) triple for sequences of length 3.

If $s$ is an $n$-ary sequence (an $n$-tuple) and $i$ is a number between 1 and $n$ inclusive (that is, $1 \leq i \leq n$) then we write $s_i$ for the $i$th coordinate of $s$. Thus $\langle 2, 5, 2 \rangle_1 = 2$, $\langle 2, 5, 2 \rangle_2 = 5$, etc[1]. If $s$ is a sequence of length $n$ then $s = \langle s_1, \ldots, s_n \rangle$. The *length* of a sequence $s$ is noted $|s|$. So $|\langle 2, 5, 2 \rangle| = 3$, $|\langle 2, 5 \rangle| = 2$, and $|\langle 2 \rangle| = 1$. The following is fundamental:

(5)  a. To define a sequence $s$ it is necessary, and sufficient, to (i) give the length $|s|$ of $s$, and (ii) say for each $i$, $1 \leq i \leq |s|$, what object $s_i$ is.

   b. Sequences $s$ and $t$ are identical iff $|s| = |t|$ and for all $i$ such that $1 \leq i \leq |s|$, $s_i = t_i$

For example, the statements in (6a,b,c,d) are all proper definitions of sequences:

(6)  a. $s$ is that sequence of length 3 whose first coordinate is the letter $c$, whose second is the letter $a$, and whose third is the letter $t$. In list notation $s = \langle c, a, t \rangle$.

   b. $t$ is that sequence of length 4 given by: $t_1 = 5$, $t_2 = 3$, $t_3 = t_2$, and $t_4 = t_1$.

   c. $u$ is that sequence of length 7 such that for all $1 \leq i \leq 7$,

$$u_i \quad = \quad \begin{cases} 3 & \text{if } i \text{ is odd} \\ 5 & \text{if } i \text{ is even} \end{cases}$$

   d. $v$ is that sequence of length 3 whose first coordinate is the word *Mary*, whose second is the word *criticized*, and whose third is the word *Bill*.

We frequently have occasion to consider sets of sequences. The following notation is standard:

**Definition 2.4.** For $A$ and $B$ sets,

a. $A \times B$ is the set of sequences $s$ of length two such that $s_1 \in A$ and $s_2 \in B$. We write

$$A \times B \quad =_{df} \quad \{\langle x, y \rangle | x \in A \text{ and } y \in B\}.$$

$A \times B$ is read "$A$ cross $B$" and called the *Cartesian product of $A$ with $B$*. Generalizing,

---

[1] In more technical literature we start counting coordinates at 0. So the first coordinate of an $n$-tuple $s$ would be noted $s_0$ and its $n$th would be noted $s_{n-1}$.

b. If $A_1, \ldots, A_k$ are sets then $A_1 \times \cdots \times A_k$ is the set of sequences $s$ of length $k$ such that for each $i$, $1 \leq i \leq k$, $s_i \in A_i$. We abbreviate $A \times A$ as $A^2$ and $A \times \cdots \times A$ ($n$ times) as $A^n$. $A^0 = \{e\}$, where $e$ is the unique (see below) sequence of length zero. $A^*$ is the set of finite sequences of elements of $A$. That is, $s \in A^*$ iff for some natural number $n$, $s \in A^n$.

$|A \times B|$, the cardinality of the set $A \times B$, is exactly the product $|A| \times |B|$. This is what accounts for the notation. We have $|A|$ many choices for the first element of a pair in $A \times B$ and $|B|$ many choices for the second. Thus we have $|A| \times |B|$ choices in toto. So $|A \times A| = |A|^2$, and more generally $|A^n| = |A|^n$.

**Exercise 2.7.**

a. Exhibit the sequences (6b,c,d) in list notation.

b. Answer the following True or False; for a false statement explain why it is false.

    a. $\langle 2, 4, 6 \rangle_2 = 2$.

    b. $|\langle 3 \rangle| > 1$.

    c. $|\langle 3, 3, 3 \rangle| = 3$.

    d. for some $i$ between 1 and 3 inclusive, $\langle c, a, t \rangle_i = b$.

    e. for some $i < j$ between 1 and 3 inclusive, $\langle c, a, t \rangle_i = \langle c, a, t \rangle_j$.

c. Let $A = \{a, b, c\}$ and $B = \{1, 2\}$. Exhibit the following sets in list notation:

    i. $A \times B$.

    ii. $B \times A$.

    iii. $B \times B$.

    iv. $B \times (A \times B)$.

Note that a sequence of length zero has no coordinates. And from (5b) there cannot be two different sequences both of length zero since they have the same length and do not differ at any coordinate. Moreover,

(7)    There is a sequence of length zero, called the empty sequence, often noted $e$. (Sometimes it is noted $\epsilon$, occasionally $\lambda$; we will use $e$.)

One widely used binary operation on sequences is *concatenation*, noted $\frown$. (Other notations for concatenation include $+$ and even $-$. Frequently the symbol for concatenation is omitted entirely.)

**Definition 2.5.** If $s$ is a sequence $\langle s_1, \ldots, s_n \rangle$ of length $n$ and $t$ a sequence $\langle t_1, \ldots, t_m \rangle$ of length $m$ then $s \frown t$ is that sequence of length $n + m$ whose first $n$ coordinates are those of $s$ and whose next $m$ coordinates are those of $t$. That is, $s \frown t =_{df} \langle s_1, \ldots, s_n, t_1, \ldots, t_m \rangle$.

For example, $\langle 3, 2 \rangle \frown \langle 5, 4, 3 \rangle = \langle 3, 2, 5, 4, 3 \rangle$. Similarly, we have that $\langle 1 \rangle \frown \langle 1 \rangle = \langle 1, 1 \rangle$.

Observe that concatenation is *associative*:

(8) $\quad (s \frown t) \frown u = s \frown (t \frown u)$.

For example, (9a) = (9b):

(9) $\quad$ a. $(\langle 3, 4 \rangle \frown \langle 5, 6, 7 \rangle) \frown \langle 8, 9 \rangle = \langle 3, 4, 5, 6, 7 \rangle \frown \langle 8, 9 \rangle = \langle 3, 4, 5, 6, 7, 8, 9 \rangle$

$\quad$ b. $\langle 3, 4 \rangle \frown (\langle 5, 6, 7 \rangle \frown \langle 8, 9 \rangle) = \langle 3, 4 \rangle \frown \langle 5, 6, 7, 8, 9 \rangle = \langle 3, 4, 5, 6, 7, 8, 9 \rangle$

So as with intersection, union, addition, etc. we omit parentheses and write simply $s \frown t \frown u$. But note that in distinction to $\cap$ and $\cup$, concatenation is not commutative. (This means when we concatenate two items, the order matters.)

$$\langle 0 \rangle \frown \langle 1 \rangle = \langle 0, 1 \rangle \neq \langle 1, 0 \rangle = \langle 1 \rangle \frown \langle 0 \rangle.$$

The empty sequence $e$ exhibits a distinctive behavior with respect to concatenation. Since $e$ adds no coordinates to anything it is concatenated with we have:

(10) For all sequences $s$, $s \frown e = e \frown s = s$.

The role that $e$ plays with regard to $\frown$ is like that which 0 plays with regard to addition ($n + 0 = 0 + n = n$) and the $\emptyset$ plays with regard to union ($A \cup \emptyset = \emptyset \cup A = A$). $e$ is called an *identity element* (sometimes a *neutral* element) with respect to concatenation, just as 0 is an identity element with respect to addition and $\emptyset$ an identity element with respect to union.

Note that just as sets can be elements of other sets, so sequences can be coordinates of other sequences. For example the sequence $s = \langle 4, \langle 3, 5, 8 \rangle \rangle$ is a sequence of length 2. Its first coordinate is the number 4, is second a sequence of length 3: $\langle 3, 5, 8 \rangle$. That is, $s_1 = 4$ and $s_2 = \langle 3, 5, 8 \rangle$. Observe:

(11)     a. $|\langle j, o, h, n, c, r, i, e, d\rangle| = 9$

         b. $|\langle\langle j, o, h, n\rangle, \langle c, r, i, e, d\rangle\rangle| = 2$

(11a) is a 9-tuple of English letters. (11b) is a sequence of length 2, each of whose coordinates is a sequence of letters. If we call these latter sequences words then (11b) is a two coordinate sequence of words, that is, an (ordered) pair of words.

**Exercise 2.8.** Answer True or False to each statement below. If False, say why.

a. $|\langle c, a, t\rangle| < |\langle\langle e, v, e, r, y\rangle, \langle c, a, t\rangle\rangle|$.

b. $|\langle a, b, a\rangle| = |\langle b, a\rangle|$.

c. $|\langle 0, 0, 0\rangle| < |\langle 1000\rangle|$.

d. $|\langle 2, 3, 4\rangle \frown e| > |\langle 1, 1, 1\rangle|$.

e. for all finite sequences $s$, $t$, $s \frown t = t \frown s$.

f. $\langle 2 + 1, 32\rangle = \langle 3, 23\rangle$.

g. For all finite sequences $s$, $t$,

    i. $|s \frown t| = |s| + |t|$; and

    ii. $|s \frown t| = |t \frown s|$.

**Exercise 2.9.** Compute stepwise the concatenations in (a) and (b) below, observing that they yield the same result, as predicted by the associativity of concatenation.

a. $(\langle a, b\rangle \frown \langle b, c, d\rangle) \frown \langle b, a\rangle$

b. $\langle a, b\rangle \frown (\langle b, c, d\rangle \frown \langle b, a\rangle)$

**Exercise 2.10.** Fill in the blanks below, taking $s$ to be $\langle 0, \langle 0, 1\rangle, \langle 0, \langle 0, 1\rangle\rangle\rangle$.

a. $s_1 =$ _____

b. $s_2 =$ _____

c. $(s_2)_2 =$ _____

d. $s_3 =$ _____

e. $(s_3)_2 =$ _____

f. $((s_3)_2)_1 =$ _____

**Subsequences** A sequence $s$ is a *prefix* of a sequence $t$ iff there is a sequence $u$, possibly empty, such that $s \frown u = t$. For example, the prefixes of $t = \langle 2, 4, 5, 1 \rangle$ are $\epsilon$ (the empty sequence), $\langle 2 \rangle$, $\langle 2, 4 \rangle$, $\langle 2, 4, 5 \rangle$ and $\langle 2, 4, 5, 1 \rangle$. We say that $s$ is a *proper prefix* of $t$ iff $s$ is a prefix of $t$ and $s \neq t$.

**Exercise 2.11.**

1. Prove that $s$ is a proper prefix of $t$ iff there is a non-empty sequence $u$ such that $s \frown u = t$.

2. Complete correctly the following definitions:

    a. $s$ is a *suffix* of $t$ iff _____

    b. $s$ is a *proper suffix* of $t$ iff _____

**Caveat** In linguistics, *prefix* and *suffix* are used with stronger meanings. A prefix is an initial segment as above, but which has a meaning, one that is used when the prefix combines with different bases. Thus *re* is a prefix of *rewrite*, but *r*, *rew*, and *rewr* are not. And *re* occurs with the meaning "repeat the action" in *rebuild*, *rethink*, *rework*, etc. But *re* is not a (linguistic) prefix of *read*, *reel*, or *repeat*. □

Returning to mathematical usage, the term *substring* is used for contiguous subsequences of a sequence. Formally: $s$ is a substring of $t$ iff there are strings $u$, $v$ such that $t = u \frown s \frown v$. We leave the definition of *proper substring* to the reader. $\langle 4, 5, 1 \rangle$ is a proper substring of $\langle 2, 4, 5, 1, 7, 5 \rangle$, $\langle 4, 5, 7 \rangle$ is not. *read* is a proper substring of *unreadable* (which has an *un* prefix and an *able* suffix).

Prefixing and suffixing are commonly used morphological processes in word formation in natural languages. Proper infixing is less common but nonetheless well attested in some language families. Thus in Tagalog (Philippines, W. Austronesian) from the root sampal 'action of hitting/slapping' we infix *um* after the initial consonant to form an active verb *sumampal* 'hits' and we infix *in* there to form a kind of passive *sinampal* 'is hit by'. See Spencer (1991, 12).

Substrings are a special case of subsequences, but the latter term has a slightly broader usage, covering cases of sequences of non-contiguous elements. Thus $\langle 2, 4, 2 \rangle$ is a subsequence of $\langle 7, 2, 9, 4, 6, 3, 2, 5 \rangle$. In comparing strands of DNA, represented as sequences of the four letters G, C, T, A for the nucleotides that compose it, their similarity is determined by the number of subsequences, not just the substrings, they share.

Do natural languages have word formation processes analogous to affixation (prefixation, suffixation, infixation) but using proper subsequences? A reasonable case here is Semitic languages (Hebrew, Arabic, Amharic) in which alternations of pairs of vowels within a triconsonantal root indicate many different classes of verbs. For example in Hebrew *Hu katav* = 'He wrote' and *Hu kotev* = 'He writes/is writing'. It is the difference in the subsequences $\langle \dots a \dots a \dots \rangle$ vs $\langle \dots o \dots e \dots \rangle$ that codes the tense difference.

## 2.3 Functions and Sequences

We have seen that a function $f$ from a set $A$ into a set $B$ associates with each $\alpha \in A$ a unique object $f(\alpha)$ in $B$. $f(\alpha)$, recall, is called the value of the function $f$ at the argument $\alpha$. If $A$ was a small set whose members had names we could define $f$ just by listing the objects $\alpha$ in $A$ and next to each we note the object in $B$ that $f$ maps $\alpha$ to, namely $f(\alpha)$. Suppose for example that $A$ is the set $\{1, 2, 3\}$ and $B$ is the set $\{1, 4, 9\}$ and that $f(1) = 1$, $f(2) = 4$, and $f(3) = 9$. Then we could define this $f$ just by listing pairs (sequences of length 2).

(12)  $f = \{\langle 1, 1 \rangle, \langle 2, 4 \rangle, \langle 3, 9 \rangle\}$

In this way we think of a function $f$ from $A$ into $B$ as a particular subset of $A \times B$, namely $f = \{\langle \alpha, f(\alpha) \rangle \mid \alpha \in A\}$. So we represent $f$ as a set of sequences of length 2. This set of pairs is called the *graph* of $f$. Consider the squaring function $SQ$ from $\mathbb{N}$ to $\mathbb{N}$. $SQ(n) =_{df} n \cdot n$, all $n \in \mathbb{N}$. (Usually $SQ(n)$ is noted $n^2$). The domain, $\mathbb{N}$, of $SQ$ is infinite, and the graph of $SQ$ is given in (13).

(13)  $SQ = \{\langle n, SQ(n) \rangle \mid n \in \mathbb{N}\}$

We could even *define* a function $F$ from a set $A$ into a set $B$ as a subset of $A \times B$ meeting the condition that for every $\alpha \in A$ there is exactly one $\beta \in B$ such that $\langle \alpha, \beta \rangle \in F$. As long as $F$ meets this condition then we can define $F(\alpha)$ to be the unique $\beta$ such that $\langle \alpha, \beta \rangle \in F$. This is what it means to say that $\beta$ is given as a function ($F$) of $\alpha$.

**Some Terminology.** A two-place function $g$ from $A$ into $B$ is a function from $A \times A$ into $B$. So such a $g$ maps each pair $\langle \alpha, \alpha' \rangle$ of objects from $A$ to a unique element of $B$. More generally an $n$-place function from $A$ into $B$ is a function from $A^n$ into $B$. We use the phraseology "$n$-place function on $A$" to refer to a function from $A^n$ into $A$. For example the addition function is a 2-place function on $\mathbb{N}$. It maps each pair $\langle n, m \rangle$ of natural numbers to the number $(n + m)$. Notice here that in writing traditional expressions we tend to write the function symbol, '+' in this case, between its two arguments.

The illustrative functions on numbers utilized so far used are defined in terms of addition, multiplication, and exponentiation. But several of the ones we used earlier to describe syntactic structure were defined in a non-trivial *recursive* way. Namely the values at small arguments were given explicitly (by listing) and then their values at larger arguments were defined in terms of their values at lesser arguments. Recall for example the function $F$ from $\mathbb{N}$ into the set of English expressions as follows:

(14)    a. $F(0) = $ *the President* and for all $n > 0$,

    b. $F(n) = \langle the \frown mother \frown of \frown F(n-1) \rangle$

So we compute that $F(2) = $ *the mother of* $F(1) = $ *the mother of the mother of* $F(0) = $ *the mother of the mother of the President*. Recursive functions of this sort are widely used in computer science. Here are two household examples, the *factorial* function **Fact** and the *Fibonacci* function **Fib**, both from $\mathbb{N}$ into $\mathbb{N}$:

(15)    a. **Fact**$(0) = 1$ and for all $n > 0$, **Fact**$(n) = n\cdot$**Fact**$(n-1)$
    (**Fact**$(n)$ is usually denoted $n!$ and read $n$ *factorial*).

    b. **Fib**$(0) = 1$, **Fib**$(1) = 1$, and for all $n > 1$,
    **Fib**$(n) = $ **Fib**$(n-1)+$**Fib**$(n-2)$.

In defining the Fibonacci sequence **Fib** above we gave its value explicitly at both 0 and 1, and then defined later values in terms of the two previous values. You might use a similar (not identical) tack in the following exercise:

**Exercise 2.12.** Let $K$ be the following set of informally given expressions:
$K = \{$a whisky lover, a whisky lover hater,
    a whisky lover hater lover, a whiskey lover hater lover hater, ...$\}$
Note that the "-er" words at the end of each expression alternate between 'lover' and 'hater'. For example, 'a whiskey lover lover' is not in the set, nor is 'a whiskey hater lover', etc. Define a one to one function from $\mathbb{N}$ onto $K$.

**Bijections.** When we define a function $F$ from some $A$ into some $B$ we specify $B$ as the codomain of $F$. The *range* of $F$, Ran$(F)$, is by definition the set of values $F$ can take, that is, $\{F(\alpha) \mid \alpha \in A\}$. If Ran$(F) = B$ then $F$ is said to be *onto* $B$ and is called *surjective* (or a *surjection*). If in addition $F$ is one-to-one (injective, an injection) then $F$ is *bijective* (a *bijection*). A *bijection* from a set $A$ to itself is called a *permutation* of $A$. In general bijections play a fundamental role in defining what we mean by *sameness* of structure. But for the moment we just consider two examples.

(16)  Let $H$ be that function from $\{a, b, c, d\}$ into itself given by the table below:

| $x$ | $a$ | $b$ | $c$ | $d$ |
|------|------|------|------|------|
| $H(x)$ | $b$ | $c$ | $d$ | $a$ |

So $H(a) = b$, $H(b) = c$, $H(c) = d$, and $H(d) = a$. Clearly $H$ is both one-to-one and onto, so $H$ is a permutation of $\{a, b, c, d\}$. Suppose we think of $a$ as the upper left hand corner of a square, $b$ as the lower left hand corner, $c$ as the lower right hand corner, and $d$ as the upper right hand corner. Then H would represent a 90 degree rotation counter-clockwise.

As a second example, define a function $\neg$ from $\mathcal{P}(\{a, b, c\})$ to itself as follows: for all subsets $A$ of $\{a, b, c\}$, $\neg(A) = \{a, b, c\} - A$.

**Exercise 2.13.** Exhibit the table of $\neg$ defined above. (So you must list the subsets of $\{a, b, c\}$—there are 8 of them—and next to each give its value under $\neg$.)

We will have much more to say about bijections in later chapters, but first we generalize the set theoretic operations of intersection and union in useful ways.

## 2.4   Arbitrary Unions and Intersections

Suppose we have a bunch of sets (we don't care how many). Then the *union* of the bunch is just that set whose members are the things in at least one of the sets in the bunch. And the *intersection* of the bunch is the set of objects that lie in each set in the bunch (if no object meets that condition then the intersection of the bunch is just the empty set). Let us state this now a little more carefully.

Given a domain (or universe) $E$ of objects under study, let $K$ be any set whose members are subsets of $E$. In such a case we call $K$ a *family* (or *collection*) of subsets of $E$. Then we define:

(17)     a. $\bigcup K =_{df} \{x \in E \mid \text{for some } A \in K, x \in A\}$

          b. $\bigcap K =_{df} \{x \in E \mid \text{for all } A \in K, x \in A\}$

$\bigcup K$ is read "union $K$" and $\bigcap K$ is read "intersect $K$".

Here is an example. Let $E$ be $\mathbb{N}$. Let $K$ be the collection of subsets of $\mathbb{N}$ which have 5 as a member. Then $\{5\} \in K$, $ODD \in K$, $\mathbb{N} \in K$, and $\{3, 5, 7\} \in K$. But $\emptyset \notin K$, nor are $EVEN$ or $\{n \in \mathbb{N} \mid n > 7\}$.

If $K$ is a finite collection of sets, say $K = \{A_1, A_2, A_3, A_4, A_5\}$, then $\bigcup K$ might be noted with a notation such as $\bigcup_{1 \le i \le 5} A_i$. We would even be likely to write simply $A_1 \cup \cdots \cup A_5$. In cases such as this the set $K$ is called an *indexed* family of sets. In this example the index set is $\{1, 2, 3, 4, 5\}$. We often use letters like $I$ and $J$ for arbitrary index sets, and when say "Let $K$ be an indexed family of sets" we mean that for some set $I$, $K = \{A_i \mid i \in I\}$. And now arbitrary unions and intersections are noted $\bigcup_{i \in I} A_i$ and $\bigcap_{i \in I} A_i$. Writing out their definitions explicitly we have:

(18)  a. $\bigcup_{i \in I} A_i =_{df} \{x \in E \mid \text{for some } i \in I, x \in A_i\}$

  b. $\bigcap_{i \in I} A_i =_{df} \{x \in E \mid \text{for all } i \in I, x \in A_i\}$

When the index set $I$ is clear from context (or unimportant) we just write $\bigcup_i A_i$ and $\bigcap_i A_i$.

## 2.5  Definitions by Closure (Recursion)

Many of our definitions of linguistic sets will use this format. There are several different ways of formulating this type of definition in the literature. The one we opt for here is not the most succinct but is the best for understanding the core idea behind the definitional technique. We present a second, very useful variant, in an Addendum to this chapter.

**Definition 2.6.** Given a set $A$, a function $f$ from $A$ into $A$, and a subset $K$ of $A$, we define the *closure of $K$ under $f$*, noted $\mathrm{Cl}_f(K)$, as follows:

  a. Set $K_0 = K$ and for all $n \in \mathbb{N}$, $K_{n+1} = K_n \cup \{f(x) \mid x \in K_n\}$.

  b. $\mathrm{Cl}_f(K) =_{df} \{x \in A \mid \text{for some } n, x \in K_n\}$. That is, $\mathrm{Cl}_f(K) = \bigcup_n K_n$.

So the idea is that we start with some given set $K$ and add in all the things we can get by applying $f$ to elements of $K$. That gives us $K_1$. Then repeat this process, obtaining $K_2$, and then continue ad infinitum. The result is all the things you can get starting with the elements of $K$ and applying the function any finite number of times. In the linguistic cases of interest $K$ will be a lexicon for a language and $f$ (actually there may be several $f$) will be the structure building functions that start with lexical items and construct more complex expressions. Here are two simple examples.

**Example 1.** Let $V = \{a, b\}$, $f$ a map from $V^*$ into $V^*$ defined by: $f(s) = a \frown s \frown b$, and $K = \{ab\}$. (Here we write simply $ab$ for the sequence $\langle a, b \rangle$; for sequences of symbols we often omit the commas and angled brackets). Then $K_0 = \{ab\}$, $K_1 = \{ab, aabb\}$, $K_2 = \{ab, aabb, aaabbb\}$, etc. Then provably $\mathrm{Cl}_f(\{ab\}) = \{a^n b^n \mid n > 0\}$.

**Example 2.** Let $V = \{a, b\}$, and let Copy be a function from $V^*$ to $V^*$ given by $\mathrm{Copy}(s) = s \frown s$, and $K = \{b\}$. Then $K_0 = \{b\}$, $K_1 = \{b, bb\}$, $K_2 = \{b, bb, bbbb\}$, etc., and $\mathrm{Cl}_{\mathrm{Copy}}(\{b\}) = \{b^{2^n} \mid n \in \mathbb{N}\}$.

A fundamental theorem concerning definitions by closure is given in Theorem 2.1.

**Theorem 2.1.** *For all functions $f$ and sets $K$, $Cl_f(K)$ has the following three properties:*

a. $K \subseteq Cl_f(K)$,

b. $Cl_f(K)$ *is closed under $f$. That is, whenever $x \in Cl_f(K)$ then $f(x) \in Cl_f(K)$, and*

c. *if $M$ is any set which includes $K$ and is closed under $f$ then $Cl_f(K) \subseteq M$. (This is what we mean when we call $Cl_f(K)$ the* least *set that includes $K$ and is closed under $f$.)*

**Fact.** $\mathbb{N}$ is the closure of $\{0\}$ under $+1$, the addition of 1 function. So if $M$ is a set with $0 \in M$ and $M$ is closed under addition of 1 then $M$ contains all the natural numbers. So to show that all numbers have some property $\varphi$ we just let $M$ be the set of numbers with $\varphi$ and show that $0 \in M$ and $M$ is closed under $+1$. This is usually called the *Principle of Induction*.

Definition by Closure as given above generalizes in several largely obvious ways. It makes obvious sense to form the closure of a set under several functions, not just one, and the functions need not be unary. We may naturally speak of the closure of a set of numbers under multiplication for example. An only slightly less obvious generalization concerns closure under partial functions, a case which arises very frequently in linguistic study.

**Definition 2.7.** A *partial function* $f$ from $A$ to $B$ is a function whose domain is a subset of $A$ and whose codomain is included in $B$.

For example, a function whose domain was the set of even numbers which mapped each one to its square would be a partial function from $\mathbb{N}$ to $\mathbb{N}$.

In defining closure under partial functions we need a slight addition to the definition of $K_{n+1}$ as follows: $K_{n+1} = K_n \cup \{f(x) \mid x \in K_n \text{ and } x \in \text{Dom}(f)\}$.

**Exercise 2.14.**

a. Let Sq be that function from $\mathbb{N}$ to $\mathbb{N}$ given by: $\text{Sq}(n) = n \cdot n$.

    i. Set $K = \{2\}$. Exhibit $K_1$, $K_2$, and $K_3$. Say in words what $\text{Cl}_{\text{Sq}}(\{2\})$ is.

    ii. Do the same with $K = \{1\}$.

    iii. Do the same with $K = \emptyset$. Is $\emptyset$ closed under Sq?

    iv. What is $\text{Cl}_{\text{Sq}}(EVEN)$.

b. Consider the set $V = \{P, Q, R, \&, \text{not}, ), (, \}$.

    i. Define a unary function NEG : $V^* \to V^*$ which prefixes 'not' to each $s \in V^*$.

    ii. Define a binary function AND which maps each pair $\langle s, t \rangle$ of elements of $V^*$ to the sequence consisting of a left parenthesis, then $s$, then the symbol $\&$, then $t$, and finally a right parenthesis.

Note that AND and NEG are functions defined on $V^*$ and so apply to any strings over that vocabulary. For example,

$$
\begin{array}{llll}
\text{NEG}(\&\&Q) & = \text{not}\frown\&\&Q & = \text{not}\&\&Q \\
\text{NEG}(\text{not}\&((P) & = \text{not}\frown\text{not}\&((P & = \text{notnot}\&((P \\
\text{AND}(\text{NEG}(RRR), \text{not}) & = (\text{NEG}(RRR)\frown\&\frown\text{not}) & = (\text{not}RRR\&\text{not})
\end{array}
$$

The functions must be defined independently of the set we form the closure of.

**Exercise 2.15.** This exercise is a continuation of the previous one, so you should use your definitions of NEG and AND. Write AF ("atomic formula") for $\{P, Q, R\}$. So $\text{AF}_0$ is $\{P, Q, R\}$. Let $C$ be the closure of AF under NEG and AND.

a. What is the least $n$ such that NEG($P$ & NEG($Q$)) is in $\text{AF}_n$?

  b. Give an explicit argument that NEG($P$ & NEG($Q$)) $\in C$. Your argument might begin: $Q \in \text{AF}_0$. So NEG($Q$) $\in \text{AF}_1$, ...

  c. Prove that for all $\varphi \in C$, the number of parentheses occurring in $\varphi$ is even. Here is how to set up the proof:
  Let

$$M \;=\; \{\varphi \in C : \text{the number of parentheses in } \varphi \text{ is even}\}$$

  Step 1: Show that AF $\subseteq M$.
  Step 2: Show that $M$ is closed under NEG and AND.

**Exercise 2.16.** Prove that for all sets $A$, $\bigcup \mathcal{P}(A) = A$.

   We conclude this chapter by stating and proving a fundamental theorem in set theory due to Georg Cantor in the late 1800s. For the linguistic material covered in subsequent chapters of this book it is not necessary to understand the proof of this theorem. But it is one of the foundational theorems in set theory, and our brief introduction actually gives us (almost) enough to follow the proof, so we give it here. The basic claim of the theorem is that *any* set is strictly smaller than its power set. So forming power sets is one way of forming new sets from old that always leads to bigger sets. In presenting the properly formal version of the theorem we do need to assume the Schröder-Bernstein Theorem mentioned earlier and stated more rigorously here (we give a proof at the end of Chapter 9):

**Theorem 2.2** (Schröder-Bernstein). *For all sets $A, B$, $A \approx B$ iff there is a bijection from $A$ to $B$.*

   (Our original definition of $\approx$ just says there is an injection from $A$ to $B$ *and* an injection from $B$ to $A$.)

**Theorem 2.3** (Cantor). *For all sets $A$, $A \prec \mathcal{P}(A)$.*

   You might try a few simple examples to see that the theorem holds for them. For example, $\emptyset \prec \mathcal{P}(\emptyset) = \{\emptyset\}$ since $|\emptyset| = 0$ and $|\{\emptyset\}| = 1$. Similarly $\{a\} \prec \mathcal{P}(\{a\}) = \{\emptyset, \{a\}\}$, as $\{a\}$ has one element, $\mathcal{P}(\{a\})$ has 2. If $A$ has just 2 elements then $\mathcal{P}(A)$ has 4 elements. If $A$ has just 3 elements $\mathcal{P}(A)$ has 8. In general for $A$ finite with $n$ elements, how many elements does $\mathcal{P}(A)$ have?
   We now prove theorem 2.3.

*Proof.* Let $A$ be an arbitrary set. We show that $A \prec \mathcal{P}(A)$. First we show that $A \preceq \mathcal{P}(A)$. Clearly the function $f$ mapping each element

$\alpha$ in $A$ to $\{\alpha\}$ is a map from $A$ into $\mathcal{P}(A)$ which is one to one. Thus $A \preceq \mathcal{P}(A)$.

Now we show that there is no surjection from $A$ to $\mathcal{P}(A)$. From this it follows that there is no bijection from $A$ to $\mathcal{P}(A)$. By Schroeder-Bernstein then $A \not\approx B$. Thus $A \prec \mathcal{P}(A)$.

Let $h$ be an arbitrary function from $A$ into $\mathcal{P}(A)$. We show that $h$ is not onto. For each $x \in A$, $h(x) \subseteq A$, so it makes sense to ask whether $x \in h(x)$ or not. Let us write $K$ for $\{x \in A \mid x \notin h(x)\}$. Trivially $K \subseteq A$, so $K \in \mathcal{P}(A)$. We show that for every $\alpha \in A$, $h(\alpha) \neq K$, whence we will infer that $h$ is not onto. Suppose, leading to a contradiction, that there is an $\alpha$ in $A$ such that $h(\alpha) = K$. Then either $\alpha \in K$ or $\alpha \notin K$ (this is a logical truth). If $\alpha \in K$ then since $\alpha \in A$ we infer by the defining condition for $K$ that $\alpha \notin h(\alpha)$. But $h(\alpha)$ is $K$, so we have a contradiction: $\alpha \in K$ and $\alpha \notin K$. Thus the assumption that $\alpha \in K$ is false. So $\alpha \notin K$. But again since $h(\alpha) = K$ then $\alpha \notin h(\alpha)$ and since $\alpha \in A$, $\alpha$ satisfies the condition for being in $h(\alpha)$. And since $h(\alpha) = K$ we infer that $\alpha \in K$, contradicting that $\alpha \notin K$. Thus the assumption that there is an $\alpha$ such that $h(\alpha) = K$ is false. So for all $\alpha$, $h(\alpha) \neq K$. Thus $h$ is not onto. Since $h$ was an arbitrary function from $A$ into $\mathcal{P}(A)$ we have that all such $h$ fail to be onto. Thus $A \not\approx B$, so $A \prec \mathcal{P}(A)$ completing the proof. $\qquad\square$

**Corollary 2.4.** $\mathbb{N} \prec \mathcal{P}(\mathbb{N})$.

This follows immediately as a special case of Cantor's Theorem.

Now let us define the following infinite sequence $H$ of sets:

(19)  $H(0) =_{df} \mathbb{N}$ and for all $n$, $H(n+1) =_{df} \mathcal{P}(H(n))$.

Thus we have an infinite sequence of increasingly large infinite sets:

(20)  $\mathbb{N} \prec \mathcal{P}(\mathbb{N}) \prec \mathcal{P}(\mathcal{P}(\mathbb{N})) \prec \cdots$.

## 2.6  Bijections and the Sizes of Cross Products

Cantor's power set theorem shows that forming power sets always leads to bigger sets, since $A \prec \mathcal{P}(A)$, for all sets $A$. It is natural to wonder whether there are other operations that always lead to bigger sets. Here are two natural candidates (neither of which works, but this is not obvious without proof).

First if $A$ and $B$ are disjoint, non-empty finite sets then $A \prec A \cup B$ and $B \prec A \cup B$. So union looks like it leads to larger sets, but this fails when $A$ or $B$ are infinite. Consider first a near trivial case: Let $A = \{a\} \cup \mathbb{N} = \{a, 0, 1, \ldots\}$. Consider the mapping in (21b), indicated informally in (21a):

(21)   a.

| $x$ | $=$ | $a$ | 0 | 1 | $\cdots$ |
|---|---|---|---|---|---|
| $F(x)$ | $=$ | 0 | 1 | 2 | $\cdots$ |

b. Define $F : A \to \mathbb{N}$ by setting $F(a) = 0$ and for all natural numbers $n$, $F(n) = n + 1$.

It is easy to see that $F$ is a bijection from $A$ into $\mathbb{N}$, thus $A \approx \mathbb{N}$ by the Schroeder-Bernstein Theorem. Still, we may wonder if the union of two disjoint infinite sets leads to sets bigger than either of those we take the union over. Again the answer is no. Here is simple, non-trivial, case:

(22)   Set $\mathbb{N}^+ = \{1, 2, \ldots\}$ and $\mathbb{N}^- = \{-1, -2, \ldots\}$. Then $\mathbb{N} \approx \mathbb{N}^+ \cup \mathbb{N}^-$. Elements of $\mathbb{N}^+$ are called *positive integers* and elements of $\mathbb{N}^-$ are *negative integers*.

A bijection from $\mathbb{N}^+ \cup \mathbb{N}^-$ into $\mathbb{N}$ is informally sketched in (23a) and given formally in (23b):

(23)   a.

| 1 | $-1$ | 2 | $-2$ | 3 | $-3$ | $\cdots$ |
|---|---|---|---|---|---|---|
| $\downarrow$ | $\downarrow$ | $\downarrow$ | $\downarrow$ | $\downarrow$ | $\downarrow$ | |
| 1 | 2 | 3 | 4 | 5 | 6 | $\cdots$ |

b. Define $F$ from $\mathbb{N}^+ \cup \mathbb{N}^-$ into $\mathbb{N}$ by:

$$F(n) = \begin{cases} 2n - 1 & \text{if } n \text{ is positive} \\ -2n & \text{if } n \text{ is negative.} \end{cases}$$

Clearly $F$ is one to one, and is in fact onto. So $\mathbb{N}^+ \cup \mathbb{N}^- \approx \mathbb{N}$. Thus taking (finite) unions does not always increase size—indeed when $A$ and $B$ are infinite $A \cup B$ has the same size as the larger of $A, B$ (that is, $A \cup B \approx A$ if $B \preceq A$, otherwise $A \cup B \approx B$).

Does forming cross products produce sets larger than the ones we form the product from? Certainly for $A$ and $B$ finite sets each with at least two elements $A \prec A \times B$ and $B \prec A \times B$ since $|A \times B| = |A| \cdot |B|$. But what about the infinite case? It doesn't seem silly to think that there are more pairs of natural numbers than natural numbers. After all, each natural number is paired with infinitely many others in forming $\mathbb{N} \times \mathbb{N}$, and there are infinitely many such sets of pairs in $\mathbb{N} \times \mathbb{N}$. But again it turns out that $\mathbb{N} \times \mathbb{N} \approx \mathbb{N}$, though it is harder to see than in the case of unions. (24a) gives an explicit bijection from $\mathbb{N} \times \mathbb{N}$ to $\mathbb{N}$, and (24b) provides a pictorial representation illustrating the bijection (Büchi, 1989, p. 22; Enderton, 1977, p. 130).

(24)   a. Define $F : \mathbb{N} \times \mathbb{N} \to \mathbb{N}$ by
$$F(x, y) = x + (x + y + 1)(x + y)/2.$$

b.

| | | 0 | 1 | 2 | 3 | 4 | 5 | $\cdots$ |
|---|---|---|---|---|---|---|---|---|
| | 0 | 0 | 2 | 5 | 9 | 14 | 20 | $\cdots$ |
| | 1 | 1 | 4 | 8 | 13 | 19 | | |
| | 2 | 3 | 7 | 12 | 18 | | | |
| $y$ | 3 | 6 | 11 | 17 | | | | |
| | 4 | 10 | 16 | | | | | |
| | 5 | 15 | | | | | | |
| | $\vdots$ | $\vdots$ | | | | | | |

We close this section by noting three basic characteristics of bijections, ones that arise often in formal studies. First, for any set $A$, let us define a function $\mathrm{Id}_A$ from $A$ to $A$ by:

(25)  For all $\alpha \in A$, $\mathrm{Id}_A(\alpha) = \alpha$.

$\mathrm{id}_A$ is the *identity* function on $A$. It is clearly a bijection. Second, for $A, B, C$ arbitrary sets,

(26)  If $h$ is a bijection from $A$ to $B$ then $h^{-1}$ (read: "$h$ inverse") is a bijection from $B$ to $A$, where for all $\alpha \in A$, all $\beta \in B$,

$$h^{-1}(\beta) = \alpha \text{ iff } h(\alpha) = \beta.$$

In other words, $h^{-1}$ maps each $\beta$ in $B$ to the unique $\alpha$ in $A$ which $h$ maps to $\beta$. (There is such an $\alpha$ because $h$ is onto, and there isn't more than one because $h$ is one to one). So $h^{-1}$ just runs $h$ backwards. The domain of $h^{-1}$ is $B$, $h^{-1}$ maps distinct $\beta$ and $\beta'$ to distinct $\alpha$ and $\alpha'$ in $A$ (otherwise $h$ would not even be a function) so $h^{-1}$ is one to one, and finally $h^{-1}$ is onto since for each $\alpha$ in $A$ there is a $\beta$ in $B$ such that $h^{-1}(\beta) = \alpha$. And thirdly,

(27)  Given a bijection $f$ from $A$ to $B$ and a bijection $g$ from $B$ to $C$ we define a bijection noted $g \circ f$ (read: "$g$ compose $f$") from $A$ to $C$ as follows: for all $\alpha \in A$,

$$(g \circ f)(\alpha) = g(f(\alpha)).$$

Clearly $g \circ f$ is one to one: if $\alpha \neq \alpha'$ then $f(\alpha) \neq f(\alpha')$ since $f$ is one to one, thus $(g \circ f)(\alpha) = g(f(\alpha)) \neq g(f(\alpha')) = (g \circ f)(\alpha')$. And since $f$

is onto, the range of $f$ is all of $B$, and since $g$ is onto the range of $g \circ f$ is all of $C$, so $g \circ f$ is onto, whence $g \circ f$ is a bijection.

So far we have just used bijections to show that two sets are the same size. Deeper uses arise later in showing the different mathematical structures are isomorphic. Even here these definitions allow us to draw a few conclusions that reassure us that we have provided a reasonable characterization of "has the same size as". For one, if $A \approx B$, i.e. there is a bijection $h$ from $A$ into $B$, then $h^{-1}$ is a bijection from $B$ into $A$, so we infer that $B$ has the same size as $A$. If our mathematical definition of *has the same size as* allowed that some $A$ had the same size as some $B$ but did not support the inference that $B$ had the same size as $A$ then our mathematical definition would have failed to capture our pretheoretical notion. Similarly the fact that the composition of two bijections is a bijection assures us that if $A$ has the same size as $B$, and $B$ the same size as $C$, then $A$ has the same size as $C$.

**Some Notation and Terminology**

1. As already noted, a set of the same size as $\mathbb{N}$ is said to be *denumerable*. A set which can be put in a one to one correspondence with a subset of $\mathbb{N}$ is called *countable*. So countable sets are either finite or denumerable. When a countable set is denumerable we tend to say it is *countably infinite*.

2. We often abbreviate the statement $x \in A$ and $y \in A$ by $x, y \in A$. And we abbreviate $A \subseteq X$ and $B \subseteq X$ by $A, B \subseteq X$.

## 2.7 A Linguistic Function

We close this chapter by illustrating a linguistic function that is not directly mathematical in character. We will call the function RPL (for Regular Plural). We assume given a list of *singular count nouns* in English – *cat, dog, witch*, etc. used to name collections of objects we can count. Such nouns have *plural* forms, often given *orthographically* (= in the written language) by appending an –*(e)s*: *cats, dogs, witches*, etc. The sound of –*(e)s* in these cases varies between /s/, /z/, and /ɪz/. *Abstract nouns*, like *courage* and *sincerity* are not count nouns and lack plural forms (\**courages*, \**sincerities*). And *mass nouns* like *hydrogen* and *dirt* do not (usually) have plurals – \**hydrogens*, \**dirts*. (Sometimes they form plurals with a "kind of" interpretation: *We had several fine wines at dinner last night*).

We define a function, RPL, which states the ways, called *productive*, that plurals of singular count nouns newly added to English are generally formed. Several classes of non-productive plurals are listed afterwards. They are often borrowed plurals or ones inherited from earlier stages of English. Our interest, here, is to illustrate a linguistic function defined by conditions.

To define RPL we note that the *sibilant* phonemes (distinctive sounds) of English are the last ones in the following six words: *bus*, *maze* ,*bush*, *mirage*, *batch*, *badge*. These are represented phonologically as /s/, /z/, /ʃ/, /ʒ/, /tʃ/, and /dʒ/ respectively. (ʒ does not occur frequently at the end of nouns in English, but is more common between vowels, as in *pleasure*, *treasure* and *leisure*).

**Definition 2.8.** For all singular count nouns $\sigma$, except those listed further below,

$$\text{RPL}(\sigma) = \begin{cases} \sigma \frown \text{iz} & \text{if } \sigma_{|\sigma|} \text{ is a sibilant} \\ \sigma \frown \text{s} & \text{if } \sigma_{|\sigma|} \text{ is not a sibilant and is voiceless} \\ \sigma \frown \text{z} & \text{if } \sigma_{|\sigma|} \text{ is not a sibilant and is not voiceless.} \end{cases}$$

Here $\sigma$ is a sequence of phonemes and $\sigma_{|\sigma|}$ is the last phoneme in $\sigma$.

Definition by conditions is typical of linguistic functions. Note that the three conditions are *exclusive* – no English noun meets more than one of them, and *exhaustive*, all English nouns satisfy at least one of them. Here is an incomplete list of non-productive plurals (just given orthographically):

1. leaf → leaves; knife → knives; life → lives; loaf → loaves

2. shelf → shelves; wolf → wolves; scarf → scarves; wharf → wharves

3. criterion → criteria; phenomenon → phenomena; automaton → automata

4. parenthesis → parentheses; thesis → theses; hypothesis → hypotheses

5. deer → deer; sheep → sheep; halibut → halibut

6. child → children; ox → oxen; woman → women; man → men

7. mouse → mice; louse → lice; die → dice

8. tooth → teeth; foot → feet

9. vertex → vertices; index → indices

Remark: We say *He caught two trout / perch* (*\*trouts / \*perches*) *yesterday* but *He caught two sharks /\*shark yesterday*. Any hypothesis as to why?

## 2.8   A Closing Reflection on *Functions*

We have presented functions as matchings – sets of pairs – where each pair is an argument of the function and the value it assigns to that argument. Let us call this set the *extension* of the function. As we have seen, the extension of many functions of syntactic interest is too big (usually infinite) to be listed in any useful way. The extension of a function contrasts with its *intension* (spelled with an *s*, note), which we think of, a little vaguely, as the "procedures" used to compute a value for an arbitrary argument. Empirically the work-a-day linguist is often faced with a finite portion of the extension of a function and asked to figure out what the function is, that is, its intension, the procedures used to yield a value at an arbitrary argument. So we generalize from a finite amount of data to new instances. If we generalize correctly we correctly predict the inclusion of new pairs in the extension of the function and the exclusion of certain other new pairs.

Our point here is that the process of generalizing to the intension of a function given a finite portion of its extension in general does not mathematically yield a unique result even when successful. We illustrate this with a hypothetical example. Suppose we are given a little black box – call it a bot. We feed our bot a tape with zero or more vertical strokes and it outputs a tape with some number of strokes. Different trials with the same input yield the same output, so our bot's behavior is not random. Our empirical task here is to generalize from our observed input-output instances so that we correctly predict the bot's outputs (values) for new inputs (arguments). This is just an instance of normal scientific hypothesis formation and testing.

For example, suppose when we input a tape with no strokes the bot outputs a single stroke. But if we give the bot 1 input stroke it outputs 4; given 2 it outputs 9, 3 it outputs 16. Looking through these values, they seem to just be the positive square numbers: 1, 4, 9, 16, ?25, ?36,...But the number squared is not the input number, but one greater than it. So we hypothesize that our bot has internalized (maybe in terms of gears and levers, or electrical circuitry and switches, or neurons and synapses) the function $f$ from $\mathbb{N}$ into $\mathbb{N}$ given in (28).

(28)   For each natural number $n$, $f(n) = (n + 1)^2$.

We try a few more cases, confirm the result and shout Huzzah! "We have figured out the (abstract) structure of the bot!".

We were doing fine up until we said *the* structure. Suppose just as we cheer our colleagues working on a bot at the other end of the table also shout Huzzah! "We got it!". The bot, they say, internalizes the function $g$ below:

(29) $g(n) = n^2 + 2n + 1$

Hmmm. Clearly, $g$ and $f$ have different intensions. $f$ says "add 1 and square". $g$ says square, then double the input and add it to the square, and then add 1. But as we recall from high school algebra, $(n+1)^2 = n^2 + 2n + 1$, all natural numbers $n$, so $f$ and $g$ have the same extension. Thus we cannot choose between these hypotheses on the basis of predicting the observed extensions. In linguistic jargon they are *descriptively adequate* to the same extent.

Similarly the linguist trying to figure out a grammar for a language works with some speakers and establishes a fair range of vocabulary items together with some more complex expressions, some of which speakers accept as grammatical and some of which they reject. The problem is to hypothesize some functions (rules) which apply to vocabulary items to yield just those strings the speakers agree are grammatical expressions in their language. If our linguist is fortunate enough to find a descriptively adequate set of functions she should rejoice, but not believe that her answer is unique. Mathematical experience does not support uniqueness (There's always that pesky guy at the other end of the table). Rather:

> If a problem has any solutions it has many solutions

Of course multiple analyses may be pared down on external criteria. Maybe one analysis is more learnable by children, or better supports a compositional semantic analysis, or is just more "elegant". (But then distinct descriptively adequate analyses simply have distinct, incomparable, merits).

## 2.9 Suggestions for Further Study

If you are interested in getting more background on set theory, we recommend Enderton (1977) and Halmos (1974).

## 2.10 Addendum 1: Russell's Paradox

In defining sets by abstraction we require that the set so defined be a subset of an antecedently given set. And we consider all the members of that set that satisfy whatever requirement we are interested in. This approach is one way to avoid what is known as *Russell's Paradox*, which we give here for the interested reader, noting that paradoxes tend to be confusing and understanding the paradox deeply is a not a prerequisite for following the rest of this book. The paradox, historically very important in the development of set theory, arises if we allow ourselves to (try to) define sets without requiring that the elements in the defined set be drawn from an antecedently given set. If we could do this then (this begins Russell's Paradox) we would consider $A$ below to be a set:

(30) $A = \{x \mid x \text{ is a set and } x \notin x\}$.

So suppose that $A$, as apparently defined, is a set. Is it a member of itself? Suppose (leading to a contradiction) that $A \in A$. Then $A$ fails the condition for being in $A$, so $A \notin A$, a contradiction. Thus the assumption that $A \in A$ is false. So, $A \notin A$. But then, since $A$ is a set by assumption, $A$ meets the conditions for being a member of $A$. That is, $A \in A$, contradiction. Thus the assumption that $A$ was a set must be false.

## 2.11 Addendum 2: An Equivalent, Useful, Definition of Closure

Given a set $A$, a function $f$ from $A$ into $A$, and a subset $K$ of $A$, we have defined *the closure of $K$ with respect to $f$*, noted $\mathrm{Cl}_f A$, as $\bigcup_n K_n$, where we set $K_0 = K$, and $K_{n+1} = K_n \cup \{f(x) \mid x \in K_n\}$. The idea behind this definition is that we start with $K_0$, the set we are given, and add in just enough elements to get to one that is closed with respect to (wrt) $f$. Suppose in some case, when we get to $K_6$ we find that it is closed wrt $f$. So for each $\alpha \in K_6$ we have that $f(\alpha)$ is also in $K_6$. That means we add no new elements in forming $K_7$, so $K_7 = K_6$. This means that $\mathrm{Cl}_f K = K_6$ and we are done. But can we be sure that by successive additions we will ever get to a set which is closed wrt $f$? The answer is that the biggest set we could get to would be $A$ itself, as all the sets we are taking unions of are subsets of $A$, and $A$ is closed wrt $f$ since $f$ is given as a function from $A$ into $A$. So for all $\alpha \in A$, $f(\alpha)$ is also an element of $A$. In a "typical" case we may have to take an infinite union – each $K_{n+1}$ has some new elements, ones not in $K_n$, but even so the union may be a proper subset of $A$ (or it may be $A$ itself).

An alternate, and often very useful, way of defining this closure is in terms of intersections rather than unions. On this approach, to get the "least" set which includes the given elements in $K$ we simply take the intersection of all the supersets of $K$ that are closed wrt $f$. That set is provably closed wrt $f$, and is a subset of any superset of $K$ that is closed wrt $f$. More formally:

**Theorem 2.5.** *Given $A, f, K$ as above, $Cl_f K = \bigcap \{M \subseteq A \mid K \subseteq M \text{ & } M \text{ is closed wrt } f\}$.*

For succinctness set $D = \{M \subseteq A \mid K \subseteq M \& M \text{ is closed wrt } f\}$. We are to prove that $\mathrm{Cl}_f K = \bigcap D$. Note (crucially) that $D$ is not empty, since $A \in D$. (Clearly $A \subseteq A$ and $K \subseteq A$ and $A$ is closed wrt $f$ as noted above). If $A$ were the only set in $D$ then $\bigcap D = \bigcap\{A\}$, and an object $x$ is in $\bigcap\{A\}$ iff for all sets $B$ in $\{A\}$, $x \in B$. But since $A$ is the only set in $\{A\}$ that comes down to saying that $x \in \bigcap\{A\}$ iff $x \in A$; that is, $\bigcap\{A\} = A$. Now let us show the equality in the theorem.

**Lemma 2.6.** $Cl_f K \subseteq \bigcap D$

We show that for all $n \in \mathbb{N}$, $K_n \subseteq \bigcap D$. Hence $Cl_f K = \bigcup_n K_n \subseteq \bigcap D$.

*Proof.* Set $W = \{n \in \mathbb{N} \mid K_n \subseteq \bigcap D\}$. We show that $\mathbb{N} \subseteq W$.

a. $0 \in W$ since every $M$ in $D$ is a superset of $K_0$, hence everything in $K_0$ is in every set we take the intersection of (and there is at least one!) and so is in the intersection (by the definition of intersection).

b. Let $n$ arbitrary in $\mathbb{N}$ and assume $n \in W$, so $K_n \subseteq \bigcap D$. We show that $n + 1 \in W$, that is, $K_{n+1} \subseteq \bigcap D$. Let $y$ in $K_{n+1}$. Then $y \in K_n$ or $y = f(x)$ for some $x \in K_n$. In the former case $y \in \bigcap D$ by assumption. In the latter case $x \in$ every $M$ in $D$. Since each such $M$ is closed wrt $f$, $f(x) = y$ is in every $M$ in $D$, hence $y \in \bigcap D$. Thus by induction $\mathbb{N} \subseteq W$, so for every $n$, $K_n \subseteq \bigcap D$, so $Cl_f K = \bigcup_n K_n \subseteq \bigcap D$.

$\square$

**Lemma 2.7.** $\bigcap D \subseteq Cl_f K$

*Proof.* We show that $Cl_f K \in D$, hence $\bigcap D \subseteq Cl_f K$. We must show that $Cl_f K$ includes $K_0$ and is closed wrt $f$.

a. $K_0 \subseteq Cl_f K$. It is one of the sets we take the union of in forming $Cl_f K$.

b. $Cl_f K$ is closed wrt $f$. Let $x \in Cl_f K$. Then for some $n$, $x \in K_n$. But then $f(x) \in K_{n+1} \subseteq Cl_f K$, so $f(x) \in Cl_f K$, so $Cl_f K$ is closed wrt $f$.

Thus $Cl_f K$ is one of the sets we took the intersection of in forming $\bigcap D$, so $\bigcap D \subseteq Cl_f K$. The theorem follows from the conjunction of lemmas 2.6 and 2.7. $\square$

**Terminology** A *lemma* is a result used in leading up to the main result, a theorem. A *corollary* is an easily shown result of a theorem.

## 2.12   Addendum 3: Some Initial Hints on Setting up Proofs

A proof is a kind of text. It is a text designed to convince a reader of a specific conclusion based on specific assumptions (called *premisses*), and typically the individual steps are justified in some way. Proofs vary as to how formal they are: there is a trade-off between readability and detail depending on the readership and the overall purpose of the proof. If you are just starting out with formal proofs, then you should feel free to include all the details that you can think of, and gradually you will learn to suppress details and steps that are routine to you and therefore to others, too.

A proof begins with a clear and explicit statement of what you are trying to prove. Then you should list your assumptions; some will be specific to what you are trying to prove, others will be generally accepted, such as axioms in whatever domain you are working in, and are understood to be in play without explicit statement. A proof is then a sequence of sentences in whatever language you are using that proceeds by sound reasoning from your assumptions to your conclusion. Each line in a proof should either be an assumption or logically follow from one or more of the previous lines or from the definition of some terms you are using. The the last line should be a (re-)statement of the overall conclusion of the argument.

Commonly, the form a proof takes depends on the syntactic form of what you are trying to prove. Here is a run-down of some common cases.

a. To prove a conjunction of two sentences, say $(\varphi \ \& \ \psi)$, prove $\varphi$, and then prove $\psi$. In other words, prove the two *conjuncts* of $(\varphi \ \& \ \psi)$. The idea is that a conjunction of sentences if true iff each of is conjuncts is true. Instead of $(\varphi \& \psi)$, texts often write $(\varphi \wedge \psi)$, but we will use the $\wedge$ sign for something else later).

b. Suppose that we wish to prove a conditional statement *if $\varphi$ then $\psi$*, often noted $(\varphi \rightarrow \psi)$ or $(\varphi \Rightarrow \psi)$. In a conditional statement the sentence to the left of the arrow $\rightarrow$ is called the *antecedent* of the conditional, and the sentence to the right the *consequent*.

   Here is a typical way to prove $(\varphi \rightarrow \psi)$.

   **Step 1:** Assume the antecedent $\varphi$.

   **Step 2:** From that assumption reason your way to the consequent, $\psi$.

**Step 3:** Infer the original conditional, if $\varphi$ then $\psi$, from no assumptions.

A second common way of proving $(\varphi \to \psi)$ is to prove (not $\psi \to$ not $\varphi$), the *contrapositive* of $(\varphi \to \psi)$. We note that $(\varphi \to \psi)$ and its contrapositive always have the same truth value, so proving one is, in effect, a proof of the other. Proving $(\varphi \to \psi)$ by proving its contrapositive (not $\psi \to$ not $\varphi$) is called *proof by contraposition*. Note that the contrapositive of a formula is a conditional, as is the original formula.

NB. A conditional $(\varphi \to \psi)$ just says that $\psi$ is true if $\varphi$ is. It does not imply or assume that $\varphi$ is true. So $(\varphi \to \psi)$ is false in just one case: when $\varphi$ is true and $\psi$ is false. In all other cases, $(\varphi \to \psi)$ is true. In particular it is true, vacuously we say, if $\varphi$ is false, regardless of the truth value of $\psi$. Speakers sometimes find this usage unnatural (in ordinary English). But there are circumstances where taking *if ... then* as a *material conditional* is sensible. Suppose someone tells you *If John isn't sick he'll come to the party.* You cannot refute the claim by asserting *But John is sick!* The original claim says nothing about what happens in that case (Maybe John will come to the party anyway).

c. To prove a disjunction, $(\varphi$ or $\psi)$, prove $\varphi$ or prove $\psi$. Note that a disjunction of sentences is true (in mathematical discourse) iff at least one of the two disjuncts, $\varphi, \psi$ is true. It may even be that both are true. So it suffices to prove $\varphi$ or to prove $\psi$. Here is another technique: Prove (not $\varphi \to \psi$), which is just a conditional statement. Note that $(\varphi$ or $\psi)$ has the same truth value as "if not $\varphi$, then $\psi$".

d. Suppose that we wish to prove $(\varphi$ iff $\psi)$, often noted $(\varphi \leftrightarrow \psi)$, or $(\varphi \leftrightarrow \psi)$, in which case the sentence is called a *biconditional*. A biconditional just says that $\varphi$ and $\psi$ have the same truth value – both true or both false. So $(\varphi \leftrightarrow \psi)$ is logically equivalent to a conjunction of conditionals: $((\varphi \to \psi) \land (\psi \to \varphi))$, so to prove $(\varphi \leftrightarrow \psi)$, it suffices to prove each of these conjuncts.

A second common option is to prove $(\varphi \to \psi)$ and (not $\varphi \to$ not $\psi$). The first of these, in effect, says that $\psi$ is true if $\varphi$ is, and the second says that $\psi$ is false if $\varphi$ is, whence $\psi$ and $\varphi$ must have the same truth value.

e. Next, suppose that we wish to prove a sentence of the form "there is an $x$ such that $Px$", where $Px$ is a sentence (or formula), possibly of considerable syntactic complexity. Sentences of the form there is an $x$ such that $Px$ are said to be *existentially quantified*, noted $\exists x Px$, where $\exists$, a backward E, is the *existential quantifier* and $x$ is a variable. They are also read as "for some $x$, $Px$". The most common way to prove an existentially quantified sentence is to find an example in the domain of objects under discussion.

Here is an illustration: Consider the language of elementary arithmetic (which we use to talk about the natural numbers $0, 1, 2, \ldots$ – so our domain of objects is $\mathbb{N}$). Let us prove: There is an $x$ such that $(x > 3)$, that is $\exists x(x > 3)$.

*Proof.* Choose $x = 7$. Then $x > 3$. (This is known from elementary arithmetic, and hence needs no additional justification.) Therefore, there is an $x$ such that $x > 3$. □

**Remark** As you can see, we often mark the end of a proof with a symbol like the square; other symbols used include a black vertical bar, or some other arbitrary symbol. In older texts we still find QED, which abbreviated the Latin *Quod erat demonstrandum* "that which was to be shown". Sometimes a little box or some such (but not the letters QED) is used to mark the end of a definition rather than a proof.

f. Proving sentences of the form "for all $x$, $Px$". Such sentences are said to be *universally quantified*, often noted $\forall x Px$, where $\forall$, an upside down A, is called the *universal quantifier*, and of course $x$ is a variable. To prove such a sentence, let $x$ denote an arbitrarily chosen object in your domain and prove $Px$. Then since $x$ was arbitrary you can infer that $P$ holds for all $x$, that is, for all $x$, $Px$ is true.

g. Proofs by *reductio ad absurdum*

To prove some statement, call it $\varphi$:

**Step 1:** assume not $\varphi$.

**Step 2:** reason your way to a sentence known to be false, or to a logical contradiction.

**Step 3:** conclude $\varphi$ from no assumptions.

Note that in distinction to our other cases above, proofs by reductio do not depend on the form of the statement to be proved.

Reductio proofs are sometimes felt to be unsatisfying since they may not tell you clearly why the original sentence is true, they just say that if it isn't, you're in trouble.

## 2.12.1 A Few Sample Proofs

We present a few very simple proofs. We do so to help the novice learn how to set up proofs, the theorems themselves are elementary.

(1) To prove: For all sets $A$, $A \subseteq A$.

*Proof.* Let $A$ be an arbitrary set. Show $A \subseteq A$. That is, show $\forall x (x \in A \rightarrow x \in A)$. Let $x$ be arbitrary. Show: $x \in A \rightarrow x \in A$. Assume $x \in A$. Then, trivially, $x \in A$. Thus, we have shown from no assumption that $x \in A \rightarrow x \in A$. Since $x$ was arbitrary, we know that for all $x$ $(x \in A \rightarrow x \in A)$. Thus $A \subseteq A$, since, by the definition of $\subseteq$, $A \subseteq A$ iff for all $x$, $(x \in A \rightarrow x \in A)$. $\square$

(2) To prove: For all sets $A$ and $B$, $(A \cap B) \subseteq A$.

*Proof.* Let $A$ and $B$ be arbitrary sets. Show $(A \cap B) \subseteq A$, that is, we show: for all objects $x$, $x \in (A \cap B) \rightarrow x \in A$. Let $x$ be arbitrary. (Show: $x \in (A \cap B) \rightarrow x \in A$).

Assume $x \in (A \cap B)$.
Then $x \in A$ and $x \in B$.                  Definition of $\cap$
Therefore $x \in A$.                            The meaning of "and"
Therefore if $x \in (A \cap B)$, then $x \in A$.     Proof of *if* sentence
 Since $x$ was arbitrary: for all $x$, $x \in (A \cap B) \rightarrow x \in A$.
Thus $(A \cap B) \subseteq A$.                  Definition of $\subseteq$

$\square$

(3) To prove: For all sets $A$, $B$, $(A \subseteq B) \rightarrow ((A \cap B) = A))$.

Fix sets $A$ and $B$ (that is, let $A, B$ be arbitrary sets). We show that $(A \subseteq B) \rightarrow ((A \cap B) = A))$.

Assume $A \subseteq B$; we show $(A \cap B) = A$. This task divides into two subtasks. First, we show: (1) $(A \cap B) \subseteq A$. After this, we turn to the second subtask: $A \subseteq (A \cap B)$.

(a) $(A \cap B) \subseteq A$. This holds for all sets $A$, $B$ by (2) (and does not depend on the assumption that $A \subseteq B$). We omit this part of the proof, since we have seen it in our text.

(b) Show: $A \subseteq (A \cap B)$. By the definition of $\subseteq$ we must show: that for all $x$, $(x \in A) \rightarrow (x \in A \cap B)$. For this, let $x$ be arbitrary. Assume $x \in A$. Now since $A \subseteq B$ is one of our assumptions, we know that for all $y$, $(y \in A) \rightarrow (y \in B)$. Turning back to $x$, we see that $x \in B$. Of course $x \in A$ also. So we can conclude that $(x \in A)$ & $(x \in B)$, and therefore that $x \in A \cap B$. This last argument holds for all $x$, showing that for all $x$, $(x \in A) \rightarrow (x \in A \cap B)$. By the definition of $\subseteq$, we see that $A \subseteq A \cap B$. In part (a) just above, we saw that $(A \cap B) \subseteq A$. And so we conclude from the antisymmetry of the inclusion relation $\subseteq$ that $A \cap B = A$.

We have shown $A \cap B = A$ from the assumption that $A \subseteq B$. Turning things around, we have shown that $(A \subseteq B) \rightarrow ((A \cap B) = A)$. Since $A$ and $B$ are arbitrary, we know have the conclusion: for all $A, B$, $(A \subseteq B) \rightarrow ((A \cap B) = A)$.

(4) We prove the converse of (3), speeding up the pace slightly:

For all sets $A, B$, $((A \cap B) = A) \rightarrow (A \subseteq B)$.

*Proof.* Let $A$, $B$ be arbitrary sets. Assume $(A \cap B) = A$ (so they have the same members). Show $A \subseteq B$. Let $x$ be arbitrary, and assume $x \in A$. Since $A = A \cap B$, we see that $x \in A \cap B$. In particular, $x \in B$.

So we have shown about $x$ that $(x \in A) \rightarrow (x \in B)$. Since $x$ was arbitrary, we have that for all $x$, $(x \in A) \rightarrow (x \in B)$. Thus $A \subseteq B$. So $((A \cap B) = A) \rightarrow (A \subseteq B)$. Finally, since $A$ and $B$ are arbitrary sets, we have the desired conclusion: for all sets $A, B$, $((A \cap B) = A) \rightarrow (A \subseteq B)$. □

(5) Prove: for all sets $A, B$, $A \subseteq B \rightarrow A - B = \emptyset$.

Here is a proof which proceeds at a faster pace than our previous proofs.

*Proof.* Let $A$ and $B$ be arbitrary and assume $A \subseteq B$. Show $A - B = \emptyset$. Assume, leading to a contradiction, that there is a $z \in A - B$. So $z \in A$ and $z \notin B$ (Def $-$). Since $z \in A$ and $A \subseteq B$, $z \in B$. So $z \in B$ and $z \notin B$, a contradiction. Thus there is no $z \in A - B$. So $A - B = \emptyset$.

Thus from no assumptions, $(A \subseteq B)$ implies that $(A - B) = \emptyset$. Since $A$ and $B$ were arbitrary, we now know that indeed for all $A$ and $B$, $A \subseteq B$ implies $A - B = \emptyset$. □

# 3

# Boolean Phonology

In this book we are primarily concerned with the mathematical properties of expressions – their combinatorial ones (syntax) and interpretative ones (semantics). But expressions are *discrete* ("digital"), we can count them. Yet what impinges on our ears in daily conversation is a *continuous* wave form with properties such as pitch, amplitude and spectral shape that vary continuously over time. Somehow we conceptually convert this continuous phenomenon to a discrete one. Representing this conversion in a rigorous way is the topic of this chapter.

Practical examples of such conversions abound. The written English you are now reading is a discrete representation of the continuous system of spoken English. It is composed of 26 letters augmented with some special symbols as well as diacritics, punctuation and the "space" between words – overall a smallish finite set. Sequences of these symbols form words and phrases, and sequences of these form sentences. Comparable claims hold for different alphabets in different languages: Greek, Russian, Hebrew, Arabic, Amharic, Vietnamese, Hindi, Korean ... When you take notes at a lecture you are converting the continuous speech of the lecturer to a discrete form, a finite sequence of finite sequences. Occasionally we "see" the conversion, as when a signer at a televised political speech converts the speech simultaneously into ASL (American Sign Language), a representational system which is more character based than alphabetic (see Baker-Shenk and Cokely, 1991). As we'll see later the representational system of mathematical logic is significantly character based, special symbols being used for fixed concepts, such as $=$ for "equals", $\forall$ for "for all", and $\exists$ for "for some/there exists". The writing systems for Mandarin Chinese and Old Egyptian are character systems as opposed to alphabetic ones.

Now the English alphabetic system might suggest that the different letters of the alphabet correspond to the distinctive sound segments we use to build words, phrases and sentences. But in fact there is a very imperfect correspondence between letters and sounds, and between sequences of letters and words. Consider for example the letter *a*. The following eight words each have exactly one occurrence of *a* and yet, in some dialects, no two occurrences are pronounced exactly the same: *trap, father, face, tall, watch, agree, image, typically*. In fact in *typically* the *a* is usually not pronounced! The pronunciation would be the same if *typically* were spelled *typikly*, with no *a* at all. Many English words contain unpronounced letters, as the *k* in *know, knot*, and *knight* and the *gh* in *night, sight*, and *light*.

Consider words that end in *ough*: *through* is pronounced like *threw* (as in *I threw the ball*); but *though* rhymes with *oh!*, *cough* with *off*, *rough* with *puff* and *bough* (*a bough of a tree*) with *ow!*. Even worse, a given written word may have more than one pronunciation, each with its own meaning. Consider *read*. In *I read that book yesterday*, *read* is pronounced like *red*, the color name, and rhymes with *said*. But in *I will read that book tomorrow*, *read* rhymes with *need*.

Conversely, a given sound sequence may correspond to different meaningful letter sequences, as already seen in *know* and *no*. The words in each of the following pairs are homophones (pronounced the same but differ in meaning): ⟨*bored, board*⟩, ⟨*made, maid*⟩, ⟨*cereal, serial*⟩, ⟨*complement, compliment*⟩, ⟨*died, dyed*⟩, ⟨*prays, praise*⟩, ⟨*won, one*⟩ and ⟨*morning, mourning*⟩. Little wonder that the U.S. has a 14% functional illiteracy rate!

So written English, however useful in practice, does not satisfy scientific standards of rigor and clarity as a representation of the sound system of English. It does have one basic desirable property however: it can represent arbitrary long expressions of English as sequences of elements drawn from a fixed finite list. So it has the global profile of a recursive system. What we would like is that the list of primitive elements represent "significant" sound segments of English, with different elements representing different segments. Then phonological and syntactic rules will tell us which sequences (of sequences) of segments are grammatical expressions of English. And of course we want to do this not just for English but for languages in general. Ultimately we want to define the notion "possible phonological system" for a natural language.

Here we begin with a study of the initial mathematical steps in converting continuous sound waves to sequences of discrete units, which we shall call *segments*. Exactly how the segments we define are empirically related to observable, measurable, properties of the speech stream is a major part of the empirical science of phonology. We do not attempt to recapitulate what is known here, noting only a few issues so the reader does not think our mathematical work has solved the major empirical issues in phonology. Very many empirical and conceptual issues are open and debated at time of writing.

## 3.1 Abstract Segmental Phonology

Our conceptual analysis of the conversion builds on a widely used mathematical construction, *equivalence relations* and the *equivalence classes* they induce. Equivalence classes are sets and thus discrete. Words and phrases may be represented as sequences of these classes. Equivalence relations also arise in syntax and semantics and are studied more abstractly in Chapter 8.

Now phonologically we distinguish linguistic sounds (unsurprisingly) according as they have different properties. Properties which are linguistically "significant" are called **features** by linguists. What makes a property of a sound "significant"? One criterion (not the only one) is that we can find expressions with distinct meanings (note the reliance on semantics here!) that differ in pronunciation by just that property.

### 3.1.1 Some American English Features

Consider the words *melted* vs *melded* (= in certain card games exhibiting a certain sequence of cards for a score). They are different words as they have different meanings. But their pronunciations are very similar, differing only by the sounds written *t* and *d*. And even these two sounds are quite similar: they both block air from exiting the mouth, and they are both formed by pressing the blade of the tongue (just behind the tip of the tongue) against the alveolar ridge (just above the upper teeth). So they have the same *point of articulation.*

They differ primarily in that in producing the *d* sound the vocal folds of the glottis are open just enough that when air passes through them they vibrate, yielding the voicing sound we hear in *d*. In contrast there is no such vibration and so no such voicing in pronouncing the *t* sound. We say that *d* is *voiced* and *t* is *voiceless*, and we treat **voice** as a *distinctive* (*phonemic*) feature of English, meaning that we can find pairs of meaningful expressions that differ just by the presence vs. absence of that feature. Such pairs are called *minimal pairs*.

**Voice** is a widely used feature in English in that we find many pairs with quite different sounds that differ solely or primarily by voicing: *pin/bin, tin/din, sip/zip, fan/van, gin/chin; coat/goat, batch/badge, thigh/thy*. Lest the reader think that the empirical problem of establishing feature inventories for a language is easy, we note that the voicing difference heard in *sip/zip* is similar to our initial example *melted/melded* but is significantly greater than that in *tin/din*. In the latter the primary voicing difference, upon careful measurement, is that the second sound, noted *i*, is voiced in both words, but its voicing onset in *din* begins slightly before that in *tin*. So there is a voicing distinction in *tin/din* but it is much less striking than that in *sip/zip*.

Our concern in this chapter is to represent features mathematically and to investigate the mathematical structure of feature sets, not to discuss the real world empirical problems in defining them. But of course we need some examples to know that there is something real we are modeling.

Before considering some other of these features let us make the empirical vs mathematical distinction clear for **voice**. *Empirically* we characterized the feature **voice** in terms of real world observations (1) how it is articulated – vocal folds vibrating, and (2) its perceptual quality[1] – the voicing sound we hear in *d* but not in *t*. *Mathematically* we represent **voice** as a two valued function from utterances – sounds you can record, to the set $\{-, +\}$. To say that an utterance *u* is voiced we write $\textbf{voice}(u) = +$. We also say that *u* is +**voice**. Similarly to say that *u* is unvoiced we write $\textbf{voice}(u) = -$, and say that *u* is −**voice**. (Later we consider features that are more than two valued).

We have so far seen that *s* and *z* (in *sip/zip*) differ with regard to voicing, as do *t* and *d* (though moreso in some contexts than others). But *s* and *z* as a group differ from *t* and *d* in another significant way. *s* and *z* expel air from the mouth, whereas *t* and *d* block it. Sounds in which the air flows continuously from the mouth are called *continuants*. We adopt this as a feature: $\textbf{continuant}(s) = \textbf{continuant}(z) = +$, while $\textbf{continuant}(t) = \textbf{continuant}(d) = -$.

Note that we have so far characterized two two valued features, **voice** and **continuant**, which enables us to define $2^2 = 4$ significant sounds – and indeed we have four such: *s, z, t, d*. So if our language consisted of just these two features and these four sounds the feature system would be *independent*. We could change the value of any feature on any distinctive sound and find another distinctive sound which had just that combination of feature values. But in fact as we adduce

---

[1]Works on phonology differ with regard to the emphasis they put on perceptual properties vs articulatory ones – which part of the tongue is raised or lowered in producing one or another vowel sound for example. This difference in emphasis can lead to quite different feature sets for a given language. Compare Jakobson et al. (1952) with Chomsky and Halle (1968/1995). For works that rely more on acoustic or perceptual properties see Dresher (2009); Hayes (2009, Ch 1.1) and Hyman (1975, Ch 2).

further features to characterize further distinctive sounds we lose the property of independence and introduce (massive) feature redundancy. Consider for example the word *lip*. It rhymes with and forms minimal pairs with *sip*, *zip*, *tip*, *dip* so there must be some feature which makes its initial sound different from the other four. A widely used one (in many languages) is **sonorant**, a property a sound has if its primary quality is resonance (as opposed for example to turbulence, which is perceived as noise). So for the *l* in *lip*, **sonorant**(*l*) = + and for all the other sounds *u* so far considered, **sonorant**(*u*) = −. Note that both *z* and *l* are +**voice** and +**continuant**, they differ (so far) just at the feature **sonorant**, as **sonorant**(*z*) = −.

We now have three features and if they were independent we could distinguish $2^3 = 8$ distinctive sounds. But in fact with these three features we cannot distinguish 8 sounds in English as any sound that is +**sonorant** must also be +**voice**. That is, our feature system now has a redundancy since distinctive sound segments in English do not vary freely according as they are sonorant and voiced. These two properties are not independent. This would commonly be expressed by a "redundancy rule" as in (1), which just means that if a sound is sonorant then it is voiced. (2) states this using our function notation.

(1)    +**sonorant** $\Rightarrow$ +**voice**

**Definition 3.1.** For all sets $A$, all functions $F, G$ from $A$ into $\{-, +\}$, $F \Rightarrow G$ iff for all $\alpha \in A$, if $F(\alpha) = +$ then $G(\alpha) = +$.

(2)    **sonorant** $\Rightarrow$ **voice**

Note that the converse of (2) fails: both *d* and *z* are +**voice** and −**sonorant**. And as we shall see, as more features are added the amount of redundancy grows frighteningly fast. To anticipate, we have appended at the end of this chapter the list of 14 features used by Giegerich (1992) to characterize the phonological systems of three dialects of English (including General American). If these features were independent and two valued we would have $2^{14} = 16,384$ significant sounds. In fact Giegerich[2] only distinguishes about 40. So the redundancy is massive. The redundancy relation $\Rightarrow$ turns out to have some basic mathematical properties of interest (below). But first, a few more features.

---

[2]Giegerich's list is not to be taken as "standard" or "generally agreed upon". It is simply one carefully thought out feature analysis for English.

### 3.1.2 Some Vowel Features

Giegerich treats **consonantal** as a feature, one an utterance has iff producing it involves a radical obstruction of the vocal tract. (Note the value judgment term "radical"). Vowels are sounds that are not consonantal. We induce features for them with minimal pair tests as for consonants. Consider the triple (*seat, set, sat*). These differ minimally in the sound between the *s* and the *t*. In *seat* that sound involves raising the tongue, in *sat*, it involves lowering the tongue, and in *set* the tongue stays in its level neutral position. It would seem natural to introduce a feature height with three values, say {**high, mid, low**}. Giegerich however introduces two two valued features, **high** and **low**. The vowel in *seat* is taken to be +**high** and −**low**, that in *sat* is −**high** and +**low**, and the mid vowel in *set* is −**high** and −**low**.

Observe that this analysis introduces an *inherent* (or *definitional*) redundancy. There can be no distinctive sounds that are simultaneously +**high** and +**low**, just as a volume of water at uniform temperature may be cold and not hot, hot and not cold, or neither hot nor cold (tepid), but it cannot be simultaneously both hot and cold. The redundancy rules may be given as:

(3)     a. +**high** ⇒ −**low**    and    b. +**low** ⇒ −**high**

But these claims are empirically vacuous. They cannot distinguish one language from another. All languages satisfy them. Contrast this with an empirically significant case: within a given height level in English we can distinguish vowels according to their place of articulation. Compare the vowels in *beat* and *boot*. In both the tongue body is raised, but in *beat* it is the front part of the tongue body that is raised while in *boot* it is the back part. So we introduce the feature **back** and say that the vowel sound in *boot* is +**back**, while that in *beat* is −**back**.

Now note that some back vowels, such as those in *boot* and *boat*, are accompanied with partial rounding of the lips (starting to put them in a circular shape) whereas the front vowels, as in *beat, bit, bet, bait* do not exhibit lip rounding (some even involve lip spreading). And the following redundancy is empirically significant:

(4)    +**round** ⇒ +**back**

So vowels with lip rounding in English are all back. But in French the vowels in *tu* 'you(fam)' and *feu* 'fire' are front, i.e. −**back**, and +**round**. So the redundancy in (4) does distinguish among languages, and informs us that there is nothing necessary about the English correlation of round vowels with back ones.

We may reasonably wonder what the effect is of adopting Giegerich's two two valued feature approach to height compared with having a single three valued feature. Given a set $F_1, \ldots, F_n$ of $n$ independent features, write $\text{val}_i$ for the number of values the $i^{\text{th}}$ feature can take. Then the total number of distinctions we can make is $\text{val}_1 \times \ldots \times \text{val}_n$. Giegerich defines just 40 "phonemes" for English, but with 14 two valued features we could have had $2^{14} = 16,384$ possible distinctive sounds, yielding a redundancy value of $16,384/40 = 4,096$. With only 12 two valued features and one three valued one we have $2^{12} \times 3 = 4,096 \times 3 = 12,288$, a redundancy reduction of about 25% ($12,288/40 = 3,072$). The absolute redundancy values given here are not particularly meaningful, but using them to compare different feature analyses is informative.

### 3.1.3 Justifying Feature Choices

Our first reason for positing features (**voice, continuant**, etc.) is classificatory: they enable us to classify and so distinguish sounds used to form distinct meaningful expressions. But we have just now seen a second justification: They enable us to distinguish regular differences between languages. This latter is quite important. In trying to define "possible phonological system" for a language we want to know what properties and what redundancies are peculiar to that language, and what ones are language general. And we have just seen that in the vowel systems of languages the association of lip rounding with backness of articulation that we find in English is not general. It fails even for genetically and historically closely related languages such as English and French.

Here is a second sort of comparative generalization, one that describes a phonetic regularity in English involving features that are not distinctive in English (they do not distinguish minimal pairs) but which we are led to notice as these features are distinctive in other languages. For example in Hindi (and Thai) we find minimal pairs which differ just by the *aspiration* of a consonant (meaning that the consonant is immediately followed by a little puff of air, indicated here by a superscript $h$). Thus in Hindi we find minimal pairs *pal* 'moment' and $p^h al$ 'fruit'; *taal* 'beat' and $t^h aal$ 'a type of plate'; *baaii* 'maid servant'; $b^h aaii$ 'brother'; *dar* 'door step' and $d^h ar$ 'to place'.

Now in English aspiration is not distinctive (phonemic). We have no minimal pairs differing just by $p$ and $p^h$ for example. Nonetheless there are some regularities associated with aspirated consonants in English. Compare for example the pronunciation differences in *pin/spin*, *ton/stun*, *kin/skin*. In the first member of each pair the initial consonant is aspirated. Native speakers of American English can feel the puff of air with their hand open in front of their mouth when they say *pin*, *ton*, etc. But this puff of air is absent in the second members of the pairs where the stop is preceded by *s*.

This generalization could be enriched, as aspiration is also present when *p*, *t*, *k* are followed by *l* or *r* and a stressed vowel, as in *play*, *pray*, *clown*, *crown* and *trap*. But our purpose here is to simply illustrate revealing generalizations, not to present, even in summary form, a full description of English phonology. Worth noting though is that our generalization covers more than just the simple monosyllabic words we have used to illustrate it. Compare (from Hayes, 2009, 123) *note*, *notable* and *notation*. In the first two the *t* segment does not precede a stressed vowel and so is not aspirated. But in *notation* the *t* sound (there is only one, despite the spelling) is followed by a stressed syllable so the *t* sound is aspirated.

We would like to state this regularity in general terms, using features, not just listing consonants *p*, *t*, *k*, etc. which exhibit the generalization. To this end it will be helpful to augment our set of features in two systematic ways. Specifically we define two functions which build features from features.

## 3.2    Enriching Feature Sets

First, given an initial feature $F$ we define $\neg F$ as that feature which maps an utterance $u$ to $+$ iff $F$ itself maps it to $-$. Note that in such a case if $(\neg F)(u) = -$ then $F(u) = +$ (otherwise $F(u) = -$, forcing $(\neg F)(u) = +$, contrary to assumption). Note that $\neg$ is a function, called *complement*, which takes a function $F$ as argument yielding a function $\neg F$ as value.

Now given a set IF of *initial features* motivated empirically as we have started doing, we define:

**Definition 3.2.** Neg(IF) is the closure of IF under $\neg$.

That is, Neg(IF) is the intersection of the sets of functions from utterances into $\{-, +\}$ that include IF and are closed under $\neg$.

**Exercise 3.1.**    a. Prove that $\neg(\neg F) = F$, $F$ any feature.

b. Prove that $F \Rightarrow \neg G$ iff $G \Rightarrow \neg F$, for $F, G$ any features.

c. Prove that Neg(IF) = IF $\cup \{\neg F \mid F \in \text{IF}\}$.

**Exercise 3.2.** Prove that Neg(IF) is closed under $\neg$.

And second we define a binary function $\wedge$, called *meet*, on features by: $(F \wedge G)(u) = +$ iff $F(u) = +$ and $G(u) = +$. And then:

**Definition 3.3.** Meet(Neg(IF)) is the closure of Neg(IF) under $\wedge$. That is, Meet(Neg(IF)) is the intersection of the function sets that include all members of Neg(IF) and are closed under $\wedge$.

**Exercise 3.3.** Prove that Meet(Neg(IF)) is closed under $\wedge$.

**Caveat** Meet(Neg(IF)) is usually not closed under $\neg$, though formally it depends on what elements are chosen to be in IF. For example, if IF were already closed under $\neg$ and $\wedge$ then Meet(Neg(IF)) = IF and so would be also be closed under $\wedge$.

## 3.3   Some Phonological Generalizations

Now we can formulate several phonological generalizations using our set of features, including the ones derived by $\neg$ and $\wedge$. To define the aspiration generalization noted above we first define:

**Definition 3.4. voiceless stop** = $\neg$**voice** $\wedge$ $\neg$**continuant**

Since **voice** and **continuant** are initial features in English, $\neg$**voice** and $\neg$**continuant** are in Neg(IF), and so their meet $\neg$**voice** $\wedge$ $\neg$**continuant** is in Meet(Neg(IF)). The primary voiceless stops in English are the $p$, $t$, $k$ sounds in *pin*, *tin*, and *kin*. So also would be the initial sound in *chin* if considered a single sound rather than a sequence of two, the first a voiceless stop $t$ and the second the "sh" sound in *she*, noted $\int$ in IPA (International Phonetic Alphabet). And here now is a statement of our generalization of interest.

**Generalization 1.** Voiceless stops are aspirated when they precede a stressed vowel and are not preceded by $s$.

In sum: voiceless stops are a natural class in English phonology, and they are definable in terms of $\neg$ and $\wedge$ beginning with initial features. That is, they are members of Meet(Neg(IF)).

A second generalization uses a feature, **nasal**, not yet considered. An utterance is +**nasal** if it requires air to exit the nose. The word *nip* contrasts with *sip*, *zip*, *tip*, *dip* and *lip* considered earlier and since these words rhyme, the initial $n$ must differ in one or more features from $s$, $z$, $t$, $d$ and $l$. So we add **nasal** to our set of initial features for English. It maps the $n$ in *nip* to $+$ and $s$, $z$, $t$, $d$ and $l$ to $-$. Adding **nasal** to IF for English increases redundancy significantly since English has no distinctive sounds which differ from $s$, $z$, $t$, $d$ or $l$ just by being +**nasal**.

Moreover, reading through Giegerich's feature list carefully we see that we could have defined nasal by:

(5)    **nasal** = **sonorant** ∧ ¬**continuant** ∧ **consonantal**

So we could have simplified our initial features and reduced redundancy by not taking **nasal** as initial. Some reasons for taking it as initial are (1) it is easy to verify its presence acoustically, whereas the cut-off points for **sonorant** and **consonantal** are a little arbitrary. (2) the ¬**continuant** feature rules out nasal vowels (see later), an issue which is somewhat unclear in English. The nasal consonants *n* and the *m* in *mat* and *bum*, and the *ng* sound in *sang* (noted ŋ in IPA) clearly block air from exiting the mouth and so are ¬**continuant**. But if we limit nasals to these consonants then additional means are needed to account for the nasal sound on the *a* sound in *camp*, *hang* and *hand*. (Appeal is made to a process called *nasal spread*). And (3) we find languages like Burmese in which there are voiceless nasals and since **sonorant** ⇒ **voice** in English the definition in (5) wouldn't hold generally. In a moment we see a further reason for taking nasal as initial in English. First we define:

**Definition 3.5. oral stop** = ¬**continuant** ∧ ¬**nasal**

**oral stop** is clearly in Meet(Neg(IF)) for English if **nasal** is in IF. If it isn't then if **nasal** is defined as a meet as in (5) then likely ¬**nasal** is not in Meet(Neg(IF)) as that set is not closed under complements.

**Generalization 2.** In monomorphemic syllables ending with a vowel followed by a nasal consonant followed by an oral stop the place of articulation of the nasal assimilates to that of the following stop.

Thus we have *limp, lent, lend, link, lunge, lunch* but not \**linp*, \**lamt*, \**lumch*, and \**linb*. (*Monomorphemic* means having just one meaningful part. *Play* is monomorphemic but *played*, while monosyllabic, is bimorphemic as *play* is one meaningful part and the past tense marking expressed by *ed* is a second. One might argue that *limped* and *dammed* end phonologically with an *mt* (*md*) sequence not showing place assimilation, but they are clearly bimorphemic.)

A third generalization concerns consonants that may constitute full syllables (a notion not defined here) of monomorphemic words. For example, *little* and *ripple* are bisyllablic (and monomorphemic), but the second syllable is expressed just with the consonant *l*. In *brother* and *butter* the second syllable may be just *r*; in *button* and *even* just *n*, and in *prism* and *bottom* just *m*. In common pronunciations of *national* both the $n$ and the $l$ are syllabic (Roach, 2009); in *literal* the $r$ and the $l$ may be both syllabic. In particular both $r$s may be syllabic. We find it difficult to find clear cases of syllabic ŋ. So we support:

**Generalization 3.** Possible monomorphemic syllabic consonants are **consonantal ∧ sonorant ∧ ¬back.**

Some further natural classes, cited from the literature but not justified here are:

(6)    a. **fricative = ¬sonorant ∧ continuant**
          (*f, v, s, z, h, ʃ (she), ʒ (treasure), θ (thigh), ð (thy)*)

       b. **approximants = sonorant ∧ continuant ∧ consonantal**
          (*ran, land, we, yes*)

## 3.4    The Mathematical Structure of Feature Sets

In general a mathematical structure is a set (or collection of sets) on which are defined various functions and relations with specified properties (axioms). We have already treated a feature set for a language by first closing some set of initial features determined empirically under complements (¬) and then closing the result under meets (∧). And recall that our features possess a natural *redundancy* relation: For $F, G$ features, $F \Rightarrow G$ iff for all utterances $u$, if $F(u) = +$ then $G(u) = +$.

> **Mathematical Note.** To define a binary relation $R$ on a set $A$ you must say for all (not necessarily distinct) choices $x, y$ of elements of $A$ whether $x$ bears the relation $R$ to $y$ or not. So we may think of $R$ as given by a set of ordered pairs $\langle x, y \rangle$, and we usually write $xRy$ rather than $\langle x, y \rangle \in R$. In our example $A$ is a set of functions (features) and $R$ is the redundancy relation $\Rightarrow$.
>
> A relation $R$ defined on a set $A$ is *reflexive* iff for all $x \in A$, $xRx$. $R$ is *antisymmetric* iff $xRy$ & $yRx$ implies $x = y$, all $x, y \in A$. And $R$ is *transitive* iff for all $x, y, z$ if $xRy$ and $yRz$ then $xRz$. $R$ is a (*reflexive*) *partial order* iff $R$ is reflexive, antisymmetric and transitive.
>
> There are also irreflexive partial orders – relations $R$ which are transitive and meet a condition stronger than antisymmetry, namely *asymmetry*: $xRy$ implies not($yRx$), all $x, y$. This guarantees irreflexivity (not($xRx$), all $x$). A *linear order* is a partial order (reflexive or not, it doesn't matter) in which for all distinct $x, y$ either $xRy$ or $yRx$. That is any two distinct items stand in the order relation.    □

Clearly the redundancy relation $\Rightarrow$ is reflexive. That just says that for any utterance $u$, if $F(u) = +$ then $F(u) = +$, which is a logical truth (of the form *If P then P*). $\Rightarrow$ is also antisymmetric: Let $F \Rightarrow G$ and $G \Rightarrow F$. Show that $F = G$. They are functions with the same domain and codomain, so we need only show they take the same value at all arguments. Let $u$ arbitrary and suppose first that $F(u) = +$. Then $G(u) = +$ since $F \Rightarrow G$. Suppose second (exhausting the cases) that $F(u) = -$. Then $G(u) = -$, otherwise $G(u) = +$ whence $F(u) = +$ since $G \Rightarrow F$, contra assumption. Finally $\Rightarrow$ is transitive: Let $F \Rightarrow G$ and $G \Rightarrow H$. Show $F \Rightarrow H$. Let $u$ arbitrary and suppose $F(u) = +$. Then $G(u) = +$ since $F \Rightarrow G$, whence $H(u) = +$ since $G \Rightarrow H$, completing the proof. Thus $\Rightarrow$ is a (reflexive) partial order. $\square$

Note too that $\wedge$ and $\neg$ interact with redundancy in regular ways:

**Exercise 3.4.** Prove for all features $F, G$

a. $(F \wedge G) \Rightarrow F$ and $(F \wedge G) \Rightarrow G$.

b. $(F \wedge G) = (G \wedge F)$.

c. $(F \wedge F) = F$.

Note too that while we have used the complement and meet structure of features to make some basic phonological generalizations one may think that Meet(Neg(IF)) contains some useless features. For example, let $F_1$ be an initial feature, so $\neg F_1$ is in Neg(IF), whence $(F_1 \wedge \neg F_1)$ is in Meet(Neg(IF)). But no sound can be assigned $+$ by both $F$ and its complement, any $F$. So $(F_1 \wedge \neg F_1)$ maps all utterances to $-$. Let's call this function $\mathbf{0}$.

$\mathbf{0}$ seems useless as it can not distinguish any two utterances. But it does turn out to be handy in evaluating redundancy. Observe:

**Exercise 3.5.** For all features, $F, G$

a. $F \Rightarrow G$ iff $(F \wedge \neg G) = \mathbf{0}$.

b. $F \wedge \mathbf{0} = \mathbf{0} \wedge F = \mathbf{0}$.

c. $\mathbf{0} \Rightarrow F$.

## 3.5  Significant Sound Segments

Suppose now that we have empirically investigated a language and formed a satisfactory set of features. How do we use them to mathematically define distinctive sound segments, temporally continuous intervals?

Our basic answer to this query is simple enough: the significant sound segments of a language are the maximal subintervals of meaningful utterances for which no feature takes more than one value. First a mathematical note:

**Mathematical Note.** (1) $X$ is a collection of *pairwise disjoint* sets iff for all distinct $A, B \in X$, $A \cap B = \emptyset$.

(2) a *partition* of a set $X$ is a collection of non-empty pairwise disjoint subsets of $X$ whose union is $X$. The sets in the partition are called *blocks*. It follows that no block is empty and for each $x \in X$, there is exactly one block that $x$ is in.                 □

To continue, a *bounded temporal interval* is, as usual, a continuous linearly ordered set of points in time with distinct endpoints. Given such an interval $T$ and distinct points $t, t' \in T$, we write $t < t'$ to say that $t$ precedes $t'$. A *subinterval* $T'$ of $T$ is simply a bounded interval which is a subset of $T$. An *interval of sound* then can be represented as a function $\sigma$ that maps a bounded temporal interval onto a continuous meaningful utterance preserving the temporal order: $t < t'$ iff $\sigma(t) < \sigma(t')$. That is, time point $t$ precedes time point $t'$ iff $\sigma(t)$ is uttered before $\sigma(t')$. Note that the $\sigma(t)$ are arguments of features, so it makes sense to say that $\mathbf{voice}(\sigma(t)) = +$ or $\mathbf{voice}(\sigma(t)) = -$. (Utterances are the kind of thing you can record, recall.)

Now an *order preserving partition* of a bounded temporal interval $T$ is a finite partition of $T$ whose blocks are ordered by the temporal order $<$. That is, for $T_1$ and $T_2$ distinct blocks, $T_1 < T_2$ iff for all $t \in T_1$ all $t' \in T_2, t < t'$. Since the partition of $T$ has just finitely many temporally ordered blocks $T_1 < \ldots < T_n$ it makes sense to ask of any two blocks whether they are adjacent or not, i.e. of the form $T_i, T_{i+1}$ . A block $T_i$ of a partition is *feature fixed* iff for all $t, t' \in T_i$, $F(\sigma(t)) = F(\sigma(t'))$, all features $F$ for $L$. If $T_i$ and $T_j$ are feature fixed blocks they are *phonemically distinct* iff they differ by some feature. That is, for some feature $F$, some $t \in T_i$ and some $t' \in T_j$, $F(\sigma(t)) \neq F(\sigma(t'))$. An order preserving partition of an utterance $\sigma(T)$ is *maximal* iff each block is feature fixed and adjacent blocks are phonemically distinct.

**Definition 3.6.** The *significant segments* of $L$ are the blocks of maximal order preserving partitions of meaningful utterances of $L$.

**Definition 3.7.** For $s, s'$ significant segments (of possibly different utterances) we say that $s \equiv s'$ (read: $s$ is *equivalent* to $s'$) iff for all features $F$, $F(s) = F(s')$. ($F(s)$ makes sense: we say $F(s) = F(\sigma(t))$, all $\sigma(t) \in s$.) We may even define the *phoneme* generated by a significant segment $s$ as the set of significant segments $s'$ such that $s \equiv s'$.

Note that in English two significant segments, hence two phonemes, may differ in length, pitch, aspiration, pre-glottalization, etc. and still be equivalent, as the features of English are not sensitive to those phonetically audible differences. The following two theorems may be helpful here.

> **Mathematical Note.** A binary relation $R$ on a set $A$ is called an *equivalence relation* iff it is reflexive, transitive and *symmetric* ($xRy$ implies $yRx$, all $x, y \in A$). Obviously $\equiv$ as defined above is an equivalence relation. Given an equivalence relation $R$, $[x]_R = \{y \in A \mid xRy\}$ is the *equivalence class* of $x$. Our phonemes are the $\equiv$ equivalence classes of the significant segments. $\qquad\square$

**Theorem 3.1.** *For $s, s'$ significant segments, $s \equiv s'$ iff they are assigned the same value under every initial feature.*

The values of $\neg F$ and $F \wedge G$ at a segment are uniquely determined by their values at the features they are built from – ultimately the initial features.

**Definition 3.8.** If $\{F_1, \ldots, F_n\}$ are the initial features (assumed two valued) of a language then a *product* is a meet of the form $J_1 \wedge \ldots \wedge J_n$, where $J_i \in \{F_i, \neg F_i\}$.

**Theorem 3.2.** *For each product $p$ as above, either $p = \mathbf{0}$ or $p$ holds of all the significant segments in exactly one phoneme.*

For example drawing on Giegerich's feature list and using his abbreviations, the phoneme $b$, usually noted /b/, is the unique phoneme in English with the following product (For $K$ a finite set of features we write $\bigwedge K$ for the meet of the features in $K$). /b/ $= \bigwedge\{\mathbf{cons}, \mathbf{ant}, \mathbf{voice}\} \wedge \bigwedge\{\neg F \mid F \in \{\mathbf{son}, \mathbf{cont}, \mathbf{cor}, \mathbf{strid}, \mathbf{rnd}, \mathbf{high}, \mathbf{low}, \mathbf{back}, \mathbf{tense}, \mathbf{nasal}, \mathbf{lat}\}\}$.

From this theorem we see that each phoneme of a language is represented by a unique product. Note that there will be $2^n$ product expressions but due to redundancy most will denote the $\mathbf{0}$ function. For example, since **round** $\Rightarrow$ **back** (in English) any product of the form $\ldots \wedge \mathbf{round} \wedge \ldots \wedge \neg\mathbf{back} \wedge \ldots = \mathbf{0}$ (in English). So the $\mathbf{0}$ property in Meet(Neg(IF)) does turn out to be useful. Observe in fact:

**Theorem 3.3.** *If no product over the initial features of is $\mathbf{0}$ then $F \not\equiv G$, all distinct initial features $F, G$.*

Note though that the converse to the theorem above fails.

**Exercise 3.6.** Let $F$, $G$, $H$ be three initial features that hold of just the elements of $A$, $B$, and $C$ respectively, where $A = \{a, c\}$, $B = \{c, d\}$, and $C = \{a, b, d\}$. The intersection of these three sets is empty, hence the product $F \wedge G \wedge H = \mathbf{0}$. But the intersection of any two of these sets is non-empty, as is the intersection of each of these sets with the complement of the others. Write out the 9 cases that show this, i.e. compute $A \cap B$, $A \cap \neg B$, $B \cap \neg A$, ... showing in each case that the intersection is not empty. (There are nine cases to consider). Hence there is no pairwise redundancy in these features, but one of their products is $\mathbf{0}$.

We should notice that phonological generalizations and the natural classes we have taken from the literature are all defined in terms of features in Meet(Neg(IF)). Is this an accident of our sample? Or does it represent a basic empirical constraint on features that natural languages use? We leave this as a query for scholars with more knowledge of phonology than we possess:

**Query.** Are feature definable generalizations always definable from those in Meet(Neg(IF))?

It is worth noting that mathematically it would be very natural to close Meet(Neg(IF)) under a further operation, *join*, noted $\vee$.

**Definition 3.9.**

  a. For $F, G$ features $(F \vee G)$ is that map from utterances into $\{-, +\}$ given by: $(F \vee G)(u) = +$ iff $F(u) = +$ or $G(u) = +$.

  b. Let Join(Meet(Neg(IF))) be the closure of Meet(Neg(IF)) under $\vee$.

**Theorem 3.4.** *Join(Meet(Neg(IF))) is closed under $\wedge$, $\vee$ and $\neg$ and is thus a boolean algebra (This theorem is sometimes called the Fundamental Theorem of Boolean Algebra; see Mendelson, 1970.)*

So far however we have not found it natural to disjunctively define phonological properties or natural classes. We should note though that some joins are already in Meet(Neg(IF)) in virtue of redundancy:

**Exercise 3.7.** For $F, G$ features, $F \Rightarrow G$ iff $(F \vee G) = G$.

Nonetheless closing Meet(Neg(IF)) under joins massively increases the number of features, even when IF is rather small. The Venn diagram pictures the subset relations involved.

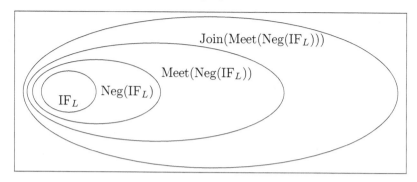

Even if we limited IF to 10 independent features the total number of elements in Join(Meet(Neg(IF))) is 2 raised to the power $2^{10} = 1,024$. This is expressed by a number with more than 302 digits (Harel, 1987, 156), unimaginably large! So the disjunctive properties we want to exclude are those in Join(Meet(Neg(IF))) that are not already in Meet(Neg(IF)).

**Concluding Observations** From the perspective of formal language theory in later chapters it is often useful to think of syntactically complex expressions as concatenations of shorter ones. In phonological detail however this is not accurate. For one thing, detailed close transcriptions of utterances will include a lot of acoustic information that is ignored by our phoneme classification, as the acoustic differences are not phonemic, that is, they are predictable from the phonological context in which they occur and do not serve to distinguish minimal pairs. Thus a voiceless stop and its aspirated counterpart, say $p$ and $p^h$ count as the same phoneme but sound a little different. Equally voiceless stops at the ends of words (Hayes, 2009, 121) are often pre-glottalized, meaning that the vocal folds close just before the stop sound is made, as in *cap, hat,* and *back.*

Secondly, while phonemes are discrete entities, adjacent phonemes (more precisely their allophones) are not completely independent. We have already seen that the place of articulation of nasal consonants assimilates to that of an oral stop at the end of a word. Equally we have noted in passing that the main vowel in a word final syllable will become nasalized when immediately followed by a nasal consonant (*camp, hand,* etc.). So we are reminded a little of Dawkins' (2006, Ch 3) genes – conceptually discrete but in reality a little spread out.

Thirdly, many properties of phonological interest are not localized on significant segments but rather on larger stretches of sound. For a case in English observe stress. Compare the two uses of *object* and

*permit* in the following sentences, with the stressed syllable underlined:
*I object to that object in the living room*; *I just got my driver's permit
but it doesn't permit me to drive a truck.* So here we have a cases
of the same segment sequence forming different words with different
stress patterns. And stress is a property of syllables, not segments.
These examples however do differ in grammatical category (Verb vs
Noun) and it could be maintained (with some difficulty) that it is the
grammatical category difference which conditions their different stress
patterns. Pairs like *abbess* and *abyss* are not subject to that criticism,
but the unstressed vowel in *abyss* differs slightly in quality from its
correspondent in *abbess*.

A more obvious suprasegmental property in many languages is *tone*.
To use a classical example: In Mandarin Chinese the segment sequence
*ma* can have five different meanings: *mother* when said with a high level
tone, *hemp* with a middle level rising tone, *horse* with a fall then rising
tone, and *scold* with a high falling tone. In addition when unstressed
and said with no distinct tone (low level) it functions as as question
particle. Many languages of SE Asia are tonal: Thai and Vietnamese
are other examples. Also many W. African languages are tonal: Yoruba
and Igbo in Nigeria are examples.

Thus to represent a particular utterance we use a linear sequence
of segments, but also an independent sequence of stress markings (in
English), a linear sequence of tone markings (in Chinese), and several
other linear sequences, called *tiers*. In particular there is a syllable tier
with association lines to the segment tier which enable us to see if two
adjacent segments are part of the same syllable or not. There will also
be a timing tier. Roca (1994, 8) points out that Polish for example has
both a ʧ which takes one timing unit and a *t+ʃ* sequence which takes
two. The tier based approach was established by Goldsmith (1976),
who cites some precursors.

**Appendix 1** A Feature List for English (Giegerich, 1992)

1. **Cons (consonantal)**. A token *t* is **cons** iff producing *t* involves
   a radical obstruction in the vocal tract.

2. **Son (sonorant)**. Production of *t* primarily involves resonance
   (not turbulence, as with *fine*, *vine*, *sign*, and *zone*).

3. **Voice** in producing *t* the vocal folds vibrate or are set in a position
   to vibrate.

4. **Nasal** in producing *t* the velum is lowered letting air pass through
   the nasal passages.

5. **Cont** (**continuant**) producing *t* does not stop the air flow in the oral cavity.

6. **Ant** (**anterior**) producing *t* involves an obstruction in front of the palatal region of the mouth. Examples are *p*, *b*, *m*, *n*, *t*, *d*, *l*, *f*, *v*, *s*, *z*, θ and ð.

7. **Cor** (**coronal**) producing *t* requires raising the blade of the tongue. E.g. *t* and *d* and *n* are coronal in English.

8. **Strid** (**strident**) producing *t* involves producing high frequency noise ("white noise") such as *s*, *z*, *f*, *v*, ʃ and ȝ.

9. **Rnd** (**round**) producing *t* requires narrowing the lip orifice (i.e. rounding the lips). The vowels in *boot*, *put*, *boat*, *caught* as well as the *w* in *we* are round.

10. **High** producing *t* requires raising the body of the tongue above its neutral position. Some high vowel sounds are those in *seat*, *sit*, *boot*, and *put*. Some high consonants are *k*, *g*, *w*, *y*, ʃ and ȝ.

11. **Low** producing *t* requires lowering the body of the tongue below its neutral position. The *h* in *help* is low, as are the vowels in *car*, *bat*, and *caught*.

12. **Back** producing *t* involves retracting the body of the tongue. The vowel sounds in *cool*, *pull*, *boat*, *but*, *cot*, and *caught* are back; those in *cat*, *fit*, *bait*, *bet*, and *bat* are not back.

13. **Lat** (**lateral**) *t* is produced by lowering the mid-section of the tongue at least on one side allowing the air to flow out of the mouth in the vicinity of the molar teeth. In English only the initial sound in *laugh* is lateral.

14. **Tense** producing *t* requires a tightening (tensing) of the articulators (lips, tongue, ... ) used in producing *t*. Tensed sounds are (relatively) clear and distinct. The vowel sounds in *beat*, *cool*, and *boat* are tense, while those in *bit*, *pull*, and *but* are not. Some tense consonants are *p*, *t*, *k*, *f*, *s*, and ʃ, while their voiced counterparts are not tense.

**Appendix 2** Speculating on Phonological Relations vs Features

*You are taller than me* is clearer and easier to verify or refute than *You are tall*. The first asserts that you and I stand in a certain relation, the second that you have a certain property – but just which property is unclear. To explicate its meaning we often construe it in terms of the relation is *taller than*: to be tall is to be taller than average, or taller than some contextually given standard.

And quite generally assertions of relations between objects are clearer and more verifiable than ascriptions of properties to single objects. In semantic studies, and to some extent syntactic ones as well, primary data that linguists want to explain are (largely) based on relational judgments. Thus a semantic theory of English should tell us that *Ed laughed loudly* **entails** *Ed laughed*, meaning simply that if the first sentence is true then the second is. As linguists we do not attempt to determine the truth conditions of *Ed laughed loudly*, we only judge relations between truth conditions: The set of states of affairs in which *Ed laughed loudly* is true is a subset of those in which *Ed laughed* is true.

Generative syntax on the other hand did start with properties as basic "Is this expression grammatical?" but has increasingly moved to judgments of relative grammaticality: Does change X in structure preserve (relative) grammaticality, (even if it lessens each instance by a little)? We note that early on Zellig Harris (1991, 203–205, 228) used preservation of grammaticality ordering as a basis for what he counted as a transformation.

Let us speculate here that generalizing from distinctive features (properties) to distinctive relations might be phonologically enlightening. A two valued property, like **voice**, can be represented as a relation: /z/**voice**/s/ iff /z/ is voiced compared to /s/. But now $n > 2$ valued "properties" are more naturally treated. Consider the four vowel heights in *beat*, *bait*, *bet*, and *bat* – represented as /i/, /e/, /ɛ/ and /æ/. Omitting angled brackets, the pairs we want in the **high** relation include: ⟨i,e⟩, ⟨i,ɛ⟩, ⟨i,æ⟩, ⟨e,ɛ⟩, ⟨e,æ⟩, and ⟨ɛ, æ⟩. (Ladefoged and Maddiesson, 1996, 289 cite Danish as having four front vowels differing just by height). This relation is transitive, as are, vacuously, the two valued ones like **voice**, as they are cross product relations $A \times B$ with $A \cap B = \emptyset$, so we never have distinct pairs ⟨x, y⟩ and ⟨y, z⟩ in $A \times B$. **Voice, high**, etc. are also asymmetric: if $xRy$ then $\neg yRx$: if $x$ is **voice** (or **high**) compared to $y$ then $y$ is not **voice** (or **high**) compared to $x$. (It follows that nothing is **voice** (or **high**) compared to itself). So possibly the distinctive relations we need are strict partial orders.

A possible advantage of distinctive relations over distinctive features concern empirical reliability. For example fairly many languages (Estonian, Tongan) make a phonemic binary vowel length distinction (and Mixe: Penutian, Mexico) makes a three way distinction (Ladefoged and

Maddiesson, 1996, 320). In English vowel length is not distinctive, but a vowel in a syllable closed with a voiceless stop is shorter than when closed with the corresponding voiced stop: *bat* vs *bad*, *bit* vs *bid*, *boat* vs *bode*, etc. But surely whether a given token in isolation is short or long can not be determined by measuring its absolute duration. Some people speak more rapidly than others, a given individual speaks at different speeds on different occasions, etc. What determines whether a token is short (mid) or long is its length *compared* to other tokens. That is, the relation is *regularly longer* than is preserved under change of speakers and speaking situations but the absolute duration of vowels is not.

It seems to us likely that several other phonemic "features" of American English might be more reliably treated as relations rather than as properties. For example, Giegerich (1992, 98) acknowledges that it is easier to establish that the vowels in *beat*/*bit* stand in the **tense** relation than to establish that the vowel in *beat* in isolation is tense. Giegerich has **cons** (**consonantal**) holding of sounds if producing them involves a radical obstruction in the vocal tract. Clearly enough, $p$ **cons** $f$ and $f$ **cons** $i$ but why should the $r$ in *run* be $+$**cons** while the $w$ in *we* and the $j$ in *yes* be $-$**cons** as Giegerich (and Spencer, 1996) claim? Surely $w$ and $j$ obstruct the oral tract more than $r$. If **cons** is merely a (strict) partial order (not required to be linear) then we need not order $r$, $w$, and $j$ though $p$ and $f$ can bear **cons** to all of them, and each can bear **cons** to all the vowels. (The relations **high** and **round** suffice to distinguish $r$, $w$, and $j$.)

# 4

---

# Syntax I: Trees and Order Relations

We think of a *language* as a set of meaningful, pronounceable (or signable) expressions. A *grammar* is a definition of a language. As linguists, we are interested in defining (and then studying) languages whose expressions are approximately those of one or another empirically given natural language (English, Japanese, Swahili, ...). If a proposed grammar of English, for example, failed to tell us that *Every cat chased every mouse* is an expression of English, that grammar would be *incomplete*. If it told us that *Cat mouse every every chased* is an expression of English, it would be *unsound*. So designing a sound and complete grammar for a natural language involves considerable empirical work, work that teaches us much about the structure and nature of human language.

And as we have seen in Chapter 1, a grammar for a natural language cannot just be a finite list of expressions: natural languages present too many expressions to be listed in any enlightening way. Moreover, a mere list fails to account for the *productivity* of natural language—our ability to form and interpret novel utterances—as it fails to tell us how the form and interpretation of complex expressions depends on those of its parts.

Consequently, a *grammar G* of a language is presented in two gross parts: (1) a *Lexicon*, that is, a finite list of expressions called *lexical items*, and (2) a set of partial functions, called *Rules*, which iteratively derive complex expressions from simpler ones, beginning with the lexical items. The language $L(G)$ generated by the grammar is then the lexical items plus all those expressions constructable from them by applying the rules finitely many times. That is, it is the closure of the Lexicon wrt the Rules.

In this chapter, we present some standard techniques and formalisms linguists use to show how complex expressions incorporate simpler ones. So here we concentrate on generative syntax, ignoring both semantic representation (see Chapters 8–12) and phonological representation. In Chapter 5, we consider a specific proposal for a grammar of a fragment of English.

## 4.1 Trees

The derivation of complex expressions from lexical items is commonly represented with a type of graph called a *tree*. Part, *but not all*, of what we think of as the *structure* of an expression is given by its tree graph. For example, we might use the tree depicted in (1) to represent the English expression *John knows every teacher* (though the tree linguists would currently use is more complicated than (1) and would indicate that *knows* is present tense, as opposed to the simple past tense form *knew*).

(1)

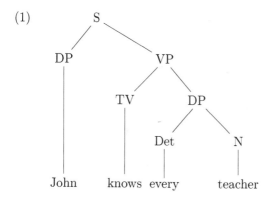

This tree is understood to represent a variety of linguistic information. First, its bottommost items *John, knows, every,* and *teacher* are presented here as underived expressions (lexical items) having the categories indicated by the symbols immediately above them. Specifically, according to this tree (given here for illustrative purposes only), *John* is a DP (Determiner Phrase), *knows* is a TV (Transitive Verb), *every* is a Det (Determiner), and *teacher* is a N (Noun).

The tree in (1) identifies not only the lexical items *John knows every teacher* is constructed from, it also defines their **pronunciation order**. Specifically, we use the convention that the word written leftmost is pronounced first, then the next leftmost item, and so on. (Other writing conventions could have been used: in Hebrew and Arabic items written rightmost are pronounced first; in Classical Chinese reading may go from top down, not left to right or right to left).

Finally, (1) identifies which expressions combine with which others to form complex ones, resulting ultimately in the expression *John knows every teacher*. The expressions a derived expression is built from are its **constituents**. (1) also identifies the grammatical category of each expression. This in (1), *every* and *teacher* combine to form a constituent *every teacher* of category DP. The TV *knows* combines with this constituent to form another constituent, *knows every teacher* of category VP. And this in turn combines with *John* of category DP to form *John knows every teacher* of category S. Note that some substrings of the string *John knows every teacher* are not constituents of it according to (1): they were not used in building that particular S. For example, *knows every* is not a constituent, and that string has no category. Similarly, *John knows* and *John knows every* are not constituents of (1).

The tree in (1) does not exhibit the rules that applied to combine various words and phrases to form constituents. In the next chapter, we formulate some such rules. Here we just suggest some candidates so that the reader can appreciate the sense in which (1) records the derivational history of *John knows every teacher*, even though some structurally relevant information has been omitted.

To build the DP *every teacher* from the Det *every* and the N *teacher*, the simplest rule would be the concatenative one whose effect is given in (2):

(2)  if $s$ is a string of category Det and $t$ is a string of category N, then $s \frown t$ is a string of category DP.

Recall that $s \frown t$ denotes the concatenation of the sequences $s$ and $t$.

Similarly, we might derive the VP *knows every teacher* by concatenating *knows* of category TV with *every teacher* of category DP. And then we might derive the S *John knows every teacher* by concatenating *John* with that VP string.

Linguists commonly assume that the trees they use to represent the derivation of expressions are in fact derived by concatenative functions of the sort illustrated in (2). Such functions will take $n$ expressions as arguments and derive an expression by concatenating the strings of those expressions, perhaps inserting some constant elements. For example, we might consider a function of two arguments, which would map *John* of category DP and *cat* of category N to *John's cat* of category DP. This function introduces the constant element *'s*.

We are not arguing here that the rules of a grammar—its structure building functions—*should* be concatenative, we are simply observing that linguists commonly use such functions. And this in turn has a limiting effect, often unintended, on how expressions can be syntactically analyzed and hence how they can be semantically interpreted. Here is an example which illustrates the use of a non-concatenative function. It introduces some non-trivial issues taken up in more detail in our later chapters on semantics.

Ss like (3) present a subtle ambiguity. (3) might be interpreted as in (a), or it might be interpreted as in (b).

(3)    Some editor read every manuscript.

      a. Some editor has the property that he read every manuscript.

      b. Every manuscript has the property that some editor read it.

One the a-reading, a speaker of (3) asserts that there is at least one editor who read all the manuscripts. But the b-reading is weaker. It just says that for each manuscript, there is some editor who read it. Possibly different manuscripts were read by different editors. Thus in a situation in which there are just two editors, say Bob and Sue, and three manuscripts, say $m_1$, $m_2$, and $m_3$, and Bob read just $m_1$ and $m_2$, and Sue read just $m_2$ and $m_3$, we see that (3) is true on the b-reading: every manuscript was read by at least one editor. But (3) is false on the a-reading, since no one editor read all of the manuscripts. Ambiguities of this sort are known as *scope ambiguities* and are taken up in Chapter 10.

One approach to representing these ambiguities originates with the work of Montague (1970a). This approach says that (3) is syntactically ambiguous – derived in two interestingly different ways. In one way, corresponding to the a-reading, it is derived by the use of concatenative functions as we have illustrated for (1). The difference this time is that the last step of the derivation concatenates a complex DP *some editor* with the VP *read every manuscript*; earlier we had used not a complex DP but rather the lexical DP *John*. The derivation of the S whose interpretation is the b-reading is more complicated. First we derive by concatenation a VP *read it* using the pronoun *it*. Then we concatenate that with the DP *some editor* to get the S *Some editor read it*. Then we form *every manuscript* by concatenation as before. In the last step, we derive *Some editor read every manuscript* by **substituting** *every manuscript* for *it*. So the last step in the derivation is a substitution step, not a concatenation step. It would take two arguments on the left in (4) and derive the string on the right.

(4)  every ms, some editor read it  $\Longrightarrow$  some editor read every ms

Let us emphasize that while the a-reading has a standard tree derivation, the b-reading does not, since *read every manuscript* is not formed solely by concatenative functions. Thus if we were to limit ourselves to the use of standard trees in representing derivations of natural language expressions, we would exclude some ways of compositionally interpreting semantically ambiguous expressions. For the record, let us formally define the core substitution operation.

**Definition 4.1.** Let $s$ be a string of length $n > 0$. Let $t$ be any string, and let $i$ be a number between 1 and $n$. Then $s(i/t)$ is the string of length $n$ whose $i^{th}$ coordinate is $t$ and whose $j^{th}$ coordinate is $s_j$, for all $j \neq i$. We call $s(i/t)$ the result of *substituting the $i^{th}$ coordinate of $s$ by $t$*.

**Exercise 4.1.** Complete the following in list notation.

a. $\langle 2, 5, 2 \rangle (2/7) = $ _____ .

b. $\langle 2, 2, 2 \rangle (2/7) = $ _____ .

c. $\langle \text{John, 's, cat} \rangle (3/\text{dog}) = $ _____ .

d. $\langle \text{every, cat} \rangle (2/\text{fat cat}) = $ _____ .

**Trees as mathematical objects**  Having presented some motivation for the linguists' use of trees, we now formally define these objects and discuss several of the notions definable on trees that linguists avail themselves of. For convenience, we repeat the tree in (1).

(5)

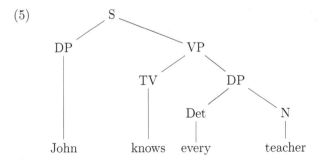

The objects presented in (5) are linguistic *labels*—names of grammatical categories, such as S, DP, VP, etc., or English expressions such as *John, knows,* etc. These labels are connected by lines, called *branches* or *edges*. We think of the labels as labeling *nodes* (or *vertices*), even though the nodes are not explicitly represented. But note, for example, that the label DP occurs twice in (5), naming different nodes. The node representing the category of *John* is not the same as that representing the category of *every teacher*, even though these two expressions have the same category. So we must distinguish nodes from their labels, since different nodes may have the same label. In giving examples of trees below, we shall commonly use numbers as nodes, in which case (5) could receive a representation as in (6).

(6)

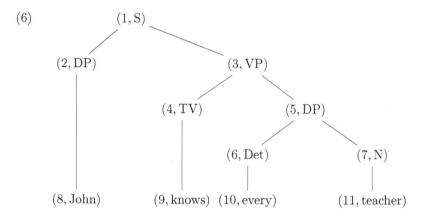

Now we can say that node 2 and node 5 have the same label, DP. Our formal definition of *tree* will include nodes, and their absence on specific occasions is just one more typical instance of simplifying a notation when no confusion results.

Now let us consider what is distinctive about the graph structure of trees. Some nodes as we see are connected to others by a line (a branch). If we can read *down* along branches from a node $x$ to a node $y$, we say that $x$ *dominates* $y$. And the distinctive properties of trees lie in the properties of this dominance relation. First, we understand that if we can move down from a node $x$ to a node $y$ (so $x$ dominates $y$), and we can move down from $y$ to a node $z$ (so $y$ dominates $z$), then we clearly can move down from $x$ to $z$, whence $x$ dominates $z$. Thus *dominates* is a *transitive* relation.

We have already seen one transitive relation, namely inclusion of subsets ($\subseteq$): given a collection of sets, we see that if $X \subseteq Y$ and $Y \subseteq Z$, then also $X \subseteq Z$. Many common mathematical relations are transitive. For example, the $\geq$ relation on natural numbers is transitive: if $n \geq m$ and $m \geq p$, then $n \geq p$. So let us define more generally.

**Definition 4.2.** $R$ is a *binary relation* on a set $A$ if $R$ is a subset of $A \times A$. Instead of writing $(x, y) \in R$, we often write $xRy$, read as "$x$ stands in the relation $R$ to $y$." To say that $x$ does not stand in the relation $R$ to $y$ we write $x \not R y$, or $\neg(xRy)$, usually omitting parentheses. Generalizing, for $n \in \mathbb{N}$, $R$ is$_{\text{def}}$ an $n$-ary relation on $A$ iff $R \subseteq A^n$. In particular $R$ is a 0-ary relation on $A$ iff $R \subseteq A^0 = \{\emptyset\}$. So the *set* of 0-ary relations on $A$ is $\{\emptyset, \{\emptyset\}\}$, often noted $\{0, 1\}$.

In general, to define a binary relation $R$ on a set $A$ we must say for each choice $x$ and each choice $y$ of elements from $A$ whether $xRy$ or not. In particular this means that we must say for each $x \in A$, whether $xRx$ or not.

In what follows we are concerned with whether various relations we define of interest are *reflexive, antisymmetric, asymmetric,* or *transitive*. These notions are defined below.

**Definition 4.3.** A relation $R$ on a set $A$ is *transitive* if for all $x$, $y$, $z \in A$, if $xRy$ and $yRz$, then $xRz$.

As we have seen, the *dominates* relation among nodes in a given tree is transitive. Further, *dominates* is "loop-free", meaning that we can never have two *different* nodes each of which dominates the other. The traditional term for "loop free" is *antisymmetric*:

**Definition 4.4.** A binary relation $R$ on a set $A$ is *antisymmetric* iff for $x, y \in A$, $xRy$ and $yRx$ jointly imply $x = y$. (Antisymmetry should not be confused with *asymmetry*, defined as follows: A binary relation $R$ on a set $A$ is *asymmetric* iff for $x, y \in A$, if $xRy$, then $yRx$ is *false*. For example the proper subset relation $\subset$ is asymmetric: if $A$ is a proper subset of $B$, $B$ is certainly not a subset of $A$, hence not a proper subset of $A$. Similarly the 'is strictly less than' relation $<$ in arithmetic is asymmetric, as is the 'is a parent of' relation on people.)

Again, $\subseteq$ is antisymmetric. If $X \subseteq Y$ and $Y \subseteq X$, then $X$ and $Y$ have the same members and are hence equal. Similarly, one checks that the arithmetical $\geq$ is antisymmetric.

Note that the antisymmetry of a relation $R$ still allows that a given element $x$ stand in the relation $R$ to itself. In what follows, we treat *dominates* as a *reflexive* relation, meaning that each node is understood to dominate itself. For the record:

**Definition 4.5.** A binary relation $R$ on a set $A$ is *reflexive* iff for all $x \in A$, $xRx$. $R$ is *irreflexive* iff for all $x \in A$, it is not the case that $xRx$. We write $\neg xRx$ in this case as well.

Now the cluster of properties that we have adduced for *dominates*, transitivity, antisymmetry, and reflexivity, is a cluster that arises often in mathematical study. We note:

**Definition 4.6.** A binary relation $R$ on a set $A$ is a *reflexive partial order* iff $R$ is reflexive, transitive, and antisymmetric. The pair $(A, R)$ is often called a *partially ordered set* or *poset*

In practice, when we refer to partial order relations, we shall assume that they are reflexive unless explicitly noted otherwise. Note that $\subseteq$ and $\geq$ are reflexive partial orders.

**Exercise 4.2.** Exhibit a binary relation $R$ on $\{a, b, c\}$ which is neither reflexive nor irreflexive.

**Exercise 4.3.** We define a binary relation $R$ on a set $A$ to be *symmetric* if whenever $xRy$ then also $yRx$. $R$ is *asymmetric* if whenever $xRy$ then it is not the case that $yRx$. Let $R$ be a reflexive partial order on a set $A$, and define another binary relation $SR$, *strict-R*, on $A$ by

$$\text{for all } x, y \in A, \ xSRy \text{ iff } xRy \text{ and } x \neq y.$$

Prove that $SR$ is irreflexive, asymmetric, and transitive. Such relations will be called *strict partial orders*.

For example, the strictly greater-than relation on numbers, $>$, is the strict-$\geq$ relation. So by this exercise, it is is a strict partial order. So is the strict-$\subseteq$ relation defined on any collection of sets. This relation is written $\subset$.

**Exercise 4.4.** Given a relation $R$ on a set $A$, we define a relation $R^{-1}$ on the same set $A$, called the *converse of R* by: $xR^{-1}y$ iff $yRx$, for all $x, y \in A$. Show that

 a. If $R$ is a reflexive partial order, so is $R^{-1}$.

 b. If $R$ is a strict partial order, so is $R^{-1}$.

In each case, state explicitly what is to be shown before you show it.

Returning to *dominates*, it has two properties that go beyond the partial order properties. First, it has a *root*, a node that dominates all nodes. In (6) it is node 1, the node labeled S.

**Observation** If $R$ is a partial order relation on a set $A$, then there cannot be two distinct elements $x$ and $y$ such that each bears $R$ to all the elements of $A$. The reason is that if both $x$ and $y$ have this property, then $xRy$ and $yRx$, whence by the antisymmetry of $R$, $x = y$, contra our assumption that they were distinct.

The second and more important property of the dominance order is that its branches never coalesce: if two nodes dominate a third, then one of those two dominates the other. We summarize these conditions below in a formal definition. The objects we define are unordered, unlabeled trees which we call *simple trees* (usually omitting 'simple'). We do not impose a left-right order on the bottommost nodes, and we do not require that nodes be labeled. For this reason, simple trees might well be called *mobiles*. Simple trees are ideal for studying pure constituent structure. Once they are understood, we add additional conditions to obtain the richer class of trees that linguists use in practice.

**Definition 4.7.** A *simple tree* $T$ is a pair $(N, D)$, where $N$ is a set whose elements are called *nodes* and $D$ is a binary relation on $N$ called *dominates*, satisfying (a) - (c):

a. $D$ is a **reflexive partial order** relation on $N$.

b. **the root condition**: There is a node $r$ which dominates every node. This $r$ is provably unique and called the *root* of $T$.

c. **chain condition** For all nodes $x, y, z$, if $xDz$ and $yDz$, then either $xDy$ or $yDx$. [1]

On this definition, the two pictures in (7) are the *same* (simple) tree. The difference in left-right order of node notation is no more significant then the left-right order in set names like '$\{2, 3, 5\}$'; it names the same set as '$\{5, 2, 3\}$'.

(7)

Unordered trees are frequently used to represent structures of quite diverse sorts – chain of command hierarchies, classification schemes, genetic groupings of populations or languages. These often do not have a left-right order encoded. For example, Figure 4.1 is a tree representing the major genetic groupings of Germanic languages.

---

[1]The reason for this name is that the chain condition as defined above is equivalent to the assertion that the set of nodes dominating any given node is a chain, that is, linearly ordered, by $D$. For the definition of a linear order, see Definition 4.14.

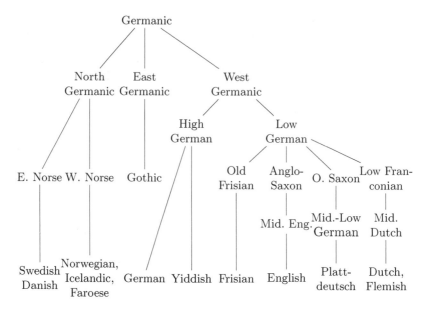

Figure 4.1: The major Germanic Languages

The root node of Figure 4.1 represents a language, Germanic, from which all other languages shown are genetically descended. The leaves (at the bottom) are languages or small groups of closely related languages. Notice that Gothic is also a leaf. To see how closely related two languages are, read up the tree until you find the first common ancestor. For example, (Modern) German and Yiddish are more closely related than either is to (Modern) English, since they are descended from High German, itself coordinate with Low German. So the least common ancestor of English and German is W. Germanic, itself a proper ancestor of High German.

And observe that the left-right order on the page of the names of the daughter languages has no structural significance. There is no sense in which Icelandic is to the left of, or precedes, English, or Dutch is to the right of English.

Let us consider in turn the three defining conditions on trees. The discussion will be facilitated by the following definitions:

**Definition 4.8.** Let $T = (N, D)$ be a tree. Then for all $x$, $y \in N$,

    a. *x strictly dominates y*, $xSDy$, iff $xDy$ and $x \neq y$.

   b. *x immediately dominates y*, $xIDy$, iff $x$ strictly dominates $y$, but there is no node $z$ such that $x$ strictly dominates $z$ and $z$ strictly dominates $y$.

In drawing pictures of trees, we just draw the *ID* relation. So in (6), $1ID2$ and $1ID3$, but $\neg 1ID4$. This last fact holds despite the fact that $1D4$ and indeed $1SD4$. Observe that when $\varphi$ is a sentence, we sometimes write $\neg\varphi$ for the sentence "it is not the case that $\varphi$".

**Definition 4.9.** A tree $T = (N, D)$ is *finite* if its node set $N$ is finite.

In this book we only consider finite trees.

Consider the dominance relation $D$ on trees. Because $D$ is an *order* relation – transitive and antisymmetric – we know that it can have no *cycles*, where a cycle is a finite sequence $\langle n_1, \ldots, n_k \rangle$ of two or more nodes such that the first and last nodes are the same and each node $n_j$ except the last immediately dominates the next one, $n_{j+1}$. For then $n_1$ would strictly dominate $n_k$ and thus be distinct from it, contradicting that the first and last nodes are the same.

Second, linguists often don't consider the case where a given node might dominate itself. Usually when we speak of $x$ dominating $y$, we are given that $x$ and $y$ are different nodes. In a case where $x$ and $y$ are intended as different but not independently given as different, it would be clearer for the linguist to say "$x$ strictly dominates $y$".

Third, our tree pictures do not include the transitivity edges – there is no edge directly from 1 to 4 in (6), for examples. Nor do we have to put in the reflexivity loops, the edges from each node to itself. We just represent the immediate dominance relation (sometimes called the *cover relation*), the rest being recoverable from this one by the assumptions of transitivity and reflexivity. Now, of the three conditions that the dominance relation $D$ must satisfy, the root condition rules out relations like those with diagrams in (8):

(8)      (*a*)                                    (*b*)

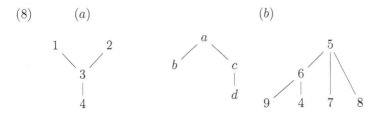

In (8a) there is clearly no root, that is no node that dominates every node. And (8b) is just a pair of trees. There is no root since no node dominates both $a$ and 5. (A graph with all the properties of a tree except the root condition is sometimes called a *forest*.) So neither (8a) nor (8b) are graphs of trees.

The truly distinctive condition on trees, the one that differentiates them from many other partial orders, is the chain condition. Consider the graph in (9), as always reading down.

(9)

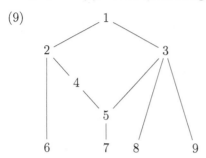

(9) violates the chain condition: for example, both 2 and 3 dominate 5, but neither 2 nor 3 dominates the other.

We present in Figure 4.2 a variety of linguistic notions defined on simple trees (and thus ones that do not depend on labeling or linear order of elements).

**Exercise 4.5.** For each graph below, state whether it is a tree graph or not (always reading down for dominance). If it is not, state at least one of the three defining conditions for trees which fails.

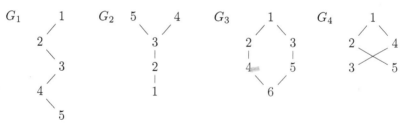

**Exercise 4.6.** Below are four graphs of trees, $T_1, \ldots, T_4$. For each distinct $i, j$ between 1 and 4, state whether $T_i = T_j$ or not. If not, give one reason why it fails.

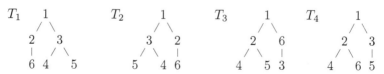

Let $T = (N, D)$ be a tree, and let $x$ and $y$ be nodes of $N$.

a. $x$ is an *ancestor* of $y$, or, dually, $y$ is a *descendant* of $x$, iff $xDy$.

b. $x$ is a *leaf* (also called a *terminal node*) iff $\{z \in N \mid xSDz\} = \emptyset$.

c. The *degree* of $x$, noted $deg(x)$, is $|\{z \in N \mid xIDz\}|$. (Some texts write *out-degree* where we write simply degree.) So if $z$ is a leaf then $deg(z) = 0$.

d. $x$ is a *n-ary branching node* iff $|\{y \in N \mid xIDy\}| = n$. We write *unary* branching for 1-ary branching and *binary* branching for 2-ary branching. $T$ itself is called *n-ary branching* if all nodes except the leaves are *n*-ary branching. In linguistic parlance, a *branching* node is one that is *n*-ary branching for some $n \geq 2$. (So unary branching nodes are not called branching nodes by linguists.)

e. $x$ is a *sister* (*sibling*) of $y$ iff $x \neq y$ and there is a node $z$ such that $zIDx$ and $zIDy$.

f. $x$ is a *mother* (*parent*) of $y$ iff $xIDy$; Under the same conditions we say that $y$ is a *daughter* (*child*) of $x$.

g. The depth of $x$, noted $depth(x)$, is $|\{z \in N \mid zSDx\}|$.

h. $Depth(T) = \max\{depth(x) \mid x \in N\}$. This is also called the *height* of $T$. Note that $\{depth(x) \mid x \in N\}$ is a finite non-empty subset of $\mathbb{N}$. (Any finite non-empty subset $K$ of $\mathbb{N}$ has a greatest element, noted $\max(K)$.)

i. $x$ is (dominance) *independent of* $y$ iff neither dominates the other. We write *IND* for *is independent of*. Clearly *IND* is a symmetric relation. This relation is also called *incomparability*.

j. A *branch* (*edge*) is a pair $(x, y)$ such that $xIDy$.

k. A *path in* $T$ is a sequence $p$ of two or more nodes, all of which are distinct, such that each one (except the last) either immediately dominates the next one or is immediately dominated by the next one.

l. $x$ *c-commands* $y$, noted $xCCy$, iff

   i. $x$ and $y$ are independent, and

   ii. every branching node which strictly dominates $x$ also dominates $y$.

We say that $x$ *asymmetrically c-commands* $y$ iff $x$ c-commands $y$ but $y$ does not c-command $x$.

Figure 4.2: Linguistic notions defined on trees.

**Exercise 4.7.** Referring to the tree below, mark each of the statements $T$ (true) or $F$ (false) correctly. If you mark $F$, say why (relevant definitions on the previous page).

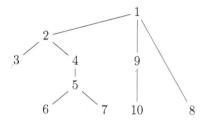

| | | |
|---|---|---|
| *a.* 4 and 9 are sisters | *b.* $2SD7$ | *c.* $1ID8$ |
| *d.* 2 and 8 are sisters | *e.* 1 is mother of 8 | *f.* 3 is a leaf |
| *g.* $depth(5) = 3$ | *h.* $depth(T) = depth(7)$ | *i.* $5IND7$ |
| *j.* $depth(8) > depth(2)$ | *k.* $depth(7) = depth(10)$ | *l.* $2CC5$ |
| *m.* $\langle 4,2,3,2 \rangle$ is a path | *n.* $\langle 7,5,4,2,3 \rangle$ is a path | *o.* $5CC3$ |
| *p.* $\langle 8 \rangle$ is a path | | |

*q.* 8 asymmetrically c-commands 3.

*r.* For all nodes $x, y$, if $x$ is mother of $y$, then $y$ is mother of $x$.

We conclude with an important fact about trees:

**Theorem 4.1.** *If $x$ and $y$ are distinct nodes in a tree $T$, then there is exactly one path from $x$ to $y$ in $T$.*

Informally, we show this as follows: Let $T$ be a tree with distinct nodes $x, y$. We give a proof by cases:

**Case 1:** $xDy$. Then since $x \neq y$ and $T$ is finite there is a finite sequence $\langle n_1, \ldots, n_k \rangle$ of nodes such that $x = n_1$, $y = n_k$ and each node in the sequence except the last immediately dominates the next one. This sequence is the unique path from $x$ to $y$.

**Case 2:** $yDx$. Then, as above, there is a unique path $\langle n_1, \ldots, n_k \rangle$ from $y$ to $x$, and its reversal, $\langle n_k, \ldots, n_1 \rangle$ is the unique path from $x$ to $y$.

**Case 3:** $x$ and $y$ are independent. Consider the set of nodes that dominate both $x$ and $y$. This set is non-empty since it contains the root node. The set is a chain by the chain condition and as it is finite it has a deepest element $z$. $z$ is the least common ancestor of $x$ and $y$. The unique path from $x$ to $z$, followed by that from $z$ to $y$ is the unique path from $x$ to $y$. Its reversal is the unique path from $y$ to $x$. $\qquad\square$

We note that in the mathematical literature on graph theory, trees are graphs that satisfy the unique path condition in Theorem 4.1. Then a *rooted tree* is defined as a tree in which one vertex is designated as a root, and then the paths from that vertex to the others ultimately determine the dominance relation in the linguists' sense. For further accessible reading in the mathematical theory of trees we have found the early chapters in Wilson (1979) and Harary (1972) helpful.

The topic of trees is standard in mathematics and computer science books (these will be on topics like graph theory, discrete mathematics or data structures). But there, the basic definition is often graph theoretic: one takes vertices and symmetric edges as primitive, and the definition of a tree is as in Theorem 4.1: between every two vertices there is a unique path.

## 4.2   C-Command

Figure 4.2 defines a number of concepts pertaining to trees. The only one of these that originates in linguistics is c-command. We want to spell out in detail the motivations for this concept. Here is one: Reflexive pronouns (*himself, herself,* and a few other *self* forms) in Ss like (10) are referentially dependent on another DP, called their *antecedent*.

(10)   *John's father embarrassed himself at the meeting.*

In (10) *John's father* but not *John* is the antecedent of *himself.* That is, (10) only asserts John's father was embarrassed, not John. A *linguistic query*: Given a reflexive pronoun in an expression $E$, which DPs in $E$ can be interpreted as its antecedent? (11) is a *necessary* condition for many expressions:

(11)   Antecedents of reflexive pronouns c-command them.

Establishing the truth of a claim like (11) involves many empirical claims concerning constituent structure which we do not undertake here. Still, most linguists would accept (12) as a gross constituent analysis of (10). (We "cover" the proper constituents of *at the meeting* with the widely used "triangle", as that internal structure is irrelevant to the point at hand.)

(12)

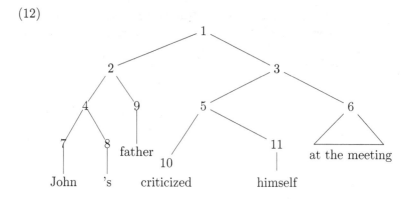

We see here that node 2, *John's father*, does c-command node 11, *himself*. Clearly 2 and 11 are independent, and every branching node which strictly dominates 2 also dominates 11 since the only such node is the root 1. In contrast, node 7, *John* does not c-command 11, since both 2 and 4 are branching nodes which strictly dominate 7 but do not dominate 11.

One might object to (11) as a (partial) characterization of the conditions regulating the distribution of reflexives and their antecedents on the grounds that there is a less complicated (and more traditional) statement that is empirically equivalent but only uses left-right order:

(13)   Antecedents of reflexive pronouns precede them

In fact for basic expressions in English the predictions made by (11) and (13) largely coincide since the c-commanding DP precedes the reflexive[2]. But in languages like Tzotzil (Mayan: see Aissen, 1987) and Malagasy (Malayo-Polynesian; Keenan, 1995) in which the basic word order in simple active Ss is VOS (Verb + Object + Subject) rather than SVO (Subject + Verb + Object) as in English, we find that antecedents follow reflexives but still c-command them. So analogous to (10), speakers of Malagasy understand that (14) only asserts that

---

[2]Some known empirical problems with the c-command condition are given by:

   i. *It is only himself that John admires.*

  ii. *Which pictures of himself does John like best?*

  iii. *The pictures of himself that John saw in the post office.*

But these expressions are derivationally complex. It may be that c-command holds in simple expressions (e.g., *John admires only himself*) and that the antecedent-reflexive relation is preserved under the derivation of more complex ones.

Rakoto's father respects himself, but says nothing about Rakoto himself. So c-command wins out in some contexts in which it conflicts with left-right order.

(14)

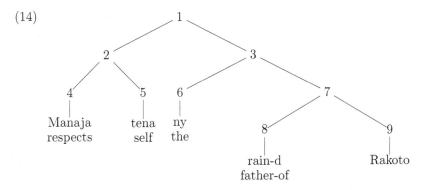

*Rakoto's father respects himself* (Malagasy)

Pursuing these observations it is natural to wonder whether c-command is a *sufficient* condition on the antecedent-reflexive relation. That is, can any DP which c-commands a reflexive be interpreted as its antecedent? Here the answer is a clear negative, though more so for Modern English than certain other languages. Observe first that in (15a), the DP *every student* is naturally represented as a sister to the VP *thinks that Mary criticized himself* and

(15)     a. *Every student thinks that Mary criticized himself*

      b. *Every student thinks that himself criticized John*

And since *himself* lies properly within that VP, we have that *every student* (asymmetrically) c-commands *himself*. But it cannot be interpreted as its antecedent. Comparable claims hold for (15b). But patterns like those in (15), especially (15b), are possible in a variety of languages: Japanese, Korean, Yoruba, even Middle English and Early Modern English:

(16) (Japanese)

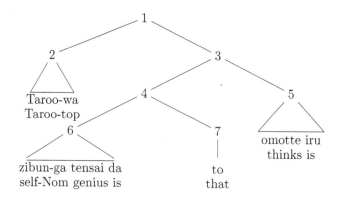

*Taroo thinks that he (Taroo) is a genius.*

(17) ...  *a  Pardonere*  ...  *seide  that  hymself  myghte  assoilen*
...  a  Pardoner  ...  said  that  himself  might  absolve
*hem   alle.*
them  all

*Piers Plowman* c.1375; Keenan (2007)

(18) *he ... protested ..., that himselfe was cleere and innocent.*
*Dobson's Drie Bobbes*, 1607; Keenan (2007)

(19) *But there was a certain man, ... which ... bewitched the people*
*of Samaria, giving out that himself was some great one.*
(*King James Bible*, Acts 8.9, 1611)

So the possible antecedents for a reflexive pronoun in English thus appear to be a subset of the c-commanding DPs with the precise delimitation subject to some language variation. See Büring (2005) for an overview discussion.

**Exercise 4.8.** For each condition below exhibit a tree which instantiates that condition:

   a. $CC$ is not symmetric.

   b. $CC$ is not antisymmetric.

   c. $CC$ is not transitive.

   d. $CC$ is not asymmetric.

In each case say why the trees show that $CC$ fails to have the property indicated. We note regarding part (c) that asymmetric c-command is a transitive relation.

**Exercise 4.9.** In any tree $(N, D)$,

    a. if $aCCb$ and $bDx$ does $aCCx$?

    b. Do distinct sisters c-command each other?

    c. c-command is irreflexive. Why?

    d. For all nodes $a$, $\{x \in N \mid xDa\} \neq \emptyset$. Why?

## 4.3 Sameness of Structure: Isomorphism

Our interest in trees concerns the structural relations between nodes – relations defined in terms of dominance – not the identity of the nodes themselves. For example the tree $T_1$ below whose nodes are the numbers 1 through 5 and $T_2$ whose nodes are the letters $a$ through $e$ are regarded as "essentially" the same. They have the same "branching structure", differing just by identity of nodes. And these, as we have noted, are normally not even noted in tree graphs used by linguists.

Thus we want a way of saying that $T_1$ and $T_2$ have the same structure, that is, are *isomorphic*, even though they fail to be identical. Then any structural claim we can make of one will hold of the other as well. For example the statement "All non-terminal nodes are binary branching" holds of both; "The total number of nodes is 9" fails of both trees. But no structural statement can hold of one but fail of the other.

    Here is the core idea of isomorphism (an idea that generalizes naturally to other types of structures used in this book, such as linear orders, context free grammars, boolean algebras, and finite state machines): Trees $T$ and $T'$ are isomorphic iff (1) we can match up their nodes one for one with none left over and (2) whenever a node $x$ dominates a node $y$ in one tree the node $x$ is matched with dominates the one $y$ is matched with in the other tree, and conversely. Formally:

**Definition 4.10.** A tree $T = (N, D)$ is *isomorphic* ($\cong$) to a tree $T' = (N', D')$ iff there is a bijection $m$ from $N$ to $N'$ satisfying:

$$\text{for all } x, y \in N, \ xDy \text{ iff } m(x)D'm(y).$$

Such a bijection is called an *isomorphism* (from $T$ to $T'$).

Thus, to prove that $T_1$ above is isomorphic to $T_2$, we must show that there is a bijection from the nodes of $T_1$ to those of $T_2$ satisfying the condition in Def 4.10. We do this by exhibiting such a bijection, $m$ below as a dotted arrow. (Recall: we establish an existential claim by exhibiting an example).

(20)  $T_1$

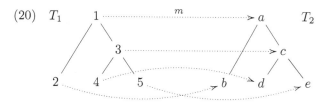

To establish that the $m$ shown in (20) is an isomorphism, we must verify (1) that $m$ is a bijection, and (2) that $m$ satisfies the condition in Def. 4.10. Visual inspection establishes that $m$ is a bijection. To visually establish that $m$ strongly preserves dominance check first that whenever $xDy$ in $T_1$ than $m(x)$ dominates $m(y)$ in $T_2$. Then you must check the converse: whenever $x'$ dominates $y'$ in $T_2$ then $m^{-1}(x')$, the node in $T_1$ that $m$ maps to $x'$, dominates $m^{-1}(y')$ in $T_1$. This verifies that $T_1$ and $T_2$ have the same dominance structure.

**Exercise 4.10.** Let **T** be any collection of trees. Each statement below is true. Say why.

 a. For all $T \in \mathbf{T}$, $T \cong T$.

 b. For all $T, T' \in \mathbf{T}$, if $T \cong T'$ then $T' \cong T$.

 c. For all $T, T', T'' \in \mathbf{T}$, $T \cong T'$ and $T' \cong T''$, then $T \cong T''$.

When two relational structures are isomorphic they have the same structurally definable properties. In particular, if two trees are isomorphic then they have the same tree definable properties. For example,

Let $(A, R)$ and $(B, S)$ be relational structures (So $R$ is a binary relation defined on the set $A$, and $S$ is a binary relation defined on $B$). Then $(A, R)$ is isomorphic to $(B, S)$, noted $(A, R) \cong (B, S)$, iff there is a bijection $h$ from $A$ into $B$ satisfying

$$\text{for all } x, y \in A, \ xRy \text{ iff } h(x)Sh(y).$$

Such an $h$ is called an *isomorphism* (from $(A, R)$ to $(B, S)$).

a. If $h$ is an isomorphism from $(A, R)$ to $(B, S)$ then $h^{-1}$ is an isomorphism from $(B, S)$ to $(A, R)$.

b. If $h$ is an isomorphism from $(A, R)$ to $(B, S)$ and $g$ is an isomorphism from $(B, S)$ to some $(C, T)$ then $g \circ h$ is an isomorphism from $(A, R)$ to $(C, T)$.

c. Every relational structure $(A, R)$ is isomorphic to itself, using the identity map $id_A : A \to A$. This map is defined by $id_A(a) = a$ for $a \in A$. An isomorphism from a structure to itself is called an *automorphism*.

Figure 4.3: Basic Facts About Isomorphisms

**Fact 1** Let $T = (N, D)$ and $T' = (N', D')$ be isomorphic trees, let $h$ be an isomorphism from $T$ to $T'$. Then, for all $a, b \in N$:

a. $aSDb$ iff $h(a)SD'h(b)$.

b. $aIDb$ iff $h(a)ID'h(b)$.

c. $deg(a) = deg(h(a))$.

d. $a$ is 3-ary branching iff $h(a)$ is 3-ary branching.

e. $leaf(a)$ iff $leaf(ha)$.

f. $depth(a) = depth(ha)$

g. $aINDb$ iff $h(a)INDh(b)$.

h. $h(root(T)) = root(T')$.

i. $aCCb$ iff $h(a)CCh(b)$.

j. $a$ and $b$ are sisters iff $h(a)$ and $h(b)$ are sisters.

k. $|N| = |N'|$.

**Remark** You don't really know what the structures of a given class are until you can tell when two such are isomorphic. Using the fundamental fact that isomorphic structures make the same sentences true we see that trees $T_1$ and $T_2$ below are not isomorphic. $T_2$ for example has one node of out-degree 2, $T_1$ has no such node.

**Fact 2** If $T$ is a simple tree with exactly four nodes, then $T$ is isomorphic to exactly one of the following:

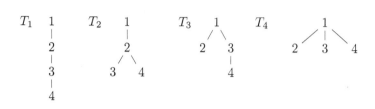

**Exercise 4.11.**

a. In (20) we exhibited an isomorphism from $T_1$ to $T_2$. Exhibit another isomorphism from $T_1$ to $T_2$ and conclude that there may be more than one isomorphism from one structure to another (in fact a very common case).

b.　 i. Give a sufficient reason why $T_2$ is not isomorphic to $T_3$.

　　 ii. Same question regarding $T_1$ and $T_4$; also $T_1$ and $T_2$.

c. Consider the tree $T^* = $
$$
\begin{array}{ccc}
 & 1 & \\
 / & & \backslash \\
3 & & 2 \\
 & & | \\
 & & 4
\end{array}
$$

Which of the trees in **Fact 2** is $T^*$ isomorphic to? Exhibit an isomorphism.

d. Exhibit a set of five-node trees with the following two properties:

　 i. no two of them are isomorphic, and

　 ii. any tree with exactly five nodes is isomorphic to one you have exhibited (Hint: the set you want has exactly 9 members).

e. The trees displayed in **Fact 2** differ with regard to how "rigid" they are, that is, how much freedom they have in allowing us to map some nodes to different nodes without changing structure. We can measure the rigidity of a tree by stating how many automorphisms it has. If it has only one then it must be the identity function, which maps each node to itself. So no changes are possible. Your problem: Say for each tree in **Fact 2** how many automorphisms it has. Two hints:

(1) $T_2$ has exactly two automorphisms.

(2) Any isomorphism $h$ from a tree $T$ to a tree $T'$ must map the root $r$ of $T$ to the root $r'$ of $T'$, since $r$ dominates all the nodes in $T$ so $h(r)$ must dominate all the nodes in $T'$ and $r'$ is the only node in $T'$ with that property.

f. A node $\alpha$ in a tree $T$ is *structurally definable* iff all automorphisms of $T$ map $\alpha$ to itself. So in all trees the root node is structurally definable. For each tree in **Fact 2** list the structurally definable nodes of that tree.

Let us now elaborate our Remark preceding **Fact 2**.

**Theorem 4.2** (A Fundamental Theorem of Model Theory).

A. *Isomorphic structures make the same (mathematical) sentences true, but*

B. *The converse may fail; there are non-isomorphic structures (of the same logical type) for which there is no sentence that is true of one but false of the other. (See Enderton, 1972; §2.2 for a formally explicit presentation).*

Both parts of this theorem are of concern to us. Part A suggests (wrongly) that it is not of interest to investigate distinct but isomorphic models of a given phenomenon. In fact looking at a problem in a new way often suggests new observations, new questions, new hypotheses, and ultimately new ways of extending our models. Our discussion in Chapter 7 of the Regular (Finite State) languages will provide an example. (See also the discussion of the Four Color Problem in Wilson, 2002.)

Part B of Theorem 4.2 touches our goals directly. For many explicit models of language processors we can find (easily) non-isomorphic ones that accept exactly the same strings. So in these cases even if we know for each string whether it is grammatical or whether it isn't we still cannot infer the structure of the processor to within isomorphism. We don't know whether this claim holds for human processors of natural languages as we do not (?yet) have a characterization of the grammars (or machines) that accept just the pretheoretically judged well formed expressions of, for example, English. That said, the prima facie case is negative. So – but this is speculation – it is likely that there are epistemological limits on our ability to infer the structure of the human language faculty just given a characterization of what expressions over the relevant alphabet are accepted and what are rejected.

### 4.3.1 Constituents

We turn to the important definition of *constituent*.

**Definition 4.11.** Let $T = (N, D)$ be a tree. For each node $b$ of $T$, we define $T_b =_{df} (N_b, D_b)$, where

   i. $N_b =_{df} \{x \in N \mid bDx\}$,

   ii. for all $x, y \in N_b$, $xD_by$ iff $xDy$.

We show that each $T_b$ as defined is a tree, called the *constituent of T generated by b*. (Note already that $N_b$ is never empty. Why?)

For example, consider the tree $T$ depicted on the left in (21); $T_3$ is depicted on the right in (21):

(21)
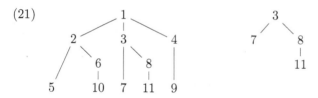

**Exercise 4.12.** Using the $T$ exhibited on the left in (21), exhibit

   a. $T_2$

   b. $T_{10}$

   c. $T_1$

**Theorem 4.3.** *Let $T = (N, D)$ be a tree. For all $b \in N$, $T_b = (N_b, D_b)$ is a tree whose root is $b$.*

**Definition 4.12.** For all trees $T = (N, D)$ and $T' = (N', D')$, $T'$ is a *constituent of T* ($T' CON\ T$) iff for some $b \in N$, $T' = T_b$.

**Theorem 4.4.** *Consider the set $T(\mathbb{N})$ of finite trees $(N, D)$ with $N \subseteq \mathbb{N}$.* CON, *the "is a constituent of" relation defined on $T(\mathbb{N})$ is a reflexive partial order relation.*

**Remark** Our mathematically clear and simple definition of *constituent* should not be confused with the empirical issue of identifying the constituents of any given expression in English. This is often far from obvious. Here are a few helpful rules of thumb given just so the reader can see that our examples of constituents are not utterly arbitrary. Suppose that an expression $s$ is a constituent of an expression $t$. Then, (1) $s$ is usually semantically interpreted (has a meaning). (2) $s$ occurs in diverse syntactic environments with the same meaning. For example, the following grammatical expressions support the naturalness of treating *pass the exam* as representing a constituent in all of them: *John wants to pass the exam*; *John said he would pass the exam and pass the exam he did.* (3) $s$ plausibly has a grammatical category and is replaceable by other expressions of that category preserving grammaticality; particularly convincing is replaceability by single lexical items. (4) $s$ may (sometimes) be deleted or be referred to by a pronoun or proverb preserving meaning: *Sue passed the exam and Ann did so too* / *and so did Ann.* (5) $s$ may form boolean compounds with *and, or,* and *neither/nor*: *He came early and left late*, *He neither came early nor left late.*

## 4.4  Labeled Trees

We now enrich the tree structures we have been considering to include ones whose nodes are labeled. The basic idea of the extension is fairly trivial; it becomes more interesting when the set of labels itself has some structure (as it does in all theories of grammar).

**Definition 4.13.** $T$ is a *labeled tree* iff $T$ is an ordered triple $(N, D, L)$ satisfying:

i. $(N, D)$ is a simple tree, and

ii. $L$ is a function with domain $N$.

**Terminology** For $x \in N$, $L(x)$ is called the *label* of $x$. When we say that a labeled (unordered) tree is a triple we imply that to define such an object there are three things to define: a set $N$ of nodes, a dominance relation $D$ on $N$, and a function $L$ with domain $N$.

Graphically we represent an (unordered) labeled tree as we represented unlabeled ones, except now we note next to each node $b$ its label, $L(b)$:

(22)

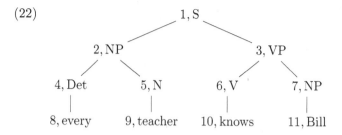

So the labeled tree represented in (22) is that triple $(N, D, L)$, where $N = \{1, 2, \ldots, 11\}$, $D$ is that dominance relation on $N$ whose immediate dominance relation is graphed in (22), and $L$ is that function with domain $N$ which maps 1 to 'S', 2 to 'DP', ..., and 11 to 'Bill'.

**Labeled bracketing** One often represents trees on the page by labeled bracketing, flattening the structure, forgetting the names of the nodes of the tree, and showing only the labels. For example, the labeled bracketing corresponding to (22) is

$$[[[\text{every}]_{\text{Det}}[\text{teacher}]_{\text{N}}]_{\text{NP}}[[\text{knows}]_{\text{TV}}[\text{Bill}]_{\text{NP}}]_{\text{VP}}]_{\text{S}}.$$

Given our discussion above, a natural question here is "Under what conditions will we say that two (unordered) labeled trees are isomorphic?" And here is a natural answer, one that embodies one possibly non-obvious condition:

(23)  $h$ is an *isomorphism* from $T = (N, D, L)$ to $T' = (N', D', L')$ iff

a. $h$ is an isomorphism from $(N, D)$ to $(N', D')$ and

b. for all $a, b \in N$, $L(a) = L(b)$ iff $L'(h(a)) = L'(h(b))$.

Condition (23a) is an obvious requirement; (23b) says that h maps nodes with identical labels to ones with identical labels and conversely. It guarantees for example that while $T_1$ and $T_2$ below may be isomorphic, neither can be isomorphic to $T_3$:

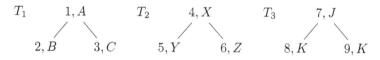

The three trees obviously have the same branching structure, but they differ in their labeling structure. In $T_3$, the two leaf nodes have the same label, '$K$', whereas the two leaf nodes of $T_1$ (and also of $T_2$) have distinct labels. Hence no map $h$ which preserves the branching structure can satisfy condition (23b) above, since $h$ must map leaf nodes to leaf nodes and hence must map nodes with distinct labels to ones with the same label.

A deficiency with (23), however, is that all current theories of generative grammar use theories in which the set of category labels is highly structured. But we have not committed ourselves to any particular linguistic theory, only considering the most general case in which nodes are labeled, but no particular structure on the set of labels is given. When such structure is given, say the set of labels itself is built by applying some functions to a primitive set of labels, then that structure too must be fixed by the isomorphisms.

Below we consider informally one sort of case based on work in GB (Government & Binding) theory (Lasnik and Uriagereka, 1988). Within GB theory category labels (we usually just say "categories") are partitioned into *functional* ones and *content* ones. The latter include Ns (like *book* and *mother*), Vs (like *sleep* and *describe*), Ps (like *for* and *with*) and As (like *bold* and *bald*). The former include categories of "grammatical" morphemes like *Poss* for the possessive marker *'s* (as in *John's book*) or *I* for the inflection which marks tense and person/number on verbs, such as the *is* in *John is running*, or the *will* in *John will sleep*.

Cross classifying with the functional content distinction is a "bar level" distinction. A basic category $C$ comes in three bar levels: $C_0$, $C_1$, and $C_2$. The bar level of a category pertains to the internal complexity of an expression having that category. Thus $C_0$'s, categories of bar level zero, are the simplest. Expressions of zero level categories are usually single lexical items like *book* and *sleep*, or grammatical morphemes like *'s* and *will*. $C_2$'s, categories of bar level 2, are complete phrasal expressions. For example *John will sleep* and *John's cat* have (different) categories of bar level 2. A category $X$ of bar level 2 is called a *phrasal* category and noted XP.

Phrasal categories combine with categories of bar level 0 to form ones of bar level one according to the tree schema below (nodes suppressed, as is common practice).

(24)

The expression of category $A_0$ in (24) is called the *head* of the entire $A_1$, and the expression of category $B_2$ is called its *Complement*. An example is the $V_1$ *describe the thief* whose head is the $V_0$ *describe* and whose complement is *the thief.* Similarly, *in the garden* is a $P_1$ headed by the $P_0$ *in.* A second type of labeled tree accepted by GB grammars is illustrated in (25).

(25)
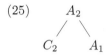

A category of level 2 which is a left sister to a one level category as in (25) is called the *Specifier* of the entire expression. The head of an expression like (25) is the head of the $A_1$ expression. In the next figure, we exhibit two expressions each illustrating (24) and (25), noting that we allow that Specifiers and Complements may be absent.

(26)  a.                     b.

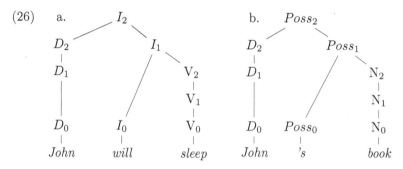

These two expressions have different categories. (26a) is an $I_2$, that is, an Inflection Phrase (IP) and (26b) is a $Poss_2$, that is, a Possessive Phrase (*PossP*). It is easy to see that (26a) and (26b) are isomorphic. Having drawn the graphs to scale we can superpose (26a) and (26b) in such a way that (1) the branching structures coincide and (2) the bar levels of labels on matching nodes coincide and (3) the labels on nodes in (26a) are distinct iff the ones they are matched with in (26b) are distinct. Note that this last condition does not follow from the others. Suppose for example that we replaced the label $N_0$ in (26b) with $D_0$ (a replacement which is not in fact sanctioned by GB grammars). Then we have not changed branching structure nor bar level of labels (since we replaced a zero level label with a zero level one) but now the distinct $D_0$ and $V_0$ nodes in (26a) correspond to two distinct $D_0$ nodes in (26b); that is, nodes with distinct labels are matched with ones having the same label and thus the trees are not isomorphic.

In addition to trees whose labels satisfy the schema in (24) and (25), we also find GB trees like those in (27), called *Adjunction structures* ($Adv_2$ is read "Adverb Phrase"):

(27)

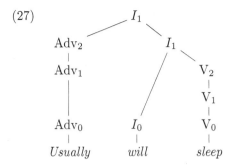

(27) has the same branching structure as (26a) and (26b). So if the labeling on these trees were erased the resulting unlabeled trees would be isomorphic. But none of those isomorphisms can preserve distinctness of node labels or their bar level. Any isomorphism from (26a) to (27) must map the root to the root and hence associate a 2 level label with a 1 level one. And since it must map daughters of the root to daughters of the root, it cannot preserve label distinctness since both root daughters in (26a) have different labels from the root label. But this is not so in (27).

We see, then, that if $h$ is an isomorphism from a GB tree $T = (N, D, L)$ to a GB tree $T' = (N', D', L')$, then, in addition to the conditions in (23), we should require:

(28) For all nodes $x$ of $T$,

    a. the bar level of $L(x)$ = the bar level of $L'(hx)$, and

    b. $L(x)$ is a functional category iff $L'(hx)$ is a functional category.

**Exercise 4.13.** For all distinct $T$, $T'$ in the set of (unordered) labeled trees below, exhibit an isomorphism between them if they are isomorphic, and give at least one reason why they are not isomorphic if they are not. (The nodes are exhibited to facilitate your task).

$T_1$    $1, e$        $T_2$    $9, a$        $T_3$    $3, a$

   $2, b$    $3, c$      $2, b$    $3, c$      $2, b$    $1, c$

$4, d$   $5, a$      $4, d$   $5, e$      $4, c$   $5, d$

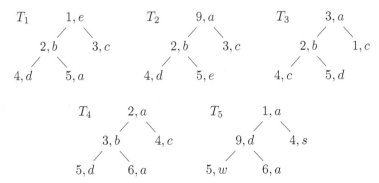

$T_4$    $2, a$        $T_5$    $1, a$

   $3, b$    $4, c$      $9, d$    $4, s$

$5, d$   $6, a$      $5, w$   $6, a$

## 4.5 Ordered Trees

As already noted, linguists use labeled trees to represent the pronunciation order of expressions. Pronounced expressions are represented by the labels on the leaf nodes of trees, and the pronunciation order is given by the left-right order in which the labels on leaf nodes are written on the page: the leftmost expression is pronounced first, then the second leftmost, etc. Thus in ordinary usage the tree graph in (22), repeated below as (29), not only represents constituents and their labels, it also tells us that *every* is pronounced before *knows*, *knows* before *Bill*, etc.

(29)

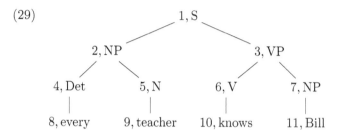

We consider more precisely the properties of the pronunciation order of expressions. Clearly it is transitive: if $x$ is pronounced before $y$, and $y$ before $z$, then, obviously, $x$ is pronounced before $z$. It is also clearly asymmetric: if $x$ is pronounced before $y$, then $y$ is not pronounced before $x$. (This also means that antisymmetry holds, albeit vacuously).

Let us write simply '$<$' for the left-right order on the leaf nodes of a tree. When $x < y$ we say that $x$ *precedes* $y$ or that $y$ *follows* $x$. And observe that for any two distinct leaves one must precede the other. That is, $<$ is a *total* (synonym: *linear*) order of the leaf nodes. Here is the definition:

**Definition 4.14.** A binary relation $R$ on a set $A$ is a *linear (total) order* iff

   i. $R$ is transitive, and

  ii. $R$ is antisymmetric, and

 iii. $R$ is total (that is, for all $x \neq y \in A$, $xRy$ or $yRx$).

**Examples** Clearly $\leq$ in arithmetic is a linear order. We have already seen that it is transitive and antisymmetric. And for totality we observe that for any distinct numbers $m$ and $n$, either $n \leq m$ or $m \leq n$. Also the strictly less than relation, $<$, is a linear order. It is obviously transitive. Since it is asymmetric ($n < m$ implies $\neg(m < n)$), it is antisymmetric. And it is total: for distinct $m$ and $n$, either $m < n$ or $n < m$. In contrast the subset relation $\subseteq$ defined on $\mathcal{P}(A)$ (the power set of $A$) for $A$ with at least two distinct elements, say $a$ and $b$, ..., is not total. There are subsets of $A$ such that neither is a subset of the other. For example $\{a\}$ and $\{b\}$ have this property. So in general the subset relation on a collection of sets is a properly partial order, not a total (or linear) order. Note further, in analogy to $<$, that the proper subset relation is irreflexive, asymmetric and transitive, and again, normally not a total order.

Using these notions we define the notion *ordered tree*. We take a conservative approach at first, defining a larger class of ordered trees than is commonly considered in linguistic work. Then we consider an additional condition usually observed in the linguistic literature but which rules out some trees which seem to have some utility in modeling properties of natural language expressions.

**Definition 4.15.** $T = (N, D, L, <)$ is a *leaf ordered labeled tree* (or lol tree) iff

    i. $(N, D, L)$ is a labeled tree, and

    ii. $<$ is a strict linear order of the terminal nodes (read as *precedes*).

The graphical conventions for representing lol trees are those we have been using, with the additional proviso that the left-right written order of leaf labels represents the precedes order $<$. The notions we have defined on trees in terms of dominance carry over without change when passing from mere unordered or unlabeled trees to lol trees. Only the definition of "constituent" needs enriching in the obvious way. Each node $b$ of a tree T determines a subtree $T_b$, the constituent generated by $b$, as before, only now we must say that nodes of the subtree have the same labels they have in $T$ and the leaves of the subtree are linearly ordered just as they are in $T$. Formally,

**Definition 4.16.** Let $T = (N, D, L, <)$ be a lol tree. Then for all $b \in N$, $T_b =_{df} (N_b, D_b, L_b, <_b)$, where

$$N_b = \{x \in N \mid bDx\} \qquad L_b(x) = L(x), \text{ all } x \in N_b$$
$$D_b = D \cap (N_b \times N_b) \qquad <_b = \{(x, y) \mid x, y \in N_b \text{ and } x < y\}$$

And one proves that $T_b$ is a lol tree, called, as before, the *constituent generated by b*.

An additional useful notion defined on lol trees is that of the *leaf sequence* of a node. This is just the sequence of leaves that the node dominates. It is often used to represent the constituent determined by the node. Formally we define:

**Definition 4.17.** For $b$ a node in a lol tree $T$, $LS(b)$ or the *leaf sequence determined by* $b$, is the sequence $\langle b_1, \ldots, b_n \rangle$ of leaves which $b$ dominates, listed in the $<$ order.

That is, the leaf sequence of a node is the string of leaf nodes it dominates.

What we have defined as lol trees differ from the type of tree most widely used in generative grammar in that we limit the precedes order $<$ to leaves. It is the labels of leaves which represent the words and morphemes that are actually pronounced and our empirical judgments of pronunciation order are highly reliable. Now the $<$ order on the leaf nodes extends in a straightforward way to certain internal (non-leaf) nodes as follows:

**Definition 4.18.** For $x, y$ nodes of a lol tree T, $x <^* y$ iff every leaf node which $x$ dominates precedes $(<)$ every leaf node that $y$ dominates.

Note that when $x$ and $y$ are leaves, then, $x <^* y$ iff $x < y$ since the leaf nodes that $x$ dominates are just $x$ and those that $y$ dominates are just $y$. When being careful, we read $<^*$ as *derivatively precedes*. But most usually we just say *precedes*, the same as for the relation $<$. By way of illustration consider (30), reading 'Prt' as particle:

(30)

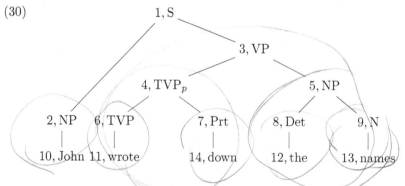

Here 4 precedes $(<^*)$ 12, since every leaf that 4 dominates, namely 11 and 14, precedes every leaf that 12 dominates (just 12 itself). Equally 4 precedes 5, 8, 9, and 13. But 4 does not precede 7: it is not so that every leaf 4 dominates precedes every leaf that 7 dominates since 4 dominates 14 and 7 dominates 14, but 14 does not precede 14 since $<$ is irreflexive. Observe now that (31) is also an lol tree:

(31)

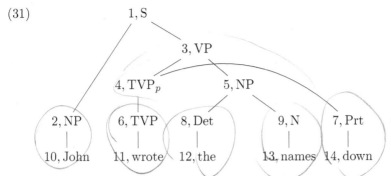

The lol trees in (30) and (31) are different, though they have the same nodes and each node has the same label in each tree. They also have identical dominance relations: $n$ dominates $m$ in (30) iff $n$ dominates $m$ in (31). But they have different precedence relations since in (30), 14 precedes 5 and everything that 5 dominates, such as 12 and 13. But in (31), 14 does not precede 5 or anything that 5 dominates. In consequence the constituents of (30) are not exactly the same as those of (31), though there is much overlap. For example (32a) is a constituent of both (30) and of (31). So is (32b)

(32) a.    b.

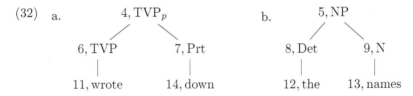

**Exercise 4.14.** Exhibit the smallest constituent of (30) that is not a constituent of (31).

The constituent $T_4$ in (31) is a classical example of a *discontinuous constituent*: its sequence of leaf nodes $\langle 11, 14 \rangle$ is not a substring of the leaf sequence $\langle 10, 11, 12, 13, 14 \rangle$ of the entire tree. (Recall that a sequence $s$ is a substring of a sequence $t$ iff there are sequences $u, v$ (possibly empty) such that $t = usv$.) Formally,

**Definition 4.19.** For all lol trees $T$ and $T'$, $T'$ is a *discontinuous constituent* of $T$ iff $T'$ is a constituent of $T$ and the leaf sequence of $T'$ is not a substring of the leaf sequence of $T$.

Note that we have here defined a binary relation between trees: *is a discontinuous constituent of*. Whether a tree like (32a) is a discontinuous constituent of a tree $T$ depends crucially on the relative linear order of leaves of (32a) with the leaves of $T$. We cannot tell just by looking at a tree $T'$ in isolation whether it is discontinuous or not.

Most work in generative grammar does not countenance discontinuous constituents so our understanding of the role they might play in linguistic description, and theory, is limited. Still, the reader should be aware that discontinuity in simple sentences is not restricted to a few cases of Particle Placement. Below we discuss four types of fairly common phenomena which help us diagnose discontinuity: (i) cooccurrence restrictions, (ii) semantic dependencies, (iii) binding, and (iv) case marking. For yet further examples see Huck and Ojeda (1987) and McCawley (1982, 1988).

i. **cooccurrence restrictions.** The simplest cases here are ones in which the possibility of occurrence of a certain word depends on the presence of another. This is naturally accounted for if the two words are introduced as a single unit, though perhaps presented in non-adjacent positions. In fact the Verb+Particle construction in (30) and (31) illustrates this case. The choice of particle, *down* in our examples, depends significantly on the choice of verb: we do not say *\*John printed/erased/memorized/forgot the names down*. One way to represent this would be to treat the ordered pair $\langle(write, \text{TV}), (down, \text{PRT})\rangle$ as a complex lexical item, the rules which combine it with a DP object like "the names" being defined in such a way as to allow the particle on either side of the DP. Formalism aside, the effect of the rules would be:

(33)  If $\langle x, y \rangle$ is a TVP-Particle pair and $z$ is a DP, then

    i. $xzy$ is a string of category VP, and

    ii. if $z$ is not a pronoun, $xyz$ is a string of category VP.

(The condition ii. blocks generating strings like *\*write down them.*)

There are many other sorts of lexical cooccurrence restrictions in English. For example observe that in humble coordinations we find that the presence of *both*, *either*, and *neither* conditions the choice or coordinator *and*, *or*, or *nor*:

(34)    a. Neither Mary nor Sue came early;

        \*Neither Mary and Sue came early

    b. Either Mary or Sue came early;

        \*Either Mary nor Sue came early

    c. Both Mary and Sue came early;

        \*Both Mary nor Sue came early

We might represent these cooccurrence restrictions by treating ⟨*both, and*⟩, ⟨*either, or*⟩, and ⟨*neither, nor*⟩ as complex lexical items and code this in our representations as in (35):

(35)

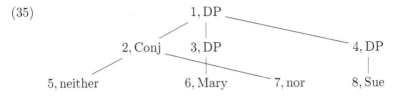

Node 5 labeled *neither* precedes 6, labeled *Mary*, but node 2, which represents the complex conjunction *neither* ... *nor* ... neither precedes nor follows 6, *Mary*.

Similarly comparatives in English illustrate cooccurrence restrictions. Compare (36a,b):

(36)  a. (Many) more students than / *as teachers came to the party.

b. (Exactly) as many students as / *than teachers came to the party.

Here the presence of *than* as opposed to *as* is conditioned by the presence of *more* in (36a). In (36b) *as many* selects *as* as opposed to *than*. This is natural if we treat *more-than* and *as-many-as* as complex constituents.

**Exercise 4.15.** Exhibit plausible tree structures for (36a,b) illustrating the discontinuity.

ii. **semantic units.** In mathematical languages the syntactic constituents of an expression are precisely the subexpressions which are assigned denotations. But it seems that in (37) and (38) the prenominal adjectives *easy* and *difficult* form a semantic unit with the postnominal *to*-phrase. Note that the (a,b) pairs are paraphrases of the right-hand ones in which the the adjective occurs postnominally and more clearly forms a constituent with the *to*-phrase.

(37)  a. an easy rug to clean

b. a rug which is easy to clean

(38)  a. an easy theorem to state but a difficult one to prove

b. a theorem which is easy to state but difficult to prove

Rugs of the sort mentioned in (37a) are understood to have the property expressed by *easy to clean*; (overtly expressed by the postnominal constituent *which is easy to clean* in (37b)). Typically the constituents of an expression are assigned a meaning. But *easy rug* in (37a) does not have a meaning, nor does *easy theorem* in (38b). It seems then that we want to think of *easy to clean* as having a semantic interpretation in (37a) and *easy to state* and also *difficult to prove* as having semantic interpretations in (38b). Assuming that only constituents are interpreted we can represent these judgments of interpretation by:

(39)

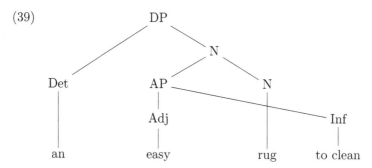

Note that ordinal numerals (*first, second, ...*) as well as *last* and *next* also seem to form a semantic unit with the postnominal modifier, as (40a,b) are synonymous:

(40)    a. the first / second / last village that we visited

         b. the village that we visited first / second / last

This pattern includes superlative adjectives as well, as in:

(41)    a. the worst movie I have ever seen

         b. the most expensive necktie that John owns

**Exercise 4.16.** Exhibit a tree structure for (40a) in which *first* and *that we visited* form a discontinuous constituent. And note that the apparent Determiner *the* exhibits strong cooccurrence restrictions with *first, ..., next* (*\*each/\*no/\*first village that we visited*) and so arguably *the first/next ... that we visited* should be a discontinuous constituent. Exhibit a relevant tree structure for this discontinuity.

iii. **binding** (Blevins, 1994). Here we consider some expression types that play an important role in current linguistic theorizing. In expressions like (42) the pronoun *his* can be understood as bound by *each teacher*, indicated here by the use of the same subscript $i$.

(42)  Each teacher$_i$ criticized many of his$_i$ students

Linguists have observed that in cases like this the antecedent *each teacher* c-commands the referentially dependent expression *his* (as well as *his students* and *many of his students*). The relevant constituency relations in (42) are given by (43):

(43)

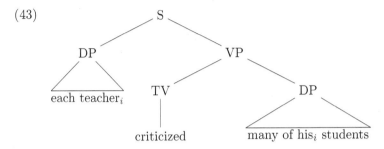

But when the c-command relations are reversed, as in (44a,b) graphed in (44c), the pronominal expressions are not naturally interpretable with *his* bound to *each teacher*.

(44)   a. *Many of his$_i$ students criticized each teacher$_i$

       b. *Which of his$_i$ students criticized each teacher$_i$?

       c.

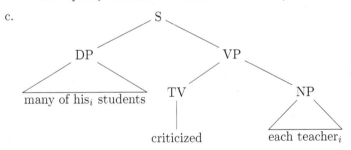

But suppose we question the object of *criticize* in (42). In such cases the interrogative DP, noted DP[+Q] here, occurs initially in the question, noted S[+Q], and the subject DP, which denotes the ones doing the criticizing, remains in place preverbally. To avoid irrelevant complications due to auxiliaries, we present the questions in an indirect context determined by the frame *I don't know* _____ .

(45)   a. I don't know which of his$_i$ students each teacher$_i$ criticized.

       b. I don't know how many of his$_i$ students each teacher$_i$ criticized.

Now under standard ways of presenting the constituent structure of (45a,b) the interrogative DPs *which of his students* and *how many of his students* would not be c-commanded by *each teacher* so we should predict that we cannot interpret these Ss in such a way that the pronominal DPs are referentially dependent on *each teacher*. But in fact we can. The judgments of referential dependency are those appropriate to the case where *each teacher* c-commands the pronominal DPs. But that would be the structure on the discontinuous constituent analysis in (46). (We only graph that part of (45a,b) following *I don't know*.)

(46)

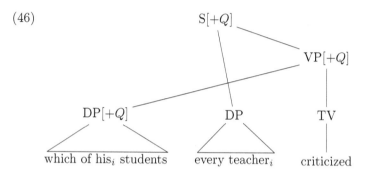

Thus the discontinuous constituent (DC) analysis preserves the generalization that quantified DP antecedents of pronominal expressions c-command them.

Our purpose here is not to claim that DC analyses can be used to represent the full range of facts concerning the distribution of referentially dependent expressions and their antecedents. Much has been discovered about these relations in the past twenty years, and we have just mentioned one of the relevant facts. No current analysis adequately represents all the (known) facts. But DC analyses have not been extensively investigated in these or other regards, and we now understand that lol trees are mathematically clear and respectable objects which allow DCs. As students of language structure, then, we have a new tool of analysis at our disposal and should feel free to use it.

iv. **case marking** enables us to use audible morphological marking on Nouns and Adjectives to construct the constituent structure needed for semantic interpretation without the relevant items occurring adjacent. The positive correlation between overt case marking and word order freedom in simple sentences is an old observation.

(47)

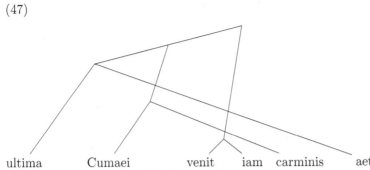

| ultima | Cumaei | venit | iam | carminis | aetas |
|--------|--------|-------|-----|----------|-------|
| final.nom.f.s | gen.s (non-fem) | come.3s | now | song.gen.n.s. | age.nom |

*The final age of the Cumaean song has now arrived.*

(Virgil, *Eclogues*, IV.4) cited from Matthews (1981, 255)

(48)

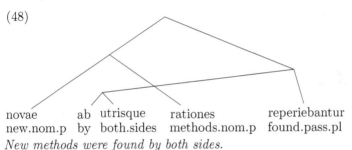

| novae | ab | utrisque | rationes | reperiebantur |
|-------|----|---------| ---------|---------------|
| new.nom.p | by | both.sides | methods.nom.p | found.pass.pl |

*New methods were found by both sides.*

(Caesar, *Civil Wars*, III.50) cited from Matthews (1981, 106)

(49)

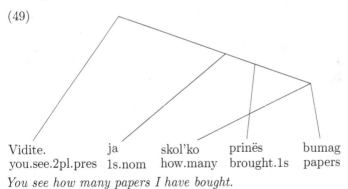

| Vidite. | ja | skol'ko | prinës | bumag |
|---------|----|---------|--------|-------|
| you.see.2pl.pres | 1s.nom | how.many | brought.1s | papers |

*You see how many papers I have bought.*

(Russian radio broadcast, 2010; Denis Paperno, personal communication)

The next two examples, from Quechua (Andean, Peru) and Warlpiri (Pama- Nyungan, Australia) illustrate enlightening cases in which non-adjacent modifier- noun constituents are identified by being in the same

morphologically marked case. The last example from Warlpiri illustrates two nouns with two modifiers separated, so the choice of case
marker is crucial.

(50)    a. *[[hatun   runa]-ta]   rikaa*
             big     man-acc   see.1s
             (Huallaga Quechua; Weber, 1989)

         *I see the big man.*

    b.

    hatun-ta   rikaa   runa-ta
    big-acc   see.1s   man-acc
    *I see the big man.*

    c.

    runa-ta   rikaa   hatun-ta
    man-acc   see.1s   big-acc
    *I see the big man.*

(51)   (Warlpiri; Bittner and Hale, 1995)

    a. *jarntu   wiri-ngki=ju       yarlku-mu*
        dog     big-erg=1s.nsubj   bit-pst
        *The big dog bit me.*

    b. *jarntu-ngku=ju     jarrlku-mu   wiri-ngki*
        dog-erg=1s.nsubj   bit-pst      big-erg
        *The big dog bit me.*

(52)  *Yakaajirri-rli   yankirri-∅   maju-manu   wita-∅      maju-ngku*
       berry-erg       emu-abs     bad-made    small-abs   bad-erg
       *The bad berries hurt the little emu.*               (Laughren, 2002)

Lastly in this category we might point out the oft noted relative order of subject and object when these functions are marked with case
markers. (53) below from Korean is illustrative. Here (53c) is naturally represented with a discontinuous constituent if we want the object
to form a constituent with the transitive verb to the exclusion of the
subject.

(53)   a. *John-i      Sam-ul     piphanhayssta*
          John-nom   Sam-acc   criticized

          *John criticized Sam. / *Sam criticized John.*

b. *Sam-ul    John-i     piphanhayssta*
   Sam-acc  John-nom  criticized

   *John criticized Sam. / *Sam criticized John.*

c. *John-ul    Sam-i     piphanhayssta*
   John-acc  Sam-nom  criticized

   *Sam criticized John. / *John criticized Sam.*

Despite the extensive variety of discontinuous constituents in the world's languages, the constituent structure trees most commonly used by linguists are required to satisfy an additional condition, called the Exclusivity Condition:

**Definition 4.20.** A leaf ordered tree $T$ satisfies the Exclusivity Condition iff for all nodes $b$, $d$, if $b$ and $d$ are independent then $b <^* d$ or $d <^* b$. (Nodes $x$ and $y$ are independent, recall, iff neither dominates the other.)

(31) fails Exclusivity since nodes 4 and 5 are independent but neither precedes the other. So the lol trees satisfying Exclusivity constitute a proper subset of the lol trees.

## 4.6  Concluding Formal Exercises on Relations and Ordered Trees

**Exercise 4.17.** On the basis of the data in (a), exhibit plausible tree graphs using discontinuous constituents for the expressions in (b). (You may hide small amounts of ignorance with little triangles). State why you chose to represent the discontinuous expressions as single constituents.

a.1. More boys than girls came to the party.
   Five more students than teachers signed the petition.
   (Many) fewer boys than girls did well on the exam.
   More than twice as many dogs as cats are on the mat.
   Not as many students as teachers laughed at that joke.

a.2. *More boys as girls came to the party.
   *Five more students as teachers signed the petition.
   *Fewer boys as girls did well on the exam.
   *More than twice as many dogs than cats are on the mat.
   *Not as many students than teachers laughed at that joke.

b.1. More boys than girls

b.2. Exactly as many dogs as cats

**Exercise 4.18.** Consider the intuitive interpretation of the Ss in (i) below:

(i.)    a. some liberal senator voted for that bill.

b. every liberal senator voted for that bill.

c. no liberal senator voted for that bill.

We can think of these three Ss as making (different) quantitative claims concerning the individuals who are liberal senators on the one hand and the individuals that voted for that bill on the other. (i.a) says that the intersection of the set of liberal senators with the set of individuals who voted for that bill is non-empty; (i.c) says that that intersection is empty; and (i.b) says that the set of liberal senators is a subset of the set of those who voted for that bill. In all cases the Adjective+Noun combination, *liberal senator*, functions to identify the set of individuals we are quantifying over (called the domain of quantification) and thus has a semantic interpretation. That interpretation does not vary with changes in the Determiner (*every*, *some*, *no*). Similarly we can replace *liberal senator* with, say, *student*, *tall student*, *tall student who John praised*, etc., without affecting the quantitative claim made by the determiners (Dets) *some*, *every*, and *no*. So the interpretation of the Det is independent of that of the noun or modified noun combination that follows it. These semantic judgments are reflected in the following constituent analysis:

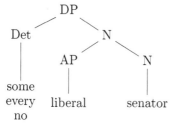

Similarly, in (i.d), the relative clause *that we interviewed* functions to limit the senators under consideration to those we interviewed and thus seems to form a semantic unit with *senator* to the exclusion of the Dets *every*, *no*, ... as reflected in the constituent structure in (i.d).

d. every senator that we interviewed; no senator that we interviewed.

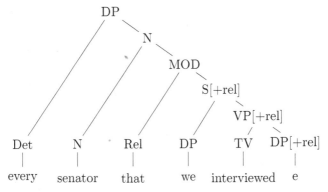

Current linguistic theories vary with regard to the categories assigned to the constituents in (i.b) and (i.d), but for the most part they agree with the major constituent breaks, specifically that the adjective and relative clause form a constituent with the common noun senator to the exclusion of the Dets *every, no,* ... But consider the expressions in (e):

e. the first man to set foot on the moon; the next village we visited; the second book written by Spooky-Pooky; the last student to leave the party

Question 1 Give a semantic reason why we should not treat the apparent adjectives (*first, next,* ... ) as forming a constituent with the following common noun (*man, village,* ...) to the exclusion of the material that follows the common noun. So your semantic reason should argue against a constituent structure of the sort below:

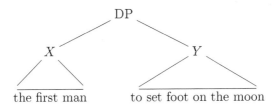

Question 2 Give a semantic reason why the apparent adjectives (*first, next,* ...) should be treated as forming a unit with the expression that follows the common noun (*man, village,* ...).

Question 3 Give a syntactic reason why the apparent Det <u>the</u> forms a syntactic unit with the apparent adjective (*first, next,* ...). Exhibit a discontinuous tree structure for these expression which embodies both the facts.

**Exercise 4.19.** Consider the DPs below:

the tallest student in the class      the fastest gun in the west
the most expensive necktie John owns   the worst movie I ever saw

a. Give a semantic reason why we do not want to treat the superlative adjective (*tallest, fastest, worst, most expensive*) as forming a constituent with the following common noun to the exclusion of the postnominal material (*in the class, in the West, . . .*).

b. Give a syntactic reason why the initial occurrence of the should form a constituent with the superlative adjective to the exclusion of the common noun.

c. Exhibit a gross constituent structure for one of these DPs which incorporates these judgments. ("gross" means you can use little triangles to avoid detailing irrelevant structure).

**Exercise 4.20.** Consider the DPs below:

John's favorite book; his latest play; my most treasured pictures

Find reasons supporting a constituent analysis compatible with (i.a) rather than (i.b)

(a)                         (b)

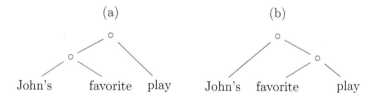

John's    favorite   play      John's   favorite      play

**Exercise 4.21.** Exhibit gross constituent structures for each of the Ss below from Spanish (Ojeda, 1987).

a. *Tu quieres poder bailar tangos.* "You want to be able to dance tangos."

b. *Quieres tu poder bailar tangos?* "Do you want to be able to dance tangos?"

c. *Quieres poder tu bailar tangos?* "Do you want to be able to dance tangos?"

d. *Quieres poder bailar tu tangos?* "Do you want to be able to dance tangos?"

**Exercise 4.22.** Provide a discontinuous tree structure for the sentence below in which *wrote down* is a constituent and *the names of my colleagues and their spouses* is a constituent. (The example is modeled on one in Chomsky, 1996, p. 324)

I wrote the names down of my colleagues and their spouses.

**Exercise 4.23.** Let $T = (N, D, L, <)$ and $T' = \langle N', D', L', <' \rangle$ be lol trees. Complete the following definition correctly (the correct definition is the same regardless of whether $T$ and $T'$ are required to satisfy Exclusivity):
A function $h : N \rightarrow N'$ is an isomorphism from $T$ to $T'$ iff _____.

**Exercise 4.24.** Let $A$ be an $n > 0$ element alphabet linearly ordered as follows: $a_1 < a_2 < \ldots < a_n$. Define the *dictionary order* on the non-empty "words" in $A^*$. That is, complete the following definition: For all non-empty $s, t$ in $A^*$, $s \leq t$ iff _____ in such a way that the order you define extends the original order on $A$. To test your definition make sure that it states that $a_2 a_3 \leq a_2 a_4$ and $a_2 a_3 \leq a_2 a_3 a_7$. The dictionary order is also called the *lexicographic* order.

**Exercise 4.25.** In their book on minimalist syntax, Lasnik et al. (2003) define c-command as follows (p. 51):

**Definition 4.21.** *A c-commands B* iff (1) and (2) both hold:

a. *A does not dominate B.*

b. *Every node that dominates A dominates B.*

This is simpler than the definition which we gave in Figure 4.2.
**Query.** Are these definitions equivalent? That is, in an arbitrary tree is it the case that a node $x$ c-commands a node $y$ using the original definition iff $x$ c-commands $y$ in the alternative sense mentioned just above. Hint: the answer is NO. Give an example illustrating the difference. Consider separately the cases in which (1) the dominance relation is taken to be reflexive, and (2) the dominance relation is irreflexive.

**Definition and Exercise** Given a binary relation $R$ defined on a set $A$, a subset $K$ of $A$ is said to be *closed wrt R* iff for all $x \in K$, all $y \in A$, if $xRy$ then $y \in K$. Your task: define $\mathrm{Cl}_R K$, the *closure of K wrt R*. (We find it most natural to use the intersection format introduced in an addendum to the previous chapter.)

**Definition 4.22.** Given $R \subseteq A \times A$, TR($R$), the *transitive closure* of $R$, $=_{\text{def}} \bigcap \{S \subseteq A \times A \mid R \subseteq S$ and $S$ is transitive$\}$.

**Exercise 4.26.** Prove that TR($R$) above is transitive.

**Exercise 4.27.** Define analogously Refl($R$), the reflexive closure of $R$.

In fact Refl($R$) is provably simply $R \cup \{\langle x, x \rangle \mid x \in A\}$. Note that when linguists exhibit a tree, only the immediate dominance relation is depicted. The full dominance relation is the reflexive transitive closure of that relation.

**Concluding Reflection.** We have seen that order relations—ones that are transitive and antisymmetric—are basic to linguistic representation. And they will recur in various guises throughout later work in this text. It is then of some interest to consider operations on relations that preserve these order properties. Here is one basic one:

**Definition 4.23.** Let $R$ be a binary relation on a set $A$. Then the *R-converse* of $R$, written $R^{-1}$, is the binary relation on $A$ defined by

$$\text{for all } x, y \in A, \langle x, y \rangle \in R^{-1} \text{ iff } \langle y, x \rangle \in R.$$

For example, consider the $\leq$ relation in arithmetic. Its converse is the $\geq$ relation: $n \geq m$ iff $m \leq n$, for all numbers $m, n$. Equally the converse of the strictly $<$ relation is the strictly $>$ relation: $m > n$ iff $n < m$. For another example, suppose we are considering the subset relation on $\mathcal{P}(\mathbb{N})$. Its converse is the superset relation: $X \supseteq Y$ iff $Y \subseteq X$. And as well the converse of the proper subset relation, $\subset$, is the proper superset relation, $\supset$.

Now let us observe the following two properties of the converse operation—that function noted $^{-1}$ which maps a binary relation $R$ to its converse:

**Theorem 4.5.** *For $R$ a binary relation on a set $A$,*

    *a. if $R$ is transitive then $R^{-1}$ is transitive, and*

    *b. if $R$ is antisymmetric then $R^{-1}$ is antisymmetric.*

*Thus we infer that if $R$ is an order relation then so is $R^{-1}$.*

*Proof.*

    a. Let $R$ be transitive. Assume that $\langle x, y \rangle \in R^{-1}$ and $\langle y, z \rangle \in R^{-1}$. We must show that $\langle x, z \rangle \in R^{-1}$. By the assumptions both $\langle y, x \rangle$ and $\langle z, y \rangle$ must be in $R$. So by the transitivity of $R$, $\langle z, x \rangle \in R$, whence by the definition of $^{-1}$, $\langle x, z \rangle \in R^{-1}$, which is what we desired to show.

b. Let $R$ be antisymmetric. Assume $\langle x, y \rangle$ and $\langle y, x \rangle$ are both in $R^{-1}$. Show that $x = y$. But by the assumptions $\langle y, x \rangle$ and $\langle x, y \rangle$ are in $R$, so $y = x$, which is what we desired to show. $\quad\square$

Suppose now that we know that the converse of a relation $R$ is transitive (antisymmetric). Can we infer that the relation $R$ itself is transitive (antisymmetric)? The answer is yes. By the theorem immediately above we see that if a relation $R^{-1}$ is transitive (antisymmetric) then its converse must be transitive (antisymmetric), and we see below that:

**Theorem 4.6.** *For $R$ a binary relation on a set $A$, $(R^{-1})^{-1} = R$.*

*Proof.* We know that for all $x, y \in A$, $\langle x, y \rangle \in R$ iff $\langle y, x \rangle \in R^{-1}$ iff $\langle x, y \rangle \in (R^{-1})^{-1}$.

Thus the pairs $\langle x, y \rangle$ in $R$ are the same as those in $(R^{-1})^{-1}$ so the two relations are the same. $\quad\square$

# 5

# Syntax II: Design for a Language

A grammar for natural language such as English, Japanese, Swahili, etc. is a definition of the set of expressions of the language. For each expression the grammar should specify three things: (1) its *syntax* – how it is constructed, (2) its *semantics* – what it means, and (3) its *phonology* – how it is pronounced (or gesturally interpreted in the case of signed languages.) In what follows we limit ourselves to syntax and semantics. Expressions will be given in some written format (*orthography*) with no attempt to provide a precise representation of their phonology, though we may refer to such strings as *phonological strings*.

We have already seen that the number of expressions in a natural language is too large to be enlighteningly listed. And even given a list we still want to know what the basis is for including for example *every dog barks* but not *dog every barks*. In consequence we shall represent the syntactic component of a grammar $G$ in two parts: A lexicon, noted $\text{Lex}_G$, and a set of rules, noted $\text{Rule}_G$. $\text{Lex}_G$ is a finite set of expressions, called *lexical items*. $\text{Rule}_G$ is a finite set of (partial) functions, called *structure building* functions (rules), that derive expressions from expressions. The *language generated by* $G$, noted $L(G)$, is the closure of $\text{Lex}_G$ under the functions in $\text{Rule}_G$. That is, $L(G)$ is the set of expressions that can be built starting with the lexical items and applying the structure building functions finitely many times. We will have much more to say about $\text{Lex}_G$ and $\text{Rule}_G$ later in this chapter.

If we design a grammar $G$ intended to generate a given natural language $L$, say $L$ = English, we say that $G$ is *sound* if $L(G) \subseteq L$. That is, everything the grammar generates is in $L$. And $G$ is said to be *complete* if $L \subseteq L(G)$, everything in the language is in the set generated by $G$. So given $L$, our goal as linguists is to define a grammar $G$ for $L$ such that $L(G) = L$; that is, $G$ is both sound and complete. Striving to meet these twin goals leads very quickly to empirical problems – how to generate everything we want without generating too much. (And the problem of semantically interpreting the expressions generated remains.)

It is not difficult to design a sound but (very) incomplete grammar for English. Just list a few expressions which are clearly English and stipulate that $L(G)$ is that set. But this is not interesting, as it does not tell us how to form new expressions and more generally it simply fails to identify the class of expressions we want. Such a grammar is said to *undergenerate*. It is equally trivial to construct a complete but very unsound grammar. Roughly, let $L(G)$ be the set of all finite sequences of English words. This includes all English expressions but also massive amounts of junk, of strings that no one accepts as English. (Try choosing five words at random from an English dictionary. The chances that that sequence of words is a well formed expression of English is close to zero.) Even if you choose on the basis of frequency of occurrence your sequence is likely (*the, the, the, the, the*). A grammar that generates expressions not in the language under study is said to *overgenerate*. A given grammar may both overgenerate and undergenerate.

We should note that at time of writing no one has a grammar for any natural language which is both sound and complete (even up to some reasonable level of approximation). Below we start to formulate a grammar for English, called ENG. ENG will be incomplete, but serve to indicate some of the formal tools we use in formulating grammars and some of the kinds of reasoning used to motivate one or another design feature. The literature contains many approaches to defining grammars, ones that differ considerably in the notation used. Here we adopt a fairly generic approach with no attempt to capture any particular linguistic theory of syntactic structure.

## 5.1 Beginning Grammar

To define our grammar $\text{ENG} = \langle \text{Lex}_{\text{ENG}}, \text{Rule}_{\text{ENG}} \rangle$ we must exhibit some lexical items of English and some rules that derive expressions starting with the lexical ones. Expressions in $L(\text{ENG})$, whether lexical or derived, will be represented as ordered pairs $(s, C)$, where $s$ is a phonological string and $C$ is a category name. Typically expressions with the same category coordinate are treated the same by the rules that derive complex expressions. They are also, usually, meaningful in similar ways. Expressions $(s, C)$ and $(t, C)$, of the same category but with different string coordinates are (usually) pronounced differently and semantically interpreted differently. For example in $L(\text{ENG})$, (laughed, $P_1$) and (cried, $P_1$) are lexical expressions of category $P_1$ (one place predicate phrase). So they have, in our grammar, the same distribution – in derived expressions they can be interchanged preserving grammaticality. But their pronunciations are not identical, nor are their semantic interpretations, though they share some general properties.

We note that including a category coordinate as part of an expression, rather than just thinking of an expression as a string of words and morphemes, enables us to distinguish conveniently between expressions with the same pronunciation but different categories. Using traditional notation for example we might treat *slice* as two expressions, (*slice*, V) and (*slice*, N), as they occur in *He will slice the pizza and help himself to a slice*. The first occurrence is a verb and has, for example, a past tense form: *He sliced the pizza*. And the second is a noun, and has for example a plural form: *He ate two slices*. A very large number of lexical strings in English exhibit this category duality: *I'll walk to school* (verb), *I'll take a walk* (noun); *I respect him a lot* (verb); *My respect for him is great* (noun). Similarly with *honor, envy, love, judge, fall, hit, catch* and hundreds of others.

However not all dual meanings can be distinguished in this way. Arguably, to take a classical case, *bank* as a noun is ambiguous according as it refers to a river bank or a financial institution. Can you think of other examples? Also, despite appearances, sometimes one or another of the nominal vs verbal uses are thought of as more basic, and the other is derived despite the absence of any overt morphological marking which indicates that. For example, some would treat the noun use of *walk* as derived from the verbal use (and call it a *deverbal noun*); in other cases, as in *He shouldered the problem without complaint* we think of the verbal use, *shouldered*, as derivative of the noun *shoulder* (and call it a *denominal verb*).

An important point regarding the nature of expressions: their choice of grammatical category is very theory dependent. Different theories – Minimalism (Radford, 2004), Categorial Grammar (Carpenter, 1997, ch. 4), Lexical Functional Grammar (Bresnan, 2001) – use different notations for naming categories. They all make some sort of nominal vs verbal distinction, and they all tend to assume that different natural languages draw their category names from a fixed stock. But perhaps most importantly, within a given theory it tends to be assumed that expressions with the *same* category are treated the same, or at least in a very similar way, by the structure building rules. So what is most important about the category of an expression is not its identity per se, but rather which other expressions in the grammar have the same category. Here we follow this practice rigorously but otherwise make up different category names for expressions with different distributions.

Our choices are, nonetheless, broadly compatible with or translatable into various widely used current theories.

## 5.2 ENG– **Towards a Grammar of English**

Below are two groups of English expressions which we will design our grammar, Eng, to generate initially. Traditionally these expressions are (*Declarative*) *Sentences* (Ss) and are the kind of expression that are True or False (in a given situation). We note shortly many important aspects of these expressions which we ignore for the moment in the interests of focusing on the core formal apparatus we use to derive them. Then of course we want to add further lexical items and further structure building rules (or generalizations of the ones we have) to more closely approach a sound and complete grammar of English.

(1)    a.  [Dana][laughed]

        b.  [Adrian] [spoke rapidly]

        c.  [Each student] [laughed]

        d.  [No student] [both laughed and cried]

        e.  [Neither Kim or Dana] [complained]

(2)    a.  [Some teacher] [criticized Dana]

        b.  [Each student] [praised each teacher sincerely]

        c.  [Ed] [congratulated each student and laughed]

        d.  [No teacher] [[both praised and criticized] each student]

        e.  [John and some policeman] [captured the thief]

To keep things fairly simple we note that all the Ss in (1) and (2) are in the simple past tense. So we do not consider present tense forms, like *Dana laughs* or *Dana is laughing*, nor future tense forms – *Dana will laugh*. We also ignore complex past tense forms which use auxiliary verbs like *has laughed*, etc.

    Now, again in traditional terms, the Ss in (1) and (2) are in subject-predicate form. The first bracketed constituent is the subject and the second the predicate. Both may be syntactically complex.

    We consider first the predicates. In (1) there is a main predicate that may stand alone (e.g. *laughed* in (1a)) to combine with a subject, such as *Dana* to form a S. We shall treat *laughed* as a lexical item (ignoring its past tense marking for now). It will have category $P_1$ (abbreviating *one place predicate*, more usually called a VP – *Verb Phrase* – in the linguistic literature). $P_1$s may be (and usually are) syntactically complex. In (1b), the $P_1$ is *spoke rapidly*, in which the adverb *rapidly* modifies the $P_1$ *spoke* to form a complex $P_1$ *spoke rapidly*. In (1d) we see that $P_1$ is a *boolean category* – meaning that its expressions may be, in general, appropriately combined with *and, or, not, neither... nor...* to form complex $P_1$s. *Some child neither laughed nor cried* would be another example. Nor are such boolean compounds limited to just two conjuncts: *John works in New York and either lives in Atlantic City or commutes from Westport.*

Consider now the predicates in (2). They consist of a lexical $P_2$ – *two place predicate*, such as *criticized* in (2a), *praised* in (2b), *captured* in (2e). $P_2$s require terms like those which served as subjects in (1) in order to form a complex $P_1$. Thus we treat *criticized* as a $P_2$ in (2a) and *criticized Dana* as a derived $P_1$. Such complex $P_1$s may also be modified by adverbs, like *sincerely*, in (2b). They also may coordinate with lexical $P_1$s, as in (2c) and are themselves boolean categories, as illustrated in (2d). Another example would be *Some teacher neither praised nor criticized each student.*

What now shall we say about the category of expression that $P_1$s combine with to form Ss (which we now also call $P_0$s)? In terms of internal syntax they seem somewhat diverse. Simple proper names such as *Kim, Dana*, etc. seem lexical in having no meaningful parts (proper constituents). But others, such as *each student, some teacher*, etc. are obviously syntactically complex consisting of a Determiner (Det) such as *each, some, no* etc. + a noun, which may itself be syntactically complex: *each industrious student, some student who I met in Chicago*, etc. And further we have the usual boolean suspects: *John and some policeman, every professor but not every student (signed the petition)*, etc. Perhaps the most common cover term for these expressions in generative grammar today is DP, abbreviating Determiner Phrase (though the term appears somewhat inappropriate for proper names and boolean compounds). A more appropriate name would be simply *Term*, as was used in early work in Relational Grammar (Perlmutter and Postal, 1983b,a,c), but here we will stick with DP for reasons of familiarity to most linguists.

Combinatorily speaking DPs combine with $P_1$s to form $P_0$s (Ss), and they combine with $P_2$s to form $P_1$s. So we shall invent a category $\langle P_0, P_1 \rangle / \langle P_1, P_2 \rangle$ for them.[1] Of course we don't know exactly how they combine with the predicates until we specify the rule. Moreover these rules vary in somewhat regular ways from language to language. Let us

---

[1] This is just a limited form of $n$-tuple categories used in Keenan and Timberlake (1988).

then begin with ENG, a mini-grammar intended to generate a fragment of English.

### 5.2.1   ENG

Here we specify a Lexicon and two rules, the language $L(\text{ENG})$ being the closure of $\text{Lex}_{\text{ENG}}$ wrt rules. We assume phonological theory has defined the set of possible phonological sequences of English, though most of these sequences, like *blik*, are not actually words or phrases in the language. A few acceptable sequences, such as *both* and *either* (in our grammar here) do get used syncategorematically in the conjunction rules. That is, they appear in the output of the rule but are not themselves expressions of any category.

In stating $\text{Lex}_{\text{ENG}}$ we use some obvious shorthands instead of writing out each lexical item separately e.g (laughed, $P_1$) $\in \text{Lex}_{\text{ENG}}$, etc. Also the category formation rules now read: if $\langle A_1, \ldots, A_n \rangle$ and $\langle B_1, \ldots, B_n \rangle$ are $n$-tuples of elements of $\text{Cat}_{\text{ENG}}$ then $\langle A_1, \ldots, A_n \rangle / \langle B_1, \ldots, B_n \rangle$ is an element of $\text{Cat}_{\text{ENG}}$. The idea here is that an expression of category $\langle A_1, \ldots, A_n \rangle / \langle B_1, \ldots, B_n \rangle$ is one that combines with expressions of category $B_i$ to form ones of category $A_i$, all $1 \leq i \leq n$. Exactly how they combine must be stated in the rules. And even when the rules just concatenate expressions, as will be our case, the relative order of $A_i$ and $B_i$ may be different from that for $A_j$ and $B_j$. Equally there are regular differences between languages as we will see. In our grammar ENG for a fragment of English, the only proper $n$-tuple category we use is $\langle P_0, P_1 \rangle / \langle P_1, P_2 \rangle$. Expressions of this category combine with $P_1$s to form $P_0$s (Sentences), and with $P_2$s to form $P_1$s. This category is usually abbreviated DP. When $A$ and $B$ are 1-tuples we write simply $A/B$ rather than $\langle A \rangle / \langle B \rangle$, using or omitting parentheses for clarity as usual. Of course we understand that $\text{Cat}_{\text{ENG}}$ is closed under the right slash function, / and so is infinite, but as will follow from our statement of $\text{Rule}_{\text{ENG}}$, for all but finitely many of the $C \in \text{Cat}_{\text{ENG}}$, $\text{PH}(C)$, the set of phrases of category $C$, is empty.

**Lex$_{\text{ENG}}$**

|         |                                            |
|---------|--------------------------------------------|
| $P_1$:  | laughed, spoke, cried, complained          |
| $P_2$:  | praised, criticized, congratulated, captured |
| DP:     | Dana, Kim, Sasha, Ed, John, Adrian, Ann    |
| N:      | doctor, lawyer, teacher, student, policeman |
| DP/N:   | each, every, some, no, the, a              |
| CJ:     | and, or, nor                               |

(Recall, to emphasize, that DP abbreviates $\langle P_0, P_1 \rangle / \langle P_1, P_2 \rangle$.) And we posit two rules MERGE and COORD, which are partial functions from

$n$-tuples of possible expressions to possible expressions (a possible expression is just a pair $(s, C)$ for $s$ an acceptable phonological string and $C$ a category name.) We write $+$ for concatenation.

$$\text{MERGE}((s, X), (t, Y)) = \begin{cases} (s + t, P_0) & \text{if } X = DP \text{ and } Y = P_1 \\ (s + t, DP) & \text{if } X = DP/N \text{ and } Y = N \\ (t + s, P_1) & \text{if } X = DP \text{ and } Y = P_2 \end{cases}$$

(Recall that DP just abbreviates $\langle P_0, P_1 \rangle / \langle P_1, P_2 \rangle$.) The order in which the arguments of MERGE are written is irrelevant. We could have written MERGE$((t,Y), (s,X))$ instead of MERGE$((s,X), (t,Y))$ above without changing the expressions on the right of the $=$ sign. So while the order in which the arguments of MERGE is fixed (as is traditional) our choice of order is arbitrary.

We note also that assigning *John, every student*, etc. to the $n$-tuple category $\langle P_0, P_1 \rangle / \langle P_1, P_2 \rangle$ is a way of expressing a linguistic generalization. DPs are expressions that reduce the rank (arity, adicity) of predicates, combining with $n+1$-place predicates to form $n$-place ones. This enables us, later, to distinguish the categories of DPs as given from reflexive DPs such as *himself* and *both himself and the teacher* as they occur in *John criticized himself* and *John criticized both himself and the teacher*. Reflexive DPs will just have category $P_1/P_2$ (and more generally $P_{n+1}/P_{n+2}$). So our grammar will not generate *Himself laughed*, where *himself* would combine with a $P_1$ to form a $P_0$. But, as we will see, it will coordinate *himself* and the (non-reflexive) DP *the teacher* to form a $P_1/P_2$. So far then the syntactic upshot of $n$-tuple categories is that *every student*, etc. has one "big" category rather than many "small" ones: $P_0/P_1$, $P_1/P_2$, ... Further advantages of this notation are discussed in Chapter 8.

**Terminology**     Pairs of possible expressions in the domain of MERGE have category coordinates of the form A/B and $B_i$, where $B_i$ either is B or is one of the coordinates of B (if B is a sequence of categories). In this context A/B will be called the *Functor* category and that of B its *Argument* category. Note that B itself may be a "slash" category C/D, in which case A/B = A/(C/D).

In what follows we progressively enrich our grammar by adding new pairs to the domain of MERGE specifying its value at that pair as "Functor First" or "Functor Last". MERGE applies Functor First to $(\langle john, DP \rangle, \langle laughed, P_1 \rangle)$ to yield $\langle John\ laughed, P_0 \rangle$. (Since DP $= \langle P_0, P_1 \rangle / \langle P_1, P_2 \rangle$ it is the functor category in this case). MERGE applies "Functor Last", when it maps $(\langle john, DP \rangle, \langle criticized, P_2 \rangle)$ to $\langle criticized\ John, P_1 \rangle$.

Our second structure building function is COORD (COORDINATION):

For all $C \in \{P_0, P_1, P_2, DP, DP/N\}$,

$$\text{COORD}((s, \text{CJ}), (t, C), (u, C)) = \begin{cases} ((\text{both}) + t + s + u, C) & \text{if } s = \text{and} \\ ((\text{either}) + t + s + u, C) & \text{if } s = \text{or} \\ (\text{neither} + t + s + u, C) & \text{if } s = \text{nor} \end{cases}$$

As expected we can illustrate the application of MERGE and COORD with trees. In (3a) below we illustrate a Function-Argument (F-A) tree for the derivation of *Sasha laughed* of category $P_0$ (S). In such trees the leaf nodes are labeled with lexical expressions and their mother nodes are labeled with the expressions built from their daughters by MERGE or COORD. In (3b) by contrast we use a "standard" tree, those commonly used in generative grammar.

(3)  a. F-A tree:

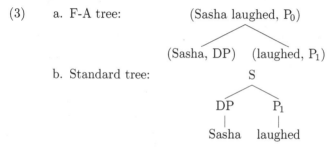

b. Standard tree:

As we have noted, F-A trees are more useful when the structure building functions (e.g. so far just MERGE and COORD) do more than merely concatenate their argument expressions. But for much of what we do concatenation is the primary operation so we use both F-A trees and standard trees. Even here though the use of discontinuous expressions such as *neither... nor...* is most naturally represented in F-A trees. Consider (4):

(4)  (Adrian neither laughed nor cried, $P_0$)

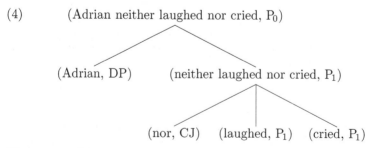

The tree in (4) summarizes the argument that the label on the root node is in the language $L(\text{ENG})$. The argument goes as follows: Each label of a terminal node is in $L(\text{ENG})$ since it is in the lexicon. Each label on a non-terminal node is derived by MERGE or COOR from the labels on its daughters. Thus by recursion the labels on all mother nodes are in $L(\text{ENG})$.

Finally (5) below is a reasonable attempt to represent the sentence in (4) using a standard tree. It does not however capture the sense in which *neither... nor...* is a constituent. (5) is the standard tree for (4).

(5)

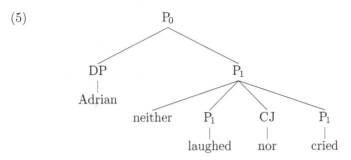

**Exercise 5.1.** Give the F-A trees for (1b,c,d) and (2a,b,c,d).

**Exercise 5.2.** We would like of course to generate Ss built from $P_3$s, such as:

i. The teacher gave every student a book.

ii. Some nurse handed the doctor a scalpel.

What additions/modification to ENG must be made so $L(\text{ENG})$ contains these Ss?

## 5.3 Word Order Variation in Other Languages

We have designed our MERGE rule so that "subjects" precede $P_1$s and "objects" follow $P_2$s. The Subject+$P_1$ order is pragmatically unmarked in many languages, roughly about 80% of the world's languages. Still 20% put the $P_1$ first. Here are 3 cases. We have chosen the languages because they exhibit further differences among themselves when $P_2$s are considered.

(6)    a. Tamazight (Berber):

immu    uryaz    n-ṭmǝṭtutt
died    man(+c)    of-woman(+c)
*The woman's husband died.*

    b. Malagasy (Austronesian; Madagascar):

      *nihomehy  Rabe*
      laughed    Rabe

      *Rabe laughed.*

    c. Hixkaryana (Carib; Brazil):

      *n-eweh-yatxhe*          *woriskomo  komo*
      3s-bathe-NONPAST.COLL  woman      COLL

      *The women are bathing.*

There is even more variation with regard to the relative order of $P_2$s and its two DPs. Here are some well attested cases:

(7)      a. Finnish (Uralic; Finland):

      *Pekka  luki   kirja-n*
      Pekka  read   book-gen

      *Pekka read the book.*

      b. Hixkaryana (Carib; Brazil):

      *toto  y-ono-ye*             *kamara*
      man  3s.3o-eat-DISTPST.COMPL  jaguar

      *The jaguar ate the man.*

(8)      a. Japanese (Altaic):

      *Yuko-ga    shimbun-o     yonda*
      Yuko-nom  newspaper-acc  read

      *Yuko read a newspaper.*

      b. Tamazight (Berber; Morocco):

      *uywy    uryaz      agrum*
      carried  man(+c)  bread

      *The man carried the bread.*

      c. Malagasy (Austronesian; Madagascar):

      *nanenjika  azy   izy*
      chased     him   he

      *He chased him.*     (he $\neq$ him)

The SOV order as illustrated by Japanese is perhaps the most common order by a slight margin. Then comes the SVO order as in Finnish and English, then the VSO order as in Berber and Welsh, then the VOS order as in Malagasy and Tzotzil and then the quite rare order OVS as in Hixkaryana.

**Exercise 5.3.** Construct a (very) mini-grammar for Malagasy using English words but modeling them on the examples in (6) and (8). Assume the lexicon just has some P$_1$s and P$_2$s, the only DPs are some lexical proper nouns (say *Rabe* and *Rasoa*), and the rules are MERGE and COORD, which you are to formulate. To keep things simple assume Malagasy lacks the analogue of *neither, both, either* and the coordinate conjunctions just occur between the strings they combine. Then provide derivation trees for your Malagasy translations of: (1) *Rabe laughed*, (2) *Rabe chased Rasoa*, and (3) *Rabe laughed and chased Rasoa*.

## 5.4 Three New Types of DPs

### 5.4.1 Simple Pronouns

We observe that *he* and *she* combine nicely with P$_1$s – *She laughed, He cried* but they do not occur as objects (\**Ann praised he/she*) so they should not have the same category as *John, Ann* or *each student*.

**Exercise 5.4.** What category should *he* and *she* have which predicts these facts? Illustrate your analysis with a tree. You will doubtless have to say how MERGE behaves at the new expressions.

**Exercise 5.5.** We have a similar problem with *him* and *her*. \**Him / Her laughed* but √*Dana praised him/her*. Again, design categories for *him* and *her* which determine these facts.

### 5.4.2 Possessive DPs

Here we just add one new lexical item, *'s*, in the category ((DP/N)/DP). It will be treated as Functor Last by the MERGE rule and not added to the coordinable categories in the domain of the CO-ORD rule. So *'s* combines with a DP to yield a Det, something that combines with a N to form a DP. And our grammar generates infinitely many new expressions. Here is a simple example:

(9)

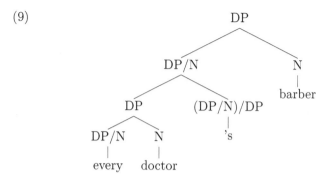

**Exercise 5.6.** Exhibit a derivation tree for (*every doctor's barber's barber*, DP).

**Exercise 5.7.** Define a one to one function from $\mathbb{N}$, the set of natural numbers, into the set of expressions of category DP in $L(\text{ENG})$ thereby showing that this class of expressions, and hence $L(\text{ENG})$ itself, is infinite.

We recall that iterated possessives become difficult to understand but we occasionally find examples. One of us recently read: *I was an MP once. I was your boss's boss's boss.* (*Not a Drill*, Lee Child 2014).

### 5.4.3 Relative Clauses

An example is the italicized portion of (10a). (10b) illustrates the distinctive part of its representation in current linguistics, and (10c) illustrates what it would be derived from there. The examples in (10) are DP strings.

(10)    a. every student *who Kim praised*

       b. every student $who_i$ Kim praised $t_i$

       c. every student [e [Kim praised wh]]

In (10a) *who* is called a *relative pronoun*. (A more sensitive analysis would write it as *whom* in this context, but for now we ignore this.) *Praised* is a $P_2$ string, but no DP follows it. In (10b) *who* carries an *index*, noted $i$ here, and following the $P_2$ *praised* is a symbol $t$, called a *trace*, co-indexed with the relative pronoun. In (10c) *who* occurs where the second argument of the $P_2$ is expected, and the symbol $e$ precedes the sentence *Kim praised who*. $e$ just indicates an empty position. Like the trace symbol $t$, it is not pronounced.

Generative grammarians commonly derive (10a) from (10c) by moving *wh* to the $e$ position leaving a co-indexed trace behind, eliminating the symbol *e*. The co-indexing of the relative pronoun and the trace is so that one can tell which moved element is tied to which trace. But in fact independent constraints on movement are strong enough that co-indexing in the examples we use is redundant, so here we omit it.

What follows the relative pronoun in relative clauses basically looks like a sentence with a trace (a gap) in a DP position. But not just any such position is available: *the teacher who either Dana criticized t or Adrian praised Sasha*. So the tricky problem is how to say rigorously just where the traces may occur. We do this using the following notation, which we exhibit first and then explain:

(11)

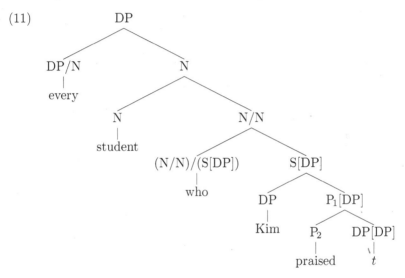

The tree in (11) illustrates two new lexical items and one new category formation rule. Previously Cat$_{\text{ENG}}$ was just the closure of a finite list of category names under the right slash function. Now we close it under an additional function, as follows:

(12)  Cat$_{\text{ENG}}$ is the least set which includes {P$_0$, P$_1$, P$_2$, N, DP, DP/N, CJ} and satisfies 1. and 2. below:

   1. If A and B are *n*-tuples of elements in Cat$_{\text{ENG}}$ then (A/B) ∈ Cat$_{\text{ENG}}$, and

   2. If A and B are in Cat$_{\text{ENG}}$ then A[B] is in Cat$_{\text{ENG}}$.

An expression of category A[B] is an "A with a gap of category B". We call such categories *gap categories*. Strings of category A[B] are like ones of category A but with a string of category B missing (represented by *t*.) So in (11), *Kim praise t* is a string of category S[DP], a sentence with a DP missing. And *praise t* is a string of category $P_1$[DP], a one place predicate with a DP missing. And the trace *t* of category DP[DP] is a DP with a DP missing. Since it is underived it is a new lexical item. Similarly (who, (N/N)/(S[DP])) and (that, (N/N)/(S[DP]) are new lexical items, ones that combine with expressions of category S[DP] to form something which combines with an N to form an N. Note that (N/N)/(S[DP]) is a slash category, not a gap category.

**New Lexical Entries in Lex$_{\text{ENG}}$**
>  DP[DP]:  *t*
>  ⟨N/N)/(S[DP]):  who, that

Now to extend our grammar we first enrich Lex$_{\text{ENG}}$ and then extend the structure building functions MERGE and COORD.

(13) To Lex$_{\text{ENG}}$ add (*t*, DP[DP]) and (who, (N/N)/(S[DP]))
  and (that, (N/N)/(S[DP])).

We extend MERGE first by adding pairs of the form

$$\langle (u, (N/N)/(S[DP])), (v, S[DP]) \rangle$$

to its domain. They are mapped in Functor First order, $(u + v)$. Then we add all other pairs of the form $\langle (A/B), B[DP] \rangle$ and $\langle (A/B)[DP], B \rangle$, which are both mapped to expressions of category A[DP], where the Functor First order is (recursively) the same as that of A/B,B.

Two important points regarding the extended MERGE rule: (1) if a pair $(\sigma, \tau)$ is in its domain then at most one of $\sigma$, $\tau$ has a DP gap. And (2), when MERGE applies to a pair one of which has a DP gap then the derived expression inherits that gap. The only way we get rid of a DP gap is by combining a relative pronoun with an S[DP], the result being the gapless N/N. We stipulate here that MERGE(N/N,N) uses Functor Last order.

We also now extend COORD by adding N/N, $P_1$[DP], $P_1$[DP] and $P_2$[DP] to the set of coordinable categories. The verbal statement of the definition of COORD is unchanged. So we combine two expressions of the same category with *and, or,* and *nor* as before, but now there are expressions of more categories to combine.

**Exercise 5.8.** Provide derivation trees for the following DPs:

  a. a student who t laughed and cried

b. a student who t laughed and who t cried

c. a student who t praised every student

d. every student who t praised every student who t praised every student

e. every student that every student who t praised every student praised t

**Some Merits of the Extended Grammar** Linguists have studied structures of the relative clause type extensively and have observed several general constraints on those in which the relative clause has a gap.[2] Many of these constraints concern the possible locations of traces. On the movement view mentioned earlier they concern the locus from which the *wh* can be moved. Most of these generalizations follow from our formulation of ENG whereas on the movement view they must be explicitly stated in addition to the formulation of the movement rule. Here are three such:

**Constraints on Relative Clause Formation**

1. *No vacuous binding* The string following the relative pronoun must contain a gap: *\*every student who some teacher laughed.* This follows on our treatment since *who* and *that* only combine with expressions of category S[DP] which must eventually contain a (t, DP[DP]).

2. The *Coordinate Structure Constraint*. We cannot relativize into just one conjunct of a coordinate structure: *\*every student who laughed and Sasha praised Dana.* But we can relativize into all the conjuncts simultaneously: *every student who Kim criticized and Sasha praised.* This follows on our formulation since a gapless sentence has category S and a gapped one S[DP] and ENG only allows us to coordinate expressions of the same category.

3. *Subjacency* (as applied to the class of expressions we consider.) Given a sentence with a relative clause we cannot relativize into that clause. So from *Kim praised the student who criticized the teacher* we cannot form *\*the teacher who Kim praised the student*

---

[2]Some languages, such as Hebrew, Arabic and spoken Czech use an overt pronoun in the trace position, depending on the position. Such pronouns are called *resumptive* pronouns, but usually (not always) have the same shape as ordinary personal pronouns in main clauses. See Keenan and Comrie (1977).

> *who criticized.* This follows on our approach since since to derive
> *t criticized t* we would have to apply MERGE to a DP[DP] and a
> $P_1$[DP], and no such pair is in the domain of MERGE.

However, our grammar is not without problems. It fails to generate
(14a) and wrongly generates (14b). So our grammar is incomplete and
unsound.

(14)  a. (every student whose teacher Kim criticized, DP)

  b. *(every student who Kim criticized t's teacher, DP)

Failure to generate (14a) means we must augment our grammar.
Wrongly generating (14b) means we must impose further constraints
on our lexicon or structure building functions. In fact the latter is not
difficult. We simply exclude from the domain of MERGE pairs of the
form ⟨('s, DP/N), (t, DP[DP])⟩. (Here *t* is trace, not just an arbitrary
phonological string.) Linguists would call such a solution *ad hoc*, indicating (rightly) that we would like to derive this condition from some
more general one, perhaps a properly generalized version of Subjacency.
The only merit of our solution is that it works (!) – it blocks the grammar from generating (14b). But the grammar still fails to generate
(14a).

**Conclusion** We shall stop here in our attempt to build a grammar
of English. Obviously we have barely touched the surface, but we
hope to have given the reader some idea what is involved in building a
grammar. Below we provide several exercises that indicate directions
in which our grammar should be further extended. For purposes of
variety and naturalness of example in doing the exercises feel free to
assume the existence of Ns, DPs, $P_1$s, etc. other than those we have
listed, e.g. (*Mary*, DP), (*house*, N), etc.

**Exercise 5.9.** How might we add to ENG ditransitive verbs such as
*show* and *give* as in *John showed Kim the house, Sasha gave Mary a
flower*, of category S? How must the category DP be enriched?

**Exercise 5.10.** Add adjectives, such as *intelligent, industrious, able*
to ENG. You must find an appropriate category. Note that they and
their coordinations precede common nouns: *an intelligent student, every industrious and intelligent student*. Do you see any overgeneration
problems with your addition?

**Exercise 5.11.** Add reflexive pronouns *himself, herself* to the grammar. Note that *\*Himself laughed, \*Herself criticized Kim*, but that *Kim
criticized himself* and *Adrian praised herself* are fine. So is *Adrian*

*praised herself and the teacher.* A natural way to add reflexives will force us to countenance an *agreement* problem: How to generate *She criticized herself* but not *She criticized himself.* (You need not attempt to solve this problem.)

**Exercise 5.12.** Add some manner adverbs like *quickly, joyfully, carefully.* What is the MERGE order for $P_1$s and these adverbs? Exhibit a derivation tree for *Kim spoke carefully.*

**Exercise 5.13.** Add PPs (Prepositional Phrases) like *at Sasha, in the garden* as they occur in *Kim smiled at Sasha, Dana praised Adrian in the garden.*

**Exercise 5.14.** Extend ENG to generate Ss like *Kim thought that Dana praised Sasha.* Assume, following standard linguistic terminology, that the constituent *that Dana praised Sasha* here has category CP ("Complementizer Phrase"). What category might we then assign to *thought, said,* and *believed?* And what category might we assign to *that?*

**Exercise 5.15.** Exhibit the derivation tree in our grammar for (14b).

**Exercise 5.16.** To generate *a student whose teacher Kim criticized* we might add *whose* as an expression that would combine with an N to form something of the same category as *who* and *that* above. Write this out explicitly.

**Exercise 5.17.** Will the augmented grammar in the previous exercise derive (*a student whose teacher's doctor praised her,* DP)? If so give a derivation tree. If not say why not.

**Exercise 5.18.** Assuming the previous exercise, how might we further extend the grammar to generate *a student whose teacher and whose barber Kim praised?*

**Exercise 5.19.** Given the exercise above, how might we prevent the grammar from generating *a student who and whose teacher Kim praised?*

**Exercise 5.20.** Most if not all theories of generative grammar incorporate some mechanisms of forming subcategories of expressions. For example, the Determiners we used all select or allow *singular* Ns: *every student, a teacher,* etc. But many Dets, such as *all, several, many* require *plural* Ns: *all students, several teachers,* etc. You might try modifying the set of basic categories so that it contains, say, $N_{sg}$ and $N_{pl}$ instead of simply N. Equally we need to subcategorize DP to $DP_{sg}$

and DP$_{pl}$. Then give the categories for the two subclasses of Dets. Note that the singular and plural features must be inherited by the DP so formed, as predicates may vary accordingly: *every student is laughing* vs. *several students are laughing*.

**Exercise 5.21.** Recall DPs such as *every friend of the President, some friend of every senator,* etc. To generate these let us add to our lexicon the following:

(15) N/DP: friend, colleague, relative, employee

Treat *of* like we treated *both* and *either*, namely as introduced by the MERGE rule and not having a category. We stipulate that MERGE applies Functor First to (N/DP, DP). Then we can derive:

(16)

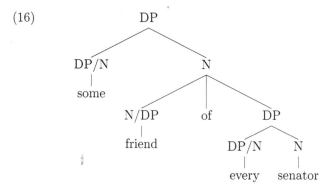

Exhibit a derivation tree for: (a friend of a friend of a senator, DP).

# 6

## A Taste of Formal Language Theory

### 6.1 Introduction

In Chapter 5 we provided several instantiations of a grammar ENG for a fragment of English. They were given in a *bottom up* (or *inductive*) format. Here we introduce a *top down* format called *context free grammars* (CFGs), which has been widely used in linguistics and computer science. (Recall from Chapter 1: *If you can't say something two ways you can't say it.* Studying an object from different points of view improves your understanding of it – and two intertranslatable formalizations may suggest different questions and generalizations).

Before formally defining the CFG format we provide some informal reasoning from this perspective. In the grammar ENG of Chapter 5 we say that *Sasha laughed* is a string of category S ($= P_0$) in $L(\text{ENG})$. We summarized that argument with an F-A tree like (1a) or, equivalently, a standard tree like (1b).

(1)    a.    (Sasha laughed, S)        b.    S

          (Sasha, $P_0/P_1$)   (laughed, $P_1$)       $P_0/P_1$    $P_1$

                                               Sasha   laughed

Reading either tree from the bottom up we infer first that *Sasha* is a string of category $P_0/P_1$ and *laughed* a string of category $P_1$, and some rule combines them to give the string in the root node, of category S.

Now reading (1b) top down, we say that an expression of category S may consist of one of category $P_0/P_1$ followed by one of category $P_1$. And a $P_0/P_1$ may be *Sasha* and one of category $P_1$ *laughed*. We express these three steps using the context free format by:

(2)    a. S $\rightarrow P_0/P_1 + P_1$

    b. $P_0/P_1 \rightarrow$ Sasha

    c. $P_1 \rightarrow$ laughed

Note that the + sign in (2) merely serves to separate two expressions (category names in the case at hand). We sometimes omit it and just leave a space to indicate the separation.

    The expressions in (2) are called *productions* (or *rules*). The upper case symbols are called *non-terminal* symbols (sometimes *variables*) and the lower case ones *terminal* symbols. Mathematically the choice of terminal and non-terminal symbols is arbitrary. In modeling grammars for natural languages we choose the non-terminals to be names of grammatical categories and the terminals to be words (roughly) in the language under study. In general the productions of a CFG are of the form in (3):

(3)    $A \rightarrow w$ (A a non-terminal symbol, $w$ a string whose coordinates may be any mix of terminal and non-terminal symbols).

The productions of a CFG, required to be finite in number, are the mechanism for deriving strings starting with non-terminal symbols. (3) says that given a string with A in it we can derive another string by replacing A with $w$ keeping everything else the same. We illustrate how this works in a simple but characteristic case. Let $G$ be a CFG whose only non-terminal is S and whose only terminal symbols are $a$ and $b$, and whose two productions are as in (4):

(4)    1. $S \rightarrow ab$    2.  $S \rightarrow aSb$

Here are three derivations of terminal strings (strings of terminal symbols) beginning with S:

| D1. | S | D2. | S | D3. | S |
|---|---|---|---|---|---|
| | ab | | aSb | | aSb |
| | | | aabb | | aaSbb |
| | | | | | aaabbb |

The first line in each of these derivations is the string whose only coordinate is S. All the other lines are derived by replacing an occurrence of S in the line immediately above with a string $w$, where $S \rightarrow w$ is a production. The last line in each derivation is a terminal string as it has no occurrences of non-terminals.

**Exercise 6.1.** Using the assumed CFG above

    a. exhibit a derivation of $a^5b^5$.

b. give a reason why aab is not derivable from S in this grammar

c. The set of terminal strings derivable from S above is $\{ a^n b^n \mid n \geqslant 1 \}$. Say informally why this is so.

## 6.2 CFGs: A Formal Definition

**Definition 6.1.** $G$ is a *context free grammar* (CFG) iff $G = \langle N, T, S, \rightarrow \rangle$, where:

$N$ is a non-empty set, whose elements are called *non-terminal* symbols.
$T$ is a set disjoint from $N$, whose elements are called *terminal* symbols.
$S$ is an element of $N$, called the *start* symbol, and
$\rightarrow$ is a finite binary relation from $N$ to $(N \cup T)^*$, that is, $\rightarrow$ is a finite subset of $N \times (N \cup T)^*$. (As usual with binary relations $R$ we write $aRb$ for $(a, b) \in R$; so here we write for example S $\rightarrow$ aSb rather than $\langle$S,aSb$\rangle \in \rightarrow$.) Elements of $\rightarrow$ are called *productions* (or *rules*.) We read A $\rightarrow w$ as "A rewrites as $w$".

This definition, given in standard format, says that to define a CFG it is necessary and sufficient to specify four things: the set of non-terminal symbols, the set of terminal symbols, the start symbol, and the productions. Often non-terminals are written in upper case, terminals in lower case. Using these conventions we can specify a CFG just by giving its productions and the start symbol, which in linguistic contexts is often S.

**Definition 6.2.** Given a CFG $G$, a *derivation* over $G$ is a sequence $u = u_1, u_2, \ldots, u_n$ of elements of $(N \cup T)^*$ such that for each $i$, $1 \leqslant i < n$, $u_{i+1}$ results from $u_i$ by replacing some non-terminal A in $u_i$ with a string $w$, where A $\rightarrow w$ is a production of $G$. (Recall the definition of substitution in Chapter 2.)

**Definition 6.3.** Given $G = \langle N, T, S, \rightarrow \rangle$ as above,

3.1 for all $w \in (N \cup T)^*$, all A $\in N$, $w$ is *derivable* from A iff there is a derivation $u_1, u_2, \ldots, u_n$ in which $u_1 = $ A and $u_n = w$.

3.2 $L(G) = \{w \in T^* \mid w$ is derivable from the start symbol$\}$. $L(G)$ is called the *language generated by* $G$,

3.3 A set $M$ of strings over some alphabet is *context free* (a *context free language* or *CFL*) iff there is a CFG $G$ such that $L(G) = M$. □

Using these definitions we can now formally define the CFG used in (4): $G_{SE} = \langle \{S\}, \{a,b\}, S, \rightarrow \rangle$, where $\rightarrow$ is given by: S $\rightarrow$ ab and

S → aSb. (5) is a derivation of $a^4b^4$. This grammar is a minimal *self embedding* grammar, where we say that $G$ is *self embedding* if there are non-empty terminal strings $u, v, w$ such that both $w$ and $u + w + v$ are derivable from the start symbol. In such a case $w$ is said to be *self embedded* in $u + w + v$. A context free stringset (= set of strings) is said to have the *self embedding* property if every CFG for that set is self embedding. $L(G_{\text{SE}})$ is a self embedding stringset. Here is a derivation of $a^4b^4$ which illustrates several instances of self embeddings.

(5)    S, aSb, aaSbb, aaaSbbb, aaaabbbb

Observe that the set of strings derivable from S in the grammar in (4) is exactly the set defined by closure in Section 2.5 of Chapter 2. In the CFG literature proving that $L(G)$ is the set of strings $\Phi$ satisfying some conditions typically uses two proofs by mathematical induction: an induction on the length of derivations shows that $L(G) \subseteq \Phi$ and an induction on the length of expressions shows that $\Phi \subseteq L(G)$. These proofs are often tedious and rather than exercise the reader with them we show in an addendum how to convert CFGs to recursively defined sets as in Chapter 2 where the proof techniques there apply.

**Exercise 6.2.** Show that $\{a^n cb^n \mid n \geqslant 1\}$ is a CFL by exhibiting a grammar $G$ such that $L(G) = \{a^n cb^n \mid n \geqslant 1\}$. (You are not asked to prove this equality.) Note that $\{a^n cb^n \mid n \geqslant 1\}$ is also a self embedding stringset.

**Exercise 6.3.**

   a. Show that $\{a^{n+1} b^n \mid n \geqslant 1\}$ is context free.

   b. Show that $\{a^n b^{n+1} \mid n \geqslant 1\}$ is context free.

**Exercise 6.4.**

   a. Show that any finite set is context free.

   b. For $V$ a finite set show that $V^*$ is context free.

     The sets in these exercises are simple examples of CFLs (context free languages). A more difficult one is $\{w \in \{a, b\}^* \mid$ the number of $a$'s in $w$ is the same as the number of $b$'s in $w\}$ (see Hopcroft et al., 2001, 181).

**Notational simplification:** In writing sequences, such as (5) for example, we often omit angled brackets and sometimes the commas between coordinates when no confusion will result. We often write X

$\rightarrow w|w'$ instead of writing separate productions $X \rightarrow w$ and $X \rightarrow w'$. Here we use this notation to specify a few CFGs. ☐

To argue that a terminal string $w$ is derivable from the start symbol of a CFG $G$ we should, in principle, present a derivation, as in (5). Here are a few simple if artificial examples of context free stringsets. We provide CFGs for them and ask the reader to illustrate a few derivations. In all cases S is the start symbol.

(6)  $\{a^n b^m \mid n, m > 0\}$     Productions: (1) S → aS | B
                                                      (2) B → b  | bB

Here is a derivation of $a^2 b^3$: S, aS, aaS, aaB, aabB, aabbB, aabbb

The grammar illustrated in (4) derives expressions of even length, as it derives all expressions consisting of one or more a's followed by the same number of b's. But many $w$ in $\{a,b\}^*$ of even length are not generated, *aa*, *abab*, for example. However the set of $w$ in $\{a,b\}^*$ of even length is context free:

**Exercise 6.5.** Define a CFG $G$ such that $L(G) = \{w \in \{a, b\}^* \mid |w| \text{ even}\}$

Here is a CFG for Sentential Logic with three atomic formulas, which uses parentheses to avoid structural ambiguity.

(7)  S → p | q | r | not S | (S & S) | (S or S)

**Exercise 6.6.** Exhibit derivations of each of the following:

a.  q                     b.  (p & (q or r))   c.  ((p & q) or r)
d.  ((p & q) or (p & r))  e.  not (p or q)     f.  (not p or q)

In the CFL defined in (7) p, q, and r are called *atomic formulas*. Ordinarily in Sentential Logic (Chapter 8) the set of atomic formulas: $P_1$, $P_2$, ... is countably infinite. It might appear that we could give a CFG for this language using rules of the form S → $P_n$ for each natural number $n$. But then we would have infinitely many rules, which is not allowed by the definition of CFG. Can you see a way to, in effect, build denumerably many atomic formulas using only finitely many rules? (Hint: Enrich the grammar so that $P_0$, $P_{10}$, $P_{110}$, etc. are formulas. These will be the atomic ones. Note that, as given, no atomic formula is a constituent of any other.)

Matching parentheses are often used in formal expressions to make constituent structure explicit in the linear string. For example in the language of elementary arithmetic $((2+3)\times 4)$ and $(2+(3\times 4))$ are distinct expressions (and denote different numbers: 20 and 14 respectively). One check on whether formal expressions are well formed is whether the parentheses are nested and matched correctly – for every left parenthesis there is a matching right parenthesis. Here is a CFG that generates the language of matching parentheses (Hopcroft et al., 2001, 192). We use *e* for the empty string (often written as an epsilon $\epsilon$ in the formal language literature).

(8)  S → SS | (S) | ()

Here is a derivation of ((()())): S, (S), ((S)), ((SS)), ((()S)), ((()())).

**Exercise 6.7.** Exhibit derivations for each of the following:
  a.  ()   b.  ((()())())   c.  (()(()()))

   A *palindrome* is a sequence which reads the same backwards as forwards. In English *Anna*, *Bob*, *Mom* and *Dad* are palindromes (ignoring capitalization.) So is the noun *radar* and the adjective *level*. Longer ones are harder to find, but two are (also ignoring punctuation): *Madam I'm Adam* and, recalling Napoleon who was exiled to Elba, *Able was I ere I saw Elba*.

**Exercise 6.8.** Exhibit a CFG whose language is the set of palindromes in {a,b}*.
Hint: You will need the production S → *e*. *e* is a palindrome, as are *a* and *b*.

   In practice linguists do not use derivations directly to show that a given string is in some $L(G)$. Rather they give a *parse tree* (or *derivation tree*).

**Parse Trees and Structural Ambiguity**

**Definition 6.4.** A parse tree for a CFG $G$ is a finite ordered labeled tree $T$ satisfying:

  a. The root node of $T$ is labeled with the start symbol of $G$.

  b. All leaf nodes of $T$ are labeled with terminal symbols.

  c. All interior (non-leaf) nodes are labeled with non-terminal symbols.

  d. If A labels an interior node which immediately dominates just the nodes labeled $w_1, w_2, \ldots, w_k$ in order then A → $w_1+w_2+\cdots+w_k$ is a production of $G$. (We use + for concatenation here.)

Here are parse trees for D1 and D2 above:

(9)   a.   S

b.   S

**Exercise 6.9.** Using the above grammar, exhibit the parse tree for *aaabbb*.

The leaf sequence of a parse tree $T$ is called the *yield* of $T$. $L(G)$ is the set of yields of the parse trees for $G$. To *parse* a string in $L(G)$ is to provide a parse tree for it.

**Fact 1.** $\{ww^R \mid w \in \{a, b\}^*\}$ is context free. ($w^R$ is $w$ in reverse order. So if $w = \langle s_1, s_2, \ldots, s_n \rangle$ then $w^R = \langle s_n, s_{n-1}, \ldots, s_1 \rangle$.)

An explicit recursive definition of $w^R$ is:

$$\text{For all } w \in V^*, w^R = \begin{cases} e & \text{if } w = e \quad (e \text{ is the empty string}) \\ b \frown y^R & \text{if } w = y \frown b \quad (\text{all } b \in V, \text{ all } y \in V^*). \end{cases}$$

**Exercise 6.10.**

a. Exhibit a CFG $G$ whose language is $\{ww^R \mid w \in \{a, b\}^*\}$. Note that the set $\{ww^R \mid w \in \{a, b\}^*\}$ is just the set of palindromes of Exercise 6.8.

b. Exhibit the parse tree for *ababbaba*.

Linguists use parse trees to give a clear characterization of how expressions are built, their constituent structure. In some interesting cases they enable us to grasp quickly certain types of structural ambiguities. Consider the ambiguous grammar G[coord] below:

(10)  G[coord] $= \langle N, T, \text{DP}, \rightarrow \rangle$, where $N = \{\text{DP}\}$, $T = \{\text{and, or, Sasha, Kim, John, Mary}\}$, DP is the start symbol, and $\rightarrow$ is given below:

DP $\rightarrow$ DP and DP | DP or DP
DP $\rightarrow$ Sasha | Kim | John | Mary

Observe that *Kim and John or Mary* is a (string of category) DP in $L(\text{G[coord]})$. In fact it has two non-isomorphic parse trees (and so two distinct derivations):

(11)   a.

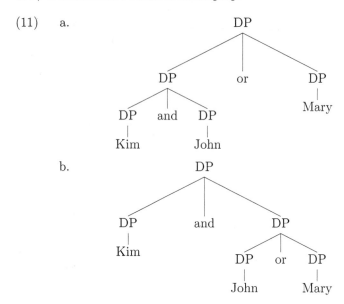

   b.

In ordinary English these two expressions have different meanings. For example the sentence *Kim and John or Mary arrived early* may have different truth values according to how we analyze the subject. Imagine that Kim didn't arrive early and that Mary did. On the analysis in (11a) the sentence is true but on the analysis in (11b) it is false. (It doesn't matter whether John arrived early or not.)

If we modified the grammar so that coordinations were flanked by matching parentheses then (11a) would appear as ((Kim and John) or Mary) and (11b) would be (Kim and (John or Mary)). While ordinary English does not use parentheses in this way the use of *both* and *either* with *and* and *or* has the same disambiguating effect: (11a) would be as in (12a), (11b) as in (12b):

(12)   a. either both Kim and John or Mary

   b. both Kim and either John or Mary

It is in part for representing structural ambiguities of this sort that linguists prefer to think of grammars as generating trees rather than simply strings. Two grammars may have the same *weak* generative capacity in the sense of generating the same string sets, but may differ radically in their *strong* generative capacity, namely the sets of parse trees they determine.

And the parse tree representation has another conceptual appeal. We may define an expression in $L(G)$, $G$ context free, to be *structurally ambiguous* if it has two or more non-isomorphic parse trees. It is less satisfying to define structural ambiguity directly in terms of derivations, as sometimes distinct derivations for the same string determine the same parse tree when the expression is not judged to be structurally ambiguous. For example:

(13)  Let $G$ with start symbol S be given by:

     a. S → AB

     b. A → a | aA

     c. B → b | bB

Here $L(G) = \{a^n b^m \mid n, m > 0\}$ for which we gave a slightly different grammar above. (14) below is one derivation of $ab$ in this grammar:

(14)  S, AB, aB, ab

**Exercise 6.11.**

    a. Give a second, distinct, derivation of $ab$.

    b. Exhibit the parse tree corresponding to each of these derivations

(Derivations are sequences and, recall, sequences are distinct iff they have different lengths or for some $i$, their $i^{\text{th}}$ coordinates are distinct.)

**Exercise 6.12.** Exhibit a CFG $G$ for $\{a^n b^m \mid n, m > 0\}$ in which every string generated has exactly one derivation (and hence exactly one parse tree.)

Exercise 6.12 prompts the following query: Does a CFL always have an unambiguous grammar? Surprisingly perhaps the answer is no (Ginsburg, 1966, 207; Kelley, 1995, 96, and Hopcroft et al., 2001, 212–14).

**Theorem 6.1** (Inherently ambiguous languages). *There exist CFLs $M$ such that every CFG $G$ for $M$ is ambiguous (i.e. for every such $G$ there is a $w \in L(G)$ such that $w$ has at least two non-isomorphic parse trees).*

The example Kelley gives is $\{a^i b^j c^k \mid i = j \text{ or } j = k\}$. The proof that every CFG for this set is ambiguous lies well beyond what we can cover here. But we note the first step in the proof as it illustrates the utility of a basic closure property of CFGs. Namely, we must show first that the stringset above is context free. To do this, consider the stringsets in (15).

(15)   a.   $\{a^i b^j c^k \mid i, j, k > 0 \text{ and } i = j\}$
       b.   $\{a^i b^j c^k \mid i, j, k > 0 \text{ and } j = k\}$

Each of these sets is easily seen to be context free using the same sort of mechanism we used in (4). Here is a grammar for (15a):

(16)   S $\to$ abC | aTbC
       T $\to$ ab | aTb
       C $\to$ c | cC

**Exercise 6.13.** Exhibit a derivation of $a^3 b^3 c^2$ using the rules in (16).

**Exercise 6.14.** Exhibit the productions of a CFG for (15b).

So the sets in (15a) and (15b) are both context free. And we now observe:

**Theorem 6.2.** *The union of two context free sets is itself context free. (That is, for G and G' CFGs, $L(G) \cup L(G')$ has a context free grammar.)*

Here is an informal proof. Let $G$ and $G'$ be CFGs. We construct a CFG $G''$ for $L(G) \cup L(G')$. We may assume that the non-terminals of $G$ are disjoint from those of $G'$ (if not, relabel them to make them disjoint.) Let S be the start symbol of $G$ and S' that for $G'$. Define the productions of $G''$ to be the union of those of $G$ with those of $G'$ together with S'' $\to$ S | S', where S'' is the start symbol for $G''$ (and not a non-terminal of $G$ or $G'$.) Clearly $L(G'') = L(G) \cup L(G')$.   □

It is the second part of the proof of Theorem 6.1 that lies beyond the scope of this chapter, namely showing that *all* grammars $G''$ for $L(G) \cup L(G')$ above have expressions with more than one parse tree. But, following Kelley, we can point out where the problem lies. Essentially we need one subset of rules to generate $L(G)$ and another to generate $L(G')$ (or sets that differ just finitely from these. See Hopcroft et al. (2001, 212–14).) This means there will be two ways to derive expressions of the form $a^n b^n c^n$, whence the inherent ambiguity.

The existence of context free languages that are inherently ambiguous is of some mathematical and epistemological interest: it places limits on our ability to characterize the structure of expressions in some languages using certain mechanisms, those given by CFGs.

There may also be a linguistic lesson to be learned here: Linguists working on grammars of natural languages often ask *What is the structure of this expression?*. But this question may not have a precise answer. If the language in question is context free and inherently ambiguous then no matter what grammar $G$ is considered there will be expressions that have more than one structure (parse tree) in $G$. A sobering thought.

Let us return now to (14). The moral of the example is that two or more occurrences of non-terminals in a line of a derivation can be rewritten in any order without changing the parse tree. So the ambiguity is an artifact of the CFG notation but does not correspond to a pretheoretically felt structural ambiguity. To avoid such multiple derivations we often stipulate that symbol replacement in a derivation always affect the leftmost (or the rightmost) non- terminal first.

Note though that while this, quite arbitrary, stipulation eliminates certain trivial cases of multiple derivations it does not eliminate structural ambiguity.

**Exercise 6.15.** Exhibit two leftmost derivations of *Kim and John or Mary* in G[coord] given in (10). Note that the two derivations still correspond to different ways of semantically interpreting the derived expression.

**Exercise 6.16.** Consider the small arithmetic grammar below and exhibit two leftmost derivations of $2+3\times4$: S $\rightarrow$ S+S | S $\times$ S | 2 | 3 | 4

Linguists' concern with the structure of expressions recalls a fundamental issue adumbrated in Chapter 1: If we think of a grammar of a natural language as representing its structure, and, as linguists are wont to do, we think of the structure of a language as (at least partially) reflecting the structure of mind, then we are quickly led to query the extent to which the set of expressions in a language determines the grammar. Suppose we have an oracle who can tell us for each string s of English words (roughly) whether s is a well formed expression of English or not. Then, to what extent does that information enable us to determine a (generative) grammar for English (possibly an ambiguous one)? In fact, given a CFG $G$ we can always find many other $G'$ that are weakly equivalent to $G$ in the sense that they generate the same set of strings. Some are trivial variants of each other to be sure. Given $G$ we could make up a trivial variant by adding some non-terminals to the grammar that were never mentioned in any production. So this would be technically a different grammar but one that generated the same expressions. Without trying to define the class of trivial variants of grammars we can nonetheless notice that it is not unreasonable to find structurally distinct grammars that generate the same expressions. Here is a candidate simply to give the reader some idea of substantive alternative analyses that arise in linguistic analysis.

(17) Let $G_1$ and $G_2$ be as below, with, in both cases, DP the start symbol and *'s, john, mary, doctor, barber* the terminal symbols:

$G_1$:  DP → DET + N          $G_2$:  DP → DP + N1
     DET → DP + 's                   N1 → 's + N
     DP → john | mary                DP → john | mary
     N → doctor | barber             N → doctor | barber

(18a) is a parse tree for *john's barber* using $G_1$, and (18b) using $G_2$.

(18)  a.          b.

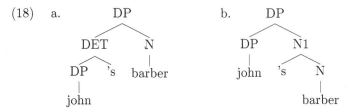

In fact linguists have provided arguments in favor of both of these analyses. So we might decide it is a case of structural ambiguity, like the coordination example above but not implying a semantic ambiguity, or we might opt for one or the other based on evidence that goes beyond mere "descriptive adequacy" – generating the expressions in question. For example, perhaps the different analyses generalize differently to new types of cases; perhaps we have evidence from semantic analysis which prefers one to the other; perhaps there is evidence from child language acquisition favoring one over the other. Sometimes competing analyses differ in "elegance", though that does not seem to be the case with $G_1$ and $G_2$ above.

**Exercise 6.17.** Provide the parse trees for *john's barber's doctor* using $G_1$ and $G_2$.

**Reference** A recent and very readable introduction to the formal study of context-free grammars as well as of finite state grammars dicussed in the next chapter is Sipser (2012).

## 6.3  How Well Do CFGs Model Natural Languages?

This is really two questions: a sufficiency one and a necessity one.

    *Sufficiency*    Can enlightening grammars for all natural languages be given in a context free format? If not we need to enrich their generative mechanisms to increase the class of languages they define.

*Necessity*   Are all languages generated by CFGs possible natural languages? If not we need to restrict their generative mechanisms to rule out certain languages.

There is modest agreement in the literature that CFGs are not sufficient, but that we do not have to enrich them much to obtain approximate models of NLs (natural languages). The necessity question is less often asked, and it does seem prima facie that many CFLs are very "unnatural".

We begin with support for the sufficiency hypothesis.

### 6.3.1   Properties of Natural Languages that are Expressible by CFGs

First, grammatical categories and the attendant substitution property are built into CFGs. By 'substitution' here we just mean that whenever some $\sigma$ of category C is a constituent of an expression $\tau$ then $\sigma$ can be replaced in $\tau$ by another expression $\sigma'$ of the came category as $\sigma$ preserving grammaticality. This enables us to represent many expressions by giving their grammatical form. For example, a Sentence consists of a DP followed by a P1. Given one S of this form we form many more (usually infinitely many more) just by replacing the DP with another DP or the P1 with another P1. Substitution applies crucially to constituents of expressions, not to strings. We have seen that *John laughed* is a sentence of English but that string is not a constituent of *The man who offended John laughed*, and that string cannot be replaced by a random sentence preserving grammaticality: *\*The man who offended now it is raining*.

Second, CFGs naturally represent constituent structure and structural ambiguities. Even operations which derive expressions from expressions by reordering parts or deleting parts are typically sensitive to constituent structure: what they move or delete are constituents.

Third, basic recursion is naturally represented in CFGs. It is unproblematic to generate *a teacher who criticized a teacher who criticized a teacher*, ... So CFGs provide a finite mechanism (the productions) for deriving infinite sets of strings.

Fourth, our definition of a CFG $G$ requires that the set of productions be finite. This is much more than a simplifying assumption, or an assumption of convenience. Were we to allow infinite sets of productions then any set whatever could be, trivially, generated by such a grammar: Let $M$ be any set and $G$ the grammar whose productions are $S \rightarrow m$ for each $m \in M$. Then $L(G) = M$, but we have said nothing about the structure of the elements of $M$.

With the finiteness restriction as we have it there are many stringsets that are provably not generable from any CFG:

**Fact 2.** Each of the sets below is not context free (has no CFG)

a. $\{a^n b^n c^n \mid n > 0\}$     b. $\{a^n b^n a^n \mid n > 0\}$

c. $\{a^m b^n a^m b^n \mid m, n > 0\}$     d. $\{a^i b^j c^k \mid i \le j \le k\}$

For proof that the set in (a) above is not context-free see Ginsburg (1966, 84); for that in (c) see Hopcroft and Ullman (1979, 128).

**Exercise 6.18.** Show $\{a^n a^n a^n \mid n > 0\}$ is context free. This set is just $\{a^{3n} \mid n > 0\}$

The examples in **Fact 2** above show that CFGs are limited in their ability to impose conditions on triples, quadruples, and in general $n$-tuples of expressions for $n > 2$. Note that 2 itself is fine: the pattern $a^n w b^n$ is a fundamental pattern in CFLs and shows up in common agreement patterns. Shortly we show how such patterns may be represented in a context free system and we also consider some apparent counterexamples in natural languages.

Fifth, to claim that natural language grammars are context free is a very strong claim: many sets, per **Fact 2** above, are not CFLs. In general linguists would like the class of grammars they can draw from in modeling a natural language to be structurally very limited. This would help explain why children learn languages rather quickly with only limited exposure to, often, imperfect data (interruptions, noisy channels, memory lapses, etc.). The idea is that learning a language requires learning a grammar for it, and the task of the learner is simplified to the extent there are few choices of possible grammars. This idea receives support from one mathematical result:

**Theorem 6.3.** *Given an arbitrary CFG G there is a mechanical procedure which tells us for each terminal string $w$ whether $w \in L(G)$ or not. (So it tells us it is in $L(G)$ if it is and it isn't if it isn't.) In short, given a CFG G, membership in $L(G)$ is decidable (Synonyms: solvable, computable, recursive).*

Many sets of expressions we work with as scholars are not decidable. For example the set of sentences provable from the (first order) axioms of arithmetic is not a decidable set. There is no procedure which looks at an arbitrary formula in arithmetic and says **yes** if that formula is a theorem and **no** if it isn't. On the other hand programming languages are decidable. Your computer has to be able to tell if your input text is a well formed program or not.

A few other linguistic questions about CFGs are decidable. In particular whether a language generated by an arbitrary CFG is empty or not, and whether it is infinite or not. But many other natural questions are not decidable – there is no mechanical procedure that answers the question. For example, it is not decidable whether $L(G) = L(G')$, given two arbitrary CFGs $G$ and $G'$. It is similarly undecidable whether $L(G) \subseteq L(G')$ and whether $L(G) \cap L(G') = \varnothing$.

Sixth, returning now to some less mathematical merits of CFGs, we see that CFGs can express a variety of cross constituent dependencies that are prominent in many natural languages. Here are two types of examples. First, *agreement* phenomena, such as subject–predicate agreement in number:

(19)    a. John daydreams. Every poet daydreams.

   b. John and Bill daydream. All poets daydream.

   c. *John daydream. *Every poet daydream.

   d. *John and Bill daydreams. *All poets daydreams

So a singular subject, like *John* or *every poet* requires a singular predicate, e.g. *daydreams* not *daydream*. Similarly plural subjects require plural predicates. In English we also find a kind of agreement (or selection) between DETs and Ns:

(20)    a.    all poets, most poets        *all poet, *most poet
   b.    every poet, a poet        *every poets, *a poets

And in these cases the DPs formed inherit the number feature, as we see in the subject-predicate agreement in (19). Below we illustrate how agreement of the sorts noted can be incorporated in a CFG.

The idea is to enrich the system of grammatical categories, annotating them with features like +pl and –pl. So a DP[+pl] is a plural DP, a DP[–pl] is a singular one. Then we enrich our productions with subcategory rules, (21), and agreement rules, (22):

(21)  DP[–pl] → John | Mary
   N[–pl] → doctor | poet
   N[+pl] → doctors | poets
   P1[–pl] → daydreams | drinks
   P1[+pl] → daydream | drink
   DP[+pl]/N[+pl] → all | most
   DP[–pl]/N[–pl] → every | a

(22)    S → DP[$\alpha$pl] + P1[$\alpha$pl]          all $\alpha \in \{+, -\}$.
   DP[$\alpha$pl] → DP[$\alpha$pl]/N[$\alpha$pl] + N[$\alpha$pl]     all $\alpha \in \{+, -\}$.
   DP[+pl] → DP[$\alpha$pl] and DP[$\beta$pl]       all $\alpha, \beta \in \{+, -\}$.

**Exercise 6.19.**

   a. Exhibit the parse tree for *John and most poets daydream*

   b. Say why *a poet daydream* is not derived from S in this grammar.

   c. Why is *each poets* not derived in this grammar?

Thus in an S consisting of a DP and a P1, both the DP and the P1 are +pl or both are –pl. Similarly when DETs combine with Ns to form DPs the DET and N agree in plurality and the DP inherits that specification.

Agreement systems (see Corbett, 1991, 2000) are much more complex than this in many languages, but still the set of agreement features in any language is always finite so enriching rewrite rules as above is in principle always possible. We are not saying that our brute force approach to agreement is the best way to represent it, only that basic agreement phenomena lie within the purview of CFGs. If one could show for example that there were agreement patterns in natural languages that could not be represented in CFGs that would be a lethal blow to claiming that natural languages are context free.

We should note that it is not uncommon across languages to find more than two agreement morphemes of the same shape, suggesting perhaps that NLs can impose identity conditions on $n$-tuples of expressions for $n > 2$. Consider (23) from Swahili (Bantu; E. Africa. See Corbett, 1991, 43):

(23)  ki*kapu*  ki*kubwa*  ki*moja*  ki*lianguka*
      basket    large      one       fell

     *One large basket fell*

Nouns in Bantu are commonly divided into 10 to 20 noun classes, marked by a prefix such as *ki* in (23). Adjectives, like "large" that modify the noun carry a copy of that prefix. The whole NP "large basket" is then in the *ki*-class of NPs and Determiners like "one" which combine with them and agree in class marking pass it along to the expression they derive. Finally when such DPs combine with predicates they trigger an agreement which is also expressed with the noun class marker occurring as a prefix on the verb, as in (23). Lest the reader think the example "exotic" we note that rich (though not identical) agreement patterns occur in Semitic (Hebrew, Arabic), Romance (French, Italian), Slavic (Russian, Polish), and many other groups. Here are a few examples:

(24)  a. *Ha-yeladim*    *ha-ktanim*    *yeshenim*
The-child.m.pl  the-small.m.pl  sleep.m.pl.
Hebrew

*The little boys are sleeping*

b. *Ha-yeladot*    *ha-ktanot*    *yeshenot*
the-child.fem.pl  the-small.fem.pl  sleep.fem.pl

*The little girls are sleeping*

In these cases the adjective "small" and the gender marked noun "child" agree in definiteness, gender and number. Linguists naturally generate this in several binary steps: (1) agreement (definiteness, gender, number) between the adjective and the NP, and (2) agreement between the DP subject (which inherits the gender and number features of its parts) with the predicate. Note finally the marked agreement in the French examples below:

(25)  a. *Les jeunes garçons sont heureux*
the   young  boys    are   happy

b. *Les jeunes filles sont heureuses*
the   young  girls  be.pl  happy.fem.pl

In both cases the definite article *les* 'the' is plural (singular masculine would be *le*, singular feminine *la*.) The *-s* on "young" and "boy/girl" marks plural (but does not change the pronunciation of the singular), *sont* is the 3$^{\text{rd}}$ person plural present tense form of "be", and *heureux* is the masculine plural form of "happy", which differs in pronunciation from the feminine plural form *heureuses* in (25b).

And in fairness let us note that while agreement phenomena are widespread in NLs, there are also many languages which present no agreement between subjects and verbs or between adjectives or determiners and nouns: Mandarin Chinese, Vietnamese, and Malagasy (Austronesian, Madagascar) are examples.

A second major type of cross constituent dependency, *filler-gap* dependencies, is illustrated by relative clause formation in Chapter 5. Copying our MERGE rules in a context free format is quite straightforward. And now we use [DP] as a feature: for C a category, C[DP] is read as "C with an DP gap", and more generally, for C′ any nonterminal, C[C′] is a "C with a C′ gap". (Below we partition the rule set for ease of comprehension.)

(26) DP/N → every | a
    N → student | poet | N + N/N
    DP → Sasha | Kim | DP/N + N
    S → DP + $P_1$
    $P_1$ → laughed | cried | $P_2$ + DP
    $P_2$ → praised | criticized

    DP[DP] → t
    S[DP] → DP[DP] + $P_1$ | DP + $P_1$[DP]
    $P_1$[DP] → $P_2$ + DP[DP] | $P_2$[DP] + DP

    (N/N)/(S[DP]) → who | that
    N/N → (N/N)/(S[DP]) + S[DP]

    C → C and C, all C ∈ {DP, S, $P_1$, $P_2$, S[DP], $P_2$[DP]}

**Exercise 6.20.** Using the grammar in (26), exhibit the parse trees for:

a. every student who Sasha praised t

b. a poet who t laughed and praised Sasha

**Exercise 6.21.** Writing $DP_{wh}$ to abbreviate (N/N)/(S[DP]) add the following productions to (26): $DP_{wh}$ → $DP_{wh}$/N + N and $DP_{wh}$/N → whose. Exhibit a parse tree for *a student whose teacher Kim praised t*.

### 6.3.2 Sufficiency: Are Natural Languages Adequately Modeled by CFGs?

By *adequately modeled* we understand that we are concerned with strong generative capacity – we must not only generate the right stringset, we must generate each string with a correct constituent analysis. This is needed both to provide the right input to complex processes – movement and deletion (and perhaps copying, see below) that build complex expressions from simpler ones. We also need the right constituent structure to provide the right input to processes of semantic and phonological interpretation.

That said, the CFG Hypothesis – that NLs are adequately modeled by CFGs – is useful even if we find NL properties not naturally expressible by CFGs. The reason is that, as we have seen, CFGs do capture several basic properties of NLs, so a given proposal for a grammar of a NL can be informatively described in terms of the ways it differs from a CFG. We turn now to some specific issues.

## Self Embedding (Center Embedding)

Self embedding (center embedding) was the first formal property of languages cited in support of the utility of CFG grammars for English (Chomsky, 1956, 1959). It is easily expressed, as per $G_{SE}$ given for (4). Certain simpler classes of grammars, called *finite state* ones which define a class of languages called *regular* languages (Chapter 7) are easily shown not to accommodate self embedding. But English appears to instantiate it:

(27)  [s That [s Ed left] surprised Mary]

Here *Ed left* is a sentence properly embedded in the S (27). But one robin doesn't make a spring. Treating *surprised Mary* as a kind of P1, let's call it a P1*, we might posit a rule for a CFG for English such as (28).

(28)  S → that + S + P1*

We could express this in a more sophisticated way, making *that+S* a kind of sentential DP and P1* the kind of P1 that combines with such DPs to make Ss. But (28) suffices here, as all we want is any rule set that in one or several steps properly embeds Ss within Ss. And such CFGs will derive Ss like (27). The problem is that they also derive (29a,b) as Ss.

(29)  a. That that Ed left surprised Mary annoyed Dan

b. That that that Ed left surprised Mary annoyed Dan pleased Sue

But the expressions in (29a,b) are not acceptable English. Suppose we decide that in structures of the form [*that* [s X] *surprised Mary*] X cannot itself have any self embeddings. Then we do not need a self embedding rule (for these cases) and we can "fake it" by invoking a new category, say S*, whose expansion rules exhibit no self embedding of any category. Then (28) becomes S → that + S* + P1*, and we capture the one level embedding without overgenerating.

Note further, the meanings of (29a,b) are naturally expressible by syntactic variants which extrapose the sentential subject:

(30)  a. It annoyed Dan that it surprised Mary that Ed left

b. It pleased Sue that it annoyed Dan that it surprised Mary that Ed left

But these expressions do not exhibit self embedding! No sentential sub-constituent has any material to its right, so it is not properly embedded. All the recursion in these cases is right peripheral and this sort of recursion can be handled with the more restricted finite state grammars (Chapter 7).

A different instance of this phenomenon is center embedding in relative clauses. Consider the frame in (31a) when we replace X with various DPs:

(31)   a.  [DP the cat that [DP X] bit t]

       b.  [DP the cat that [DP my dog] bit t]

       c.  [DP the cat that [DP the dog I chased t] bit t]

       d.  [DP the cat that [DP the dog that [DP the man I saw t] chased t] bit t]

Here (31c) results from replacing X in (31a) with *the dog I chased*. It is at the limit of comprehensibility. One more replacement, as in (31d), crosses that line. And again right peripheral recursion on DP is more comprehensible:

(32)   a.  the dog that t bit X

       b.  the dog that t bit the child who t called me

       c.  the dog that t bit the child who t called the man who t was smiling

Patterns such as these make one hesitate to say that self embedding is a basic property of English. It seems not to iterate easily. However, maybe that is just an accident of the specific examples we chose. Perhaps there are others that are better. And indeed even the problematic (29a,b) can be improved (somewhat) if we use the sentential subjects as complements of nouns:

(33)   a.  The fact that Ed left surprised Mary

       b.  The claim that the fact that Ed left surprised Mary was denied

       c.  The oft-made claim that the belief that the Earth is flat was widely discussed in the Middle Ages has recently been disputed

Here (33b) is much more comprehensible than (29a), and (33c) has the same level of embedding as (33b) but is merely a little long, not incomprehensible. Further, it is possible that self embedding is more tolerated in other languages. Recall example (26) in Chapter 1 from Nepali. It exhibits two levels of proper self-embedding and is, impressionistically, less problematic than (29a) above in English. So we shall continue to require that natural language grammars allow self embedding.

**Copying vs Mirror Image**

We begin this section with a thought experiment. We're going to type a sequence of five letters and numbers and ask you to read it once, close your eyes and repeat it. Here it is: 7, Q, 5, B, N. Now close and repeat. Likely you were successful. In general human beings seem competent to repeat phrases that lie within their immediate memory span. But now, glance at it again: then repeat it backwards. If you are like us you probably repeat in your mind the whole thing and say the last letter, then you repeat again the first four items and say the last one of that, and so on until you are done. In short, humans seem good at repetition but bad at making palindromes, repeating backwards.

To find longish palindromes – *Able was I ere I saw Elba* – we sought examples from the literature as we couldn't make up any interesting ones off the top of our head. But the set of palindromes over a finite alphabet is easy to generate using a CFG. Phonological copying however is not. The top down format + context freeness (free substitutivity of items with the same category) of CFGs blocks us from building new strings from already derived strings. But we claim that NLs make productive use of copying – copying of phonological strings which embody a non-trivial amount of morphological and syntactic structure. Here we review a few examples, as the copying processes are not well attested in English but are in many other languages so they are something that a specification of "possible human language" must take into account.

First, as is well known, certain kinds of word and phrase repetition – reduplication – are widely used in natural languages, often to indicate pluralization, intensification, repetition, or indefinitization. For example in Malay from *akar* '(a) root' ⇒ *akar-akar* 'many kinds of roots'; *bunga* 'flower(s)' ⇒ *bunga-bunga* 'all sorts of flowers', *perempuan* 'woman' ⇒ *perempuan-perempuan* 'women'. Expressions in virtually all categories except prepositions appear to undergo reduplication, even various indefinite pronouns: *siapa* 'who' ⇒ *siapa-siapa* 'whoever, anyone; *apa* 'what' ⇒ *apa-apa* 'whatever, whichever, any'. Reduplication is sufficiently common that it is often indicated in texts with a superscript on the word: $baju^2$ = *baju-baju* 'clothes'.

Of course if only lexical items, finite in number, could be reduplicated this would not prevent the language from being context free. We could simply add each reduplicated item to the lexicon as a separate word, nearly doubling its size but still remaining finite. But this approach fails to be linguistically revealing. It ignores a regular way of deriving words whose meaning is understood as a function of what they are derived from. *Bunga* 'flower' and *bunga-bunga* 'all sorts of flowers' are semantically related, unlike two independent lexical items, say *bunga* and *perempuan* 'woman'. Merely listing reduplicated forms as separate lexical entries does not enable us to predict that when a new noun is borrowed speakers can use its reduplication even though that may not even exist in the donor language.

Reduplication as in Malay is widespread in Austronesian (Tagalog, Malagasy) and also prominent in Mandarin Chinese. We note that verbal reduplication in Mandarin and in Malagasy often has an attenuating effect rather than an intensifying one. From Mandarin (Li and Thompson, 1981):

(34)  jiāo 'teach' ⇒ jiāo-jiao 'teach a little' (second copy neutral tone)
      bèi 'recite' ⇒ bèi-bei 'recite a little'
      yánjiū 'research' ⇒ yánjiū-yánjiū 'research a little' (not reduce tone)

(35)  a.  *mitsiky  izy*          b.  *mitsikitsiky  izy*
          smile    3s                 smile a bit    3s
          "He is smiling"             "He is smiling a bit"

Classical reduplication is largely limited (but see Blust, 2001) to single words or even roots. In general it does not iterate: from *mitsikitsiky* 'smiles a bit' we cannot form *mitsikitsikitsikitsiky* 'smiles just a tiny tiny bit'. Productive reduplication would provably take us outside the class of CFLs. But even the more limited kind that is well attested in NL is unnatural in a CFL. We can "fake" it by entering each reduplicated verb and adjective as its own entry in the Lexicon, but that misses the generalization that we build novel expressions by copying, and we semantically interpret the result as a function of what was copied. For example, the Malagasy borrowed *latabatra* 'table' from French, using it to mean 'table', and when hearing its reduplicated form *latabatabatra* they do not wonder if it means "blind unicorn", they infer immediately that it means "something that is sort of a table, say something that is functioning as a table but wasn't really made as a table". So the Reduplication function in Malagasy is one that has a finite domain, but still a large one – numbering in the thousands, as essentially all content words – Nouns, Verbs, Adjectives and even some quantifiers reduplicate. Speakers do not learn the meanings of the reduplicated forms independently of those of the forms they are derived from. Our interest here however goes well beyond classical reduplication. We consider first some cases where a certain amount of complex syntactic structure is reduplicated. One well known case is A-not-A question formation in Mandarin Chinese (Li and Thompson, 1981, Radzinski, 1990).

(36)  a.  *ta  zai  jia*          b.  *ta  zai  jia    bu   zai  jia?*
          3s   at   home              3s   at   home  not   at   home

          S/he is at home           Is s/he at home?

      c.  *ni   xihuan  ta  de  chenshan  bu   xihuan  ta  de*
          you  like    3s  gen  shirt          not  like    3s  gen
          *chenshan?*
          shirt

          Do you like his/her shirt?

Both Bambara (Niger-Congo; W. Africa) and Malagasy (Austronesian; Madagascar) have a construction which copies common noun phrases yielding a whatever reading. From Bambara (Culy, 1985) we see the repetition in (37a), and in (37b) that non-repetition is ungrammatical. (38a,b) show that the repeated items are productively formed. (We have added the hyphens to mark morpheme boundaries.)

(37)  a.  *wulu  o  wulu*          b.  *\*wulu  o  malo*
          dog    o  dog                \*dog    o  rice

          whatever dog

(38)  a.  *wulu-nyinina  o  wulu-nyinina*
          dog-searcher   o  dog-searcher

          whatever dog searcher

      b.  *wulu-nyinina-nyinina   o   wulu-nyinina-nyinina*
          dog-searcher-searcher  o   dog-searcher-searcher

          whoever searches for dog searchers

In Malagasy (see Rajemisa-Raolison, 1971, 73; Dez, 1990; Paul, 2005) copying builds on interrogatives, the simplest cases reminiscent of Malay above:

(39)  a.  *na  iza  na  iza*        b.  *na  inona  na  inona*
          or  who  or  who             or  what   or  what

          whoever/anyone              whatever/anything

(40) (Dez, 1990)

> | *na* | *fanafody* | *inona* | *na* | *fanafody* | *inona* | *no* | *omena* | *azy,* |
> |------|-----------|---------|------|-----------|---------|------|---------|--------|
> | or | medicine | what | or | medicine | what | foc | given | him |
>
> whatever medicine is given to him, . . .

In both Malagasy and Bambara these copy expressions are subject to performance limitations: the acceptability of copying decreases with the length of the expression.

Culy claims that the Bambara construction can be iterated and presents a mathematically correct argument that Bambara with this unbounded iteration is not a CFL. In the Malagasy case, where we have been able to consult with several Malagasy linguists[1] we have clear judgments that the items governed by *na* in (39) and (40) are limited to lexical items and perhaps some fixed expressions. So again the structures do not iterate but still use thousands of interrogative phrases with lexical heads.

We note further that Malagasy does present a richer copy paradigm with expressions of the form: Predicate + Prt + Predicate, where we have two choices of Particle: *dia* indicating intensification and *fe* indicating attenuation (again thanks to joint work with Ralalaoherivony and Razanamompionona).

(41)  a. *nianatra*      *dia*   *nianatra*      *Rabe*
         past.act.study  dia    past.act.study  Rabe
         *Rabe really studied*

      b. nianatra fe nianatra Rabe
         *Rabe just sort of studied*

This copying admits some syntactic complexity aside from that in the bound morphology above. Thus transitive verb + indefinite objects work easily:

(42) | *mamboatra* | *trano* | *dia/fe* | *mamboatra* | *trano* | *Rabe* |
     |-------------|---------|----------|-------------|---------|--------|
     | repair | house | dia/fe | repair | house | Rabe |

     Rabe is really / sort of repairing houses

However richer predicates with PP modifiers seem not to copy:

(43)  a. | *Mamy* | *dia* | *mamy* | *toy* | *ny* | *tantely* | *ity* | *paiso* | *ity* |
         |--------|-------|--------|-------|------|----------|-------|---------|-------|
         | sweet | dia | sweet | like | det | honey | this | peach | this |

         This peach is sweet like honey

---

[1] Our Malagasy judgments here and further below rely on the work of the Malagasy linguists Baholy Ralalaoherivony and Ravaka Razanamompionona

b. *Mamy toy ny tantely dia mamy toy ny tantely
   sweet like det honey dia sweet like det honet
   ity paiso ity
   this peach this

A third structure type that not uncommonly uses overt phonological copying is the formation of reciprocal constructions (each other; one another.) We find this in Russian (drug drug), Dyirbal (Pama-Nyungan; Australia) and with possessors (each other's wives) in Abkhaz (NW Caucasian: Hewitt, 1979).

Below is a striking example from Amele (Trans-New Guinea; New Guinea; Roberts, 1987). The predicate in (44b) is a complex serial verb construction in which different-subject (ds) marking is present on both parts, as is the local (singular) subject agreement, the whole predicate followed by dual agreement.

(44)   a. *Dana ale qo-co-b qo-oo-b esi-a*
       man 3.dual hit-ds-3s hit-ds-3s 3.dual-today.past
       The two men hit each other

     b. *Age eeta eh-i le-ce-b eh-i le-ce-b*
       3p yam take-pred go-ds-3s take-pred go-ds-3s
       *eig-a*
       3p-today.pst
       They took each other yams

     c. *Ege tanaw-udo-co-b tanaw-udo-co-b oq-a*
       1p pacify-3s-ds-3s pacify-3s-ds-3s 1p-today.past
       We made peace with each other

Of more import to us are cases where copying seems to have more of a syntactic or structural function rather than a direct semantic interpretation: We note two types of case. The first, from Mandarin Chinese (Li and Thompson, 1981, Ch 13): in certain sentences of the form Subject+TV+DO+Adverb, where TV is a transitive verb and the DO (direct object) is either indefinite or at least not both referential and animate, the transitive verb must be repeated.

(45)   a. *tā niàn – shū de hěn kuài*
       3s read – book prt very fast
       S/He reads very quickly

     b. *tā niàn – shū niàn de hěn kuài*
       3s read – book read prt very fast
       S/He reads very quickly

(46)    a. *\*wǒ  pāi   –  le     shǒu  liǎng  cì*
           1s    clap    perf  hand  two    time

           I clapped (my) hands twice

    b. *wǒ  pāi   –  le     shǒu  p=ai  liǎng  cì*
          1s    clap    perf  hand  clap  two    time

          I clapped (my) hands twice

The second case seems widespread in W. Africa. (47) is from Yoruba (Nigeria; Kobele, 2008) and (48) from Wolof (Senegal; Torrence and Tamba, 2014).

(47)    a. *Jimọ  ọ    ra    adie*
           Jimo  hts  buy  chicken

          Jimo bought a chicken       (hts = high tone syllable)

    b. *Rira     ti    Jimọ  ọ    ra    adie*
          red.buy  rel   Jimo  hts  buy  chicken

          The fact/way Jimo bought a chicken / Jimo's buying a chicken

    c. *Rira     adie   ti    Jimọ  ọ    ra    adie*
          Red.buy  chicken  rel   Jimo  hts  buy  chicken

          The fact/way Jimo bought a chicken / Jimo's buying a chicken

We note that in the (b) and (c) sentences the verb *ra* is copied to the front and itself reduplicated by the formula CV ⇒ CiCV, (C = consonant, V vowel). See also Aboh and Dyakonova (2009).

    Similar examples are laid out in Kandybowicz (2008) for Nupe.

(48)    a. *Ayda  teg-na    xaalis  ci    taabal*
           Ayda  put-fin.3s  money  Prep  table
           (Wolof; Senegal)

          Ayda put money on the/a table

    b. *teg   bi       Ayda  teg  xaalis  ci    taabal  dafa*
          put   rel/Comp  Ayda  put  money  Prep  table   focus
          *bette*
          surprising

          The fact that Ayda put money on a table is surprising

c. *teg    xaalis   ci    taabal   bi           Ayda   teg   xaalis*
  put    money   prep   table   rel/Comp   Ayda   put   money
  *ci       taabal   dafa   bette*
  prep   table   foc    surprising

The fact that Ayda put money on the table is surprising

We see then that cross linguistically copying is a widely used process in forming novel utterances, though of limited utility in English. (Occasionally repetition indicates intensity – *My love is like a red red rose, He talked on and on,* and a curious usage seems to be growing involving noun repetition: "I don't mind a little consulting work, but I'd rather have a JOB job".)

Worth noting too is the other side of the copy coin. Just as CFGs cannot naturally enforce copying, so they cannot not naturally block it either – which is overall good, as a given string can often be used twice in a row with an independent contribution to the meaning in each case. Recall cases like *the mother of the mother of the President.* But in cases with coordination of DPs it seems worse than just redundant (as we have previously noted): *He visited the White House and the Library of Congress* is fine, but *\*?He visited the Library of Congress and the Library of Congress, \*?He visited neither the Library of Congress nor the Library of Congress* sound a little unearthly. But in a CFG the distribution of all but listably many expressions is decided by their category, not their string part. (*sing,* V) and (*dance,* V) distribute in very similar ways, but are pronounced and semantically interpreted differently.

### 6.3.3   Discontinuous Constituents

Discontinuous constituents have been illustrated in Chapter 4. And observe:

**Fact 3.** The parse trees of a CFG satisfy the Exclusivity Condition (Chapter 4: Definition 4.20).

Thus CFGs cannot represent the trees with crossing branches we used for the constituent structure of expressions such as *wrote the names down, an easy rug to clean,* I don't know *which of his students every teacher criticized.* These constitute just a very small sample of expressions with apparent discontinuous constituents. A few others are illustrated in the x' examples below:

(49)    a. [a review of Chomsky's new book][ has just appeared]

      a'. a review has just appeared of Chomsky's new book

    b. [ John [has already visited the Louvre]]

    b'. Has John already visited the Louvre?

    c. I [looked up] [the information that was in the phone book]

    c'. I [looked [the information that was in the phone book] up]

    c''. I looked the information up that was in the phone book.

**Exercise 6.22.** Provide a tree structure for (49c''). It should have two instances of crossing branches

We might note that linguists are well aware of the discontinuity patterns above. Our point is that to handle them mechanisms must be employed that are not naturally given in a context free format.

Much early work in generative grammar used grammars consisting of two components: a Base and a set of Transformations. The Base was treated often as a CFG. The transformational component took as input the structures determined by the Base and modified them by moving and deleting constituents, thereby providing an account of many apparently discontinuous constituents.

That tradition carries over to current work but with many conceptual changes. Still grammarians would derive many expressions having what we have called discontinuous constituents by starting with ones with no discontinuities and then moving constituents around creating the discontinuity. Our point here is that these mechanisms are not naturally stated in a context free format.

### Cross Serial Dependencies

These dependencies have been noted in the grammars of certain Germanic languages (see Shieber, 1985, Manaster-Ramer, 1987 and references cited there.) We begin by noting the following structure type in English:

(50)    a. Ann helped Bill walk

       b. Ted persuaded Ann to help Bill walk

       c. Kim helped Ted persuade Ann to help Bill walk

In (50) the grammatical case of subjects is nominative – *she* or *he* in $3^{rd}$ person singular pronouns, whereas objects of verbs are accusative – *him* or *her*. Pronominalizing the DPs in (50b) yields <u>*He*</u> *persuaded* <u>*her*</u> *to help* <u>*him*</u> *walk*. But in German some transitive verbs, like *helfen* 'to help' and *beibringen* 'to teach' take dative case objects (*ihm* in $3^{rd}$ sg masc.) and others take accusative (*ihn*).

In the English example above the recursion is right peripheral. A rough constituent bracketing of (50c) is:

(51)  Kim [helped Ted [persuade Ann [to help Bill [walk]]]]

(51) instantiates basic English word order: SVO (Subject + [Verb + Object]). But consider the pattern in an SOV language. In fact there are several. The one in standard German subordinate clauses, which have SOV order, is seen in (52).

(52)  a.  *[Der      Mann    [den     Jungen   schwimmen]  sieht]*
          the$_{nom}$  man    the$_{acc}$  boy     swim$_{inf}$      sees
          *The man sees the boy swim*

      b.  *[Sie     [den     Mann    [dem     Jungen   schwimmen]*
          she$_{nom}$  the$_{acc}$  man   the$_{dat}$  boy     swim$_{inf}$
          *beibringen]  sieht]*
          teach$_{inf}$      sees
          *She sees the man teach the boy to swim*

In (52a) *the man* is the subject of *sees* and *the boy* is subject of *swim*, so the pattern in (52) is a self embedding one, as indicated in our bracketing. Nonetheless the grammatical case of *boy* is determined by the final verb. *See* takes accusative, as indicated, but *teach* 'beibringen' takes dative, as illustrated in (52b), which also illustrates a further level of self embedding, 3 case marked DPs followed by three verbs. So this pattern is the $\{a^n b^n \mid n > 0\}$ one. Had the deepest P1, *swim*, consisted of a DP object and a transitive verb, as in *She sees the man teach the boy to paint the house* we would have 4 DPs followed by three verbs, still a self embedding pattern.

Of interest now is that Swiss German (Shieber, 1985) has a verb order which mirrors the DP order, rather than using the self embedding mirror image order. And at least pronoun and proper noun arguments are overtly case marked, helping us identify which DPs are governed by which verbs.

(53)  ... *mer      em Hans   es       huus      hälfed     aaströche*
      ... we$_{nom}$  Hans$_{dat}$  the     house$_{acc}$  helped     paint
      ... *we helped Hans paint the house*

The verb *hälfed* 'helped' takes a dative case argument so *em Hans...hälfed* forms a discontinuous constituent. If we replace *hälfed* with *lönd* 'let' then *Hans* must be in the accusative form *de Hans*. If we connect the object DPs in (53) with the verbs that govern their case we see that the dependencies "cross". We indicate this below with indexing:

(54)  ... mer [em Hans]$_j$   [es huus]$_k$   [hälfed]$_j$   [aastriiche]$_k$

Joining co-indexed constituents with lines clearly leads to crossing lines. Finally, Shieber notes that this construction iterates:

(55)  ... *mer  d'chind        em Hans   es    huus      lönd  hälfe*
      ... we   the children$_{acc}$  Hans$_{dat}$  the   house$_{acc}$  let   help
      *aastriiche*
      paint

      ... *we let the children help Hans paint the house*

Dutch exhibits similar cross serial dependencies (Bresnan et al., 1982) but has insufficient case marking on the DPs, so Ss with $n$ (or $n+1$) DPs followed by $n$ verbs could be derived context freely by self embedding, even though a DP and the transitive verb that governs it would not be generated in the same step, which might make compositional semantic interpretation difficult. For this reason Bresnan et al. suggest that a CFG for Dutch might get the stringset right but not the parse trees needed for semantic interpretation and so fail to be strongly context free.

### 6.3.4  Necessity: Are All CFLs Possible Natural Languages?

Here our question of concern is whether CFGs are not, in some sense, too strong. Do they allow us to represent properties not present in or not characteristic of NLs? The answer here is a clear yes, but this just means we need constraints on form other than those built into CFGs to characterize NLs. This is hardly surprising, given that CFGs as given have nothing to say about phonological or semantic properties of NL. But as we will see, even at the level of syntax they allow derivational operations that seem decidedly unnatural to the linguist.

As we have seen grammars of languages provide many cases of copying of lexical and phrasal material, albeit with bounds on how complex the copied material can be. But searching grammars we do not find productive morphosyntactic use of palindromes. So speakers do not regularly derive expressions by saying some sequence $w$ and then saying its mirror image. We can, as we have done, find expressions which accidentally have this form, but it is never a regular part of the morphology or syntax of a NL.

A second, more obvious, objection is our earlier remark that any finite set has a CFG. For any such set $K$ let the productions of $G$ be $\{S \to w \mid w \in K\}$. Then $L(G) = K$. But surely the set of sequences of the word *cat* of length less than 10 billion is not a possible human language. This point is less uninteresting than it seems. What it suggests is that grammars of NLs must have some iterative mechanisms that enable generating arbitrarily many expressions, even if they get too long to be usable in practice. So this prompts us to look for the kinds of recursion characteristic of NLs.

Some more systematic objections concerning the excessive generative capacity of CFGs are given in the section below on *Closure Properties*.

## Closure Properties

Closure properties are mathematically very helpful ways of characterizing classes of sets, such as the set of CFLs. As a simple example, consider how we distinguish even and odd numbers. The even numbers are the multiples of 2 – numbers of the form $2n$ for some natural number $n$, The odd numbers are ones of the form $2n + 1$. Now observe that the set EVEN of even numbers is closed under addition $(+)$. That is, for all natural numbers $n, m$ if $n$ and $m$ are both even then so is $(n + m)$. By contrast ODD is not closed under addition. For example, 3 and 5 are odd but $3+5 = 8$ is not. (Indeed, for all odd $n, m$ we have that $n+m$ is not odd.) On the other hand, EVEN and ODD are similar in that both are closed under multiplication.

Now consider the class of CFLs. We have seen that it is closed under (finite) unions. That is, if $U$ and $V$ are CFLs so is $U \cup V$. $U \cup V$ is often noted $U + V$ in formal language theory. Note though:

**Fact 4.** The set of CFLs is not closed under arbitrary unions.

*Proof.* Let $K$ be a stringset which is not context free. For every $w \in K$ define $G[w]$ to be that CFG whose only production is S $\rightarrow w$. So each $G[w]$ is context free and $L(G[w]) = \{w\}$. But the union of all the $L(G[w])$ is $K$, which is not context free, so the set of CFLs is not closed under arbitrary unions. $\square$

Earlier we used closure under (finite) union to show that a certain "tricky" set was in fact context free. And as budding mathematicians we naturally ask if the set of CFLs is closed under other set theoretical operations. What about $\cap$ for example? The answer is negative:

**Theorem 6.4.** *The set of CFLs is not closed under intersection.*

*Proof sketch (relies on some earlier unproven claims).* We have seen that
$\{a^m b^n c^m \mid n, m > 0\}$ and $\{a^m b^n c^n \mid n, m > 0\}$ are both context free. But their intersection, $\{a^n b^n c^n \mid n > 0\}$, is not. $\square$

Given a CFG $G$ over a finite $V$, $\neg L(G)$, the *complement* of $L(G)$ $=_{\text{def}} V^* - L(G)$. It follows from the facts above that:

**Theorem 6.5.** *The set of CFLs over a finite $V$ is not closed under complements.*

*Proof.* $\cap$ is definable in terms of $\cup$ and $\neg$: $X \cap Y = \neg(\neg X \cup \neg Y)$. So if the set of CFLs were closed under $\neg$ it would be closed under $\cap$, but it isn't. $\qquad \square$

**Theorem 6.6.** *The set of CFLs is closed under (finite) cross products. If $X$ and $Y$ are CFLs then so is $X \times Y = \{ww' \mid w \in X, w' \in Y\}$. $X \times Y$ is often noted $X \cdot Y$ in the formal language theory literature.*

*Proof sketch.* Let $G$ and $G'$ be CFGs generating X and Y respectively. We may assume they have disjoint sets of non-terminals. Let S and S' be the start symbols for $G$ and $G'$. Form a new grammar $G''$ with start symbol S'' and whose productions are the union of those of $G$ and $G'$ plus S'' $\rightarrow$ S S'. Then $L(G'') = $ X $\cdot$ Y. $\qquad \square$

**Theorem 6.7.** *The set of CFLs is closed under star. I.e. if $L$ is context free so is $L^*$.*

*Proof.* Let $G$ generate $L$ with start symbol S. Form $G'$ with start symbol S', not a non-terminal of $G$. The productions of $G'$ are S' $\rightarrow$ SS | $e$ plus those of $G$. Clearly $L(G') = (L(G))^*$. $\qquad \square$

We mention one last closure property which has proven quite useful in linguistic contexts to show that certain stringsets associated with a natural language are not context free. (For further closure properties see Hopcroft and Ullman, 1979, 131–7.) We state the closure condition and then define one new notion used in it.

**Theorem 6.8.** *The intersection of a CFL with a finite state language is context free.*

The finite state languages are most intuitively defined either as those accepted by finite state machines or those denoted by so called *regular expressions*. (And then called *regular languages*.) Both these notions are defined and studied in the next chapter. Here we give an equivalent definition in terms of the context free apparatus we already have. The definition suffices to make sense of Theorem 6.8, but may seem lacking in intuitive motivation. But it does make explicit certain relations between regular languages and context free ones.

**Definition 6.5.** A CFG $G$ is *right linear* iff all productions are of the form: A → $w$B or A → $u$, where A and B are non-terminals and $w, u$ are terminal strings.

**Definition 6.6.** The *regular* stringsets are just the $L(G)$ for $G$ a right linear grammar.

**Example** Write **a(ba)**\* for the set of strings consisting of an $a$ followed by any number (including zero) of copies of $ba$. $a$ and $abababa$ are in this set, $b$ and $abab$ are not. Here is a right linear grammar for **a(ba)**\*:

$$S → aT, \ T → baT \mid e.$$

**Exercise 6.23.** Exhibit a derivation of $ababa$ using the grammar above.

**Exercise 6.24.**

  a. Complete the following definition: A CFG $G$ is *left linear* iff _____

  b. Exhibit a left linear grammar for **a(ba)**\*.

  Let us see that the image of a CFL under a string homomorphism is itself a CFL. We define:

**Definition 6.7.** Given vocabularies $V$ and $U$, a function $h$ from $V^* →$ $U^*$ is a *string homomorphism* iff it satisfies conditions (a) and (b) below:

  (a) $h(e) = e$ and

  (b) $h(w) = h(y) ⌢ h(b)$ if $w = y ⌢ b$, any $y ∈ V^*$, any $b ∈ V$.

  Obviously the values of a string homomorphism h as above are given by its values on the elements of $V$. So to define such a function it suffices to say what its values are at the elements of $V$. Then we extend $h$ to a function $h'$ from sets of strings over $V^*$ as follows:

**Definition 6.8.** If $h$ is a string homomorphism from $V^*$ to $U^*$ and $K$ is any subset of $V^*$, then $h'(K) = \{h(k) \mid k ∈ K\}$. When no confusion results we write $h(K)$ instead of $h'(K)$.

**Theorem 6.9.** *For $G$ a CFG with terminal vocabulary $V$, for any string homomorphism h from $V^*$ to any $U^*$, $h(L(G))$ is context free.*

**Exercise 6.25.** Say informally why the theorem immediately above holds.

Theorems 6.8 and 6.9 are frequently invoked in showing that certain languages we are interested in are not context free. This is so for example for the Bambara claim (Culy, 1985) and the Swiss German claim (Shieber, 1985).

These theorems also enable us to see the interest of working with artificial languages with very small vocabularies. If we start with a language with a large vocabulary (e.g. a model of English), a homomorphism may map the language to one with a very small alphabet by being massively not one to one, e.g. by mapping many of its lexical strings to the same element of $U^*$ (perhaps the $e$ string). Then this very artificial language may be easily proven to be not context free, hence the original one must fail to be context free by the theorems. On the other hand, the closure facts do suggest properties that do not seem characteristic of NLs. We do not expect to be able to paddle up the Amazon and find some tribe whose utterances are exactly those in the cross product of English, Malagasy, Mandarin, Turkish and Yoruba. But as earlier, the problems here may relate in part of ones concerning phonology and semantics.

### 6.3.5 Inferring Structure from Strings: Normal Form Theorems

We have insisted that evaluating a proposal for the adequacy of a class of grammars as models of NLs involves crucially assessing its strong generative capacity, not just its weak generative capacity, that is, the set of strings it generates. Some results in CFGs serve to highlight this point. It has been useful in developing proofs that certain string sets are, or are not, context free to show that an arbitrary CFG can be transformed to one all of whose rules are in a certain form. Here are two well known useful cases:

(56) Chomsky Normal Form
Given a CFG $G$ we can construct a CFG $G'$ with the property that:

1. $L(G) = L(G')$ and

2. All productions of $G'$ are of one of the two forms:

A. A → BD, where B and D are non-terminal symbols, and

B. A → $w$, $w$ a terminal string.

(57) Greibach Normal Form
Given a CFG $G$ we can construct a CFG $G'$ such that:

1. $L(G) = L(G')$ and

2. All productions are of the form: A → a$\alpha$, where a is a terminal symbol and $\alpha \in (N \cup T)^*$.

Now considered jointly these two theorems tell us that merely given the set of strings a grammar generates is not sufficient to determine the form of the rules of the grammar (even limiting them to context free ones) as the form of the rules in Chomsky Normal Form and in Greibach Normal Form are not the same.

We turn now to the study of a more restrictive class of grammars, those of the regular or finite state languages. The stringsets they can parse are a proper subset of those parsable by context free grammars. Nonetheless grammars of this form have proven useful as morphological parsers, even for languages with elaborate and complex morphology (Hankamer, 1986 and Creider et al., 1995, and references cited there.)

**Addendum 1.** How to convert $L(G)$, $G$ context free, into an inductive (bottom up) definition by recursion.

Let $G = \langle N, T, S, \rightarrow \rangle$ be context free. We show how to define $L(G)$, the language generated by $G$, in an ordinary bottom up way, one to which our ordinary proofs by recursion apply.

To facilitate the conversion we define an *unconstrained grammar* $G$ to be a four-tuple: $\langle \text{Cat}_G, V_G, \text{Lex}_G, \text{Rule}_G \rangle$, as follows (omitting subscripts when no confusion results.) Elements of $\text{Cat}_G$ are called *grammatical categories*, elements of $V_G$ are called *phonological strings*. A *possible expression* is an ordered pair (s,C), where s is a phonological string and C $\in$ Cat. We note this set $\text{PE}_G$, the set of *possible expressions* of $G$. Formally $\text{PE}_G$ just abbreviates $(V_G^* \times \text{Cat}_G)$. $\text{Lex}_G$ is finite subset of $\text{PE}_G$ called the Lexicon of $G$, and $\text{Rule}_G$ is a finite set of partial functions from $\text{PE}_G^*$ to $\text{PE}_G$. So $\text{Lex}_G$ is just a finite set of possible expressions, and an $F \in \text{Rule}_G$ is simply a partial function from sequences of possible expressions to possible expressions. Then of course we define $L(G)$, the *language* generated by $G$, to be the closure of $\text{Lex}_G$ wrt $\text{Rule}_G$.

Given a CFG $G = \langle N, T, S, \rightarrow \rangle$ we build an unrestricted $G$ as follows: $G = \langle N, T, \text{Lex}_G, \text{Rule}_G \rangle$ where:

Step 1:  $\text{Lex}_G = \{\langle w, A \rangle \mid A \rightarrow w \text{ in } G, \text{ where } w \in T^*\}$     and

Step 2:  Each production P of $G$ not of the form $A \rightarrow w$ as above has the following form:

P is : $A \rightarrow w_0 A_1 w_1 \ldots w_n A_n w_{n+1}$, where the $A_i \in N$ and the $w_j \in T^*$

NB: The $w_i$ here are fixed terminal strings, like *neither* and *nor* in a rule like: VP → *neither* VP *nor* VP, used in deriving *neither laughed nor cried*.

For each such P we define $F(P)$ in $\text{Rule}_G$ as below, and then set $\text{Rule}_G$ to be $\{F(P) \mid P$ a non-lexical production of $G$, as above$\}$.

    a. The domain of $F(P)$ is $\{(u_1, A_1), \ldots, (u_n, A_n) \mid u_i \in T^*\}$   and

    b. $F(P)$ maps each $n$-tuple $(u_1, A_1), \ldots, (u_n, A_n)$ in its domain to $w_0 u_1 w_1 \ldots w_n u_n w_{n+1}$.

By way of example, consider the CFG $G$ given by: S → ab, S → aSb. Converting it to an unrestricted grammar $G'$ gives us a Lexicon $\{(ab, S)\}$ and the single rule F with domain $\{(u, S) \mid u \in \{a, b\}^*\}$ given by: F(u,S) $= (a \frown u \frown b, S)$.

To prove that $L = \{(a^n b^n, S) \mid n > 0\} \supseteq L(G)$ we note that $(ab, S) \in L$ and $L$ is closed wrt F: if $(w, S) \in L$ then for some $k$, $w = (a^k b^k, S)$, so F(w,S) $= (aa^k b^k b, S) = (a^{k+1} b^{k+1}, S) \in L$. Thus $L$ is one of the sets we took the intersection of in forming $L(G)$. Going the other way show that $K = \{n \in \mathbb{N} \mid n > 0 \Rightarrow (a^n b^n, S) \in L(G')\} = \mathbb{N}$, so for all $n$, $(a^n b^n, S) \in L(G')$. Clearly $0 \in K$ (vacuously) and $1 \in K$, and $n+1$ is if $n$ is, so $\mathbb{N} \subseteq K$, whence equality holds. Thus we see that w is derivable from S in $G$ iff (w, S) is an element of $L(G')$.    □

# 7

---

# Finite State Automata

*Mathematical linguistics* usually refers to a field common to mathematics and linguistics where one studies *formal languages*. We have already introduced mathematical linguistics in our last chapter, when we studied *context-free languages*. We saw that context-free languages are a reasonable formalism for natural language syntax. True, there are constructions and phenomena that cannot be captured using context-free grammars. Even more, the parse trees of context-free grammars also do not seem to be the right tool for investigating long-distance dependencies. But keeping in mind these limitations, there is still *something right* about CFG's, something worth knowing and studying. Perhaps a good rough analogy would be with physics. Nobody believes that classical Newtonian physics can explain the universe as well as its successors. On the other hand, Newtonian physics does well for many phenomena. And in learning physics, one cannot really omit it.

In this chapter, we study a mathematical model that is *less expressive* than CFGs. The class of languages here are the *regular languages*. Every regular language is context-free, but not vice-versa. There will be an associated type of grammars, called *simple grammars*. So all of the negative points about how CFGs are inadequate for various things are even more applicable to simple. Even more, there is a solid argument why languages with center-embedding cannot be considered as regular.

With this said, you might wonder why regular languages are treated in this book at all. The fact is that in many areas like morphology and phonology, especially in the computational parts of those subjects, the methods of this chapter are more useful than context-free grammars. (See our quote at the end of this chapter from Terence Langendoen.) And even for syntax, the relation between automata, grammars, and regular expressions is something that all linguists with formal interests should see.

The progression of ideas in this chapter is indicated in Figure 7.1. We begin in Section 7.1 with *finite-state automata*, and then in Section 7.2 we turn to *regular expressions*. These give us two ways to define formal languages. We'll see yet a third way in Section 7.3, when we consider a simple form of the grammars which we saw in Chapter 4. Naturally, we'll call these *simple grammars*. Now whenever we have more than one way to define something, it is natural to ask whether one way is more powerful than another. In this chapter, we therefore want to know whether finite-state automata are more powerful than regular expressions, and also how both of these compare to simple grammars. As it happens, all of these formalisms define the same class of languages. There is small wrinkle that the languages of grammars do not contain the empty word, and so we shall need to adjust the other formalisms to keep track of this (slightly annoying) fact.

We shall convert $\epsilon$-free regular expressions into simple grammars in Section 7.3. Then in Section 7.4 we turn simple grammars into finite automata whose start state is not accepting. Finally, in the same section we see how to take such an automaton and read off its language as a regular$^+$ expression. At the end, we indicate in Section 7.5 why center-embedding cannot be accommodated with the formalisms of this chapter, and we conclude in Section 7.6 with a classic argument that English is not a regular language.

We have tried to make this chapter more classroom-friendly by making it possible to omit Section 7.4. If one is only interested in seeing what the three formalisms are like, they may end this chapter after Section 7.3. Finally, Section 7.5 may be read after Section 7.1.

## 7.1 Finite-State Automata

A *finite-state automaton* is a mathematical object that is easy to grasp as a picture and then to remember the definition afterwards. For example, here is a picture of an automaton:

(1)

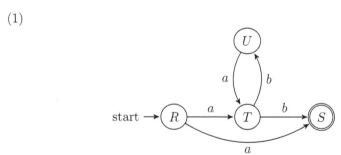

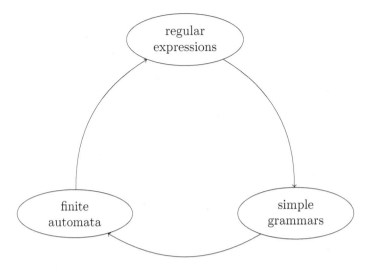

Figure 7.1: This chapter deals with several ways to define languages.

We'll call this $\mathcal{A}$. It has four *states*: $R$, $S$, $T$, and $U$. $R$ is called the *start state*, indicated by the arrow. $S$ is the *accepting state*, indicated by the double circle.

We want to take words on our alphabet and ask whether or not it is possible to read the letters beginning at the start state and ending at the accepting state of $\mathcal{A}$, following the arrows. We can make a chart to give some examples, using $\sqrt{}$ for "yes" and $\times$ for "no".

| word | accepted? |
|------|-----------|
| $a$ | $\sqrt{}$ |
| $b$ | $\times$ |
| $aa$ | $\times$ |
| $ab$ | $\sqrt{}$ |
| $ba$ | $\times$ |
| $bb$ | $\times$ |

| word | accepted? |
|------|-----------|
| $aba$ | $\times$ |
| $abb$ | $\times$ |
| $abaa$ | $\times$ |
| $abab$ | $\sqrt{}$ |
| $ababab$ | $\sqrt{}$ |
| $abababab$ | $\sqrt{}$ |

To be accepted, a word only needs one path to an accepting state. It may take some trial-and-error to see if a word actually is accepted by a given automaton, or not. For example, $ab$ is accepted because we can go from $R$ first to $T$ and then to $S$; it is irrelevant that we can go from $R$ to $T$ and then to (the non-accepting state) $U$. All of this is a little like parsing with a grammar: one only needs *some* appropriate parse to make a sentence with some grammar.

The *language of an automaton* $\mathcal{A}$ is the set of words which *are* accepted by $\mathcal{A}$ in the sense above. We write this as $\mathcal{L}(\mathcal{A})$.

For the automaton in (1), the language is

(2)
$$\{a, ab, abab, ababab, abababab, \ldots\}$$
$$= \underline{a} + (\underline{a} \cdot \underline{b})^+$$

We are going to discuss *regular expressions* such as the one at the end of (2) a little later, in Section 7.2. But for now, you can take $\underline{a} + (\underline{a} \cdot \underline{b})^+$ in (2) to say: "either an $a$, or a non-empty finite concatenation of $ab$'s."

**Exercise 7.1.** What is the language of this automaton?

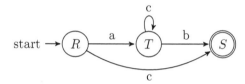

That is, write three words that are in the language, three that are not, and then give a regular expression for it, as we did in (2).

As can be easily seen the automaton below accepts just the strings of even length from $\{a, b\}*$:

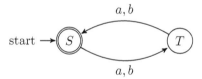

(We write an arrow with label $a, b$ rather than writing two arrows, one labeled $a$ and the other labeled $b$).

**Automata may have more than one accepting state** So far this chapter, we only dealt with automata with *one* accepting state. But automata can have more than one accepting state.

(3)

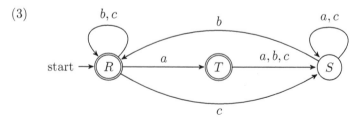

This automaton has two accepting states, $R$ and $T$. It accepts both $a$ and $b$ (in different states). Of course, it accepts many other words as well.

**Exercise 7.2.** Exhibit a two state automaton that accepts just the strings of odd length from $\{a, b\}^*$.

**Exercise 7.3.** Exhibit an automaton whose language is:

$$\{\text{the President}\} \cup \{\text{the (mother of)}^n \text{ the President} \mid 1 \leq n\}.$$

Here is a summary of where we are.

**Definition 7.1.** Let $A$ be an alphabet (an arbitrary set, for us a finite set). A *finite-state automaton* over $A$ is a tuple

$$\mathcal{A} \quad = \quad (\mathcal{S}, start, \langle \overset{a}{\rightarrow} \rangle_{a \in A}, Acc)$$

consisting of (1) a finite set $\mathcal{S}$ of *states*; (2) a special state called *start*; (3) for each alphabet symbol $a$, a relation $\overset{a}{\rightarrow}$ on $\mathcal{S}$; and (4) a set *Acc* of *accepting states*. Given an automaton $\mathcal{A}$ and a world $w \in A^*$, we say that $\mathcal{A}$ *accepts* $w$ if it is possible to read $w$ into $\mathcal{A}$, starting in the start state and following the arrows in the word $w$ from left to right, and ending in one of the accepting states.

**Exercise 7.4.** Construct an automaton for each of the following sets:

a. $\{ab, acb, ad\}$.

b. $\{a^{2n} \mid 0 \leq n\}$.

c. $\{ab^n a \mid 1 \leq n\}$.

d. $\{b, ba, bac, bacc, baccc, \ldots, bac^n, \ldots\}$.

e. $\{a^n b^m \mid n, m \geq 0\}$.

**Exercise 7.5.** In our definition of a finite-state automaton, we insisted that the set of states be finite. To see why we did this, show that if we allowed infinite state sets, then every language would be $\mathcal{L}(\mathcal{A})$ for some $\mathcal{A}$.

**Exercise 7.6.** Here is a somewhat harder exercise. Let $A = \{a, b, c\}$, and let $L$ be the language of all words with no repeated letters. Construct a finite automaton whose language is $L$.

**Exercise 7.7.** Let $A = \{\text{John}, \text{Mary}, \text{Sam}, \text{knows}, \text{that}\}$. Notice that the "words" on this "alphabet" $A$ include strings such as

Sam that that knows Sam knows

Yet some of the words on $A$ are proper sentences in English, and as we have just seen, some are not. Construct an automaton whose language is he set of *all* words on $A$ that *are* English sentences.

**Exercise 7.8.** Do a similar exercise, but start with

$$A = \{\text{every}, \text{boy}, \text{girl}, \text{knows}, \text{sees}, \text{who}\}.$$

and only use *subject relative clauses*. So we can have *every boy who sees every girl who knows every girl sees every boy*. But for the purposes of this exercise, we do not want *every girl who every boy sees sees every girl* because the relative clause *who every boy sees* is "missing its object" rather than its subject.

**Definition 7.2.** Let $A$ be an alphabet. A *language over $A$* is a subset $L$ of $A^*$, the set of all words on $A$, including the empty word $\epsilon$. If $L$ does not contain $\epsilon$, it is said to be *$\epsilon$-free*. A language $L$ is *finite-state* if there is a finite-state automaton $\mathcal{A}$ such that $L = \mathcal{L}(\mathcal{A})$, where

$$\mathcal{L}(\mathcal{A}) \quad = \quad \{w \in A^* \,|\, w \text{ is accepted by } \mathcal{A}\}.$$

The rest of this section deals with this definition, and with some fine points, variants and alternatives.

One of the interesting things about the definition of *finite-state automaton* and hence of the definition of a finite-state language is that an automaton might be "non-deterministic". Here is the relevant definition.

**Definition 7.3.** An automaton $\mathcal{A}$ is *deterministic* if for every state $X$ and every alphabet symbol $a$, there is one and only one arrow out of $S$ labeled with $a$. Otherwise, $\mathcal{A}$ is *non-deterministic*.

As an example, consider

(4)

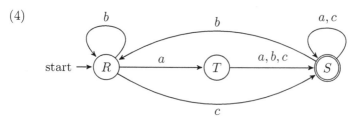

This is deterministic, but the one below is not.

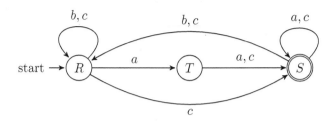

One problem is that from state $S$ there are two arrows labeled $c$: one goes to $R$, and the other back to $S$ itself. Another problem is that there is no $b$-arrow from $T$.

Now the interesting fact is that the notion of a *finite-state language* would not change if we changed the definition to require acceptance by a *deterministic* automaton.

**Theorem 7.1.** *For non-deterministic automaton, say $\mathcal{A}$, there is a deterministic automaton, say $\mathcal{B}$ with the same language as $\mathcal{A}$.*

*Proof.* We are going to give the construction after we illustrate it. But we'll omit the central verification in the proof since it uses induction. Here is a non-deterministic automaton, call it $\mathcal{A}$:

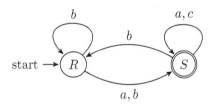

The alphabet is $\{a, b, c\}$. Note that this automaton is non-deterministic because we can go from $R$ to itself on input $b$, and also from $R$ to $S$ on input $b$. Further, there is no $c$ edge from $R$. For our deterministic variant, we use as states the set of all subsets of $\{R, S\}$. As you know, there are $2^2 = 4$ such subsets: $\emptyset$, $\{R\}$ $\{S\}$ and $\{R, S\}$.

The start state of our new automaton $\mathcal{B}$ will be $\{R\}$. The accepting states will be all sets of states containing the accepting state $S$: so they will be $\{S\}$ and $\{R, S\}$. And here is a description of the arrows. Given two subsets, say $X$ and $Y$, and an alphabet symbol $d$, we say

(5) $\qquad X \xrightarrow{d} Y \qquad$ iff $\quad$ if $Y$ is the set of all states reachable
$\qquad\qquad\qquad\qquad\qquad\qquad$ from some state in $X$ by a $d$-arrow

So for example, $\{R\} \xrightarrow{b} \{R, S\}$. This is because from $R$ we can go via a $b$-arrow to $R$ and to $S$. Similarly, $\{R\} \xrightarrow{a} \{S\}$, and $\{R\} \xrightarrow{c} \{\emptyset\}$. So our new automaton is

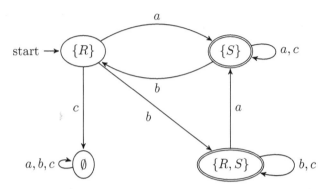

You should check that the two automata pictured in this proof have the same language by trying out a reasonable number of examples. Of course, no number of examples constitutes a proof. But examples do help one to find the ideas behind a proof. See Example 7.11 for more on this.

So far, we have merely illustrated the general construction. And so now we'll state that general construction. Let $\mathcal{A}$ be an automaton. We construct a new automaton $\mathcal{B}$ as follows: the state set of $\mathcal{B}$ is the set of all subsets of the state set of $\mathcal{A}$. The accepting states of $\mathcal{B}$ are the sets which have at least one member which is accepting in $\mathcal{A}$. The arrows in $\mathcal{B}$ are given by (5). □

The construction in Theorem 7.1 is called the *power-set construction* in automata theory.

**Exercise 7.9.** As practice, draw any two-state automaton over a four-letter alphabet $\{a, b, c, d\}$. Then carry out the construction in Theorem 7.1.

**Exercise 7.10.** Why does the power-set construction actually give us a deterministic automaton?

**Exercise 7.11.** Here is the crux of the matter as to why the power-set construction in Theorem 7.1 works. Let $X$ be any set of states in $\mathcal{A}$. Let $w \in A^*$. If we read $w$ into $\mathcal{B}$ starting in the state $X$, we get to some state, call it $Y$. $Y$ is unique because $\mathcal{B}$ is deterministic. Show that $Y$ is the set of states of $\mathcal{A}$ which we can possibly get to by starting in some element of $X$ and following arrows in $\mathcal{A}$.

**Exercise 7.12.** Suppose that $\mathcal{A}$ is deterministic to begin with. What happens when we apply the power-set construction to it?

**Exercise 7.13.** Our definition of a finite-state language insists on having one start state. Let us call a *multi-start* automaton one which might have more than one start state. Prove an analog of Theorem 7.1 for multi-start automata. [Hint: given a multi-start automaton $\mathcal{A}$, the idea would be to add a fresh new state, say $Z$, to get $\mathcal{B}$. The hard part would then be figuring out what the arrows from this new state $Z$ are.]

**Exercise 7.14.** Suppose that $L$ and $M$ are both finite-state languages. Use Exercise 7.13 to show that $L \cup M$ is a finite-state language.

**Exercise 7.15.** Suppose that $\mathcal{A}$ is a *deterministic* automaton, and suppose that we make a new automaton $\mathcal{B}$ by using the same states as $\mathcal{A}$, the same start state, and the same arrows; the only difference is that the accepting states of $\mathcal{B}$ are exactly the *non-accepting states* of $\mathcal{A}$. Show that the language of $\mathcal{B}$ is the complement of the language of $\mathcal{A}$. Be sure that your argument used the assumption that $\mathcal{A}$ is deterministic. And give an example where $\mathcal{A}$ is non-deterministic and where the language of $\mathcal{B}$ is not the complement of the language of $\mathcal{A}$.

**Exercise 7.16.** Suppose that $L$ and $M$ are both finite-state languages. Use other Exercises in this set to show that $L \cap M$ is a finite-state language. [Hint: also use de Morgan's Law]

## 7.2 Regular Expressions and Languages

Here we introduce the language of *regular expressions* which denote just the stringsets accepted by finite state automata. The expressions in this language are called *regular* expressions, and the stringsets they denote *regular* sets. This new notation provides a succinct way to specify these stringsets and makes apparent several algebraic properties they have. For "cumbersome" stringsets we might need FSAs with hundreds of states, which are not only hard to draw but are hard to understand. On the other hand FSAs remain quite useful for purposes of proving theorems concerning which stringsets are or are not regular.

**Background: The Algebra of Languages** For this discussion, we fix an alphabet set $A$, and we consider the set of all (formal) languages $L$ over $A$. Each such language is a (possibly infinite) subset of $A^*$.

We specify two operations on languages, called $+$ and $\cdot$. The $+$ operation is set union. In describing $L \cdot M$ and in formal language theory more generally, we use the operation of putting one word in front of another. This is called *concatenation*, and we have seen it earlier (see page 37). For example, $aab \cdot bbab = aabbbab$. Given any two languages on the same alphabet, say $L$ and $M$, we define

$$
\begin{aligned}
L + M &= \text{the union } L \cup M \\
L \cdot M &= \{v \cdot w \,|\, v \in L, w \in M\}
\end{aligned}
$$

Frequently one omits the symbol $\cdot$ and just writes $LM$ instead of $L \cdot M$.

We note some special languages. For any alphabet symbol, say $a \in A$, $\underline{a}$ is the language with just one word: the one-term sequence $a$. So $\underline{a} = \{a\}$ for all alphabet symbols $a$.

**The Empty Language and the Language $\{\epsilon\}$** We know about the empty set $\emptyset$ from Chapter 2. It is the set with no elements. It is also like zero for union:

$$
\emptyset \cup X = X
$$

for all sets $X$.

When it comes to languages, we write 0 for $\emptyset$. We therefore have

$$
L + 0 = L = 0 + L
$$

for all languages $L$.

But $\{\epsilon\}$ is different from $\emptyset$. The reason is simple: $\{\epsilon\}$ has an element, while $\emptyset$ has no elements.

Here is the main property of the language $\{\epsilon\}$. Recall that for all $w$, $w \cdot \epsilon = w = \epsilon \cdot w$. Thus, for all languages $L$, $L \cdot \{\epsilon\} = L = \{\epsilon\} \cdot L$. So $\{\epsilon\}$ serves as the neutral element for language multiplication: nothing happens. As a short notation, we therefore write 1 for $\{\epsilon\}$.

**The Star Operation $*$ on Languages** For any language $L$, $L^*$ is the set of words which we can make by concatenating zero or more elements of $L$.

For example, let $L = \{a, bb\}$. Then

$$
\{a, bb\}^* = \{\epsilon, a, bb, abb, bba, bbbba, bbaaabb, bbabbaabbabb, \ldots\}.
$$

In words, $\{a, bb\}^*$ will have all the words consisting of only $a$s and $b$s, and with the property that the consecutive strings of $b$'s always have even length.

**The Operation $^+$** We define an operation $+$ on regular expressions by setting $L(r^+)$ to be $L(r^*) - \{\epsilon\}$. Thus $L(r^+)$ is the set of concatenations of non-empty strings in $L(r)$.

**Regular Expressions** We now come to one of the two important definitions of this section. Fix an alphabet $A$. A *regular expression* is something you can write out of symbols $\underline{a}$, for $a \in A$; fresh symbols 0 and 1; binary function symbols $+$ and $\cdot$, and a unary function symbol $*$. For examples, we mention $\underline{a}$, $\underline{a} + \underline{b}$, $\underline{b} + \underline{a}$, $\underline{a}^*$, and $\underline{b} + (\underline{a}^* \cdot (\underline{c}^*)^*)$. These are syntactic expressions, and at this point we think of $\underline{a} + \underline{b}$ and $\underline{b} + \underline{a}$ as *different regular expressions*. We use letters like $r$ and $s$ to denote regular expressions, and we let $R$ be the set of all regular expressions on our alphabet $A$.

A bit more formally, given an alphabet set $A$, the set $RE(A)$ of *regular languages* over $A$ is defined to be the least set with the following properties:

a. 0 and 1 are in $RE(A)$

b. Each $a \in A$, $\underline{a}$ is in $RE(A)$.

c. If $s, t$ are in $RE(A)$ then $(s + t)$, $(s \cdot t)$ and $s^*$ are in $RE(A)$.

We define a function $\mathcal{L} : R \to \mathcal{P}(A^*)$, giving for each regular expression $r$ its *denotation language* $\mathcal{L}(r)$. This function is defined as follows:

$$
\begin{array}{rcl}
\mathcal{L}(0) & = & 0\,(= \emptyset) \\
\mathcal{L}(1) & = & 1\,(= \{\epsilon\}) \\
\mathcal{L}(\underline{a}) & = & \{a\} \\
\mathcal{L}(r + s) & = & \mathcal{L}(r) \cup \mathcal{L}(s) \\
\mathcal{L}(r \cdot s) & = & \mathcal{L}(r) \cdot \mathcal{L}(s) \\
\mathcal{L}(r^*) & = & (\mathcal{L}(r))^*
\end{array}
$$

Here are some examples with $A = \{a, b, c\}$:

| regular expression $r$ | its associated language $\mathcal{L}(r)$ |
|---|---|
| $\underline{a}$ | $\{a\}$ |
| $\underline{a} + \underline{b}$ | $\{a, b\}$ |
| $(\underline{a} + \underline{b}) \cdot \underline{a}$ | $\{aa, ba\}$ |
| $(\underline{a} + \underline{b})^*$ | $\{\epsilon, a, b, aa, ab, ba, bb, \ldots\}$ |
| $\underline{c} \cdot (\underline{a} + \underline{b})^*$ | $\{c, ca, cb, caa, cab, cba, cbb, \ldots\}$ |

Each regular expression *denotes* a language, as we have seen. The set $Reg(A)$ of *regular languages on* $A$ are defined to be the set of all denotations of regular expressions:

$$
Reg(A) \quad = \quad \{\mathcal{L}(r) \mid r \in R\}.
$$

$\mathcal{L}$ is a function from regular expressions to the set of languages. The regular languages are defined as the image set of this function $\mathcal{L}$. Here is a picture of the situation:

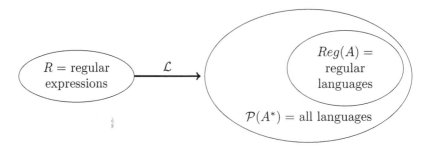

**Exercise 7.17.** Is $\mathcal{L}$ is a one-to-one function from regular expressions to languages?

**Exercise 7.18.** Let $A = \{a, b, c\}$. Write regular expressions for the languages described below.

 a. The language of all words on $A$ which begin with $b$.

 b. The language of all words on $A$ which have even length.

 c. The language of all words on $A$ which have length at least 2.

 d. The language of all words on $A$ which do not have two $a$'s in a row. (This last one is harder than the others!)

**Exercise 7.19.** This exercise is a variation on Exercise 7.7. Let

$$A = \{\text{John, Mary, Sam, knows, that}\}.$$

Write a regular expression that denotes the set of *all* words on $A$ that *are* English sentences.

**Equality Again** Often one writes $r = s$ when $\mathcal{L}(r) = \mathcal{L}(s)$. For example, one would usually write

$$\underline{a} + \underline{b} \;=\; \underline{b} + \underline{a},$$

since

$$\mathcal{L}(\underline{a} + \underline{b}) \;=\; \underline{a} \cup \underline{b} \;=\; \{a, b\} \;=\; \underline{b} \cup \underline{a} \;=\; \mathcal{L}(\underline{b} + \underline{a}).$$

(For those who have solved Exercise 7.17: does this make you reconsider your answer?) But it is important to see that there is a difference between an expression $r$ and the language $\mathcal{L}(r)$ it denotes.

**But isn't it pedantic to use all those underlines?** In a way, it is. Certainly most authors identify $a$ and $\underline{a}$, and we encourage you to do this if you prefer. But early in our book we emphasized the difference between an object and its singleton set (in this case, this is the distinction between $a$ and $\{a\}$). And so to be careful, we use two different notations.

**Why are we interested in regular expressions?** First, regular expressions are a very simple form of grammar. There is the tantalizing possibility that one could take

$$A \quad = \quad \text{the set of words of English}$$

and write a single (huge) regular expression that would give the set of all English sentences.

The notion of regular expressions also has a practical value: grammar checkers on a computer are based on regular expressions.

We are also interested in them because they enable us to see many natural algebraic properties of regular sets such as:

$$
\begin{aligned}
L + M &= M + L \\
L \cdot (M_1 + M_2) &= (L \cdot M_1) + (L \cdot M_2) \\
(L^*)^* &= L^* \\
(L \cdot M) \cdot N &= L \cdot (M \cdot N)
\end{aligned}
$$

that (in the first two cases) remind us of laws about numbers.

**Definition 7.4.** A *regular*$^+$ *expression* over a set $A$ is an expression built from the symbols $\underline{a}$ for $a \in A$, and also $0$, $1$, $+$, $\cdot$, and $^+$. (But unlike our earlier regular expressions, it should not have $*$.)

**An Interesting Fact** If we have a regular expression $r$, and it just so happens that $\epsilon \notin \mathcal{L}(r)$, then we can find a regular$^+$ expression $s$ such that $\mathcal{L}(s) = \mathcal{L}(r)$.

For example: let $r$ be $(\underline{a}^* \cdot \underline{b}) + (\underline{a} \cdot \underline{b}^*)$. Then

$$\mathcal{L}(r) \quad = \quad \{a, b, ab, aab, aaab, \ldots, abb, abbb, \ldots\}.$$

It is any non-empty sequence of $a$'s followed by any non-empty sequence of $b$'s. The point is that it is also $\mathcal{L}(s)$, where

$$s \quad = \quad (\underline{a}^+ \cdot \underline{b}) + (\underline{a} \cdot \underline{b}^+) + (\underline{a} + \underline{b}),$$

and this last expression used $^+$ instead of $^*$.

**Exercise 7.20.** let $r$ be $(\underline{a}^* \cdot \underline{b}) + (\underline{a} \cdot \underline{b}^*)$. What is the language $\mathcal{L}(r)$? Can you find a regular expression $s$ using $^+$ instead of $^*$ such that $\mathcal{L}(s) = \mathcal{L}(r)$?

For example: $\underline{a} + \underline{b} = \{a\} \cup \{b\} = \{a, b\}$. And $\underline{a} \cdot \underline{b} = \{a\} \cdot \{b\} = \{ab\}$. Finally, $(\underline{a} + \underline{b}) \cdot \underline{c} = \{a, b\} \cdot \{c\} = \{ac, bc\}$.

**Exercise 7.21.** Let $L = \underline{a}^*$.

a. Write $L$ out in pseudolist notation.

b. Check that $L + L = L$.

c. What language is $L \cdot L$? Is it the same as $L + L$?

**Exercise 7.22.** Try writing some languages in list notation, then if possible describing them in English.

a. $(\underline{a} + \underline{b})^*$

b. $\underline{a} \cdot (\underline{a} + \underline{b})^*$

c. $(\underline{a} + \underline{b}) \cdot (\underline{a} + \underline{b})^*$

d. $(\underline{a} + \underline{b})^* \cdot \underline{c}$

e. $(\underline{a}^*)^*$

**Exercise 7.23.** What are $0 \cdot L$ and $1 \cdot L$? What are $0 + L$ and $1 + L$? What is $0^*$? What is $1^*$?

**Exercise 7.24.** Let $r$ be a regular expression over $A$. Suppose that $\epsilon \notin \mathcal{L}(r)$. We claimed above that there is a regular$^+$ expression $s$ such that $\mathcal{L}(s) = \mathcal{L}(r)$. The actual proof of this would be *by induction on the regular expression* $r$, and in this exercise we give the main points of that proof.

Suppose that $r$ and $s$ are regular expressions. Recall that $1 = \{\epsilon\}$.

a. If $\epsilon \notin \mathcal{L}(r)$ and $\epsilon \notin \mathcal{L}(s)$, then $\mathcal{L}(r \cdot s) - 1 = (\mathcal{L}(r) - 1) \cdot (\mathcal{L}(s) - 1)$.

b. If $\epsilon \notin \mathcal{L}(r)$ and $\epsilon \in \mathcal{L}(s)$, then

$$\mathcal{L}(r \cdot s) - 1 \;=\; ((\mathcal{L}(r) - 1) \cdot (\mathcal{L}(s) - 1)) + (\mathcal{L}(r) - 1).$$

c. State a similar fact for when $\epsilon \in \mathcal{L}(r)$ and $\epsilon \notin \mathcal{L}(s)$, and another fact for when $\epsilon \in \mathcal{L}(r)$ and also $\epsilon \in \mathcal{L}(s)$.

d. Now the main fact that we are driving towards is that for every regular expression $r$ there is a regular$^+$ expression $s$ such that $\mathcal{L}(s) = \mathcal{L}(r) - 1$. If you know about induction, you might try to prove this fact by induction on $r$.

e. Use the previous part to prove the statement in the beginning of this exercise: if $\epsilon \notin \mathcal{L}(r)$, then there is a regular$^+$ expression $s$ such that $\mathcal{L}(s) = \mathcal{L}(r)$.

At this point in the chapter, we have discussed finite-state languages and also regular languages. Examples from automata suggest that every finite-state language is actually regular. But we have not proven this. And we have not discussed the converse at all. We shall eventually clear up these matters. In Section 7.3 just below, we discuss a third way of presenting language, via a simple form of the grammars which we studied in Chapter 4. This is independently interesting, as were automata and regular expressions. And after this we connect all three ways to define languages.

## 7.3 Simple Grammars

What we want to do at this point is to take am $\epsilon$-free regular language and write a grammar for it in the style of Chapter 4. As an first example of what we are trying to do, consider $\underline{a}^+$ as a language over the alphabet $A = \{a, b, c\}$. We take a basic category $S$. This will be our only basic category. We take as the lexicon

$$(a, S), (a, S/S).$$

(Actually, the lexicon *set* with these two elements, but in this chapter we shall omit the set braces.) And we take $S$ to be our top-level category. So now we have a grammar that we'll call $\mathcal{G}(a^+)$. We can check that $\mathcal{L}(\mathcal{G}) = \underline{a}^+$.

Here is a second example, a grammar for $(\underline{a} \cdot \underline{b})^+$. We take a basic category $S$, and also a category $T$. (We have complete freedom over what basic categories to take. We usually use $S$ as our "top level" category, but this is not strictly required. And we can name our categories $A$ and $B$; they do not have to be named $N$, $DP$, $S$, $T$, etc.) Here is our lexicon:

$$(a, S/T) \qquad (b, T) \qquad (b, T/S)$$

Let's call this grammar $\mathcal{G}_2$. To see that it works, here is a parse of *abab*. We are not drawing the tree the way we have done it earlier, mostly to show you a different notation for parse trees.

$$\cfrac{a : S/T \quad \cfrac{b : T/S \quad \cfrac{a : S/T \quad b : T}{ab : S}}{bab : T}}{abab : S}$$

It would be worthwhile to try examples and convince yourself that the language of our grammar really is $(ab)^+$.

**Definition 7.5.** A grammar is *simple* if all the categories in the lexicon are either basic categories, or else $X/Y$, where $X$ and $Y$ are basic categories. Moreover, we insist that in a simple grammar, we combine words *functor first*. An $SG$ is a simple grammar with a specified choice of a "top-level" category. Usually, we'll denote this category by $S$, but occasionally other letters will be used.

We are driving towards the following general fact:

**Theorem 7.2.** *Let $A$ be an alphabet. Let $r$ be a regular$^+$ expression over $A$. Then there is a simple grammar $\mathcal{G}(r)$ such that*

  a. $\mathcal{L}(\mathcal{G}(r)) = \mathcal{L}(r)$. *In words, the set of words over $A$ which can be parsed in $\mathcal{G}(r)$ as $Ss$ is exactly $\mathcal{L}(r)$, where $S$ is the top-level symbol of $\mathcal{G}(r)$.*

  b. *All categories in the lexicon of $\mathcal{G}(r)$ are either basic categories, or are of the form $X/Y$ for basic categories $X$ and $Y$.*

The proof actually gives a method of coming up with $\mathcal{G}(r)$ from $r$. We go *bottom-up*. That is, if we drew the regular expression as a tree, we would be literally going bottom-up.

Theorem 7.2 also gives us the following result.

**Corollary 7.3.** *Let $L$ be an $\epsilon$-free regular language. Then $L$ is the language of a simple grammar.*

*Proof.* Let $L$ be as in our statement. We observed in Exercise 7.24 that $L$ is the language of some regular$^+$ expression. And now our result follows from Theorem 7.2. □

**The simplest case, when $r$ is $\underline{a}$ for some $a \in A$** We take a basic category $S$, a lexicon $\{(a, S)\}$, and declare $S$ to be the top-level symbol. This gives a grammar $\mathcal{G}$. Clearly $\mathcal{L}(\mathcal{G}(r)) = \{a\} = \mathcal{L}(r)$.

**Combining Grammars $\mathcal{G}(r)$ and $\mathcal{G}(s)$ to get a Grammar $\mathcal{G}(r+s)$**
Suppose we have $\mathcal{G}(r)$ for $r$, and also $\mathcal{G}(s)$ for $s$. Here is how to combine these to get a grammar $\mathcal{G}(r + s)$ for $r + s$.

    a. Re-name all the basic categories in $\mathcal{G}(r)$ and $\mathcal{G}(s)$ so that the grammars have no categories in common. Make sure that $S$ is *not* a basic category in either grammar.

    b. Call the top-level symbol of $\mathcal{G}(r)$ $T$, and call $U$ the top-level symbol of $\mathcal{G}(s)$.

    c. Put the lexicons together in one big set.

    d. Add entries to the lexicon: If it has $(a, T)$, add $(a, S)$. If it has $(a, T/X)$, add $(a, S/X)$. If it has $(a, U)$, add $(a, S)$. If it has $(a, U/X)$, add $(a, S/X)$.

    e. Declare $S$ to be the top-level symbol of the new grammar.

**Combining Grammars $\mathcal{G}(r)$ and $\mathcal{G}(s)$ to get a Grammar $\mathcal{G}(r \cdot s)$**
Suppose we have $\mathcal{G}(r)$ for $r$, and also $\mathcal{G}(s)$ for $s$. Here is how to combine these to get a grammar $\mathcal{G}(r \cdot s)$ for $r \cdot s$.

    a. Re-name all the basic categories in $\mathcal{G}(r)$ and $\mathcal{G}(s)$ so that the grammars have no categories in common.

    b. Let $S$ be the top-level symbol in $\mathcal{G}(r)$.

    c. Let $T$ be the top-level symbol in $\mathcal{G}(s)$.

    d. Put the lexicons together in one big set.

    e. Make *changes* to the lexicon: If $X$ is a basic category in $G(r)$ and the lexicon has $(a, X)$, then change this entry to $(a, X/T)$.

    f. Declare $S$ to be the top-level symbol of the new grammar.

**Changing $\mathcal{G}(r)$ to get $\mathcal{G}(r^+)$** Suppose we have $\mathcal{G}(r)$ for $r$. Here is how to modify it to get a grammar $\mathcal{G}(r^+)$ for $r^+$.

    a. Let $S$ be the top-level symbol in $\mathcal{G}(r)$.

    b. Make a few *additions* to the lexicon: If $X$ is a basic category in $G(r)$ and the lexicon has $(a, X)$, then *add* $(a, X/S)$.

    c. Declare $S$ to be the top-level symbol of the new grammar.

**An Example: A Grammar for** $(\underline{a}\cdot\underline{b})^+ + \underline{c}^+$. We build our grammar from the bottom-up. First, we know how to construct grammars $\mathcal{G}(\underline{a})$, $\mathcal{G}(\underline{b})$, and $\mathcal{G}(\underline{c})$. Our last point tells us how to get a grammar $\mathcal{G}(\underline{c}^+)$: we would take a basic category $S$, a lexicon $\{(c : S), (c : S/S)\}$, and of course use $S$ as the top-level symbol.

Second, we combine $\mathcal{G}(\underline{a})$ and $\mathcal{G}(\underline{b})$ as follows. Rename $S$ to $T$ in $\mathcal{G}(\underline{b})$, change the lexicon entry $(a : S)$ to $(a : S/T)$, and put the lexicons together. We get

$$(a : S/T), (b : T)$$

with $S$ as the top-level symbol.

Third, to get $\mathcal{G}((\underline{a}\cdot\underline{b})^+)$, add the entry $(a : T/S)$ to the last lexicon.

Finally, we make additions for the overall $^+$ operation. We get the grammar below:

(6)

| | |
|---|---|
| $(a, T/X)$ | $(c, Y)$ |
| $(a, S/X)$ | $(c, Y/Y)$ |
| $(b, X)$ | $(c, S)$ |
| $(b, X/T)$ | $(c, S/Y)$ |

Once again, our top-level symbol is $S$.

**Review and a Definition** Given a regular expression $r$, we found a simple grammar $\mathcal{G}(r)$ which generated $\mathcal{L}(r)$.

**Exercise 7.25.** Although we indicated the steps in constructing $\mathcal{G}(r)$ from $r$, we did not actually prove that $\mathcal{L}(\mathcal{G}(r)) = \mathcal{L}(r)$. If you know about induction, prove that indeed $\mathcal{L}(\mathcal{G}(r)) = \mathcal{L}(r)$.

**Exercise 7.26.** We saw context-free grammars in Chapter 5, and now is a good time to show that the language of every simple grammar is context-free. We will not prove this in detail. But you can glean the idea from this problem. Here is the lexicon of a simple grammar.

| | | |
|---|---|---|
| $(a, S/T)$ | $(b, U)$ | $(b, U/U)$ |
| $(b, T)$ | $(b, U/S)$ | $(c, T)$ |
| $(b, T/S)$ | $(b, T/U)$ | $(c, T/S)$ |

The top-most symbol is $S$. Find a CFG whose language is the same as the language of this grammar. You will need to decide on what the non-terminals are, and also the productions. If you do this in a general way, you will have the idea for the general case. [Hint: the language involved is $(\underline{a} \cdot (\underline{b}^+ + \underline{c}))^+$.]

Our next goal is to show that the language of an SG, is always an $\epsilon$-free regular language. That is, we'll take an SG $\mathcal{G}$ and (after many steps) come up with a regular$^+$ expression with the property that $\mathcal{L}(r) = \mathcal{L}(\mathcal{G})$.

## 7.4 Closing the Circle

At this point in the chapter we have several ways of defining languages. First, we saw finite-state languages; these are the languages of finite automata. We then looked at regular languages, and following that the languages of SGs. We close the circle of equivalences by showing two results: every SG gives rise to a finite-state automaton with the property that the start state is not accepting, and the language of every such finite-state automaton is a regular$^+$ language.

**From Grammars to Automata** Here is how to take an SG $\mathcal{G}$ and associate a finite-state automaton $\mathcal{A}(\mathcal{G})$ to it:

a. The states of automaton $\mathcal{A}(\mathcal{G})$ are the basic categories of the grammar $\mathcal{G}$, plus a new state that we'll call $R$.

b. The top-level state of the $\mathcal{G}$ is the initial state of $\mathcal{A}(\mathcal{G})$.

c. If the lexicon has $(a, X)$, then add an arrow from $X$ to $R$ labeled by $a$.

d. If the lexicon has $(a, X/Y)$, then add an arrow from $X$ to $Y$ labeled by $a$.

e. The new state $R$ is the accepting state of $\mathcal{A}(\mathcal{G})$.

As an example, consider our grammar for $(\underline{a} \cdot \underline{b})^+ + \underline{c}^+$ from (6) above. The automaton for it is shown below:

(7)

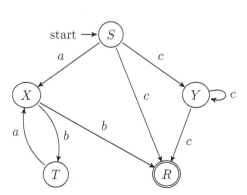

One should observe that when we make an automaton from an SG, the accepting state is different from the start state.

**Proposition 7.4.** *In the notation above, the language of the automaton is the one we started with:*

$$\mathcal{L}(\mathcal{G}) \quad = \quad \mathcal{L}(\mathcal{A}(\mathcal{G})).$$

To prove this result, we shall take an automaton, and then turn it into an "algebra problem." We use scare quotes here because this will be different from the kinds of problems one finds in high school algebra. In that subject, we typically solve equations for *numbers*; here we want to solve equations for languages. And want those solutions to be $\epsilon$-free regular languages.

For example, look back at the automaton in (7) above. Here is the associated system of equations:

(8)

$$
\begin{aligned}
X_R &= 1 \\
X_Y &= cX_Y + cX_R \\
X_U &= bX_T + bX_R \\
X_T &= aX_U \\
X_S &= aX_U + cX_R + cX_Y
\end{aligned}
$$

Here and below, $X_S$ and $X_T$ are *variables ranging over languages.* We'll have one variable for each state of the automaton, and one equation per variable. We got each equation $X_S$ by looking at the *outgoing edges from* $S$. We changed the state $X$ to $U$ to avoid the terrible notation $X_X$.

We get a *system of equations* in the variables. The idea is that $X_S$ is the set of words $w$ which when read in at state $S$ could lead by some path to the accepting state $R$. (And similarly for the other variables.) So $X_R = 1$, since $1 = \{\epsilon\}$, and this is the only word which, when started in $R$, leads back to $R$ itself. And the equation for $X_S$ means that a word $w$ could be read in at state $S$ to get to $R$ if and only if

$w = av$, where $v$ can be read in at $U$

or $w = cv$, where $v$ can be read in at $R$

or $w = cv$, where $v$ can be read in at $Y$

**Solving a System** Here is the most basic observation: We wish to solve

(9) $$X = vX + w,$$

where $w$ is a word, and $w$ is any expression that does not involve $X$. (Note: $w$ might involve other variables besides $X$.)

**Lemma 7.5.** *The solution of (9) is*

$$X = v^* \cdot w$$

*That is, the only language $X$ such that $X = vX + w$ is $v^*w$.*

But to use this lemma, the equation has to have a special form. On the left we have to have a variable, and that variable cannot occur in $w$.

In addition, you can work in a similar manner to what you do in algebra: substitute partially done work, use laws of algebra to simplify expressions.

**A Worked Example** We return to (8), shown again below.

$$\begin{aligned} X_R &= 1 \\ X_Y &= cX_Y + cX_R \\ X_U &= bX_T + bX_R \\ X_T &= aX_U \\ X_S &= aX_U + cX_R + cX_Y \end{aligned}$$

$X_R$ is already solved. So we go back and rewrite a few of the equations:

$$\begin{aligned} X_R &= 1 \\ X_Y &= cX_Y + c{\cdot}1 &&= cX_Y + c \\ X_U &= bX_T + b{\cdot}1 &&= bX_T + b \\ X_T &= aX_U \\ X_S &= aX_U + c{\cdot}1 + cX_Y &&= aX_U + c + cX_Y \end{aligned}$$

We see first that $X_Y = c^* \cdot c = c^+$. We can plug this in to the equation for $X_S$:

$$\begin{aligned} X_R &= 1 \\ X_Y &= c^+ \\ X_U &= bX_T + b \\ X_T &= aX_U \\ X_S &= aX_U + c + c \cdot c^+ \end{aligned}$$

We then plug the right-hand side of the $X_T$ equation in for $X_T$ in the right-hand side of the $X_U$ equation:

$$
\begin{aligned}
X_R &= 1 \\
X_Y &= c^+ \\
X_U &= b(aX_U) + b &&= (ba)X_U + b \\
X_T &= aX_U \\
X_S &= aX_U + c + c(c^+)
\end{aligned}
$$

We solve for $X_U$ in one step; it is $(ba)^*b$. So we get

$$
\begin{aligned}
X_R &= 1 \\
X_Y &= c^+ \\
X_U &= (ba)^*b \\
X_T &= a(ba)^*b \\
X_S &= a(ba)^*b + c + c(c^+)
\end{aligned}
$$

And then we get

$$
\begin{aligned}
X_S &= a(ba)^+b + c + (c \cdot c^+) \\
&= a(ba)^*b + c^+
\end{aligned}
$$

The overall variable that we are interested in is the *start state* of the automaton. In this case, it is $X_S$. So the language $\mathcal{L}(\mathcal{A})$ of this automaton $\mathcal{A}$ is

$$a(ba)^*b + c^+.$$

An equivalent (and better) way to write this answer is to notice that $a(ba)^*b = (ab)^+$. So we may simplify our answer above to $(ab)^+ + c^+$. This is a check on our work, since we got $\mathcal{A}$ from a SG for $(ab)^+ + c^+$.

Here is a summary of what we have done in this section. It is a famous result in automata theory due to Stephen Kleene in 1956.

**Theorem 7.6** (Kleene's Theorem). *Let $\mathcal{A}$ be a finite-state automaton. Then $\mathcal{L}(\mathcal{A})$ is a regular language. Moreover, if the start state of $\mathcal{A}$ is not an accepting state, then $\mathcal{L}(\mathcal{A})$ is $\epsilon$-free.*

*Proof.* Here is a sketch. Given $\mathcal{A}$, we write its equations down using the general formula

$$X_T = c_1 X_{U_1} + c_2 X_{U_2} + \cdots + c_n X_{U_n} \; (+1)$$

We use this when $T$ is a state with a $c_1$-transition to the state $U_1$, a $c_2$-transition to $U_2$, etc., and no other outgoing arrows. The $(+1)$ at the end means that we add 1 to the expression if and only if the state $T$

is an accepting state. (If $T$ has no outgoing arrows, we get 0 when it is a non-accepting state and 1 when it is an accepting state.) This gives a finite system of equations. We can solve this system by eliminating variables. The key point here is Lemma 7.5. And when we do this repeatedly, we eventually get a regular expression for every variable in the system. (That is, we eliminate the variables from the right-hand sides.) □

**A summary of what we have done**  The progression of ideas is indicated back in Figure 7.1. We have gone

$$\text{regular language} \implies \text{SG} \implies \text{finite-state automaton} \implies \text{regular language}$$

To be a little more precise, we needed to adjust the picture a little because the language of an $SG$ should not contain the empty string. So to get an exact match of concepts, we begin with an $\epsilon$-free regular language, convert it to an $SG$, then associate to the grammar a systems of language equations, and finally solve the language system and take the solution corresponding to the top-level symbol of the grammar.

**Exercise 7.27.**  Consider the automaton below.

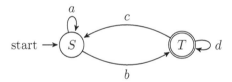

Write the system of equations, and solve it. In this way, you'll get $\mathcal{L}(\mathcal{A})$, the language of this automaton.

Exercises 7.28-7.32 have to do with the language $\mathcal{L}(r)$, where

$$r \;=\; (\underline{a} \cdot (\underline{b}^+ + \underline{c}))^+.$$

**Exercise 7.28.**  Find a simple grammar $\mathcal{G}$ such that $\mathcal{L}(\mathcal{G}) = \mathcal{L}(r)$. That is, you should come up with a set of basic categories, find a lexicon for $a$, $b$, and $c$, and finally say what your top-level category is.

**Exercise 7.29.**  Take the grammar that you found in Exercise 7.28, and turn it into an automaton. Be sure to indicate which is your "start state", and also which state is your accepting state.

**Exercise 7.30.**  Take the automaton from Exercise 7.29, and find the corresponding system of equations.

**Exercise 7.31.** Take the system of equations from Exercise 7.30, and find a regular expression for the set of words accepted when we read them in, beginning in the start state of the automaton from Exercise 7.29. [This means that you solve the system using the version of algebra presented in the notes.]

**Exercise 7.32.** If you did all the previous problems correctly, your answer to Exercise 7.31 should be the original regular expression, $(\underline{a} \cdot (\underline{b}^+ + \underline{c}))^+$. Check that it is. [As a hint, you might find it useful to note that for all words $u$ and $v$,

$$(u \cdot v)^* \cdot u \;\; = \;\; u \cdot (v \cdot u)^*.$$

That is, use a special case of this, with a well-chosen $u$ and $v$.]

**Exercise 7.33.** The *reversal* of any language $L$ is the set of elements in $L$ written backwards. For example, the reversal of $ab = \{ab\}$ is $ba$. Write a regular expression for the *reversal* of $\mathcal{L}(r)$, where $r$ again is $(\underline{a} \cdot (\underline{b}^+ + \underline{c}))^+$.

**Exercise 7.34.** Prove that the reversal of every regular language is regular.

## 7.5  $a^n b^n$ is not a Regular Language

In this section we show that there are context free languages that are not regular. We have already seen that the stringset displayed below is generable by a context free grammar. Here we show it is not a regular set, whence that set cannot be the language of a finite state machine or the language generated by a simple grammar as we have defined them.

$$\{a^n b^n \mid n \geq 1\}$$
$$= \;\; \{ab, aabb, aaabbb, \ldots, a^n b^n, \ldots\}$$

We are going to assume that $a^n b^n$ *is* regular, and then get a contradiction. Since regular languages can be presented in three ways, we have presentations of $a^n b^n$ in all three. We thus would have a finite automaton, say $\mathcal{A}$, whose language $\mathcal{L}(\mathcal{A})$ was exactly $a^n b^n$.

(Recall that $\mathcal{L}(\mathcal{A})$ is the set of words which can be read in from the start state of $\mathcal{A}$ and have a path leading to the accepting state of $\mathcal{A}$.)

$\mathcal{A}$ is finite, and so it has some number of states. Let's say that $M$ is that number. One of the words in $a^n b^n$ is $a^{M+1} b^{M+1}$. When we read $a^{M+1} b^{M+1}$ in to $\mathcal{A}$, we begin at the start state, follow some path or other, and somehow end up at the accepting state. But this word is longer than the number of states, so there must be a *loop* somewhere.

In fact, there has to be a loop while reading the $a$'s. Let's say that when after $i$th and $j$th $a$'s were read in, the automaton was in the very same state. Call this state $X$, and call the accepting state $Y$.

| letter | $a$ | | $a$ | $\cdots$ | $a$ | $\cdots$ | $a$ | $\cdots$ | $a$ | $b$ | $b$ | $\cdots$ | $b$ |
|---|---|---|---|---|---|---|---|---|---|---|---|---|---|
| state | start | | | | $X$ | $\cdots$ | $X$ | $\cdots$ | | | | | $Y$ |

Since we have a loop in the states, we can *repeat* the $a$'s between the $X$'s, except for the last one:

| letter | $a$ | | $a$ | $\cdots$ | $a$ | $\cdots$ | $a$ | $\cdots$ | $a$ | $b$ | $b$ | $\cdots$ | $b$ |
|---|---|---|---|---|---|---|---|---|---|---|---|---|---|
| state | start | | | | $X$ | $\cdots$ | $X$ | $\cdots$ | $X$ | $\cdots$ | | | $Y$ |

Notice the two sequences of states indicated by $\cdots$ on this bottom line. These are exactly the same. Notice also that the word one the top line just above is

$$a^{M+j-i+1}b^{M+1}.$$

Since $j > i$, this word is *not* in the language $a^n b^n$. But it *is* accepted by $\mathcal{A}$. So we have a contradiction. And our proof is done.

(The point, informally, is that since our original word was read in using a loop in the states, we can go around the loop twice. The automaton "has no memory," and so it must accept the longer word.)

We just saw that $a^n b^n$ cannot be the language of any finite automaton, and it follows that we cannot write an SG for it. But if we allow ourselves the full power of context free grammars (CFGs), we *can* write a grammar for it. We need only use

$$S \to aSb \qquad S \to a \qquad S \to b.$$

And this formulation shows what is going on: the CFG derivations exhibit a kind of "memory" in the sense that going down the spine of any derivation tree results in the same number of $a$s on the left as $b$s on the right. This isn't a conscious memory, but it implicitly behaves like one. The point of our work earlier in this section is that simple grammars do not have any method, even a clever one, for implicitly constructing a memory.

We asked earlier: Are context-free grammars (CFGs) more powerful than simple grammars (SGs)? We now know that the answer to this is Yes. We next want to ask the question of whether SGs are powerful enough to handle a natural language like English.

**Exercise 7.35.** What is the solution to $X = aXb + 1$?

## 7.6 An Argument Why English is Not Regular

Regular languages are useful for representing certain kinds of recursion, as we have seen. Also, they useful in areas such as computational linguistics. But regular languages have their limits. Certain kinds of iterations which are arguably present in natural languages are provably not expressible by any regular language, as we now show.

Suppose towards a contradiction that English were regular. Consider $L$ defined by

$$L \quad = \quad \text{English} \cap \{\text{the}, \text{boy}, \text{girl}, \text{saw}, \text{ran}\}^+$$

Since the intersection of two regular languages is regular (see Exercise 7.16), this language $L$ must also be regular.

Here are some sentences in $L$:

> the boy ran
> the boy the girl saw ran
> the girl the girl saw ran
> the boy the girl *the girl saw* saw ran
> the boy the girl *the girl* **the girl saw** *saw* saw ran

Sentences don't really have underlining, italics or boldface, and we only have added those to make it easier to parse the sentences. We know that nobody can possibly understand this last sentence, but there are reasons why linguists want to take it to be part of *ideal English*.

The list above goes on, so $L$ is infinite. The main things about $L$ are that

(1) No sentence has two "the"s in a row.

(2) No sentence has two "boy"s in a row, or two "girl"s.

(3) the sentence has exactly as many "girl"s as "see"s.

Now we repeat the proof that $a^n b^n$ is not regular. We know now that $L$ is regular, so for some automaton, say $\mathcal{A}$, $L = \mathcal{L}(\mathcal{A})$. Let $M$ be the number of states in $\mathcal{A}$.

Consider

> the girl the girl the girl $\cdots$ saw saw $\cdots$ saw ran

We would have one more "girl" than "saw". But by considering loops in $\mathcal{A}$ again, this automaton must also accept a string of words with more stuff in the first part of the sentence.

As a result $\mathcal{A}$ would accept a string that violated one of our points (1)–(3) above. And this string would definitely *not* be an English sentence, hence not in $L$. So this proves that $\mathcal{L}(\mathcal{A}) \neq L$.

**Exercise 7.36.** Show that every finite language $L \subseteq A^*$ is regular. (The regular expression or automaton is likely to be as big as the cardinality of $L$, depending on how you measure the size.) So if someone believes that English is a finite language, what will they make of the argument in this section?

**Exercise 7.37.** A *palindrome* is a word that reads the same way backwards as forwards. Adapt the work of this section to show that the set of palindromes on $\{a, b\}$ is not a regular language. And as a review of our earlier work, show that this language is context-free.

## 7.7 Two Final Observations on Finite State Automata

**1.** Given a finite vocabulary $\Sigma$ and a subset $L$ of $\Sigma^*$, what tests can we apply to decide if $L$ is a regular language or not? We have already, in effect, given some tests for the positive case: $L$ is regular if $L$ is the set of strings accepted by a FSA, or it is denotable by a regular expression. What about tests to show that $L$ is not regular? If we fail to find a FSA or a regular expression, we cannot conclude that $L$ is not regular, perhaps we have simply not been clever enough in our search. The Myhill-Nerode theorem below does provide a useful negative test.

We begin with a preliminary which, again, uses equivalence relations in an important way.

**Definition 7.6.** For $\Sigma$ a finite vocabulary and $L \subseteq \Sigma^*$, define, for all $u, v \in \Sigma^*$, $u$ is *L-equivalent* to $v$, noted $u \equiv_L v$, iff for all $w \in \Sigma^*$, $uw \in L$ iff $vw \in L$. (That is, either both $uw$ and $vw$ are in $L$ or neither are).

**Exercise 7.38.** Say informally why $\equiv_L$ is an equivalence relation.

**Theorem 7.7** (Myhill-Nerode Theorem (M-N)). *For $\Sigma$ finite and $L \subseteq \Sigma^*$, $L$ is regular iff the number of equivalence classes of $\equiv_L$ is finite.*

Using M-N we can show that a stringset $L$ is not regular by showing that its $L$- equivalence relation has infinitely many equivalence classes.

For example, let us (re)show that $L = \{a^n b^n \mid 0 < n\}$ is not regular. Here $\Sigma = \{a, b\}$. Consider the set $\{a^n \mid 0 < n\}$. This set is clearly infinite (say why), and no two elements are $L$-equivalent. For let $a^j \neq a^k$, so $j \neq k$. But $a^j b^j \in L$ and $a^k b^j \notin L$. Hence when $j \neq k$, $[a^j]_L \neq [a^k]_L$. And since there are infinitely many pairs of distinct positive integers there are infinitely many $L$-equivalence classes. Thus by M-N, $\{a^n b^n \mid 0 < n\}$ is not regular.

We refer the reader to Hopcroft and Ullman (1979, 65–66) for a proof of Myhill-Nerode. Here we give the left to right direction, which is all we need for the example above. Let $\Sigma$ and $L$ be given. Assume $L$ is regular, whence it is the set of strings over $\Sigma$ accepted by some DFA (Deterministic Finite Automaton), $D$. Assume first that $L$ is finite, say $|L| = k$. Now since every $L$-equivalence class is $[u]_L$, the set of expressions $L$-equivalent to $u$, for some $u$) then the number of such classes is at most the number of expressions in $L$, which is finite, so the number of such classes is finite.

Now let $L$ be infinite. Let $D$ have $n$ states $s_1, s_2, \ldots, s_n$. Write string($s_i$) for the set of strings $u$ which are such that when $D$ reads them it ends in state $s_i$. Observe that for all $u, v \in \Sigma^*$, if $u$ and $v$ are both in string($s_i$) then for any string $z$, if each of $u$ and $v$ are followed by $z$, $D$ is in the same state, since whether it reads $u$ or $v$ it gets to $s_i$ and then reads the fixed string $z$, from which it can get to only one state, call it $s_j$, since $D$ is deterministic. If $s_j$ is a final state then $uz$, $u$ followed by $z$, and $vz$, $v$ followed by $z$, are both in $L$, and if $s_j$ is not a final state then $uz$ and $vz$ are both not in $L$, whence $u$ and $v$ are $L$-equivalent.

Now let $S = \{\text{string}(s_i) \mid 1 \leq i \leq n \,\&\, \text{string}(s_i) \neq \emptyset\}$. (A string($s_i$) can be empty if $s_i$ is a state that can't be reached by any input string). $S$ is finite, having at most $n$ members. Now we define a function $F$ from $S$ into the set of $L$-equivalence classes by setting $F(\text{string}(s_i)) = [u]_L$ iff $u \in \text{string}(s_i)$. (This is a well definition since none of these string($s_i$) are empty and if both $v$ and $u$ are in string($s_i$) then $v$ and $u$ are $L$-equivalent, so $[v]_L = [u]_L$). Note that every string $u$ in $\Sigma^*$ is in some (in fact exactly one) string($s_i$) since $D$ must end in some state after reading $u$ and can't end in more than one as $D$ is deterministic. Thus every string $u$ in $\Sigma^*$ is in exactly one $F(\text{string}(s_i))$. Thus $\{F(\text{string}(s_i)) \mid \text{string}(s_i) \neq \emptyset\}$, the range of $F$, is the set of $L$-equivalence classes, and this set must be finite as the domain of $F$ is finite. Trivially $F$ is onto its range (Every function is!) and if $F$ is one to one then $|\text{Ran}(F)| = |\text{Dom}(F)|$, which is finite, and if $F$ is not one to one, its range is smaller than its (finite) domain, and so is finite. $\square$

The proof of Myhill-Nerode in the other direction begins with an $L$ whose equivalence relation $\equiv_L$ has just finitely many equivalence classes. Then we construct a DFA whose states correspond one for one to these classes. And as a corollary we get:

**Corollary to Myhill-Nerode** Given finite $\Sigma$ with $L \subseteq \Sigma^*$, if $\equiv_L$ has just finitely many equivalence classes then the smallest DFA whose acceptance language is $L$ has just that many states. Moreover this DFA is unique up to isomorphism (meaning that any other minimal DFA for $L$ is isomorphic to this one).

**Exercise 7.39.** Use Myhill-Nerode to show that $\{ww \mid w \in \{a, b\}^*\}$ is not regular.

## 2. Structural and Behavioral Equivalence of DFAs

Using an earlier vocabulary, let us call $L(D)$, the set of strings accepted by a DFA $D$, its extension. It is reasonable to ask whether two DFAs (over the same alphabet) with the same extension have the same structure (are isomorphic). We expect (correctly) that the answer is NO. But to show this we must say explicitly what is meant by saying that two DFAs are isomorphic. Recall from chapter 4 on trees that we don't fully understand the structures of a given type (e.g. terminally ordered unlabeled trees, etc.) until we can say when two such structures are isomorphic (have the same structure). And thus it goes with DFAs.

In defining a DFA $D$ we assumed a fixed alphabet and then specified four things: the set of states of $D$, the *start* state, the *accepting* states, and, crucially, the transition function: for each state $s$, and each input symbol $b$, the state $D$ moves to when it is in state $s$ and reads $b$. And we say that automata $D$ and $D'$ over a given $\Sigma$ are *isomorphic* iff there is a bijection $h$ from the states of $D$ to those of $D'$ such that: (1) $h$ maps the start state of $D$ to the start state of $D'$, (2) $s$ is an accepting state of $D$ iff $h(s)$ is an accepting state of $D'$, and (3) $D$ moves from $s$ to $t$ on input $b$ iff $D'$ moves from $h(s)$ to $h(t)$ on input $b$. From this it follows that if $D$ and $D'$ are isomorphic automata over some $\Sigma$ then they have the same extension (accept the same strings). It is the converse of this which interests us, as it fails.

**Fact** The two automata below are clearly not isomorphic. They do not even have the same number of states. Nonetheless the extension of each is $\{a, b\}^*$.

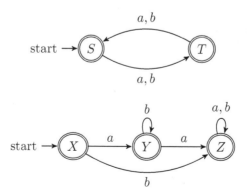

Our example also shows that there is not even a strong homomorphism from one of these automata to the other. (A strong homomorphism is

like an isomorphism but is not required to be injective). Two strongly homomorphic automata over the same alphabet do have the same extension, but, as we see above, the converse fails: so same extension does not imply strongly homomorphic. We note though that the two automata exhibited above are each strongly homomorphic to the one state automaton with $a$- and $b$-arrows from that state to itself. (That state is the start state and also an accepting state.)

**Exercise 7.40.**

   a. Exhibit two two state automata over $\{a, b\}$ with the same states, the same transitions and the same accepting states but which differ as to which is the start state. Exhibit a non-empty string accepted by one and not the other. This justifies that isomorphisms should identify start states; i.e., that the choice of start state is part of the structure of the automaton.

   b. Exhibit two two state automata over $\{a, b\}$ with the same states, the same transitions and the same start state but different accepting states. Again, exhibit a non-empty string accepted by one but not the other. This justifies that the designation of which states are accepting is structural.

   c. Linguistically it is natural to say that two grammars are structurally the same if they differ just with regard to choice of vocabulary. Imagine two automata that are identical except that the alphabet of one is $\{a, b\}$ and that of the other is $\{\alpha, \beta\}$ and that in the transitions, wherever the one has $a$ the other has $\alpha$, and analogously for $b$ and $\beta$. Clearly such automata have the same structure (and we can give a word for word translation of one language to that of the other).

**Your task** Generalize the definition of isomorphism of DFAs so that the case of different alphabets is covered.

**Sources** Much of the material in this chapter is standard, including work on finite-state automata and regular expressions, Kleene's Theorem 7.6, and also the fact that $a^n b^n$ is not regular. A more general fact that can be used to show that various languages are not regular is called the Pumping Lemma. You may find all of this in any book on automata theory, and in nearly every book on theoretical computer science at the undergraduate or graduate level. We believe that the work on simple grammars is new here; the standard treatment of the subject does not include solving systems of equations for languages.

The argument of Section 7.6 is due to Chomsky (1956). According to Langendoen (2003):

> For the most part, linguists accepted Chomsky's argument, and their interest in the theory of finite-state languages and grammars, which was never great in the first place, languished.

However, certain aspects of a natural language, at least, are completely analyzable using finite-state methods, in particular its phonotactics (the determination of legitimate sequences of sounds in natural language; Johnson, 1970, Kaplan and Kay, 1994), and its morphology excluding compound formation (Koskenniemi, 1983). Despite the fact that in principle morphological rules can give rise to sets of words that cannot be generated by a finite-state grammar, no such system for natural languages has ever been discovered (Langendoen, 1981). Consequently in the areas of speech (and orthographic) analysis and of morphological analysis, finite-state methods have become standard.

The use of finite-state methods in syntax and semantics was somewhat slower to develop, in large measure due to the belief that these aspects of linguistic structure are not fully analyzable in those terms. However, partial syntactic and semantic analyses have been carried out using finite-state methods beginning with the Transformation and Discourse Analysis Project at the University of Pennsylvania in the late 1950s (Joshi and Hopely, 1999). The first serious proposal that finite-state methods are fully adequate for syntactic analysis was made by Krauwer and des Tombe (1981), and a sophisticated (augmented) finite-state grammar that handles discontinuous elements was developed by Blank (1989). For recent surveys of what is now a vast and rapidly growing field, see Roche and Schabes (1997), Kornai (1999), Nederhof (2000), and Beesley and Karttunen (2003).

# 8

# Semantics I: Compositionality and Sentential Logic

In this chapter we consider first some of the goals of a semantic analysis for a language and we illustrate a semantic analysis for a particularly simple language, that of Sentential Logic (SL). Then we enrich our analysis to include a language with some (not all) of the linguistic complexity studied in Chapter 5.

## 8.1 Compositionality and Natural Language Semantics

### 8.1.1 Goals of Semantic Analysis

**Compositionality.** Our primary way of understanding a complex novel expression is understanding what the lexical items it is composed of mean and how expressions built in that way take their meaning as a function of the meanings of the expressions they are built from (beginning with the lexical items). We illustrate this conceptually with our semantics for Sentential Logic.

**Semantic characterization of syntactic phenomena.** In practice syntactic and semantic analysis are partially independent and partially dependent. So a variety of cases arise where the judgments that an expression is grammatical seem to be decided on semantic grounds (See Chapters 9, 11 and 12). Here are three examples. First, negative elements like *not* and *n't* license the presence of *negative polarity items* (npi's) within the $P_1$ they negate:

(1)    a. Sue hasn't <u>ever</u> been to Pinsk.

   b. *Sue has <u>ever</u> been to Pinsk.

However some subject DPs also license npi's, as in (2a) but not (2b):

(2)    a. No student here has <u>ever</u> been to Pinsk.

    b. *Some student here has <u>ever</u> been to Pinsk.

These judgments give rise to two linguistic problems: (1) How to define the class of subject DPs which, like *no student*, license npi's in their $P_1$. This class must be defined in order to define a grammar for English. And (2) what, if anything, do these DPs have in common with *not* and *n't*? The best answer we have to date is stated in semantic terms, specifically in terms of the denotations of the Dets used in the subject DP.

Second, a long standing problem in generative grammar is the characterization of the DPs which occur naturally in Existential-There contexts:

(3)    a. Are there *more than two students* in the class?

    b. *Are there *most students* in the class?

Again the best answers that linguists have found are semantic in nature: they are those DPs built from Dets whose denotations satisfy a certain condition.

Third, which DPs occur naturally in plural, count partitive contexts such as: *two of* _____? *Two of those students, two of the ten students*, and *two of John's students* are natural. But *two of no students*, **two of most students*, and **two of all but three students* are decidedly less good.

**Issues of expressive power**  Given an adequate semantic analysis of a class of expressions in natural language we can study that analysis to uncover new purely semantic regularities about the language. For example, we can show that natural languages present quantifier expressions which are not definable in first order logic (Chapter 10), and we can show that Det denotations quite generally satisfy a logically and empirically non-trivial condition known as Conservativity (Chapter 12).

### 8.1.2  Semantic Facts

Crucial to each of the three goals above is that we have a clear sense of the facts that a semantic analysis of natural language must account for[1]. That is, we need a way of evaluating whether a proposed semantic

---

[1] This problem arises in syntactic study as well, but it is less pressing as we begin with a large range of syntactic facts our theory should predict. Namely facts of the form *Every cat chased every dog* is an expression of English whereas *Cat dog every every chased* is not. As we pursue syntactic analysis more deeply than was done in Chs 4 and 5 further non-trivial methodological issues arise, but we do not pursue them in this book.

analysis is adequate or not. The facts we rely on are the judgments by competent speakers that a given expression has, or fails to have, a certain semantic property. More generally a semantic analysis of a language must explicitly predict that two (or more) expressions stand in a certain semantic relation if and only if competent speakers judge that they do. Pre-theoretically to say that a property $P$ of expressions is *semantic* is just to say that competent speakers decide whether an expression has $P$ or not based on the *meaning* of $P$. Similarly a relation between expressions is semantic just in case whether expressions stand in that relation depends on the meaning of the expressions. The best understood semantic relation in this sense is *entailment*, introduced briefly in Chapter 5. We repeat and expand that definition:

**Definition 8.1.** A sentence $P$ *entails* ($\models$) a sentence $Q$ iff $Q$ is true in every situation (model) in which $P$ is true. More generally a set $K$ of sentences *entails* a sentence $Q$ iff $Q$ is true in every situation (model) in which the sentences in $K$ are simultaneously true.

Consider the following examples using manner adverbs:

(4)     a. Rick is singing loudly. $\models$ Rick is singing.

  b. Ed walked rapidly to the post office. $\models$ Ed walked to the post office.

  c. Sue smiled mischievously at Peter. $\models$ Sue smiled at Peter.

In a situation in which *Sue smiled mischievously at Peter* is true then, obviously, in that situation, it is true that *Sue smiled at Peter*. Our judgments of entailment here are good, even though we may be unclear about precisely what a smile must be like to be mischievous. But the judgment of entailment doesn't require that we know precisely the truth conditions of the first sentence, it just requires an assessment of *relative* truth conditions. *If* a situation suffices to make the first true, does it also suffice to make the second true? For example, we may not be able to assess the truth of *John loves Marsha* in every situation, but we are certain that if the sentence *It is Marsha who John loves* is true in some situation $s$, then *John loves Marsha* must also be true in $s$. That is, our judgment that *It is Marsha who John loves* entails *John loves Marsha* is solid even when our judgment of absolute truth is not.

Observe further that, like manner adverbs, many predicate modifiers function to simply add information to the situation depicted in a simple Subject+Predicate construction. Thus (5a) is judged to entail (5b) and (6a) to entail (6b).

(5)     a. Max opened the can with a screwdriver.

        b. Max opened the can.

(6)     a. Sue is laughing in the kitchen.

        b. Sue is laughing.

But (7a) below does not entail (7b), though its syntactic form seems comparable to that of (6a):

(7)     a. Sue is laughing in Ben's picture.

        b. Sue is laughing.

Somehow the phrase *in Ben's picture* identifies a situation (model) and (7b) doesn't, so we seem to revert to some default situation, perhaps the one we are having the discussion in. So our judgments of entailment here tell us something of interest about the nature of PPs like *in the kitchen* vs. *in Ben's picture*.

As a further instance of the utility of entailment to elucidate meaning consider that either sentence in (8a) below entails (8b). But the comparable entailment in (9) fails, indicating that quantifiers like *all* and *no* have something common that makes them different from *some* and *at least two* (see Chapter 12).

(8)     a. All / No poets daydream.

        b. $\models$ All / No female poets daydream.

(9)     a. Some / Most poets daydream.

        b. $\not\models$ Some / Most female poets daydream.

Note too that the entailment in (8) also depends on the choice of adjective. *All diamonds are valuable* entails *All pretty diamonds are valuable* but does not entail *All fake diamonds are valuable*.

Thus one adequacy condition on a semantic analysis of English is that it predict the entailments in (4). More generally, an adequate semantic analysis of English must tell us that an English sentence $P$ entails an English sentence $Q$ if and only if competent speakers judge that it does. Thus an adequate semantic analysis must correctly predict the judgments of entailment and non-entailment by competent speakers.

Our observations here incorporate an important assumption concerning the nature of truth, one of our fundamental semantic primitives. Namely we treat truth as a relation between a sentence in a language and "the world" or "the situation we are talking about", notions we shortly represent more formally as "models". The truth value—True or False—of a given sentence may vary according to how the world is. A simple sentence such as *Some woodworker likes mahogany* is true in some situations and false in others. It depends on what woodworkers there are in the situation and what they like. This is why our definition of entailment quantifies over situations (models). It says that for $P$ to entail $Q$ it must be so that in *each* situation in which $P$ is true $Q$ is true.[2]

### 8.1.3 Further Adequacy Criteria for Semantic Analysis

**Semantic ambiguity.** Not uncommonly an expression is felt to express two or more distinct meanings. In such a case obviously all the meanings must be represented. To take a classical example, the sentence *Flying planes can be dangerous* is semantically ambiguous. On the one hand the subject phrase *flying planes* can refer to the act of flying planes, and so is presumably dangerous to those who fly them. On this interpretation the subject phrase is grammatically singular, as is evident in the choice of singular *is* in *Flying planes is dangerous*. But the original sentence has another interpretation on which it means that planes that are flying are dangerous, presumably to those in their vicinity. In this case the subject phrase is plural, as seen in *Flying planes are dangerous*. In our original example, *Flying planes can be dangerous*, the Predicate Phrase is built with a modal *can*. (Some other modals, of which there are about 10 in English, are *might, may, must, should, will, would* and *could*). Modals in English neutralize verb agreement. One says equally well *Johnny can read* and *the children can read* with no change in the form of the predicate despite the first having a singular subject and the second a plural one.

**Exercise 8.1.** Each of the expressions below is semantically ambiguous. In each case describe the ambiguity informally.

a. The chickens are ready to eat.

b. France fears America more than Russia.

c. John thinks he's clever and so does Bill.

---

[2] The instances of entailment we have provided use expression types we study in later chapters. Here are two further ones, which are less obvious and more titillating (the first adapted from de Morgan, the second from George Boolos):

(i)    All poets are vegetarians $\models$ All mothers of poets are mothers of vegetarians

(ii)   Everybody loves my baby and my baby loves no one but me. $\models$ I am my baby.

   d. Ma's home cooking.

   e. John and Mary or Sue came to the lecture.

   f. John didn't leave the party early because the children were crying.

In our mini-grammars in Chapter 5 we had at one point, two ways of deriving (Kim smiled, S). On one, *Kim* had category NP, on the other it had category S/(S/NP). But the English sentence is not felt as semantically ambiguous, so if we keep both analyses (we ultimately decided to drop the first, but we ignore that for the moment) we must be sure that a semantic interpretation of the language interprets them the same. Note that many syntactically distinct expressions are semantically equivalent: *Uruguay's declaration of war against Brazil surprised us* and *Uruguay's declaring war against Brazil surprised us*.

And second, recall DP scope ambiguities in Ss like *Some student praised every teacher*. In this chapter we represent the object narrow scope reading. The object wide scope reading, *Every teacher has the property that some student praised him* is treated in Chapter 10. A related type of ambiguity is the transparency/opacity (= *de re / de dicto*) one in Ss like (10):

(10) Sue thinks that the man who won the race was Greek.

On the opaque (*de dicto*) reading of *the man who won the race* we understand that Sue thinks that the winner was Greek. Sue may have no direct knowledge of who the winner was, she may just know that all the contestants were Greek men so obviously the winner was Greek. On the transparent reading of this DP, (10) is interpreted like *The man who won the race has the property that Sue thinks that he was Greek*. Here Sue has an opinion about a certain individual, namely that that individual is Greek, but she may not even know that he won the race.

Variations on this type of ambiguity are rife in the analysis of expressions involving sentence complements of verbs of thinking and saying, especially in the philosophical literature where such verbs are said to express *propositional attitudes*. It is among the reasons we do not attempt a quick semantic analysis here. These problems have no fully agreed upon solution in the literature.

**Selection restrictions.** For most of the expression types considered in $\mathcal{L}$(Eng) we find that choices of the slash category expression semantically constrain the choice of expression in the denominator category. Here are some examples.

*Adjective + Noun.* It makes sense to speak of a skillful or accomplished writer, but not of a skillful or accomplished faucet. Faucets are not the kinds of things that can be skillful or accomplished—those adjectives require that the item modified denote something animate at least. We say that adjectives *select* (impose *selection restrictions* on) their N arguments.

*Predicate modifiers.* These exhibit similar selection properties as adjectives. We use # to indicate a selection restriction violation and a check ✓ for selection restriction satisfaction.

(11)    a. He solved the problem ✓ in an hour / # for an hour.

b. He knocked at the door # in an hour / ✓ for an hour.

Thus a repetitive or durative action can be modified by durational phrases such as *for an hour* but not by modifiers like *in an hour*. In contrast an accomplishment or achievement predicate like *solve the problem*, which is over in an instant when it is over, can sensibly take modifiers like *in an hour* but not duratives like *for an hour* (see Dowty, 1982).

*Determiners + Noun.* Dets also place some selection requirements on the Ns they determine. *Many students* is natural, #*Many gold* is senseless. In contrast *Much gold* is sensible and #*Much students* is not. Ns like *gold, butter, hydrogen* are called *mass nouns*, whereas ones like *student, brick*, and *number* are called *count nouns*. And Dets may at least select for mass or count. Many abstract nouns, like *honesty, sincerity* and *honor* behave like mass nouns in this respect.

*Predicates + Argument.* $P_1$s impose selection restrictions on their subjects: *The witness lied* is fine, but #*The ceiling lied* is bizarre since ceilings aren't the kind of thing that can lie—they are too low on the chain-of-being hierarchy. Also $P_2$s impose selection restrictions on their object arguments. It makes sense to say that *John peeled an orange* or *a grape*, but not that *he peeled a puddle* or *a rainstorm*. Such anomalies are sometimes called *category mistakes* in the philosophical literature.

Beyond pointing out their existence we do not study selection restrictions in this text. Our examples are in general chosen to satisfy selection restrictions.

**Sense dependency.** Sense dependency is a phenomenon inversely related to selection restrictions whereby the interpretation of the slash category expression is conditioned by the denotation of the denominator category expression. Consider again Adjective + Noun constructions. When we speak of a flat road or table top we interpret *flat* to mean "level, without bumps or depressions". But when we speak of flat beer or champagne we mean "having lost its effervescence". And a flat tire is one that is deflated, a flat voice is one that is off-key. So the precise interpretation of *flat* is conditioned by its argument.

Predicates also have their interpretation conditioned by the nature of their arguments. In *cut your finger*, *cut* means to make an incision in the surface of. But in *cut the roast* or *the cake*, *cut* means to divide into portions for purposes of serving. In *cut prices* or *working hours*, *cut* means to reduce along a continuously varying dimension.

Sense dependency is not one of the well studied semantic relations in the linguistic literature, but dictionaries note them. The examples here are taken from Keenan (1979).

**Presupposition.** Presupposition is a well studied relation, one which plays an important role in many current semantic and pragmatic studies. Informally we say that a sentence $P$ (*logically*) *presupposes* a sentence $Q$ iff $Q$ is an entailment of $P$ which is preserved under Yes-No questioning and "natural" negation. Consider for example the classical (12a).

(12)    a. The king of France is bald.

      b. France has a king.

      c. Is the king of France bald?

      d. The king of France isn't bald.

Clearly (12a) entails (12b)—if the king of France is bald then France must indeed have a king. And that information is not questioned in (12c) or denied in (12d), hence (12b) is a presupposition of (12a).

Presupposition can be used to distinguish meanings of predicates. Consider first:

(13)    a. It is true that Fred took the painting.

      b. Fred took the painting.

      c. Is it true that Fred took the painting?

      d. It isn't true that Fred took the painting.

Though (13a) entails (13b), (13b) is not presupposed by (13a). The information in (13b) is questioned in (13c). Someone who asks (13c) is asking whether the embedded S, (13b), is true or not. And similarly (13d) does deny the information in (13b). We can replace *true* with *false* or *probable* and argue, even more easily, that they do not presuppose the b-sentence either. By contrast consider (14a).

(14)    a. It is strange that Fred took the painting.

    b. Fred took the painting.

    c. Is it strange that Fred took the painting?

    d. It isn't strange that Fred took the painting.

Here (14a) does seem to entail (14b). And in (14c) we are not asking whether Fred took the painting, we are accepting that and asking whether that fact is strange or not. Similarly in (14d) we are just denying the strangeness of the fact, but not the fact itself. It seems then that (14a) does presuppose (14b). Moreover *strange* can be replaced by dozens of other presuppositional adjectives: *amazing, unsurprising, pleasing, ironic,* etc.

There is then a systematic difference between the predicates in (13) and those in (14), one that is revealed by observing that they behave differently with regard to whether the embedded S is presupposed or not.

This factivity distinction is also present with sentential objects. Observe that *Jack thought/believed/was sure that his wife was wealthy* does not entail the object clause, *His wife was wealthy.* Jack might simply have been mistaken. But in *Jack regretted/resented/didn't realize that his wife was wealthy* we do infer that that his wife was wealthy. So *regret, resent, realize* tend to presuppose their sentential objects.

In general presupposition is a relation that is most useful is discerning how information is packaged in a sentence, as opposed to the absolute quantity of information. To see this compare (15a) and (15b):

(15)    a. John is the one doctor who signed the petition.

       b. John is the only doctor who signed the petition.

       c. Exactly one doctor signed the petition.

Each of (15a) and (15b) entails the other, which means that they are true in the same situations and so in that sense they express the same absolute information. They both entail (15c) for example. But (15a) and (15b) present their information somewhat differently. Compare their natural negations:

(16)    a. John isn't the one doctor who signed the petition.

       b. John isn't the only doctor who signed the petition.

Now (16a) still entails (15c), it only denies that John is that doctor. But (16b) denies that John was the only doctor who signed, implying thereby that there was an additional doctor who signed. So (16b) does not entail (15c). And it seems then that (15a) and (15b), while logically equivalent, differ in that (15a) presupposes (15c) whereas (15b) does not. Questioning or denying (15b) does not preserve that information. For further discussion of presupposition see Heim and Kratzer (1998). See also the section on Presupposition in the *Stanford Encyclopedia of Philosophy* (Beaver and Geurts, 2014).

Now, as we have seen, Ss in natural language are syntactically complex objects, and there are normally infinitely many of them. So we cannot just list the set of Sentence interpretations in English. Rather we must show for each S how its interpretation is constructed from the interpretation of the lexical items which occur in it. Those we can list—that is what *dictionaries* do—since the number of lexical items in a natural language is finite. Otherwise the recursive construction of interpretations follows the same steps as the recursive construction of the expressions themselves. We illustrate this first with an artificial language, Sentential Logic, and then with some of our small fragments of English.

### 8.1.4   A Basic Example of Compositionality

Our grammar Eng in Chapter 5 allows us to form coordinations of Ss using *and* and *or* (and with some modification, *neither ... nor ...*). Such syntactically complex Ss are called *boolean compounds* of the ones they are built from. *And, or, neither ... nor ...* and *not* are called *boolean connectives*.

Now in a given situation, the truth value of a boolean compound of Ss is uniquely determined by—is a function of— the truth values in that situation of the Ss it combined. That is, the boolean connectives are *truth functional*. In a situation in which $P$ is true and $Q$ is true we infer *Both P and Q* is true, *Either P or Q* is true, and *Neither P nor Q* is false. Many subordinate conjunctions that build an S from two others are not truth functional. Imagine a situation in which *John left the party early* and *The children were crying* are both true. The sentence *John left the party early because the children were crying* may still be either true or false. So its truth value is not determined by the truth of its component sentences. Thus *because* is not a truth functional connective. *Sentential Logic* is used by logicians and philosophers to study the meanings of boolean (truth functional) connectives. Below we present it explicitly as it illustrates in a simple form how we may define a language and compositionally interpret it. And as a result it provides a convenient vehicle for studying basic issues in both syntax and semantics.

## 8.2 Sentential Logic

The language SL of *Sentential Logic* (also called *Propositional Logic*) consists of denumerably many *atomic formulas* $P1, P2, \ldots$ closed under combinations with *and, or* and *not*. So for example $((P1$ and not $P5)$ or $(P5$ and not $P1))$ is an element of SL, whose members in general are called *formulas*. Here is a more precise definition. Recall that for $V$ a set, $V^*$ is the set of finite sequences of elements of $V$.

### 8.2.1 The Syntax of SL

**Definition 8.2.** $\text{AF} =_{df} \{\langle 'P', n \rangle \mid n \in \mathbb{N}\}$.

We usually write simply $P_n$ for $\langle 'P', n \rangle$. By '$P$' we just mean the letter $P$. Elements of AF are called *atomic formulas*.

**Definition 8.3.** $\text{V} =_{df} \text{AF} \cup \{\text{and}, \text{or}, \text{not}, ), (\}$

We define one unary function NEG on $\text{V}^*$ and two binary functions AND, OR on $\text{V}^*$ as follows (writing simply $uv$ for $u \frown v$).

**Definition 8.4.** $\text{NEG}(\varphi) = \text{not } \varphi, \text{AND}(\varphi, \psi) = (\varphi \text{ and } \psi)$, $\text{OR}(\varphi, \psi) = (\varphi \text{ or } \psi)$.

**Definition 8.5.** SL is the closure of AF under NEG, AND, and OR.

Thus SL is the set of strings that can be built starting with the atomic formulas and applying the NEG, AND, and OR functions any finite number of times. An explicit definition of this closure, on the model of our earlier one for $\text{Cat}_{\text{Eng}}$, is given below. Here (and elsewhere) we write $x, y \in A$ as a shorthand for "$x \in A$ and $y \in A$".

(17)    i. Set $\text{SL}_0 = \text{AF}$, and

   ii. for all natural numbers $n$,
   $\text{SL}_{n+1} = \text{SL}_n \cup \{\text{NEG}(\varphi) \mid \varphi \in \text{SL}_n\}$
   $\cup \{\text{AND}(\varphi, \psi) \mid \varphi, \psi \in \text{SL}_n\} \cup \{\text{OR}(\varphi, \psi) \mid \varphi, \psi \in \text{SL}_n\}$.

   iii. Then $\text{SL} =_{df} \{\tau \in \text{V}^* \mid \text{for some } n, \tau \in \text{SL}_n\}$.
   So $\text{SL} =_{df} \bigcup_{n \in \mathbb{N}} \text{SL}_n$.

Then SL provably has the following three basic properties:

**Theorem 8.1.**

   *a. $AF \subseteq SL$.*

   *b. SL is closed under NEG, AND, OR. That is, if $\varphi, \psi \in SL$ then $NEG(\varphi)$, $AND(\varphi, \psi)$ and $OR(\varphi, \psi)$ are in SL as well.*

   c. *If a set K includes all the atomic formulas and is closed under NEG, AND, and OR then SL ⊆ K. (This is what is meant by saying that SL is the* least *subset of V\* which includes the atomic formulas and is closed under NEG, AND, and OR).*

## Some abbreviations.

   i. We often write & instead of *and*.

   ii. Ss of the form $(\varphi \ \& \ \psi)$ are called *conjunctions*; $\varphi$ and $\psi$ are its *conjuncts*.
Ss of the form $(\varphi$ or $\psi)$ are called *disjunctions*; $\varphi$ and $\psi$ are its *disjuncts*.

   iii. For $\varphi, \psi \in$ SL we use $(\varphi \to \psi)$ to abbreviate ((not $\varphi$) or $\psi$). $(\varphi \to \psi)$ is called a *conditional* formula; $\varphi$ called its *antecedent* and $\psi$ its *consequent*.

   iv. Similarly we write $(\varphi \leftrightarrow \psi)$ to abbreviate $((\varphi \to \psi) \ \& \ (\psi \to \varphi))$. Formulas of the form $(\varphi \leftrightarrow \psi)$ are called *biconditionals*.

In what follows it will be useful to be able to refer to the atomic formulas which occur one or more times in a given formula $\varphi$. Here is an explicit recursive definition, one that illustrates the recursive format:

**Definition 8.6.** For all $\varphi, \psi \in$ SL,

   a. $\text{AF}(Pn) = \{Pn\}$ for all atomic formulas $Pn$,

   b. $\text{AF}(\text{NEG}(\varphi)) = \text{AF}(\varphi)$,

   c. $\text{AF}(\text{AND}(\varphi, \psi)) = \text{AF}(\varphi) \cup AF(\psi)$, and

   d. $\text{AF}(\text{OR}(\varphi, \psi)) = \text{AF}(\varphi) \cup AF(\psi)$.

$\text{AF}(\varphi)$ is the set of atomic formulas which occur in $\varphi$.

   AF here is a recursively defined function from SL into $\mathcal{P}(\text{SL})$, the power set of SL, since it associates with each formula of SL a set of formulas. That AF is *well defined* depends on the fact that NEG, AND, and OR are *unambiguous*. Imagine for example that there was a formula $\sigma$ such that $\sigma = NEG(\tau)$ for some $\tau \in$ SL and also that $\sigma = \text{OR}(\varphi, \psi)$ for some $\varphi, \psi \in$ SL. Then Definition 8.6 would say that $\text{AF}(\sigma) = \text{AF}(\tau)$ and also that $\text{AF}(\sigma) = \text{AF}(\varphi) \cup \text{AF}(\psi)$. Likely these two sets are not the same, so AF would not be a function, it would associate two different values with $\sigma$. But in fact this situation provably does not arise:

**Theorem 8.2.** *SL is syntactically unambiguous. That is, (a)–(c) below hold:*

a. *Each generating function NEG, AND, OR is one to one,*

b. *The ranges of any two of NEG, AND, OR are disjoint, and*

c. *AF and the range of any of NEG, AND, and OR are disjoint.*

Thus no formula gets into SL in more than one way. Here is a stepwise computation using Definition 8.6:

(18) $\mathrm{AF}((\mathrm{not}\ P2\ \mathrm{or}\ P3)\&(P3\ \mathrm{or}\ P4))$
$= \mathrm{AF}(\mathrm{not}\ P2\ \mathrm{or}\ P3) \cup \mathrm{AF}(P3\ \mathrm{or}\ P4)$
$= \mathrm{AF}(\mathrm{not}\ P2) \cup \mathrm{AF}(P3) \cup \mathrm{AF}(P3) \cup \mathrm{AF}(P4)$
$= \mathrm{AF}(P2) \cup \{P3\} \cup \{P3\} \cup \{P4\}$
$= \{P2\} \cup \{P3, P4\}$
$= \{P2, P3, P4\}$

**Exercise 8.2.** Compute stepwise each of the following:

a. $\mathrm{AF}(P5\ \mathrm{or}\ \mathrm{not}\ P5)$

b. $\mathrm{AF}(\mathrm{not}\ (P5\ \mathrm{or}\ P6))$

c. $\mathrm{AF}(P6 \leftrightarrow P6)$

d. $\mathrm{AF}((P1 \rightarrow P9)\ \mathrm{or}\ (P1 \rightarrow \mathrm{not}\ P9))$

(Replace the defined formulas here with the ones that define them.)

### 8.2.2  The Semantics of SL

To simplify notation in what follows consider the two element set $\{T, F\}$ whose elements we call *truth values*, with $T = $ true, and $F = $ false. This set is commonly noted $\{0, 1\}$ in the literature, with $0 = $ false and $1 = $ true, but here we stick with $\{T, F\}$ for mnemonic reasons. We define one unary function called *complement* noted $\neg$ on $\{T, F\}$ and two binary functions, *meet* $\wedge$ and *join* $\vee$ by giving their tables:

(19)  a.

| $X$ | $\neg X$ |
|---|---|
| $T$ | $F$ |
| $F$ | $T$ |

b.

| $X$ | $Y$ | $X \wedge Y$ | $X \vee Y$ |
|---|---|---|---|
| $T$ | $T$ | $T$ | $T$ |
| $T$ | $F$ | $F$ | $T$ |
| $F$ | $T$ | $F$ | $T$ |
| $F$ | $F$ | $F$ | $F$ |

If a formula $\varphi$ in our logic has truth value $X$ then its negation has truth value $\neg X$. And if formulas $\varphi$, $\psi$ have truth values $X$ and $Y$ respectively then their conjunction has truth value $(X \wedge Y)$ and their disjunction has truth value $(X \vee Y)$. More formally we define:

**Definition 8.7.** A *model* for SL is a function $v : \text{AF} \to \{T, F\}$. $v$ is often called a *valuation*.

**Definition 8.8.** For each model $v$ we define a function $v^*$ from SL into $\{T, F\}$ by setting:

    a. $v^*(Pn) = v(Pn)$, for all atomic formulas $Pn$,

    b. $v^*(\text{NEG}\varphi) = \neg(v^*(\varphi))$,

    c. $v^*(\text{AND}(\varphi, \psi)) = v^*(\varphi) \wedge v^*(\psi)$, and

    d. $v^*(\text{OR}(\varphi, \psi)) = v^*(\varphi) \vee v^*(\psi)$.

$v^*$ is called an *interpretation* of SL.

We note without argument that for each $v$, $v^*$ is a function, one which extends $v$. That is, $Dom(v) \subseteq Dom(v^*)$ and for all $\varphi \in Dom(v)$, $v^*(\varphi) = v(\varphi)$. Further, each function from SL into $\{T, F\}$ which satisfies conditions (b)–(d) extends some valuation $v$, that is, it is an interpretation of SL.

The informal idea behind this semantics is that the atomic formulas represent *independent* claims we can make about the world. If we are in a model in which $P5$ is true we have no predictability of the truth of any other atomic formula. $P7$ for example might be true or it might be false. That is, there are models $v$ in which $v(P5) = T$ and $v(P7) = T$ and other models $v'$ in which $v'(P5) = T$ and $v'(P7) = F$. However once we are given a model $v$—so we know the truth value of each atomic formula, then the truth values of the syntactically complex formulas are uniquely determined by the stipulations in (b)–(d).

We emphasize that our definition of interpretation is fully *compositional*. The interpretation (truth value) of a complex formula is uniquely determined by the interpretations (truth values) of the formulas it is built from.

A seemingly obvious property of SL is that the truth of a formula depends *only* on the truth of the atomic formulas which occur in it. Formally we have:

**Theorem 8.3** (The Coincidence Lemma). *For all $\varphi \in SL$ and all models $v$ and $u$, if $v(Pn) = u(Pn)$ for all atomic formulas occurring in $\varphi$ then $v^*(\varphi) = u^*(\varphi)$.*

*Proof.* By induction on formula complexity. The main idea is: we let $K$ be the set of formulas in SL for which the theorem holds. Then we show that $K$ contains all the atomic formulas and is closed under the functions AND, OR, and NEG. Then by Theorem 8.1c, SL $\subseteq K$, proving the theorem.

More explicitly now, set

$$K = \{\varphi \in \text{SL} \mid \text{for all models } u, v \text{ if } u(P) = v(P)$$
$$\text{for all } P \in \text{AF}(\varphi) \text{ then } u^*(\varphi) = v^*(\varphi)\}.$$

**Step 1:** All atomic formulas are in $K$. Let $Pm$ be an arbitrary atomic formula. Then $\text{AF}(Pm) = \{Pm\}$, so if $u, v$ are models that assign the same value to the elements of $\text{AF}(Pm)$ then, trivially, $u^*(Pm) = v^*(Pm)$ since $u^*(Pm) = u(Pm) = v(Pm) = v^*(Pm)$.

**Step 2:** Show that $K$ is closed under NEG. Let $\varphi \in K$, show that $\text{NEG}(\varphi) \in K$. Let $u, v$ be arbitrary models, assume they assign the same values to $Pn$ in $\text{AF}(\text{NEG}(\varphi))$. We must show that

$$u^*(\text{NEG}(\varphi)) = v^*(\text{NEG}(\varphi)).$$

But $\text{AF}(\text{NEG}(\varphi)) = \text{AF}(\varphi)$. Hence, by the induction hypothesis, $\varphi \in K$, so $u^*(\varphi) = v^*(\varphi)$. Therefore

$$u^*(\text{NEG}(\varphi)) = \neg u^*(\varphi) = \neg v^*(\varphi) = v^*(\text{NEG}(\varphi)).$$

**Step 3:** Show that $K$ is closed under AND. Let $\varphi, \psi \in K$. Show that $\text{AND}(\varphi, \psi) \in K$. Now $\text{AF}(\text{AND}(\varphi, \psi)) = \text{AF}(\varphi) \cup \text{AF}(\psi)$. So if $u$ and $v$ agree on all the $Pn$ in $\text{AF}(\text{AND}(\varphi, \psi))$ then they agree on the $Pn$ in $\text{AF}(\varphi)$ and on the $Pn$ in $\text{AF}(\psi)$. Thus by the induction hypothesis $u^*(\varphi) = v^*(\varphi)$ and $u^*(\psi) = v^*(\psi)$. So

$$u^*(\text{AND}(\varphi, \psi)) = u^*(\varphi) \wedge u^*(\psi) = v^*(\varphi) \wedge v^*(\psi) = v^*(\text{AND}(\varphi, \psi)).$$

**Step 4:** Show analogously to Step 3 that $K$ is closed under OR. Thus, since $K$ contains all the atomic formulas and is closed under NEG, AND, and OR, we infer that SL $\subseteq K$, proving the theorem.  □

**Terminology**   Many authors write *inductive hypothesis* where we have written *induction hypothesis*.

We turn now to the definition of *entailment* and related notions on SL.

**Definition 8.9.**

a. For $\varphi, \psi \in \mathrm{SL}$, $\varphi \models \psi$ (read: $\varphi$ *entails* $\psi$) iff for all models $v$ for SL, if $v^*(\varphi) = T$ then $v^*(\psi) = T$.
$\varphi \models \psi$ is often read "$\varphi$ logically implies $\psi$".

b. For all $K \subseteq \mathrm{SL}$, all $\varphi \in \mathrm{SL}$, $K \models \varphi$ iff for all models $v$,
if $v^*(\tau) = T$ for all $\tau \in K$ then $v^*(\varphi) = T$.

Note that Definition 8.9a is just the special case of Definition 8.9b where $K$ is the unit set $\{\varphi\}$. We normally write $\varphi \models \psi$ rather than $\{\varphi\} \models \psi$.

**Definition 8.10.** For $\varphi \in \mathrm{SL}$, $\varphi$ is *logically true* (*valid*, a *tautology*) iff for all models $v$, $v^*(\varphi) = T$. To say that $\varphi$ is logically true we write $\models \varphi$.

**Theorem 8.4.** *For $\varphi \in SL$, $\varphi$ is logically true iff $\emptyset \models \varphi$.*

The significance of Theorem 8.4 is that logical truth (validity) is definable in terms of entailment, so we don't have two independent semantic notions.

**Definition 8.11.** For $\varphi, \psi \in \mathrm{SL}$, $\varphi$ is *logically equivalent* to $\psi$, noted $\varphi \equiv \psi$, iff for all models $v$, $v^*(\varphi) = v^*(\psi)$.

**Theorem 8.5.** *For $\varphi, \psi \in SL$,*

a. $\varphi \equiv \psi$ iff $\varphi \models \psi$ and $\psi \models \varphi$,

b. $\varphi \equiv \psi$ iff $\models (\varphi \leftrightarrow \psi)$,

c. $\varphi \models \psi$ iff $\models (\varphi \rightarrow \psi)$.

From Theorem 8.5c we carefully distinguish $\models$ from $\rightarrow$. A conditional formula $(\varphi \rightarrow \psi)$ may be true in some interpretations and false in others. But $\varphi \models \psi$ is simply true or false. For example the formula $(P1 \rightarrow P3)$ is true in a model $v$ in which $v(P1) = F$ or $v(P1) = v(P3) = T$. But it is false in models $v'$ in which $v'(P1) = T$ and $v'(P3) = F$. In contrast $P1 \models P3$ is simply false, since it is not the case that $P3$ is interpreted as $T$ in every model in which $P1$ is interpreted as $T$. The models $v'$ just mentioned are examples.

Note that to prove a formula of the form $(\varphi \rightarrow \psi)$ in mathematical discourse it suffices to consider the case when $\varphi$ is true and then prove that $\psi$ is true. If $\varphi$ is false then $(\varphi \rightarrow \psi)$ is true no matter what truth value $\psi$ has.

**Equivalence Relations.** In Definition 8.11 we defined a semantic relation, *logical equivalence*, noted ≡, on the formulas of Sentential Logic. This relation is representative of a class of widely used relations in mathematical discourse called *equivalence relations*. Roughly, an equivalence relation $R$ defined on a set $A$ relates objects $x$ and $y$ in $A$ if they are identical in some respect or another. In the limit they may be identical in every respect, that is, they are the exact same object. Indeed, absolute equality $=$ is an equivalence relation. But the utility of equivalence relations lies in the fact that we can ignore certain differences between objects, as we did with ≡ above. If we are just interested in studying the entailments (logical consequences) that a formula may have then there is no need to distinguish between (not $P$ & not $Q$) on the one hand and not$(P$ or $Q)$ on the other, since they have the same entailments as they are logically equivalent (always have the same truth value). Formally we define a relation to be an equivalence relation as follows.

**Definition 8.12.** A binary relation $R$ on a set $A$ is an *equivalence relation* iff:

a. $R$ is reflexive (for all $x \in A$, $xRx$),

b. $R$ is symmetric (for all $x, y \in A$, $xRy \Rightarrow yRx$), and

c. $R$ is transitive (for all $x, y, z \in A$, $(xRy$ & $yRz) \Rightarrow xRz$).

**Exercise 8.3.**

a. State explicitly the three conditions that must be met for ≡ (the relation of logical equivalence defined above) to be an equivalence relation.

b. We define the equi-cardinality relation ≈ on $\mathcal{P}(\mathbb{N})$ by: $A \approx B$ iff there is a bijection from $A$ to $B$ (that is, $A$ and $B$ have the same cardinality). State explicitly the three things you must show to prove that ≈ is an equivalence relation. For each of these three say what justifies its truth.

c. Consider the isomorphism relation ≅ defined on the set of simple trees with nodes drawn from $\mathbb{N}$. Is ≅ an equivalence relation? If so, say why it is reflexive, symmetric, and transitive.

d. Which property of equivalence relations makes them distinct from partial order relations (such as $\leq$ in arithmetic, or $\subseteq$ on sets, or *dominates* on nodes of a tree)?

Given an equivalence relation $R$ on a set $A$, we may group equivalent objects together and, often, just study the behavior of these *equivalence classes*.

**Definition 8.13.** Given an equivalence relation $R$ and an object $x \in A$, we set $[x]_R = \{b \in A \mid xRb\}$. $[x]_R$ is called the *equivalence class of $x$ modulo $R$*.

When $R$ is clear from context we simply write $[x]$. $[x]$ is a subset of $A$ but it is never $\emptyset$. Why not?

**Theorem 8.6.** *For all $x, y \in A$, $[x] = [y]$ iff $xRy$.*

*Proof.* ($\Longrightarrow$) Let $[x] = [y]$. We must show that $xRy$. Since $x \in [x]$ because $xRx$ and $[x] = [y]$ we have that $x \in [y]$. So by the definition of $[y]$ it follows that $yRx$. Thus, because $R$ is symmetric we conclude that $xRy$

($\Longleftarrow$) Suppose $xRy$. We must show that $[x] = [y]$. Let $z$ be arbitrary in $[x]$. Then $xRz$, so $zRx$, whence by the transitivity of $R$ we have that $zRy$. Since $R$ is symmetric it follows that $yRz$, and so $z \in [y]$. Since $z$ was arbitrary, $[x] \subseteq [y]$. By analogous reasoning, $[y] \subseteq [x]$, so equality holds. $\square$

**Corollary 8.7.** *For $R$ an equivalence relation on $A$, $\{[x] \mid x \in A\}$ is a partition of $A$.*

A *partition* of a set $A$ is a collection of non-empty subsets of $A$ such that each element $x$ in $A$ is in exactly one of the subsets. So any two of the subsets are disjoint. The corollary follows immediately from Theorem 8.6 given that $[x]$ is never empty.

Returning to Sentential Logic again, observe first that the entailment relation $\models$ is reflexive since any formula entails itself. This relation is also transitive, but it is not antisymmetric, since for any formula $\varphi$, $\varphi \models$ not not $\varphi$ and conversely, but $\varphi$ and not not $\varphi$ are not the same formula. But consider now what happens when we take the corresponding relation on the equivalence classes of formulas.

**Definition 8.14.** For all formulas $\varphi, \psi$ in Sentential Logic, $[\varphi] \leq [\psi]$ iff $\varphi \models \psi$.

We purport here to define the relation $\leq$ on the set of equivalence classes of formulas (under the logical equivalence relation) in terms of the relation $\models$ on the formulas themselves. We must be careful in such cases. Suppose for example we could find some $\varphi' \in [\varphi]$ such that $\varphi'$ failed to entail some $\psi$ even though $\varphi$ did entail $\psi$. Then we would be claiming that $[\varphi] \leq [\psi]$ and $[\varphi] \not\leq [\psi]$, which is to say that the $\leq$ relation would not be well-defined. Fortunately this cannot happen, since $\varphi \models \psi$ means that every valuation that makes $\varphi$ true also makes $\psi$ true. And the valuations that make $\varphi$ true are exactly those that make $\varphi'$ true since they are logically equivalent. So in defining the $\leq$ relation as we did, we see that whether it holds or not does not depend on the choice of representative we pick from $[\varphi]$ (or from $[\psi]$).

Observe now that the $\leq$ relation is a partial order; in particular it is antisymmetric since if $[\varphi] \leq [\psi]$ then $\varphi \models \psi$. And if $[\psi] \leq [\varphi]$ then $\psi \models \varphi$, so $\varphi$ and $\psi$ are logically equivalent (if one could be true under some valuation in which the other was false the one would fail to entail the other). So once we have traded in the entailment relation on formulas for the $\leq$ relations on the equivalence classes of formulas we are then working with a familiar ordering relation. More about this order can be found in Chapter 9.

**Decidability.** Sentential Logic has the pleasing property that there is a general mechanical procedure (an *algorithm*) for deciding whether an arbitrary formula $\varphi$ is logically true or not. The procedure is called a *Decision Procedure* and SL is said to be *decidable*. Similarly there is a procedure for deciding whether arbitrary formulas $\varphi$, $\psi$ are logically equivalent, or whether one entails the other. The procedures all use truth tables, illustrated below.

Consider the formula $((P2 \ \& \ P5) \text{ or } (\text{not } P2 \ \& \ \text{not } P5))$. To test whether it is logically true we must evaluate its truth under all interpretations. But by the Coincidence Lemma we need only consider a model $v$ in so far as it assigns truth values to $P2$ and $P5$, the atomic formulas occurring in it. Any two interpretations which assign the same values to $P2$ and to $P5$ must assign the same value to the formula $((P2 \ \& \ P5) \text{ or } (\text{not } P2 \ \& \ \text{not } P5))$. Now there are just two ways we can assign truth values to $P2$, and for each of those there are two ways to assign truth values to $P5$. So there are a total of 4 combinations of truth values that $P2$ and $P5$ can take jointly. So let us list all cases, writing under each atomic formula the value we assign it and then computing the truth value of the entire formula by writing the truth value of a derived formula under the connective $(\&, \text{or}, \text{not})$ used to build it. Here is what this procedure yields in this case:

| (20) | $P2$ | $P5$ | $((P2$ | $\&$ | $P5)$ | or | $(\text{not}P2$ | $\&$ | $\text{not } P5))$ |
|---|---|---|---|---|---|---|---|---|---|
| | $T$ | $T$ | | $T$ | | $T$ | $F$ | $F$ | $F$ |
| | $T$ | $F$ | | $F$ | | $F$ | $F$ | $F$ | $T$ |
| | $F$ | $T$ | | $F$ | | $F$ | $T$ | $F$ | $F$ |
| | $F$ | $F$ | | $F$ | | $T$ | $T$ | $T$ | $T$ |

The first line in this truth table says that if $P2$ and $P5$ are both true then the entire formula is a disjunction of a true formula with a false one, and thus is true. The second line says that if $P2$ is interpreted as true and $P5$ as false then the entire formula is a disjunction of a false formula with a false one and thus is false. Lines 3 and 4 are computed similarly. Thus $((P2 \ \& \ P5)$ or $(\text{not } P2 \ \& \ \text{not } P5))$ is not logically true as it is not true under all assignments of truth values to the atomic formulas occurring in it. To show that it is not logically true it suffices to exhibit line 2 or line 3 in the truth table.

Generalizing, since any formula in SL is built from just finitely many atomic formulas (Theorem 8.5) we can decide the validity of any such formula by constructing a truth table.

Similarly to show that two formulas are not logically equivalent it suffices to illustrate one line of their truth table in which they have different values. If they have the same value for all lines then they are logically equivalent. And finally to show that some $\varphi$ entails some $\psi$ you must show that for each line of the truth table for $\varphi$ which makes it true, $\psi$ is also true in that case. To falsify the entailment claim it suffices to find one assignment of truth values to the atomic formulas of $\varphi$ which make $\varphi$ true but $\psi$ false.

**Exercise 8.4.** Establish the claims below by exhibiting an assignment of truth values to the atomic formulas in the left hand formula which make it true and the right hand formula false. We write $\nvDash$ for *does not entail*.

   a. $(\text{not } P4$ or $P7) \nvDash (\text{not } P7$ or $P4)$

   b. $((P4$ or $P7) \ \& \ (P8$ or $P7)) \nvDash (P4$ or $P8)$

   c. $((P1 \ \& \ P2)$ or $P3) \nvDash (P1 \ \& \ (P2$ or $P3))$

**Exercise 8.5.** For each pair of formulas below show that they are logically equivalent if they are and exhibit a line of their truth table at which they differ if they are not.

| | | | | |
|---|---|---|---|---|
| a. | i. | $((P \ \& \ Q)$ or $(\text{not } P \ \& \ \text{not } Q))$ | ii. | $(P \leftrightarrow Q)$ |
| b. | i. | $(P \rightarrow Q)$ | ii. | $(\text{not } Q \rightarrow \text{not } P)$ |
| c. | i. | $(P \ \& \ Q)$ | ii. | $(Q \ \& \ P)$ |
| d. | i. | $(P \rightarrow Q)$ | ii. | $((P \ \& \ Q) \leftrightarrow P)$ |
| e. | i. | not not $P$ | ii. | $P$ |
| f. | i. | $((P \ \& \ Q)$ or $P)$ | ii. | $P$ |
| g. | i. | $(P \ \& \ (Q$ or $R))$ | ii. | $((P \ \& \ Q)$ or $(P \ \& \ R))$ |

### 8.2.3 Some Reflections on the Syntax and Semantics of SL

**Syntax.** We first consider an easily established point which (1) illustrates how to prove claims about SL, and (2) may counteract a confusion students occasionally make.

**Theorem 8.8.** *For all $\varphi \in SL$, $AF(\varphi)$ is finite.*

(So SL itself is an infinite set, but each element of it is built from just a finite number of atomic formulas).

*Proof.* Set $K =_{df} \{\varphi \in SL \mid AF(\varphi) \text{ is finite}\}$.

(1) We show first that $AF \subseteq K$. That is, each atomic formula $Pn$ is in $K$. This is so since $AF(Pn) = \{Pn\}$ which has just one element and so is finite.

(2)   a. $K$ is closed under NEG.
        Suppose $\varphi \in K$. We must show that $NEG(\varphi) \in K$. But $AF(NEG(\varphi)) = AF(\varphi)$ and thus is finite since $\varphi \in K$ so $AF(\varphi)$ is finite.

      b. $K$ is closed under AND and OR.
        Let $\varphi, \psi \in K$. Show that $AND(\varphi, \psi) \in K$. $AF(AND(\varphi, \psi))$ $= AF(\varphi) \cup AF(\psi)$, which is finite since the union of two finite sets is finite (if the first has exactly $k$ elements and the second exactly $m$ then the union has at most $k + m$ and so is finite). That $AF(OR(\varphi, \psi))$ is finite is shown similarly.

So by Theorem 8.1 $SL \subseteq K$. And since $K \subseteq SL$ then $K = SL$, that is, each formula in SL contains just finitely many atomic formulas.  □

**The Syntactic Role of Parentheses: Polish Notation.** Let $\varphi, \psi$ and $\chi$ be formulas in SL. Then (21a,b) are different formulas, whose derivations may be represented by the trees in (22a,b).

(21)  a. $((\varphi \ \& \ \psi) \text{ or } \chi)$        b. $(\varphi \ \& \ (\psi \text{ or } \chi))$

(22)  a.                                           b.

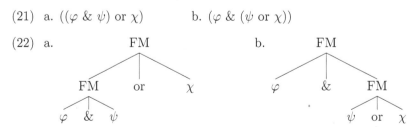

The structures in (22a,b) together with our definition of interpretation make it clear that formulas of these two forms are not logically equivalent. For example in any model in which $\varphi$ is interpreted as $F$ and $\chi$ as $T$ (22a) will be True as it is a disjunction of a true formula with something; in contrast (22b) will be False, as it is a conjunction of a false formula with something.

Now the constituency (derivational history) represented by (21a,b) is coded by the use of parentheses in (20a,b). And (finite) ordered labeled trees satisfying Exclusivity can always be represented this way (subscripting parentheses with labels when necessary). It is natural to wonder if we could simplify the linear representation by eliminating parentheses. The short answer is No. If we omitted all parentheses from (20a,b) then the resulting expressions would be identical and thus would be semantically ambiguous—possibly True, possibly False depending on how we thought the expression was built. However, a parenthesis-free notation is available if we write the boolean connectives (not, and, or, ...) always on the left of the formulas they combine with (called *Polish* notation; *reverse Polish* puts all the connectives after the formulas they combine with). The notation we used is *infix* notation, as the binary connectives occur between their arguments. Here is what the syntax of Polish SL would look like, given less formally than in our original syntax for SL. We use $A$ for *and*, $O$ for *or*, and $N$ for *not* and otherwise assume the abbreviations we gave for the infix notation.

(23)  $SL_{Pol}$ is the least set such that (a) and (b) below hold:

    a. $AF = \{P1, P2, \ldots\} \subseteq SL_{Pol}$.

    b. If $\varphi, \psi \in SL_{Pol}$ then $A\varphi\psi$, $O\varphi\psi$ and $N\varphi \in SL_{Pol}$.

Then (21a,b) translate from our infix notation to (24a,b) respectively in Polish:

(24)    a. $((\varphi \,\&\, \psi) \text{ or } \chi) =_{\text{trans}} OA\varphi\psi\chi$

        b. $(\varphi \,\&\, (\psi \text{ or } \chi)) =_{\text{trans}} A\varphi O\psi\chi$

**Exercise 8.6.** Draw the derivation trees for each of the Polish formulas in (24).

**Exercise 8.7.** Translate each of the formulas below from infix SL into $SL_{Pol}$.

    a. $(\varphi \to \psi)$               b. $((\text{not}\varphi \,\&\, \text{not } \psi) \text{ or } (\varphi \,\&\, \psi))$

    c. $((\varphi \,\&\, \text{not}\psi) \text{ or } (\text{not}\varphi \,\&\, \psi))$    d. $(\text{not}\varphi \leftrightarrow \text{not}\psi)$

**Exercise 8.8.** Translate the formulas below from $SL_{Pol}$ into infix notation.

   a. $NA\varphi\psi$        b. $AN\varphi\psi$

   c. $AAA\varphi\psi\chi\tau$     d. $OAO\varphi\psi\chi\tau$

   e. $O\varphi A\psi O\chi\tau$    f. $A\varphi O\psi A\chi\tau$

**Exercise 8.9.** Compare the derivation trees for (c) in Exercise 8.8 above with that for your translation into infix notation. Is there any difference between the trees in terms of degree of center embedding as opposed to left or right branching?

We should emphasize here that $SL_{Pol}$ is syntactically unambiguous. That is, the analogue of Theorem 8.2 given earlier holds when we set $AND(\varphi, \psi) = A\varphi\psi$, $NEG(\varphi) = N\varphi$, etc. So our recursive definition of interpretation in a model carries over as before.

Naively it seems natural to consider that it is the use of *matching* parentheses in infix notation that accounts for the non-ambiguity of its expressions. Matching parentheses conveniently identify the constituents we interpret in building an interpretation of an entire expression. And one of the (partial) automated checks of syntactic well-formedness is a parity check that rejects a string of symbols if the number of left and right parentheses is different. (They must be the same in any formula of SL since whenever a structure building rule (function) puts in a left parenthesis it also puts in a right one, and conversely.

**Exercise 8.10.**

   a. Show that the set of Polish SL formulas is context free.

   b. Show that the set of Polish SL formulas is not regular.

   c. Show the comparable claims for SL in infix notation.

Informed now about parenthesis-free notation fixing the boolean connectives formula initially, we can prove that a syntax like our infix one but which only introduces left parentheses also leads to unambiguous expressions. Here the AND an OR functions would be: $AND(\varphi, \psi) = (\varphi \ \& \ \psi$, and $OR(\varphi, \psi) = (\varphi \text{ or } \psi$. These expressions look odd, and to our knowledge no one has ever proposed a syntax for SL just like this, but it is easy to do so. In fact, suppose we modified these AND and OR functions so that they introduce their first argument with different shaped parentheses—say round ones for AND and square brackets for OR, thus:

(25)  a. AND$(\varphi, \psi) = (\varphi\psi$        b. OR$(\varphi, \psi) = [\varphi\psi$

Clearly this grammar is just a notational variant of Polish notation where the ( plays the role of $A$ and [ the role of $O$.

**Semantics**  Here we note some standard results concerning semantic properties of SL. In some cases explicit definitions and proofs would recapitulate a significant amount of mathematical logic. It is not our intent to do anything like that. Rather, what the reader should take from section is that given an explicit syntax and interpretation for SL we can in fact make interesting, non-obvious, *linguistic* claims about SL.

**Theorem 8.9** (Decidability). *SL is decidable.*

We have already noted that there is an algorithm (mechanical process) which will tell us for any $\varphi \in$ SL that it is true in all models if it is and that it isn't if it isn't. The algorithm essentially says that given any $\varphi$ write down its truth table and check that each line is $T$. In a similar way we can mechanically check whether $\varphi \models \psi$ or not (We just check whether (not$\varphi$ or $\psi$) is true in all models).

This decidability result should not however go to our heads. To be sure, given any $\varphi$ it contains only finitely many, say $n$, atomic formulas so we write them all down, compute all possible combinations of truth values and see if $\varphi$ is true in each (or that $\varphi$ is false in one of them). But a moment's reflection tells us that given $n$ atomic formulas, since each one is two valued (either $T$ or $F$) the number of "possible combinations" above is $2^n$. So the number of lines in the truth table quickly gets too large to realistically compute and the problem is said to be *intractable*. For example, for $n = 100$ the number of lines in the truth table, $2^{100}$, is a 31 digit number, much greater than the number of microseconds since the Big Bang; see Harel (1987).

**Theorem 8.10** (Compactness). *For $S \subseteq$ SL and $\varphi \in$ SL, $S \models \varphi$ iff there is a finite subset $K$ of $S$ such that $K \models \varphi$.*

Compactness tells us that in SL the truth of a claim $\varphi$ cannot depend on infinitely many premises. If $\varphi$ follows from some infinite set then there is a finite subset from which it follows. This theorem seems more mathematical than linguistic. But when we look at first order logical representations for English we see that it fails for English.

**Theorem 8.11** (Interpolation). *For $\varphi, \psi$ non-trivial (neither is true in all models or false in all models), if $\varphi \models \psi$ then there is a $\tau \in$ SL such that $\varphi \models \tau$ and $\tau \models \psi$ and $AF(\tau) \subseteq AF(\varphi) \cap AF(\psi)$.*

So if a formula non-trivially entails another that fact just depends on the interpretations of the atomic formulas they have in common (see Craig, 1957, van Dalen, 2004, p. 48).

We write $S \vdash \varphi$ to say that there is a proof of $\varphi$ from premises in $S$. Crucial here is that the notion *proof* is purely syntactic. A proof of $\varphi$ from premises $S$ is a finite sequence of formulas ending in $\varphi$, each of which is drawn from $S$ and marked as a premise or is derived by some syntactic rule from earlier formulas in the sequence.

There are just finitely many rules: Here are some candidates: *Conjunction Elimination*: If $(\psi \,\&\, \chi)$ is a line in a proof then we can add $\psi$ to the end; also we can add $\chi$ to the end. *Modus Ponens*: if $(\psi \to \chi)$ and $\psi$ are both lines in the proof then we can add $\chi$ to the proof. See Mates (1972) and Enderton (1972) for presentations of proof rules. There is an algorithm which tells us for any (finite) sequence of formulas whether it is a proof or not.

**Theorem 8.12** (Soundness). *For all $S \subseteq SL$, all $\varphi \in SL$, if $S \vdash \varphi$ then $S \models \varphi$.*

**Theorem 8.13** (Completeness). *For all $S \subseteq SL$, all $\varphi \in SL$, if $S \models \varphi$ then $S \vdash \varphi$.*

The completeness property of SL tells us that in SL we can syntactically characterize the entailment relation. Whenever $S \models \varphi$ there is a proof from $S$ to $\varphi$. Moreover the proof meets the soundness condition that whenever we syntactically derive some $\psi$ from some premises then those premises really entail $\psi$. Thus in SL we can syntactically characterize the entailment relation.

It is of interest to wonder whether natural languages have the four properties we have adduced in this section. In a later chapter we review these properties for a much richer logic, *First Order Predicate Logic*.

We now take our leave from Sentential Logic and consider the semantic interpretation of a small fragment of English, equipped now conceptually with what we expect a semantic interpretation to be.

## 8.3   Interpreting a Fragment of English

Interpreting predicates and their arguments is more challenging than merely interpreting compounds of Ss ($P_0$s). These are, as in Sentential Logic (SL), interpreted as members of the set $\{T, F\}$ with *and*, *or*, and *not* interpreted as meet ($\wedge$), join ($\vee$), and complement ($\neg$) as before. So the set $\{T, F\}$, of *truth values*, is one of the semantic primitives of a model. But now a model $\mathcal{M}$ contains a second primitive, a set

$E_\mathcal{M}$, called the *domain* (or *universe*) of the model and usually, for convenience not necessity, taken to be non-empty. Different models may have different universes, but the set $\{T, F\}$ is the same for all models (and commonly is not listed among the primitives, being "universally" assumed). Further, as with SL, a model must tell us how the syntactically underived (= lexical) expressions are interpreted. (Then the syntactically derived expressions are interpreted recursively beginning with the interpretations of the lexical ones). Formally:

**Definition 8.15.** A *model* $\mathcal{M}$ for a language $L$ is a pair $\langle E_\mathcal{M}, [\![\cdot]\!]_\mathcal{M} \rangle$, where $E_\mathcal{M}$ is a non-empty set and $[\![\cdot]\!]_\mathcal{M}$ is a function assigning an appropriate denotation to each expression of $L$. (The subscript $\mathcal{M}$ is often dropped when clear from context.)

$[\![\cdot]\!]_\mathcal{M}$ is recursively defined: denotations are assigned to lexical items with some freedom (as in SL in which the atomic formulas are interpreted as truth values freely), and then denotations are assigned compositionally to derived expressions as a function of the denotations assigned to their constituents. Thus a definition of $[\![\cdot]\!]_\mathcal{M}$ comes in two parts: (1) an explicit specification of the values it assigns to the finitely many lexical items, and (2) its recursive specification on derived expressions (which is what is meant by a *compositional* interpretation). We treat these in turn.

### 8.3.1 Interpreting Lexical Items

**Interpreting $P_n$s and DPs**      We assume a grammar like ENG in Chapter 5.

First we consider $P_n$s. $P_0$s, of which there are none in the lexicon, will be interpreted as truth values, elements of $\{T, F\}$, as in Sentential Logic. $P_1$s are interpreted as functions from $E$ into $\{T, F\}$. We shall call such functions *properties* (of individuals). Thus $[\![(\text{smiled}, P_1)]\!]$ maps each entity $b$ to a truth value, $[\![(\text{smiled}, P_1)]\!](b)$. In general for $C$ a category of expression in our grammar, we write $\text{DEN}_\mathcal{M}(C)$ for the set in which expressions of category $C$ denote in the model $\mathcal{M}$. Thus $\text{DEN}_\mathcal{M}(P_1) = [E_\mathcal{M} \to \{T, F\}]$. $P_2$s denote functions from $E_\mathcal{M}$ into $\text{DEN}_\mathcal{M}(P_1)$. And in general $P_{n+1}$s denote functions from $E_\mathcal{M}$ into $\text{DEN}_\mathcal{M}(P_n)$. (For simplicity we do not consider here $n$-place predicates for $n > 2$.)

**Two Notational Simplifications**

1. Possible expressions in $L(\text{ENG})$ are pairs $(s, C)$ for $s$ a phonological string and $C$ a category name. But we have in fact designed ENG so that no string $s$ has more than one category. So we can

write $s$ for $(s, C)$ unambiguously. For example we shall write simply *smiled* instead of (*smiled*, $P_1$).

2. Noting $[\![s]\!]_{\mathcal{M}}$ for the interpretation of an expression $s$ with the bracket notation $[\![\cdot]\!]_{\mathcal{M}}$ is standard but hard to read when the recursive interpretation of complex expressions is given. So often we note denotations of expressions in small caps instead. And when a model $\mathcal{M}$ is clear from context, we write simply SMILE for $[\![\text{smiled}]\!]_{\mathcal{M}}$, omitting also the past tense *-ed* on verbs as we have not interpreted tense marking (distinguishing *smiled* from *smiles* for example).

With these simplifications we turn to the interpretation of lexical DPs, such as *Dana*, *Bob*, etc. These are called *proper nouns* (or *names*) and classically interpreted as elements of $E$. Then a sentence such as *Bob laughed* is interpreted as whatever truth value the function denoted by LAUGH assigns to the entity denoted by BOB. But to interpret boolean compounds of DPs such as *Bob and some student*, *neither Bob nor any other student*, as well as more complex DPs such as *Every student but Bob*, it is natural to treat proper nouns and properly quantified DPs as denoting in the same big set. Here we treat them both as denoting functions from $P_{n+1}$ denotations to $P_n$ ones. So *Bob* has the same denotation in *Bob laughed*, *Bob and some student laughed* and *Kim praised Bob*.

The denotation of proper nouns at $P_1$ denotations – functions from $E$ into $P_0$ denotations, $\{T, F\}$, are called *individuals* and are defined below.

**Definition 8.16.** Given a model $(E, \{T, F\})$ we define for each $b \in E$, the function $I_b$ from $E$ into $\{T, F\}$ by: $I_b(p) = p(b)$, all $p \in \text{DEN}_{\mathcal{M}}(P_1)$. And more generally, for $p$ a $P_{n+1}$ denotation, a function from $E$ into $\text{DEN}_{\mathcal{M}}(P_n)$, $I_b(p) = p(b)$.

Note then that thinking of *John* as denoting an individual $I_j$ and *laugh* as LAUGH, $I_j(\text{LAUGH}) = \text{LAUGH}(j)$, just the classical analysis. Similarly *Mary criticized John* will be interpreted as $I_m(I_j(\text{CRITICIZE}))$, which computes to $I_m(\text{CRITICIZE}(j)) = (\text{CRITICIZE}(j))(m)$, again just the classical analysis. Of course we must say in general how expressions such as *John laughed* and *Mary criticized John* built by MERGE are interpreted:

**Interpreting Derived Expressions**     Interpreting expressions derived by MERGE is straightforward as one of it arguments (the first coordinate in our definition of MERGE in Chapter 5) is interpreted as a function and the other as one of its arguments. The entire expression is interpreted as the value of that function at that argument:

(26) $[\![\text{MERGE}(\sigma, \tau)]\!]_{\mathcal{M}} = [\![\sigma]\!]_{\mathcal{M}}([\![\tau]\!]_{\mathcal{M}})$

Thus in a model $\mathcal{M}$ in which *John* is interpreted as an individual $I_j$ and *laugh* as LAUGH, *John laughed* is interpreted as $I_j(\text{LAUGH})$, which by the definition of individual, is just $\text{LAUGH}(j)$. And *Mary criticized John* is interpreted as $I_m(I_j(\text{CRITICIZE}))$, which $= I_m(\text{CRITICIZE}(j)) = (\text{CRITICIZE}(j))(m)$, given that *Mary* is interpreted as $I_m$. So formally things work out as informally claimed above.

Let us illustrate a sample model $\mathcal{M}$. Suppose, to start, that our lexicon just contains *Adam, Ben, laughed, cried,* and *praised* in the obvious categories. Choose the universe $E$ of $\mathcal{M}$ to be $\{a, b, c\}$ and let $[\![\cdot]\!]$ be the following interpreting function (in streamlined notation):

(27) ADAM $= I_a$; BEN $= I_b$;

| $x$ | LAUGH$(x)$ | CRY$(x)$ | PRAISE$(a)(x)$ | PRAISE$(b)(x)$ | PRAISE$(c)(x)$ |
|---|---|---|---|---|---|
| $a$ | $T$ | $F$ | $F$ | $T$ | $T$ |
| $b$ | $T$ | $T$ | $F$ | $F$ | $T$ |
| $c$ | $F$ | $T$ | $T$ | $T$ | $T$ |

To show that *Ben cried* is true in this model we compute, stepwise:

(28) $\quad [\![\text{Ben cried}]\!]_{\mathcal{M}} \quad = \quad [\![\text{Ben}]\!]_{\mathcal{M}}([\![\text{cried}]\!]_{\mathcal{M}})$
$\qquad\qquad\qquad\quad = \quad \text{BEN}(\text{CRY})$
$\qquad\qquad\qquad\quad = \quad I_b(\text{CRY})$
$\qquad\qquad\qquad\quad = \quad \text{CRY}(b)$
$\qquad\qquad\qquad\quad = \quad T$

**Exercise 8.11.**

   a. Compute stepwise that *Adam cried* is false in this model.

   b. Compute stepwise the truth value of *Adam praised Ben* in this model.

   c. Compute stepwise the truth value of *Ben praised Adam* in this model.

A model $\mathcal{M}'$ may differ from $\mathcal{M}$ in two ways. One, its universe $E_{\mathcal{M}'}$ may be different. Perhaps $E_{\mathcal{M}'} = \{b, c, d, e\}$, or even $\mathbb{N}$. And two, even if $E_{\mathcal{M}'} = E_{\mathcal{M}}$, $\mathcal{M}'$ may differ from $\mathcal{M}$ in interpreting some of the lexical items differently. Perhaps $[\![\text{Adam}]\!]_{\mathcal{M}'} = b$, or $[\![\text{cry}]\!]_{\mathcal{M}'}(b) = F$, etc. We desire that a given expression may have different interpretations in different models: *Ben cried* may be true in some and false in others. This is what accounts for the strength of the entailment relation. $\varphi$ entails ($\models$) $\psi$ recall, iff $\psi$ is true in all models in which $\varphi$ is true.

**Interpreting Coordinations**     We begin, again, with the interpretation of $P_n$s. Conjunctions and disjunctions of $P_0$s are interpreted as in SL (Sentential Logic). So [[Bob laughed and Adam cried]] = [[Bob laughed]] $\wedge$ [[Adam cried]], and [[Bob laughed or Adam cried]] = [[Bob laughed]] $\vee$ [[Adam cried]] where $\wedge$ and $\vee$ are binary functions defined on truth values as before. Moreover this interpretation "lifts" pointwise to coordinations of $P_n$s generally.     Specifically, given a model, the interpretation of (*both*) *laughed and cried* is [LAUGH $\wedge$ CRY], that function from $E$ into $\{T, F\}$ which maps each $b \in E$ to LAUGH($b$) $\wedge$ CRY($b$), where of course LAUGH($b$) and CRY($b$) are truth values. Similarly (*either*) *laughed or cried* is interpreted as [LAUGH $\vee$ CRY], which maps each $b$ to LAUGH($b$) $\vee$ CRY($b$).

Similarly coordinations of $P_2$s are interpreted pointwise (meaning that the conjunction and disjunction of $P_2$s are interpreted as the meets and joins of their values at the "points", the elements of $E$.) So (*both*) *praised and criticized* is interpreted as PRAISE $\wedge$ CRITICIZE, which maps each $b$ in $E$ to PRAISE($b$) $\wedge$ CRITICIZE($b$), itself a meet of $P_1$ functions, as defined above. Similarly PRAISE $\vee$ CRITICIZE maps each $b$ to PRAISE($b$) $\vee$ CRITICIZE($b$).

**Exercise 8.12.** Using the model $\mathcal{M}$ above, compute stepwise

   a. Adam praised Ben and laughed.

   b. Ben praised Adam and cried.

Finally, coordinations of DPs behave similarly, that is, the conjuncts distribute over the predicates. Observe the following logical equivalences:

(29)     a. Both John and Bill smiled $\equiv$ John smiled and Bill smiled

   b. Either John or Bill praised Ed $\equiv$ John praised Ed or Bill praised Ed

The same pattern holds when the DPs are properly quantified (see below). So the (x, x$'$) pairs below are logically equivalent and we give a uniform semantics here to avoid repetition later.

(30)     a. Every student and some teacher objected.

   a$'$. Every student objected and some teacher objected.

    b.  Either every student or some teacher objected.

    b'.  Every student objected or some teacher objected.

A conjunction of DPs is interpreted as the meet of the interpretations of the conjuncts and dually for disjunctions and joins.

(31)  For $F, G \in \text{DEN}_{\mathcal{M}}(\text{DP})$, and $p \in \text{DEN}_{\mathcal{M}}(\text{P}_{n+1})$,
$(F \wedge G)(p) = F(p) \wedge G(p)$ and $(F \vee G)(p) = F(p) \vee G(p)$.

**Interpreting Quantified DPs**    Now enrich ENG with some common nouns, Ns, such as *student, teacher*, etc. as well as some Dets (DP/N), such as *every/all, some, no, at least two, the (one)*, and *most*. We treat Ns as denoting sets of entities (subsets of $E$):

(32)  For all models $\mathcal{M}$, $\text{DEN}_{\mathcal{M}}(\text{N}) = P(E_{\mathcal{M}})$, the power set of $E_{\mathcal{M}}$.

And of course different models, even with the same universe, may differ as to what set they assign to a given common noun. Many frequent Dets on the other hand have a fixed denotation over a given universe. We note that Det is a "slash" category, DP/N, and in general:

(33)  For $A/B$ a slash category, $\text{DEN}_E(A/B)$ is a set of functions from $\text{DEN}_E B$ into $\text{DEN}_E A$. (When $A$ and $B$ are $n$-tuples of categories for $n > 1$, $\text{DEN}_E(A/B)$ is a set of functions mapping each $\text{DEN}_E B_i$ into $\text{DEN}_E A_i$),

having category DP/N, Dets are interpreted by functions from N denotations, subsets of $E$, to DP denotations, functions from $\text{P}_{n+1}$ denotations to $\text{P}_n$ denotations. But *all* for example doesn't denote just any function in this set, its meaning is logically fixed at ALL, defined below (in two steps):

(34)  for all $A \subseteq E$, all $p \in \text{DEN}_{\mathcal{M}}(\text{P}_1)$, $\text{ALL}(A)(p) = T$ iff
$A \subseteq \{b \in E \mid p(b) = T\}$.

So *All poets daydream* is true (in $\mathcal{M}$) iff POET $\subseteq \{b \in E \mid \text{DAYDREAM}(b) = T\}$. Here are the denotations of some other Dets for the case where they combine with an N to build a DP that takes a $\text{P}_1$ as argument:

(35)    a.  $\text{SOME}(A)(p) = T$ iff $A \cap \{b \in E \mid p(b) = T\} \neq \emptyset$.

        b.  $\text{NO}(A)(p) = T$ iff $A \cap \{b \in E \mid p(b) = T\} = \emptyset$.

        c.  $(\text{AT LEAST TWO})(A)(p) = T$ iff $|A \cap \{b \in E \mid p(b) = T\}| \geq 2$.

        d.  $(\text{THE(ONE)})(A)(p) = T$ iff $|A| = 1$ and
$A \subseteq \{b \in E \mid p(b) = T\}$.

        e.  $\text{MOST}(A)(p) = T$ iff $2 \cdot |A \cap \{b \in E \mid p(b) = T\}| > |A|$.

These cases are straightforwardly given just using naive set theory. But these cases only tell us how to interpret quantified DPs when they function as subjects, that is, combine with $P_1$s to form $P_0$s.

How do we interpret them when they combine with $P_2$s to form $P_1$s, as in *Jan admires all poets*? This question has provoked much discussion in the semantics literature: Montague (1970b), van Benthem (1986, Ch 7), Heim and Kratzer (1998), Keenan (1989, 2016). But, curiously, the values DPs take at $P_{n+1}$ denotations are determined by their values at properties, possible $P_1$ denotations. To state this succinctly let us write $\textsc{admire}_b$ for that property that maps an entity $d$ to the truth value $\textsc{admire}(d)(b)$. Then we say that $(\textsc{all poet})$ maps $(\textsc{admire})$ to that $P_1$ denotation given by:

(36) $((\textsc{all poet})(\textsc{admire}))(b) = (\textsc{all poet})(\textsc{admire}_b)$

So it is clear that the value that $(\textsc{all poet})$ maps $\textsc{admire}$ to is determined by the values that $\textsc{all poet}$ takes at properties (functions from $E$ into $\{T, F\}$) since $\textsc{admire}_b$ is such a function. Then, interpreting *Jan* as $I_j$,

(37) $\llbracket$Jan admires all poets$\rrbracket = I_j((\textsc{all poet})(\textsc{admire}))$
$= ((\textsc{all poet})(\textsc{admire}))(j)$
$= (\textsc{all poet})(\textsc{admire}_j)$
$= T$ iff $\textsc{poet} \subseteq \{d \mid \textsc{admire}(d)(j) = T\}$
$= T$ iff for each $d \in \textsc{poet}, \textsc{admire}(d)(j) = T$.

Generalizing (slightly):

(38) The functions $F \in \textsc{den}_\mathcal{M}(\text{DP})$ are those that map $\textsc{den}_\mathcal{M}(P_{n+1})$ to $\textsc{den}_\mathcal{M}(P_n)$ satisfying the condition that for all $R \in \textsc{den}_\mathcal{M}(P_2)$, $F(R)$ is that element of $\textsc{den}_\mathcal{M}(P_1)$ given by: $F(R)(b) = F(R_b)$.

Using (38) we see that to define a $D$ in $\textsc{den}_\mathcal{M}(\text{DP})$ we need only give its values on the $P_1$ denotations, as we have in (38). (The same verbiage works for the case where $R$ is a $P_{n+1}$, interpreting $b$ now as an $n$-tuple of entities, not just a single entity (a one-tuple). So when $b = (b_1, \ldots, b_n)$, $R_b = \{d \in E \mid R(d)(b_1) \ldots (b_n) = T\}$.

**Exercise 8.13.** Compute $\llbracket$Jan admires $d$ poet$\rrbracket$, for each choice $d$ of quantifiers defined in (35). Here is the case for $d = \textsc{some}$ to illustrate the pattern:

$$\begin{aligned}
[\![\text{Jan admires some poet}]\!] &= I_j((\text{SOME POET})(\text{ADMIRE})) \\
&= ((\text{SOME POET})(\text{ADMIRE}))(j) \\
&= (\text{SOME POET})(\text{ADMIRE}_j) \\
&= (\text{SOME POET})(\{d \mid \text{ADMIRE}(d)(j)\}) \\
&= T \text{ iff } \text{POET} \cap \{d \mid \text{ADMIRE}(d)(j)\} \neq \emptyset.
\end{aligned}$$

Write out the cases for $d = $ NO, AT LEAST TWO, THE(ONE), and MOST.

**Exercise 8.14.** Below we exhibit a model $\mathcal{M}'$. You are asked to mark the sentences a. – q. as True or False in this model. You are not asked to provide the compositional interpretation of the sentences. We include a few negative Ss even though we have not formally included negation in our syntax of ENG (as yet).

$\mathcal{M}'$ the domain $E_{\mathcal{M}'} = \{a, b, c, d, e\}$

STUDENT $= \{a, c, e\}$ ADAM $= a$

ATHLETE $= \{a, b\}$ BARRY $= b$

| $x$ | LAUGH$(x)$ | CRY$(x)$ | FAINT$(x)$ | SMILE$(x)$ |
|---|---|---|---|---|
| $a$ | $T$ | $F$ | $T$ | $T$ |
| $b$ | $T$ | $T$ | $F$ | $T$ |
| $c$ | $F$ | $T$ | $F$ | $T$ |
| $d$ | $F$ | $T$ | $T$ | $F$ |
| $e$ | $T$ | $F$ | $F$ | $T$ |

a. Every athlete laughed.

b. Every athlete cried.

c. Every athlete both laughed and cried.

d. Some athlete both laughed and cried.

e. No athlete cried.

f. Exactly two students laughed.

g. Exactly two students fainted.

h. Exactly one athlete laughed.

i. Most students fainted.

j. Every athlete either laughed or cried.

k. Not every athlete either laughed or cried.

l. No student is an athlete.

m. Barry is Adam.

n. Barry fainted.

o. Some student is an athlete.

p. At least one student both laughed and cried.

q. Not every student smiled.

**Doubly quantified Ss** are directly interpreted by our DP semantics:

(39) [every child admires some poet] = (EVERY CHILD)((SOME POET)(ADMIRE))

$= \mathrm{T}$  iff  CHILD $\subseteq \{d \mid ((\text{SOME POET})(\text{ADMIRE}))(d) \neq \emptyset\}$

  iff  for all $x \in$ CHILD, $x \in \{d \mid ((\text{SOME POET})(\text{ADMIRE}))(d) \neq \emptyset\}$

  iff  for all $x \in$ CHILD, $((\text{SOME POET})(\text{ADMIRE}))(x) \neq \emptyset$

  iff  for all $x \in$ CHILD, $(\text{SOME POET})(\text{ADMIRE}_x) \neq \emptyset$

  iff  for all $x \in$ CHILD, POET $\cap \{b \mid \text{ADMIRE}(b)(x) = T\} \neq \emptyset$

  iff  for all $x \in$ CHILD, there is a $y \in$ POET, ADMIRE$(y)(x) = T$

So for Ss built from transitive verbs with both arguments quantified our semantics captures the subject wide scope (SWS) reading. Often enough this reading is the only one available, as (40a,b,c) or the clearly preferred one. See Keenan (2016) for overview support for this claim, and Steedman (2012) and Szabolcsi (1997) for much more thorough discussion of such scope ambiguities.

(40)  a. No student answered every question correctly.
$\neq$ Every question has the property that no student answered it correctly.

  b. Every pupil read more poems than plays.
$\neq$ More poems than plays are such that every pupil answered them correctly.

  c. Most of the pupils read exactly two plays.
$\neq$ Exactly two plays have the property that most of the pupils read them.

**Exercise 8.15.** As in (39) above compute the interpretation of *No pupil admires every poet.*

**A Common Alternative Notation.** Many texts treat $P_1$ denotations as subsets of the universe $E$. So on that approach we say that *John walks* is true in $\mathcal{M}$ iff the object *John* denotes in $\mathcal{M}$ is an element of the set *walks* denotes in $\mathcal{M}$. That approach is equivalent to the one given here. Each subset $K$ of $E$ corresponds to a function $\mathrm{CH}_K$ from $E$ into $\{T, F\}$ which maps to $T$ just the elements of $K$. $\mathrm{CH}_K$ is called the *characteristic function* of $K$. So for anything that can be said about $K$ on the set approach we can formulate a comparable statement about $\mathrm{CH}_K$ on the function approach. For example to say that some object $b \in K$ we just say $\mathrm{CH}_K(b) = T$. Conversely, the functions $g$ from $E$ into $\{T, F\}$ correspond one to one to the subsets of $E$. To each such $g$ we associate its *truth set* $T_g$, namely $\{x \in E \mid g(x) = T\}$. So any statement about $g$ can be translated into a statement about its truth set on the set approach.[3]

Similarly the set oriented approach interprets a $P_2$ as a set of ordered pairs of entities. But consider how we presented the function ADMIRE above. We interpret *Jan admires Mary* by $I_j(I_m(\text{ADMIRE}))$, where *admires Mary* denotes the $P_1$ function $I_m(\text{ADMIRE})$. The more traditional approach would interpret ADMIRE as a set of ordered pairs and *Jan admires Mary* is true iff $\langle j, m \rangle \in \text{ADMIRE}$. The two approaches are intertranslatable but we prefer our function approach as it assigns a denotation to *admires Mary*, which linguists agree does form a constituent. The ordered pair approach treats the subject-object pair as a unit, but they do not form a constituent.

**Lexical Constraints on Interpretations.** In natural languages it happens often that lexical items are not interpreted freely in their denotation set: the interpretation of one lexical item may constrain that of another. If one is built from another, e.g. *slowly* from *slow*, we expect by Compositionality that the interpretation of the derived expression is not independent of that of the one from which it is derived. But many morpho-syntactically independent lexical items also exhibit interpretative dependencies. For example:

(41) Antonyms:

    a. Kim is awake iff Kim is not asleep.

    b. Kim is male iff Kim is not female.

    c. The door is open iff it is not closed.

---

[3] In the next chapter we see that $[E \to \{T, F\}]$ and $P(E)$ are boolean lattices which are isomorphic, implying that they make the same sentences true.

Thus acceptable interpretations of lexical items for English cannot freely interpret *awake* and *asleep*, *male* and *female*, etc. Treating them as $P_1$s for simplicity here we must require of interpretations in a model that *meaning postulates* like those in (42) hold:

(42)  For all $x \in E_{\mathcal{M}}$,

    a.  if $[\![\text{alive}]\!]_{\mathcal{M}}(x) = T$ then $[\![\text{dead}]\!]_{\mathcal{M}}(x) = F$, and

    b.  if $[\![\text{male}]\!]_{\mathcal{M}}(x) = T$ then $[\![\text{female}]\!]_{\mathcal{M}}(x) = F$, and

    c.  if $[\![\text{open}]\!]_{\mathcal{M}}(x) = T$ then $[\![\text{closed}]\!]_{\mathcal{M}}(x) = F$.

The study of these interpretative dependencies is part of *Lexical Semantics*. It covers much more than simple antonyms. Consider for example that *kill* and *dead* are not interpretatively independent: If $x$ *killed* $y$ then $y$ *is dead*. In our formalism we require:

(43)  For all models $\mathcal{M}$, if $[\![\text{kill}]\!]_{\mathcal{M}}(y)(x)$ then $[\![\text{dead}]\!]_{\mathcal{M}}(y) = T$.

Finally, while often we have considerable freedom in deciding what element of its denotation set a given lexical item denotes sometimes the denotation is fixed, meaning we have no freedom at all. This is often the case for Determiner denotations, as we have seen. And at the lower level of $P_1$ and $P_2$ denotations we have a few candidates. For example we might require that:

(44)  For all models $\mathcal{M}$, all $x \in E$, $[\![\text{exist}]\!]_{\mathcal{M}}(x) = T$.

Similarly among the $P_2$s we find that *is* is not freely interpreted. For example, usually a $P_2$ does not require that its two NP arguments denote the same entity. While it is quite possible for someone to praise himself, typically an assertion of *John praised Bill* invites the inference that *John* and *Bill* are different people, and in any event they are certainly not required to be the same person. But *is* combines with two NPs to form a sentence and *John is Bill* precisely asserts that *John* and *Bill* are the same individual and doesn't assert anything further. So we might reasonably require of interpretations of English that

(45)  For all models $\mathcal{M}$, $[\![\text{is}]\!]_{\mathcal{M}}(y)(x) = T$ iff $x = y$.

This will yield the correct result for *John is Bill*. It also yields correct results for *John is a student* and *John is no student*. For most choices of quantified DP however Ss built from *is* are bizarre (though interpretable). *John is every student* implies that there is just one student, John. *John is exactly two students* is necessarily false, etc.

Lastly here, and curiously, it seems that $P_3$ present no "logical" members analogous to *exists* among the $P_1$s or *is* (*be*) among the $P_2$s. The presence of an underived verb meaning *give* is quite general (?universal) across languages so the category $P_3$ is universally available. Yet no language to our knowledge has a $P_3$ *blik* where *Blik(Dana,Kim,Robin)* would be true iff Dana = Kim = Robin. We return now to models of $\mathcal{L}$(Eng).

**Interpreting Modifiers.** In exercises we added two types of predicate modifiers to ENG: manner adverbs such as *joyfully* and *tactfully* of category $P_1/P_1$, and adjectives such as *tall* and *clever*, of category N/N.

**Interpreting Predicate Modifiers.** By (33) manner adverbs are interpreted by functions from $P_1$ denotations to $P_1$ denotations. These functions are chosen from the restricting ones (see Keenan and Faltz, 1985) which guarantees the basic entailment relation illustrated in (4). To define this notion we observe first that the set of possible $P_1$ denotations in a model $\mathcal{M}$, namely $[E_\mathcal{M} \to \{T, F\}]$, possesses a natural partial order, which we note $\leq$ and define by:

**Definition 8.17.** For all $p, q \in [E_\mathcal{M} \to \{T, F\}]$, $p \leq q$ iff for all $b \in E_\mathcal{M}$, if $p(b) = T$ then $q(b) = T$.

**Theorem 8.14.** $\leq$ *as defined above is a reflexive partial order.*

*Proof.* Clearly $p \leq p$, since if $p(b) = T$ then, trivially, $p(b) = T$. Regarding transitivity, assume that $p \leq q$ and $q \leq r$. We must show that $p \leq r$. For $b$ arbitrary, suppose $p(b) = T$. Then $q(b) = T$ since $p \leq q$, and thus, since $q \leq r$, $r(b) = T$, which is what we desired to show. Regarding antisymmetry suppose $p \leq q$ and $q \leq p$. We must show that $p = q$. We know that $p$ and $q$ are functions with the same domain and codomain, so it suffices to show that they assign each $b \in E_\mathcal{M}$ the same truth value. For $b$ arbitrary, suppose first that $p(b) = T$. Then $q(b) = T$ since $p \leq q$. So they have the same value in this case. Suppose now that $p(b) = F$. Then $q(b) = F$, otherwise $q(b) = T$, whence $p(b) = T$, contrary to assumption, since $q \leq p$. This covers all the cases, so $p$ and $q$ are the same function, that is, $p = q$. □

**Definition 8.18.** Let $(A, \leq)$ be an arbitrary partially ordered set (poset). That is, $A$ is a set and $\leq$ is a partial order on $A$. Then a function $f$ from $A$ into $A$ is *restricting* iff for all $p \in A$, $f(p) \leq p$.

**Exercise 8.16.** Let $A$ be a set. Then $(\mathcal{P}(A), \subseteq)$ is a poset.

a. Let $B$ be a subset of $A$. Define $f_B$ from $\mathcal{P}(A)$ to $\mathcal{P}(A)$ by setting: $f_B(K) = K \cap B$. Prove that $f_B$ is restricting.

b. Let $b \in A$. Define $f_b$ from $\mathcal{P}(A)$ to $\mathcal{P}(A)$ by: $f_b(K) = K - \{b\}$. Prove that $f_b$ is restricting.

Returning now to $P_1$ modifiers, we require of interpretations $[\![\cdot]\!]_\mathcal{M}$ that

(46) For all models $\mathcal{M}$, for all $(s, P_1/P_1)$ in $\text{Lex}_{\text{Eng}}$, $[\![(s, P_1/P_1)]\!]_\mathcal{M}$ is a restricting function (from $[E_\mathcal{M} \to \{T, F\}]$ into $[E_\mathcal{M} \to \{T, F\}]$).

Imposing condition (46) on interpretations does guarantee the entailment facts in (4):

(47) Suppose that Kim laughed joyfully. We show that it follows that Kim laughed. Let $\mathcal{M}$ be arbitrary, and using our streamlined notation, let $\text{KIM} = I_k$, for some $k \in E_\mathcal{M}$. Then,

$$
\begin{aligned}
(\text{kim laughed joyfully})_\mathcal{M} &= \text{KIM}(\text{LAUGHED JOYFULLY}) \\
&= I_k(\text{LAUGHED JOYFULLY}) \\
&= (\text{LAUGHED JOYFULLY})(k) \\
&= \text{JOYFULLY}(\text{LAUGH})(k) \\
&\leq \text{LAUGH}(k) \\
&= I_k(\text{LAUGH}) \\
&= (\text{kim laughed})_\mathcal{M}
\end{aligned}
$$

Thus if the first line $= T$ so does the last, proving the entailment.

In a richer fragment of English than that of $\mathcal{L}(\text{Eng})$ we might include $P_1$ modifiers that are not restricting, though the examples we are aware of all seem to introduce other complications which lie well beyond the scope of this introduction. Still here are a few candidates. Consider *almost* and *nearly*, as they occur in (48).

(48) a. Kim almost failed the exam.    b. John nearly fell off his chair.

Clearly these items are not restricting: (48a) does not entail that Kim failed the exam. Indeed it rather suggests that Kim didn't fail. Similarly (48b) does not entail that John fell off his chair. So if we treat *almost* and *nearly* as $P_1$ modifiers they will not denote restricting functions. Syntactically however these expressions differ somewhat from manner adverbs—they naturally occur before the predicate, not after (*??Kim laughed almost, ??John fell off his chair nearly*) and they seem to assume a much deeper analysis of $P_1$s than we have offered so far. Namely they introduce a notion of process, whereby an action can be partially but not totally completed. So *Kim almost failed the exam* suggests that Kim took the exam and received a grade that was just good enough to pass.

Another candidate class of non-restricting $P_1$ modifiers are words like *apparently* and *possibly*, as in (49).

(49) a. Gore apparently won the election.
  b. John possibly ran out of bounds.

Apparently (possibly) winning an election does not entail winning it, so these "-ly" adverbs are not restricting. But like *almost* and *nearly* they don't pattern positionally with the manner adverbs.

**Interpreting Noun Modifiers.** Since nouns such as (student, N) are interpreted as subsets of the universe $E_{\mathcal{M}}$, we infer from (33) that noun modifiers, of category N/N, are interpreted by functions from $P(E_{\mathcal{M}})$ into $P(E_{\mathcal{M}})$. And since a power set is partially ordered by $\subseteq$ it makes sense to ask if noun modifiers, like $P_1$ modifiers, are interpreted by restricting functions. And in basic cases they are. A clever student is a student, a female lawyer is a lawyer, etc. So, analogous to (46) we impose the following condition on interpretations in a model:

(50) For all models $\mathcal{M}$, all lexical items $(s, \text{N/N})$, $[\![(s, \text{N/N})]\!]_{\mathcal{M}}$ is a restricting function from $\mathcal{P}(E_{\mathcal{M}})$ to $\mathcal{P}(E_{\mathcal{M}})$.

This condition on interpretations accounts for facts such as those in (51) once expressions of the form Det + N are interpreted:

(51) *Every clever student is a student* is true in all models $\mathcal{M}$; so is *If Kim is a female lawyer then Kim is a lawyer.*

## A Concluding Speculation

Treating the sequence of $n$-place predicates as a single object (the argument of DPs) is somewhat novel. It is natural to wonder whether there are other structure building operations which avail themselves of this generalization. Here are a few prima facie plausible suggestions.

**Locative PPs as $P_n$ Modifiers** (Keenan, 1981; Keenan and Faltz, 1985). Consider the entailment paradigms in (52)–(55) below. In all cases the source locative *from the attic* predicates a location of one or another argument, the subject in (52a), whence the entailment of (52b). But in (53) it is the object argument and not the subject which the location is predicated of.

(52) a. John sang / shouted / fell from the attic.

  b. $\models$ John was in the attic.

(53) a. John took /removed / withdrew the trunk from the attic.

  b. $\models$ The trunk was in the attic.

  c. $\not\models$ John was in the attic.

These data can be accounted for if we treat *from the attic* as combining with either a $P_1$ or a $P_2$ and predicating location of its argument. In (54) we just treat *from the attic* as combining with the complex $P_1$ *watched Bill* (*attacked Bill*, etc.). So the PP is sensitive to the type of $P_2$; it can tell the difference between *take, remove*, etc. on the one hand and *watch, attack*, etc. on the other.

(54) a. John watched / attacked / studied Bill from the attic.

  b. $\models$ John was in the attic.

  c. $\not\models$ Bill was in the attic.

And finally, in (55) we can represent the ambiguity according as *from the attic* combines with the $P_2$ *shoot, grab*, etc. thus predicating of Bill, or it combines with the complex $P_1$ *shot Bill, grabbed Bill*, etc. predicating of its subject John.

(55) John shot / grabbed / called Bill from the attic.
  (Ambiguous according as John or Bill was in the attic. If it was Bill then he is understood to have moved or be intended to move from the attic).

**Passives.** A variety of languages present a strict morphological passive formed by affixing the active form of the verb (see Keenan and Dryer, 2007). The derived, passive, predicate has one fewer arguments than the active one it is built from. In the most widely cited cases the active verb is a $P_2$ and the passive one a $P_1$. However languages which have such passives—Latin, Turkish, Kinyarwanda (and Eastern Bantu quite generally) also always allow passive morphology on $P_3$s forming $P_2$s. So if a language can say *The door was opened* it can also say either

*Sue was given the key* or *The key was given to Sue* (and perhaps both). Less well known is that in some of these languages passive morphology also applies to $P_1$s creating $P_0$s. Turkish (Perlmutter and Postal, 1983c, Özkaragöz, 1986), and Latin are examples. (In Turkish the passive suffix is *-ın* following laterals, *-n* after vowel-final stems, and *-ıl* elsewhere. Vowels exhibit front-back harmony surfacing as *-ül* or *-ün*.)

(56) Turkish:

    a. Active $P_2$:

        *Hasan   bavul+u      açtı*
        Hasan   suitcase+acc  open+past
        'Hasan opened the suitcase.'

    b. Passive $P_2 \Rightarrow P_1$:

        *Bavul    (Hasan   tarafından)   aç-ıl-tı*
        suitcase  (Hasan   by)          open+pass+past
        'The suitcase was opened (by Hasan).'

    c. Passive $P_1 \Rightarrow P_0$:

        *Burada   düş-ül-ür*
        here       fall-pass-aorist
        'Here one falls.'

    d. Passive twice: $P_2 \Rightarrow P_0$:

        *Bu   oda-da      döv-ül-ün-ür*
        this   room-loc   hit-pass-pass-aorist
        'One is beaten (by one) in this room.'

**Causatives** It is generally recognized (Comrie, 1985) that there are languages with a causative affix that derives $P_2$s from $P_1$s, and often also applies to $P_2$s to derive $P_3$s. (57) and (58) illustrate these ordinary cases from Malagasy (Austronesian). It is less common but still attested that a given causative affix may iterate at least once, deriving a $P_3$ from a $P_1$. (59) from Tsez (Daghestanian; Comrie, 2000) is illustrative.

(57)    a. *Mihomehy  izy     ireo*
          laugh      3nom  dem+pl
          'They are laughing.'

        b. *Mampihomehy  azy    ireo    aho*
          make+laugh    3acc  dem+pl  1s.nom
          'I am making them laugh.'

(58)   a. *manenjika   ny   ankizy   Rabe*
        chase        the   children   Rabe
        'Rabe is chasing the children.'

      b. *mampanenjika   an-dRabe   ny   ankizy   aho*
        make+chase      acc-Rabe   the   children   1s.nom
        'I am making Rabe chase the children.'

(59)   *učitel-ā       uži-q      kidb-eq     kec'*
      teacher-erg   boy-poss   girl-poss   song-abs
      *q'aλi-r-er-si*
      sing-caus-caus-past+witnessed
      'The teacher made the boy make the girl sing a song.'

We turn now to a generalized treatment of the boolean connectives and the surprisingly extensive role played by boolean lattices in natural language semantics.

# 9

---

# Semantics II: Coordination, Negation and Lattices

This chapter provides a unified interpretation for expressions built from the boolean connectives *(both) and, (either) or, neither nor*. This task is challenging since these connectives are properly *polymorphic*: they combine with expressions in almost any (content) category to form further expressions in that category. We provide a semantic basis for polymorphism and speculate on a deeper explanation for it. We first review (at the risk of repetition) the extensive variety of categories which host coordination:

(1)   $P_0$ (Sentence) Coordination:

    a. Either John came early or Mary stayed late.

    b. Neither did John come early nor did Mary stay late.

    c. Kim insulted Dana and Dana insulted Kim.

(2)   $P_1$ Coordination:

    a. Kim bought a puppy and either laughed or cried.

    b. He neither laughed nor cried.

(3)   $P_2$ Coordination:

    a. Kim either praised or criticized each student.

    b. Kim neither praised nor criticized each student.

(4)   $P_3$ Coordination:

    a. Jim either gave or sold Mary his watch.

    b. She neither showed nor handed me the jewels.

(5)   CP (Complementizer Phrase) Coordination:

   a. Kim believes either that there is life on Mars or that there isn't (life on Mars).

   b. Ted thinks (both) that the election was rigged and that the state is corrupt.

(6)   DP Coordination:

   a. Most poets and all musicians daydream often.

   b. Either Kim or some student insulted every teacher.

   c. Kim interviewed half the male candidates and all the female ones.

   d. Neither every student nor every teacher attended the meeting.

(7)   Det Coordination:

   a. Most but not all students read the Times.

   b. John interviewed either exactly two or exactly three candidates.

(8)   AdvP (Adverb Phrase) Coordination:

   a. John drives rapidly and recklessly.

   b. He drives neither rapidly nor recklessly.

   c. He works slowly but not carefully.

(9)   Preposition Coordination:

   a. She lives neither in nor near New York City.

   b. The water was flowing over, under and around the car.

(10)  PP (Prepositional Phrase) Coordination:

   a. He was either at the office or on the train when the accident occurred.

   b. He works with Martha and with Bill but not with Ann.

(11)  AP (Adjective Phrase) Coordination:

   a. No intelligent or industrious student.

   b. An attractive but not very well built house.

**Question** Do these diverse uses of *and* (*or, neither... nor...* ) have anything semantic in common? Is there any reason to expect boolean connectives to be polymorphic?

For example, surely the meaning of *or* when it combines P$_2$s is not completely different from its meaning when it combines DPs, etc. Our task in this chapter is to show just what the different usages have in common, answering both parts of the query and exhibiting a non-obvious, possibly deep, generalization about natural language.

## 9.1 Coordination: Syntax

Here is essentially the coordination rule we add to the grammar of the previous chapter.

(12)  Coord :

$$(s, \mathrm{Conj})(t, C)(u, C) \longrightarrow \begin{cases} (\mathrm{both} \frown t \frown s \frown u, C) & \text{if } s = \text{and} \\ (\mathrm{either} \frown t \frown s \frown u, C) & \text{if } s = \text{or} \\ (\mathrm{neither} \frown t \frown s \frown u, C) & \text{if } s = \text{nor,} \end{cases}$$

where $C$ is any of the categories in (1–11), henceforth called *coordinable* categories.

Here is a sample derivation of an expression in standard tree form.

(13)

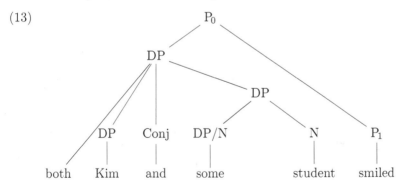

In general we do not need to mark which rules applied as that information is recoverable: the rules (structure building functions) of Eng have the property that if a rule $F$ maps a tuple of expressions to an expression $u$ then $F$ is the only rule that maps that tuple to $u$.

**Remarks on Syntax.**

1. *both, either,* and *neither* are not assigned categories on this syntax; they are introduced *syncategorematically* by the rules.

2. We add (himself, P$_1$/P$_2$) and (herself, P$_1$/P$_2$) to Lex$_{\mathrm{Eng}}$.

**Exercise 9.1.** Provide syntactic analysis trees for each of the following.

a. Either Kim or Sasha laughed.

b. Dana criticized both herself and every teacher.

**A typological regularity.** In examples we often omit *both* and *either* for simplicity. But a two part expression of coordination is not uncommon; often we just repeat the conjunction, as in Russian and French *et Jean et Marie* "and John and Mary", *ou Jean ou Marie* "or John or Mary", and *ni Jean ni Marie* "neither John nor Mary". This is the normal order in V-initial and SVO languages. In V-final languages the order is postpositional: *John-and Mary-and*, as in (14) from Tamil (Corbett, 1991, p. 269).

(14)  *raaman-um    murukan-um    va-nt-aaka*
      Raman-and    Murugan-and   come+past+3.pl.rational
      'Raman and Murugan came.'

**Exercise 9.2.** The subject DP in *Mary and Sue or Martha can read Greek* is logically ambiguous. Using *both* and *either*, exhibit two DPs each of which unambiguously represents a different interpretation of the subject DP. Describe in words a situation in which one of the Ss they build is true and the other false.

## 9.2   Coordination: Semantics

Here we provide an answer to our initial Question by showing that the sets in which expressions in coordinable categories denote are ones with a particular kind of partial order, a *(Boolean) lattice* order. And the core generalization we seek is that no matter what the category of expression coordinated, a conjunction of expressions denotes the *greatest lower bound* of the denotations of its conjuncts, and a disjunction of expressions denotes the *least upper bound* of its disjuncts. So *and* is a greatest lower bound operator, *or* a least upper bound operator. We now define these notions.

**Definition 9.1.** For $(L, \leq)$ a poset ($L$ always assumed non-empty), then for $x \in L$ and $K \subseteq L$,

a.  i. $x$ is a *lower bound* (lb) for $K$ iff for all $y \in K$, $x \leq y$.

   ii. $x$ is a *greatest lower bound* (glb) for $K$ iff $x$ is a lb for $K$ and for all lb's $y$ for $K$, $y \leq x$.

b.  i. $x$ is an *upper bound* (ub) for $K$ iff for all $y \in K$, $y \leq x$.

   ii. $x$ is a *least upper bound* (lub) for $K$ iff $x$ is an ub for $K$ and for all ub's $y$ for $K$, $x \leq y$.

**Proposition 9.1.** *If a subset $K$ of a poset has glb it has just one.*

*Proof.* Let $x$ and $x'$ be glb's for $K$. Then they are both lb's for $K$ and $x \leq x'$ since $x'$ is a greatest lower bound. Similarly since $x$ is a glb we have that $\bar{x}' \leq x$. So by antisymmetry, $x = x'$. □

**Notation** If $K$ has a glb it is noted $\bigwedge K$, read as "meet $K$" or the *infimum* (inf) of $K$. $\bigwedge \{x, y\}$ is usually written $(x \wedge y)$, read as "$x$ meet $y$". Note: $(x \wedge y)$ is an element of the poset; trivially $(x \wedge y) \leq x$ since $(x \wedge y)$ is a lb for $\{x, y\}$.

**Exercise 9.3.** Prove that if a subset $K$ of a poset has a lub it is unique (i.e. it has just one).

**Notation** If $K$ has a lub it is noted $\bigvee K$ and read "join $K$" or the *supremum* (sup) of $K$. $\bigvee \{x, y\}$ is usually written $(x \vee y)$, read as "$x$ join $y$".

**Two important logical abbreviations.** Expressions such as "For all $x \in A, \varphi$", as in the right hand side of Definition 9.1a-i and b-i, are short for "For all $x$, if $x \in A$ then $\varphi$". Thus every element $x$ of the poset $L$ above is a lower bound for $\emptyset$ since this just requires that for all $y \in \emptyset$, $x \leq y$. That is, "for all $y$, if $y \in \emptyset$ then $x \leq y$" is true, since for each $y$ the antecedent $y \in \emptyset$ is false, so the if-then claim is (vacuously) true. In contrast, when we say "for some $x \in A, \varphi$" we are stating a conjunction not a conditional claim. So a claim of the form "For some $x \in \emptyset, \varphi$" means "There is an $x \in \emptyset$ and $\varphi$" and this claim is false, no matter what sentence $\varphi$ is, since the first conjunct, $x \in \emptyset$, is false.

**Definition 9.2.** A *lattice* is a partially ordered set $(L, \leq)$ which satisfies: for all $x, y \in L$, $\{x, y\}$ has a greatest lower bound and $\{x, y\}$ has a least upper bound.

These conditions may be given by saying "for all $x, y \in L$, $x \wedge y$ and $x \vee y$ exist".

Small lattices are often represented by their Hasse (pronounced: "Hassuh") diagrams, as (15a–d) below. In such diagrams a point (node, vertex) $x$ is understood to bear the lattice order $\leq$ to a point $y$ iff either $x$ is $y$ or you can move up from $x$ along edges and get to $y$. (15a) is called the *diamond* lattice, (15b) a *chain* lattice, (15c) the *pentagon* lattice, and (15d) is, up to isomorphism, a power set lattice.

(15) a.      b.      c.      d.

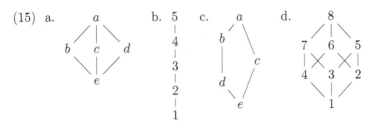

**Exercise 9.4.** Compute the meets and joins for the lattices as indicated

(15a) i. $(b \wedge d)$    ii. $(a \wedge c)$    iii. $b \wedge (c \wedge d)$    iv. $\bigvee \{e, b, c, d\}$

(15b) i. $(4 \wedge 4)$    ii. $\bigwedge \{3\}$    iii. $2 \vee \bigwedge \{5, 3, 4\}$    iv. $((5 \vee 4) \vee 3) \vee 4$

(15c) i. $b \wedge (d \vee c)$    ii. $(e \vee c) \wedge d$    iii. $(d \vee c \vee b) \wedge d$    iv. $\bigvee \emptyset$

(15d) i. $8 \wedge 6 \wedge 3$    ii. $(7 \wedge (3 \vee 2)) \vee 6$    iii. $(7 \wedge 3) \vee (7 \wedge 1)$    iv. $\bigwedge \emptyset$
v. $\bigwedge \{7, \bigvee \{7, (7 \wedge 2)\}\}$    vi. $\bigvee \{1, 2, 3, 4, 5, 6, 7, 8\}$
vii. $\bigwedge \{1, 2, 3, 4, 5, 6, 7, 8\}$

**Exercise 9.5.** For each Hasse diagram below say whether it is a lattice; if not, give a reason.
a.      b.      c.

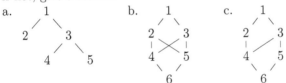

**Exercise 9.6.** Is $(\mathbb{N}, \leq)$ a lattice (where $\leq$ is the ordinary $\leq$ in arithmetic)? If so, what is $m \wedge n$ and $m \vee n$, any $m, n \in \mathbb{N}$?

### 9.2.1 Some Important Examples of Lattices

**Proposition 9.2.** *For $A$ any set, $(\mathcal{P}(A), \subseteq)$ is a lattice.*

*Proof.* Clearly for all $X \in \mathcal{P}(A)$, $X \subseteq X$, so $\subseteq$ is reflexive. And for $X, Y, Z \in \mathcal{P}(A)$, if $X \subseteq Y$ and $Y \subseteq Z$ then $X \subseteq Z$, so $\subseteq$ is transitive. Finally for $X, Y \in \mathcal{P}(A)$, if $X \subseteq Y$ and $Y \subseteq X$ then $X = Y$ since neither has a member the other doesn't. So $(\mathcal{P}(A), \subseteq)$ is a poset. Now, let $X, Y \in \mathcal{P}(A)$, we must show (a) and (b):

   a. $\{X, Y\}$ has a glb in $\mathcal{P}(A)$. But since $X, Y \in \mathcal{P}(A)$, $X \cap Y \in \mathcal{P}(A)$. Clearly $X \cap Y \subseteq X$ and $X \cap Y \subseteq Y$, so $X \cap Y$ is a lb for $\{X, Y\}$. Now let $Z$ be a lower bound for $\{X, Y\}$. Then $Z \subseteq X$ and $Z \subseteq Y$, so any element $z \in Z$ is an element of $X$ and an element of $Y$

and thus an element of $X \cap Y$. Since $z$ was arbitrary, $Z \subseteq X \cap Y$, which is to say that $X \cap Y$ is the greatest lower bound of $\{X, Y\}$, as was to be shown.

b. $X \cup Y$ is the least upper bound of $\{X, Y\}$. $\qquad\qquad$ □

**Exercise 9.7.** Prove (b) above.

Thus our familiar power sets are posets with additional structure, a lattice structure. Here for example is the Hasse diagram of $\mathcal{P}(\{a, b, c\})$:

(16)

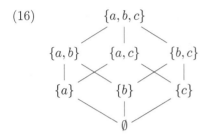

**An important abstraction step.** Earlier we defined intersection and union standardly in terms of set membership. We have now characterized those notions in a purely order theoretic way: $X \cap Y = X \wedge Y$, the greatest lower bound of $\{X, Y\}$ in $\mathcal{P}(A)$, and $X \cup Y = X \vee Y$, the least upper bound of $\{X, Y\}$. The whiff of generalization is in the air.

**Proposition 9.3.** $(\{T, F\}, \leq)$ *is a lattice, defined by the Hasse diagram below:*

$$T$$
$$|$$
$$F$$

So we understand here that $T \leq T$, $F \leq F$ and $F \leq T$. But $T \not\leq F$. This two element lattice is often represented as $\{0, 1\}$, using 0 for $F$ and 1 for $T$. It is called the lattice **2**.

The $\leq$ relation defined on the truth values $T$ and $F$ above is easily seen to be a partial order. Since both $T \leq T$ and $F \leq F$, the relation is obviously reflexive. It is antisymmetric since if $x$ and $y$ are distinct elements of $\{T, F\}$, then it is not possible for each to stand in the $\leq$ relation to the other; thus antisymmetry is vacuously satisfied. For transitivity, suppose that for $x, y, z \in \{T, F\}$ that $x \leq y$ and $y \leq z$. We must show that $x \leq z$. The only way this could fail is if the consequent is false and the antecedent true. For the consequent to be false $x = T$ and $z = F$. But if $x = T$ and $x \leq y$, then we must have $y = T$. And since $y \leq z$, then $z = T$, contrary to our assumption. So transitivity holds. Notice too that our truth table for conjunction shows that $x \wedge y$ is the glb of $\{x, y\}$; similarly $x \vee y$ is the lub of $\{x, y\}$.

So not only is $(\{T, F\}, \leq)$ a poset, it is a lattice. For all $x, y \in \{T, F\}$ the greatest lower bound of $\{x, y\}$ is $x \wedge y$ and its least upper bound is $x \vee y$.

(17)

| $x$ | $y$ | $x \wedge y$ | $x \vee y$ |
|---|---|---|---|
| $T$ | $T$ | $T$ | $T$ |
| $T$ | $F$ | $F$ | $T$ |
| $F$ | $T$ | $F$ | $T$ |
| $F$ | $F$ | $F$ | $F$ |

Reading the second line of (17) let us verify that $F$ is the glb of $\{T, F\}$. Clearly $F$ is a lower bound, since for all $x \in \{T, F\}$, $F \leq x$. Now suppose that some $z \in \{T, F\}$ is a lb for $\{T, F\}$. Then in particular $z \leq F$, showing that $F$ is greatest of the lower bounds for $\{T, F\}$.

**Useful remark.** For $x, y \in \{T, F\}$, to show that $x \leq y$ it suffices to show that if $x = T$ then $y = T$, since if $x = F$ then $x \leq y$ no matter what $y$ is. So there is only one case to consider. Similarly to show that a statement of the form "if $P$ then $Q$" is true it suffices to consider the case where $P$ is True. Then we must show that $Q$ is true. If $P$ is False then the statement "if $P$ then $Q$" is vacuously true. "If $P$ then $Q$" is false only when $P$ is True and $Q$ False. The conditional statement "if $P$ then $Q$" is often symbolized $(P \rightarrow Q)$.

**A fundamental abstraction.** The glb column in (17) gives the standard truth table for conjunction! A sentence of the form $(P$ and $Q)$ is interpreted as True iff both $P$ and $Q$ are. In all other cases $(P$ and $Q)$ is interpreted as False. Similarly the lub table gives the truth table for disjunction: A disjunction $(P$ or $Q)$ is interpreted as True iff either $P$ is or $Q$ is (possibly both). Thus, for $P$ and $Q$ sentences and $\mathcal{M}$ a model,

(18)  a. $[\![(P \text{ and } Q)]\!]_{\mathcal{M}} = [\![P]\!]_{\mathcal{M}} \wedge [\![Q]\!]_{\mathcal{M}}$

   b. $[\![(P \text{ or } Q)]\!]_{\mathcal{M}} = [\![P]\!]_{\mathcal{M}} \vee [\![Q]\!]_{\mathcal{M}}$

So (18) says that a conjunction of Ss always denotes the glb of the denotations of its conjuncts; a disjunction of Ss denotes their lub. And this is the property of *and* and *or* that generalizes to other categories and answers our initial Question:

(19) For $P$ and $Q$ expressions of any coordinable category $C$, the equations in (18) hold.

We must of course state what lattices are the denotation sets for the other categories $C$. Almost all the other cases are covered by:

**Proposition 9.4.** *If $(A, \leq_A)$ is a lattice and $B$ a set, $([B \to A], \leq)$ is a lattice, with $\leq$ defined by: $f \leq g$ iff for all $b \in B, f(b) \leq_A g(b)$. Such lattices are said to be defined* pointwise.

*Proof.* Let us see that $([B \to A], \leq)$ is, in fact, a lattice. First we must show that $\leq$ as defined is a partial order. Clearly for all $f \in [B \to A]$, $f \leq f$ since for all $b \in B, f(b) \leq_A f(b)$ because $\leq_A$ is reflexive. In a similar way the transitivity and antisymmetry of $\leq$ is inherited from $(A, \leq_A)$. To show the existence of meets let us define for all functions $f, g \in [B \to A]$ a function $h_{f,g}$ from $B$ into $A$ by setting:

$$h_{f,g}(b) = f(b) \wedge g(b).$$

We claim that $h_{f,g}$ is the glb of $\{f, g\}$. Clearly $h_{f,g} \leq f$ since for all $b$, $h_{f,g}(b) = f(b) \wedge g(b) \leq_A f(b)$. Similarly $h_{f,g} \leq g$, so $h_{f,g}$ is a lower bound for $\{f, g\}$. To see that it is greatest of the lower bounds, let $k$ be a lb for $\{f, g\}$. So $k \leq f$ and $k \leq g$, so for all $b$, $k(b) \leq_A f(b)$ and $k(b) \leq_A g(b)$, whence $k(b)$ is a lower bound for $\{f(b), g(b)\}$, so $k(b) \leq_A f(b) \wedge g(b) = h_{f,g}(b)$. So $k \leq h_{f,g}$, whence $h_{f,g}$ is greatest of the lower bounds for $\{f, g\}$. So $h_{f,g} = f \wedge g$ as was to be shown. $\square$

**Notational simplification.** In noting pointwise lattices $([B \to A], \leq)$ we can usually omit the subscript on $\leq_A$ since in writing $x \leq y$ we know that if $x, y \in A$ then $x \leq_A y$ is intended.

**Exercise 9.8.**

   a. Prove that $\leq$ in $([B \to A], \leq)$ is transitive.

   b. Prove that $\leq$ in $([B \to A], \leq)$ is antisymmetric.

   c. Prove that for all $f, g \in [B \to A]$, $\{f, g\}$ has a least upper bound.

### 9.2.2   The Use of Pointwise Lattices in Semantics

Given a model $\mathcal{M}$ with domain $E$ (we omit the subscript on $E$), the denotation set for expressions of category S/NP $= P_1$ was given as $[E \to \{T, F\}]$. But this set is the domain of a pointwise lattice, since $\{T, F\}$ is a lattice. And conjunctions of $P_1$s are interpreted by (19) as the glb of the conjuncts, and disjunctions as the lubs of their disjuncts.

(20)

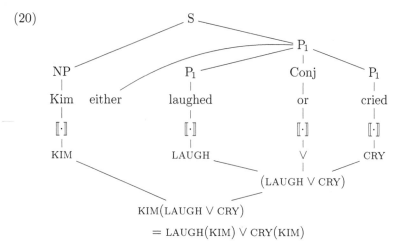

$$\text{KIM}(\text{LAUGH} \vee \text{CRY})$$
$$= \text{LAUGH}(\text{KIM}) \vee \text{CRY}(\text{KIM})$$

Thus we have shown that in each model $\mathcal{M}$ *Kim laughed or cried* and *Kim laughed or Kim cried* are interpreted as the same truth value.

Moreover our semantics from Chapter 8 supports that in general (EVERY $A$) does not map $(P \vee Q)$ to (EVERY $A$)$(P) \vee$ (EVERY $A$)$(Q)$. Observe first that this claim accords with our semantic intuitions of entailment based on ordinary English. Compare:

(21)    a. Every student either laughed or cried.

       b. Either every student laughed or every student cried.

Imagine a model with 5 students, three laughed but didn't cry and the other two cried but didn't laugh. In such a case (21a) is true: no matter what student you pick, that student either laughed or cried. But (21b) is false; it is not true that every student laughed, and it is not true that every student cried. And to see that our semantics guarantees this result consider that (21a) is interpreted as in (22) below:

(22)  (EVERY(STUDENT))(LAUGH OR CRY)
$$= T \text{ iff STUDENT} \subseteq \{x \in E \mid (\text{LAUGH OR CRY})(x) = T\}$$
$$= T \text{ iff STUDENT} \subseteq \{x \in E \mid \text{LAUGH}(x) \vee \text{CRY}(x) = T\}$$
$$= T \text{ iff for each } x \in \text{STUDENT}, x \text{ laughed or } x \text{ cried}.$$

And this last statement can be true in a situation in which just some of the students laughed and the others cried. But in contrast (21b) is a disjunction of Ss and is true if and only if one of the disjuncts is true. The first disjunct says that all the students laughed, the second that they all cried. As both conditions fail in the scenario given above it is false in some models in which (21a) is true, hence (21a) does not entail (21b).

**Exercise 9.9.** Exhibit an informal model in which sentence (a) below is true and sentence (b) is false. Say why it is false and conclude that (a) does not entail (b). Again this follows on our semantics for SOME given earlier plus that of conjunctions of $P_1$s given here.

 a. Some student laughed and some student cried.

 b. Some student both laughed and cried.

The bottommost line in (20) represents directly the denotation of *Either Kim laughed or Kim cried*. Thus (23a,b) below are logically equivalent, where we define:

**Definition 9.3.** Expressions $s$ and $t$ are *logically equivalent* iff for each model $\mathcal{M}$ they have the same denotation in $\mathcal{M}$ (that is, $[\![s]\!]_{\mathcal{M}} = [\![t]\!]_{\mathcal{M}}$).

(23)    a. Kim either laughed or cried.

      b. Either Kim laughed or Kim cried.

**Exercise 9.10.** Analogous to (20) exhibit the semantic interpretation trees for (a) and (b) below, concluding that they too are logically equivalent.

 a. Dana both laughed and cried.

 b. Dana laughed and Dana cried.

Now, once we have seen that $\text{DEN}_{\mathcal{M}}(P_1)$ is a (pointwise) lattice we can infer that $\text{DEN}_{\mathcal{M}}(P_2)$ is as well, as it is given as the set $[E \rightarrow [E \rightarrow \{T, F\}]]$, the set of functions from $E$ into a lattice. (And in general $\text{DEN}_{\mathcal{M}}(P_{n+1}) = [E \rightarrow \text{DEN}_{\mathcal{M}}(P_n)]$ is a lattice pointwise). In the case of $P_2$s observe the semantic computation in (24), again crucially using proper NPs not arbitrary DPs.

(24)

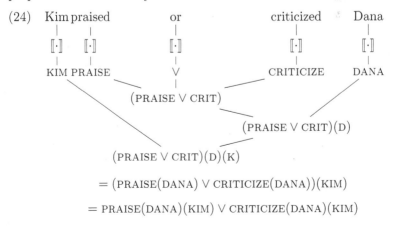

$$= (\text{PRAISE}(\text{DANA}) \vee \text{CRITICIZE}(\text{DANA}))(\text{KIM})$$

$$= \text{PRAISE}(\text{DANA})(\text{KIM}) \vee \text{CRITICIZE}(\text{DANA})(\text{KIM})$$

The last two lines just multiply out the pointwise definition of join at the $P_2$ and $P_1$ levels. And as the last line is the interpretation of (25b) below we see that our semantics shows that (25a,b) are logically equivalent.

(25)    a. Kim either praised or criticized Dana.

        b. Either Kim praised Dana or Kim criticized Dana.

We see then that the denotation set for a slash category $A/B$ assumes pointwise the lattice structure of $\text{DEN}_{\mathcal{M}} A$ , the set in which the functions take their values.

(26)  **Functional Projection (FP)**: For all categories $A, B$,
$\text{DEN}_{\mathcal{M}}(A/B) = [\text{DEN}_{\mathcal{M}}(B) \to \text{DEN}_{\mathcal{M}}(A)]$, assumes the structure of $\text{DEN}_{\mathcal{M}}(A)$ pointwise.

Functional Projection covers many more cases than just the $n$-place predicates. A basic case is $P_0/P_1$, that is, $S/(S/NP)$ in unabbreviated form. Now $\text{DEN}_{\mathcal{M}}(P_0)$ is a lattice so we take $\text{DEN}_{\mathcal{M}}(P_0/P_1)$ to be the pointwise lattice built from it. This guarantees logical equivalences like the (a,b) pairs below (which shows that Boolean compounds of DPs "distribute" over $P_n$s):

(27)    a. Every student and some teacher laughed joyfully.

        b. Every student laughed joyfully and some teacher laughed joyfully.

(28)    a. Either John or some teacher took your car.

        b. Either John took your car or some teacher took your car.

Similarly the pointwise definitions mapping $P_2$ denotations to $P_1$ denotations predict, correctly, the following equivalences:

(29)    a. John interviewed every bystander and a couple of storeowners.

        b. John interviewed every bystander and interviewed a couple of storeowners.

(30)    a. He wrote a novel or a play.

        b. He wrote a novel or wrote a play.

In fact for essentially all slash categories, conjunctions and disjunctions behave pointwise. So without detailed justification we note the following equivalences.

(31)  Det: most but not all students ≡ most students but not all
      students

(32)  ($P_1/P_1$): He spoke softly and quickly. ≡ He spoke softly and
      spoke quickly.

(33)  P: He lives in or near NY City. ≡ He lives in NY City or near
      NY City.

### 9.2.3  Revisiting the Coordination Generalization

We pursued our semantic analysis of coordinate expressions by interpreting a conjunction of expressions as the glb of the denotations of its
conjuncts, and a disjunction as the lub of the denotation of its disjuncts.
This has led us naturally towards a system in which at least certain
types of expressions, boolean compounds, are directly interpreted, as
we have illustrated above. Thus we independently derive and interpret (23a) and (23b) and then prove that they are logically equivalent,
always denoting the same truth value.

But early work in generative grammar suggested a more syntactic
approach to these equivalences. The idea was that there is only one
*and* (*or*, *nor*), the S or "propositional" level one. It just combines
with Ss to form Ss. Apparent coordinations of non-Ss are treated as
Ss, "syntactically reduced" and *and*, *or*, and *nor* are still interpreted
propositionally. So the $P_1$ coordination in (23a) would be derived by
some Conjunction Reduction rules from the S (23b) and it would receive
the same interpretation as (23b).

This syntactic approach to the initial Question thus states that
what the different uses of a boolean connective have in common is that
they all denote the meaning they have when they conjoin Ss. Initially
this solution seems semantically appealing, since (23a) and (23b) are
logically equivalent. So the reduction rules seem to satisfy Compositionality: the interpretation of the derived expression (23a) is a function
(the identity function) of the one it is derived from, (23b).

But as we have seen in (21) and Exercise 9.9, this equivalence fails
for most DP subjects. The relevant pairs in (34) for example are certainly not logically equivalent:

(34)  a.  Some student both laughed and cried.

      a′.  Some student laughed and some student cried.

      b.  Most of the students both laughed and cried.

      b′.  Most of the students laughed and most of the students
           cried.

If just one student laughed and just one, a different one, cried, (34b) is true and (34a) is false. Similarly replacing *some student* everywhere by *no student, exactly four students, more than four students, . . .* and infinitely many other DPs yields sentence pairs that are not logically equivalent, though a few cases do work: *every student*, and *both Mary and Sue* preserve logical equivalence in (34) (but not if *and* is replaced by *or*).

Thus Ss derived by Conjunction Reduction are not regularly related semantically to their sources: sometimes the pairs are logically equivalent, sometimes one entails the other but not conversely, and sometimes they are *logically independent* (neither entails the other). In addition the precise formulation of the Reduction rules has not been worked out and it seems quite complicated. Note that a sentence may contain many Boolean compounds:

(35)  Neither did most of the teachers write a novel or two poems or review at least one book and four plays in or near NY City nor did most of the grad students (write a novel or two poems or review at least one book and four plays in or near NY City) over the vacation.

**Exercise 9.11.** From our Coord rule above it follows that for every $n > 0$ there is a DP in English with more than $n$ constituents of category DP. Prove this by induction on $n$ and conclude that English has infinitely many Boolean compounds of DPs.

For all these reasons then we recommend directly deriving and interpreting Boolean compounds rather than deriving all from sentential sources where the Boolean connectives would be interpreted.

## 9.3   Negation and Additional Properties of Natural Language Lattices

The lattices we use as denotation sets have three further properties: they are *bounded, distributive,* and *complemented. not* and *neither. . . nor. . .* are interpreted by complements, which presupposes boundedness.

**Definition 9.4.** A lattice $(L, \leq)$ is *bounded* iff it has a least element and a greatest element. $x \in L$ is *least* iff for all $y \in L, x \leq y$; $x$ is *greatest* iff for all $y \in L, y \leq x$.

**Fact**  Let $(L, \leq)$ be a bounded lattice. Then it has just one least element noted 0 read *the zero* (*bottom*), and just one greatest element, noted 1 read *the unit* (or *top*). (If $x$ and $x'$ are both least then $x \leq x'$ and $x' \leq x$ so by antisymmetry $x = x'$. If $(L, \leq)$ is bounded then $1 = \bigvee L$ and $0 = \bigwedge L$. Every finite lattice is bounded, since if $L$ is finite with $n$ elements say $a_1, \ldots, a_n$ then $\bigwedge L = (a_1 \wedge a_2 \wedge \cdots \wedge a_n)$ and similarly $\bigvee L = (a_1 \vee a_2 \vee \cdots \vee a_n)$. Most of the lattices exhibited so far are finite and thus bounded. But many non-finite lattices are unbounded.

**Theorem 9.5.**

   *a.* $(\mathcal{P}(A), \subseteq)$ *is bounded with* $A$ *greatest and* $\emptyset$ *least, no matter how large* $A$ *is.*

   *b.* *If* $(L, \leq)$ *is bounded then the pointwise lattice* $[E \to L]$ *is bounded. The 0 function maps each* $x \in E$ *to* $0_L$, *the zero of* $L$, *and the unit function maps each* $x \in E$ *to* $1_L$.

**Proposition 9.6.** *In any lattice* $(L, \leq)$, $x \vee 0 = x$.

*Proof.* Since $x \leq x$ and $0 \leq x$ we have that $x$ is an ub for $\{x, 0\}$. And for $z$ an ub for $\{x, 0\}$, $x \leq z$, so $x$ is least of the ub's, as was to be shown. $\square$

**Exercise 9.12.** Show in analogy to the fact above that in any lattice, $x \wedge 1 = x$.

**Definition 9.5.** A lattice $(L, \leq)$ is *distributive* iff for all $x, y, z \in L$, (a) and (b) hold:

   a. $x \wedge (y \vee z) = (x \wedge y) \vee (x \wedge z)$, and

   b. $x \vee (y \wedge z) = (x \vee y) \wedge (x \vee z)$.

One proves in any lattice that (a) and (b) are equivalent in the sense that if either holds the other does. Moreover the right hand side of (a) stands in the $\leq$ relation to its left hand side in any lattice. So to prove that a lattice is distributive it suffices to show that $x \wedge (y \vee z) \leq (x \wedge y) \vee (x \wedge z)$, all $x, y, z \in L$. Dually, the left hand side of (b) is $\leq$ the right hand side in any lattice, so to prove a lattice distributive it suffices to show that $(x \vee y) \wedge (x \vee z) \leq x \vee (y \wedge z)$.

**Theorem 9.7.**

   *a.* *The* $\{T, F\}$ *lattice is distributive.*

b. *All power set lattices are distributive.*

c. *If $(L, \leq)$ is distributive then so is the pointwise lattice $[E \rightarrow L]$.*

An example of a non-distributive lattice consider (15c), the pentagon lattice. There $b \wedge (d \vee c) = b \wedge a = b \neq (b \wedge d) \vee (b \wedge c) = d \vee e = d$, so distributivity fails.

**Exercise 9.13.** Show that the diamond lattice, (15a) fails to be distributive.

**Definition 9.6.** A lattice $(L, \leq)$ is *complemented* iff $(L, \leq)$ is bounded and for every $x \in L$ there is a $y \in L$ such that $(x \wedge y) = 0$ and $(x \vee y) = 1$.

**Notation** To say that complements are unique in a lattice $(L, \leq)$ is to say that for every $x \in L$ there is exactly one $y \in L$ satisfying the complement axioms $(x \wedge y) = 0$ and $(x \vee y) = 1$. In such a case this unique $y$ is noted $\neg x$, read as "complement $x$".

**Theorem 9.8.** *If a complemented lattice is distributive then complements are unique.*

*Proof.* Suppose that $(x \wedge y) = 0$ and $(x \vee y) = 1$, and also that $(x \wedge z) = 0$ and $(x \vee z) = 1$.
Show: $y = z$.

1. $y = y \wedge 1 = y \wedge (x \vee z) = (y \wedge x) \vee (y \wedge z) = 0 \vee (y \wedge z) = y \wedge z$, whence $y \leq z$.

2. $z = z \wedge 1 = z \wedge (x \vee y) = (z \wedge x) \vee (z \wedge y) = 0 \vee (z \wedge y) = z \wedge y$, whence $z \leq y$, so by antisymmetry $y = z$.

$\square$

Note that the third equality in each line uses distributivity. And since each $x$ has at least one complement ($y$ as above) we now know each $x$ has exactly one, which we may denote $\neg x$. Here is a simple proof of the double complements law using uniqueness of complements:

**Theorem 9.9.** *For all $x$ in a boolean lattice, $x = \neg(\neg x)$.*

*Proof.* By commutativity and axiom we have: $\neg x \wedge x = 0$ and $\neg x \vee x = 1$, Hence by uniqueness of complements, $x = \neg(\neg x)$. $\square$

**Exercise 9.14.** A lattice may be complemented but not uniquely complemented (and so not distributive by Theorem 9.8). For example the pentagon lattice (15c) is complemented but the element $c$ has two complements. One is $b$, since $b \wedge c = 0$ (the zero element is $e$) and $b \vee c = 1$, the unit element $a$. What is the other complement of $c$?

**Definition 9.7.** A *boolean* lattice is a lattice that is distributive and complemented.

All DEN$_\mathcal{M}(C)$ for $C$ coordinable are boolean with negation denoting the complement operation, just as *and* and *or* denote the meet and join functions. The denotation for *neither... nor...* is sometimes noted $\downarrow$, defined by $x \downarrow y =_{df} (\neg x \wedge \neg y)$. Of course $(\neg x \wedge \neg y) = \neg(x \vee y)$. So *neither John nor Bill* denotes the complement of the denotation of *either John or Bill*. We now assume Eng enriched with a Negation rule:

(36) Negation: $(\text{not}, \text{NEG}) + (s, C) \to (\text{not } s, C)$

**Fact**

1. In the $\{T, F\}$ lattice, $T$ is the top or unit element, $F$ is the bottom or zero element, and provably $\neg T = F$ and $\neg F = T$.

2. In any power set lattice $\mathcal{P}(A)$, for each $X \subseteq A$, $\neg X$ is provably $A - X$, the set of elements in $A$ that are not in $X$.

3. In a pointwise boolean lattice $[E \to L]$, for each $f \in (E \to L)$, $\neg f$ provably maps each $x \in E$ to $\neg(f(x))$. For example interpreting *not* as the complement operator in the pointwise $[\text{P}_1 \to \text{P}_0]$ lattice we have:

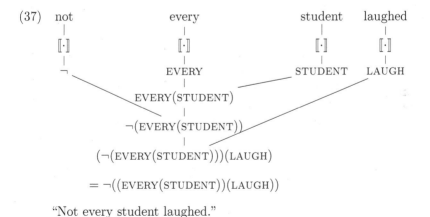

"Not every student laughed."

**Remark** In each lattice $L$ above, the complement operation is not simply added to $L$, rather, the partial order provably is a bounded distributive lattice with the property that for each $x$ there is a unique $y$ such that $x \wedge y = 0$ and $x \vee y = 1$. Then we *define* $\neg x$ to be that unique $y$. For example in the $\{T, F\}$ lattice with the implication order, $F$ is provably least and $T$ greatest, and $T \wedge F = F$, the zero, and $T \vee F = T$, the unit, so we infer that $F$ is the complement of $T$, that is, $F = \neg T$.

Interpreting negation as complement generally yields reasonable results in terms of judgment of entailment and logical equivalence. And it answers the query analogous to the one we raised for *and* and *or*. Namely, the uses of negation with expressions in different categories do have something in common: they denote the boolean complement of the denotation of the expression they negate. But they appear to combine with somewhat fewer categories than *and* and *or* and to exhibit more category internal restrictions.

The most easily negated expressions across languages are $P_1$s (despite a tradition that calls it "sentential" negation). In English the expression of this negation is fully natural, but complicated. It requires the presence of an auxiliary verb, an appropriately tensed form of *do*, as in (38b).

(38)   a. Just two skaters fell.

   b. Just two skaters didn't fall.

   c. It is not the case that just two skaters fell.

Note that (38c) is not at all logically equivalent to (38b). In a situation with exactly four skaters, just two of whom fell both (38a) and (38b) are true, and (38c) is false, so (38b) does not entail (38c). And in a situation with six skaters, exactly three of whom fell, (38c) is true and (38b) false, so (38c) fails to entail (38b). The point of this observation is that the information contained in the subject of the $P_1$ is not in general understood to be under the scope of $P_1$ negation.

Equally many DPs negate easily, as in (39), but also many don't, as in (40).

(39)   a. Not a creature was stirring, not even a mouse.

   b. Not more than a couple of students will answer that question correctly.

   c. Not one student in ten knows the answer to that.

   d. Not every student came to the party.

(40)   a. *Not John came to the party.

   b. *Not the students I met signed my petition.

   c. *Not each student came to the party.

On the other hand sometimes apparently unnegatable DPs can be forced to negate in coordinate contexts, as in *So Sue and not Jill will represent us at the meeting.*

Finally we note that it is usually quite difficult to interpret negation as taking a mere P$_2$ (or P$_3$) in its scope. *John didn't criticize every teacher* does not mean that John stands in the not-criticize relation to every teacher, which would mean that every teacher has the property that John didn't criticize him. Rather the sentence most naturally means simply that John lacks the property expressed by *criticized every teacher.*

## 9.4 Properties versus Sets: Lattice Isomorphisms

We have already said (Chapter 4) what it means for two relational structures, in particular two (boolean) lattices, to be isomorphic: you must be able to match the elements of the their domains one for one in such a way that elements stand in the order relation in one if and only if their images stand in the order relation in the other. Now for the lattices we have considered there is one interesting and possibly not obvious, instance of an isomorphism that is used often in the literature, often without explicit mention. Namely, a power set lattice $(\mathcal{P}(A), \subseteq)$ is isomorphic to the corresponding pointwise "property" lattice $([A \rightarrow \{T, F\}], \leq)$. To show this we exhibit an isomorphism. Let $K$ be any subset of $A$ and define $h_K$ from $A$ into $\{T, F\}$ by

(41)  $h_K(a) = T$ iff $a \in K$.

Now we claim that the function $h$ mapping each subset $K$ of $A$ to $h_K$ is an isomorphism. Here is an informal proof using the Hasse diagrams of the lattices. First the power set lattice, repeating (16).

(42)

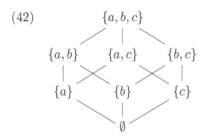

And now consider the Hasse diagram for the $h_K$:

(43)

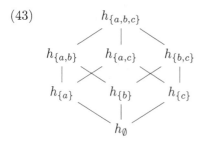

Now it is clear that the map $h$ sending each $K$ in (42) to $h_K$ in (43) is a bijection. But two queries still arise. First, how do we know that all the maps from $A$ into **2** (we often write **2** for $\{T, F\}$ recall) are exhibited in (43)? The answer is easy: for any $g$ from $A$ into **2** let $T[g]$ be $\{a \in A \mid g(a) = T\}$, the set of elements of $A$ that $g$ is true of. Then clearly $h_{T[g]}$ is $g$, since $h_{T[g]}$ is true of exactly the elements of $T[g]$, so $h_{T[g]}$ and $g$ are true of exactly the same objects. And second, how do we know that we have correctly represented the $\leq$ relation in (43)? Well, we see that in moving up along lines from some $h_K$ to some $h_{K'}$ it must be so that $K \subseteq K'$, whence the set of things $h_K$ maps to $T$ is a subset of those that $h_{K'}$ maps to $T$; that is, for all $a \in A$, if $h_K(a) = T$ then $h_{K'}(a) = T$, and this suffices to show that $h_K \leq h_{K'}$, completing the proof.

Now, given that a power set lattice and its pointwise counterpart are isomorphic, why should we care? One practical reason is that authors differ with regard to how they represent properties of objects. Often we find it natural to think of a property of objects $X$ as a function that looks at each element of $X$ and says True (or False). So we treat the set of properties of objects $X$ as $[X \to \{T, F\}]$. And in such a case when $b$ is an object and $p$ a property we write $p(b)$ to say that the object $b$ has property $p$. But other times we just treat a property of elements of $X$ as the set of objects which have it. So here the set of properties is $\mathcal{P}(X)$, and we write $b \in p$ to say that $b$ has property $p$.

But from what we have just seen, $\mathcal{P}(X)$ and $[X \to \{T, F\}]$ are isomorphic, and we write $\mathcal{P}(X) \cong [X \to \{T, F\}]$. That means that the order theoretic claims we can make truly of one are exactly the ones we can make about the other. Whenever one says $b \in p$ the other says $p(b)$ and conversely. In fact within a given text an author may shift back and forth between notations, acknowledging that there is no logical point in distinguishing between isomorphic structures.

We close with two further properties which the boolean lattices we use have but which are not present in all boolean lattices.

**Definition 9.8.** A lattice $(L, \leq)$ is *complete* iff every subset has a glb and a lub, that is, $\bigwedge K$ and $\bigvee K$ exist for all $K \subseteq L$.

**Fact** All finite lattices are complete. If $K = \{k_1, \ldots, k_n\} \subseteq L$ then $\bigwedge K = k_1 \wedge \cdots \wedge k_n$ and $\bigvee K = k_1 \vee \cdots \vee k_n$. $\bigwedge L$ is the zero element of $L$ and $\bigvee L$ is the unit.

**Definition 9.9.**

   a. An element $\alpha$ of a lattice is an *atom* iff $\alpha \neq 0$ and for all $x$, if $x \leq \alpha$ then $x = 0$ or $x = \alpha$

   b. A lattice $(B, \leq)$ is *atomic* iff for all $y \neq 0$ there is an atom $\alpha \leq y$. Write ATOM($B$) for the set of atoms of $B$.

In a power set boolean lattice the unit sets are the atoms.

**Theorem 9.10.** *A boolean lattice $(B, \leq)$ is complete and atomic iff it is isomorphic to $\mathcal{P}(ATOM(B))$.*

The map sending each $y$ to $\{\alpha \in \text{ATOM}(B) \mid \alpha \leq y\}$ is the desired isomorphism. Thus $|B| = |\mathcal{P}(\text{ATOM}(B))| = 2^{|\text{ATOM}(B)|}$.

**Theorem 9.11.** *All finite boolean lattices are complete and atomic. So each finite boolean lattice is isomorphic to the power set of its atoms, and so isomorphic to a power set.*

There are complete atomic distributive lattices that are not boolean, as they are not complemented. Here is one that arises in certain semantic studies.

(44) Let $A$ be a non-empty set and $EQ(A)$ the set of equivalence relations on A. So $R \in EQ(A)$ iff $R \subseteq A \times A$ and $R$ is reflexive, symmetric and transitive. Define a binary relation, called *refines*, on $EQ(A)$ by setting $R \leq S$ iff for all $x, y \in A$, $xRy \Rightarrow xSy$. So whenever $x$ is $R$-equivalent to $y$ then it is also $S$-equivalent to $y$.

The above definition implies that every $S$-equivalence class is a union of $R$-equivalence classes. Furthermore, the definition of $\leq$ basically says that $R \subseteq S$, so we know then that $\leq$ is reflexive, antisymmetric and transitive.

**Fact** $\langle EQ(A), \leq \rangle$ is a poset.

Further, since each equivalence relation over $A$ is reflexive we have that $ID_A = \{\langle x, x \rangle \mid x \in A\}$ is a subset of every $R$ in $EQ(A)$. And since $ID_A$ is itself an equivalence relation (antisymmetry and transitivity are vacuously satisfied) we have that $ID_A$ is least. That is, the 0 of $EQ(A)$ is $ID_A$. Similarly $A \times A$ is the unit 1 of $EQ(A)$ since it is an equivalence relation on $A$ and all (equivalence) relations on $A$ are subsets of $A \times A$. So $EQ(A)$ is a bounded poset. What is slightly less obvious is that $EQ(A)$ is a lattice. Glbs are actually intuitive since:

**Theorem 9.12.**

    a. *For all $R, S \in EQ(A)$ we have that $R \cap S$ is an equivalence relation in $EQ(A)$. Generalizing,*

    b. *For $I$ an index set, if $R_i \in EQ(A)$ for each $i \in I$, then $\bigcap_i R_i$ is an equivalence relation (so $\bigcap_i R_i \in EQ(A)$ ).*

*Proof.* We prove the general case by showing that $\bigcap_i R_i$ is reflexive, symmetric, and transitive.

**Reflexivity.** Let $x \in A$ be arbitrary. Then for each $i$, $\langle x, x \rangle \in R_i$ so it is in their intersection, thus $\bigcap_i R_i$ is reflexive.

**Symmetry.** Let $\langle x, y \rangle \in \bigcap_i R_i$. So $\langle x, y \rangle$ is in each $R_i$. Since each $R_i$ is symmetric, $\langle y, x \rangle$ is in each $R_i$, so it is in $\bigcap_i R_i$ showing that $\bigcap_i R_i$ is symmetric.

**Transitivity.** Similarly if $\langle x, y \rangle$ and $\langle y, z \rangle$ are both in $\bigcap_i R_i$ then they are both in each $R_i$ so $\langle x, z \rangle$ is in each $R_i$ since each $R_i$ transitive. Thus $\langle x, z \rangle \in \bigcap_i R_i$, showing that the latter is transitive. Thus $\bigcap_i R_i$ is an equivalence relation. We already know it is glb for $\{R_i \mid i \in I\}$.    □

The trickier part is to show that any collection of equivalence relations on $A$ has a least upper bound. That lub would be the union of the collection if that union were an equivalence relation, but often isn't. For example, let $x, y, z$ be distinct element of $A$. Then,

(45)     a. $R = ID_A \cup \{\langle x, y \rangle, \langle y, x \rangle\}$ is an equivalence relation over $A$.

    b. $S = ID_A \cup \{\langle y, z \rangle, \langle z, y \rangle\}$ is an equivalence relation over $A$.

    c. $R \cup S$ is not an equivalence relation as it contains $\langle x, y \rangle$ and $\langle y, z \rangle$ but not $\langle x, z \rangle$ so it fails transitivity.

But in fact any collection of equivalence relations over $A$ has a lub in $EQ(A)$, but that relation is larger than the union of the $R_i$ in the collection. Here is a standard way to build it.

**Definition 9.10.** Given an index set $I$ with $R_i \in EQ(A)$ for each $i \in I$, let $K$ be the following set:

$$\bigcap \{S \in EQ(A) \mid \text{for all } i \in I, R_i \subseteq S\}.$$

Clearly $K$ is an equivalence relation over $A$ by the proof of Theorem 9.12. It is obviously the least equivalence relation that includes each $R_i$ (meaning, as usual, that it is a subset of each equivalence relation over $A$ which includes each $R_i$; this is so because the intersection of a bunch of sets is always a subset of any set in over which the intersection was taken. So $K$ is the least upper bound for $\{R_i \mid i \in I\}$. Thus $(EQ(A), \leq)$ is a complete bounded lattice.

$(EQ(A), \leq)$ is not however a boolean lattice, as in general its elements lack complements. For example, for $A$ with at least three distinct elements $x, y, z$ the relation $R$ in (45a) lacks a complement in $EQ(A)$. If some $R^*$ were its complement then its intersection with $R$ must be $ID_A$, so $R^*$ must lack $\langle x, y \rangle$ and $\langle y, x \rangle$. If it lacks any other pair then its union with $R$ will not be $A \times A$. So it must then have the pairs $\langle x, z \rangle$ and $\langle z, y \rangle$, whence by transitivity it has $\langle x, y \rangle$, a contradiction.

Thus we have shown that $(EQ(A), \leq)$ is a complete lattice which in general is not boolean. In fact more can be said:

**Exercise 9.15.**

a. Show that $(EQ(A), \leq)$ is atomic and exhibit an atom.

b. Show that $(EQ(A), \leq)$ is distributive.

## 9.5    Theorems on Boolean Lattices

We conclude this chapter with some basic regularities that hold in all boolean lattices. For those that are named, the names are in common use and should be learned.

**Theorem 9.13.** *For* $(B, \leq)$ *a boolean lattice and any* $x, y, z$ *in* $B$,

a. $x \wedge y = y \wedge x$, and $x \vee y = y \vee x$.　　　　　(Commutativity)

b. $x \wedge (y \vee z) = (x \wedge y) \vee (x \wedge z)$, and　　　(Distributivity)
$x \vee (y \wedge z) = (x \vee y) \wedge (x \vee z)$.

c. $x \wedge (y \wedge z) = (x \wedge y) \wedge z$, and　　　(Associativity)
$x \vee (y \vee z) = (x \vee y) \vee z$.

d. $x \vee 0 = x$, and $x \wedge 1 = x$.　　　　　(Identity elements)

e. $x \vee \neg x = 1$, and $x \wedge \neg x = 0$.     (Complement Laws)

f. $x \wedge x = x$, and $x \vee x = x$.     (Idempotency)

g. $\neg\neg x = x$.     (Double Complements)

h. $\neg(x \wedge y) = \neg x \vee \neg y$, and     (de Morgan's laws)
  $\neg(x \vee y) = \neg x \wedge \neg y$.

i. $x \wedge (x \vee y) = x$, and $x \vee (x \wedge y) = x$.     (Absorption)

j. $x \leq y$ iff $(x \wedge y) = x$, and $x \leq y$ iff $(x \vee y) = y$.

k. $x \leq y$ iff $x \wedge \neg y = 0$, and $x \leq y$ iff $\neg x \vee y = 1$.

l. $x \wedge y \leq x \leq x \vee y$.

m. $x \leq y$ iff $\neg y \leq \neg x$.

n. $x \leq y$ implies $(x \wedge z) \leq (y \wedge z)$, and $x \leq y$ implies $(x \vee z) \leq (y \vee z)$.

**Exercise 9.16.** Let $(A, R)$ be a relational structure. Define a binary relation $R^{-1}$ on $A$ by setting $xR^{-1}y$ iff $yRx$. $R^{-1}$ is called the *converse* of $R$. We often use symbols like $\leq$, $\preceq$, $\subseteq$ for partial orders, and $\geq$, $\succeq$, $\supseteq$ for their converses.

  a. Prove that when $(A, R)$ is a poset then $(A, R^{-1})$ is a poset. $(A, R^{-1})$ is called the *dual* of $(A, R)$.

  b. Same as (a) above with 'lattice' replacing 'poset'.

  c. Given a boolean lattice $(A, R)$ prove that the complement function from $A$ to $A$ is an isomorphism from $(A, R)$ to its dual $(A, R^{-1})$.

## 9.6   Some (Possibly) Unexpected Boolean Lattices

The boolean lattices we have seen so far are ones that have been defined in terms of the linguistic expression of boolean expressions. But many others sets that have arisen in our study also turn out to have a boolean structure. It is for example interesting to classify classes of formal languages – each one is a set of expressions – according as they are closed under the boolean set operations or not. First let us define:

**Definition 9.11.** A boolean *set* algebra is a boolean algebra whose elements are subsets of a given set A and whose operations are ∩, ∪ and ¬ (complement relative to A). The algebra may fail to contain all the subsets of A and hence is a proper subset of $P(A)$.

For example:

**Theorem 9.14.** *Let $\Sigma$ be a finite vocabulary.*

1. *Set $FSL(\Sigma) =_{def} \{K \subseteq \Sigma^* \mid K = L(A) \text{ for } A \text{ some finite state automaton}\}$. Then $\emptyset$ and $\Sigma^*$ are in $FSL(\Sigma)$ and $FSL(\Sigma)$ is closed under $\cap$, $\cup$, and $\neg$. So $FSL(\Sigma)$ is a boolean set algebra.*

2. *Set $CFL(\Sigma) =_{def} \{K \subseteq \Sigma^* \mid K = L(G) \text{ for } G \text{ some context-free grammar}\}$. $CFL(\Sigma)$ is closed under $\cup$ but not under $\cap$ or $\neg$ and so is not a boolean set algebra.*

**Definition 9.12** (informal). A subset $R$ of $\mathbb{N}^n$ (the set of $n$-tuples of natural numbers) is *computable* (synonym: *decidable, solvable*) iff there is an algorithm (mechanical procedure) which for each $n$-tuple $\sigma$ of numbers computes in a finite number of steps YES if $\sigma \in R$ and NO if $\sigma \notin R$.

For example (See Loveland et al., 2014, Ch 4) the set of primes is a computable subset of $\mathbb{N}^1$. $\{\langle x, y \rangle \mid x > y\}$ is a computable subset of $\mathbb{N}^2$ and the set of Pythagorean triples $\{\langle a, b, c \rangle \mid a^2 + b^2 = c^2\}$ is a computable subset of $\mathbb{N}^3$.

**Theorem 9.15** (informal). *The set of computable subsets of $\mathbb{N}^n$ includes $\emptyset$ and $\mathbb{N}^n$ and is closed under $\cap$, $\cup$ and $\neg$ and so is a boolean set algebra. It is a (very) proper subset of $P(\mathbb{N}^n)$.*

## 9.7 A Concluding Note on Point of View

We have presented lattices in an order theoretic way: $x \wedge y$ and $x \vee y$ are defined as greatest lower bounds and least upper bounds. Another widely used approach, perhaps the most widely used, is one in which a lattice is given as a triple $(L, \wedge, \vee)$, with $\wedge$ (meet) and $\vee$ (join) binary functions on $L$ satisfying commutativity, associativity, and absorption. Then we define $\leq$ by: $x \leq y$ iff $x \wedge y = x$. Sets with functions defined on them are algebras, so on this view a lattice is an algebra of a certain sort, and a boolean lattice is called a boolean algebra, named after George Boole (1854) who first constructed them. The two approaches, the relational one and the functional one, are interdefinable and serve to illustrate different ways of accomplishing the same goal. Recall,

If you can't say something two ways you can't say it.

**Boole's Speculation.** Boolean algebra has developed explosively since Boole initiated it. But Boole's original work still merits reading, especially for its motivation. Boole was not interested in inventing a type of algebra per se, rather he was trying to formulate with mathematical precision and rigor the thought steps he took in clear reasoning, hence his title *The Laws of Thought*. This was a marvelously ambitious enterprise, and while we may reasonably think there is more to thought than the kinds of reasoning that can be carried out within boolean algebra, might not Boole's intuitions give us a deeper account of the polymorphism of *and, or,* and *not?* Their meanings indeed are not tied to any particular type of denotation – truth value, property, relation, restricting modifiers, generalized quantifiers, ... and this suggests that the boolean operators express *properties of mind*, more the way we think about things, how we conceptualize them, than properties of things themselves. This suggestion is to be sure speculative.

But there is one additional linguistic observation that is nicely compatible with it. Namely, if the Boolean connectives have a meaning independent of the categories of expression they combine with, as we have supported here, then it is perhaps not surprising that they have some capacity to create meaningful constituents for which there is little or no independent syntactic support. We have already noted cases like (46a,b):

(46)    a. *So not Jill will represent us at the meeting.

        b. So Sue and not Jill will represent us at the meeting.

Similarly in (47a) the right branching constituency of the subject DP is natural, but a left branching constituency can be forced by coordination.

(47)    a. [Most [female [doctors]]] support healthcare reform.

        b. [[Most female] and [almost all male]](doctors) support healthcare reform.

Right node raising cases like (48b) and Gapping as in (49b) are further instances:

(48)    a. [John [bought a turkey]] and [Bill [cooked it]].

        b. [[John bought] and [Bill cooked]] the turkey.

(49)    a. John [[handed Bill] a snake].

        b. John [handed [Bill a snake] and [Fred a scorpion]].

Steedman and Baldridge (2007) provide derivations of various "non-constituent coordinations" within the framework of Combinatory Categorial Grammar. Here we offer no such derivational mechanisms, we simply notice that however such coordination and negation is derived, it is the Boolean connectives that induce or allow it.

## 9.8 Further Reading

See Payne (1985) and Horn (1989) for typological discussion of negation; see Keenan and Faltz (1985) for extensive discussion of boolean structure in natural language semantics. And see Winter (2001) for an analysis of the interaction of Boolean structure with plurals and collectives, as well as issues concerning wide scope phenomena (which we consider in Chapter 10).

## 9.9 Appendix: Tarski-Knaster and Schröder-Bernstein

**The Tarski-Knaster Fixed Point Theorem** For $L$ a complete lattice and $F$ an isotone (= monotone increasing, $\uparrow$) function from $L$ into $L$, $F$ has a fixed point. (That is, there is an $x \in L$ such that $F(x) = x$).

*Proof.* Set $K = \{a \in L \mid a \leq F(a)\}$. We show that $\bigvee K$ is a fixed point of $F$.

For each $a \in K$, $a \leq \bigvee K$, so for each such $a$, $F(a) \leq F(\bigvee K)$ because $F$ is $\uparrow$. And since $a \leq F(a)$ then $F(\bigvee K)$ is an upper bound for $K$, so (1) $\bigvee K \leq F(\bigvee K)$. Thus $F(\bigvee K) \leq F(F(\bigvee K))$, so $F(\bigvee K) \in K$, thus (2) $F(\bigvee K) \leq \bigvee K$. (1) and (2) establish the theorem. □

**Notation** When $f$ is a function with domain $X$ and $Z \subseteq X$, we write $f[Z]$ or $f(Z)$ indifferently for $\{f(z) \mid z \in Z\}$.

**The Schröder-Bernstein Theorem** For $A, B$ sets, if $F : A \to B$ and $G : B \to A$ are both one to one then there is a bijection $H : A \to B$.

*Proof.* First we find $A_0 \subseteq A$ such that $G[B - F(A_0)] = A - A_0$. Then we define $H$ by:

$$H(a) = \begin{cases} F(a) & \text{if } a \in A_0 \\ G^{-1}(a) & \text{if } a \in A - A_0. \end{cases}$$

Define $k : \mathcal{P}(A) \to \mathcal{P}(A)$ by: $k(X) = A - G[B - F(X)]$.

**Fact**: $k$ is isotone. Let $X \subseteq Y \subseteq A$. Then $F(X) \subseteq F(Y)$. So $B - F(Y) \subseteq B - F(X)$, so $G[B - F(Y)] \subseteq G[B - F(X)]$, so $A - G[B - F(X)] \subseteq A - G[B - F(Y)]$, so $k(X) \subseteq k(Y)$, whence $k$ is isotone.

By Tarski-Knaster, let $A_0$ be a fixed point of $k$. So $A_0 = A - G[B - F[A_0]]$. Define $H$ as above. We show that $H$ is a bijection.

NB: for $a \in A$, $a \in A_0$ iff $a \notin G[B - F(A_0)]$, iff $a \neq G(b)$, any $b \in B - F(A_0)$.

1. $\mathrm{Dom}(H) = A$. Trivial from the definition of $H$.

2. $H$ is one to one. Let $a \neq a' \in A$.

    Case 1: $a, a' \in A_0$. Then $H(a) = F(a) \neq F(a') = H(a')$.

    Case 2: $a \in A_0$ and $a' \in A - A_0$, so $a' \notin A_0$, so $a' \in G[B - F(A_0)]$, so $G^{-1}(a') \notin F(A_0)$ so $H(a') = G^{-1}(a') \neq F(a)$.

    Case 3: $a, a' \in A - A_0$. Then $G^{-1}(a) \neq G^{-1}(a')$ since $G^{-1}$ is one to one since $G$ is.

3. $H$ is onto. Let $b \in B$. If $b \in F(A_0)$ then $b = H(a)$ for some $a \in A_0$. So suppose $b \notin F(A_0)$. Then $b \in B - F(A_0)$, so $G(b) \in A - A_0$, and $H(G(b)) = G^{-1}(G(b)) = b$, so $H$ is onto. □

**Reference** Richard Kaye, *The Mathematics of Logic*, 2007: pp 176–7. Cambridge: Cambridge University Press.

# 10

---

# Semantics III: Logic and Variable Binding Operators

Generalized quantifiers and boolean lattices are powerful conceptual tools for representing aspects of natural language semantics. We pursue them more extensively in Chapters 11 and 12. Here we address two independent semantically significant topics that are enlighteningly treated within standard logic and its extensions. These concern scope ambiguities and "binding" phenomena. The tool we use from standard logic is *variable binding operators* (VBO's).

This chapter is presented in three parts: Section 10.1 contains the syntax and semantics of standard first order logic (FOL), together with basic examples of its utility in "translating" expressions from ordinary English. Section 10.2 steps back and summarizes a variety of general linguistic properties of FOL. The idea is to give the reader a feel for the "linguistic" character of work in logic, as well as to present several of the major results logicians have achieved. This section is intended for reference and is not presupposed by the subsequent sections and chapters of this book. Finally, Section 10.3 presents the syntax and semantics of the lambda operator, an enormously useful conceptual tool in the representation of semantic properties of natural language.

## 10.1 Translation Semantics

It is only recently[1] that the direct interpretation of natural language expressions has become feasible. More traditionally the semantic analysis of natural language proceeded by translation into logic, usually some variant of FOL. Such an approach is helpful because FOL is well understood, so translating English say into a first order language has

---

[1] The direct interpretation tradition can be said to have begun with Montague (1970b).

the merit of representing something we are trying to understand in terms of something we already understand.

### 10.1.1 Semantic Phenomena Motivating the Use of Variable Binding Operators

**Scope ambiguities**

Scope ambiguities have already been seen in simple examples like (1), which can be understood on the *object narrow scope* (ONS) reading in (1a), a reading our direct interpretation analysis already captures, and on the *object wide scope* (OWS) reading in (1b), which our analysis to date does not capture.

(1)   Some student praised every teacher.

      a. ONS: There is at least one student who praised every teacher.

      b. OWS: For every teacher there is a student who praised him (possibly different teachers were praised by different students).

So on the OWS reading the students may vary with the teachers. But on the ONS reading a student is chosen independently of the teachers and it is asserted that that student stands in the PRAISE relation to each teacher. (It is not ruled out that there is more than one student with this property). It is easy to imagine a situation in which (1) is true understood on the OWS reading but false on the ONS reading. Imagine a situation with just two students, John and Mary, and just two teachers. John praises one of the teachers and no one else, and Mary praises the other teacher and no one else. Then for each teacher there is a student who praised him, so (1b), the OWS reading of (1), is true. But no one student praised each teacher, so (1a), the ONS reading, is false.

In mathematical discourse scope ambiguities would be intolerable, whence the utility of variable binding notation there. Compare the strikingly different meanings of the two scope readings of (2) for example, into which we introduce an informal use of variables.

(2)   Some number is greater than every number.

      a. ONS: There is a number $x$ such that for every number $y$, $x > y$.

      b. OWS: for every number $y$ there is a number $x$ such that $x > y$.

In elementary arithmetic (2b) is true: given $y$, choose $x$ to be $y + 1$. But (2a) is false, a number greater than every number would be greater than itself, an impossibility.

Our concern in this chapter is with scope ambiguities involving pairs of DPs as illustrated here. But scope ambiguities arise for other expression types as well. For example (3) is ambiguous according to the scope of negation:

(3)   John didn't leave because the children were crying.

     a. John stayed, because the children were crying.

     b. John left, but not because the children were crying.

On the reading in (3a) the subordinate clause, *because the children were crying*, is not in the scope of the negation. Rather that clause modifies *didn't leave* and the sentence means roughly *Because the children were crying John didn't leave*. In (3b) the subordinate clause modifies *leave* and the entire modified predicate is negated, so the subordinate clause in particular is in the scope of *didn't*. (3b) doesn't deny that *John left*, it only denies that the children crying was the reason for his leaving.

## Binding

There is an ambiguity in (4), not entirely dissimilar to the scope ambiguity in (2):

(4)   Each of the children loves his mother.

On one reading *his* is understood as *bound* to *each of the children* and (4) would be true in a situation with several children as long as each one loves his own mother—Johnny loves his mother, Amy loves her mother, etc. So on this reading the mothers may vary with the children. (This does not force a reading on which different children have different mothers; some of the children may be brothers and sisters).

But (4) has a second reading, less apparent than the first when, as here, no context is provided. On this reading *his* refers to some male whose existence has been previously established in the discourse. Imagine that we have been discussing Billy, whose mother is the local kindergarten teacher beloved by all the children. Then an assertion of (4) might be used to assert that each child in the discourse loves Billy's mother. So on this reading context provides a denotation for *his*, and the choice of mothers does not vary with the choice of children.

Compare the use of *his* in (4) with that of *its* in the more mathematical (5).

(5)    Every number is less than or equal to its square.

       a. For every number $x$, $x$ is less than or equal to $x$ squared.

       b. For every number $x$, $x$ is less than or equal to $y$ squared.

Out of context the natural reading of (5) is (5a), in which the pronoun *its* is bound to *every number*. On this reading (5) implies that 3 is less than or equal to 3 squared (usually written $3 \leq 3^2$), $13 \leq 13^2$, and in general, for each number $n$, $n \leq n^2$.

Notice that the portion of (5a) following the quantifier phrase *for every number x*, uses the same variable $x$ twice. This is what tells us that we compare 3 with $3^2$, 13 with $13^2$, etc. The two occurrences of $x$ are said to both be *bound* by the quantifier phrase *for every number x*. In contrast, in (5b) we have used different variables in the portion following the quantifier phrase. Here the first occurrence, $x$, is bound by the quantifier phrase since its variable matches $x$. But the second variable $y$ is not bound by the quantifier phrase. This reading of (5) is comparable to the non-bound reading of *his mother* in (4), where context identifies a referent for the phrase and it does not vary with the choice of child. In (5) $y$ denotes some number fixed in context, but (5) itself provides no context to help us figure out the denotation of $y$.

This completes our illustration of the phenomena we are to represent. We turn now to an informal presentation of first order logic.

### 10.1.2    First Order Logic (with Equality)

First Order Logic (FOL) defines a class of languages, called *first order languages*, and states how expressions in each of these languages is semantically interpreted. So FOL is a kind of universal grammar. Different first order languages differ by their choices of lexical items, specifically their $n$-place predicate symbols and $n$-place function symbols (individual constants are 0-place function symbols). For example, in the language of Set Theory we would take a single two place predicate symbol, $\in$ , as primitive (and then of course state many axioms that use the predicate); in the language of Elementary Arithmetic we might have two two place function symbols, $+$ and $\cdot$, as primitive; in Euclidean geometry we would have a two place predicate symbol $\|$ read as *is parallel to* and a three place predicate symbol $B$ read as *is between*. In linguistic parlance these are the *parameters* of the language, and are called *non-logical constants*. Once given, all first order languages form complex expressions in the same ways (below).

## Syntax:

**Terms** are expressions which, when interpreted, denote elements in the domain $E_{\mathcal{M}}$ of a model $\mathcal{M}$ (defined shortly). Syntactically unanalyzable terms are either *individual variables*: $x, y, z, x_1, y_1, \ldots,$ of which there are always denumerably many ($=$ natural number many), or *individual constants* such as '0', '1', etc., of which there are usually just a few, sometimes none. Then complex terms are built recursively by combining function symbols, such as '+' in the language of arithmetic, with an appropriate number of terms to form a complex term. We usually write two place function symbols between their arguments, writing $(0 + 1)$ in preference to $+(0, 1)$. Since we use infix notation some parentheses are needed to rule out pernicious ambiguities. For example, $2 \cdot (3 + 4) = 14 \neq (2 \cdot 3) + 4 = 10$ so if we eliminated all parentheses we would have ambiguously denoting expressions (as we saw earlier in discussing the placement of boolean connectives).

**Formulas** are the sort of expression which we think of as True or False under an interpretation, and they come in three syntactic types: *Atomic Formulas*, *Boolean Compounds*, and *Quantified Formulas*.

**Atomic Formulas** are built by combining an $n$-place predicate symbol $P$ with n terms, $t_1, \ldots, t_n$, the result being noted $P(t_1, \ldots, t_n)$, which is called an *atomic* formula (even when the terms themselves are syntactically complex). Often when $P$ is a two place predicate symbol we write $(t_1 \, P \, t_2)$ rather than $P(t_1, t_2)$. So usually we write $(0 \leq 1)$ rather than $\leq (0, 1)$, and we write $(t_1 = t_2)$ instead of $= (t_1, t_2)$. Note that the standard syntax for first order languages treats $P_2$s as combining directly with pairs of expressions to form a $P_0$ (formula) rather than combining with just one to form a $P_1$, which in turn combines with one term to form a $P_0$. In the pair notation the "subject" argument is written first. So using English expressions, *Kim praised Amy* would be represented as *praise(Kim, Amy)*, whereas we have been writing *((praise Amy) Kim)*, with *praise Amy* a constituent of category $P_1$.

**Boolean Compounds** of formulas are formulas. Here we write '&' for 'and', 'or' for 'or', $-$ for 'not', $\rightarrow$ for 'if...then...' and $\leftrightarrow$ for 'if and only if'. Different authors use different variants of this notation. So if $P$ and $Q$ are formulas so are $(P \,\&\, Q)$, $(P \text{ or } Q)$, $-P$, $(P \rightarrow Q)$ and $(P \leftrightarrow Q)$. First order languages don't allow direct boolean compounds of $P_1$s (or $P_n$s for any $n > 0$), though expressive power would not be changed if we added this in.

**Quantified Formulas** are ones formed by concatenating a quantifier symbol followed by a variable, followed by a formula. There are two quantifier symbols: $\forall$, the universal quantifier symbol, read as "for all", and the existential quantifier symbol $\exists$, read as "for some", or "there exists". For example, in the language of elementary arithmetic $\forall x(x < x + 1)$ is a universally quantified formula read as "For all numbers x, x is less than x plus one". And $\exists x(Prime(x) \,\&\, Even(x))$ is an existentially quantified formula read as "There is a number x such that x is prime and x is even". Note that there is nothing in the formulas themselves that tells us what we are using the quantifiers to quantify over the natural numbers. It was the stipulation that these Ss were drawn from the language of elementary arithmetic that guarantees this in this case, since that language is just used to speak about the natural numbers.

**Semantics** (informal): Individual constants denote elements of the domain of a model. A derived term $F(t_1, \ldots, t_n)$ denotes the value of the function denoted by $F$ at the $n$-tuple of objects denoted by the $n$ terms $(t_1, \ldots, t_n)$. An atomic formula $P(t_1, \ldots, t_n)$ is true in a model $\mathcal{M}$ iff the $n$-tuple of objects denoted by the $n$-ary sequence $(t_1, \ldots, t_n)$ terms stands in the relation denoted by $P$. An equivalent approach treats '$P$' as denoting a function mapping $n$-tuples of objects from the domain $E$ into $\{T, F\}$. The symbol '$=$', a logical constant, denotes the identity relation, $\{\langle b, b \rangle \mid b \in E\}$.

Boolean compounds of formulas are interpreted as expected: A conjunction of formulas $(P \,\&\, Q)$ is interpreted as $T$ iff each conjunct is $T$, a disjunction is interpreted as $T$ iff at least one disjunct is $T$. A conditional $(P \to Q)$ is interpreted as $T$ iff $P$ is interpreted as $F$ or both $P$ and $Q$ are interpreted as $T$. $(P \leftrightarrow Q)$ is interpreted as $T$ iff $P$ and $Q$ are interpreted as the same truth value (both $T$ or both $F$).

For quantified formulas, $\forall x \varphi$ is interpreted as $T$ iff $\varphi$ is interpreted as $T$ no matter what object in the domain we let $x$ denote. $\exists x \varphi$ is interpreted as $T$ iff there is an object $b$ in the domain of the model such that $\varphi$ is interpreted as $T$ when we set $x$ to denote that $b$. To say this in a formally rigorous way we will need a mechanism which lets the denotations of variables vary holding constant the denotations of the other lexical items (the predicate and function symbols).

For example, in the first order language of Elementary Arithmetic the formula $\forall x(x \leq x^2)$ is true in the model whose domain is $\mathbb{N}$. No matter what $n \in \mathbb{N}$ we choose, $x \le x^2$ is true when $x$ is set to denote $n$. Similarly $\exists x(x = x^2)$ is true since letting $x$ denote 1 the formula $x = x^2$ is true. That formula is also true when $x$ is set to denote 0, but it is false when $x$ denotes any $n > 1$.

Crucially in a *first order language* $\mathcal{L}$ we may have symbols denoting functions or relations (on the domain of the model), but we cannot use quantifiers with variables ranging over such functions or relations. Thus (6a) is a first order sentence. It says that the function '$h$' denotes is one to one. But (6b), which says that there is a one to one function is not a first order sentence.

(6)  a. $\forall x \forall y (h(x) = h(y) \rightarrow x = y)$

b. $\exists h \forall x \forall y (h(x) = h(y) \rightarrow x = y)$

Similarly (7a), which says that $R$ is a symmetric relation, is first order, but (7b), which defines symmetry, is not:

(7)  a. $\forall x \forall y (xRy \leftrightarrow yRx)$

b. $\forall R (R \ is \ symmetric \ \leftrightarrow \forall x \forall y (xRy \leftrightarrow yRx))$

### 10.1.3  Representing English in First Order Logic

Representing English in FOL takes practice (and is not always possible, as we see below). The major artificiality is that DPs such as *every student*, *some student*, etc. do not occur as arguments of predicates. Consider the natural first order translations of the English Ss below:

(8)  a. John criticized every student.

b. $\forall x (\text{STUDENT}(x) \rightarrow \text{CRITICIZE}(\text{JOHN}, x))$

c. For every object $x$, if $x$ is a student then John criticized x.

(8b) is a standard first order rendition of (8a), though we would often abbreviate JOHN simply as '$j$'. A literal read-out of (8b) is (8c), which makes it clear that we are quantifying over all objects in the domain, not just the students. Moreover no constituent of (8b) or (8c) corresponds to *every student* in (8a). Compare (8a) with (9a) below:

(9)  a. John criticized some student.

b. $\exists x (\text{STUDENT}(x) \ \& \ \text{CRITICIZE}(\text{JOHN}, x))$

c. There is an object $x$ such that $x$ is a student and John criticized x.

Again, (9b), as made clear in (9c), quantifies over the entire domain of objects, not just the students. And the constituent *some student* in (9a) does not correspond to any constituent in (9b). Note too that both (8b) and (9b) introduce VBO's, $\forall x$ and $\exists x$ respectively, and in each case two occurrences of a variable in the following formula are bound, even though nothing in (8a) or (9a) indicates that binding is required (they contain no pronouns or DP gaps for example). Equally both (8b) and (9b) introduce a boolean operator, $\rightarrow$ in the case of (8b) and & in the case of (9b). The difference in boolean operator correlates with the difference in the choice of quantifier, $\forall$ vs. $\exists$. But that there are such differences at all is surprising. After all (8a) and (9a) appear to be syntactically isomorphic, differing just by a choice of lexical item, *every* vs. *some*.

These "unnaturalness" facts highlight that translations of English into FOL are not syntactically driven. The criterion of good translation is whether it gets the entailment properties right. Compare (8a) and (9a) with (10a) below, also apparently isomorphic to the first two.

(10)   a.   John criticized no student.

     b.   $-\exists x(\text{STUDENT}(x)\,\&\,\text{CRITICIZE}(\text{JOHN}, x))$

     b'.  $\forall x(\text{STUDENT}(x) \rightarrow -\text{CRITICIZE}(\text{JOHN}, x))$

     c.   It is not the case that for some object $x$, $x$ is a student and John criticized $x$.

     c'.  For all objects $x$, if $x$ is a student then it is not the case that John criticized $x$.

Here both (10b) and (10b') are reasonable translations of (10a) as they have the same, correct, truth conditions, hence the same entailments. And in general as the English sentences increase even slightly in complexity we find that the syntactic complexity of the FOL translations often skyrockets. Here are a few illustrative examples (shortening 'JOHN' to '$j$').

(11)   a.   John criticized two students.

     b.   $\exists x \exists y(\text{STUDENT}(x)\,\&\,\text{STUDENT}(y)\,\&$
        $-(x = y)\,\&\,\text{CRITICIZE}(j, x)\,\&\,\text{CRITICIZE}(j, y))$

So while (11a) appears syntactically isomorphic to (10a), its FOL translation uses two VBO's and five conjunctions. Further (11b) is true in any model in which John criticized at least two students, in particular ones in which he criticized a dozen students. To force an upper bound on the number criticized English can use little words like *only*, *exactly*, and *just* which effect only a modest increase in syntactic complexity. But consider (12a) and a reasonable FOL translation, (12b), which we may literally read as (12c).

(12)    a. John criticized exactly one student.

   b. $\exists x(\text{STUDENT}(x) \,\&\, \text{CRITICIZE}(j, x)$
      $\&\, \forall y((\text{STUDENT}(y) \,\&\, \text{CRITICIZE}(j, y)) \to y = x))$

   c. John criticized a student, and every student who John criticized is that one.

**Exercise 10.1.** Provide reasonable FOL translations for each of the following:

a. John criticized three students.

b. John criticized just two students.

c. John criticized a student and a teacher.

d. Every student criticized John.

e. Not every student criticized every student.

Now let us turn to some of the cases that motivate our interest in VBO's. Consider first the representation of each of the readings of (13)

(13) Some student praised every teacher.

   a. ONS: There is at least one student who praised every teacher.

   a′. $\exists x(\text{STUDENT}(x) \,\&\, \forall y(\text{TEACHER}(y) \to \text{PRAISE}(x, y)))$

   b. OWS: For every teacher there is a student who praised him.

   b′. $\forall y(\text{TEACHER}(y) \to \exists x(\text{STUDENT}(x) \,\&\, \text{PRAISED}(x, y))$

We have observed that (13b′) does not entail (13a′). Here is an informal model which shows this: Let TEACHER = {Mary, Sue}, and let STUDENT = {Manny, Moe, Jack}. Lastly, let Manny PRAISE Mary, and both Moe and Jack PRAISE Sue and no one else PRAISEs anyone else. Then for every teacher $y$ we can find a student $x$ such that $x$ praised $y$. In fact in Sue's case we can find two such $x$. However there is no student $x$ in this model who stands in the PRAISE relation to both Mary and Sue, hence (13a′) is false in this model. A rather more typical case for Ss with scope ambiguities is that neither scope reading entails the other.

294 / *Mathematical Structures in Language*

**Exercise 10.2.** Exhibit FOL translations of the two scope readings for the S displayed below. Then exhibit an informal model on which the ONS is true and the OWS false, showing that ONS↛ OWS. Then exhibit another model in which the OWS reading is true and the ONS one false, showing that OWS ↛ ONS.

Two students criticized two teachers.

Notice that coordinate $P_1$s in English must be translated into first order $\mathcal{L}$s with coordination at the S = $P_0$ level.

(14)   a. Some student both laughed and cried.
         $\exists z(\text{STUDENT}(z) \,\&\, \text{LAUGH}(z) \,\&\, \text{CRY}(z))$

       b. Some student laughed and some student cried.
         $\exists z(\text{STUDENT}(z) \,\&\, \text{LAUGH}(z)) \,\&\, \exists x(\text{STUDENT}(x) \,\&\, \text{CRY}(x))$

Clearly (14a) entails (14b) since if $x$ is a student who both laughed and cried then $x$ laughed, whence some student laughed, and also $x$ cried, whence some student cried, so (14b) is the conjunction of two true Ss and thus is true. But (14b) does not entail (14a). If John and Bill are the only students, John laughed but didn't cry and Bill cried but didn't laugh then (14b) is true and (14a) false.

**Exercise 10.3.** Exhibit FOL translations of (a) and (b). Say why (b) entails (a) and exhibit an informal model which shows that (a) does not entail (b).

    a. Each student either laughed or cried.

    b. Either each student laughed or each student cried.

**Exercise 10.4.** Exhibit the two scope readings in FOL translation of *No student likes every teacher.* (In practice speakers do not normally use this S intending the OWS reading. See Szabolcsi (1997), Steedman (2012) and Keenan (2016) for discussion of the availability of various scope readings.)

We now consider some cases of binding and non-binding. Such examples can be tricky. Compare first the two readings of (15). We assume here that *'s mother* is a one place function mapping each individual $x$ to $x$'s mother.

(15)  Every child loves his mother.

       a. $\forall x(\text{CHILD}(x) \to \text{LOVE}(x, x\text{'S MOTHER}))$
       b. $\forall x(\text{CHILD}(x) \to \text{LOVE}(x, y\text{'S MOTHER}))$

An occurrence of a variable $x$ in a formula $\varphi$ is said to be *bound* if it occurs in a constituent of $\varphi$ of the form $Qx\psi$, where $Q = \forall$ or $\exists$ (or any other VBO). Otherwise that occurrence of $x$ is *free* in $\varphi$. All occurrences of $x$ in (15a) and (15b) are bound. But the occurrence of $y$ in (15b) is free. Also we note a technical usage here. In logical parlance *sentences* are the special case of formulas with no free occurrences of variables.

A similar binding vs free pattern is seen in (16a) and (16b) below. Typically argument occurrences of reflexive pronouns (*himself, herself,* etc.) in English correspond to bound occurrences of variables in their FOL translations.

(16)　　a. Some student criticized himself.
　　　　　$\exists u(\text{STUDENT}(u)\ \&\ \text{CRITICIZE}(u,u))$

　　　　　b. Some student criticized him.
　　　　　$\exists u(\text{STUDENT}(u)\ \&\ \text{CRITICIZE}(u,x))$

In contrast pronouns like *him, her,* etc. correspond to free or to bound variables depending on the syntactic context in which they occur. They must be free when their antecedents would be "too close", as in (16b). But when their antecedents are farther away they can be free or bound. So (17a) and (17b) are acceptable FOL translations of (17).

(17)　Every teacher likes every student who likes him

　　　　　a. $\forall x(\text{TEACHER}(x) \rightarrow \forall y((\text{STUDENT}(y)\ \&\ \text{LIKE}(y,x)) \rightarrow \text{LIKE}(x,y)))$

　　　　　b. $\forall x(\text{TEACHER}(x) \rightarrow \forall y((\text{STUDENT}(y)\ \&\ \text{LIKE}(y,z)) \rightarrow \text{LIKE}(x,y)))$

We note that FOL does not provide a means of directly treating individual constants as VBO's. So its simplest translation of Ss like (18a) is as in (18b), though (18c) has the same truth conditions.

(18)　　a. John criticized himself.

　　　　　b. $\text{CRITICIZE}(j,j)$

　　　　　c. $\exists x(\text{CRITICIZE}(x,x)\ \&\ j = x)$

(18b) is awkward since English does not really like repeated proper nouns as arguments of P$_2$s. *John criticized John* is felt to be awkward. Speakers tend to say that the two occurrences of *John* refer to different individuals (exactly what we don't represent in (18b)!). Similarly (19a) is not quite adequately translated as (19b), since a free occurrence of

$x$ can denote any object in the domain. It might "accidentally" denote John. But English speakers tend to feel that in (19a) the two arguments of *admire* must be different in reference, not simply not necessarily the same.

(19)  a. John admires him.

   b. ADMIRE($j, x$)

Interestingly however repeated occurrences of quantified DPs is not judged awkward: *some student criticized some student, just one student praised just one student*, etc. are natural. Observe of course a stark meaning difference, as indicated in the different FOL translations:

(20)  a. Every student criticized every student.

   a′. $\forall x(\text{STUDENT}(x) \rightarrow (\forall y(\text{STUDENT}(y) \rightarrow \text{CRITICIZE}(x, y))))$

   b. Every student criticized himself.

   b′. $\forall x(\text{STUDENT}(x) \rightarrow \text{CRITICIZE}(x, x))$

**Exercise 10.5.** Exhibit an informal model in which (20b′) above is true and (20a′) false, showing that on the translations given, (20b) does not entail (20a). Note that (20a′) does entail (20b′).

**Exercise 10.6.** For each S below provide at least one FOL translation. In some, perhaps many, your translations will be syntactically quite different than the original English S.

   a. No one likes everyone who likes himself.

   b. John criticized some student other than himself.

   c. Every student criticized every student but himself.

   d. John criticized every student who did not criticize him.

   e. Every teacher either praised or criticized John.

   f. At least two students criticized each other.

   g. John is a teacher who admires himself.

   h. The only person who John criticized was Mary.

   i. Every student admires only himself.

   j. Only Lucifer admires only himself.

**Exercise 10.7.** Provide a FOL translation for the S below and argue that it is logically false (= false in every model). (Example due to Bertrand Russell).

> There is a barber who shaves just those barbers who do not shave themselves.

## First Order vs Second or Higher Order Logics

The distinguishing feature of first order logic (and languages) is that we can only quantify over the domain of a model. Second order logic quantifies over subsets of the domain and more generally over functions and relations on the domain, third order logic quantifies over sets of subsets of the domain, etc. Recall for example the sentences we used to define partial orders:

(21) For all binary relations $R$ (over a given domain $E$)

    a. $R$ is reflexive iff $\forall x(xRx)$

    b. $R$ is antisymmetric iff $\forall x \forall y(xRy \to yRx)$

    c. $R$ is transitive iff $\forall x \forall y \forall z((xRy \,\&\, yRz) \to xRz)$

(21) is a second order sentence since it quantifies over relations over the domain. A *monadic* second order sentence is one that just quantifies over subsets of the domain. For example, the version of mathematical induction we have been assuming is monadic second order: *For all sets $K$, if $0 \in K$ and $K$ is closed under addition of 1 then $\mathbb{N} \subseteq K$.*

## 10.1.4 Interpreting First Order Expressions

We indicated informally how the three types of first order formulas are interpreted. Now we are going to be more explicit about that, as there is one crucial interpretative mechanism we have quietly glossed over. The core idea is that the interpretation of an expression is relativized to "contexts", which we can think of as functions which interpret the free variables in the expression. That is, just as the interpretation of an English sentence such as *She is clever* depends on what the context tells us that *she* refers to, similarly the interpretation of a formula like $3 \leq x$ depends on what the context tells us that $x$ denotes. "Contexts" are technically called *assignments (of values to the variables)*. For the moment we are only using individual variables, ones that range over the domain of a model, so an assignment is simply a function from the set VAR $= \{x_1, x_2, \ldots\}$ of variables into $E$, the domain of the model. We assume an arbitrary first order language $\mathcal{L}$ is given.

**Definition 10.1.** For all sets $E$, $A_E$ is $[\text{VAR} \rightarrow E]$, the set of functions from the variables into $E$.

And for $\mathcal{M}$ a model with domain $E$, we design the interpreting function $[\![\cdot]\!]_{\mathcal{M}}$ so that expressions denote functions from the set $A_E$ of assignments into the appropriate denotation set. An expression with no free variables will denote a constant function, that is, its interpretation does not vary with the context (assignment). For example a lexical $P_1$ like *laugh* has no free variables and so will denote a constant function from $A_E$ into $[E \rightarrow \{T, F\}]$. On our old way of interpreting *laugh* it simply denoted an element of $[E \rightarrow \{T, F\}]$, so making it a function which associates a fixed element of $[E \rightarrow \{T, F\}]$ with all the contexts is not really very different. The important difference shows up with expressions that have free occurrences of variables.

A formula like $x$ *laughed* will denote, not a truth value, but a function from contexts (assignments) to truth values. And its truth value may vary with the assignment (context). For example if $\alpha$ is an assignment that maps $x$ to John and $\beta$ is one that maps $x$ to Jane then the denotation of $x$ *laughed* might map $\alpha$ to $T$ (if John laughed) and $\beta$ to $F$ (if Jane didn't laugh). In this way the interpretation of "open" expressions—ones with free variables—may vary with the context according to what the free variables denote.

And the crucial place where these assignments come into play is with the interpretation of quantified formulas. To give the main idea we first define:

**Definition 10.2.** For all assignments $\alpha$ and $\beta$, all variables $x$, $\beta$ is an *x-variant* of $\alpha$ iff $\beta(y) = \alpha(y)$ for all variables $y \neq x$. So $\beta$ may assign a different value to $x$ than $\alpha$ does (though it doesn't have to) but it assigns the same value as $\alpha$ does to all the other variables. For $b$ in the domain of the model $\mathcal{M}$, we write $\alpha^{x \rightarrow b}$ for that $x$-variant of $\alpha$ which maps $x$ to $b$. Formally

$$\alpha^{x \rightarrow b}(y) =_{df} \begin{cases} \alpha(y) & \text{if } y \neq x \\ b & \text{if } y = x. \end{cases}$$

Note that for each variable $x$, the binary relation *is an x-variant of* is an equivalence relation on $A_E$. (Reflexivity and symmetry are trivial. For transitivity let $x$ be an arbitrary variable and suppose that $\alpha$ is an $x$-variant of $\beta$ and $\beta$ an x-variant of $\gamma$. We must show that $\alpha$ is an $x$-variant of $\gamma$. Let $y$ be a variable other than $x$. Then $\alpha(y) = \beta(y)$ by the first assumption, and $\beta(y) = \gamma(y)$ by the second. So by the transitivity of $=$, $\alpha(y) = \gamma(y)$ showing that $\alpha$ is an $x$-variant of $\gamma$). Now we give the truth conditions for quantified formulas as follows:

**Definition 10.3.** For all models $\mathcal{M}$ with domain $E_{\mathcal{M}}$, and all assignments $\alpha$,

a. $[\![\forall x\varphi]\!]_{\mathcal{M}}(\alpha) = T$ iff for all $b \in E_{\mathcal{M}}$, $[\![\varphi]\!]_{\mathcal{M}}(\alpha^{x \to b}) = T$, and

b. $[\![\exists x\varphi]\!]_{\mathcal{M}}(\alpha) = T$ iff for some $b \in E_{\mathcal{M}}$, $[\![\varphi]\!]_{\mathcal{M}}(\alpha^{x \to b}) = T$.

Thus $\varphi$ universally quantified maps a context $\alpha$ to $T$ iff $\varphi$ maps to $T$ every context that differs from $\alpha$ at most by what it assigns to the variable $x$. Similarly $\varphi$ existentially quantified is true in a context $\alpha$ iff $\varphi$ is true of some assignment that differs from $\alpha$ at most in what it assigns to $x$. In both cases the interpretation of the quantified formula is done compositionally: $[\![Qx\varphi]\!]_{\mathcal{M}}$ is defined in terms of $[\![\varphi]\!]_{\mathcal{M}}$, all $Q = \forall$ or $\exists$.

For later reference we give a comprehensive formal definition of model and entailment for first order languages. (Some readers may want to skip this definition on first reading.)

**Definition 10.4.** For $\mathcal{L}$ an arbitrary first order language a model $\mathcal{M}$ is a pair $(E, [\![\cdot]\!]_{\mathcal{M}})$, where $E$ is a non-empty set, the domain of $\mathcal{M}$, and $[\![\cdot]\!]_{\mathcal{M}}$ is a function mapping each expression of $\mathcal{L}$ to a function from the assignments over $E$ satisfying:

a. Lexical conditions:

    i. For $P$ an $n$-place predicate symbol, $[\![P]\!]_{\mathcal{M}}$ is a constant function from $A_E$ into $[E^n \to \{T, F\}]$.

    ii. For $c$ an individual constant $[\![c]\!]_{\mathcal{M}}$ is a constant function from $A_E$ into $E$.

    iii. For $F$ an $n > 0$ place function symbol, $[\![F]\!]_{\mathcal{M}}$ is a constant function from $A_E$ into $[E^n \to E]$.

    iv. $[\![=]\!]_{\mathcal{M}}$ is a constant function sending each $\alpha$ to $\{\langle b, b\rangle \mid b \in M\}$.

b. Term conditions:

    i. For $x$ a variable $[\![x]\!]_{\mathcal{M}}$ maps each assignment $\alpha$ to $\alpha(x)$ (So in a context $\alpha$ a variable denotes what the context says it denotes)

    ii. For $F$ an $n$-place function symbol and $t_1, \ldots, t_n$ terms, $[\![F(t_1, \ldots, t_n)]\!]_{\mathcal{M}}$ maps each assignment $\alpha$ to $[\![F]\!]_{\mathcal{M}}(\alpha)([\![t_1]\!]_{\mathcal{M}}(\alpha), \ldots, [\![t_n]\!]_{\mathcal{M}}(\alpha))$.
    (That is, $[\![F(t_1, \ldots, t_n)]\!]_{\mathcal{M}}$ maps each assignment $\alpha$ to the object that the function $F$ is interpreted as in $\alpha$ maps the $n$-tuple of objects that the $n$ terms are interpreted as in $\alpha$.)

c. Atomic formula conditions:

    i. For $P$ an $n$-place predicate symbol and $t_1, \ldots, t_n$ terms, $[\![P(t_1, \ldots, t_n)]\!]_{\mathcal{M}}$ maps each assignment $\alpha$ to $[\![P]\!]_{\mathcal{M}}(\alpha)([\![t_1]\!]_{\mathcal{M}}(\alpha), \ldots, [\![t_n]\!]_{\mathcal{M}}(\alpha))$.

d. Boolean conditions:
Boolean compounds are interpreted pointwise on the assignments

    i. $[\![\varphi \,\&\, \psi]\!]_{\mathcal{M}}(\alpha) = [\![\varphi]\!]_{\mathcal{M}}(\alpha) \wedge [\![\psi]\!]_{\mathcal{M}}(\alpha)$.

    ii. $[\![\varphi \text{ or } \psi]\!]_{\mathcal{M}}(\alpha) = [\![\varphi]\!]_{\mathcal{M}}(\alpha) \vee [\![\psi]\!]_{\mathcal{M}}(\alpha)$.

    iii. $[\![-\varphi]\!]_{\mathcal{M}}(\alpha) = \neg[\![\varphi]\!]_{\mathcal{M}}(\alpha)$.

    iv. $[\![\varphi \to \psi]\!]_{\mathcal{M}}(\alpha) = \neg[\![\varphi]\!]_{\mathcal{M}}(\alpha) \vee [\![\psi]\!]_{\mathcal{M}}(\alpha)$.

    v. $[\![\varphi \leftrightarrow \psi]\!]_{\mathcal{M}}(\alpha) = T$ iff $[\![\varphi]\!]_{\mathcal{M}}(\alpha) = [\![\psi]\!]_{\mathcal{M}}(\alpha)$.

e. Quantifier conditions:
Quantified formulas are interpreted as in Definition 10.3 above. An equivalent statement is:

    i. $[\![\forall x \varphi]\!]_{\mathcal{M}}(\alpha) = \bigwedge \{[\![\varphi]\!]_{\mathcal{M}}(\alpha^{x \to b}) \mid b \in E\}$
    (Recall, for $K$ a non-empty subset of $\{T, F\}$, $\bigwedge K = T$ iff $K = \{T\}$.)

    ii. $[\![\exists x \varphi]\!]_{\mathcal{M}}(\alpha) = \bigvee \{[\![\varphi]\!]_{\mathcal{M}}(\alpha^{x \to b}) \mid b \in E\}$
    (Recall, for $K \subseteq \{T, F\}$, $\bigvee K = T$ iff $T \in K$.)

So the universal quantifier, like *and*, is a glb operator, and the existential quantifier, like *or*, is a lub operator. Given a context, $\forall x \varphi$ denotes the greatest lower bound of the set of truth values denoted by $\varphi$ when we let $x$ denote successively the elements of $E$. (If all those values are $T$ then the set is $\{T\}$ and its glb is $T$. But if one of those values is $F$ then the set is $\{F\}$ or $\{F, T\}$ and in each case its glb is $F$). In a similar way existential quantification is a least upper bound operator. $\exists x \varphi$ denotes the least upper bound of the set of truth values denoted by $\varphi$ when we let $x$ denote successively the elements of $E$. If one those values is $T$ then the set is $\{T\}$ or $\{T, F\}$ and in each case its lub is $T$. If none of its values is $T$ then the set is $\{F\}$ and its lub is $F$.

**Notational variants.** Texts often write $[\![\varphi]\!]_{\mathcal{M}}^{\alpha}$ or $[\![\varphi]\!]^{\mathcal{M}, \alpha}$ instead of $[\![\varphi]\!]_{\mathcal{M}}(\alpha)$ and read it as "the interpretation of $\varphi$ in the model $\mathcal{M}$ at the assignment $\alpha$". We will stay with our function-argument notation but the reader should realize that anything that can be said with one notation can be said with the other. Also we often omit the brackets, writing $\varphi_{\mathcal{M}}$ instead of $[\![\varphi]\!]_{\mathcal{M}}$.

Now to define truth in a model and entailment it simplifies matters to use the Coincidence Lemma below, which guarantees that we can ignore assignments when dealing with expressions that have no free variables. We first define what we mean by a *free variable* in $\varphi$: FV will be a function mapping each expression $\varphi$ to the set of variables which occur free in $\varphi$:

**Definition 10.5.**

a. $\mathrm{FV}(c) = \emptyset$ if $c$ is an individual constant,

b. $\mathrm{FV}(x) = \{x\}$ if $x$ is a variable,

c. $\mathrm{FV}(H(t_1, \ldots, t_n)) = \mathrm{FV}(t_1) \cup \cdots \cup \mathrm{FV}(t_n)$ if $H$ is an $n$-place function or predicate symbol and $t_1, \ldots, t_n$ are terms,

d. $\mathrm{FV}(-\varphi) = FV(\varphi)$,

e. $\mathrm{FV}(\varphi\, c\, \psi) = \mathrm{FV}(\varphi) \cup \mathrm{FV}(\psi)$ for $c = \&, \mathrm{or}, \rightarrow$, or $\leftrightarrow$, and

f. $\mathrm{FV}(\forall x \varphi) = \mathrm{FV}(\exists x \varphi) = \mathrm{FV}(\varphi) - \{x\}$ for $x$ any variable.

**Theorem 10.1** (The Coincidence Lemma). *For $\varphi$ a first order formula, $\mathcal{M}$ a model and $\alpha$ and $\beta$ assignments, if $\alpha(x) = \beta(x)$ for all variables $x \in FV(\varphi)$, then $[\![\varphi]\!]_{\mathcal{M}}(\alpha) = [\![\varphi]\!]_{\mathcal{M}}(\beta)$.*

**Corollary 10.2.** *If $\varphi$ has no free variables ($FV(\varphi) = \emptyset$) then for all assignments $\alpha$, $\beta$, $[\![\varphi]\!]_{\mathcal{M}}(\alpha) = [\![\varphi]\!]_{\mathcal{M}}(\beta)$.*

**Definition 10.6.** For $\varphi$ a formula, $\mathcal{M} = (E, [\![\cdot]\!]_{\mathcal{M}})$ a model and $\alpha$ an assignment,

a. $\varphi$ is *True in $\mathcal{M}$ at $\alpha$* iff $[\![\varphi]\!]_{\mathcal{M}}(\alpha) = T$. In such a case we also write $\mathcal{M} \models_\alpha \varphi$ and say that $\mathcal{M}$ *satisfies* $\varphi$ at $\alpha$.

b. If $\varphi$ is a sentence (no free variables recall), $\varphi$ *is True in $\mathcal{M}$*, noted simply $[\![\varphi]\!]_{\mathcal{M}} = T$, iff for some $\alpha$, $[\![\varphi]\!]_{\mathcal{M}}(\alpha) = T$. In such a case we write simply $\mathcal{M} \models \varphi$ and say that $\mathcal{M}$ *satisfies* $\varphi$. (If a sentence $\varphi$ is True at some $\alpha$ it is True at all, by the Coincidence Lemma). $\varphi$ is said to be *satisfiable* iff there a model $\mathcal{M}$ such that $\mathcal{M} \models \varphi$ and $\varphi$ is *logically true* (*valid*) iff for all models $\mathcal{M}$, $\mathcal{M} \models \varphi$.

c. A set $K$ of sentences *entails* ($\models$) a sentence $\psi$ iff for all $\mathcal{M}$, $\bigwedge\{[\![\varphi]\!]_{\mathcal{M}} \mid \varphi \in K\} \leq [\![\psi]\!]_{\mathcal{M}}$. (This just says that $\psi$ is true in all models in which the $\varphi$ in $K$ are simultaneously True). We say that a sentence $\varphi$ *entails* a sentence $\psi$ iff $\{\varphi\} \models \psi$. And sentences $\varphi$ and $\psi$ are *logically equivalent*, noted $\varphi \equiv \psi$, iff each entails the other.

### 10.1.5   Remarks

**Notational simplification.** Generalizing our convention in Definition 10.6b above, we write simply $[\![\varphi]\!]_{\mathcal{M}}$ instead of $[\![\varphi]\!]_{\mathcal{M}}(\alpha)$ when $\varphi$ of any category is *closed*, that is, has no free variables and thus denotes a constant function on the assignments. And when $\varphi$ is syntactically simple we often omit the double brackets, writing simply $\varphi_{\mathcal{M}}$ instead of $[\![\varphi]\!]_{\mathcal{M}}$. For example if EVEN is a one place predicate symbol in a language (say, the language of elementary arithmetic) we would write EVEN$_{\mathcal{M}}$ instead of $[\![\text{EVEN}]\!]_{\mathcal{M}}$.

**Some simple logical equivalences.** Here are some useful logical equivalences involving the quantifiers and negation:

(22)    a. $\forall x \varphi \equiv -\exists x - \varphi$

       b. $\exists x \varphi \equiv -\forall x - \varphi$

       c. $-\forall x \varphi \equiv \exists x - \varphi$

       d. $-\exists x \varphi \equiv \forall x - \varphi$

The universal and existential quantifiers are *duals* of each other, just as *and* and *or* are (and just as $\Box$ (necessity) and $\Diamond$ (possibility) are in modal logic). The interpretations of *and, all,* $\Box$ are meet operations, and those for *or, some,* and $\Diamond$ are join operations.

The rules which prefix a quantifier to a formula $\varphi$ do not require that the variable they use occur in $\varphi$ (much less occur free). In linguistic parlance first order languages allow *vacuous quantification*. It is sometimes held that natural languages disallow it. In any event, (23a,b) are well formed formulas in the language of first order arithmetic:

(23)    a. $\forall x(0 < 1)$

       b. $\exists x(0 > 1)$

Moreover such formulas pose no interpretative problem, not even a special case. If $x$ has no free occurrences in $\varphi$ then

$$[\![\forall x \varphi]\!]_{\mathcal{M}} = [\![\exists x \varphi]\!]_{\mathcal{M}} = [\![\varphi]\!]_{\mathcal{M}}.$$

This follows from our truth definition for quantified formulas (and uses the Coincidence Lemma). Still Ss such as (23a,b) seem useless, so why don't we restrict the syntax of FOL to require that $Qx$ can only combine with a $\varphi$ in which $x$ occurs free? The answer is that such a restriction would force us to make many unenlightening restrictions on meta-theorems. For example it is a meta-theorem that universal quantification distributes over conjunction:

$$\forall x(\varphi \,\&\, \psi) \equiv (\forall x\varphi \,\&\, \forall x\psi).$$

Now if $x$ was not free in $\varphi$ but was in $\psi$ it would occur free in $(\varphi \,\&\, \psi)$. So the formula on the left of $\equiv$ is well formed, but the one on the right is not, since $\forall x\varphi$ is not a formula. So the natural distributivity meta-theorem doesn't hold in the more restrictive syntax, and the reason does not seem enlightening.

**Alphabetic variants.** Every first order formula has infinitely many *alphabetic variants*, all logically equivalent to it. For example (24a,b,c) differ just by choice of bound variable, they are alphabetic variants and logically equivalent. Definition 10.7 is the explicit definition.

(24)   a. $\forall x(Px \to Qx)$

   b. $\forall y(Py \to Qy)$

   c. $\forall z(Pz \to Qz)$

**Definition 10.7.** For $\mathcal{L}$ a first order language with $V$ its basic vocabulary and VAR its set of individual variables, let $\pi$ be a permutation of VAR (so $\pi$ is a bijection from VAR onto VAR). Extend $\pi$ to $V$ by putting $\pi(d) = d$, all $d \in V$. Extend $\pi$ to all sequences of symbols $s = \langle s_1, \ldots, s_n \rangle$ over $V \cup$ Var by setting $\pi(s) = \langle \pi(s_1), \ldots, \pi(s_n) \rangle$. Then we define a formula $\psi$ to be an *alphabetic variant* of a formula $\varphi$ iff for some such $\pi$, $\psi = \pi(\varphi)$.

**Exercise 10.8.** Show that the *is an alphabetic variant of* relation on expressions is an equivalence relation.

One shows by induction on formula and term complexity that any two alphabetic variants are logically equivalent. Here is the induction principle on formulas that would be used:

**Definition 10.8.** Let $\mathcal{L}$ be the set of expressions of some first order language. Then if $K \subseteq \mathcal{L}$ satisfying conditions (a)–(c) below then all formulas of $\mathcal{L}$ are in $K$:

   a. All atomic formulas are in $K$.

   b. $K$ is closed under the formation of boolean compounds. That is, if $\varphi, \psi \in K$ then $-\varphi$, $(\varphi \,\&\, \psi)$, $(\varphi$ or $\psi)$, $(\varphi \to \psi)$ and $(\varphi \leftrightarrow \psi)$ are all in $K$.

c. $K$ is closed under universal and existential quantification. That is, if $\varphi \in K$ then for all variables $x$, $\forall x \varphi$ and $\exists x \varphi \in K$.

Thus to prove that all formulas have some property $P$ let $K$ be the set of formulas with $P$ and show that all atomic formulas are in $K$ and that $K$ is closed under the formation of boolean compounds and quantification.

We turn in Section 10.3 to one extension to the class of VBO's—the *lambda* operator—which makes the logic a more natural vehicle for representing natural language. But let us note some general linguistic properties of FOL. Little that we do later in this book presupposes this material, but FOL is well studied and has many appealing linguistic properties, to the point where it is not foolish to think of mathematical logic as a mode of linguistic analysis—but the languages studied are mathematical ones (the language of Set Theory, Euclidean Geometry, Elementary Arithmetic for example) and increasingly programming languages in computer science.

## 10.2 Some General Linguistic Properties of First Order Logic (FOL)

Three of the four general properties of SL (Sentential Logic) we presented in Chapter 8 generalize to FOL, though the generalizations involve significant enrichments in some cases.

**Proposition 10.3.** *Both SL and any first order language are compact: whenever a set $K$ of sentences entails a sentence $\varphi$ then some finite subset of $K$ entails $\varphi$.*

Both SL and all first order languages satisfy *interpolation*, though its statement must be enriched to take into account the richer syntax of FOL (which includes the logical constant $=$) and its proof is significantly more complex (see Boolos and Jeffrey, 1980, Ch. 23 and Monk, 1976, Ch. 22):

**Proposition 10.4** (Craig's Interpolation Lemma). *For $\mathcal{L}$ a first order language and $\varphi, \psi$ sentences of $\mathcal{L}$, if $\varphi \models \psi$ then there is a sentence $\tau$ of $\mathcal{L}$ such that*

a. $\varphi \models \tau$ *and* $\tau \models \psi$ *and*

b. *all non-logical constants occurring in $\tau$ occur in both $\varphi$ and $\psi$.*

As in SL the Craig Lemma is a kind of relevancy condition on entailment. It says that whether some $\psi$ is entailed by some $\varphi$ depends just on what they have in common.

**Soundness and Completeness** generalize to the FOL case. Since we have a greater diversity of syntactic structures in FOL (predicates and arguments, quantifiers) we must extend the (syntactically defined) deduction system with more derivational rules. For example, if we have a line in a proof of the form $\forall x(Px)$ and $t$ is a term in our language, then we must be able to infer $P(t)$. But logicians have formulated (in several ways) the deduction system(s) we need, yielding the following elegant theorem, where $S \vdash \varphi$ says that there is a proof of $\varphi$ from premises in $S$:

(25) $S \models \varphi$ iff $S \vdash \varphi$

So again the semantic relation, entailment, is syntactically characterized by $\vdash$ relation. The left to right direction of (25) is *completeness*: if $\varphi$ follows from $S$ then there is a proof of $\varphi$ from premises in $S$. The right to left direction is *soundness*—whenever we can derive $\varphi$ from a set of premises $S$ then indeed $S$ really does entail $\varphi$. Also (25) enables us to give a linguistically useful equivalent statement of compactness. Namely,

(26) For any set $K$ of sentences in a first order language $\mathcal{L}$, $K$ has a model iff every finite subset of $K$ has a model.

(A set of sentences has a model $\mathcal{M}$ iff every $\varphi \in K$ is true in $\mathcal{M}$ (that is $[\![\varphi]\!]_{\mathcal{M}} = T$)). To prove (26) from compactness as we defined it, note that the left to right direction above is trivial: if some $\mathcal{M}$ makes every sentence in $K$ true then for any finite subset $K'$ of $K$, every sentence in $K'$ is true in $\mathcal{M}$. Going the other way, suppose that every finite subset of $K$ has a model. And leading to a contradiction assume that $K$ itself does not have a model. Then (vacuously) $K \models \exists x(x \neq x)$, the latter sentence having no models, so by completeness $K \vdash \exists x(x \neq x)$, and since proofs are finite sequences of formulas only finitely many of the sentences in $K$ were used in the proof. Let $K'$ be such a set. So $K' \vdash \exists x(x \neq x)$ whence by soundness $K' \models \exists x(x \neq x)$. But that means that $K'$ has no model since any model of it would also have to be a model of $\exists x(x \neq x)$. And this contradicts our assumption that every finite subset of $K$ has a model. Thus compactness entails the displayed sentence above (and in fact is equivalent to it, but we only need the entailment case later).

**Definability (Is English first order?).** Here we are concerned with whether the semantic analysis of English (or any other natural language) can be given in the first order apparatus we spelled out above. Coming at this question cold a "Yes" answer would seem discouraging.

Thorough grammars of natural languages run to several hundreds of pages, and they don't even pretend to enumerate just the expressions competent speakers accept, nor, despite semantic insights, do they provide a systematic semantic interpretation of the sort we gave for FOL above in just a few pages. Is it really plausible that we only need a page and a half of semantic interpretation to represent what it takes us hundreds of pages to spell out in the syntax? Nonetheless at a certain point in the history of generative grammar linguists tended to assume that something close to a first order semantics for a natural language would suffice (see Chomsky and Lasnik, 1977 for such an assumption, albeit one that played no important role in their conclusions in that article). Then several scholars debated whether certain (sometimes subtle) aspects of English were or were not first order definable (Barwise, 1979, Hintikka, 1974, Gabbay and Moravcsik, 1974, Guenthner and Hoepelmann, 1974, Fauconnier, 1975, Boolos, 1981). Below we offer a non-subtle argument that English is not first order: we exhibit a class of naturally expressible quantifiers which provably cannot be defined in FOL.

But first, idle curiosity aside, "Why should we care whether English semantics can be expressed in first order?". One reason is that FOL has many very nice properties, of which we have begun to cite a few. So if the syntax and semantic interpretation of English (or any other natural language) can be given in first order that means that English and presumably natural languages in general have these nice properties. Perhaps more important scientifically, FOL is well studied and well understood. So if we succeed in formulating English semantics in first order we will have succeeded in representing something we are trying to understand in terms of something we already understand. To some extent,

Knowledge is translation from the unknown to the known.

Thirdly, as we have noted above, many mathematical theories have or admit of first order axiomatizations (meaning that the axioms of the theory are first order sentences). Set theory is a crucial case in point, as it is often held that most of mathematics can be coded in set theory. Now regardless of the precise status of this latter claim, it is clear that we can express a lot in first order formulas, so it would be of interest to learn whether the semantic analysis of natural languages forces us beyond that or not. To support such claims, we must first be clear about what it means to be first order definable. Let us give some examples, both pro and con.

(27)   a. *There exist at least n things* can be said in first order (for
         each $n \in \mathbb{N}$), but

      b. *There exist just finitely many things* is not sayable in first
         order, nor is *There are infinitely many things*.

Here is how we say *There are at least 3 things*. Let $\varphi$ be defined by

$$\varphi = \exists x \exists y \exists z (x \neq y \,\&\, x \neq z \,\&\, y \neq z).$$

$\varphi$ is clearly a first order sentence and for all models $\mathcal{M}$, $[\![\varphi]\!]_{\mathcal{M}} = T$ iff
$|E_{\mathcal{M}}| \geq 3$. A common way of putting this would be,

(28)   for all models $\mathcal{M}$, $\mathcal{M} \models \varphi$ iff $3 \leq |E_{\mathcal{M}}|$.

So the models that satisfy $\varphi$ are just those whose domains have at
least three elements. And in general for any $n \in \mathbb{N}$ , we can say *There
are at least n things* in a comparable way: we begin with $n$ existential
quantifiers using distinct variables and form the conjunction of all the
non-equals sentences using all distinct pairs of these variables. So all
we need is the logical predicate $=$.

Now consider (27b). First we show that *There are infinitely many
things* is not first order definable (FOD). From this it follows that *There
are just finitely many things* is not FOD. For if it were, its negation,
*There are not just finitely many things* would be a first order definition of *There are infinitely many things*. Now it looks as though we
might construct a definition of this latter sentence starting with some
disjunction of the form: *There is at least one thing or there are at least
two things or ... there are at least n things or ....* But this "sentence"
would be an infinite disjunction, and all expressions in a first order
language are of finite length. So this is not a first order definition. And
in fact our sentence has no first order definition. Here is a proof using
compactness:

*Proof.* Let $\Phi = \{\varphi_n \mid n \in \mathbb{N}\}$, where $\varphi_n$ is the sentence *There exist
at least n things*. Let $\psi$ be the sentence *There exist just finitely many
things*. Then any finite subset $K$ of $\Phi \cup \{\psi\}$ has a model. Just choose
$E_{\mathcal{M}}$ to be $\{1, 2, \ldots, n\}$ where $n$ is the largest number such that $\varphi_n \in K$.
The model is finite so $\psi$ is true (whether it is in $K$ or not) and each $\varphi_m$
in $K$ is true in $\mathcal{M}$. Thus every finite subset of $\Phi \cup \{\psi\}$ has a model, so
by compactness (if our language is first order) the entire set $\Phi \cup \{\psi\}$ has
a model $\mathcal{M}$. But it doesn't since if $\psi$ holds $\mathcal{M}$ is finite, of cardinality
m say, so $\varphi_{m+1}$ is false in $\mathcal{M}$ so $\mathcal{M}$ is not a model for $\Phi \cup \{\psi\}$. So a
language which can say *There are just finitely many things* is not first
order. $\qquad\square$

And from these observations it is a small step to show that the quantifiers in (29) are not first order definable:

(29)    a. *Just finitely many* sentences have fewer than ten words.

       b. *Infinitely many* sentences have more than ten words.

       c. *All but finitely many* sentences have more than ten words.

Let us say explicitly what it means for an English-type quantifier (including the mathematical ones above) to be first order definable. In the simplest cases in English quantifiers such as *all, some, no, most, several, not all, most but not all, nearly forty and infinitely many others* (Chapter 12) are Determiners which combine with a common noun such as *poet* to form a DP, which combines in the basic case with a $P_1$ to form a $P_0$, as in *All (most, no, some) poets daydream*.

**Definition 10.9.** For $D$ a functional which associates with each domain $E$ a function $D_E$ from $\mathcal{P}(E)$ into $[\mathcal{P}(E) \to \{T, F\}]$, $D$ is *first order* iff there is a sentence $\varphi$ in a first order language $\mathcal{L}$ whose only non-logical constants are two one place predicate symbols $P,Q$ such that for all models $\mathcal{M}$ for $\mathcal{L}$,

$$\mathcal{M} \models \varphi \text{ iff } D_{E_\mathcal{M}} P_\mathcal{M} Q_\mathcal{M} = T.^2$$

For example to see that *exactly one* is first order definable, set

$$\varphi = \exists x ((Px \,\&\, Qx) \,\&\, \forall y ((Py \,\&\, Qy) \to y = x)).$$

And taking EXACTLY ONE to map sets $A, B$ to $T$ iff $|A \cap B| = 1$ we can prove that $(\text{EXACTLY ONE})_E P_M Q_M = T$ iff $[\![\varphi]\!]_\mathcal{M} = T$, showing that $\varphi$ defines this quantifier.

If the only English quantifiers that lay beyond the first order boundary used technical notions like *(in)finite* we might not, as linguists, regard the boundary as very constraining. So we note a few additional cases, the first showing that first order definability may be subtle in appearance (unlike the unsubtle appearance of words like *finite*, etc.).

First, quantifying over natural numbers is usually not first order definable and some statements that do that do not do it in an obvious way. Adapting informally an example from Kolaitis (2006) to whom we refer the reader for a precise statement and proof, let us consider the set $T[r, b]$ of trees with $r$ the root and $b$ a leaf node distinct from $r$. Let $\varphi_n$ be the statement *There is no path of length n or less from r to b.*

---

$^2$ $P_\mathcal{M}$ here is the set of $b \in E$ that $[\![P]\!]_\mathcal{M}$ maps to $T$ (under any assignment). Analogously for $Q_\mathcal{M}$.

Set $\Phi = \{\varphi_n \mid n \in \mathbb{N} \ \& \ n > 1\}$ and let $\psi$ say For all distinct nodes $x, y$ there is a path from $x$ to $y$ or a path from $y$ to $x$. (Recall that a path was defined to be a finite sequence of distinct nodes satisfying certain (first order) conditions). Let $K$ be any finite subset of $\Phi \cup \{\psi\}$. Clearly $K$ has a model: just choose the tree to be a chain with $n$ distinct nodes between $r$ and $b$. The path from $r$ to $b$ has length $n + 1$ and that is the only path from $r$ to $b$ so there is no path of length $n$ from $r$ to $b$. Further $\psi$ obviously holds in every chain. By compactness $\Phi \cup \{\psi\}$ should have a finite model. But it doesn't, as $\Phi \cup \{\psi\} \models \varphi_n$ for every $n > 0$. (Kolaitis shows a stronger result—connectivity is not first order definable even over finite models).

Our last examples are again drawn from natural language proper. The first concerns proportionality quantifiers like *most* in the sense of *more than half*. Such quantifiers include fractional and percentage expressions such as *a third of*, *seventy per cent of*, as well as a variety of constructions whose meaning is proportional but are not constructed with *of* as partitives are: *seven out of ten (sailors smoke Players), not one student in ten (knows the answer to that question)*. Now Barwise and Cooper (1981) provide a summary argument that *more than half* is not first order definable (even limiting ourselves to finite domains). The techniques introduced in Westerståhl (1989) can also be used. And in general when D is properly proportional (D is not a boolean function of 100% (= ALL) and 0% (= NO), and the truth of $D(A)(B)$ depends on the proportion of $A$s that are $B$s) D is not first order definable. Without reconstructing the "back and forth" methods used in the proof, we may help convince the reader of the non-first-orderizability of *most* and its kin by observing that we could explicitly enumerate the cases of *Most As are Bs* if there were just finitely many $A$s and we knew how many. For example, for $|A| = 5$, *Most As are Bs* is true iff *at least three of the five As are Bs*. And *at least 3 of the 5*, and more generally *at least n of the m*, for $n, m \in \mathbb{N}$, are first order definable. So intuitively *most* could be expressed by a disjunction of the form: *at least two of the three or at least three of the four or at least three of the five,...* but, as with *finite*, we cannot form an infinite disjunction in first order. So we see that proportionality quantifiers pose problems comparable to those of more mathematical predicates.

Moreover the proportionality cases also serve to show that cardinal comparisons are not definable in first order. Such comparatives are illustrated in (30). Note that they combine with two Nouns and a $P_1$ and so denote functions mapping three subsets of the domain into $\{T, F\}$.

(30)    a. *More* students *than* teachers came to the party.

   b. John interviewed *exactly as many* men as women.

   c. *More than twice as many* men *as* women get drafted.

If *more...than...* were first order definable then we could define *most* by saying *Most As are Bs* iff *More As that are Bs than As that are not Bs exist*. But since *most* in this sense is not first order definable neither is *more...than...* or the infinitely many other cardinal comparatives.

**Decidability** however does not fully carry over from SL to FOL. There is no algorithm that tells us for an arbitrary first order sentence $\varphi$ that it is true in all models if it is, and that it isn't, if it isn't (Church, 1936, Turing, 1936). On reflection this is not surprising. Many quite non-trivial mathematical theories, such as Set Theory, Group Theory, and Elementary Arithmetic, have or can be given axioms in first order. And many proofs from these axioms seem non-obvious, ingenious, or complicated. So it would be surprising to learn that we could program a computer to look at any first order formula we wrote down and tell us that it is true if it is and that it is false if it isn't.

On the other hand, while validity is not decidable in FOL, it does have a weaker property—that of being *semi-decidable* (Enderton, 1985), also called in this case *recursively enumerable*. By the completeness of FOL we know that if a first order $\varphi$ is valid then there is a proof of $\varphi$ (from no premises). A proof is a finite sequence of formulas and whether a finite sequence of formulas is a proof or not is decidable. Thus there is a mechanical procedure which tells us that an arbitrary $\varphi$ is valid if it is, but no procedure which tells us that $\varphi$ is not valid if it isn't. We note that if a set, say the set of valid formulas in some first order language, is recursively enumerable and its set theoretic complement is also then the set itself is decidable (also called *recursive*).

In fact, not only is validity (truth in all models) undecidable in FOL, so is satisfiability: there is no algorithm that will say of an arbitrary first order sentence whether it has a model or not.

There are however some special cases, of some linguistic interest, in which decidability is restored. Here are two:

(31)    a. FOL with at most two variables is decidable (Mortimer, 1975, Grädel et al., 1997). Decidability is lost when we allow even three variables (Kahr et al., 1962).

   b. Monadic First Order Logic is decidable (Boolos and Jeffrey, 1980, Ch. 25) but FOL with even one $n > 1$ place predicate is not decidable (Boolos and Jeffrey, 1980, Ch. 22).

Concerning (31a), some axioms for familiar theories crucially use formulas in three variables. The statement of *distributivity* in the defining conditions for boolean lattices is one such. Recall, that a lattice $(L, \leq)$ is distributive iff

(32)   a. $\forall x, y, z(x \wedge (y \vee z)) = ((x \wedge y) \vee (x \wedge z))$, and

   b. $\forall x, y, z(x \vee (y \wedge z)) = ((x \vee y) \wedge (x \vee z))$.

Similarly the claim that an order relation is transitive, (21c) or that a binary function (like $\cap$, $\wedge$) is associative $((A \cap B) \cap C) = (A \cap (B \cap C))$ uses three variables in an essential way. And impressionistically when verifying that a given mathematical structure satisfies various conditions–say that some given partial order relation meets the conditions for being a boolean lattice—it is the conditions using three variables which are the hardest to verify. (31a) is a logical correlate of this impression.

Concerning (31b), a language $\mathcal{L}$ is *monadic* first order if all its predicates are at most unary (so it has no $n$-place predicate symbols for $n > 1$). For such an $\mathcal{L}$ there is an algorithm which tells us for any sentence $\varphi$ in $\mathcal{L}$ whether it is valid or not. Decidability here hinges on the fact that Monadic FOL has the *finite model property*: If $\varphi$ is false in some model then it is false in a model with a finite domain, where an upper bound on the size of the domain can be computed as a function of the syntactic structure of $\varphi$—$2^k \cdot r$ will do, $k$ the number of unary predicates in $\varphi$ and $r$ the number of variables (Boolos and Jeffrey, 1980). So to verify $\varphi$ we "merely" check the finite number of models of that size or less. If $\varphi$ is not false in any of them then it is valid (logically true). Otherwise it is not.

This apparently technical fact is of some linguistic interest. One might have thought that the reason it is harder to evaluate whether a formula is valid in FOL compared to SL is due to the quantifiers, which allow us to make claims about arbitrarily many objects, in particular about infinitely many. And doubtless this is where some of the complexity of FOL comes from. But not all of it. Monadic FOL has the full range of quantifiers and variables as in full FOL and validity is decidable. But adding a single two place predicate symbol to Monadic FOL results in a loss of decidability (Boolos and Jeffrey, 1980, Chs. 22, 25).

So we see that having two (and greater) place predicates in our language significantly increases logical complexity. And in the syntactic and semantic analysis of natural language many of the phenomena we study are only, or primarily, significant when transitive (and ditransitive) verbs are considered. For example, the basic concern of Binding

Theory is mostly of interest when we are binding co-arguments of a given predicate. If English had only one place predicates reflexive pronouns would probably not exist. *Himself walks* is ungrammatical, it seems, as is *Himself criticized Dana*, but *Dana criticized himself* is fine, as are *Dana sent himself flowers* and *He often treats himself to a fine cognac after dinner*[3]. Equally morphological causatives (Turkish, Malagasy, Tsez) primarily make $P_2$s from $P_1$s (and also often $P_3$s from $P_2$s):

(33) Malagasy; Austronesian:

    a. *mihomehy izy*
       laugh     3nom
       'He is laughing.'

    b. *mampihomehy azy izy*
       cause+laugh   3acc  3nom
       'He is making him laugh.'

Similarly Passive primarily derives $P_1$s from $P_2$s and $P_2$s from $P_3$s. In some languages (German, Turkish, Latin) it may in addition derive $P_0$s from $P_1$s. (34) and (35) exhibit $P_1$ and $P_2$ derivations by Passive in Kinyarwanda (Bantu).

(34)   a. *umugore* [$_{P_2}$ *a-ra-andik-a*]  *ibaruwa*
       woman   she-pres-write-asp  letter

      'The woman is writing a letter.'

    b. *Ibaruwa* [$_{P_1}$ *i-ra-andik-w-a*]  *(n'umugore)*
       letter   it-pres-write-Pass-asp  (by'woman)

      'The letter is being written (by the woman).'

---

[3] The problem is not that the previous starred sentences are ungrammatical, it is that *himself* is not interpretable as an anaphor there. Keenan (1988b) cites (i) from Irish dialects of English and (ii) from Japanese, where, in both cases an item that can be interpreted anaphorically when an object may occur grammatically as a subject but is not interpreted as locally bound there.

(i)     Herself is getting herself ready.             (Irish English)

(ii)     a. *Hanako-ga*  *zibun-o*   *utagatte-iru*
        Hanako-nom   -acc   doubts
        (Japanese)

      *Hanako doubts herself* or *Hanako doubts Speaker*

    b. *Zibun-ga*   *Hanako-o*   *utagatte-iru*
        -nom   Hanako-acc   doubts

      *Speaker doubts Hanako* / *Hanako doubts speaker*

(35)   a. *umugabu*  [$_{P_3}$ *y-a-haa-ye*]   *umugore   igitabo*
       man          he-past-give-asp  woman    book

'The man gave the woman the book.'

   b. *umugore*  [$_{P_2}$ *y-a-haa-w-e*]       *igitabo   (n-umugabo)*
      woman      she-past-give-Pass-asp  book    (by man)

'The woman was given the book (by the man).'

   c. *igitabo*  [$_{P_2}$ *cy-a-haa-w-e*]       *umugore   (n'umugabo)*
      book       it-past-give-Pass-asp   woman    (by man)

'The book was given to the woman by the man.'

And lastly, case marking and verb agreement paradigms, while serving a variety of functions, are most prominent with $P_2$s and $P_3$s, where understanding requires that speakers be able to identify which DPs bind which arguments of the predicate. There is no issue if the predicate is monadic—one DP, one argument to bind. But with $P_2$s if what we hear in some language is *praise Mary Sue* we need a way to decide if it means *Sue praised Mary* (per the word order conventions in Fijian and Tzotzil (Mayan)) or it means *Mary praised Sue* (per the word order conventions in Berber and Maasai). In languages with extensive case marking, such as Latin, Warlpiri (Australia) and even Japanese, word order may be fairly free preverbally, and it is the case marking conventions we rely on to associate DPs with semantic arguments of the predicates.

**The non-utility of limiting ourselves to finite models.** We might have expected that we could simplify the task of semantic evaluation and restore decidability by limiting ourselves to finite models (ones whose domains are finite). Surely part of the undecidability results is suggested by the fact that to evaluate the truth of a quantified sentence we may have to search through an infinite domain. But it turns out that restricting ourselves to finite domains doesn't help:

**Theorem 10.5** (Trakhtenbrot, 1950). *Neither validity nor satisfiability are decidable in FOL even if we restrict attention just to models with finite domains.*

In fact matters get worse. Trakhtenbrot's theorem tells us that there isn't even a proof procedure for the set of formulas true in all finite models. So the set of first order formulas true in all finite models is not even recursively enumerable. See Lassaigne and de Rougement (1993, pp. 177–180) for an exposition.

We end this section by discussing a characterization of FOL which shows that we can not significantly increase its expressive power without losing some of its "nice" properties, such as compactness or completeness and Löwenheim-Skolem (below).

**Theorem 10.6** (Löwenheim-Skolem). *For $K$ a set of first order sentences, if $K$ has an infinite model then $K$ has models in every cardinality greater than or equal to $|K|$.*

Loosely this theorem says that first order formulas can't discriminate among different infinite cardinals. (Recall that $|\mathbb{N}| < |\mathcal{P}(\mathbb{N})| < |\mathcal{P}(\mathcal{P}(\mathbb{N}))| < \cdots$). This is not surprising given that we can't even define infinite in first order. Our interest in the theorem is partly the role it plays in the Lindström theorems (see below) but also its utility in showing directly that some quite natural English constructions imply cardinal comparison and thus are not first order. The following, surprising, observation is due to Boolos (1981):

**Theorem 10.7.** *There are in English on place predicates $A, B$ such that the sentence* "For every $A$ there is a $B$" *is not expressible in first order logic.*

An illustrative example from Boolos is *For every philosopher that has studied Spinoza thoroughly, there is one that hasn't even read the Ethics.* A catchy example (which Boolos credits to E. Fisher) is *For every drop of rain that falls a flower grows.* Boolos points out that *For every A there is a B* is not correctly represented by the first order formula $\forall x(Ax \to \exists yBy)$ which just says (on reflection) that if there is an $A$ then there is a $B$. It is logically equivalent to $(\exists xAx \to \exists yBy)$. Moreover we understand the association that *For every A there is a B* enforces between the $A$s and the $B$s to be one to one. Different drops of rain correspond to different flowers (though there may be some flowers unrelated to any drop of rain). Thus in effect *For every A there is a B* says that there is a one to one map from the set of $A$s into the set of $B$s, that is, $|A| \leq |B|$. And the direct proof of Theorem 10.7 is as follows.

*Proof.* Let $\varphi(n)$ be *There are at least $n$ Bs* (which we have already seen how to represent in first order). Suppose, leading to a contradiction, that $\psi(A, B)$ is a first order sentence expressing that $|A| \leq |B|$. So $-\psi(A, B)$ says that $|A| > |B|$. Set $K = \{\varphi(n) \mid n \in \mathbb{N}\} \cup \{-\psi(A, B)\}$. Clearly any finite subset $K'$ of $K$ has a model: for $n$ the largest number such that $\varphi(n)$ is in $K'$ choose $B$ to be the $n$-membered set $\{1, 2, \ldots, n\}$ and choose $A = \{1, 2, \ldots, n, n+1\}$, so $|A| > |B|$. So by compactness

$K$ itself has a model. But $|K| = |\mathbb{N}|$ so by Löwenheim-Skolem $K$ has a model $M$ with universe $E_M$ whose cardinality is $|\mathbb{N}|$. So $|B| \leq |\mathbb{N}|$ and sine each $\varphi(n)$ is true in $M$, $|\mathbb{N}| \leq |B|$ so equality holds. Since $A \subseteq E_M$, then $|A| \leq |\mathbb{N}| = |B|$ so $|A| \not> |B|$, whence $-\psi(A, B)$ is false, the desired contradiction. □

In fact the same technique here can be used to show that proportional *most* (in the sense of "more than half" is not first order. We note first that

(36)  $\text{MOST}(A)(B) = T$ iff $|A \cap B| > |A - B|$, iff $\neg(|A - B| \geq |A \cap B|)$.

Now we go through Boolos' proof working with $\psi(A - B, A \cap B)$ instead of $\psi(A, B)$. Specifically, let $\varphi(n)$ be the first order formula expressing *There are at least $n$ As that are not Bs*. For $n = 3$ for example

$$\begin{aligned} \varphi(n) \;=\; & \exists x \exists y \exists z (x \neq y \,\&\, x \neq z \,\&\, y \neq z \\ & \&\, Ax \,\&\, Ay \,\&\, Az \,\&\, \neg Bx \,\&\, \neg By \,\&\, \neg Bz). \end{aligned}$$

Then set $K = \{\varphi(n) \mid n \in \mathbb{N}\} \cup \{\neg\psi(A, B)\}$ where $\psi(A, B)$ says *Most As are Bs* and is assumed expressible in FOL (leading to a contradiction). To see that each finite subset of $K$ has a model choose $n$ maximal such that $\varphi(n) \in K$ and set $A = \{1, 2, \ldots, 2n + 1\}$ and set $B = \{n + 1, \ldots, 2n + 1\}$. Then $B$ lacks the first $n$ elements of $A$ so $|A - B| = n$. $A \cap B$ contains just the remaining $n+1$ elements of $A$ so $|A \cap B| = n+1 > |A - B|$. So *Most As are Bs* is true in this model. By compactness then $K$ itself has a model. And since $K$ is clearly denumerable $K$ has a model of cardinality $|\mathbb{N}|$ by Löwenheim-Skolem. But $K$ entails that for every $n$ there are at least $n$ elements of $A - B$, so that set has cardinality $|\mathbb{N}|$. But $A \cap B$ is a subset of the domain of cardinality $|\mathbb{N}|$ and so cannot have cardinality greater than $|\mathbb{N}|$ contradicting that $|A \cap B| > |A - B|$. Thus *Most As are Bs* is not expressible in first order after all.

We close with a statement of the fundamental Lindström (1969) theorems (quoted from Flum, 1975).

1. First-order logic is a maximal logic with respect to expressive power satisfying compactness and Löwenheim-Skolem.

2. First-order logic is a maximal logic with respect to expressive power satisfying completeness and Löwenheim-Skolem.

This ends our excursus into the linguistic properties of FOL. Let us return now to the use of variable binding operators in representing English.

## 10.3 Extending the Class of VBO's: The Lambda Operator

The merits of FOL as a translation target for English have been amply attested in the literature. Its ability to represent binding and scope ambiguities has proven enlightening. But as a language in which to represent the meaning system of a natural language we want better, preserving its merits of course. On the one hand it seems unenlightening to destroy basic constituents of English structure. If phrases like *every student, some student*, etc. have no logical meaning why does English use them? If we needed to tear apart English DPs to interpret Ss containing them why don't we speak in a language closer to FOL to begin with? And second, we know that the expressive power of FOL is limited. It cannot express proportionality quantifiers or cardinality comparison. *I have more seashells than you do* is not a first order sentence.

So we return to $\mathcal{L}$(Eng), enriching it with the *lambda* operator $\lambda$ yielding a language in which we can handle binding and scope ambiguities but retain the presence of DP constituents like *all/most/no students* which are directly semantically interpreted. We first enrich the syntax of our language, and then say how the new expressions are interpreted. Individual variables $x, y, z, \ldots$ are added in the category NP.

(37) $\lambda$ abstraction (restricted)

syntax: If $d$ is an expression of category $C$ and $x$ an individual variable then $\lambda x.d$ is an expression of category $C/\mathrm{NP}$. We also often write $\lambda x(d)$ for $\lambda x.d$.

semantics: $[\![\lambda x.\varphi]\!]_{\mathcal{M}}$ maps each assignment $\alpha$ to a function with domain $E_{\mathcal{M}}$ whose value at each $b \in E_{\mathcal{M}}$ is $[\![\varphi]\!]_{\mathcal{M}}(\alpha^{x \to b})$.

So $\lambda x$ is a function creator: whatever type of object $\varphi$ denotes, $\lambda x.\varphi$ denotes a function mapping entities to those objects (when $\lambda x.\varphi$ has no free variables—defined as before, but with the clause $\mathrm{FV}(\lambda x.\varphi) = \mathrm{FV}(\varphi) - \{x\}$ added). Later we remove the restriction that the lambda variable range just over the domain of the model. Thus, informally, in the language of arithmetic $\lambda x.(x > 5)$ denotes a function mapping a number $n$ to $T$ if $n > 5$ and to $F$ otherwise. $\lambda x.(x \ \mathrm{CRITICIZE} \ x))$ maps *John* to $T$ iff "$x$ criticized $x$" is true when $x$ is set to denote John. So it is true iff John criticized himself. Thus lambda allows us to bind variables without introducing any universal or existential commitment. Here are examples representing binding in $\mathcal{L}$(Eng) with the lambda operator.

(38)   a.  Every worker criticized himself.

     a$'$.  (EVERY WORKER)$\lambda x.(x$ CRITICIZE $x)$

     b.  Most students respect themselves.

     b$'$.  (MOST STUDENT)$\lambda x.(x$ RESPECT $x)$

In (38a$'$) $x$ *criticize* $x$ has category $P_0$, so $\lambda x.x$ CRITICIZE $x$ has category S/NP $= P_1$. *every worker* has category $P_0/P_1$ so it combines with it to yield (38a$'$) of category $P_0$. And as $\lambda x.x$ CRITICIZE $x$ denotes the property of criticizing oneself (e.g. it holds of John iff John criticized himself) our previous semantics tells us that (38a$'$) is true iff WORKER $\subseteq \{b \in E \mid$ CRITICIZE$(b)(b) = T\}$, that is, each worker is an object that criticized himself. Note too that (38a) and (38b) have the same syntactic form (except for plural marking in (38b)), and their logical representations are syntactically isomorphic as well. This isomorphism is maintained by the Ss resulting from replacing *every* in (38a) by other Dets, such as *some, no, most*, etc. So quantified DPs are directly interpreted, not destroyed as in standard FOL translation semantics.

This approach also has the advantage that we can represent cases in which antecedents of anaphors, such as *every worker* in (38a) and *most students* in (38b), are not representable at all in first order, as is the case with *most students*.

## Quantification and variable binding are independent operations.

Shortly we turn to some more complicated cases of binding and then of scope ambiguities, indicating the very significant utility of the lambda operator. But let's pause for a moment to wonder whether we have not lost something in eliminating the classical universal and existential quantifiers in favor of GQs. We have clearly gained something, the ability to represent binding by DPs like *most students*. But the classical semantics for universal and existential quantifiers made their boolean nature (glb, lub) apparent, whereas our set theoretic interpretations, repeated in (39), are not so directly boolean.

(39)   a.  EVERY$(A)(p) = T$ iff $A \subseteq \{b \in E \mid p(b) = T\}$

     b.  SOME$(A)(p) = T$ iff $A \cap \{b \in E \mid p(b) = T\} \neq \emptyset$

However these definitions have simpler equivalent formulations which are directly boolean (Keenan and Faltz, 1985) and indeed prove to be more useful than those above in certain contexts:

(40)    a. EVERY$(A) = \bigwedge\{I_b \mid b \in A\}$

  b. SOME$(A) = \bigvee\{I_b \mid b \in A\}$

Recall that $I_b$s are individuals—denotations of proper nouns, like *John*, and are defined by:

(41)  For all properties $p \in [E \to \{T, F\}]$, all $b \in E$, $I_b(p) =_{df} p(b)$.

So in a given model, EVERY$(A)$ in (40a) would denote the same function as *John and Mary and Sue...* where the proper names run through the individuals in $A$. And the definition in (40a) yields the same result when applied to a property $p$ as our earlier set theoretic definition:

(42) EVERY$(A)(p) = (\bigwedge\{I_b \mid b \in A\})(p)$     Def EVERY in (40a)

$\qquad\qquad\;\; = \bigwedge\{I_b(p) \mid b \in A\}$     Pointwise meets

$\qquad\qquad\;\; = \bigwedge\{p(b) \mid b \in A\}$     Def individual

$\qquad\qquad\;\; = T$ iff for every $b \in A$,     Def glb in $\{$T,F$\}$

$\qquad\qquad\;\;\;\;\; p(b) = T$

$\qquad\qquad\;\; = T$ iff $A \subseteq \{b \in E \mid p(b) = T\}$ Set Theory

The last line above is exactly the truth conditions for EVERY$(A)(p)$ on our earlier definition in (39a). And in a similar way (40b) shows that *some A* denotes the same as *John or Mary or Sue...* where the proper names run through the individuals with property $A$. Thus existential DPs behave denotationally like arbitrary disjunctions.

**Exercise 10.9.** Fill in the lines below proving that our two definitions of SOME are equivalent.

SOME$(A)(p)\quad = (\bigvee\{I_b \mid b \in A\})(p)$

$\qquad\qquad\; =$

$\qquad\qquad\;\; \vdots$

$\qquad\qquad\; = T$ iff $A \cap \{b \in E \mid p(b) = T\} \neq \emptyset$

We turn now to some (slightly) more complicated cases of binding. Observe that (43a) is ambiguous according as Bill is a threat to himself, (43b), or John is a threat to Bill, (43c).

(43)    a. John protected Bill from himself.

  b. $\lambda y.$(JOHN PROTECTED $y$ FROM $y$)(BILL)

  c. $\lambda y.$($y$ PROTECTED BILL FROM $y$)(JOHN)

**Exercise 10.10.** On the informal pattern of (43) use lambda binding to represent the binding in each of the Ss below.

a. Some doctor protected himself from himself.

b. Some doctor didn't protect himself from himself.

c. Some woman protected every patient from himself.

d. John protected himself from himself and so did Bill.

**Exercise 10.11.** Using lambda represent the two readings of the S displayed below. On one *his* is bound to *every child* and on the other it isn't bound at all.

Every child loves his mother.

We note that lambda can be used to bind long distance (across clause boundaries) as well:

(44)   a. Each student thinks that every teacher likes him.

       b. (EACH STUDENT)($\lambda x.(x$ THINKS EVERY TEACHER LIKES $x$))

We turn now to the use of lambda in representing scope ambiguities, as in (45a). Recall that our mode of direct interpretation (Chapter 8) with DPs interpreted in the position in which they occur in natural English captured the ONS (Object Narrow Scope) reading directly. But we didn't provide a way to represent the OWS (Object Wide Scope) reading. Now we can.

(45)   a. Some student praised every teacher.

       b. OWS: (EVERY TEACHER)($\lambda x.$(SOME STUDENT PRAISED $x$))

### 10.3.1   Generalizing the Use of the Lambda Operator

Our examples so far have just combined $\lambda x$ with $P_0$s (formulas) to form a $P_1$. But we find instances of binding and scope ambiguities in expressions of other categories. For example, let us add nominals like *friend of*, *colleague of*, etc. to $\mathcal{L}$(Eng) as expressions that combine with a DP on the right to form an N, as in (46a).

(46)   a. [SOME[FRIEND-OF[EVERY SENATOR]]]

       b. (EVERY SENATOR)($\lambda x.$SOME FRIEND OF $x$)

In (46a) FRIEND OF EVERY SENATOR denotes a property, one that someone has iff he is a friend of every senator. And as usual with existentially quantified expressions, (46a) denotes the least upper bound of the individuals with that property.

But the wide scope reading of *every senator* in (46b) might be read as *for every senator, some friend of his*. It denotes the greatest lower bound of *some friend of* $x_1$, *some friend of* $x_2$, ... where the $x_i$ run through the individuals with the senator property. The interesting fact here is that the ambiguity seems local to the DP, rather than being an essential S-level ambiguity.

More widely used in linguistic description are cases where lambda binds a variable of type other than the type of individuals. This allows for more complicated lambda expressions than we have used so far, so it will be useful to introduce a widely used *type* notation which helps us check both the well formedness of lambda expressions and their semantic interpretation. Type will be a set whose elements are used to index expressions in such as way as to identify the set in which they denote (in a given model). Here first is a standard, minimal, set of types.

**Definition 10.10.** Type is the least set satisfying:

a. e ∈ Type and t ∈ Type, and

b. if $a, b$ are both in Type then $(a, b) \in$ Type.

An expression of Type t will denote in the set $\{T, F\}$ of truth values, noted $\mathrm{DEN}_E(\mathsf{t}) = \{T, F\}$. An expression of Type e will denote in the domain $E$ of a model, so $\mathrm{DEN}_E(\mathsf{e}) = E$. So the primitive Types correspond to the semantic primitives of the language. And in general an expression of Type $(a, b)$ will denote a function from the denotations of Type $a$ to those of Type $b$. That is, $\mathrm{DEN}_E(a, b) = [\mathrm{DEN}_E(a) \to \mathrm{DEN}_E(b)]$. For example, an expression of Type $(\mathsf{e}, \mathsf{t})$ is just a property, a map from $E$ into $\{T, F\}$. Common nouns like *doctor* and $\mathrm{P_1}$s like *laugh* have this Type in our treatment (which has not represented tense which usually shows up on $\mathrm{P_1}$s but not on Ns). An expression of Type $(\mathsf{e}, (\mathsf{e}, \mathsf{t}))$ denotes a binary relation, one of Type $((\mathsf{e}, \mathsf{t}), \mathsf{t})$ the Type of subject DPs, such as *he* and *she*, and $((\mathsf{e}, (\mathsf{e}, \mathsf{t})), (\mathsf{e}, \mathsf{t}))$ the Type of object DPs, such as *him*, *her*, *himself*, and *herself*. Here is a "Type tree" for the $\mathrm{P_0}$ *Kim praised Sasha* from $\mathcal{L}(\mathrm{Eng})$ assuming *Kim* and *Sasha* are NPs (not DPs) here.

(47)

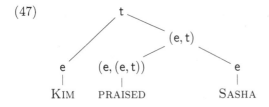

Note that assigning a type to DPs treated polymorphically as we have done appears problematic, with our minimal set Type, since as subjects DPs map $P_1$s to $P_0$s and should have type $((e, t), t)$ like *he* and *she*, but as grammatical objects they map $P_2$s to $P_1$s and should thus have type $((e, (e, t)), (e, t))$, like *him* and *himself*. So we shall extend the (standard) type notation above by adding $(p_{n+1}, p_n)$, where $n$ varies over the natural numbers. Expressions of this type denote maps from the union of the $p_{n+1}$ denotations into the union of the $p_n$ denotations as given in Chapter 8. Then *every student praised every student* is succinctly typed as in (48), writing t for $p_0$.

(48)

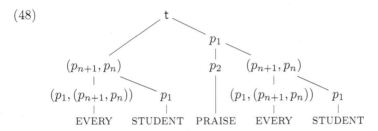

**Exercise 10.12.**

a. What type would you assign to manner adverbs (*slowly, gleefully,* etc.) given that they combine with $P_1$s to form $P_1$s?

b. Exhibit a plausible type tree for *Ruth talks rapidly.*

c. Exhibit a type tree for the $P_0$ *every student criticized himself.*

d. Make a sensible guess at a type tree for *John criticized both himself and the teacher*. Assuming *himself* has type $(p_2, p_1)$, what change must we make to the Coordination rule to accommodate this?

e. How might we assign types to Prepositions (*to, for, from, with,* ...) so that they combine with DPs to form predicate modifiers such as *with every teacher* in *Kim spoke with every teacher*. Using your type assignment exhibit a type tree for the (i), (ii) and (iii) below, and then say why we have no type for (iv).

   i. Kim spoke with every teacher.

   ii. Kim spoke with him.

   iii. Kim talks to himself.

   iv. *Kim talks to he.

We have so far used the lambda operator to bind variables of type e in expressions of type t. Here is a simple illustrative type tree using the lambda operator in this way:

(49)

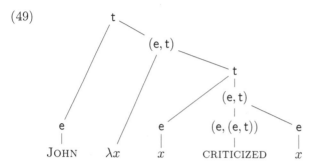

In (49) $\lambda x$ combined with an expression $x$ *criticized* $x$ of type t to form an expression of type (e,t). Note that (49) assumes we interpret *john* as an element $b$ of the universe $E$. If we interpret it as an individual $I_b$ it would have type ((e,t),t) or more generally $(p_{n+1}, p_n)$. The rest of the type tree in (49) remains unchanged under this substitution.

We now generalize the use of lambda so that it can bind variables of any type $\sigma$ in expressions of any type $\tau$, forming expressions of type $(\sigma, \tau)$.

**Exercise 10.13.** Consider the use of the lambda operator in the $P_0$ below. What is the type of the expression it combines with and what type does it build?

[Mary[Dana[$\lambda x$[PROTECTED $x$ FROM $x$]]]]

The more general use of the lambda operator allows variables of all types. To know what type is intended we either say it explicitly in the text or we subscript the variable with its type. Thus the property of criticizing oneself which we represented above as $\lambda x(x$ CRITICIZED $x)$ would now be represented as $\lambda x_e(x$ CRITICIZED $x)$. It has type (e,t). In general if $x$ is a variable of type $\sigma$ and $d$ an expression of type $\tau$ then $\lambda x.d$ has type $(\sigma, \tau)$. For the formal record,

**Definition 10.11** (Lambda Abstraction (unrestricted)).

a. **Syntax:** For $x$ a variable of type $\sigma$ and $d$ an expression of type $\tau$ $\lambda x.d$ is of type $(\sigma, \tau)$.

b. **Semantics:** For each model $\mathcal{M}$, each assignment $\alpha$ and each $b \in \text{DEN}_E(\sigma)$, $[\![\lambda x.d]\!]_{\mathcal{M}}(\alpha)(b) = [\![d]\!]_{\mathcal{M}}(\alpha^{x \to b})$.

The definition in 10.11 assumes that we have denumerably many variables of all types and that an assignment $\alpha$ maps each variable of each type to the denotation set associated with that type.

Now English presents a variety of expressions in which we bind expressions of type other than e, so the more general use of lambda is enlightening. Consider for example the use of the "pro-verb" *so do* in (50a). We might represent this binding as in (50b)

(50)  a. John laughed and so did Bill.

  b. $\lambda q_{(e,t)}(\text{JOHN } q \text{ AND BILL } q)(\text{LAUGH})$

To verify that (50b) is of type t and thus a truth value denoting expression, here is its type tree:

(51)

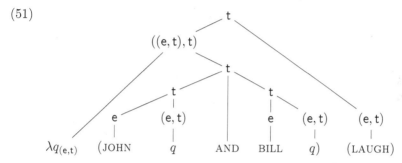

As lambda expressions become more complicated sketching their type tree is a useful way to verify that our expressions are well formed and have the type we want them to. For example in the next exercise some of the sisters to lambda expressions are themselves lambda expressions.

**Exercise 10.14.** Exhibit lambda representations for each of the following. Give two representations in cases where the expression is marked as ambiguous:

  a. John didn't laugh and neither did Bill.

  b. John criticized himself and so did Bill.

  c. No philosopher thinks he's clever and Bill doesn't either.
    (not ambiguous with *he* bound to *no philosopher*)

  d. John thinks he's clever and so does Bill.
    (Two readings, with *he* bound in both)

  e. The woman that every Englishman likes best is his mother.
    (with *his* bound to *every Englishman*)

## Simplifying Lambda Expressions

The increasing complexity of lambda expressions can be lessened by various reduction operations. Here are three widely used techniques.

First, it is often useful to "rename variables", that is, to replace a lambda expression with an alphabetic variant. This is sometimes referred to as α-*conversion*, and is occasionally necessary when applying other reduction mechanisms discussed below.

Second, if we syntactically combine a lambda expression $\lambda x.\varphi$ with an expression $b$ of the same type as the variable $x$ introduced by $\lambda$ and usually written after the lambda expression $(\lambda x.\varphi)(b)$, our semantics tells us that, with one restriction (Trap 2 below), this expression is logically equivalent to the one we get by replacing all free occurrences of $x$ in $\varphi$ with $b$, noted $\varphi[x\backslash b]$. For example:

(52) $(\lambda x.$MARY PROTECTED $x$ FROM $x$'S FATHER$)(b)$
   $\equiv ($MARY PROTECTED $x$ FROM $x$'S FATHER$)[x\backslash b]$
   $=$ MARY PROTECTED $b$ FROM $b$'S FATHER.

This process of substitution is called β-*conversion* (or β-*contraction*, and sometimes in linguistic contexts, λ-*conversion*) here noted $\Rightarrow$.

**Exercise 10.15.** For each expression below give the step by step result of applying β-conversion. The first case is done to illustrate the step by step process. The last two examples involve vacuous binding.

  a. $(\lambda x.(\lambda y.[[$LOVE $x]y])(j))(m)$
    $\Rightarrow (\lambda y.[[$LOVE $m]y])(j)$
    $\Rightarrow [[$LOVE $m]j]$
    ("john loves mary")

  b. $(\lambda y.(\lambda x.[[$LOVE $x]y])(j))(m) \Rightarrow$

  c. $(\lambda x.[$SLEEP $(j)])(m) \Rightarrow$

  d. $(\lambda x.(\lambda x.[[$LOVE $x]x])(j))(m) \Rightarrow$

In general if $x$ is not among the free variables of $\varphi$ then $\lambda x.\varphi(b) \Rightarrow \varphi$.

In reasoning with complex expressions using many lambdas the use of β-conversion may be helpful in reducing their level of variable binding complexity (but not always). But in using β-conversion there are two traps you must be aware of:

**Trap 1.** $\beta$-conversion cannot apply when the variable and the replacing expression have different types. For example in (53a) we cannot replace the $x$'s, of type e, with *some student*, taken here for illustrative purposes to be of type $((e,t),t)$. If we do substitute we obtain (53b) which does not have the same meaning as (53a), and we intend of course that $\beta$-conversion preserve meaning.

(53)  a. (SOME STUDENT)$\lambda x_e(x$ LAUGHED AND $x$ CRIED)

  b. *(some student laughed and some student cried)

**Trap 2.** The expression we replace the variable with must not itself contain free variables that would, after the substitution, occur in the scope of an expression already present in the host expression. For example, using variables $p$ of type t, (54a) $\beta$-converts to (54b), but we cannot apply $\beta$-conversion to (55a), as the variable $x$ in 'dance$(x)$' would become bound by a quantifier already present in the host expression.

(54)  a. $(\lambda p_t(\exists x(\text{SANG}(x)\,\&\,p)))(\text{DANCED}(y))$

  b. $\Rightarrow \exists x(\text{SANG}(x)\,\&\,\text{DANCED}(y))$

(55)  a. $(\lambda p_t(\exists x(\text{SANG}(x)\,\&\,p)))(\text{DANCED}(x))$

  b. $\not\Rightarrow \exists x(\text{SANG}(x)\,\&\,\text{DANCED}(x))$

Some authors (see Hindley and Seldin, 1986) allow conversion in cases like (54) building in that we trade in the host expression for an alphabetic variant with a totally new variable thereby avoiding the unintentional binding problem. We can always do this since we have infinitely many variables and each formula only uses finitely many. For example if we trade in the host expression $(\lambda p_t(\exists x(\text{SANG}(x)\,\&\,p)))$ in (54a) for $(\lambda p_t(\exists z(\text{SANG}(z)\,\&\,p)))$ then we can correctly derive the $\beta$-reduced form $\exists z(\text{SANG}(z)\,\&\,\text{DANCED}(x))$.

**Exercise 10.16.** Represent each of the expressions using lambda binding and then present the result of applying $\beta$-conversion. I illustrate with the first example.

a. John said he would pass the exam, and pass the exam he did (Topicalization)

  $\lambda x.((x$ SAY $x$ PASS THE EXAM) $\&$ $(\lambda p_{(e,t)}(p(x))(\text{PASS THE EXAM}))(j)$
  $\Rightarrow j$ say $j$ pass the exam and $(\lambda p_{(e,t)}(p(j))(\text{PASS THE EXAM})$
  $\Rightarrow j$ say $j$ pass the exam and $j$ pass the exam

b. John said he would punish himself and punish himself he did

c. Bill I really like but Fred I don't

d. What John is is proud of himself (Pseudocleft)

e. John bought and Bill cooked the turkey (RNR)

f. John interviewed the President and Bill the Vice President (Gapping)

**Exercise 10.17.** Which of the following expressions can be $\beta$-converted? In each case if your answer is "yes" exhibit the result of $\beta$-conversion. If your answer is "no", say why conversion does not apply. Then perform a change of variables so that conversion does apply and exhibit the result. Assume $w$, $x$, $y$, and $z$ are all variables of type e, *love* is of type (e,(e,t)).

a. $(\lambda x.(\lambda y.[[\text{LOVE } x]y])(z))(w)$

b. $(\lambda x.(\lambda y.[[\text{LOVE } x]y])(x))(y)$

c. $(\lambda x.(\lambda y.[[\text{LOVE } x]y])(y))(x)$

**Exercise 10.18.**

a. Draw the type tree for (i) below. Its root node should be (e,t). Then apply $\beta$-conversion and draw the type tree for the result. Its root node should also be (e,t).

  i. $\lambda F_{(e,t)}(\lambda x_e(Fx))(G_{(e,(e,t))}(y_e))$

  ii. $\Rightarrow$

b. Can we apply $\beta$-conversion to iii. below? If we do what result do we get? That result does have the right type, (e,t), but does not denote the same function as the expression in ii.

  iii. $\lambda F_{(e,t)}(\lambda x_e(Fx))(G_{(e,(e,t))}(x_e))$

A last reduction process, at times quite useful, is:

$$\lambda x_a.F_{(a,b)}x \Rightarrow F_{(a,b)}.$$

This reduction, called *eta* reduction, is reasonable since the value of the function denoted by $\lambda x_a.F_{(a,b)}x$ at an argument $d$ is the same as that denoted by $F$ at $d$, whence $\lambda x_a.F_{(a,b)}x$ and $F$ are the same function.

## $\lambda$ Definitions of Quantifiers

We have been treating Dets, such as *every, some, no,* and *most* as having type $((e,t),((e,t),t))$. (We just need to define them in this type, as we have already said how the interpretation is extended to maps from $n + 1$-ary relations to $n$-ary ones, $n > 0$). And for Dets which are first order definable we can find a first order formula such that by lambda abstracting twice over property denoting variables will indeed yield an expression of type $((e,t),((e,t),t))$. For example we might define *every* of this type by:

(56)  every $=_{df} \lambda p_{(e,t)}(\lambda q_{(e,t)}(\forall x_e(p(x) \to q(x))))$

Using the definition in (56) the type tree for (57a) can be given as in (57b):

(57)    a. every student laughed.

   b.

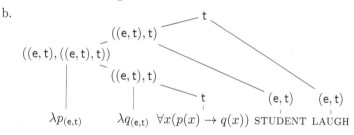

**Exercise 10.19.** On the pattern in (56) define:

a. some

b. no

c. exactly one

We illustrate this way of representing quantifiers as the student may encounter it in the literature, but we will not use it in what follows since our set theoretical definitions are both notationally much simpler and, crucially, more general. For example they treat proportionality quantifiers such as *most* comparably to *all, some,* and *no* despite not being first order definable.

### 10.3.2   Concluding Reflection on Scope and Compositionality

The lambda operator gives us a means of representing the object wide scope (OWS) reading of sentences like (58a), again using upper case for denotations in a model.

(58)    a. Every student knows some teacher.

b. ONS reading:
(EVERY(STUDENT))(SOME(TEACHER)(KNOW))

c. OWS reading:
(SOME(TEACHER))$\lambda x$.((EVERY(STUDENT))(KNOW($x$)))

Naively the ONS reading in (58b) is natural in that it just interprets constituents of the expression it interprets. In particular *some teacher* is assigned a meaning, and so is *knows some teacher*. But in (58c) in order to get *some teacher* interpreted with scope over *every student* we have destroyed the $P_1$ constituent *knows some teacher* by lambda abstracting over the object of *know* and forming an (e,t) type expression, namely $\lambda x$.((EVERY(STUDENT))(KNOW($x$))). This is unnatural as we trade in the expression we are interpreting (58a) for a different one, one with different c-command relations. In effect, we are interpreting *every student knows* as a property, one that holds of an entity $b$ just in case (EVERY(STUDENT))(KNOW($b$)) = $T$. And to do this we have introduced the expression $\lambda$ and two occurrences of the variable $x$, none of which have an obvious exponent in English.

Are we free to lambda abstract freely when interpreting English expressions? With no constraints this would make expressions with many DPs massively ambiguous. A sentence like *Some dean thought every student gave each teacher two apples* would be 24 ways ambiguous according to which of the four DPs had widest scope, then which of the three remaining had next widest scope, etc. In general an expression with $n$ quantified DPs would be $n!$ ways ambiguous if all scope interpretations are possible. But while scope ambiguities do exist, as in the examples we have cited earlier, it does seem that in English Ss of the form Subject+Verb+Object, there is an interpretative asymmetry: the ONS reading is essentially always available and the object OWS reading only available in limited cases. For example competent speakers of English do not assert (59a,b) intending the OWS reading roughly paraphrased in (59a′,b′).

(59)    a. No student answered every question correctly.

a′. *OWS: Every question has the property that no student answered it correctly.

b. Each student answered no question correctly.

b′. *OWS: No question has the property that each student answered it correctly

Just how best to characterize object wide scope readings is, at time of writing, still an actively researched question. One additional possibility we offer for consideration here is function composition. Recall that when $F$ and $G$ are functions with the range of $G$ included in the domain of $F$ then $F \circ G$ is that function with domain $G$ and codomain that of $F$, given by: $(F \circ G)(b) = F(G(b))$. We can think of the composition operator, $\circ$, as a storage operator (Cooper, 1982). It holds first $F$, then also $G$ in store until it gets an argument to which one may apply yielding a value that the other can apply to. Compare the two ways of interpreting *most male doctors* in (60):

(60)    a. (MOST(MALE(DOCTOR)))

       b. (MOST $\circ$ MALE)(DOCTOR) = MOST(MALE(DOCTOR))    def $\circ$

In (60a) we have just applied Function Application, in keeping with how we have been interpreting binary branching constituents in general. But note that MOST and MALE can compose, since MALE maps properties to properties, and MOST maps properties to functions from properties to truth values, so MOST $\circ$ MALE is a function mapping properties to functions from properties to truth values, just the one we'd obtain if we applied the functions one at a time just using Function Application. So there would seem no motivation in (61a) for interpreting *most* and *male* by function composition. But in (61b) there is motivation, since no proper argument of MALE forms a constituent with it.

(61)    a. Most male doctors object to that.

       b. Most male and all female doctors object to that.

In (61b) it seems that the use of *and* has forced *most male* as well as *all female* to be constituents. But they are not of the right type to be interpreted by Function Application. They can however be interpreted by Function Composition, and then they have the type of Dets and so their conjunction (and disjunction) can be interpreted pointwise, just as *most but not all students = most students but not all students*. That is,

(62) (MOST MALE AND ALL FEMALE)(DOCTOR) =
     ((MOST $\circ$ MALE) $\wedge$ (ALL $\circ$ FEMALE))(DOCTOR) =
     (MOST $\circ$ MALE)(DOCTOR) $\wedge$ (ALL $\circ$ FEMALE)(DOCTOR) =
     MOST(MALE(DOCTOR)) $\wedge$ ALL(FEMALE(DOCTOR))

This use of function composition then allows us to interpret "forced" constituents like that in (61b) derived by "Right Node Raising" (RNR) from a structure in which the noun *doctor* is repeated. RNR: *most male doctors and all female doctors* → [*most male and all female*] *doctors*, it being understood that the semantic interpretation of the derived expression is the same as the one it is derived from. We make these two modes of interpretation explicit:

(63)   a. **Interpretive Principle 1 (IP1)**
          Branching constituents are interpreted by Function Application.

       b. **Interpretive Principle 2 (IP2)**
          Adjacent expressions may be interpreted by Function Composition when their semantic types permit.

IP2 enables us (so far) to maintain the view that we just interpret what we hear rather than invoking syntactically richer underlying structures. It is Cooper's (1982) *Wholeweat syntax* (*unenriched with inaudibilia*). How far this approach can be pushed is a matter of empirical investigation.

Our specific interest in IP2 is that it provides a way of obtaining object wide scope readings of Ss like *every student knows some teacher* without invoking inaudible operators (such as lambda abstraction). *Every student* and *knows* do not form a constituent in this sentence, but they can compose: KNOW maps entities to properties, and EVERY STUDENT maps properties to truth values, so their composition is of type $(e, t)$, a property, mapping entities to truth values. SOME TEACHER, by FA, takes this property as argument and maps it to true iff for some $t \in$ TEACHER, (EVERY(STUDENT))(KNOW($t$)), which is what we want.

So it is possible to obtain object wide scope readings without invoking hidden syntactic structure, but just how far this program can be carried out is still open. For significant progress in this direction see Jacobson (1999, 2008).

**Exercise 10.20.** Illustrate how to interpret *Bill I like* without lambda abstraction, just function composition and function application.

Returning now to object wide scope readings, we see that we can insightfully use function composition here as well. Taking *every student* to be of the lowest type it can have, $((e,t),t)$ and *know* to be of type $(e,(e,t))$ we see (64a,b) that EVERY(STUDENT) composes with KNOW to yield a function of type $(e,t)$, given below:

(64)   a. [every student] [knows [some teacher]]

b.

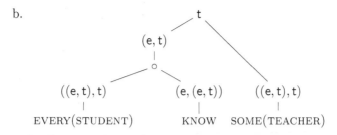

In (64a) *every student* asymmetrically c-commands *some teacher*. But in the type tree (64b) for its semantic interpretation, we have interpreted the adjacent expressions *every student* and *know* by function composition (they do not form a constituent and are not sisters). So in the type tree, SOME(TEACHER) asymmetrically c-commands EVERY(STUDENT). So interpreting adjacent expressions by function composition allows a syntactically c-commanded DP to take semantic scope over a c-commanding one. Further SOME(TEACHER) is a sister to the property (EVERY(STUDENT))∘KNOW and by Function Application maps it to a truth value. Consider now just what property is denoted by ((EVERY(STUDENT)) ∘ KNOW. Its value at an entity $b$ is given by:

(65)  ((EVERY(STUDENT)) ∘ KNOW))($b$)
  $=$ (EVERY(STUDENT))(KNOW($b$))                    Def ∘
  $= (\lambda x.((\text{EVERY}(\text{STUDENT}))(\text{KNOW}(x))))(b)$          $\beta$-conversion

In other words, the composition of EVERY(STUDENT) with KNOW is the same function as that obtained by lambda abstraction in

$$\lambda x.((\text{EVERY}(\text{STUDENT}))(\text{KNOW}(x))).$$

Thus in this case we obtain the same semantic result but without using the lambda operator or bound variables. Once again Occam's Razor cuts our way. To summarize the differences in the two approaches:

(66)    a. The lambda abstraction approach gets the object wide scope reading of Ss like (58a) by assigning the English expression two different syntactic representations, each one compositionally interpreted (just by Function Application).

    b. The function composition approach does not change the logical syntax of the expression—it only interprets what we see, but it is non-compositional in allowing non-constituents to be interpreted (just by function composition).

**Exercise 10.21.** Provide a type tree just using function composition and function application for

(67) John bought and Bill cooked the turkey.

To conclude, we are not claiming that function composition is the best way to represent scope ambiguities. We are only illustrating the use of a mathematical tool which seems enlightening in some cases. Its range of uses is a matter of further empirical investigation. Here is a last suggestive case different in character from the syntactically oriented ones above.

Several languages (German, French, Spanish, Italian, Greek, Hebrew) admit phonological words which are naturally interpreted as the composition of a Preposition denotation with a definite article (*the*) denotation. (68) from German illustrates the, roughly, optional contraction of *an* 'on' + *dem* (the: neuter sg.) to *am*:

(68) *Ich habe mich* { *an dem* / *am* } *Regal*
     I    have  me   { on   the:dat / on+the } bookshelf
     *verletzt*
     hurt

    'I hurt myself on the bookshelf.'

German admits of about ten such combined forms. Ones like *am* above can perhaps be treated as optional "contractions", the interpreted form just being the uncontracted *an+dem*. So to interpret the S with *am* we would modify its syntax, replacing *am* with *an dem*. However, we could directly interpret *am* by listing it as a lexical item and specifying its semantic interpretation as AN ∘ DEM. The latter approach seems more strongly motivated when the "contraction" is obligatory, as is the case with such forms in French and Hebrew. Thus in French *á* + *le* 'to the:m.sg' is obligatorily realized as *au* (/o/). And 'from the:m.sg' is obligatorily *du* rather than *de+le*. In contrast no short form is available with the feminine sg. article *la*, as we see in (69a).

(69)  a. *Je rentre à la       maison à midi*
        I  return to the:fem.sg house  at noon
        'I return home at noon.'

      b. *Le           bureau est fermé le   soir*
         the:masc.sg office is  closed the evening
         'The office is closed in the evening.'

c. *Je   vais   au*        *(\*à   le)*        *bureau   à   huit*
   I    go    to+the:m.sg   (\*to   the:m.sg)   office   at   eight
*heures   le    matin*
hours    the   morning
'I go to the office at 8 o'clock in the morning.'

Here it would seem a simple matter to enter *au* and *du* in the French lexicon with the meanings A∘LE and DE∘LE. In a similar way in Hebrew 'to the' is obligatorily *la*, whose meaning is Lə ∘ HA, the composition of the denotation of the goal locative *lə* with that of the definite article *ha*. Similarly 'at + the' is obligatorily *ba* = Bə ∘ HA. (70a,b,c) illustrate the goal locative case.

(70)   a. *ha-more      moxer   sfarim   lə-studentim*
          the-teacher   sells   books   to+students
          'The teacher sells books to students.'

       b. *ha-studentim   lo    baim   mukdam*
          the-students   not   come   early
          'The students don't come early.'

       c. *ha-more      moxer   sfarim   la-studentim*
          the-teacher   sells   books   to+the-students
          'The teacher sells books to the students.'

To conclude, we note that the linguistic literature concerning scope ambiguities, binding and compositional interpretation is massive, well beyond the scope of a text such as this. For a sample of approaches we refer the reader to Heim and Kratzer (1998), Szabolcsi (1997), Barker and Jacobson (2007), Moortgat (2011), and Steedman and Baldridge (2007).

# 11

# Semantics IV: DPs, Monotonicity and Semantic Generalizations

In this chapter we focus on semantically based generalizations concerning English DPs. An important, even tantalizing, role is played by *monotonicity* properties.

## 11.1 Negative Polarity Items

We begin with a classical observation in generative grammar which concerns the distribution of *negative polarity items* (*npi's*) like *ever* and *any*. Klima (1964) observed that npi's do not occur freely but require negative contexts, such as *n't* or *not*, as in:

(1)      a. John has*n't ever* been to Pinsk.

         b. *John has *ever* been to Pinsk.

(2)      a. John did*n't* see *any* birds on the walk.

         b. *John saw *any* birds on the walk.

However, certain DPs in subject position also license npi's:

(3)      a. No student here has *ever* been to Moscow.

         b. *Some student here has *ever* been to Moscow.

(4)      a. Neither John nor Mary know *any* Russian.

         b. *Either John or Mary know *any* Russian.

(5)      a. Neither student answered *any* question correctly.

         b. *Either student answered *any* question correctly.

(6)      a. None of John's students has *ever* been to Moscow.

         b. *One of John's students has *ever* been to Moscow.

The *a*-expressions are grammatical, the *b*-ones are not. But the pairs just differ with respect to their initial DPs, not the presence vs. absence of *n't* or *not*.

**Two Linguistic Problems:**

1. Define the class of DPs which license npi's, as above, and

2. State what, if anything, the licensing DPs have in common with *n't/not*.

A syntactic attempt (see for example Linebarger, 1987) to solve both problems would be to say that just as *n't* is a reduced form of *not*, so *neither... nor...* is a reduced form of [*not (either... or...)*], *none* is a reduction of *not one*, and *no* of *not a*. The presence of *n* in the reduced forms is explained as a remnant of the original *not*[1]. So on this view the licensing DPs above "really" contain a *not*, and that is what they have in common with *n't*. Note in support of this claim that DPs overtly built from *not* do license npi's:

(7)  a. Not a single student here has *ever* been to Moscow.

   b. Not more than five students here have *ever* been to Moscow.

But this solution seems insufficiently general (Ladusaw, 1983): The initial DPs in the *a*-Ss below license npi's; those in the *b*-Ss do not. But neither contains an *n*-word.

(8)  a. Fewer than five students here have *ever* been to Moscow.

   b. *More than five students here have *ever* been to Moscow.

(9)  a. At most four students here have *ever* been to Moscow.

   b. *At least four students here have *ever* been to Moscow.

(10)  a. Less than half the students here have *ever* been to Moscow.

   b. *More than half the students here have *ever* been to Moscow.

(11)  a. At most 10% of the players here will *ever* get an athletic scholarship.

   b. *At least 10% of the players here will *ever* get an athletic scholarship.

---

[1] In fact this *n*- derives historically from Anglo-Saxon *ne* (ultimately Proto-Indo European *ne*). The initial *n* in *not* is this same *n*.

Ladusaw supports a more comprehensive, semantic, answer: the licensing DPs are just the *downward entailing* ones, as defined informally below. First, the definition of *upward entailing*.

**Definition 11.1.** Let $X$ be a DP. $X$ is *upward entailing* iff the following argument type is valid (meaning the premises entail the conclusion):

Premise 1: All $P$s are $Q$s

Premise 2: $X$ is a $P$

Conclusion: $X$ is a $Q$

For example, Proper Names are upward entailing: if all $P$s are $Q$s and Mary is a $P$ we can infer that Mary is a $Q$. For example, if all students are vegetarians and Mary is a student then Mary is a vegetarian. (This is just an Aristotelian syllogism).

Note that if $X$ is a plural DP then the appropriate form of Premise 2 above is "$X$ are $P$s", and the appropriate form of the conclusion is "$X$ are $Q$s". For example, *at least two doctors* is upward entailing since if all $P$s are $Q$s and at least two doctors are $P$s then those two doctors are $Q$s, so we can infer that *at least two doctors* are $Q$s.

(12) Some upward entailing DPs:

    a. he, she, John, Mary

    b. DPs of the form [Det + N], where Det = some, more than ten, at least ten, most, at least/more than half the, infinitely many, all, every, several, at least/more than two out of three, at least/more than 10% of (the), at least/more than a third of (the), the ten, the ten or more, John's, John's ten (or more), both,

    c. Partitive DPs like [Det of John's students], where Det is as in (b) above.

And here are two ways of building syntactically complex upward entailing DPs:

**Facts:**

1. If $X$ and $Y$ are upward entailing then so are ($X$ and $Y$) and ($X$ or $Y$). But (not $X$) and (neither $X$ nor $Y$) are not upward entailing (when $X$ and $Y$ are non-trivial[2]).

---

[2]There are just two DP denotations which are both increasing and decreasing: **0**, which maps all sets to $F$, and **1**, which maps all sets to $T$. These are expressible by *fewer than zero students* and *either all students or else not all students* respectively. One computes $\neg \mathbf{0} = \mathbf{1}$ and $\neg \mathbf{1} = \mathbf{0}$, so the complements of these trivial denotations are themselves trivial and thus both increasing and decreasing.

2. If $X$ is upward entailing then so are possessive DPs of the form $[X$'s N$]$.

From Fact 1 *either John or some official* is upward entailing since *John* is, and, by (12b), *some official* is. Fact 2 implies that *every player's agent* is upward entailing, since *every player* is by (12b). And this is correct: if all $P$s are $Q$s and every player's agent is a $P$ then every player's agent is a $Q$.

We now turn to downward entailing DPs.

**Definition 11.2.** Let $X$ be a DP. $X$ is *downward entailing* iff the following argument is valid:

Premise 1: All $P$s are $Q$s

Premise 2: $X$ is a $Q$

Conclusion: $X$ is a $P$

For example, *no student* is downward entailing, since if all $P$s are $Q$s and no student is a $Q$ then no student is a $P$. For example, if all poets are vegetarians and no student is a vegetarian then indeed no student is a poet. The following Venn diagram is helpful here. It correctly reflects the set inclusion of Premise 1, and the fact that the student set does not intersect $Q$ shows that no student is a $Q$. The inference that no student is a $P$ is obvious, since if the student set intersected $P$ it would have to intersect $Q$, and it doesn't.

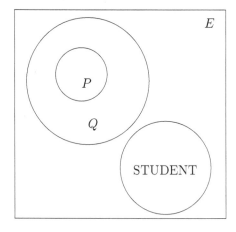

(13) Some downward entailing DPs:

a. Ones of the form [Det + N], where Det = no, neither, less/fewer than five, at most five, less than/at most half the, less than 10% of the/john's, less than one . . . in ten,

b. Partitive DPs, like [Det of John's students], where Det is as in (a) above.

And here are some ways of building complex downward entailing DPs:

**Facts:**

3. If $X$ and $Y$ are upward entailing then *neither $X$ nor $Y$* is downward entailing.

4. If $X$ is upward entailing then *not $X$* is downward entailing.

5. If $X$ and $Y$ are downward entailing then so are $(X$ and $Y)$ and $(X$ or $Y)$.

6. If $X$ is downward entailing then so are possessive DPs of the form $[X$'s N].

From Fact 3 we infer that *neither John nor Mary* is downward entailing since both *John* and *Mary* are upward entailing. And it is: if all $P$s are $Q$s and neither John nor Mary is a $Q$ then clearly neither can be a $P$. Fact 4 implies, correctly, that DPs like *not more than ten boys* and *not more than half the women* are downward entailing. Fact 5 tells us that *no student and not more than two teachers* is downward entailing. And finally the more interesting Fact 6 tells us that *no child's doctor* is downward entailing since *no child* is. And this is correct: if all $P$s are $Q$s and no child's doctor is a $Q$ then, clearly, no child's doctor can be a $P$. Specifically, if all poets are vegetarians and no child's doctor is a vegetarian then, indeed, no child's doctor is a poet.

**Exercise 11.1.** Show that Fact 6 entails that *no actor's agent's doctor* is downward entailing.

And now we can offer an answer to the first linguistic question above:

(14) The subject DPs that license npi's are just the downward entailing ones.

## 11.2 Monotonicity

(14) is a substantive semantic generalization. But it does not answer the second question: what do downward entailing DPs have in common with *n't/not*?

To provide an answer to this question we shall generalize the notions of upward and downward entailing so that they apply to categories of expressions other than DP. To this end recall that a poset is a pair $(A, \leq)$ with $A$ a non-empty set and $\leq$ a reflexive, antisymmetric and transitive binary relation on $A$. We saw that $(\{T, F\}, \leq)$ is a poset, where $\leq$ is the implication order (for all $X, Y \in \{T, F\}$, $X \leq Y$ iff if $X = T$ then $Y = T$). And the set of possible $P_1$ denotations, $[E \to \{T, F\}]$ is a poset pointwise.

Now DPs denote Generalized Quantifiers (GQs), that is, functions from $[E \to \{T, F\}]$ into $\{T, F\}$. So GQs are functions from a poset to a poset. And we generalize:

**Definition 11.3.** Let $(A, \leq)$ and $(B, \leq)$ be posets. Let $F$ be a function from $A$ into $B$. Then

    a. $F$ is *increasing* iff for all $x, y \in A$, if $x \leq y$ then $F(x) \leq F(y)$.
Increasing functions are also called *isotone* and are said to *respect the order*.

    b. $F$ is *decreasing* iff for all $x, y \in A$, if $x \leq y$ then $F(y) \leq F(x)$.
Decreasing functions are also called *antitone*, and are said to *reverse the order*.

    c. $F$ is *monotone* iff $F$ is increasing or $F$ is decreasing.

Increasing functions are often, redundantly, called *monotone increasing*; decreasing ones *monotone decreasing*. (And occasionally *monotone* by itself is used just to mean monotone increasing).

Now the DPs we called upward entailing above are just those that denote increasing functions from $[E \to \{T, F\}]$ into $\{T, F\}$. Compare the two formulations:

(15) The DP *some student* is upward entailing:

    Premise 1: All $P$s are $Q$s

    Premise 2: Some student is a $P$

    Conclusion: Some student is a $Q$

(16)  The GQ SOME STUDENT is increasing:

if $p \leq q$ then if (SOME STUDENT)$(p) = T$

then (SOME STUDENT)$(q) = T$.

(Recall that for $p, q$ $P_1$ denotations, $p \leq q$ iff for all $b \in E$, if $p(b) = T$ then $q(b) = T$).

Clearly (15) and (16) say the same thing. "All $P$s are $Q$s" just says that the denotation $p$ of $P$ is $\leq$ the denotation $q$ of $Q$. And semantically the second line says that (SOME STUDENT)$(p) = T$. To conclude that (SOME STUDENT)$(q) = T$ just says then that SOME STUDENT is increasing. (15) and (16) just differ in that the former talks about expressions and the latter talks about their denotations. Similarly downward entailing DPs are just those that denote decreasing functions.

**Exercise 11.2.** Analogous to (15) and (16) above, show that the claim that *no student* is downward entailing is the same claim as that its denotation is decreasing.

We could now reformulate (14) to say that the DPs which license npi's are just the decreasing ones. But let us generalize a little further:

(17)  The Ladusaw-Fauconnier Generalization (LFG)
      Negative polarity items only occur within the arguments of
      decreasing expressions.

The LFG enables us to see what decreasing DPs have in common with negation: they both denote decreasing functions. Consider $n't/not$ as a $P_1$ level function. Semantically it maps a property $p$ to $\neg p$, that property which maps $b$ to $T$ iff $p$ maps $b$ to $F$. This function is a map from a poset $[E \to \{T, F\}]$ to a poset $[E \to \{T, F\}]$ and is easily seen to be decreasing:

**Proposition 11.1.** *For $p, q \in [E \to \{T, F\}]$, if $p \leq q$ then $\neg q \leq \neg p$.*

*Proof.* Assume the antecedent and let $(\neg q)(b) = T$. We must show that $(\neg p)(b) = T$. But since $(\neg q)(b) = T$ we infer that $q(b) = F$, whence $p(b) = F$ since $p \leq q$ (if $p(b) = T$ then $q(b) = T$, a contradiction). And since $p(b) = F$ then $(\neg p)(b) = T$, as was to be shown.  □

Recall that in any boolean lattice $x \leq y$ iff $\neg y \leq \neg x$, so this proposition is just a special case of a general boolean regularity. And the claim that negation is decreasing does not depend on taking it to be a $P_1$ level operator as long as it denotes the boolean complement function in the appropriate denotation set. For example, taking *not* to be a sentence level operator (as in classical logic, but not with much motivation in English) it would denote the truth functional $\neg$ which maps $T$ to $F$ and $F$ to $T$. That $\neg$ is clearly decreasing.

**Exercise 11.3.**

a. Prove: For all $X, Y \in \{T, F\}$ if $X \leq Y$ then $\neg Y \leq \neg X$.

b. Prove: For an arbitrary boolean lattice $B$ that for all $x, y \in B$, if $x \leq y$ then $\neg y \leq \neg x$.

Observe, (12b,c) and (13a,b), that for DPs of the form Det + N, the monotonicity of the DP is decided by the Det. But there are many monotone DPs that are not of the form Det + N. Names are increasing for example, *neither John nor Mary* is decreasing, and (where grammatical) negations of monotone DPs are monotone.

**Exercise 11.4.** In each case below say informally why the claim is true.

a.1 *more than two students* is increasing.

a.2 *fewer than two students* is decreasing.

b.1 *every student but John* is not increasing.

b.2 *every student but John* is not decreasing.

c.1 *either John or some student* is increasing.

c.2 *neither John nor any student* is decreasing.

d. *most but not all students* is neither increasing nor decreasing.

e. *exactly three students* is neither increasing nor decreasing.

f. *between five and ten students* is neither increasing nor decreasing.

g. *several students but no teachers* is neither increasing nor decreasing.

One observes that a conjunction or disjunction of an increasing DP with a decreasing one results in a non-monotonic DP (except where the result is trivial).

**Proper Nouns.** Proper nouns such as (Kim, $P_0/P_1$) were interpreted in Chapter 5 as the sort of Generalized Quantifier (GQ) called *individuals*. We repeat that definition here.

**Definition 11.4.** Given a domain $E$, for all $b \in E$ we define the GQ $I_b$, the *individual generated by $b$*, by: for all $p \in [E \to \{T, F\}]$, $I_b(p) = p(b)$. A generalized quantifier $D$ is an *individual* iff for some $b \in E, D = I_b$.

Proper noun DPs, such as (Dana, $P_0/P_1$), not only satisfy the upward entailing paradigm in (15), their denotations, the individuals $I_b$, are clearly increasing. For suppose that $p \leq q$ and show that $I_b(p) = T$ implies that $I_b(q) = T$. But from the definition of $I_b$, if $I_b(p) = T$ then $p(b) = T$, whence $q(b) = T$, since $p \leq q$, so $I_b(q) = T$.

**Exercise 11.5.** Let $I_E$ be the set of individuals over $E$. That is,

$$I_E = \{I_b \mid b \in E\}.$$

Define a bijection from $I_E$ to $E$ and conclude that $|I_E| = |E|$ (even if $E$ is infinite).

Below we note some unexpected properties of (boolean compounds) of proper noun denotations so the reader should verify that he or she understands how to compute interpretations of boolean compounds involving proper nouns. Here is one illustration:

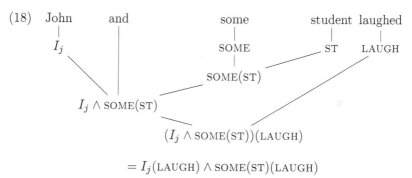

(18)

$$= I_j(\text{LAUGH}) \wedge \text{SOME}(\text{ST})(\text{LAUGH})$$

**Exercise 11.6.** Exhibit, as in (18), interpretation trees for each of the following:

a. Either Mary or Sue laughed.

b. Neither John nor Mary cried.

c. Kim interviewed Sasha but not Adrian.

**Exercise 11.7.** Given $E = \{j, b, d\}$ we display the 8 properties over $E$, classifying them by the sets of objects they map to $T$. We exhibit the individuals $I_j$ and $I_b$. You are to complete the table. Using the completed table say why $(I_j \wedge I_b)$ is not an individual.

| $p$ | $I_j(p)$ | $I_b(p)$ | $I_d(p)$ | $(I_j \wedge I_b)(p)$ | $(I_j \vee I_d)(p)$ | $(I_j \wedge \neg I_d)(p)$ |
|---|---|---|---|---|---|---|
| $\{j, b, d\}$ | $T$ | $T$ | | | | |
| $\{j, b\}$ | $T$ | $T$ | | | | |
| $\{j, d\}$ | $T$ | $F$ | | | | |
| $\{b, d\}$ | $F$ | $T$ | | | | |
| $\{j\}$ | $T$ | $F$ | | | | |
| $\{b\}$ | $F$ | $T$ | | | | |
| $\{d\}$ | $F$ | $F$ | | | | |
| $\emptyset$ | $F$ | $F$ | | | | |

Observe that for $E = \{j, b, d\}$ there are just three individuals but $2^3 = 8$ properties, functions from $E$ into $\{T, F\}$. This is an instance of the first Counting Fact, given shortly. But first we observe that individuals, in distinction to other possible DP denotations, commute with the boolean functions. First, informally, we acknowledge the judgments in (19) of logical equivalence on English:

(19)  a. Boris doesn't smoke. $\equiv$ It is not the case that Boris smokes.

  b. Kim either laughed or cried. $\equiv$ Either Kim laughed or Kim cried.

  c. Sue both jogs and writes poetry. $\equiv$ Sue jogs and Sue writes poetry.

  d. Bob neither slept nor worked. $\equiv$ Neither did Bob sleep nor did Bob work.

We have seen such judgments in earlier chapters, and we have also seen that various non-individual denoting DPs fail one or another of the paradigms above. For example, we lose logical equivalence if we replace *Sue* everywhere in (19c) by *some student*; we lose equivalence in (19b) replacing *Kim* with *every student*. A case we haven't looked at yet is negation, in (19a).

**Exercise 11.8.** Exhibit an informal model in which (a) and (b) below have different truth values:

  a. More than two students didn't pass the exam.

  b. It is not the case that more than two students passed the exam.

Once we think of proper names as DP functions mapping the set of functions $[E \to \{T, F\}]$ into $\{T, F\}$ the apparently trivial pattern in (19) becomes more interesting. Observe:

**Theorem 11.2.** *Individuals commute with all the boolean operations.*

*Proof.* Given a domain $E$, let $b$ arbitrary in $E$. Then, for all properties $p, q \in [E \to \{T, F\}]$,

$$
\begin{array}{lllr}
\text{a.} & I_b(\neg q) & = (\neg q)(b) & \text{Def } I_b \\
& & = \neg(q(b)) & \text{Pointwise } \neg \\
& & = \neg(I_b(q)) & \text{Def } I_b \\
\text{b.} & I_b(p \vee q) & = (p \vee q)(b) & \text{Def } I_b \\
& & = p(b) \vee q(b) & \text{Pointwise } \vee \text{ in } [E \to \{T, F\}] \\
& & = I_b(p) \vee I_b(q) & \text{Def } I_b \quad \square
\end{array}
$$

**Exercise 11.9.** On the pattern in part (b) above prove that individuals commute with $\wedge$.

**Definition 11.5.** For $\mathbf{A} = (A, \leq)$ and $\mathbf{B} = (B, \leq)$ boolean lattices, a function $h$ from $A$ into $B$ is a *homomorphism* from $\mathbf{A}$ to $\mathbf{B}$ iff $h$ respects meets, joins, and complements, where

a. $h$ *respects* $\wedge$ iff for all $x, y \in A$, $h(x \wedge y) = h(x) \wedge h(y)$.
   When we write $x \wedge y$ above we are referring to the greatest lower bound of $\{x, y\}$ in $A$, since $x, y$ are elements of $A$. And on the right, since $h(x)$ and $h(y)$ are elements of $B$, $h(x) \wedge h(y)$ is the glb of $\{h(x), h(y)\}$ in $B$. A longer winded but sometimes helpful way of saying that $h$ respects $\wedge$ is: if $z$ is the glb of $\{x, y\}$ in $A$ then $h(z)$ is the glb of $\{h(x), h(y)\}$ in $B$.

b. $h$ *respects* $\vee$ iff for all $x, y \in A$, $h(x \vee y) = h(x) \vee h(y)$.

c. $h$ *respects* $\neg$ iff for all $x \in A$, $h(\neg x) = \neg(h(x))$.

**Terminology.** A one to one (injective) homomorphism from $\mathbf{A}$ into $\mathbf{B}$ is called an *embedding* (also a *monomorphism*). A surjective (onto) homomorphism is called an *epimorphism* and a bijective homomorphism is called an *isomorphism*.

**Exercise 11.10.** For $\mathbf{A} = (A, \leq)$ and $\mathbf{B} = (B, \leq)$ boolean lattices and $h$ a map from $A$ to $B$,

a. Prove that if $h$ respects $\wedge$ and $\neg$ then $h$ respects $\vee$.

b. Prove the dual of (a): if $h$ respects $\vee$ and $\neg$ then $h$ respects $\wedge$.

346 / *Mathematical Structures in Language*

c. Prove: if $h$ is a homomorphism then

   i. for all $x, y \in A$, $x \le y \Rightarrow h(x) \le h(y)$.
   (We often write $\Rightarrow$ for *if... then...*)

   ii. $h(0_A) = 0_B$ and $h(1_A) = 1_B$.

**Exercise 11.11.** We define the binary *neither... nor...* function $\downarrow$ in any boolean lattice by $x \downarrow y =_{df} \neg x \wedge \neg y$.
Your task: For $\mathbf{A} = (A, \le)$ and $\mathbf{B} = (B, \le)$ boolean lattices, $h$ a map from $A$ into $B$,

a. Say what it means for $h$ to respect $\downarrow$.

b. Prove: if $h$ is a homomorphism then $h$ respects $\downarrow$.

c. Prove: if $h$ respects $\downarrow$ then $h$ is a homomorphism.

We see then that the individuals among the GQs are homomorphisms. Does the converse hold? That is, are all homomorphisms from $P_1$ denotations into $P_0$ denotations individuals? Surprisingly perhaps, and with one technical nuance, the answer is yes. First the nuance:

**Definition 11.6.** For $\mathbf{A}$ and $\mathbf{B}$ complete boolean lattices (so in each case every subset has a glb and every subset has a lub). Then a homomorphism $h$ from $A$ to $B$ is said to be *complete* iff it respects all glbs and lubs. That is,

a. for all subsets $K$ of $A$, $h(\bigwedge K) = \bigwedge\{h(k) \mid k \in K\}$, and

b. for all subsets $K$ of $A$, $h(\bigvee K) = \bigvee\{h(k) \mid k \in K\}$. [3]

In fact each of conditions (a) and (b) implies the other, so to show that a homomorphism $h$ is complete it suffices to show just one of them.

**Theorem 11.3.** *Let* $\mathbf{B} = (B, \le)$ *be a boolean lattice. Then if every subset of $B$ has a glb then every subset has a lub.*

*Proof.* Assume every subset of $B$ has a glb. Then for $K$ an arbitrary subset of $B$ show that the lub of $K$ is the glb of $\mathrm{UB}(K)$, the set of upper bounds for $K$. Dually, if all subsets have a lub, show that for any $K$, the glb of $K$ is the lub of the set of lower bounds for $K$. We write this out more carefully in the Appendix to this chapter. $\square$

---

[3] The usual definition is slightly more general. It does not require the algebras to be complete and just says that whenever a subset $K$ of $A$ has a glb then $\{h(x) \mid x \in K\}$ has a glb in $B$ and $h(\bigwedge K) = \bigwedge\{h(x)|x \in B\}$.

**Exercise 11.12.** State and prove the dual to Theorem 11.3.

**Theorem 11.4.** *A function $h$ is a complete homomorphism*

$$h : [E \to \{T, F\}] \to \{T, F\}$$

*iff $\exists b \in E$ such that $h = I_b$.*

A proof of Theorem 11.4 is given in the Appendix.

Theorem 11.4 would allow us to define denotations for proper nouns of category $P_0/P_1$ without mentioning $E$. They would just be the complete homomorphisms from $\text{DEN}_E(P_1)$ into $\text{DEN}_E(P_0)$.

**Counting Facts.**

1. $|[A \to \{T, F\}]| = |\mathcal{P}(A)| = 2^{|A|}$

2. $|[A \to B]| = |B|^{|A|}$

Since we are going to be comparing the sizes of sets let us see why the first Counting Fact is true ($A$ assumed finite, the case of interest). We have already shown, Chapter 9, that $|[A \to \{T, F\}]| = |\mathcal{P}(A)|$. This is so since each function $g$ from $A$ into $\{T, F\}$ determines a unique subset $T_g$ of $A$, namely the set of elements in $A$ which $g$ maps to $T$. Different $g$ correspond to different $T_g$, and each subset $K$ of $A$ is a $T_g$ for some $g$. So the map sending each $g$ to $T_g$ is a bijection, so $|[A \to \{T, F\}]| = |\mathcal{P}(A)|$.

To see the idea behind the claim that $|\mathcal{P}(A)| = 2^{|A|}$ we give an induction argument. When $|A| = 0$, and so $A = \emptyset$, $\mathcal{P}(A) = \{\emptyset\}$ and so has cardinality $1 = 2^0$. Assume now that when $|A| = n$, $|\mathcal{P}(A)| = 2^n$. Then let us add one new element $b$ to $A$ forming a set $A \cup \{b\}$ of cardinality $n + 1$. This set has double the number of subsets of $A$ since each old subset $K$ of $A$ is a subset of $A \cup \{b\}$, and in addition for each old subset $K$ we now have one new subset, $K \cup \{b\}$. So the number of subsets of $A \cup \{b\}$ is $2 \cdot 2^n = 2^{n+1}$. Thus for all $n \in \mathbb{N}$ if $|A| = n$ then $|\mathcal{P}(A)| = 2^n$, as was to be shown.

Observe that the number of individuals over a domain $E$ of cardinality $n$ is a vanishingly small number of $\text{GQ}_E$, the set of generalized quantifiers over $E$. Since the individuals over $E$ correspond one for one with the elements of $E$, we have that $|E| = |\{I_b \mid b \in E\}|$. By Counting Fact 1 the number of properties of elements of $E$, $|[E \to \{T, F\}]|$ is $2^{|E|}$. And thus by Counting Fact 1 again the number of generalized quantifiers over $E$ is $|[[E \to \{T, F\}] \to \{T, F\}]| = 2^{2^{|E|}}$

Thus in a model with just four entities, there are 4 individuals, $2^4 = 16$ properties and $2^{16} = 65,536$ GQs. Keenan and Stavi (1986) show that over a finite universe all GQs are actually denotable by English DPs. That is, for each GQ we can construct an (admittedly cumbersome) English DP which could denote that GQ. But the number of these GQs denotable by proper nouns is insignificant, just 4 out of 65,536 in the example above.

Counting Fact 2 is very useful and covers the first one as a special case. We are often interested in imposing linguistically motivated conditions on the elements of some $[A \rightarrow B]$ and want to evaluate how many of the functions in that set are ruled out by the conditions. Now, we see that Fact 2 holds when $|A| = 1$, since then there is one function for each element $\beta$ of $B$ (the one that maps the unique $\alpha$ in $A$ to $\beta$). Suppose now the fact holds for all $A$ of cardinality $n$, and we show it holds for any $A$ with $|A| = n+1$. So $A$ is some $X \cup \{a\}$ for $|X| = n$ and $a \notin X$. By our assumption there are $|B|^n$ functions from $X$ into $B$. And each of those functions corresponds to $|B|$ many new ones from $A$ into $B$, according to the $|B|$ many ways each such $f$ can take its value on the new $\alpha$. Thus there are $|B| \cdot |B|^n = |B|^{n+1} = |B|^{|A|}$ functions from $A$ into $B$, which is what we desired to show.

## 11.3   Semantic Generalizations

We turn now to some semantic generalizations we can make about English using our interpretative mechanisms as developed so far.

**Generalization 1.** Lexical DPs are always monotonic; almost always increasing, in fact almost always individual denoting.

Here is a snapshot of the lexical DPs of English: they include one productive subclass, the Proper Nouns: *John, Mary, ... Siddartha, Chou en Lai, ...*. By "productive" we mean that new members may be added to the class without changing the language significantly. Lexical DPs also include listable sprinklings of (i) personal pronouns: *he/him*, and their plurals *they/them*; (ii) demonstratives: *this/that* and *these/those*; and more marginally (iii) possessive pronouns: *mine/his/hers .../theirs*; and (iv) indefinite pronouns *everyone, everybody; someone/body*; and *no one, nobody*, though these latter appear syntactically complex. We might also include some DP uses of Dets, as *A good time was had by all, Some like it hot*, and *Many are called but few are chosen*, though we are inclined to interpret them as having an understood N *people* to account for their +human interpretation (a requirement not imposed by the Dets themselves).

Clearly the unequivocal cases of lexical DPs are increasing, mostly proper nouns. The only candidates for non-increasing lexical DPs are *few* and the "*n*" words (*no one, nobody*) and they are decreasing.

**Query:** Is there any reason why the simplest DPs should denote individuals? Is there any sense in which individuals are more basic that other DP denotations?

We make two suggestions towards an answer to the Query. First, there are many functions that a novel DP could denote—some 65,536 of them in a world of just 4 objects. But the denotations of syntactically complex DPs can be figured out in terms of the denotations of their parts. So the real learning problem for expressions concerns lexical ones, which have no parts and must be learned by brute force. Clearly learning is greatly simplified if the language learner can assume that lexical DPs denote individuals. In our model with 65,536 generalized quantifiers, only four (!) of them are individuals.

Second, the individuals do have a very special algebraic status among the GQs. Namely, every GQ can be expressed as a boolean function (ones defined in terms of meet, join and complement) of individuals! In other words, there is a sense in which all GQs are decomposable into individuals and the boolean operations. Moreover the boolean connectives are, as we have seen, polymorphic: for almost all categories $C$ they combine expressions of category $C$ to form further expressions in that category. So the denotation set of *most C* is a set with a boolean structure. This suggests that the boolean operations are not ones specific to one or another semantic category (one or another $\text{DEN}_{\mathcal{M}}(C)$) but rather represent, as Boole (1854) thought, properties of mind—ways we think about things rather than properties of things themselves.

This consideration is speculative. But the claim that all GQs are constructable by applying boolean operations to individuals is not. It is a purely mathematical claim whose proof we sketch here. In fact we have already seen, Exercise 11.7, that boolean functions of individuals may yield GQs that are not themselves individuals. All that is at issue is how many of these non-individuals are expressible in this way, and in fact all are. (To improve readability, slightly, we write 1 for $T$ ("True") and 0 for $F$ ("False"), as is standard).

Leading up to the proof, consider, for $p$ a property, $\bigwedge\{I_b \mid p(b) = 1\}$. This GQ maps a property $q$ to 1 iff every individual which is true of $p$ is true of $q$, that is, iff $p \leq q$. (So this GQ is, in effect, "Every(p)".)

Now we want to build a boolean function of individuals which is, in effect, "No non-$p$". Taking the meet of that GQ with "Every($p$)" will yield a GQ that holds just of $p$. Now "some non-$p$" is just $\bigvee\{I_b \mid (\neg p)(b) = 1\}$, so "no non-$p$" is the complement of that, namely $\neg \bigvee\{I_b \mid (\neg p)(b) = 1\}$, which is the same as $\bigwedge\{\neg I_b \mid (\neg p)(b) = 1\}$. (See

Appendix). It holds of a property $q$ iff for every $b$ such that $(\neg p)(b) = 1$, $(\neg I_b(q)) = 1$, that is, $I_b(\neg q) = 1$, so $(\neg q)(b) = 1$. Thus it holds of $q$ iff for every $b$, if $(\neg p)(b) = 1$ then $(\neg q)(b) = 1$, that is, iff $\neg p \leq \neg q$, which is equivalent to $q \leq p$. Combining these two results we have:

(20)  $(\bigwedge\{I_b \mid p(b) = 1\} \wedge \bigwedge\{\neg I_b \mid (\neg p)(b) = 1\})(q) = T$
    iff $\bigwedge(\{I_b \mid p(b) = 1\})(q) = 1$ and $\bigwedge(\{\neg I_b \mid (\neg p)(b) = 1\})(q) = 1$
    iff $p \leq q$ and $q \leq p$
    iff $p = q$.

For convenience call this GQ $F_p$. It is that GQ which holds just of $p$ and it is a boolean function of individuals. And one sees easily that for any GQ $H$,

(21)  $H = \bigvee\{F_p \mid H(p) = T\}$.

*Proof.* Note that by the pointwise behavior of lubs, the join of a bunch of GQs maps a property $q$ to 1 iff one of the GQs over which the join was taken maps $q$ to 1. Now let $q$ be an arbitrary property. We show that the functions on either side of the equation sign in (21) assign $q$ the same value and are hence the same function. Suppose first that $H(q) = 1$. Then $F_q$ is one of the $F_p$ in the set over which the join is taken on the right, and since $F_q$ maps $q$ to 1 then the join does as well. So in this case the functions yield the same value. Suppose secondly that $H(q) = 0$. Then $F_q \notin \{F_p \mid H(p) = 1\}$, hence each of the $F_p$ in that set maps $q$ to 0, so their lub maps $q$ to 0. So in this case as well $H$ and $\bigvee\{F_p \mid H(p) = 1\}$ take the same value at q. As this covers all the cases our proof is complete.  □

Thus any generalized quantifier is expressible as a boolean function of individuals. Of course (21) is not a definition of $H$. It is simply a truth about $H$, one that shows that an arbitrary GQ is identical to a boolean function of individuals.[4] We state this as a theorem:

**Theorem 11.5.** *For all universes $E$ (including infinite ones), each function from possible $P_1$ denotations, $[E \to \{0,1\}]$, to possible $P_0$ denotations, $\{0,1\}$, is a boolean function of individuals.*

Returning to Earth, Generalization 2 is a non-trivial empirical claim and also simplifies the learning problem for a language:

---

[4]What we have shown is that the set of individuals over $E$ is a set of complete generators for $GQ_E$. If $E$ is finite it is provably a set of free generators for $GQ_E$. And actually Keenan and Faltz (1985) show more: any complete homomorphism from the set of individuals into any complete and atomic algebra extends to a complete homomorphism from $GQ_E$ into that algebra.

**Generalization 2.** Lexical Dets generally form monotonic DPs, almost always increasing.

Now many types of DPs are not monotonic:

(22) Some non-monotonic DPs: exactly five men, between five and ten students, about a hundred students, every/no student but John, every student but not every teacher, both John and Bill but neither Sam nor Mary, most of the students but less than half the teachers, either fewer than five students or else more than a hundred students, more boys than girls, exactly as many boys as girls.

Thus the kinds of GQs denotable by the DPs in (22) are not available as denotations for DPs built from lexical Dets. So Generalization 2 is a strong semantic claim about natural language.

To support Generalization 2 observe that of the lexical Dets in (12) and (13), most clearly build increasing DPs: *each, every, all, some, my, the, this, these, several, a, both, many, most*. But *no, neither* and *few* build decreasing DPs. And opinions are less clear regarding bare numerals like *two*. In cases like *Are there two free seats in the front row?* we interpret *two free seats* as *at least two...*, which is increasing. In contexts like *Two students stopped by while you were out* the speaker seems to be using *two students* to designate two people he could identify, and as far as he himself (but not the addressee) is concerned he could refer to them as *they* or *those two students*. So this usage also seems increasing. Note that this usage is not paraphrasable by *Exactly two students stopped by while you were out.*

But in answer to *How many students came to the lecture?—Two*, the sense is "exactly two students", which is non-monotonic. We suggest here that the "exactly" part of this interpretation is due to the question, which in effect means "Identify the number of students that came to the lecture" rather than "Give me a lower bound on that number". So we favor Generalization 2 without the qualification "generally". Bare numerals are understood as increasing, and additional information provided by context can impose an upper bound on the number, forcing an "exactly", and thus a non-monotonic, interpretation.

But even if we take as basic the "exactly" interpretation of bare numerals it remains true that the GQs denotable by DPs of the form [Det + N], with Det lexical, are a proper subset of the set of denotable GQs. Reason: GQs denotable by DPs of the form *exactly n A's* are expressible as a conjunction of an increasing DP and a decreasing one: *Exactly n A's* denotes the same as *At least n A's and not more than*

$n$ $A$'s, and Thysse (1983) has shown that the functions denotable by such DPs are just the convex [5] ones.

**Definition 11.7.** A GQ $F$ is *convex* iff for all properties $p, q, r$, if $p \leq q \leq r$ and $F(p) = F(r) = T$ then $F(q) = T$.

So monotonic increasing DPs are special cases of convex ones. But many DPs are not convex. Typical examples are disjunctions of increasing with decreasing DPs (*either fewer than six students or else more than ten students*) or disjunctions of properly convex ones (*either exactly two dogs or exactly four cats*). Also DPs like *more male than female students* are not convex. Thus in analogy with the distinction between lexical vs complex DPs we also see that there are functions denotable by complex Dets which are not denotable by lexical ones, examples being the functions denotable by *more male than female* and *either fewer than ten or else more than a hundred*.

**The LFG: A Case Study in Generalization** The LFG, (17), is given with a pleasing level of generality. It makes sense to seek npi licensers in most categories, since, as it turns out, expressions in most categories are interpreted as maps from posets to posets. For example certain Prepositions license npi's, (23), and some Dets do within their N argument, (24).

(23)     a. *He did it with *any* help.

         b. He did it without *any* help.

(24)     a. *Some student who has *ever* been to Pinsk really wants to return.

         b. No student who has *ever* been to Pinsk really wants to return.

         c. Every student who has *ever* been to Pinsk really wants to return.

But we do not pursue the empirical generalization here. Rather we are interested in the mathematical basis of the generalization itself. We sought, and found, a property that DP denotations shared with negation (whether S level or $P_1$ level). Note that their denotation sets share no elements. Negation denotes a map from a set to itself, and DPs denote maps from $P_1$ denotations to $P_0$ denotations. The common property was not some fixed element that they shared (such as deriving from Anglo-Saxon *ne*) but was the more abstract property of "being an order reversing (decreasing) function". The specific orders that *n't* and *at most two students* reverse are quite different.

---

[5]Thysse calls them *continuous*, but we prefer *convex*.

## 11.4 Historical Background

Our treatment of negative polarity items draws on Ladusaw (1983), which in turn benefited from Fauconnier (1975). See also Zwarts (1981). Klima (1964) is the pioneering study of npi's. For more recent work see Nam (1994), Zwarts (1996), de Swart (1998), Chierchia (2004), Giannakidou (2011), and Homer (2012). Our work on the boolean structure of natural language owes much to Keenan (1981) and Keenan and Faltz (1985). Montague (1970a) and Lewis (1970) were the first to treat DPs (our terminology) as generalized quantifiers (a term not used by him).

Recent overviews of work in generalized quantifier theory are Keenan (1996) and Keenan and Westerståhl (2011), Westerståhl (1985), Peters and Westerståhl (2006) and Keenan (2008). Useful collections of articles in this area are van der Does and van Eijck (1996), Kanazawa and Piñón (1994), Gärdenfors (1987), and van Benthem and ter Meulen (1985).

## Appendix

**Theorem 11.3.** *Let* $\mathbf{B} = (B, \leq)$ *be a boolean lattice. Then if every subset of $B$ has a glb then every subset has a lub.*

*Proof.* Let $K \subseteq B$ be arbitrary. Define the set $\mathrm{UB}(K)$ of upper bounds of $K$ as follows.

$$\mathrm{UB}(K) = \{b \in B \mid b \text{ is an upper bound for } K\}.$$

So for $b \in \mathrm{UB}(K)$, for every $k \in K$, $k \leq b$. By the definition of glb then $k \leq \bigwedge \mathrm{UB}(K)$. $\mathrm{UB}(K)$ has a glb by by assumption that all subsets of $B$ do. Therefore $\bigwedge \mathrm{UB}(K)$ is an upper bound for K. Now let $b$ be an upper bound for $K$. So $b \in \mathrm{UB}(K)$. Trivially $\bigwedge \mathrm{UB}(K) \leq b$, so $\bigwedge \mathrm{UB}(K)$ is the least of the upper bounds for $K$, that is, $\bigwedge \mathrm{UB}(K) = \bigvee K$. □

**Theorem 11.4.** *The complete homomorphisms from $[E \to \{T, F\}]$ into $\{T, F\}$ are exactly the individuals $\{I_b \mid b \in E\}$.*

*Proof.*
($\Longleftarrow$) We have already seen that each $I_b$ is a homomorphism. To show that such an $h$ is complete we have: for any indexed family of $P_1$ denotations $\{p_j \mid j \in J\} \subseteq [E \to \{T, F\}]$,

$$
\begin{aligned}
I_b(\textstyle\bigvee_{j \in J} p_j) &= (\textstyle\bigvee_{j \in J} p_j)(b) && \text{Def } I_b \\
&= \textstyle\bigvee_{j \in J}(p_j(b)) && \text{Pointwise meets in } [E \to \{T, F\}] \\
&= \textstyle\bigvee_{j \in J}(I_b(p_j)) && \text{Def } I_b
\end{aligned}
$$

($\Longrightarrow$) Now let $h$ be a complete homomorphism. We show that for some $b \in E$, $h = I_b$. Let $p_b$ be that element of $[E \to \{T, F\}]$ that maps $b$ to $T$ and all other $b' \in E$ to $F$. $h$ must map one of these $p_b$ to $T$. If it maps all to $F$ then it maps their lub to $F$. But $\bigvee_{b \in E} p_b$ is the unit element since it maps all $b \in E$ to $T$ and as a homomorphism, $h$ must map the unit to the unit, which is $T$, a contradiction. So for some $b$, $h(p_b) = T$. And for $q$ a map from $E$ into $\{T, F\}$, $p_b \leq q$ iff $q(b) = T$. So $h$ maps to $T$ all the $q$ that $I_b$ maps to $T$. And if $q(b) = F$ then $h(q) = F$, otherwise $h(p_b \wedge q) = h(0) = T$. Thus $h = I_b$ since it holds of a $q$ iff $q(b) = T$. $\qquad \Box$

**The Infinite de Morgan's Laws.** The proofs of (20) used an infinitary form of the de Morgan's laws. We prove these below, but first some lemmas.

**Lemma 11.5.** *For all boolean lattices $B$, all $x, y \in B$,*

$$x = x \wedge 1 = x \wedge (y \vee \neg y) = (x \wedge y) \vee (x \wedge \neg y).$$

**Lemma 11.6** (The Finite de Morgan's Laws).

   *1. $\neg(x \vee y) = \neg x \wedge \neg y$, and*

   *2. $\neg(x \wedge y) = \neg x \vee \neg y$.*

*Proof.* We show (1) $\neg(x \vee y) = \neg x \wedge \neg y$.

$$
\begin{aligned}
\text{a. } (x \vee y) \wedge (\neg x \wedge \neg y) &= (x \wedge (\neg x \wedge \neg y)) \vee (y \wedge (\neg x \wedge \neg y)) \\
&= 0 \vee 0 \\
&= 0. \\
\text{b. } (x \vee y) \vee (\neg x \wedge \neg y) &= x \vee (y \vee (\neg x \wedge \neg y)) \\
&= x \vee ((y \vee \neg x) \wedge (y \vee \neg y)) \\
&= x \vee ((y \vee \neg x) \wedge 1) \\
&= x \vee \neg x \vee y \\
&= 1 \vee y \\
&= 1.
\end{aligned}
$$

Thus by Uniqueness of complements (Theorem 9.8),

$$(\neg x \wedge \neg y) = \neg(x \vee y). \qquad \Box$$

We leave the dual lemma $\neg(x \vee y) = (\neg x \vee \neg y)$ as an exercise for the reader.

Note the following definition of a *dual*.

**Definition 11.8.** If $\varphi$ is a statement in the language of boolean lattices then $dual(\varphi)$ is the statement that results from simultaneously replacing all '$\wedge$' signs with '$\vee$' and all '$\vee$' with '$\wedge$', replacing all occurrences of '0' with '1' and '1' with '0', and all occurrences of '$\leq$' with '$\geq$' and all '$\geq$' with '$\leq$'.

**Meta-Theorem: Duality.** For $\varphi$ a statement in the language of boolean lattices, $\varphi \equiv dual(\varphi)$.

The reason that Duality holds is that the dual of every axiom of boolean lattices is an axiom (though we didn't take $1 \neq 0$ as an axiom, but it obviously is logically equivalent to $0 \neq 1$). So whenever we have a proof of some $\psi$ from the axioms then replacing each line in the proof by its dual is a proof of $dual(\psi)$.

**Lemma 11.7.** *For all $x, y$ in a boolean lattice $B$, $x \leq y$ iff $\neg y \leq \neg x$.*

*Proof.*

| | | | |
|---|---|---|---|
| $x \leq y$ | iff | $(x \wedge y) = x$ | From def of glb |
| | iff | $\neg(x \wedge y) = \neg x$ | Uniqueness of complements |
| | iff | $(\neg x \vee \neg y) = \neg x$ | de Morgan's Laws |
| | iff | $\neg y \leq \neg x$ | From def of lub $\qquad\square$ |

**Lemma 11.8** ((Weak) Infinite Distributivity). *In any complete boolean lattice,*

$$x \wedge \bigvee_{j \in J} y_j = \bigvee_{j \in J} (x \wedge y_j).$$

*Proof.* To enhance readability write when convenient $y$ for $\bigvee_{j \in J} y_j$.

($\Longleftarrow$) For each $j$, $y_j \leq y$, so $x \wedge y_j \leq x \wedge y$, so $x \wedge y$ is an ub for $\{x \wedge y_j \mid j \in J\}$ thus

$$\bigvee_{j \in J} (x \wedge y_j) \leq x \wedge y = x \wedge \bigvee_{j \in J} y_j.$$

($\Longrightarrow$) We show that $x \wedge y \leq$ every upper bound for $\{x \wedge y_j \mid j \in J\}$. Let $u$ be such an ub. Then for each $j$, $y_j = (x \wedge y_j) \vee (\neg x \wedge y_j) \leq u \vee \neg x$. This is because $(x \wedge y_j) \leq u$ and $(\neg x \wedge y_j) \leq \neg x$. Thus $u \vee \neg x$ is an ub for $\{y_j \mid j \in J\}$ so $y \leq u \vee \neg x$, whence $x \wedge y \leq x \wedge (u \vee \neg x) = x \wedge u \leq u$. Since u was an arbitrary ub for $\{x \wedge y_j \mid j \in J\}$ we have that

$$x \wedge y \leq \bigvee_{j \in J} (x \wedge y_j),$$

proving equality. $\qquad\square$

There are stronger forms of distributivity but they do not hold in all complete boolean lattices.

**Theorem 11.9** (The Infinitary de Morgan's Laws.).

1. $\neg \bigvee_{k \in K} k = \bigwedge_{k \in K} \neg k$.

2. $\neg \bigwedge_{k \in K} k = \bigvee_{k \in K} \neg k$.

*Proof.*

1. ($\Longrightarrow$)For each $k \in K$, $k \leq \bigvee_{k \in K} k$, so $\neg \bigvee_{k \in K} k \leq \neg k$, so $\neg \bigvee_{k \in K} k$ is a lb for $\{\neg k \mid k \in K\}$, so

$$\neg \bigvee_{k \in K} k \leq \bigwedge_{k \in K} \neg k.$$

($\Longleftarrow$) Write $d$ for $\bigwedge_{k \in K} \neg k$. We are to show that $d \leq \neg \bigvee_{k \in K} k$. Observe that for each $k \in K$, $k \wedge d = 0$, since $k \wedge d \leq k \wedge \neg k = 0$. Thus (using the general boolean fact that $x \leq y$ iff $x \wedge \neg y = 0$) $k \leq \neg d$. Since $k$ was arbitrary in $K$, $\bigvee_{k \in K} k \leq \neg d$, whence

$$d = \bigwedge_{k \in K} \neg k \leq \neg \bigvee_{k \in K} k,$$

as was to be shown.

2. The proof of the dual statement is left to the reader. □

# 12

---

# Semantics V: Classifying Quantifiers

In this chapter we present several semantically defined subclasses of *declarative count* Determiners in English and establish a variety of empirical and mathematical generalizations about them. Some of these concern the semantic characterization of syntactic phenomena, others are purely semantic. At various points we note properties they share with *interrogative quantifiers* (1b), *mass quantifiers* (1c) and *adverbial quantifiers* (1d), classes that are less well understood than the Dets (1a) we focus on.

(1)    a. *All / Most / No* poets daydream.

       b. *How many / Which / Whose* children are laughing?

       c. There was *(too) much / (not) enough* salt in the soup.

       d. I *always / usually / often / rarely / never* work on weekends.

Useful sources of information about the expression of quantification in diverse languages are Bach et al. (1995), Gil (1993), Matthewson (2008), and Keenan and Paperno (2012, to appear). The content of this chapter draws on Keenan and Stavi (1986), Keenan and Westerståhl (2011), and Peters and Westerståhl (2006).

**A notational preliminary.** Following the lead of most work in Generalized Quantifier Theory we treat $P_1$s simply as subsets of a domain $E$ rather than as functions from $E$ into $\{T, F\}$. Up to isomorphism they are the same thing, recall. And more generally $n$-ary relations on $E$ are treated as subsets of $E^n$.

Further we refer to DPs (*Mary, Most poets*, ... ) as denoting functions of type (1), called *generalized quantifiers*, rather than using

$((e,t),t)$ which gets cumbersome when quantifiers of higher type are studied (as here.) A quantifier of type (1) is a function from subsets of $E^1$ into $\{T, F\}$. Dets like *all, most,* etc. are of type (1,1), mapping subsets of $E$ to functions of type (1). Quantifiers of type (2) map binary relations—subsets of $E^2$—into $\{T, F\}$. And quantifiers of type ((1,1),1) map pairs of subsets of $E$ to functions of type (1). This type notation derives from Lindström (1966). The interpretation of (2a) below is now given as (2b):

(2)  a. Most poets daydream.

   b. (MOST(POET))(DAYDREAM).

Here both POET and DAYDREAM are subsets of the domain. (We see shortly though that the role of the noun property, POET, in the interpretation (2a) is quite different from that of the predicate property DAYDREAM.) POET in these cases is sometimes called the *restriction* (of the quantifier). Using this set notation[1] here are some further definitions of English quantifiers of type (1,1). We have already seen most of them. Read the first line in (3) as "some $A$'s are $B$'s iff the intersection of the set of $A$'s with the set of $B$'s is not empty". The other lines are read analogously.

(3)  a. SOME$(A)(B) = T$     iff $A \cap B \neq \emptyset$
   b. NO$(A)(B) = T$     iff $A \cap B = \emptyset$
   c. (EXACTLY TWO)$(A)(B) = T$   iff $|A \cap B| = 2$
   d. (ALL BUT ONE)$(A)(B) = T$   iff $|A - B| = 1$
   e. MOST$(A)(B) = T$     iff $|A \cap B| > |A|/2$
   f. (THE $n$)$(A)(B) = T$     iff $|A| = n$ and $A \subseteq B$

---

[1]The "set" approach we take does force us to ignore the value judgment Dets such as *too many, not enough, surprisingly few,* etc. in the Appendix. Such Dets are inherently intensional and so cannot be treated a functions whose domain is simply the sets of objects with given properties.

For example in a model in which it happens that the doctors and the lawyers are the same individuals Ss (a) and (b) below can still have different truth values:

   a. Not enough doctors attended the meeting.

   b. Not enough lawyers attended the meeting.

Imagine for example that we are discussing a meeting of the American Medical Association. 500 doctors are required for a quorum, but only one lawyer is required, to take the minutes. And suppose that just 400 doctor-lawyers show up. (a) is true and (b) is false. Note that if *not enough* is replaced we by *every* (making the nouns singular) the resulting Ss must have the same truth value. This says that *every* is extensional, meaning that it can be treated as a function whose arguments are the extensions of the property denoting expressions, that is, the sets of individuals which have the property.

We turn now to the semantic classification of English Dets. We offer a field guide to English Dets in an appendix to this chapter. Those Dets serve to indicate the syntactic and semantic diversity of the expressions of interest here.

## 12.1 Quantifier Types

The most widely studied quantifiers in English are those of type (1,1). We distinguish four subcases, illustrated in (4a,b,c,d), according to what we need to know to evaluate the truth of the sentences they build:

(4)    a. *Some* students read the Times.

       b. *All* students read the Times.

       c. *Most* American teenagers read the Times.

       d. *The four* students read the Times.

To determine the truth of (4a) it suffices to have at hand the intersection of the set of students with the set of people who read the Times. If that set is empty (4a) is false, otherwise it is true. To establish the truth of (4a) we need know nothing about students who didn't read the Times, nor anything about people who read the Times who are not students. But knowing which students read the Times does not decide the truth of (4b). For that we must know about the set of students who don't read the Times. If that set is non-empty then (4b) is false, otherwise it is true. And to evaluate the truth of (4c) we must know both about the students who read the Times and also about the students who don't, to verify that the former outnumber the latter. Lastly, (4d) requires that we know the cardinality of the restrictor STUDENT and that the set of students who don't read the Times is empty. Note that merely knowing the cardinality of the set of students who read the Times does not suffice. These observations determine the *intersective* (or *generalized existential*), *co-intersective* (or *generalized universal*), *proportional* and *definite* classes of Dets respectively.

### 12.1.1    Intersective Dets

**Definition 12.1.** *Intersective* (or *generalized existential*) Dets are ones whose denotations $D$ satisfy:

$$D(A)(B) = D(X)(Y) \text{ whenever } A \cap B = X \cap Y.$$

This *invariance* condition is a way of saying that the value $D$ assigns to $A, B$ just depends on $A \cap B$. This value is unchanged (invariant) under replacement of $A$ by $X$ and $B$ by $Y$ provided $X$ has the same intersection with $Y$ as $A$ does with $B$. It is easy to see that SOME is intersective. Given $A \cap B = X \cap Y$ then either both intersections are empty and $\text{SOME}(A)(B) = \text{SOME}(X)(Y) = F$, or both are non-empty and $\text{SOME}(A)(B) = \text{SOME}(X)(Y) = T$.

But Definition 12.1 is more general than meets the eye since it does not make any commitment as to precisely what type of value $D$ assigns to a pair $A, B$. Mostly here we think of it as a truth value, but on richer semantic theories in which Ss denote *propositions*, functions from possible worlds to truth values, $D(A)(B)$ would denote a proposition. And for some of our examples below we see that $D(A)(B)$ is whatever it is that questions denote. A Venn diagram might be helpful in understanding Definition (12.1).

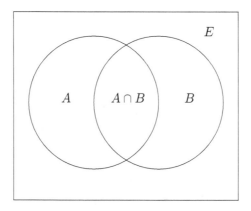

So to say that a Det is intersective is to say that when it looks at a pair of sets $A, B$ it makes its decision just by considering the area where they overlap, $A \cap B$. Theorems 12.1a,b are often helpful in establishing the intersectivity of a Det. ($E$ as always is the understood domain.)

**Theorem 12.1.**

    a. *$D$ is intersective iff for all sets $A, B$ $DAB = D(A \cap B)(E)$.*
       *We may read "$D(A \cap B)(E)$" as "$D$ As that are Bs exist".*

    b. *$D$ is intersective iff for all sets $A, B$ $DAB = D(E)(A \cap B)$.*
       *We may read "$D(E)(A \cap B)$" as "$D$ individuals are both As and Bs".*

*Proof.*
($\Longrightarrow$) Given $D$ intersective the right hand side of the "iff" above holds since $(A \cap B) \cap E = A \cap B$, as $A \cap B$ is a subset of $E$.

($\Longleftarrow$) Going the other way, assume the right hand side and suppose that $A \cap B = X \cap Y$. But then $D(A)(B) = D(A \cap B)(E)$ by the assumption, which equals $D(X \cap Y)(E)$ since $A \cap B = X \cap Y$, and equals $D(X)(Y)$ again by the assumption, so $D$ is intersective. $\square$

**Exercise 12.1.** Prove Theorem 12.1b.

The Dets in (5) are intersective since the $(x,x')$ pairs are logically equivalent.

(5)   a. Some students are vegetarians.

     a$'$. Some students who are vegetarians exist.

     b. Exactly ten boys are on the team.

     b$'$. Exactly ten individuals are boys on the team.

     c. How many athletes smoke?

     c$'$. How many individuals are athletes who smoke?

     d. Which students sleep in class?

     d$'$. Which individuals are students who sleep in class?

Intersective Dets are the most widely distributed of the English Dets. Here are some examples, in which we include the interrogative Dets *Which?* and *How many?*, though most intersective Dets are declarative.

(6)   Some intersective Dets: *some, a/an, no, several, more than six, at least six, exactly six, fewer than six, at most six, between six and ten, just finitely many, infinitely many, about a hundred, a couple of dozen, practically no, nearly twenty, approximately twenty, not more than ten, at least two and not more than ten, either fewer than five or else more than twenty, that many, How many?, Which?, more male than female, just as many male as female, no ... but John*

The intersective Dets present some interesting semantic subcategories, but first let us see that there are many Dets that are not intersective. *Every* for example is not:

(7)   Let $A = \{2,3\}$, $B = \{1,2,3,4\}$ and let $A' = \{1,2,3\}$ and $B' = \{2,3,4\}$. Then clearly $A \cap B = \{2,3\} = A' \cap B'$. But since $A \subseteq B$ we have that $\text{EVERY}(A)(B) = T$. But $A' \nsubseteq B'$ so $\text{EVERY}(A')(B') \neq T$. Thus EVERY is not intersective.

**Exercise 12.2.** For each Det below exhibit an informal model as in (7) which shows that it is not intersective.

a. all but two        b. most       c. the two

The productivity of the intersectivity class of Dets prompts us to wonder just how many of the possible Det denotations—maps from $\mathcal{P}(E)$ into $[\mathcal{P}(E) \to \{T, F\}]$—are intersective. That is, just how strong is the intersectivity condition? The answer is somewhat surprising. Here are two observations leading up the relevant result.

First, recall that the set of possible Det denotations is a boolean lattice with the operations given pointwise. This predicts, correctly, the following logical equivalences:

(8)    (Some but not all) cats are black.
     $\equiv$ (Some cats but (not all) cats) are black.
     $\equiv$ (Some cats but (not (all cats))) are black.
     $\equiv$ Some cats are black but (not (all cats)) are black.
     $\equiv$ Some cats are black but not (all cats are black).

And it turns out that the set of intersective functions in this class is closed under these boolean operations. That is, if $D$ and $D'$ are intersective, so are $(D \wedge D')$, $(D \vee D')$, and $\neg D$. So *at least two and not more than ten* is intersective since *at least two* and *more than ten* are. Generalizing, the set $\mathrm{INT}_E$ of intersective functions over $E$ is a boolean lattice. This result appears a little "abstract" but in fact it is easy to prove (though for reasons of space in this chapter we will not be concerned to prove such results.) Let us see for example, as claimed above, that the join of two intersective functions is itself intersective:

**Fact 1.** Given $E$, let $D$ and $D'$ be intersective Dets. We show that $(D \vee D')$ is intersective.

*Proof.* Let $A \cap B = X \cap Y$. We must show that

$$(D \vee D')(A)(B) = (D \vee D')(X)(Y).$$

We calculate:

$$
\begin{aligned}
(D \vee D')(A)(B) &= (D(A) \vee D'(A))(B) & \text{Pointwise } \vee \text{ in Det} \\
&= (D(A)(B) \vee D'(A)(B)) & \text{Pointwise } \vee \text{ in GQ}_E \\
&= (D(X)(Y) \vee D'(X)(Y)) & D, D' \text{ are intersective} \\
&= (D(X) \vee D'(X))(Y) & \text{Pointwise } \vee \text{ in GQ}_E \\
&= (D \vee D')(X)(Y) & \text{Pointwise } \vee \text{ in Det}
\end{aligned}
$$

The first and last lines establish that $(D \vee D')$ is intersective.    □

**Exercise 12.3.** Using a "pointwise" argument as in Fact 1, show that $INT_E$ is closed under (a) meets, and (b) complements.

Thus we see that $INT_E$ is a boolean lattice (a sublattice of the lattice of Det functions of type (1,1).) And we have the somewhat surprising result (Keenan, 1993):

**Theorem 12.2.** *For any domain E, $INT_E$, the set of intersective functions of type (1,1), is isomorphic to $GQ_E$, the set of functions of type (1). The map sending each intersective D to D(E) is the desired isomorphism*

So, semantically, the isomorphic image of *some* is *some individual*, of *less than ten*, *less than ten individuals*, etc. This result is surprising, as possible Det denotations map $\mathcal{P}(E)$ into $GQ_E$, and so in general vastly outnumber $GQ_E$. But when we limit ourselves to intersective Det denotations we see that, up to isomorphism, they are just the familiar generalized quantifiers. Recalling that isomorphic structures are elementarily equivalent, that is, they make the same sentences true, we can say:

(9)  The intersective Dets and the generalized quantifiers over an $E$ have the same logical expressive power.

So if the only Dets in English were intersective there would be little logical point in distinguishing between them and generalized quantifiers. But as we have seen, English presents many non-intersective Dets.

Finally, using the Counting Facts of the previous chapter we can see what portion of the logically possible Det denotations (functions of type (1,1)) are intersective:

**Fact 2.** Given $|E| = n$, the number of logically possible (declarative) Det denotations is

$$|[\mathcal{P}(E) \to [\mathcal{P}(E) \to \{T, F\}]]| = 2^{4^n}.$$

In contrast,

$$|GQ_E| = |[\mathcal{P}(E) \to \{T, F\}]| = 2^{2^n}.$$

So in a model with just two individuals, $|E| = 2$, there are $2^4 = 16$ distinct generalized quantifiers and so by Theorem 12.1 just $2^4 = 16$ intersective functions. But there are $2^{16} = 65,536$ logically possible (declarative) Det denotations.

Now observe that most of the Dets in (6) satisfy a condition stronger than intersectivity, they are *cardinal*: their value depends not on which objects lie in the intersection of their arguments but merely on *how many* objects lie in that intersection.

**Definition 12.2.** A possible Det denotation $D$ is *cardinal* iff for all properties $A, B, X, Y$

$$DAB = DXY \text{ if } |A \cap B| = |X \cap Y|.$$

Dets such as *some, no, practically no, more than / less than / exactly ten, between ten and twenty, just finitely many, infinitely many, about a hundred, How many?* are cardinal. SOME is cardinal. (A definition equivalent to (3) is SOME$(A)(B) = T$ iff $|A \cap B| > 0$.) The intersective Dets include "vague" ones, such as *about twenty* and *practically no*, since, while we may be uncertain concerning precisely how many sparrows must be on your clothesline in order for there to be about twenty, it does seem clear that

(10) If the number of sparrows on my clothesline is the same as the number of students in my yoga class then *About 20 sparrows are on my clothesline* and *About 20 students are in my yoga class* must have the same truth value.

Further, boolean compounds of cardinal Dets are themselves cardinal. So at *least two and not more than ten* is cardinal since *at least two* and *more than ten* are. And CARD$_E$, the set of cardinal (declarative) Dets over $E$, is a very small subset of INT$_E$.[2]

**Theorem 12.3.** *For* $|E| = n$, $|CARD_E| = 2^{n+1}$.

For example given an $E$ with just 3 elements, there are $2^8 = 256$ intersective Dets, but only $2^4 = 16$ cardinal ones. Indeed, almost all the Dets in (6) are cardinal, so it is reasonable to ask whether English has any Dets that are intersective but not cardinal. Our best examples are those in (11), where only (11a) is syntactically simple:

(11) a. *Which* students attended the lecture?

b. *No* student *but John* came to the lecture.

c. *More male than female* students came to the lecture.

Clearly (11a) asks us to identify the students who attended, not merely to say how many there were. So if we just know how many students attended the lecture we do not have enough information to answer (11a) or to decide the truth of (11b) or (11c). (11b) is not unreasonably represented by the discontinuous Det *no ... but John*, as in (12):

---

[2] Assume that $E$ is finite with cardinality $n$. Then there are $n + 1$ functions of the form (EXACTLY $k$) where $0 \leq k \leq n$. Each cardinal Det = a join ("disjunction") of functions of the form (EXACTLY $k$), so there are as many of them as there are subsets of this set of $n + 1$ functions. That is, there are $2^{n+1}$ cardinal Det functions.

(12)

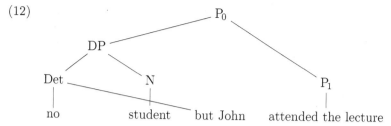

And we may interpret *no ... but John* as in:

(13) $(\text{NO} \ldots \text{BUT JOHN})(A)(B) = T$ iff $A \cap B = \{John\}$.

That is, "No $A$ but John is a $B$" says that the $As$ who are $Bs$ consist just of John. So the value of this Det at a pair $A, B$ is decided by its intersection, but it has to see that the intersection is $\{John\}$, not for example $\{Mary\}$, and not merely how many objects are in the intersection. So *no ... but John* is intersective but not cardinal. Similarly *more male than female* is not cardinal, since in (11c) its value depends not simply on how many students came to the lecture, but rather on how many male students came and how many female students came.

We turn now to some classes of non-intersective Dets.

### 12.1.2 Co-Intersective Dets

Co-intersective (generalized universal) Dets depend on $A - B$, the $As$ that are not $Bs$, just as intersective Dets depend on $A \cap B$. They are defined formally below, and exemplified in (14).

**Definition 12.3.** A Det $D$ is *co-intersective* iff

$$DAB = DXY \text{ whenever } A - B = X - Y.$$

(14)  a. $\text{ALL}(A)(B) = T$          iff $A - B = \emptyset$
      b. $\text{ALL-BUT-SIX}(A)(B) = T$      iff $|A - B| = 6$
      c. $\text{ALL-BUT-FINITELY-MANY}(A)(B) = T$   iff $A - B$ is finite
      d. $\text{EVERY} \ldots \text{BUT-JOHN}(A)(B) = T$      iff $A - B = \{j\}$

Note that for any sets $A, B$ $A \subseteq B$ iff $A - B = \emptyset$, so the definition of ALL above is as previously defined though the definitions are stated differently. And we may define the *co-cardinal* Dets as those $D$ satisfying $DAB = DXY$ whenever $|A - B| = |X - Y|$. The Dets in (14a,b,c) are co-cardinal, that in (14d) is not.

**Theorem 12.4.** *The set $CO\text{-}INT_E$ and $CO\text{-}CARD_E$ of co-intersective and co-cardinal functions over $E$ are both closed under the pointwise boolean operations and thus form boolean lattices. They have the same size as $INT_E$ and $CARD_E$ respectively.*

Thus *not all* and *all but two or all but four* are co-intersective since the items negated and disjoined are.

The value of a co-intersective Det at properties $A, B$ is decided by a single property, $A - B$. So again the map sending each co-intersective $D$ to $D(E)$ is an isomorphism from the co-intersective functions to the set of generalized quantifiers, whence the intersective and the co-intersective Dets are isomorphic). But even taken together $\text{INT}_E$ and $\text{CO-INT}_E$ constitute a minuscule proportion of the possible Det denotations: e.g. for $|E| = 2$ just 30 of the 65,536 functions from $\mathcal{P}(E)$ into $\text{GQ}_E$ are either intersective or co-intersective. We note that the two trivial Dets, **0** and **1**, which map all $A, B$ to $F$ and all $A, B$ to $T$ respectively are the only Det denotations which are both intersective and co-intersective.

The co-intersective Dets are structurally less diverse than the intersective ones. They are basically just the universal quantifier with exception phrases, including *almost all*[3]. Also we seem to find no clear examples of interrogative Dets which are co-intersective. Our best example is *All but how many?* as in (15a), of dubious grammaticality. It means the same as the natural (15b) built from the intersective *How many?*.

(15)    a. ??All but how many students came to the party?

      b. How many students didn't come to the party?

### 12.1.3   Proportionality Dets

A third natural class of Dets that take us well outside the generalized existential and universal ones are the proportionality Dets.

Proportionality Dets decide $DAB$ according to the proportion of $A$s that are $B$s. So, they yield the same value at $A, B$ as they do at $X, Y$ when the proportion of $A$s that are $B$s is the same as the proportion of $X$'s that are $Y$'s. Some examples first, then the definition, then some illustrative denotations:

(16)    a. *Most* poets daydream.

      b. *Seven out of ten* sailors smoke Players.

      c. *Less than half* the students here got an A on the exam.

---

[3]If $A$ and $B$ are largish finite sets we agree that *almost all As are Bs* is true if all but one $A$ is a $B$. E.g. if there are exactly 100 students in the model and precisely 99 read the Times then *almost all students read the Times* is clearly true. But if there are just two students and exactly one reads the Times this judgment is not convincing. So *almost all* might require a condition of minimum cardinality on its first argument.

d. *At most ten per cent of* the students passed the exam.

e. *Between a third and two thirds of* the students are vegetarians.

f. *All but a tenth of* the students are vegetarians.

g. *Not one student in ten* can answer that question.

**Definition 12.4.** A Det $D$ is *proportional* iff

$$DAB = DXY \text{ whenever } |A \cap B|/|A| = |X \cap Y|/|X|.$$

(17)  a.  SEVEN-OUT-OF-TEN$(A)(B) = T$  iff $10 \cdot |A \cap B| = 7 \cdot |A|$
      b.  AT-MOST-10%$(A)(B) = T$  iff $10 \cdot |A \cap B| \leq |A|$
      c.  ALL-BUT-A-TENTH$(A)(B) = T$  iff $10 \cdot |A - B| = |A|$
      d.  NOT-ONE … IN-TEN$(A)(B) = T$  iff $10 \cdot |A \cap B| < |A|$

Co-proportional Dets such as *all but a tenth* are covered by Definition 12.4 since the proportion of $A$s with $B$ is uniquely determined by the proportion that lack $B$: *All but (at most) a tenth* means the same as *(At least) nine out of ten*, so (18a,b) are logically equivalent.

(18)    a. All but at most a tenth of the students read the Times.

        b. At least nine out of ten students don't read the Times.

Fractional and percentage Dets, ones of the form *n out of m, n ≤ m*, and the discontinuous *less than/more than/just one … in ten* are proportional. They have been little studied. Our best candidates for interrogative proportional Dets are *What percentage / proportion of*?

Proportionality Dets are "typically" neither intersective nor co-intersective, but there are a few exceptions: *exactly zero per cent* means *no* and *more than zero per cent* means *at least one*, so both are intersective; *a hundred per cent* means *all* and *less than a hundred per cent* means *not all*, so both are co-intersective. So the proportionality Dets have a small non-empty intersection with the (co)-intersective Dets.

The three classes of Dets so far discerned are "booleanly natural" in that boolean compounds of Dets in the class yield Dets in the class. But the classes are non-exhaustive: there are Dets in English which fall in none of these classes. The definite Dets defined below (based on Barwise and Cooper, 1981) in general lie outside the classes so far discerned. They are also not booleanly natural. Some examples[4] first:

---

[4]Other Dets such as *these* and *your* can be subsumed under our definition of *definite plural*, but their deictic character (the interpretative dependency on the context of utterance) would introduce a very non-trivial dimension to our definition

368 / Mathematical Structures in Language

(19)  a. THE-TWO$(A)(B) = T$      iff $|A| = 2$ and ALL$(A)(B) = T$

b. THE-TWO-OR-MORE$(A)(B) = T$
iff $|A| \geq 2$ and ALL$(A)(B) = T$

c. JOHN'S-TWO$(A)(B) = T$ iff $|A$ WHICH JOHN HAS$| = 2$ and
ALL$(A$ WHICH JOHN HAS$)(B) = T$

(Note that $A$ WHICH JOHN HAS is a subset of $A$.)

Now we define, tediously:

**Definition 12.5.**

a. A possible Det denotation $D$ is *definite* iff for all $A \subseteq E$, either
$DAB = F$ all $B$, or $DA = $ ALL$(C)$, some non-empty $C \subseteq A$.
$D$ is called *definite plural* if the $C$ in this last condition must
always have at least two elements.

b. A Det $d$ is *definite (plural)* iff there are models $\mathcal{M}$ in which $[\![d]\!]_{\mathcal{M}}$
is non-trivial and for all such $\mathcal{M}$, $[\![d]\!]_{\mathcal{M}}$ is definite (plural).

Note that *all* is not definite. It is non-trivial but it fails the disjunction "$DAB = F$ all $B$, or $DA = $ ALL$(C)$, some non-empty $C \subseteq A$". It fails the first disjunct since for every $A$, ALL$(A)(A) = T$. It fails the second since for $A = \emptyset$ there is no non-empty subset $C$ of $A$.

In contrast the reader can compute that *the five* and *John's five* are definite plural.

**A syntactic query:** Which DPs occur naturally in the post *of* position of partitives of the form: *two of___*?

For example, *two of the ten students* and *two of John's five cats* are natural, whereas *two of most students*, *two of no students* certainly are not. Also this position seems closed under conjunctions and disjunctions but not under negation or *neither ... nor ...* : *two of John's poems or (of) Mary's plays were accepted*; *several of the students and (of) the teachers attended*. But *two of not the ten students* and *two of neither the ten students nor the ten teachers*. The same pattern of acceptability obtains replacing *two* by other plural, count Dets like *several, more than ten, all but ten, a majority of*, etc. So we propose to answer the query above with (20).

---

of interpretation in a model, one that we lack the space, and knowledge, to present here.

Note that (THE TWO) $=$ (EXACTLY TWO) $\wedge$ ALL; (THE TWO OR MORE) $=$ (AT LEAST TWO) $\wedge$ ALL. So extensionally these definite Dets are meets of intersective with co-intersective ones. But they differ in that *the two cats* presupposes that there exist two cats rather than merely asserting it, as given in (EXACTLY TWO) $\wedge$ ALL.

(20)  The DPs occurring in *two of* ___ are just those in the closure
      under conjunction and disjunction of the DPs of the form
      Det + N, with Det definite plural as above.

We defined our frame with *two of* ___ because some Dets allow a mass
interpretation with a singular terms in the post-of position (but are
understood as count terms with plural DPs. Compare *All / Most of
the house was unusable after the flood* versus *All / Most of the houses
were unusable after the flood.* See Higginbotham (1994) and references
cited there for a conceptually pleasing treatment of mass terms.

### 12.1.4  "Logical" Dets

Dets such as *John's ten, no ... but John,* and *more male than female*
lack the "logical" character of classical quantifiers and some might hesitate to call them quantifiers. But terminology aside, the challenging
question here is whether we can characterize what is meant by a "logical" character. We can. This character is captured by the idea that the
interpretations of "logical" expressions (not just Dets) remain invariant
under structure preserving maps of the semantic primitives of a model.
Such maps are the isomorphisms from a structure to itself, called *automorphisms.* For example an automorphism of a boolean lattice $(B, \leq)$
is a bijection $h$ of $B$ which fixes the $\leq$ relation: $x \leq y$ iff $h(x) \leq h(y)$).
The primitives of a standard model $\mathcal{M} = \langle E_{\mathcal{M}}, \{T, F\} \rangle$ are just its
domain $E_{\mathcal{M}}$ and the boolean lattice of truth values $\{T, F\}$. The only
automorphism of $\{T, F\}$ is the identity map, as it is the only bijection
on $\{T, F\}$ which fixes the implication order. The automorphisms of $E$
are all the permutations (bijections) of $E$ as $E$ is not endowed with
any relations or functions, so any permutation of $E$ preserves "all"
its structure. Thus an automorphism of $(E, \{T, F\})$ is in effect just
a permutation of $E$ (we omit the subscript $\mathcal{M}$.) Moreover each such
automorphism $h$ lifts to an automorphism of the denotation sets built
from $E$ and $\{T, F\}$ in a standard way: an automorphism $h$ maps each
subset $K$ of $E$ to $\{h(k) \mid k \in K\}$; it maps an ordered pair $(x, y)$ of
elements of $E$ to $(h(x), h(y))$, and it maps a binary relation $R$ on $E$ to
$\{h(x, y) \mid (x, y) \in R\}$, etc.
    An object in any denotation set is called *automorphism invariant* if
it is mapped to itself by all the automorphisms. These are the objects
you cannot change without changing structure. They are the ones with
a "logical" character. For example the only subsets of $E$ which are
automorphism invariant are $E$ and $\emptyset$, the denotations for *exist* and
*not exist.* The invariant binary relations are $\emptyset$, $E \times E$, $\{(x, x) \mid x \in E\}$
and $\{(x, y) \in E^2 \mid x \neq y\}$, these latter two being the denotation of *is* (or

*equals*) and *not equals*, respectively. Proceeding in this way (Keenan and Westerståhl, 2011) we see that

(21) The denotations of Dets such as *every, some, no, the two, most, all but five, two thirds of the,* etc. are automorphism invariant, those of *John's five, every ... but John, more male than female* may denote functions which are not automorphism invariant.

We'll see shortly that automorphism invariance improves our understanding of the relation between intersective and cardinal Dets, as well as that between co-intersective and co-cardinal ones. For later reference we note:

**Theorem 12.5.** *The set of type (1,1) functions,*

$$[\mathcal{P}(E) \to [\mathcal{P}(E) \to \{T, F\}]],$$

*is a boolean lattice pointwise. The subset of automorphism invariant (AI) functions is a sublattice of it. That is, the AI functions are closed under $\wedge$, $\vee$, and $\neg$.*

## 12.2 Generalizations Concerning Det Denotations

Surveying the Dets considered so far we see that a few, namely the intersective ones, make their truth decision at a pair $A, B$ of sets just by checking $A \cap B$; a few others just check $A - B$; yet others, the proportionality Dets, check both $A \cap B$ and $A - B$, and finally the definite Dets consider both $A$ and $A - B$, and partitive Dets check $A$ and then otherwise behave like intersective, universal, or proportional Dets, as in: *two / all / most of the ten*. We can generalize from these observations to the claim that in English, evaluating the interpretation of Det *As are Bs* does not require that we look outside the *As*. This observation is formalized in the literature by two independent conditions: *Domain Independence* and *Conservativity*, both of which are non-trivial semantic properties of Det denotations.

### 12.2.1 Domain Independence

Domain Independence (DI) is a global condition on Dets, comparing their denotations in different universes. It was first proposed as a semantic universal of natural language in van Benthem (1984a)[5]. It is prominent in Data Base Theory (see Abiteboul et al., 1995, p. 77) and rules out putative Det denotations like BLIK below, which we think of as associating with each domain $E$ a type (1,1) function BLIK$_E$ on $E$:

---

[5]Van Benthem stated this condition slightly differently; calling it *Extension*.

(22) For all $E$, $\text{BLIK}_E(A)(B) = T$ iff $|E - A| = 3$.

Were Blik an English Det then *Blik cats can fly* would be true iff the number of non-cats was three. And we could change the truth value of the S merely by adding some non-cats to the domain, which is unnatural. Note though that (22) assumes that with each $E$, BLIK associates a single quantifier. But, anticipating slightly as in Keenan and Westerståhl (2011), some Dets, like *John's two*, can have several denotations over a given domain varying with the individual *John* denotes and the things he "has". So we define:

**Definition 12.6** (Domain Independence (DI)). A functional $D$ associating each domain $E$ with a family of functions of type (1,1) is *domain independent* iff for all $E \subseteq E'$, all $A, B \subseteq E$,

a. each $f \in D_E(A)(B)$ extends to an $f'$ in $D_{E'}(A)(B)$ and

b. each $f' \in D_{E'}(A)(B)$ is an extension of some $f$ in $D_E(A)(B)$.

Recall that to say that $f'$ extends $f$ above just says that it takes the same values at subsets of $E$ as $f$ does. And to say that English Dets are domain independent just says that they determine domain independent functionals. BLIK above fails DI since $\text{BLIK}\emptyset\emptyset = T$ when $E = \{a, b, c\}$ but $\text{BLIK}\emptyset\emptyset = F$ for $E' = \{a, b, c, d\}$. We note:

**Theorem 12.6.** *For each domain independent Det $d$ and each model $\mathcal{M}$ over a finite domain $E_M$,*

a. $[\![d]\!]_{\mathcal{M}}$ *is cardinal iff $[\![d]\!]_{\mathcal{M}}$ is both intersective and automorphism invariant, and*

b. $[\![d]\!]_{\mathcal{M}}$ *is co-cardinal iff $[\![d]\!]_{\mathcal{M}}$ is both co-intersective and automorphism invariant.*

### 12.2.2 Conservativity

Conservativity[6] (CONS) is a local constraint, limiting the maps from $\mathcal{P}(E)$ into $\text{GQ}_E$ which can be denotations of Dets. Specifically it requires that in evaluating $D(A)(B)$ we ignore the elements of $B$ which do not lie in $A$. Formally,

**Definition 12.7.** A function $D$ from $P_E$ into $[P_E \to X]$, $X$ any set, is *conservative* iff for all $A, B, C \subseteq E$,

$$D(A)(B) = D(A)(C) \text{ whenever } A \cap B = A \cap C.$$

---

[6] The term *conservative* dates from Keenan (1981); it was called *lives on* in Barwise and Cooper (1981) and *intersective* in Higginbotham and May (1981).

**Theorem 12.7.** *The set of conservative maps from $\mathcal{P}(E)$ into $GQ_E$ is closed under the pointwise boolean operations.*

**Theorem 12.8.** *$D$ from $P_E$ to $[P_E \to X]$ is conservative iff for all $A, B \subseteq E$, $DAB = D(A)(A \cap B)$.*

Theorem 12.8 is the usual definition of Conservativity. The reader may use it to verify that the Dets in (23) are conservative by verifying that $(23x, x')$ are logically equivalent.

(23)    a.   All swans are white.

       a'.   All swans are swans and are white.

       b.   Most bees buzz.

       b'.   Most bees are bees that buzz.

       c.   No dogs purr.

       c'.   No dogs are dogs that purr.

       d.   John's pupils work hard.

       d'.   John's pupils are pupils and work hard.

       e.   Which states have no taxes?

       e'.   Which states are states with no taxes?

       f.   Whose two bikes are in the yard?

       f'.   Whose two bikes are bikes in the yard?

       g.   Neither John's nor Bill's abstracts were accepted.

       g'.   Neither John's nor Bill's abstracts were abstracts that were accepted.

The equivalences in (23) are felt as trivial because the predicate repeats information given by the noun. But surprisingly, Conservativity is a very strong constraint:

**Theorem 12.9** (Keenan and Stavi, 1986). *The number of logically possible Det denotations is $|[P_E \to GQ_E]|$, namely $2^{4^{|E|}}$. The total number of these functions which are conservative is $2^{3^{|E|}}$.*

Thus in a two element domain $E$ there are $2^{16} = 65,536$ maps from properties to GQs. Just $2^9 = 512$ are conservative! (And only 16 are (co-)intersective, of which 8 are (co-)cardinal.) Functions like the Härtig quantifier $H$ in (24), are not conservative: choose $A$ and $B$ to be disjoint singleton sets. Then $|A| = |B|$ but $|A| \neq |A \cap B|$.

(24) $H(A)(B) = T$ iff $|A| = |B|$.

Note that DI and CONS are independent: $\mathrm{BLIK}_E$ above is CONS but not DI; the Härtig quantifier is DI but fails CONS in each $E$. It seems then that

(25) Natural Language Dets are both domain independent and conservative.

Ben-Shalom (2001) and Keenan and Westerståhl (2011) independently provide different single conditions which capture the combined effect of domain independence and conservativity.

Thus CONS is a strong condition, ruling out most maps from $\mathcal{P}(E)$ into $\mathrm{GQ}_E$ as possible Det denotations. But it still lets through many that lie outside the INT and CO-INT classes, e.g. the proportional Dets and the definite Dets. Are there others? Can we impose a local constraint stronger than CONS on possible Det denotations? If not, is there any reason to expect that the denotable Det functions should be just those admitted by CONS? Concerning stronger constraints Keenan and Stavi (1986) show that over any finite $E$ any conservative function from $\mathcal{P}(E)$ into $\mathrm{GQ}_E$ can be denoted in the sense that we can construct an English expression (albeit a cumbersome one) which can be interpreted as that function. We also have a (more speculative) answer to the last question: Namely, consider that in general boolean compounds of intersective and co-intersective Dets lie in neither class. So the Dets italicized below are neither intersective nor co-intersective:

(26)  a. *Some but not all* students read the Times.

   b. *Either all or else not more than two* of the students will pass that exam.

   c. *Either just two or three or else all but a couple of* students will pass that exam.

But these Dets are conservative since they are boolean compounds of conservative ones (by Theorem 12.7.)

**Theorem 12.10** (Keenan, 1993). *The set of conservative functions over $E$ is the boolean closure of the intersective together with the co-intersective functions.*

That is, the set of functions obtained from INT and CO-INT by forming arbitrary meets, joins and complements is exactly the set of conservative functions. Recall our earlier remarks that the boolean connectives (*and, or, not, neither ... nor ...* ) are not semantically tied to any particular category or denotation set, but rather express ways we have of conceiving of things—properties, relations, functions, etc.—regardless of what they are. Thus given that we need intersective and co-intersective functions as denotations for expressions we expect the class of CONS functions to be denotable just because we can form boolean compounds of expressions denoting (co)intersective functions.

There is a last property related to CONS and which distinguishes natural language quantifiers from their standard logical counterparts. Namely some Dets do not make critical use of the noun argument (the *restrictor*) to restrict the domain of quantification, but can be paraphrased by replacing the noun argument by one that denotes the whole domain, forming a new predicate by some boolean compound of the original noun and predicate argument. For example, as we saw, *Some As are Bs* says the same as *Some individuals are both As and Bs,* where in the second S we are quantifying over all elements of the domain, not just those in $A$, as in the first S. Indeed it is this conversion that is learned when we teach beginning logic students to represent *Some men are mortal* by "For some $x$, $x$ is a man and $x$ is mortal". The variable $x$ here precisely ranges over the entire universe of objects under consideration. Similarly *All men are mortal* gets represented as "For all objects $x$, if $x$ is a man then $x$ is mortal".

Dets which admit of the elimination of the noun argument in this way will be called *sortally reducible*, and our key observation here is that English presents many Dets which are not sortally reducible. In fact the Dets that are sortally reducible are just the intersective and co-intersective ones. Let us more formally define:

**Definition 12.8.** $D$ is *sortally reducible* iff for all $A, B \subseteq E$,

$$D(A)(B) = D(E)(\ldots A \ldots B \ldots),$$

where "$(\ldots A \ldots B \ldots)$" is a boolean function of $A$ and $B$.

"Boolean functions" are ones definable solely in terms of the boolean connectives *and, or, not*, etc. In the formalism used here this just means that $(\ldots A \ldots B \ldots)$ is defined in terms of set intersection ($\cap$), union ($\cup$) and complement ($\neg$). We use $A \to B$ to abbreviate $\neg A \cup B$.

**Theorem 12.11.**

    *a. If $D$ is intersective then $D$ is sortally reducible, by*

$$DAB = D(E)(A \cap B).$$

    *This follows from the fact that $A \cap B = E \cap A \cap B$ plus the fact that $D$ is intersective.*

b. *If D is co-intersective then D is sortally reducible, by*

$$DAB = D(E)(A \to B).$$

*Note that* $E - (A \to B) = E \cap \neg(\neg A \cup B) = A \cap \neg B = A - B).$

**Theorem 12.12** (Keenan, 1993). *For D a function of type (1,1) over a domain E, D is sortally reducible iff either D is intersective or D is co-intersective.*

So, in general, proportionality Dets are not sortally reducible, they make essential use of the noun argument. Let us see that the reductions in Theorem 12.11 don't work for *most*. Theorem 12.11a doesn't, since *Most students are vegetarians* is not logically equivalent to *Most entities are both students and vegetarians*: given an $E$ consisting of a hundred vegetarians only ten of whom are students, the first sentence is true and the second false. For the inadequacy of the if-then type reduction we show that (27b) does not entail (27a):

(27)  a. Most students are vegans.

  b. Most entities are such that if they are students then they are vegans.

Let $|E| = 100$ with just 15 students, no vegans. Then (27a) is false: none of the students are vegans. But (27b) is true: the if-then clause is satisfied by 85 of the 100 entities.

We have covered a variety of English Dets, all of the type that take two property denoting expressions as arguments to yield a truth value (or question meaning). But English arguably presents Dets of other types.

## 12.3  *k*-Place Dets

Following Keenan and Moss (1985) the italic expressions in (28) are Det$_2$s: they combine with two Ns to form a DP and semantically map pairs of sets to GQs.

(28)  a. *More / Fewer* students *than* teachers came to the party.

  b. *Exactly / almost / not as many* students *as* teachers ...

  c. *More than ten times as many* students *as* teachers ...

  d. *How many more* students *than* teachers were arrested?

  e. *The same number of* students *as* teachers ...

  f. *A larger / smaller number of* students *than* teachers ...

(28a) gives the denotation of the Det$_2$ *more ... than ...* , with the N arguments in the easy-to-read order. Most of the other denotations in (28) are defined similarly. Read (29) as "More As than Bs have C iff the number of As with C exceeds the number of Bs with C".

(29) (MORE $A$ THAN $B$)$(C) = T$ iff $|A \cap C| > |B \cap C|$.

**Exercise 12.4.** On the pattern in (29) exhibit the denotations of the Det$_2$s below:

   a. exactly as many ... as ...

   b. more than twice as many ... as ...

   c. no more ... than ...

   d. the same number of ... as ...

Expressions such as *more students than teachers* which we treat as built from Det$_2$s are not usually treated as DPs in their own right. So it is worth noting that they share many distributional properties with standard DPs (Keenan, 1987):

(30)   a. John interviewed more men than women.

      b. He sent flowers to more teachers than students.

      c. She believes more students than teachers to have signed the petition.

      d. More students than teachers are believed to have signed the petition.

      e. More teachers than deans interviewed more men than women.

      f. Most instructors and many more students than professors signed the petition.

      g. Ann knows more Danes than Germans but not more Danes than Swedes.

      h. More students' than teachers' bicycles were stolen.

There is also an interesting semantic fact naturally represented on a view which treats *more ... than ...* , etc. as a Det$_2$ taking an ordered pair of nouns as arguments. Namely, modifiers of the pair naturally behave coordinate-wise applying to each property:

(31)  More students than teachers at UCLA attended the rally.
= More students at UCLA than teachers at UCLA attended the rally
= (AT UCLA)$(p, q)$ = ((AT UCLA)$(p)$, (AT UCLA)$(q)$)

Generalizing now, we can think of a Det$_k$ as combining with a $k$-tuple of Ns to form a DP. Semantically it would map $k$-tuples of sets to GQs. Does English present Det$_k$s for $k > 2$? Perhaps. It is reasonable for example to treat *every ... and ...* as a $k$-place Det, all $k > 0$. (Think of *every* as the form it takes when $k = 1$.) (32) interprets *every ... and ...* as a Det$_3$.

(32)   a. Every man, woman and child jumped overboard.

b. (EVERY ... AND ...)$(A, B, C)(D)$ = EVERY$(A \cup B \cup C)(D)$

The *and* in (32a) is not simple coordination, otherwise (32a) would mean that every object which was simultaneously a man, woman and child jumped overboard, which is empirically incorrect. The pattern whereby the value of a Det$_k$ built from a Det$_1$ and *and* maps the $n$ noun properties to whatever the Det$_1$ maps their union to, is quite general:

(33)  For $D \in [P_E \to \mathrm{GQ}_E]$, $(D \ldots \mathrm{AND} \ldots)$ maps $(P_E)^k$ into GQ$_E$, all $k$, defined by:

$$(D \ldots \mathrm{AND} \ldots)(A_1, \ldots, A_k) = D(\bigcup_{1 \leq i \leq k} A_i).$$

(34)   a. About fifty men and women jumped overboard.
(ABOUT FIFTY ... AND ... )$(A, B)(D)$
= (ABOUT FIFTY)$(A \cup B)(D)$

b. The sixty boys and girls laughed at the joke.
(THE SIXTY ... AND ... )$(A, B)(D)$ =
(THE SIXTY)$(A \cup B)(D)$

c. Which boys and girls came to the party?
(WHICH ... AND ... )$(A)(B)(D)$ = WHICH$(A \cup B)(D)$

The most convincing case that we have Det$_2$s in English comes from (28) as they do not lend themselves to a syntactic or semantic reduction to compounds of Dets of lesser arity.

The Det$_2$s in (28) are all cardinal (and thus intersective): the value of the DP they build at a predicate property $B$ is decided by the cardinality of the intersection of $B$ with each noun property. Defining conservativity, (co-)intersectivity, etc. for $k$-place Dets involves no real change from the unary case: a cardinal $\text{Det}_k$ decides truth by checking the cardinality of the intersection of the predicate property with each of the $k$ noun properties. A conservative $\text{Det}_k$ checks the intersection of that property with each noun property, etc[7].

Comparative quantifiers (Beghelli, 1992, 1994, Smessaert, 1996) assume a variety of other forms in English as well. Those in (35) combine with a single noun property but two predicate properties to form a S.

(35)    a. More students came early than left late.

       b. Exactly as many students came early as left late.

       c. The same number of students came early as left late.

       d. The same students as came early left late.

Enriching our type notation we treat the Dets in (28) as of type $((1,1),1)$: they map a pair of noun properties to a function from properties to truth values. The Dets in (35) then perhaps have type $(1,(1,1)))$, mapping a triple of properties to a truth value. Note that the string *more students* in (35a) is not a DP and cannot be replaced by one.

(36)    a. *All/*Most/*No students came early than left late.

       b. *Exactly ten/*Most students came early as left late.

The quantifiers of type $((1,1),1)$ and $(1,(1,1))$ we have considered are all cardinal in their type. We do not seem to find any co-cardinal two place Dets. There are however proportional Dets of type $((1,1),1)$ as in (37) and of type $(1,(1,1))$, as in (38).

(37)    a. A greater/smaller percentage of students than (of) teachers signed the petition.

       b. The same proportion of students as of teachers signed the petition.

---

[7] The extended definitions would proceed as follows:

**Definition 12.9.** For all $k$, all functions $D$ from $k$-tuples of properties over $E$ into $[P_E \to X]$,

   a. $D$ is *cardinal* iff for all $k$-tuples $A, A'$ of properties and all properties $B, B'$, if $|A_i \cap B| = |A_i' \cap B'|$, all $1 \leq i \leq k$, then $DAB = DA'B'$.

   b. $D$ is *conservative* iff for all $k$-tuples $A = \langle A_1, \ldots, A_k \rangle$ and all properties $B, B'$, if $A_i \cap B = A_i \cap B'$, all $1 \leq i \leq k$, then $DAB = DAB'$.

Define *intersectivity* for $\text{Det}_k$s by eliminating from (a) the cardinality signs; *co-cardinal* and *co-intersective* for $\text{Det}_k$s by replacing $A_i \cap B$ with $A_i - B$. For some additional types of Dets see Keenan and Westerståhl (2011).

(38)   a. A greater / smaller percentage of students came early than
            left late.

       b. The same percentage of students came early as left late.

And the Dets in (39) plausibly have type (1,1,1,1), or perhaps
((1,1),(1,1)). We only find natural cardinal examples:

(39)   a. More students came early than teachers left late.

       b. Just as many students came early as teachers left late.

Quantifiers in these high types have not, at time of writing, been sub-
jected to any intensive study. Here we note simply two entailment
paradigms which at least indicate that there is some logical behavior
to study here. The first is due to Zuber (2008).

(40)   a. More poets than linguists are vegetarians.   (type ((1,1),1)

       b. More vegetarians are poets than are linguists.

                                              (type (1,(1,1))

And in general,

(41)   MORE $A$ THAN $A'$ ARE $B$ ↔ MORE $B$ ARE $A$ THAN ARE $A'$

(42)   a. More poets than painters live in NY.

       b. ≡ More poets who are not painters than painters who are
            not poets live in NY.

**Exercise 12.5.** Exhibit an informal model in which (a) is true and (b)
is not.

   a. The students who arrived early also left late.

   b. The same students as arrived early left late.

## 12.4   Crossing the Frege Boundary

We have treated GQs as mapping $P_1$ denotations to S (= $P_0$) denotations and we extended them to maps from $P_{n+1}$ denotations to $P_n$
denotations in such a way that their values at $n + 1$-ary relations were
determined by their values at the unary relations. This yielded the object narrow scope reading of Ss like *Some student praised every teacher*.
The object wide scope reading was shown to be representable with the
use of the lambda operator:

   (EVERY TEACHER)$\lambda x$(SOME STUDENT PRAISED $x$).

We also showed that we could effect an Object Wide Scope reading by interpreting the subject and the transitive verb by function composition rather than function application (FA).

$$((\text{EVERY TEACHER}) \circ (\text{PRAISED}))(\text{SOME STUDENT})$$

Now, a suggestive aspect of our "extensions" approach is that it leads us to look for new types of DP denotations. Obviously there are many more maps from binary relations to unary relations over $E$ ($|E| > 1$) than there are from unary relations to truth values. Can any of these new functions be denoted by expressions in English? In fact many can. Consider *himself* in (43a), interpreted as SELF in (43b) and *everyone but himself* in (44a) interpreted as in (44b):

(43)   a. Every poet admires himself.

   b. $\text{SELF}(R) = \{b \in E \mid b \in R_b\}$

(44)   a. No worker criticized everyone but himself.

   b. $(\text{ALL BUT SELF})(R) = \{b \in E \mid R_b = E - \{b\}\}$

Recall that $R_b$ is $\{y \in E \mid R(y)(b) = T\}$, the set of objects $y$ which $b$ bears the relation $R$ to.

And provably these sorts of referentially dependent functions are not the extensions of any GQs to binary relations:

**Theorem 12.13** (Keenan, 1989). *There is no GQ whose restriction to binary relations is* SELF *or* ALL BUT SELF *(for $|E| > 1$).*

The same holds for other DPs with ordinary pronominal forms bound to the subject, e.g. *his mother* in *Everyone$_i$ loves his$_i$ mother*.

Even more challenging are cases like (45) in which the pairs of italic expressions are felt to stand in some sort of mutual referential dependency relation.

(45)   a. *Different people* like *different things*.

   b. *Each student* answered a *different question* (on the exam).

   c. John criticized Bill but *no one else* criticized *anyone else*.

And in fact (Keenan, 1992), there are no GQs $F,G$ such that $F(G(\text{LIKE}))$ always has the same truth value as (45a), all binary relations LIKE. But the pair (DIFFERENT PEOPLE, DIFFERENT THING) can be treated directly as a type (2) quantifier, one mapping binary relations to truth values. So such dependent pairs determine yet another type of quantification in natural language. In the same spirit, Moltmann (1996) notes inherently type (2) quantifiers like the exception constructions in (46).

(46)    a. Every man danced with every woman except John with Mary.

        b. No man danced with any woman except John with Mary.

## 12.5    A Classic Syntactic Problem

Linguists since Milsark (1977) have puzzled over which DPs occur naturally in Existential There (ET) contexts, as in (47) and (48):

(47)    a. There are at most three undergraduate students in my logic class.

        b. Isn't there at least one student who objects to that?

        c. Aren't there more than five students enrolled in the course?

        d. There were more students than teachers arrested at the demonstration.

        e. Just how many students were there at the party?

        f. Were there the same number of students as teachers at the party?

        g. There weren't as many students as teachers at the lecture.

The examples in (47) are all built from cardinal Dets. Of note is that cardinal $Det_2$s as in (47f,g), not traditionally considered in this (or any) context, build DPs fully acceptable in ET contexts.

**Exercise 12.6.** On the basis of examples like those in (47)

    a. Exhibit four structurally distinct boolean compounds of DPs acceptable in ET contexts and show that they themselves are also acceptable in ET contexts.

    b. Exhibit some ungrammatical boolean compounds of DPs built from cardinal Dets. Can you suggest any regularities limiting the formation of such DPs?

    c. Can you find any DPs acceptable in ET contexts whose boolean compounds are grammatical in general but not acceptable in ET contexts? If not this argues that ET contexts do not impose any special restrictions on boolean compounding.

There are many pragmatic issues involved with judgments of acceptability of DPs in ET constructions, but a good (but not perfect, see below) approximation to a proper characterization of the acceptable DPs here is that they are just those built from intersective Dets

(Det$_1$s or Det$_2$s) and their boolean compounds. So, like the definite plural DPs, we characterize a class of DPs in terms of the Dets that build them. The Dets in (47) are cardinal, those in (48) are intersective but not cardinal. Those in (49) are not intersective and the resulting Ss are marginal to bad:

(48)    a. Aren't there *as many male as female students* in the class?

       b. There was *no student but John* in the building.

       c. Just *which students* were there at the party anyway?

       d. There were *only two students besides John* at the lecture.

(49)    a. *There are *most students* in my logic class.

       b. *Isn't there *the student* who objects to that?

       c. ??Aren't there *seven out of ten students* enrolled in your course?

       d. *Isn't there *every student* who gave a talk at the conference?

       e. *Was there *neither student* arrested at the demonstration?

       f. ??*Which of the two students* were there at the demonstration?

See Reuland and ter Meulen (1987) for several articles discussing DPs in Existential There contexts. Keenan (2003) is a recent proposal which entails the intersectivity claim above. Peters and Westerståhl (2006, pp. 214–238) is a more recent in depth review of the literature and notes (at least) two problems with the intersectivity thesis above. Namely, partitives, as in (50) and possessives, as in (51).

(50)   I believe that there are at least two of the five supervisors that favor that bill.

Treating the Det in (50) as *at least two of the five* it will fail to be intersective as it is not symmetric: setting

$$D = (\text{AT LEAST TWO OF THE FIVE}),$$

we have that $D(A)(B)$ is true if $|A| = 5$, $|B| = 10$ and $|A \cap B| \geq 2$. But then $D(B)(A)$ is false since $|B| \neq 5$. And seemingly all options of analysis must enforce an asymmetry between $A$ and $B$ with $|A|$ required to be 5 and $|B|$ not so required.

(51)    a. There is *some neighbor's dog* that barks incessantly.

       b. *There is *each neighbor's dog* that barks incessantly.

Possessives are difficult both syntactically and semantically. The most thorough semantic treatment is in fact that given in Chapter 7 of Peters and Westerståhl (2006). Possessive Dets may fail to be symmetric hence they fail to be intersective: it may be true that John's doctor is a lawyer but false that John's lawyer is a doctor. Possibly possessive Dets are (sometimes) properly intensional, like *too many* and *not enough* noted in footnote 1. But that won't explain the judgments in (51a,b) as the sense of possession is the same in the two cases.

We conclude with a brief look at some tantalizing but less well understood instances of A(dverbial)-quantification in English, as opposed to the D(eterminer)-quantification (Partee, 1995) we have been considering.

## 12.6   Adverbial Quantification

A(dverbial)-quantification is expressible with independent adverbs or PPs: Lewis (1975), Heim (1982), de Swart (1996, 1994).

(52)     a. John *always / usually / often / occasionally / rarely / never* trains in the park.

         b. John took his driver's exam *twice / (more than) three times.*

         c. Mary brushes her teeth *every day / twice a day.*

There is a striking semantic correspondence between the adverbial quantifiers underlined above and the D-Dets presented earlier. *Always* corresponds to *all, never* to *no, twice* to *two, usually* to *most, occasionally / sometimes* to *some,* and *often* and *rarely* to *many* and *few.* Similarly Bittner (1995) lists pairs of A- and D-quantifiers (translating *always, mostly, often, sometimes*) in Greenlandic Eskimo formed from the same root but differing in adverbial vs nominal morphology. And Evans (1995) lists pairs of semantically similar D- and A-quantifiers in Mayali (Australia).

In general what we quantify over in the D-cases is given by the Ns the Det combines with. But in A-quantification there is often no such clear constituent, and precisely what we are quantifying over is less clear. One influential approach to A-quantification follows up on the unselective binding approach in Lewis (1975). Examples that illustrate A-quantifiers best and which seem empirically most adequate are ones lacking independent D-quantifiers. (53) is from Peters and Westerståhl (2006, p. 352).

(53)     a. Men are usually taller than women.

b. $\text{MOST}_2(\{\langle x, y \rangle \mid x \in \text{MAN}$
$\&\ y \in \text{WOMAN}\}, \{\langle x, y \rangle \mid x \text{ TALLER } y\}) = T$

c. iff
$$\frac{|(\text{MAN} \times \text{WOMAN}) \cap \text{TALLER}|}{|(\text{MAN} \times \text{WOMAN})|} > \frac{1}{2}$$

On this interpretation (53a) is true iff the proportion of (man,woman) pairs in the *taller than* relation is more than half the (man,woman) pairs. So $\text{MOST}_2$ is of type (2,2), mapping a pair of binary relations MAN × WOMAN and TALLER as arguments to truth values, as it does in simpler cases like *Most colleagues are friends*. Its semantics is that of MOST given earlier, but now the sets it intersects and compares cardinalities of are sets of ordered pairs. In general for $D$ any of our original Det functions, $D_k$, the $k$-resumption of $D$, is that function like $D$ except that its arguments are $k$-ary relations. Peters and Westerståhl (2006) call this lifting operation *resumption*. It is one way A-quantifiers are characterized in terms of D-quantifiers. Thus it is immediate how to interpret the Ss differing from (53a) by replacing *usually* with *always*, *sometimes*, and *never*.

Now, to what extent can we represent A-quantification by resumption? We don't know at time of writing, but one more case that has been widely treated as unselective binding (resumption) is biclausal constructions built from *when/if* clauses and generic or indefinite DPs (constructed with the indefinite article *a/an*), as (54). See Kratzer (1995).

(54)   a. (Always) when a linguist buys a book he reads its bibliography first.

   b. $\text{ALL}_2(R, S)$, where
   $R = \{\langle x, y \rangle \mid x \in \text{LINGUIST}, y \in \text{BOOK}, x \text{ BUY } y\}$ and
   $S = \{\langle x, y \rangle \mid x \text{ READ } y\text{'s BIBLIOGRAPHY FIRST}\})$

   c. $= T$ iff $R \subseteq S$

$\text{ALL}_2$ is just ALL with binary not unary relation arguments. (54c) says that (54a) is true iff for all linguists $x$, all books $y$, if $x$ buys $y$ then $x$ reads $y$'s bibliography first, which seems right. *Always* can be replaced by *Sometimes*, *Never*, and *Not always*, interpreted by $\text{SOME}_2$, $\text{NO}_2$, and $\neg\text{ALL}_2$ with the intuitively correct truth conditions. However further extensions to Ss in which A- and D-quantification interact have not been successful. A much studied example is the Geach "donkey" sentence (Geach, 1962), as in (39a) with *it* anaphoric to *donkey*. Kamp (1981) and Heim (1982) among others have tried to interpret it with resumptive quantification as in (55b).

(55)   a. Every farmer who owns a donkey beats it.

     b. $\text{ALL}_2(\{\langle x,y\rangle \mid x \in \text{FARMER}, y \in \text{DONKEY} \ \& \ x \ \text{OWN} \ y\},$
$\{\langle x,y\rangle \mid x \ \text{BEAT} \ y\})$

This yields the "strong" interpretation on which every farmer who owns a donkey beats every donkey he owns. Several linguists either accept this interpretation or at least feel that it is the closest clear statement of the truth conditions of (55a). But most choices of initial quantifier do not yield correct resumptive interpretations. Kanazawa (1994) notes that the resumptive reading of (56a) would, incorrectly, be true in a model in which there are just two farmers, one owns one donkey and doesn't beat it, the other owns two and beats them both.

(56)   a. At least two farmers who own a donkey beat it.

     b. Most farmers who own a donkey beat it.

Rooth (1987) notes the comparable problem for (56b) in which say all but one of ten farmers owns just one donkey and beats it, but the last farmer owns 100 donkeys and doesn't beat any of them. This problem is now called the *proportion* problem, a misnomer since, per Kanazawa, it arises with non-proportional Dets like *at least two* as well. Indeed Peters and Westerståhl (2006) attribute to van der Does and van Eijck (1996) the claim that only *all*, *some* and their complements don't lead to a proportion problem. In addition Chierchia (1992) cites cases in which Ss like (57a) get a "weak" or "existential" reading, not a universal one.

(57)   a. Everyone who has a credit card will pay his bill with it.
       (Cooper, 1979)

     b. Everyone who has a dime will put it in the meter.
       (Pelletier and Schubert, 1989)

Evans (1977), Cooper (1979) and, in a different way, Heim (1990), try to handle the "dangling" *it* in donkey Ss with E-type pronouns, in effect replacing it by a full DP such as *the donkey he owns*, where *he* refers back to *farmer*. But the results are less than satisfactory when some farmers own more than one donkey. From our perspective these proposals do not so much invoke new quantifiers as establish the scope of familiar quantifiers. Later proposals by Groenendijk and Stokhof (1991), Chierchia (1992), Kanazawa (1994) and de Swart (1994) invoke dynamic logic in which natural language expressions are represented in a logical language and variables not in the syntactic scope (the c-command domain) of a VBO can nonetheless be bound by it.

So far we have not considered the domain of the resumptive quantifier in a systematic way. In (53a) the two Ns *man* and *woman* are part of different DP constituents, yet the domain of the quantifier is the cross product of their denotations. In (54a) it was the subordinate *when* clause in which we abstracted twice to form a binary relation denoting expression. Now returning to our initial example, repeated as (58a), we don't find naturally constructable binary relations of the relevant sorts. Rather, following de Swart (1996), it seems that we are comparing the "times" (or "occasions") John trains with the times he trains in the park.

(58)     a. John always / usually / ... trains in the park.

         b. ALL({$t$ | John trains at $t$}, {$t$ | John trains in the park at $t$})

So the Ss in (58a) compare the set of times John trains with the set of times he trains in the park. ALWAYS says that the first set is included in the second; NEVER says they are disjoint; SOMETIMES says they are not; USUALLY says that the set of times he trains in the park number more than half of the number of times that he trains, etc. So here A-quantification is handled as D-quantification over times. This approach is not unnatural given A-quantifiers which overtly mention times as *sometimes, five times, most of the time, from time to time*. Moreover it enables us to test whether the properties we adduced for D-quantifiers extend to their corresponding A-ones. And several do, as de Swart (1996) shows.

The cases in (58) are trivially Conservative. For any A-quantifier $Q$,

(59)  $Q$(TRAIN)(TRAIN IN THE PARK)
      $= Q$(TRAIN)(TRAIN $\cap$ TRAIN IN THE PARK).

They are also Domain Independent: if more times are added to the model but the two arguments of an A-Quantifier are unchanged then the value $Q$ assigns them is unchanged. Further some A-Quantifiers are intersective: SOMETIMES, NEVER; some are co-intersective: ALWAYS, WITH JUST TWO EXCEPTIONS, (60a); and some properly proportional, (60b): USUALLY, MORE THAN TWO THIRDS OF THE TIME. (As with D-quantifiers the notion of proportion is clearest when the arguments are finite and non-empty.)

(60)     a. With two exceptions, John has always voted for a Democrat for President.

         b. More than two thirds of the time when John prayed for rain it rained.

De Swart (1996) also handles some subordinate temporal clauses with *before* and *after* which are not mere place holders for quantificational domains in the way that *when* and *if* clauses may be.

(61)   a. Paul *always* takes a shower just before he goes to bed.

   b. Paul *never* exercises immediately after he has had dinner.

(61a) says that the times just before Paul goes to bed are all among those when he takes a shower. (61b) says that the times immediately after he has had dinner are disjoint from the times he exercises. *Usually*, *always*, *sometimes* and *never* are interpretable by their corresponding D-Det. Using *when* as an argument slot definer we see that the A-quantifiers above have the monotonicity properties of their D-counterparts. Like *all*, *always* is increasing on its second argument, decreasing on its first, so the inferences in (62) are valid and npi's are licensed in the first argument but not the second, (63).

(62)   a. Always when John travels he reads a book.

   b. $\Longrightarrow$ Always when John travels he reads something.

   c. $\Longrightarrow$ Always when John travels by train he reads a book.

(63)   a. Always when *anyone* travels he reads a book.

   b. *Always when John travels he reads *any* book.

Lewis (1975) cautioned against a "times" approach noting that donkey Ss refer more to a continuing state than an event, and Ss like *A quadratic equation usually has two different solutions* lack a time coordinate altogether. This is certainly true, though it leaves unexplained why it is natural to use the temporal metaphor in discussing mathematical Ss. A logician might say that a set of sentences is semantically consistent if they can be simultaneously true. Lewis himself notes that Russell and Whitehead (1910) use *always* and *sometimes* in explaining their introduction of the now standard universal and existential quantifier: $(x).\varphi x$ means $\varphi x$ *always*, $(\exists x).\varphi x$ means $\varphi x$ *sometimes*. It would not seem problematic to interpret Ss as functions taking "abstract times" as arguments, with truly "timeless" Ss denoting constant functions, as with vacuous quantification generally. Artstein (2005), building on Pratt and Francez (2001) treats *before* and *after* phrases (*after the meeting*, *after John left*) as temporal generalized quantifiers—they map properties of time intervals to $\{T, F\}$.

## 12.7   Concluding Remarks

D-quantification over count domains is the best understood type of quantification in natural language. Our knowledge in this domain has grown enormously beginning in the 1980s. And we see that it proves helpful in understanding mass and A-quantification, both areas currently being researched and in which many empirical and conceptual issues remain unexplored, even unformulated.

## 12.8 Historical Background

Quantification has been a major topic of both syntactic and semantic investigation in natural language for some time. In addition to articles cited in the body of this chapter, some good collections or overview articles are: van Benthem and ter Meulen (1985), van Benthem (1984a), Reuland and ter Meulen (1987), van der Does and van Eijck (1996), Gärdenfors (1987), Kanazawa and Piñón (1994). Westerståhl (1989) overviews this work up to 1987; Keenan and Westerståhl (2011) cover the later work; Keenan (1996) and Keenan (2008) are more linguistically oriented overviews. Peters and Westerståhl (2006) is the most comprehensive and in depth work to date. More purely mathematical work stimulated in part by this activity is: van Benthem (1984b), Westerståhl (1985), Keenan (1993), Kolaitis and Väänänen (1995), and the recent collection Krynicki et al. (1995). Szabolcsi (1997) is an excellent source for issues concerning scope, branching, and distributivity in natural language. Unselective binding and adverbial quantification are being investigated by several people. See for example Partee (1985) and de Swart (1994). Verkuyl and van der Does (1996), Lønning (1996), Winter (1998) discuss plurals and collectives. Doetjes and Honcoop (1997) and Krifka (1989, 1990) are good sources for work on event quantification. See Groenendijk and Stokhof (2011) and Gutierrez-Rexach (1997) for recent work on questions and quantification.

## 12.9 Appendix: Some Types of English Determiners

We present a variety of subclasses of Dets below. The classes are only informally indicated and are not exclusive, some Dets appear in several classes. The intent here is to give the reader some idea of the syntactic and semantic diversity of English Dets. As the reader will see, we are generous with what we call a Det, since generalizations that we make about the entire class will remain valid if some of our Dets are syntactically reanalyzed in other ways. Had we chosen a too narrow class initially some of our generalizations might be vitiated simply by bringing up new Dets not considered.

(64) We begin with examples of $\mathbf{Det_1}$'s: These are Dets which combine with one (possibly complex) Noun to form a $P_0/P_1$—a generalized quantifier denoting expression. These include the

Dets we have already considered, like *every*, *some*, *no*, etc. and many others:

**Lexical Dets:** every, each, all, some, a, no, several, neither, most, the, both, this, my, these, John's, ten, few, many, a few, a dozen,

**Cardinal Dets:** exactly ten, approximately/more than/fewer than/at most/only ten, infinitely many, two dozen, between five and ten, just finitely many, an even/odd/large number of

**Approximative Dets:** almost all/no, practically no, approximately/about/nearly/around fifty, a hundred plus or minus ten

**Definite Dets:** the, that, this, these, my, his, John's, the ten, these ten, John's ten

**Exception Dets:** all but ten, all but at most ten, every ... but John, no ... but Mary

**Bounding Dets:** exactly ten, between five and ten, most but not all, exactly half the, just one ... in ten, only SOME (=some but not all; upper case = contrastive stress), just the LIBERAL, only JOHN'S

**Possessive Dets:** my, John's, no student's, either John's or Mary's, neither John's nor Mary's

**Comparative Possessives:** more of Mary's than of Ann's (articles were cited)

**Value Judgment Dets:** too many, too few, a few too many, (not) enough, surprisingly few, ?many, ?few, more ... than we expected

**Proportionality Dets:** most, two out of three, (not) one ... in ten, less than half the (these, John's), exactly/more than/about/nearly half the, (more than) a third of the, ten per cent of the, every second

**Partitive Dets:** most/two/none/only some of the ten / of John's, more of John's than of Mary's, not more than two of the ten

**Negated Dets:** not every, not all, not a (single), not more than ten, not more than half, not very many, not quite enough, not over a hundred, not one of John's, not even two per cent of the

**Conjoined Dets:** at least two but not more than ten, most but not all, either fewer than ten or else more than a hundred, both John's and Mary's, at least a third and at most two thirds of the, neither fewer than ten nor more than a hundred

**Adjectively Restricted Dets:** John's biggest, more male than female, most male and all female, the last ... John visited, the first ... to set foot on the Moon, the easiest ... to clean, whatever ... are in the cupboard, the same ... who came early

**Logical Dets:** every, no, most, the two, all but two, exactly two, most but not all, just two of the ten, not more than ten, at least two and not more than ten, seven out of ten, not one ... in ten

(65)  We next turn to **Det₂'s**; these combine with two Ns to form a DP, as in *more students than teachers (came to the party)*.

**Cardinal comparatives:** more ... than ... , fewer ... than ... , exactly as many ... as ... , five more ... than ... , twice as many ... as ... , the same number of ... as ...

**Coordinate extensions:** every ... and ... , no ... or ..., the more than twenty ... and ... , some ... and ...

The three dots above indicate the locus of the N arguments. E.g. in *not one student in ten* we treat *not one ... in ten* as a discontinuous Det. In general we have two reasons for positing discontinuous analyses. One, often the N+postnominal material, such as *student in ten* in *not one student in ten*, has no reasonable interpretation, and so is not naturally treated as a constituent (which, by Compositionality, should be interpreted.)

And two, the presence of the postnominal and prenominal material may fail to be independent. If in *not one student in ten* we treated *student in ten* as a N which combines with the Det *not one*, how would we block *the/this/John's student in ten? So there are sensible reasons for treating the complex expressions above as Dets, though this proposal is not without problems of its own (Lappin, 1996, Rothstein, 1988) and very possibly some of our cases will find a non-discontinuous analysis (see von Fintel, 1993, Lappin, 1996, Moltmann, 1996 on exception Dets.)

# 13

---

# Linguistic Invariants

Work in generative grammar extends beyond the simple grammars we have proposed in our earlier chapters. One major difference is that it extends the rules to ones which move, copy and delete. Our chapter covering relative clauses did show how one important type of movement could be represented without movement by feature inheritance (percolation), as we saw with the feature [DP]. But many other sorts of movements exist, such as the one relating Ss like *I like beans* and *Beans I like*. Similarly the sort of deletion purportedly used in Conjunction Reduction Rules can be effected by directly combining expressions of most categories directly with *and, or, neither... nor....* So (a good thing) we don't need to try to derive *Some child both laughed and cried* from *Some child laughed and some child cried.* But many other types of deletion (ellipsis) phenomena are known: *Martin owns a Caddy and Felix a Jag.* And we have not proposed any rules that overtly copy expressions.

A second major difference is that grammatical categories are commonly endowed with various subcategory features. We want for example to distinguish singular from plural DPs as indicated earlier. Similarly gender classes, even in English, are needed to generate *She criticized herself* but not *\*She criticized himself.*

And in addition to trying to formulate rules adequate for a grammar of particular languages, like English, Finnish, Malagasy, etc. we want to state our grammar with sufficient generality to support general, ideally universal, structural claims that adequate grammars of all natural languages meet. The broad conceptual approach that generative grammarians have taken here is to formulate the structure building rules with sufficient generality that those in specific grammars can be seen as special cases. Perhaps the rules are even "parameterized" along certain dimensions so that different values for the parameters yield different language types (the Principles and Parameters approach – see

Jaeggli and Safir, 1989 and Freidin, 1992). Work along these lines has led to an enormous increase in our knowledge of language structure over the last two generations, but we are still far from having a rigorous statement of a universal with parameters that is empirically supported. Natural languages are complicated objects and it is rare that one parameter value varies completely independently of others.

Here we suggest a different approach to structural generalization – one not empirically incompatible with the principles and parameters one but which is cognitively nonetheless quite different. It allows grammars of different languages to be quite different – not all special cases of some general statement – and pushes us to generalize over the particular grammars thus formulated.

In this chapter, which owes much to Keenan and Stabler (2003), we consider some models of languages in which morphology plays a significantly greater structural role than in English. It enables those languages to ignore the c-command generalization on anaphors mentioned in Chapter 4. To represent this linguistic variation we present a notion of *structural invariant* of a grammar which enables us to generalize across non-isomorphic grammars. It also enables us to show that morphology and lexical items may be "structural" in exactly the same sense in which properties like *is a VP* and relations like *c-commands* are. We draw on notions of invariance used elsewhere in physical science (Chemistry: Cotton, 1990; Vision: Mundy and Zisserman, 1992). See Gardner (2005) and references cited there for a more general study. Weyl (1952) is a foundational work in the study of invariants in physics. Then we hypothesize and provide support for (1) below:

(1) Anaphora Universals:
 For $G$ an adequate grammar for a natural language,

 a. the property of being an anaphor is structurally invariant in $G$, and

 b. the Anaphor-Antecedent relation is a structural invariant of $G$.

Of course these claims assume a language independent definition of *anaphor*, the *Anaphor-Antecedent* relation, and *structural invariant*. We turn to the latter task first.

We begin with a simple example showing how elements of a structure can be characterized (or not) by the structural relations which hold between them. Our examples of interest, grammars, will be more complicated, but the principles are the same. Thus consider the four isomorphism types of 4-node (unordered, rooted) trees given in Chapter 4:

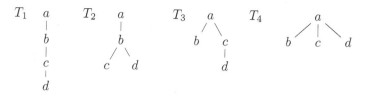

No two of these trees are isomorphic, and any 4-node (unordered, rooted) tree is isomorphic to one of them. So, reasonably, they represent the different structure types of 4-node unordered, rooted trees.

Here now is a way of characterizing the extent to which a node of a tree is structurally determined. Namely, to what extent can an isomorphism $h$ of the tree with itself (called an *automorphism* recall) map that node to some other one without changing the dominance relation: That is, $n$ dominates $m$ iff $h(n)$ dominates $h(m)$? In T1 each node has a unique property defined in terms of dominance so no node can be mapped to any other by a structure preserving operation (an automorphism). So T1 has only one automorphism, the identity function.

But consider T2. Here the root must get mapped to itself as it dominates everything so whatever it is mapped to must dominate everything, and the root is the only node with that property. Similarly, as in T1, $b$ must get mapped to itself, as it is the only node immediately dominated by the root. But $c$ and $d$ do not differ with respect to dominance: each strictly dominates no nodes and both are strictly dominated by the same two nodes. So an automorphism can interchange them. So T2 has two automorphisms: the identity map and the map that fixes $a$ and $b$ but interchanges (*transposes*) $c$ and $d$.

Reasoning in this way the reader should be able to show that T3, like T1, has only the identity map as an automorphism. But T4 has six automorphisms, all the functions that fix the root and permute $b$, $c$, and $d$. So in T4 all three terminal nodes are structurally equivalent. As an analogue at the level of grammars, we might expect that *John* and *Sam* are structurally equivalent in that given a grammar of English we can transpose them without changing how expressions are constructed. But we anticipate.

## 13.1  A Model Grammar and Some Basic Theorems

We present a model grammar ENG for English with co-argument anaphora. It is a reduced version of the grammar in Chapter 5, with just enough structural diversity to cover the basic (and a few not so basic) instances of reflexive anaphora in English. It derives sentences like (2) with the constituent bracketing indicated and so satisfies the c-command condition.

(2)    a. [John [criticized [himself]]]

     b. [John [criticized [both himself and Bill]]]

Then we present similarly simple models for two languages in which morphology rather than constituency relations controls the distribution of anaphors. We show how to compositionally interpret the morphology permitting anaphors to asymmetrically c-command their antecedents. So the structure of simple sentences in these languages is not isomorphic to those of English.

We exhibit our grammars in a theory-neutral format. We intend that grammars given within any particular theory – HPSG (Pollard and Sag, 1994), LFG (Bresnan, 2001), Feature-Value Grammars (Sag et al., 2003), Categorial Grammar (Carpenter, 1997, Morrill, 2011), and Minimalism (Stabler, 1997, Lasnik et al., 2003) – can be expressed in our format in the same sense in which much of mathematics can be expressed (however tediously) in the notation of set theory.

**Definition 13.1.** A *grammar* $G$ is a four-tuple $\langle V_G, \text{Cat}_G, \text{Lex}_G, \text{Rule}_G \rangle$, where (omitting subscripts) $V$ and Cat are non-empty sets—the *vocabulary* and *category indices* respectively. The set of *possible expressions* is $V^* \times$ Cat, noted $\text{PE}_G$. Lex, the set of *lexical items* of $G$, is a finite subset of $\text{PE}_G$, and Rule is a set of *structure building* partial functions of bounded arity from $\text{PE}_G^*$ into $\text{PE}_G$. (A function $F$ is of *bounded arity* iff for some $n$, all $s \in \text{Dom}(F)$ are of length $\leq n$.) $\mathcal{L}(G)$, the *language generated by* $G$, is the closure of $\text{Lex}_G$ under the $F \in \text{Rule}_G$.

### 13.1.1 The Grammar ENG'

We present an illustrative grammar modeled on our earlier ENG, but which eliminates some lexical items for simplicity and adds another. (The eliminated ones can be re-added unproblematically, allowing us to generate a more interesting class of expressions, but the simplified grammar ENG' suffices to illustrate the basis for comparing ENG', which satisfies the c-command requirement on anaphors, with those of Batak and Korean which do not (for interestingly different reasons).

**V:** laughed, cried, sneezed, praised, criticized, punished, congratulated, John, Bill, Sam, Dan, himself, and, or, nor, both, either, neither

**Cat:** $P_0$, $P_1$, $P_2$, $\langle P_0, P_1 \rangle / \langle P_1, P_2 \rangle$, $P_1/P_2$, CJ

**Lex: $P_1$:** laughed, cried, sneezed    (i.e. (laughed, $P_1$) $\in$ $\text{Lex}_{\text{ENG}'}$, etc.)

$P_2$: praised, criticized, punished, congratulated

$\langle \mathbf{P_0}, \mathbf{P_1} \rangle / \langle \mathbf{P_1}, \mathbf{P_2} \rangle$: John, Bill, Tom, Dan

$\qquad\qquad\qquad\quad (\langle P_0, P_1 \rangle / \langle P_1, P_2 \rangle$ is often noted DP)

$\mathbf{P_1}/\mathbf{P_2}$: himself

**CJ:** and, or, nor

**Rule:** {Merge, Coord}, defined below for $s$ and $t$ arbitrary elements of $V^*$.

**Merge:**

$$(s, A), (t, B) \to (s \frown t, P_0) \quad A = \langle P_0, P_1 \rangle / \langle P_1, P_2 \rangle, B = P_1,$$
$$(s, A), (t, B) \to (t \frown s, P_1) \quad A \in \{P_1/P_2, \langle P_0, P_1 \rangle / \langle P_1, P_2 \rangle\}, B = P_2.$$

We understand from this notation (here and later) that Merge is a two place function. Its domain is the set of pairs of possible expressions mentioned on the left above. Its value at each argument is given at the head of the arrow. The Function-Argument tree in (3) summarizes the argument that (John laughed, $P_0$) is in $\mathcal{L}(\text{ENG}')$.

(3) $\qquad\qquad$ Merge: (John laughed, $P_0$)

$\qquad$ (John, $\langle P_0, P_1 \rangle / \langle P_1, P_2 \rangle$)    (laughed, $P_1$)

The leaf nodes are lexical items and since $\mathcal{L}(\text{ENG}')$ is closed under Merge, which applies to the pair of leaf nodes, we infer that (John laughed, $P_0$) $\in \mathcal{L}(\text{ENG}')$. The tree is just a pictorial representation of the argument that (John laughed, $P_0$) $\in \mathcal{L}(\text{ENG}')$. It has no status in our definition of grammar. Our second rule is Coordination:

**Coord:**

$$(\text{and}, \text{CJ})(s, C)(t, C) \to (\text{both } s \text{ and } t, C) \quad C \in \text{Cat} - \{\text{CJ}\},$$
$$(\text{and}, \text{CJ})(s, C)(t, C') \to (\text{both } s \text{ and } t, P_1/P_2) \quad C \neq C', \text{ and}$$

$$C, C' \in \left\{ \begin{matrix} P_1/P_2, \langle P_0, \\ P_1 \rangle / \langle P_1, P_2 \end{matrix} \right\}.$$

Note that we now allow ourselves to coordinate expressions of (slightly) different categories, such as *himself*, $P_1/P_2$ with *John* of category

$\langle P_0, P_1 \rangle / \langle P_1, P_2 \rangle$ (i.e. DP). (*Himself* has the restricted category so that we do not derive \**Himself laughed* or *Himself criticized Bill*, of category S.)

(4)   Merge: (Dan criticized both himself and Bill, $P_0$)

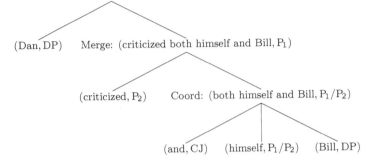

**Exercise 13.1.**

a. Write out the rules introducing *either... or...* and *neither... nor...*.

b. Exhibit function-argument derivation trees for:

   i. John both laughed and criticized either himself or Bill.

   ii. Dan neither criticized himself nor punished both himself and Bill.

   iii. Neither John nor Bill criticized both himself and Dan.

Note that *John* and *himself* differ in category. (himself cried, $P_0$) $\notin$ $\mathcal{L}(\text{ENG}')$, nor is (both himself and John cried, $P_0$).

**13.1.2  Some General Syntactic Notes**

1. Different grammars may use different categories. In ENG' they are ad hoc but mnemonic: '$P_n$' is "$n$-place predicate". Expressions of category $P_0$, zero place predicates (they require 0 arguments to make a sentence) are interpreted as True or False.

2. For an expression $s = (w, C) \in \text{PE}_G, \text{Cat}(s) =_{df} s_2$, the second coordinate of $s$, and $\text{string}(s) =_{df} s_1$. This notation facilitates defining the $F \in \text{Rule}$ and renders trivial the identification of the category of an expression. Also it avoids much lexical ambiguity; e.g. (respect, N) and (respect, V) are distinct lexical items—same string coordinate but different category coordinates. Analogously for *honor, judge, desire, envy, love*, etc. Also, some

rules, such as rules deriving deverbal nouns and denominal verbs
$((shoulder, N) \rightarrow (shoulder, V))$ just target the category coordinate. Others may primarily affect the string coordinate, such
as Reduplication (Malagasy), Preposition + Article fusion (German: *in* + *das* = *ins* 'in the'; Hebrew: *bə* + *ha* = *ba* 'in the',
Italian: *de* + *il* = *del* 'of-the', Greek *se* + *to* = *sto* 'to-the', etc.)
and like-form constraints (Spanish: *Les* 'them.dat' $\rightarrow$ *se* when
immediately followed by a *l*-initial pronoun: *\*Les la di* $\rightarrow$ *Se la
di* 'to.them it I-gave'.

**3.** We require a compositional semantics, so derived expressions are
interpreted as a function of the interpretations of what they are
derived from and the functions used to derive them. For most
lexical items we must learn their meanings de novo, and only
finitely many independent meanings can be so learned, so Lex is
finite.

**4.** The *complexity hierarchy* is the chain

$$\mathrm{Lex}_0 \subseteq \mathrm{Lex}_1 \subseteq \cdots$$

given by:

$\mathrm{Lex}_0 = \mathrm{Lex}_G$, and for all $n$,
$\mathrm{Lex}_{n+1} = \mathrm{Lex}_n \cup \{F(s) \mid F \in \mathrm{Rule}_G \ \& \ s \in \mathrm{Lex}_n^* \cap \mathrm{Dom}(F)\}.$

So $\mathrm{Lex}_1$ is $\mathrm{Lex}_0 (= \mathrm{Lex}_G)$ plus all expressions obtained by applying Merge and Coord to appropriate sequences of expressions
in $\mathrm{Lex}_0$. $\mathrm{Lex}_2$ is $\mathrm{Lex}_1$ plus all expressions obtained by applying
Merge and Coord to appropriate sequences of expressions from
$\mathrm{Lex}_1$, etc. We then define

$$\mathcal{L}(G) \quad = \quad \bigcup_{n \in \mathbb{N}} \mathrm{Lex}_n.$$

**Theorem 13.1.** *$\mathrm{Rule}_G$ is finite $\rightarrow$ each $\mathrm{Lex}_n$ is finite.*

We turn now to the crucial notion of an *automorphism* of a grammar. Informally, an automorphism of $G$ is a way of substituting expressions for expressions without changing how expressions are derived.
The substitution must map distinct expressions to distinct expressions,
and each expression in $\mathcal{L}(G)$ must have something mapped to it.

### 13.1.3 Introducing Structural Invariants

Pretheoretically a (*structural*) *invariant* of a grammar $G$ is a linguistic object that cannot be changed without changing the structure of expressions. A linguistic object may be an expression itself, or, more usually, a property of expressions, or a relation or function between expressions. It turns out for example that relations like *is a constituent of*, *c-command*, *is a sister of*, and other commonly used formal relations used by linguists, appropriately defined in the new setting (see p. 427), are provably structural invariants of all grammars satisfying our unconstrained definition 13.1. This is encouraging. Regarding properties of expressions, the property of being (*un*)*grammatical* is always invariant (a triviality) and ones like *is of category C*, *is a lexical item* typically are, though these are properly empirical claims concerning particular grammars, and depend greatly on the degree of overt subcategorization of categories. Keenan and Stabler (2003) for example make up a model of mini-Spanish in which masculine and feminine nouns have different categories, but they can be interchanged preserving grammaticality (provided there is a corresponding interchange in agreement morphemes; we also need to have the same number lexical masculine and feminine nouns, an otherwise linguistically irrelevant condition). Finally even single expressions may be structurally invariant. Suppose for example a language had only one nominal plural marker, or only one ergative case marker. Then those expressions could not be changed with anything without changing structure (of the expressions they occur in), so they would be invariant.

We turn now to the definition of invariant. It is built on the concept of a structure preserving function (an *automorphism*). Formally,

**Definition 13.2.** An *automorphism* of a grammar $G$ is a bijection $h : \mathcal{L}(G) \to \mathcal{L}(G)$ which does not change how expressions are derived. That is, whenever a rule $F$ derives an expression $w$ from some tuple $u$ of expressions, so $F(u) = w$, then $F$ also derives $h(w)$ from $h(u)$, that is, $F(h(u)) = h(w)$. (NB: if $u = \langle u_1, \ldots, u_n \rangle$ is a sequence then $h(u) = \langle h(u_1), \ldots, h(u_n) \rangle$).

Pictorially this says that given that the tree on the left below represents a derivation of $w$ from $u_1$, $u_2$ by $F$, then the tree on the right is a derivation of $h(w)$ from $h(u_1)$ and $h(u_2)$ by the same function $F$.

(5)

We note immediately several consequences of the definition of automorphism which will prove useful, and are often used silently, in establishing invariants of grammars (a notion we have not yet defined). We write $\text{Aut}_G$ for the set of automorphisms of $G$. We use variables in $h$ to range over elements of $\text{Aut}_G$.

Assume an arbitrary grammar $G$ with $F \in \text{Rule}_G$ (so $F$ is one of the structure building functions of $G$). Note that if a tuple $u = \langle u_1, \ldots, u_n \rangle$ is in $\text{Dom}(F)$, then since $h(F(u)) = F(h(u))$ we see that $h(u)$ is in $\text{Dom}(F)$, $h$ any automorphism. This tells us that $h(\text{Dom}(F)) =_{\text{def}} \{h(u) \mid u \in \text{Dom}(F)\} \subseteq \text{Dom}(F)$. In fact by the lemma below equality holds:

**Lemma 13.2.** *For $A \subseteq \mathcal{L}(G)$, if for all $h \in \text{Aut}_G$, $h(A) \subseteq A$ then for all $h \in \text{Aut}_G$, $h(A) = A$.*

*Proof.* Assume the antecedent and let $h$ arbitrary in $\text{Aut}_G$. Then $h^{-1}(A) =_{\text{def}} \{h^{-1}(a) \mid a \in A\} \subseteq A$. So $h(\{h^{-1}(a) \mid a \in A\}) \subseteq h(A)$, since $h$ is a function, and $h(\{h^{-1}(a) \mid a \in A\}) = \{h(h^{-1}(a)) \mid a \in A\} = \{a \mid a \in A\} = A$. So $A \subseteq h(A)$ and $h(A) \subseteq A$, proving equality for arbitrary $h$. □

**Corollary 13.3.** *Given $G$ and $F \in \text{Rule}_G$, $h(\text{Dom}(F)) = \text{Dom}(F)$, all automorphisms $h$.*

In fact the structure building functions $F$ are themselves invariant. Think of such an $F$ as an $n+1$ tuple $\langle u_1, \ldots, u_n, w \rangle$ where the $n$-tuple $u = \langle u_1, \ldots, u_n \rangle \in \text{Dom}(F)$ and the value of $F$ at that tuple is $w$. So $w = F(u_1, \ldots, u_n)$. Then we know that for any aut $h$, $h(u) \in \text{Dom}(F)$, and $h(w) = h(F(u_1, \ldots, u_n)) = F(h(u_1), \ldots, h(u_n))$. So we have:

(6)  $\langle u_1, \ldots, u_n, w \rangle \in F \Rightarrow h(\langle u_1, \ldots, u_n, w \rangle) \in F$, all automorphisms $h$. That is, for all auts $h$, $h(F) \subseteq F$. Whence by the lemma, for all auts $h$, $h(F) = F$. (Note, again, that $h(F)$ is just the set of values of $h$ at the $n+1$ tuples in $F$).

**Notation**  To say $\langle a, b \rangle \in f$, for $f$ a function, is just the set theoretical way of saying $f(a) = b$. So writing $\langle u_1, \ldots, u_n, w \rangle \in F$ above just says that $F(u_1, \ldots, u_n) = w$.

Thus we could have defined the automorphisms of a Grammar $G$ as the bijections $h$ on $\mathcal{L}(G)$ satisfying $h(F) = F$, all $F \in \text{Rule}_G$. As it is we defined them as the bijections which commuted with each $F \in \text{Rule}_G$: $h \circ F = F \circ h$. But this amounts to the same thing.

**Theorem 13.4.** *For all $F \in \text{Rule}_G$, $h(F) = F$, all $h \in \text{Aut}_G$, iff $h \circ F = F \circ h$, all $h \in \text{Aut}_G$.*

*Proof.*

$\Rightarrow (h \circ F)(u) = h(F(u)) = F(h(u)) = (F \circ h)(u)$. Thus $h \circ F = F \circ h$.

$\Leftarrow h(F)(h(u)) = h(F(u))$, def $h$ on $F$, $= (h \circ F)(u) = (F \circ h)(u) = F(h(u))$, thus, since $h$ is onto, $h(F)$ and $F$ take the same values at all tuples in $\text{Dom}(F)$ and thus are the same function. $\square$

**Notation**   Some texts note $n$-tuples with symbols like $\bar{u}$ or $\vec{u}$, though we shall not use that notation here.

We define invariants in terms of automorphisms, as they are the structure preserving functions on $\mathcal{L}(G)$. But first a few notional and notational preliminaries regarding automorphisms. Observe that in cases of interest $\mathcal{L}(G)$ is infinite so an automorphism of $G$ is a bijection from an infinite set to itself, so there might seem to be hugely many of them. But in general this is not so.

**Fact**   An automorphism $h$ of $G$ is defined by giving its values on the lexical items and there are only finitely many of those. The value of $h$ on a derived expression, $F(u_1, \ldots, u_n)$, is determined as $F(h(u_1), \ldots, h(u_n))$.

So to define an automorphism $h$ we only need to state its values on finitely many expressions, the lexical ones. In typical models automorphisms map lexical items to lexical items, in which case $|\text{Aut}_G| \leq |\text{Perm}(\text{Lex}_G)| = |\text{Lex}_G|!$ which is finite. We might require by definition that an automorphism h map lexical items to lexical items, guaranteeing thus that the property of being a lexical item is a structural invariant. But any condition we impose on unrestricted grammars will have empirical consequences and should not be imposed without some empirical investigation.

In this case though we note mathematically that if a lexical item $s$ is mapped by an automorphism $h$ to a non-lexical item $h(s)$, then $h(s)$ has the form $F(u)$, where $F$ is a structure building function and $u$ a tuple of expressions. That means that $s = h^{-1}(F(u)) = F(h^{-1}(u))$, so $s$ itself is derived. This naively violates our intuition that lexical items are selected as underived. So if we impose this reasonable methodological requirement on Lex for NLs then it follows that all automorphisms map lexical items to lexical items and hence $\text{Aut}_G$ is finite. We shall assume this in what follows (without nonetheless in any way forbidding investigation of what languages would look like if derived expressions were also lexical items). We should note that our assumption has one, not unreasonable, formal consequence:

**Theorem 13.5.**   *If all elements of $\text{Lex}_G$ are underived then $\text{id}_{\mathcal{L}(G)} \notin \text{Rule}_G$.*

Here $\mathrm{id}_{\mathcal{L}(G)}$ is just the identity function on $\mathcal{L}(G)$. So we cannot derive each expression from itself. We saw earlier that while English usually distinguishes singular from plural count nouns there are a few nouns, such as *deer* and *sheep*, that do not mark the distinction. Nonetheless those that do justify making a category distinction between singular and plural nouns, and if in general we derive the plurals from the singulars (not given a priori), we would still derive (*deer*, $\mathrm{N_{pl}}$) from (*deer*, $\mathrm{N_{sg}}$) and these are different expressions as they have different category coordinates. The case is similar to syntactic ones in which *student* in *The student laughed* is assigned category N and then builds *student* of category N′. Again we just have two expressions with the same string coordinate.

Pullum (1976) considers "Duke of York" derivations, mostly in phonology, in which a given string is in several steps apparently derived from itself. But (see McCarthy, 2003) the intermediate steps in the derivation are not independently well formed, so the derivations are questionable (but the observations tantalizing nonetheless). See Keenan and Stabler (2003, 161) for an analysis of one example.

To get a feel for what the automorphisms of a grammar behave like we review some basic facts about (algebraic) groups, as $\mathrm{Aut}_G$ is a group.

**Definition 13.3.** A *group* **A** is a four-tuple $\langle A, \cdot, e, ^{-1} \rangle$, where $A$ is a set, the *domain* of **A**, $\cdot$ is a binary function on $A$, $^{-1}$ is a unary function on $A$, and $e$ is an element of $A$, which satisfy the three conditions below for all $x, y, z \in A$:

a. Associativity: $((x \cdot y) \cdot z) = (x \cdot (y \cdot z))$,

b. Identity: $(x \cdot e) = (e \cdot x) = x$, and

c. Inverses: $((x^{-1} \cdot x) = (x \cdot x^{-1}) = e$.

**Theorem 13.6.** *$\mathrm{Aut}_G$ contains the identity map $\mathrm{id}_G$ on $\mathcal{L}(G)$ and is closed under function composition and inverses and is thus a group.*

So whenever $h \in \mathrm{Aut}_G$ then so is $h^{-1}$ (which maps $y$ to $x$ iff $h$ maps $x$ to $y$), and whenever $g, h \in \mathrm{Aut}_G$ so is $h \circ g$, which maps $x$ to $h(g(x))$. $\mathrm{Aut}_G$ is called the *automorphism group of* $G$ and also the *symmetry group of* $G$.

Here are some more examples of groups. The first is infinite, but our interest lies in finite groups since generally $\mathrm{Aut}_G$ is finite for any grammar $G$.

(7)  The set $\mathbb{Z}$ of integers (positive, negative and 0) with $\cdot = +$, $e = 0$, and $n^{-1} = -n$. To verify this claim we check that $+$ is associative: $((n + m) + p) = (n + (m + p))$; 0 is an identity element: $n + 0 = 0 + n = n$; and $-$ is the inverse $^{-1}$: $n + -n = -n + n = 0$.

(8)  The set $\{1, -1\}$ with $\times$ (multiplication) as the binary operation. What is the identity element? For each $n \in \{1, -1\}$, what is $n^{-1}$?

(9)  Consider a regular pentagon $P$ (regular = all angles the same, all sides the same length) with vertices named $a, b, c, d, e$ in counterclockwise order. A *rotation* of $P$ rotates $P$ around the geometric center moving each vertex a given multiple of 72 deg so that each vertex moves to the spot where another vertex was. There are clearly just 5 rotations, $r_0, r_1, \ldots, r_4$ where each $r_i$ maps each node $i$ vertices ahead. We may represent the five rotations in the table below.

| $x =$ | $a$ | $b$ | $c$ | $d$ | $e$ |
|---|---|---|---|---|---|
| $r_0(x) =$ | $a$ | $b$ | $c$ | $d$ | $e$ |
| $r_1(x) =$ | $b$ | $c$ | $d$ | $e$ | $a$ |
| $r_2(x) =$ | $c$ | $d$ | $e$ | $a$ | $b$ |
| $r_3(x) =$ | $d$ | $e$ | $a$ | $b$ | $c$ |
| $r_4(x) =$ | $e$ | $a$ | $b$ | $c$ | $d$ |

So each $r_i$ is a a permutation of the vertices (but there are $5! = 120$ permutations of the vertices, so most permutations are not rotations). In fact the set of the $r_i$ is a group, where $r_j \cdot r_i$ informally is first apply $r_i$ then apply $r_j$.

**Exercise 13.2.** For the rotation group in the above example,

a.   i. Define the $\cdot$ operation explicitly.

ii. Which $r_i$ is the identity element?

iii. For each $r_i$, what is its inverse?

b. For each vertex $v$ let $f_v$ be the permutation of $P$ obtained by reflecting the pentagon around the line bisecting the angle subtended by $v$. The bisecting line meets the opposite side perpendicularly. For example, $f_a$ is given by:

| $x =$ | $a$ | $b$ | $c$ | $d$ | $e$ |
|---|---|---|---|---|---|
| $f_a(x) =$ | $a$ | $e$ | $d$ | $c$ | $b$ |

i. Complete the table, giving values for $f_b(x), f_c(x), f_d(x),$ and $f_e(x)$.

ii. The set of these reflections does not form a group under function composition. Give a sufficient reason why not.

iii. If we add the five reflections to the set of five rotations we do get a group (called a dihedral group). Exhibit by table each of the following: $r_1 \circ f_a$, $f_a \circ r_1$, $r_2 \circ f_b$, and $f_a \circ f_a$.

**Exercise 13.3.** Let $\mathbb{Q}^+$ be the set of positive fractions, and let $\cdot =$ $\times$ (multiplication). What choice can we make for e and the inverse function so that the result is a group?.

**Exercise 13.4.** Let $A$ be a non-empty set and $\text{Perm}(A)$ the set of permutations of $A$. We claim that $\text{Perm}(A)$ is (the domain of) a group, where $\cdot = \circ$ (function composition), $e = \text{id}_A$, the map sending each $a \in A$ to itself, and $^{-1}$ is function inverse (that is, by definition $h^{-1}$ maps $a$ to $b$ iff $h$ itself maps $b$ to $a$).

a. State the three things you must prove to show that $\text{Perm}(A)$ above is a group.

b. Prove each of those three statements.

**Theorem 13.7** (Cayley). *Every group is isomorphic to a group of permutations of a set A. (Though this group may just be a proper subset of Perm(A).)*

**Exercise 13.5.** Let $A$ be an arbitrary group. Prove each of the following (always understood as universally quantified). We often do half the problem, which serves as a hint about how to do the other half. We sometimes write $xy$ for $x \cdot y$.

a. Right cancellation: $xa = ya \rightarrow x = y$,
   Proof: Assume $xa = ya$. Then

$$(xa) \cdot a^{-1} = (ya) \cdot a^{-1} \quad (\cdot \text{ is a function})$$
$$x(a \cdot a^{-1}) = y(a \cdot a^{-1}) \quad (\cdot \text{ is associative})$$
$$xe = ye \quad (\text{axiom on inverses})$$
$$x = y \quad (\text{axiom on } e )$$

b. State and prove the left cancellation law.

c. Prove that $e^{-1} = e$.

d. Uniqueness of $e$. Let $z$ satisfy condition 2 in Definition 13.3, that is, for all $x$, $x \cdot z = z \cdot x = x$. We show that $z = e$. Since $xz = x$, all $x$, then $xz = xe$, so by left cancellation, $z = e$. Your problem: Suppose that $zx = x$, all $x$. Show that $z = e$.

e. Uniqueness of inverses. We show more: namely, for each $x \in A$ there is a unique $y$ such that $x \cdot y = e$. Let $x$ be given. Suppose that $x \cdot y = e$. Then $x \cdot y = x \cdot x^{-1}$, so by left cancellation $y = x^{-1}$, which is what we wanted to show. Your problem: Show that for each $x \in A$ there is a unique $y$ such that $y \cdot x = e$.

f. Prove that $(x^{-1})^{-1} = x$.

g. Prove that $(x \cdot y)^{-1} = y^{-1} \cdot x^{-1}$.

**Definition 13.4.** We define a binary relation $\simeq$, *is structurally equivalent to*, on $\mathcal{L}(G)$ by:

$$s \simeq t \text{ iff there is an } h \in \text{Aut}_G \text{ such that } h(s) = t.$$

So expressions $d$ and $d'$ in some $\mathcal{L}(G)$ have the same structure iff there is an $h \in \text{Aut}_G$ which maps $d$ to $d'$ (whence $h^{-1}$ maps $d'$ to $d$). Since by definition automorphisms do not change the structure building functions this is a pretheoretically reasonable way to characterize sameness of structure. It also decides some cases which our pretheoretical intuitions leave undecided: Compare the sentences in (10).

(10)    a. John criticized Bill.

b. John criticized himself.

In ENG' these expressions are derived in the same way, differing just by a lexical item. But no automorphism can map one of (10) to the other. The reason (omitting several steps) is because no automorphism can map a DP, say (Bill, DP), to (himself, $P_1/P_2$) since such an automorphism or a variant of it would provably map (Bill laughed, $P_0$) to (himself laughed, $P_0$), which is not in $\mathcal{L}(\text{ENG}')$, contradicting that the range of an automorphism of ENG' is $\mathcal{L}(\text{ENG}')$. We note the following theorem.

**Theorem 13.8.** *The relation $\simeq$ is an equivalence relation. Writing $[s]_G$ for the equivalence class of $s$, we have $[s]_G =_{df} \{t \in \mathcal{L}(G) \mid s \simeq t\}$.*

So $[s]_G$ is the set of expressions which are structurally equivalent to $s$. Equivalence relations are studied more explicitly in Chapter 8. Here we just note that to say that $\simeq$ is an equivalence relation means: (1) for all $s \in \mathcal{L}(G)$, $s \simeq s$; (2) for all $s, t \in \mathcal{L}(G)$, $s \simeq t \to t \simeq s$, and (3) for all $s, t, u \in \mathcal{L}(G)$, $((s \simeq t \ \& \ t \simeq u) \to s \simeq u)$. These are all natural properties for a "sameness of structure" relation to have. Note that we have defined sameness of structure between expressions without saying what "the" structure of any expression is. We turn now to the crucial notion of an invariant.[1]

**Definition 13.5.** A linguistic object $d$ over $G$ is *structurally invariant* iff for all $h \in \mathrm{Aut}_G$, $h(d) = d$. (We generalize this definition slightly later).

**Definition 13.6.** A *linguistic object* over $G$ is an element of $\mathcal{L}(G)$, a subset of $\mathcal{L}(G)$ (that is, a property of expressions), a relation on $\mathcal{L}(G)$, a (partial) function from $\mathcal{L}(G)^*$ to $\mathcal{L}(G)$, etc.

**Definition 13.7.** A *fixed point* of a function $F$ is an object $b$ in its domain such that $F(b) = b$.

**Definition 13.8.** The *invariants* of a grammar are the *fixed points* of its syntactic *automorphisms*.

**Theorem 13.9.** *For all* $C \in Cat_{\mathrm{ENG}'}$ $PH(C) = \{s \in \mathcal{L}(\mathrm{ENG}') \mid Cat(s) = C\}$ *is invariant.*

*Proof.* Observe that there are expressions in $\mathcal{L}(\mathrm{ENG}')$, even $\mathrm{Lex}_{\mathrm{ENG}'}$ such that

(a) $\langle (s, \mathrm{DP}), \mathrm{Merge}((t, \mathrm{DP}), (u, \mathrm{P}_2)) \rangle \in \mathrm{Dom(Merge)}$

To preserve Dom(Merge), an aut $h$ must map $(u, \mathrm{P}_2)$ to a $\mathrm{P}_2$ or a $\mathrm{P}_1$. If the latter then again to preserve Dom(Merge) it must map $(t, \mathrm{DP})$ to a DP, whence the second coordinate in (a) is $\mathrm{Merge}(h(t, \mathrm{DP}), h(u, \mathrm{P}_2))$ of category $\mathrm{P}_0$. But no expression of category $\mathrm{P}_0$ is a coordinate in Dom(Merge), hence $\mathrm{Cat}(h(u, \mathrm{P}_2))$ must be $\mathrm{P}_2$. That is, for all auts $h$, $h(u, \mathrm{P}_2) \in \mathrm{PH}(\mathrm{P}_2)$. So $\mathrm{PH}(\mathrm{P}_2)$ is invariant. Further it follows immediately that $\mathrm{PH}(\mathrm{P}_1)$ is invariant since to preserve Dom(Merge) it could only be mapped by an aut $h$ to a phrase of category $\mathrm{P}_1$ or $\mathrm{P}_2$, and $\mathrm{P}_2$ is not possible since then $h^{-1}$ would map a $\mathrm{P}_2$ to a $\mathrm{P}_1$, which we

---

[1] In many classical algebras the relation *is automorphic to* is an equivalence relation which is also a *congruence relation*. That would entail that whenever a tuple $u$ was automorphic to $v$ and both were in the domain of some rule $F$, then $F(u)$ is automorphic to $F(v)$. But we have models of natural language grammars where this fails, so perhaps this is one way in which the algebraic structure of natural languages differs from that of classical algebras. Further exploration of this issue would go beyond the introductory nature of this work.

just ruled out. Hence PH($P_1$) is also invariant. Further since there are pairs $\langle(s, DP), (v, P_1)\rangle \in$ Dom(Merge) and any aut maps $P_1$s to $P_1$s, to preserve Dom(Merge) it must map DPs to DPs. Hence PH(DP) is invariant. This then entails that PH($P_1/P_2$) is invariant, as the only category triples in Dom(Merge) are $\langle DP, P_1\rangle$, $\langle DP, P_2\rangle$, and $\langle P_1/P_2, P_2\rangle$. No aut can map a $P_1/P_2$ to a DP since then its inverse would map a DP to something not a DP, which we have just ruled out. Hence for all auts $h$, $h(w, P_1/P_2)$ has category $P_1/P_2$, so PH($P_1/P_2$) is invariant.

Also PH(CJ) is invariant since there are triples $\langle(s, CJ), (t, DP), (u, DP)\rangle \in$ Dom(Coord) and DPs must be mapped to DPs, so for any aut $h$, $h(s, CJ)$ must have category CJ to preserve Dom(Coord). Finally PH($P_0$) is invariant since for any $(s, P_0)$, the triple $\langle(u, CJ), \text{Merge}((v, DP), (w, P_1)), (s, P_0)\rangle \in$ Dom(Coord) and the category of $h(\text{Merge}((v, DP), (w, P_1)))$ is $P_0$, so $h(s, P_0)$ must have category $P_0$ to preserve Dom(Coord).

This covers all $C$ such that PH($C$) $\neq \emptyset$. Note that $h(\emptyset) = \{h(x) \mid x \in \emptyset\} = \emptyset$, so $\emptyset$ is always invariant (and in general will not be considered in what follows). □

**Theorem 13.10.** *Lex*$_{\text{ENG}'}$ *is invariant.*

*Proof.* Suppose for some $s \in \text{Lex}, h(s) \notin \text{Lex}$. Then $h(s)$ is the value of Merge or Coord at some arguments, hence $h^{-1}(h(s)) = s$ is also the value of Merge or Coord at some arguments, hence its string coordinate is a concatenation of two or more vocabulary items. But that is false, no element of Lex$_{\text{ENG}'}$ has such a string coordinate. Hence $h(s) \in \text{Lex}$, proving the lemma. □

**Exercise 13.6.** Prove that all Lex$_n$ are invariant. To set the proof you might go as follows: Set $W = \{n \in \mathbb{N} \mid \text{Lex}_n \text{ is invariant}\}$. We know that $0 \in W$ since Lex$_0$ is by definition Lex$_{\text{ENG}'}$ shown above. So assume $n \in W$ and show $n + 1 \in W$ and you are done. □

**Theorem 13.11.** *Automorphisms preserve the* $\subseteq$ *relation (and hence all notions definable in terms of* $\subseteq$*, such as* $\cap$*). Specifically, let* $A, B \subseteq \mathcal{L}(G)$ *with* $A \subseteq B$*. Then for all* $h \in Aut_G$*,* $h(A) \subseteq h(B)$*.*

*Proof.* Let $x \in h(A)$. So $x = h(a)$, some $a \in A$. But since $A \subseteq B$, $a \in B$, so $x = h(b)$ for some $b \in B$. Since $x$ was arbitrary, $h(A) \subseteq h(B)$. □

**Exercise 13.7.**

a. For $A, B$ subsets of $\mathcal{L}(G)$, show $h(A \cap B) = h(A) \cap h(B)$.

b. For $I$ an index set, suppose for each $i \in I$, $A_i \subseteq \mathcal{L}(G)$. Show $h(\bigcap_i A_i) = \bigcap_i h(A_i)$.

c. Show, for all $A \subseteq \mathcal{L}(G)$, $h(\mathcal{L}(G) - A) = h(\mathcal{L}(G)) - h(A) = \mathcal{L}(G) - h(A)$.

**Corollary 13.12.** *(himself, $P_1/P_2$) is invariant.*

*Proof.* $PH(P_1/P_2) \cap \mathrm{Lex}_{\mathrm{ENG}'} = \{(\text{himself}, P_1/P_2)\}.$ ☐

**Exercise 13.8.** Show that $\langle \{A \subseteq \mathcal{L}(G) \mid A \text{ is invariant}\}, \subseteq \rangle$ is a power set boolean lattice. What is the unit element? The zero? What are the atoms?

## 13.2 A Semantic Definition of Anaphor

Studying ENG' we see that (himself, $P_1/P_2$) shares many properties with DPs. They all combine with $P_2$s to form $P_1$s. And they coordinate with each other. Still, *himself* (we omit the category coordinate when unnecessary) in distinction to DPs, does not combine with $P_1$s to form $P_0$s. Now we intend that *himself* is an anaphor. But suppose we were Martians just discovering English—how would we know that it was an anaphor, and not simply a DP with a slightly restricted distribution— though the restriction extends to boolean compounds which contain it: (*neither himself nor John* also does not combine with $P_1$s to form $P_0$s). What we need is a way of identifying expressions as anaphors independently of their category name or syntactic distribution on pain of making claims about their distribution circular. We now provide such a way.

### 13.2.1 Generalized Quantifiers

Given a domain $E$, a *generalized quantifier* $F$ over $E$ maps $\mathcal{P}(E)$, the power set of $E$, into {False, True}, usually noted $\{0, 1\}$. $F$ extends *accusatively* to maps $F_{\mathrm{acc}}$ from $\mathcal{P}(E \times E)$ to $\mathcal{P}(E)$ by $F_{\mathrm{acc}}(R) = \{a \in E \mid F(aR) = 1\}$, where $aR =_{df} \{b \in E \mid (a, b) \in R\}$. For example,

(11) For $A$ and $B$ subsets of $E$, EVERY$(A)$ maps $B$ to 1 (True) iff $A \subseteq B$. So *Every poet daydreams* is True iff POET $\subseteq$ DAYDREAM, that is, the set of poets is a subset of the set of daydreamers.

Similarly SOME$(A)$ maps $B$ to 1 iff $A \cap B \neq \emptyset$; NO$(A)(B) = 1$ iff $A \cap B = \emptyset$ and MOST$(A)(B) = 1$ iff $|A \cap B| > |A|/2$ ($A$ assumed finite and non-empty).

In general R-expressions, which we call *Referentially Autonomous* expressions, denote generalized quantifiers, and their value at a binary relation (denoted say by a transitive verb phrase) is determined by the values they assign to the subsets of $E$, as given in above. The maps $F_{\text{acc}}$ below are just those that satisfy the Accusative Extensions Condition (AEC) (Keenan, 1988b, 1989).

**The Accusative Extensions Condition (AEC):** For all $a, b \in E$, all $R, S \subseteq E \times E$, if $aR = bS$ then $a \in F(R)$ iff $b \in F(S)$.

The denotation of the higher order *most of John's students* in (12a) satisfies the AEC:

(12)   a. Sam criticized most of John's students.

   b. Sam criticized himself.

If the people Sam criticized are just those who Bob praised then *Sam criticized most of John's students* has the same truth value as *Bob praised most of John's students*.

But the denotation of *himself* fails the AEC: if Sam criticized just Fred, Mark, Bob and Ben, and those are just the people Bob praised, then *Sam criticized himself* is False and *Bob praised himself* is True. But the denotation of *himself* does satisfy the weaker Accusative Anaphor Condition (AAC) below:

**The Accusative Anaphor Condition (AAC):** For all $a \in E$, all $R, S \subseteq E \times E$, if $aR = aS$ then $a \in F(R)$ iff $a \in F(S)$

An appropriate denotation for *himself* in $\mathcal{L}(\text{ENG}')$, as well as the grammars we provide for Korean and Toba Batak shortly, is SELF:

(13)   $\text{SELF}(R) = \{a \in E \mid (a, a) \in R\}$

One verifies that for any $E$ with $|E| \geq 2$, SELF satisfies the AAC and fails the AEC. So will the denotation of conjunctions and disjunctions of *himself* with proper nouns in all those languages. This yields a language independent semantic definition of anaphor.

**Definition 13.9.**

   a. A function $\alpha$ from possible $P_2$ denotations, $[E \to [E \to \{0,1\}]]$, to possible $P_1$ denotations is *anaphoric* iff $\alpha$ satisfies the AAC but fails the AEC.

   b.   i. An expression is an *essential anaphor* iff it always denotes an anaphoric function.

      ii. An expression is *referentially autonomous* (an R-expression) if its denotation always satisfies the AEC.

iii. (Very tentative) an expression is *pronominal* if some occurrences denote anaphoric functions and others are referentially autonomous.

It will turn out that in ENG' *himself* is provably an anaphor as it denotes the function SELF given above. By pointwise interpretations of boolean compounds it follows that *both himself and Bill* is an essential anaphor. (We often omit the category coordinate of expressions when it is predictable from the string coordinate.) We thus have the following:

**Theorem 13.13.** *The set of essential anaphors of* $\mathcal{L}($ENG'$)$ *is* $PH(P_1/P_2)$.

**Corollary 13.14.** *In* $\mathcal{L}($ENG'$)$ *the property of being an anaphor is a structural invariant.*

The Corollary follows from the fact that all $PH(C)$ are invariant in $\mathcal{L}($ENG'$)$.

In usual linguistic parlance anaphors are regarded as lexical, and if we find it useful we may note that in $\mathcal{L}($ENG'$)$ the only lexical anaphor is (himself, $P_1/P_2$). It is also perhaps worth noting that even in the very limited grammar ENG' we can find lexical anaphors arbitrarily far from their "antecedents" (a notion we have not defined):

(14)  John either praised Dan or both laughed and criticized both himself and Bill.

**Some Merits and Shortcomings of our Definitions**  Our definitions of *anaphor* and *R-expression* are properly semantic. They are defined in terms of properties of their denotations. But our definitions are obviously too restricted. They apply in what we may consider the core case of anaphors, objects of transitive verbs, but they obviously occur in many other positions as well:

(15)  a. Every worker's criticism of *himself.*

b. John needs to protect *himself* from *himself.*

There are also an interesting range of complex anaphors we have not considered (Keenan, 1988a):

(16)  a. Each student criticized *everyone but himself / no one but himself.*

b. John tackled a problem that only *himself and the teacher* could solve.

c. No one likes to compete against *anyone smarter than himself.*

Moreover there are several languages, such as Polish, Russian, Norwegian and Latin where designated Determiners function to build complex anaphoric DPs:

(17)    a. Per hat sin bok    "Per has his own book"    (Norwegian)

    b. Per hat hans bok    "Per has his book" (likely someone else's book)

## 13.2.2    The Anaphor-Antecedent (AA) Relation

At the beginning of this chapter we also claimed that the AA relation was a structural invariant of natural languages – just meaning that in any given language we can structurally characterize the possible antecedents for any given anaphor in an expression. In $\mathcal{L}(\text{ENG}')$ this is indeed possible – in fact it is rather trivial and begs the genuinely important question. First the facile answer:

**Claim**   In $\mathcal{L}(\text{ENG}')$ $s$ is a possible antecedent for an anaphor $t$ in an expression $u$ iff $s$ is a DP and is sister to a $P_1$ constituent $v$ of which $t$ is a proper constituent.

Clearly then in ENG' antecedents of anaphors asymmetrically c-command them. However our claim above is totally ad hoc. We have offered no semantic definition of *antecedent* or the AA relation and then shown that our syntactic characterization identifies them. (In contrast we did give a semantic definition of anaphor and then claimed that we could syntactically characterize them – so it is non-trivial to claim that the set of expressions we syntactically defined are just those interpreted by anaphoric functions). Here would be an attempt along conceptually correct lines (though its empirical adequacy can certainly be challenged):

**Hypothesis**   A DP $s$ is a possible antecedent of an anaphor $t$ in $u$ iff $s$ is accessible to $t$ in the least constituent containing them both.

The Hypothesis is obviously not explicit until we have defined *accessible*, and before attempting that we should observe many more instances in a diversity of languages (including English). It seems likely that constituency relations as well as voice and case marking interact with the relevant notion of accessibility. Compare for example the classical (18a,b) with an educated guess as to the gross constituency relations:

(18)    a. [John [[promised Bill][ to teach himself LaTeX]]]

    b. [John [told [Bill to teach himself LaTeX]]]

In (18b) *Bill* would be the antecedent of *himself* as [*Bill to teach himself LaTeX*] would be the least constituent containing a DP accessible to the anaphor. Crucial here, and not mentioned in the definition, is that the constituent *Bill to teach himself* is, in some sense, not "anaphoric". *To teach himself* is, in the sense that it contains an "unresolved" anaphor. *Bill* in the next constituent up does resolve it. In (18a) the antecedent would be *John* assuming that *Bill*'s forming a constituent with *promised* prevents it from being accessible to *himself*. Obviously we have made many assumptions here that have not been justified. Further even the "minimal constituent" analysis needs work with Ss in which anaphors can have multiple antecedents, as in *Ted protected himself from himself*. Arguably here *Ted* antecedes the leftmost *himself*, which in turn antecedes the last one.

We turn now to models of two languages, Korean and Toba Batak, in which case marking and voice marking seem to play a decisive role in the distribution of anaphors and their antecedents.

## 13.3   A Model of Korean

We turn now to a model Kor of Korean illustrating a different, but still structurally invariant way of presenting anaphors.

Kor models case marking and word order in Korean: Verbs are final in their clauses and DPs are suffixed with (here) one of two case markers, *-nom* and *-acc*. The resulting phrases we call Kase Phrases (KPs). KPs are freely ordered preverbally with no topicality difference. Kor illustrates how morphology can be directly structural in lieu of c-command. The anaphor asymmetrically c-commands its antecedent in (19b).

(19)   a.

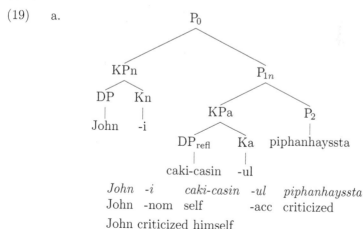

John   -i      caki-casin  -ul    piphanhayssta
John   -nom  self             -acc   criticized
John criticized himself

b.

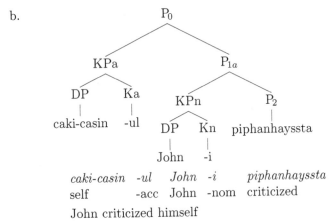

|            |            |           |            |
|------------|------------|-----------|------------|
| caki-casin | -ul        | John -i   | piphanhayssta |
| self       | -acc       | John -nom | criticized |

John criticized himself

To get a better sense of the basic role of morphology here let us see first that the *acc*-first order in (19b) differs dramatically from English object-first orders as in *Himself John likes (but no one else)*. For one, in English object-first orders with reflexives are not very natural with non-individual denoting arguments such as quantified or interrogative ones. But in both (19a) and (19b) *John* can be replaced preserving naturalness with *nwuka* 'who?' or *motun haksayng-tul* 'all the students'.

(20)  a. *Caki-casin-ul   nwuka-nun   /  motun   haksayng-tul-i*
           self-acc          who-top      /  all       student-pl-nom
           *piphanhayssta*
           criticized
           Who criticized himself? / All the students criticized themselves

      b. ??Himself who criticized?

      c. ??Himself every student criticized.

Secondly, the object-first order in English is largely a root clause phenomenon. We cannot for example relativize the subject after fronting the object:

(21)  a. Himself the man likes

      b. *the man who himself likes

But relativizing from a reflexive first order in Korean is natural:

(22)  a. *Caki-casin-ul   John-i        hoyuy-eyse     piphanhayssta*
           Self-acc          John-nom   meeting-loc    criticized
           John criticized himself at the meeting

b. *[Caki-casin-ul   John-i      piphanhay-n   hoyuy-ka]*
   Self-acc         John-nom    criticize-sub  meeting-nom
   *ecey*            *iss-ess-ta*
   yesterday        be-pst-decl
   There was a meeting yesterday at which John criticized
   himself

(Nom marking in Korean is *-i* with consonant final Nouns, *-ka* with
vowel final ones. Acc marking *-ul* vs *-lul* is similarly conditioned, as is
topic marking *-un* vs *-nun*.)

Third, topicalization effects in Korean are achieved by morphological means with a topic marker *-(n)un* rather than syntactic fronting:

(23)  *John-i      Bill-un      piphanhayssta*
      John-nom    Bill-top     criticized
      John criticized BILL

Finally, while the relative preverbal order of case marked arguments
is free, what we can't naturally change is the morphological marking:

(24)  *\*Motun    haksayng-tul-ul   caki-casin   -i      piphanhayssta*
      All       student-pl-acc    self         -nom    criticized
      All the students criticized themselves

Also the result of replacing *motun haksayng-tul-ul* 'all the students -acc'
with other accusatively marked arguments such as *nukwu-lul* 'who-acc?'
or *john-ul* 'John-acc' remains ungrammatical.

The moral of these observations is that naively Korean syntax uses
bound morphology, case and topic marking, in a way not present in English. So the observable syntax of simple clauses in these two languages
is systematically different.

Here is a grammar of minimal main clauses with reflexives, comparable to ENG′, which illustrates case marking invariants and direct
compositional interpretation of Ss with anaphors c-commanding their
antecedents. Note that we have "dissimilated" the $P_1$ categories so that
once a KP in a certain case combines with a $P_2$ then no KP in that
same case can combine with the resulting $P_1$.

### 13.3.1   The Grammar Kor

**Cat:** DP, $DP_{refl}$, Ka, Kn, KPa, KPn, $P_2$, $P_{1a}$, $P_{1n}$, $P_0$, CJ

**Lex: DP:** John, Bill, Sam, Kim

$DP_{refl}$: self

**Kn:** -nom

**Ka:** -acc

**CJ:** and

$\mathbf{P}_{1n}$: laughed, cried sneezed

$\mathbf{P_2}$: praised, criticized, teased

**Rule:** CM (Case Mark), PA (Predicate-Argument), Coord

**CM:**

| Domain | | Value | Conditions |
|---|---|---|---|
| $(\text{-nom,Kn})(t, \mathrm{DP})$ | $\to$ | $(t\text{-nom}, \mathrm{KPn})$ | none |
| $(\text{-acc,Ka})(t, C)$ | $\to$ | $(t\text{-acc}, \mathrm{KPa})$ | $C \in \{\mathrm{DP}, \mathrm{DP_{refl}}\}$ |

**PA:**

| Domain | | Value | Conditions |
|---|---|---|---|
| $(s, \mathrm{KP}x)(t, \mathrm{P}_{1x})$ | $\to$ | $(s \frown t, \mathrm{P_0})$ | $x \in \{n, a\}$ |
| $(s, \mathrm{KP}x)(t, \mathrm{P_2})$ | $\to$ | $(s \frown t, \mathrm{P}_{1y})$ | $x \neq y \in \{n, a\}$ |

**Coord:**

| Domain | Value | Conditions |
|---|---|---|
| $(\text{and}, \mathrm{CJ})(\text{t,C})(\text{u,C})$ $\to$ | $(t \frown \text{ and } \frown u, C)$ | $C \in \left\{ \begin{array}{l} \mathrm{DP}, \mathrm{DP_{refl}}, \\ \mathrm{P_0}, \mathrm{P}_{1n}, \\ \mathrm{P}_{1a}, \mathrm{P_2} \end{array} \right\}.$ |
| $(\text{and}, \mathrm{CJ})(\text{t,C})(\text{u,}C') \to$ | $(t \frown \text{ and } \frown u, \mathrm{DP_{refl}})$ | $C \neq C' \in \left\{ \begin{array}{l} \mathrm{DP}, \\ \mathrm{DP_{refl}} \end{array} \right\}.$ |

So (self-acc john-nom praised, $\mathrm{P_0}$) and (john-nom self-acc praised, $\mathrm{P_0}$) $\in \mathcal{L}(\mathrm{Kor})$.

### 13.3.2  Some Invariants of Kor

a. $(\text{-nom}, \mathrm{Kn})$, $(\text{-acc}, \mathrm{Ka})$ and $(\text{self}, \mathrm{DP_{refl}})$ but not $(\text{bill}, \mathrm{DP})$. So the case marking suffixes are structural in Korean, as linguists naively assume. Thus our formal account captures our basic intuitions here.

b. For all $C \in \mathrm{Cat}, \mathrm{PH}(C)$.

c. For each $n$, $\mathrm{Lex}_n$.

d. Anaphors (as defined semantically earlier). Provably the anaphors in Kor are just the expressions $s$ with $\mathrm{Cat}(s) = \mathrm{KPa}$ and $(\text{self}, \mathrm{DP_{refl}})$ as a constituent.

e. The AA relation, where: for $s, t$ constituents of $u$, $s$AA$t$ in $u$ iff $t$ is an anaphor, Cat$(s) = $ KPn and for some constituent $v$ of $u$, either

   i. $v$ has category $P_{1n}$, $s$ is a sister of $v$ and $t$ is a constituent of $v$, or

   ii. $v$ has category KPa, $t$ is a constituent of $v$ and for some $w$ of category $P_{1a}$, $v$ is a sister of $w$ and $s$ is a constituent of $w$.

We omit proofs for reasons of space, but we emphasize that whether a linguistic object of a grammar is invariant is a matter of proof, not pretheoretical intuition. One does not ponder long and hard to conclude "Hmmm. I can get (-nom, Kn) as invariant".

Notice too that, comparable to (4) in English, (25) contains a complex anaphor anteceded by John-nom.

(25)  (John-nom [[[Bill and self ]-acc] [criticized]])

On the other hand, $\mathcal{L}$(Kor) presents an anaphoric possibility not present in $\mathcal{L}$(ENG$'$): what we are calling a $P_{1a}$ (an accusative taking $P_1$) in (19b) can coordinate:

(26)  *Caki-casin   -ul   [John-i       piphanha-ko   Bill-i*
     Self          -acc  John-nom  criticize-and  Bill-nom
     *chingchanhayssta]*
     praised
     John criticized and Bill praised himself

Here both *John-i* and *Bill-i* are antecedents of *caki-casin-ul*. An analogous type of binding in English would be Right Node Raising sentences, as in (27b) (if grammatical).

(27)  a. [John bought but Bill cooked] [the turkey]

    b. ?[John punished but Bill congratulated][himself]

Note lastly an essential similarity between the distribution of anaphors in $\mathcal{L}$(ENG$'$) and $\mathcal{L}$(Kor). In ENG$'$ anaphors can combine with two place predicates to make one place ones, but can not combine with one place ones to form Sentences (truth bearing expressions). In $\mathcal{L}$(Kor) the analogous restriction is given by case marking: Anaphors can be case marked accusative, but not nominative[2] in main clauses. Hence they cannot combine to form main clauses with intransitive predicates. In this sense then Korean handles morphologically a constraint that English handles syntactically.

---

[2]This holds for main clauses, but as is well known, bare *caki* can occur nominatively in a complement clause, bound to the subject of the matrix verb.

### 13.3.3  Interpreting Anaphors in $\mathcal{L}(\mathbf{Kor})$

We interpret (self, $\mathrm{DP_{refl}}$) as SELF, as with (himself, $\mathrm{P_1/P_2}$) in $\mathcal{L}(\mathrm{ENG'})$. We interpret (-*acc*, Ka) as an identity function, so (John-*acc*, KPa) denotes the same individual that (John, DP) denotes. A KPn maps $\mathcal{P}(E)$ to truth values as expected, but maps binary relations $R$ to maps taking type-1 functions into $\{0,1\}$ by: $F(R)(G) = F(G(R))$. So $(\mathrm{KIM\text{-}nom}(R))(\mathrm{SELF}) = (\mathrm{KIM\text{-}nom})(\mathrm{SELF}(R))$, the correct interpretation. (-*nom*, Kn) maps DP denotations to KPn denotations. So the entire complication here rests with the interpretation of a grammatical formative, (-*nom*, Kn).

## 13.4  Toba Batak

Toba Batak (see Schachter, 1984, Cole and Hermon, 2008, Keenan, 2009) is a simple example of a structure type characteristic of West Austronesian languages (Tagalog in the Philippines, Malagasy in Madagascar). The languages are verb initial and voice marking, "dual" to case marking. Voice affixes (primarily *maN-* and *di-* in Toba) combine with verbal roots determining the structure of the clause. Anaphors may asymmetrically c-command their antecedents (29b).

(28)  a. *[mang-ida  si  Ria]  si  Torus*
        AF-see    art  Ria  art  Torus

        Torus sees Ria

    b. *[di-ida  si  Torus]  si  Ria*
        PF-see  art  Torus  art  Ria

        Torus saw Ria

(29)  a. *[mang-ida  dirina]  si  Torus*
        AF-see    self    art  Torus

        Torus sees himself

   a′. *mang-ida si Torus dirina

    b. *[di-ida  si  Torus]  dirina*
        PF-see  art  Torus  self

        Torus saw himself

   b′. *di-ida dirina si Torus

(30)   a.

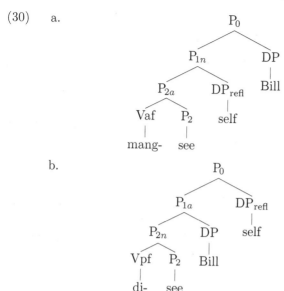

b.

The papers in Schachter (1984) provide very strong support for the major constituent break in (30a-b). We note that both *mang-ida* and *di-ida* require two arguments. And with both verbs the immediate postverbal argument cannot be separated from the verb by adverbs like *nantoari* 'yesterday'. More dramatically, the immediate postverbal DP cannot be relativized or questioned by movement, only the clause final DP above can. Consider the paradigm below (which holds mutatis mutandis in Tagalog and Malagasy).

(31)   a. *Manjaha  buku   guru    i*
          read         book  teacher  Det
          'The teacher reads the book'

       b. *Dijaha  guru    buku   i*
          read        teacher  book   Det
          'The teacher read the book'

       c. *guru     na     manjaha  buku   i*
          teacher  lnk    read        book   Det
          'the teacher who is reading a book'

       d. *buku   na     dijaha  guru     i*
          book   lnk    read       teacher  Det
          'the book the teacher read'

e. \**buku    na    manjaha    guru      i*
   book    lnk    read    teacher    Det

f. \**guru    na    dijaha    buku    i*
   teacher    lnk    read    book    Det

Judgments on (31e-f) are strong and immediate. They reflect the basic interpretative mechanisms of simple clauses, not just arbitrary constraints on what can be extracted. (31f) for example can only mean the teacher that a book read, which is nonsense. Finally Emmorey (1984) provides spectographic evidence for the major constituent break in (30a-b). She shows that the verb, whether a *mang-* or a *di-* one, plus its following DP form an intonation group in which the nuclear pitch accent falls on the stressed syllable of the last lexical item in the Predicate Phrase (PredP). Pitch accent placement identifies the immediate post-verbal DP in *mang-* and *di-* verbs as the last lexical item in their PredP's. In conjoined PredP's both conjuncts receive this accent (Emmorey op.cit.):

(32)    a. *[[Manuhor    baoang]    jala    [mangolompa    mangga]]    halak*
          Buy          onions    and    cook          mangos      man

          *an*
          Det

          The man buys onions and cooks mangos

        b. *[[Dituhor    si    Ore]    jala    [dilompa    si    Ruli]]    mangga*
           di-buy    art    Ore    and    di-cook    art    Ruli    mangos

           Ore buys and Ruli cooks mangos

### 13.4.1    A Grammar for Toba Batak

**Cat:** Vaf, Vpf, $P_2$, $P_{2a}$, $P_{2n}$, $P_{1a}$, $P_{1n}$, $P_0$, DP, $DP_{refl}$, CJ

**Lex: Vaf:** mang-

   **Vpf:** di-

   $P_2$: praised, criticized, saw

   $P_{1n}$: laughed, cried

   **DP:** john, bill

   $DP_{refl}$ self

   **CJ:** and, or

**Rule:** VM (Verb Mark), PA (Predicate-Argument), Coord

**VM:**

| Domain | | Value | Conditions |
|---|---|---|---|
| (mang, Vaf)$(t, P_2)$ | $\rightarrow$ | (mang$\frown t, P_{2a}$) | none |
| (di, Vpf)$(t, P_2)$ | $\rightarrow$ | (di$\frown t, P_{2n}$) | none |

**PA:**

| Domain | | Value | Conditions |
|---|---|---|---|
| $(s, P_{2x})(t, DP)$ | $\rightarrow$ | $(s \frown t, P_{1y})$ | $x \neq y \in \{n, a\}$ |
| $(s, P_{1x})(t, DP)$ | $\rightarrow$ | $(s \frown t, P_0)$ | $x \in \{n, a\}$ |
| $(s, P_{2a})(t, DP_{refl})$ | $\rightarrow$ | $(s \frown t, P_{1n})$ | none |
| $(s, P_{1a})(t, DP_{refl})$ | $\rightarrow$ | $(s \frown t, P_0)$ | none |

**Coord:**

Domain · Value · Conditions

$$(\text{and}, CJ)(t, C)(u, C) \rightarrow (t \frown \text{ and } \frown u, C) \qquad C \in \left\{ \begin{array}{l} DP, DP_{refl}, \\ P_0, P_{1n}, P_{1a}, \\ P_2 \end{array} \right\}.$$

$$(\text{and}, CJ)(t, C)(u, C') \rightarrow (t \frown \text{ and } \frown u, DP_{refl}) \quad C \neq C' \in \left\{ \begin{array}{l} DP, \\ DP_{refl} \end{array} \right\}.$$

### 13.4.2 Some Invariants of Toba Batak

We write $x$ *con* $y$, here and later, for $x$ *is a constituent of* $y$.

a. (*mang-*, Vaf), (*di-*, Vpf) and (*self*, $DP_{refl}$). So as with Korean, the bound morphemes are structural invariants, coinciding again with our intuitions as linguists.

b. Lex; in fact all $Lex_n$.

c. For $C \in$ Cat, PH($C$).

d. The set of anaphors in Toba. (We note without proof that the set of anaphors in Toba is just PH($DP_{refl}$)).

e. $sAAt$ in $u$ iff Cat$(s)$ = DP and either there is a constituent $v$ of $u$ with Cat$(v) = P_{1n}$, $s$ sister $v$ and $t$ con $v$ or there is a $t'$ con $v$ with Cat$(v) = P_{1a}$ and $t$ con $t'$ and $s$ con $v$.

### 13.4.3 Interpreting Anaphors in Toba Batak

Briefly: (*self*, $DP_{refl}$) denotes SELF, as expected, the rest is determined by the denotations of the voice affixes: MANG$(R)(G)(F) = F(G(R))$ and DI$(R)(G)(F) = G(F(R))$. So e.g. DI(SEE)(JOHN)(SELF) = JOHN(SELF(SEE)). So as in Kor, interpreting Ss with asymmetrically c-commanding anaphors is unproblematic.

## 13.5 Some Mathematical Properties of Grammars and their Invariants

There are at least two reasons for presenting grammars in a mathematically explicit way. One, it enables us to formulate clearly pretheoretical notions that motivate our work as linguists. And two, we can study mathematically explicit models of grammars, proving theorems about them, thereby extending our knowledge of language structure. Often a precise mathematical formulation of an issue allows us to ask new questions, ones we could not have really formulated without the mathematical notions and notation at hand. In the first category we suggest the following three ideas.

### 13.5.1 Degree of Grammaticization

The *degree of grammaticization* of a linguistic object is the percent of automorphisms that fix it. Since $Aut_G$ is generally finite it makes sense to speak of percentage here. So it makes sense to say that Prepositions and Conjunctions in English are more grammaticized than common nouns but less grammaticized than personal pronouns.

### 13.5.2 Historical Grammaticization

Commonly, grammatical morphemes derive historically from content words, such as common nouns and verbs. In several languages such as Basque, Hausa, Georgian and Tamazight Berber the content word *head* came to be interpreted as *self* (see Heine and Kuteva, 2002). We might (partially) characterize that evolution as a progressive decrease in the percentage of automorphisms that "move" the item (that is, map it to something else). At the end point of change no automorphisms would move it, that is, all would fix it.[3] So in Berber "his head" sometimes means *himself* and sometimes *his head*. For further reading, see Givon (1971), Hopper and Traugott (1993), Bybee et al. (1994), von Fintel (1995).

### 13.5.3 Grammatical Morphemes

We have proposed a rigorous characterization of grammatical morphemes as ones fixed by all the automorphisms of the grammar. Here we generalize that idea, prompted by an observation in Keenan and Stabler (2003) concerning masculine and feminine noun classes in Spanish.[4] Adjectives and determiners take agreement markers which vary

---

[3]A more precise statement would be more complicated. As is well acknowledged (Hopper, 1991, Heine and Reh, 1984) a grammaticized item may also retain its original meaning.

[4]We are indebted to Philippe Schlenker (pc) for pushing us on this point.

with the noun class of noun they combine with and it turns out that for some natural choices of lexicon some automorphisms systematically interchange masculine and feminine nouns (also interchanging the agreement markers). But we still want to say that the property of being a masculine (feminine) noun is a structural property even though not all automorphisms fix it. So we shall distinguish between variable automorphisms and non-variable ones, which we call *stable*.

**Definition 13.10.** For $f$ and $g$ functions,

a. $g$ is a *restriction* of $f$ iff $\mathrm{Dom}(g) \subseteq \mathrm{Dom}(f)$ and for all $x \in \mathrm{Dom}(g), g(x) = f(x)$.

b. $f$ *extends* $g$ iff $g$ is a restriction of $f$.

c. If $B \subseteq \mathrm{Dom}(f)$, $f|B$ is that restriction of $f$ with domain $B$.

**Definition 13.11.** For $G = \langle V_G, \mathrm{Cat}_G, \mathrm{Lex}_G, \mathrm{Rule}_G \rangle$,

a. For each $S \subseteq V_G \times \mathrm{Cat}_G$, $G[S] =_{df} \langle V_G, \mathrm{Cat}_G, \mathrm{Lex}_G \cup S, \mathrm{Rule}_G \rangle$. When $S$ is a singleton $\{s\}$ we write simply $G[s]$ for $G[\{s\}]$.

b. For $s \in V_G \times \mathrm{Cat}_G$, $G$ is *free* for $s$ iff $s \notin \mathcal{L}(G)$ and there is an $h \in \mathrm{Aut}_{G[s]}$ such that for some $t \in \mathrm{Lex}_G$, $h$ interchanges $s$ and $t$ and fixes all other $u \in \mathrm{Lex}_{G[s]}$. The intuition: $G$ being free for $s$ means we can add $s$ to $G$ without changing any of the pre-existing structural relations between the elements of $\mathcal{L}(G)$[5].

c. $G$ is *free* for $S \subseteq V_G \times \mathrm{Cat}_G$ iff for all $s \in S$, $G$ is free for $s$ and $G[s]$ is free for $S - \{s\}$. (Note that all $G$ are free for $\emptyset$).

d. $h \in \mathrm{Aut}_G$ is *stable* iff for all finite $S$ for which $G$ is free there is a $k \in \mathrm{Aut}_{G[S]}$ such that $k$ extends $h$.

e. A linguistic object $d$ over $G$ is a *stable invariant* iff $h(d) = d$, for all stable $h \in \mathrm{Aut}_G$.

We note that the automorphisms of $\mathcal{L}(\mathrm{Span})$ which can interchange the masculine and feminine Nouns and the agreement markers are not free for $(\mathrm{poet}, \mathrm{N_{fem}})$ and thus are not stable. Observe also that the stable invariants of $G$ are always a superset (not necessarily proper) of the invariants of $G$ since they are only required to be fixed under a subset of the automorphisms of $G$, namely the subset of stable automorphisms.

---

[5]Adding new lexical items typically results in new derived expressions. Recall that the structure building functions are defined on $V^* \times \mathrm{Cat}$.

**Thesis 13.1.** *The grammatical morphemes of a grammar are the lexical items which are stable invariants.*

**Theorem 13.15.** *The set of stable automorphisms of a grammar $G$ contains the identity function, are closed under inverses and composition, and thus form a subgroup of $Aut_G$.*

Our second motivation for presenting grammars mathematically is that by proving theorems about them we gain knowledge of their formal structure. Theorem 13.15 above is already one example. We exhibit some others below.

## 13.6 Invariants of Type 0

The *type 0 invariants* of a grammar $G$ are the expressions fixed by the stable automorphisms. Are there any *universal* invariants of type 0? To find some we might look for uniformly defined semantic objects, like the function SELF, and see if we feel that an expression in any natural language which denotes one of those objects is a stable invariant. Negation is a candidate. We have defined the notion *boolean complement*, often (but not exclusively) denoted in English by *not* or *n't*. We call an expression a *negation* if it always denotes boolean complement. Then we claim:

(33)  Claim: For all natural languages $G$, if $d \in \mathcal{L}(G)$ is a negation then $d$ is a stable invariant.

Note that (33) does not claim that all natural languages have an overt expression denoting negation. This is largely true, but, it seems, not quite always. Old Tamil can express negation just by eliminating the tense morpheme on the verb (see Pederson, 1993). (Thanks to Steve Levinson, p.c., for this observation.)

Equally several languages (French, Hausa, Middle English) may use discontinuous expressions of negation, whose interpretation would have to be studied carefully—are the parts independently meaningful? Or is it just one expression which is very superficially split into two phonological parts? Note too that (33) just claims that if $d$ is a negation in a language then it is syntactically distinguished, but it doesn't say that its syntactically distinctive properties are the same in different languages, just as the coding of anaphors may be distinctive in different languages (some may code it in terms of case marking, others in terms of voice marking, etc).

In a way similar to negation we feel that other boolean operators are conditional invariants. Namely, boolean greatest lower bound operators (see Chapter 9) denoted in English by *and* and *every/all*, and least upper bound operators, denoted by *or* and *some*.

(34)  Claim: For all natural languages $G$, if $d \in \mathcal{L}(G)$ always denotes a boolean greatest lower bound (least upper bound) operator then $d$ is a stable invariant.

There seem to us a variety of other semantically defined operations which are commonly expressed as type 0 invariants (though we have studied none of these in detail as yet): monomorphemic expressions of case, voice, tense, number, gender, cause, verbal nominalization (e.g. gerundive *-ing*). This claim assumes, non-trivially, language independent definitions of these notions and then of course detailed investigation of the grammars of many languages.

Finally, the candidates for type 0 invariants proposed above are all *empirical invariants* in the sense that none of them (not even the boolean ones) follow from our definition of invariant. But below we see there are some invariants of types 1 and 2 which are universal in this sense, that is, they hold of all $G$ regardless of whether $G$ is a candidate for modeling a natural language or not. We call these *uniform invariants* as opposed to empirical invariants.

## 13.7   Invariants of Type (1)

Invariants of type (1) are subsets of $\mathcal{L}(G)$, that is, properties of expressions.

### 13.7.1   Universal Uniform Invariants (INV$_1$)

These follow from our definitions of grammar, automorphism, and invariant.

**Theorem 13.16.** *For all grammars $G$:*

a. *$\emptyset$ and $\mathcal{L}(G)$ are invariant.*

b. *For all $F \in Rule_G$, $Dom(F)$ and $Ran(F)$ are invariant. Intuitively much "structure" is imposed by what the structure building functions can apply to.*

c. *$[s]_G$ is invariant, for all $s \in \mathcal{L}(G)$. No non-empty proper subset of $[s]_G$ is invariant.*

d. *If no $s \in Lex_G$ is derived ($Lex_G \cap Ran(F) = \emptyset$ for all $F \in Rule_G$) then each $Lex_n \in INV_1$.*

e. *(Closure Conditions) INV₁ is closed under relative complement and arbitrary unions and intersection. So it is a complete atomic Boolean algebra, (See Chapter 9.) For example, if the properties of being a feminine Noun and of being a plural Noun are invariant then so are the properties of being a feminine plural Noun and a feminine non-plural Noun.*

**Exercise 13.9.** Describe the atoms of $INV_1$ for arbitrary $G$. (Assumes some knowledge of Boolean Algebra. See Chapter 9.)

### 13.7.2  Universal Empirical Invariants

These are ones that hold for models $G$ for a natural language NL but may fail for artificially constructed $G$ that satisfy our definitions.

(35)  Claim: The set of anaphors of NL is a stable invariant.

In general it is interesting to determine which semantically defined sets of expressions are "coded in syntax", i.e. invariant.

(36)  The set $K$ of nouns denoting aquatic mammals in English is not invariant. We find no grammatical difference between *porpoise* and *shark*, so there is an automorphism $h$ of English which switches them, so $h(K) \neq K$.

(37)  Is the set of polar (Yes/No) questions in English invariant? We don't know. A Yes answer would mean that whenever $\varphi$ is a polar question so is $h(\varphi)$, for all automorphisms $h$ of English. And do we expect that in any NL the property of being a polar question is invariant?

(38)  Is the set of monotone decreasing DPs in English invariant? Very possibly. Such DPs (Keenan, 1996, Chapter 11 here) include *no doctor, neither John nor Mary, at most ten students, fewer than ten students, no student's doctor, not more than ten boys, neither applicant.*

### 13.7.3  On the Role of Categories

For $C \in \text{Cat}_G$, $\text{PH}(C)$, the set of phrases of category $C$, may fail to be invariant, per our discussion of gender classes of Nouns in Spanish (but also Latin, Kinyarwanda).

Theorem 13.17 below however does yield one condition, which arises in the study of formal languages and models of artificial languages (Propositional Logic, First Order Logic), which does imply that each $\text{PH}(C)$ is invariant.

**Definition 13.12.** $G$ is *category functional* iff for each $F \in \text{Rule}_G$, each $u \in \mathcal{L}(G)^* \cap \text{Dom}(F)$, $\text{Cat}(F(u))$ is a function of the categories of $u_1, \ldots, u_{|u|}$.

So the category of a derived expression is predictable from the function $F$ used to derive it and the categories of the arguments of $F$.

**Theorem 13.17.** *Given $G$, if each $Lex(C)$, the lexical expressions of category $C$, is invariant, and $G$ is category functional then all $PH(C)$ are invariant.*

Otherwise, the most we can claim is that sameness of category is invariant:

**Definition 13.13.** $G$ is *category uniform* iff for all $s, t \in \mathcal{L}(G)$, if $\text{Cat}(s) = \text{Cat}(t)$ then for all $h \in \text{Aut}_G, \text{Cat}(h(s)) = \text{Cat}(h(t))$.

Category Uniformity does not follow from our definition of invariant, but it is a condition on the role of categories that seems to us satisfied in many cases. We tentatively propose it as an axiom that NL grammars must satisfy.

**Exercise 13.10.** Show that Category Uniformity can be strengthened to an "if and only if".

When $G$ is category uniform each $h \in \text{Aut}_G$ lifts to a permutation $h'$ of $\{\text{PH}(C) \mid C \in \text{Cat}\}$, where $h'(\text{PH}(C)) = \text{PH}(C')$ iff for some $s \in \text{PH}(C), h(s) \in PH(C')$.

Automorphisms which uniformly permute sets of expressions represent natural *linguistic symmetries*. And an important syntactic role of grammatical categories is to provide the structural means of expressing these regularities. That is, if an automorphism h maps one member of some $\text{PH}(C)$ to a member of some $\text{PH}(C')$, then $h$ must map all $s \in \text{PH}(C)$ to $\text{PH}(C')$. Gender classes are a common linguistic symmetry. And we observe (Corbett, 1991) that languages with gender classes normally exhibit gender agreement of various kinds: Adj+Noun, Det+Noun, Subject+Predicate, etc. "Why, after all, would a language have many noun classes and not use them for anything?" Latin and Russian have three gender classes, and more noun classes when the imperfect cross product with declension classes is taken into account. Kinyarwanda (Kimenyi, 1980), typical for Central Bantu, has 16 noun classes, several the plurals of others.

Natural languages present many symmetries in addition to noun classes. **Conjugation** classes in Romance come to mind. Thus along with many irregular verbs, Spanish has three regular verb classes distinguished according as their infinitives end in *-ar*, *-er*, *-ir*. Structurally deeper however are *voice* classes—active vs passive. In W. Austronesian (Tagalog, Malagasy) there may be a half dozen voice distinctions, not just a twofold active/passive one. *Mood* classes—indicative vs subjunctive, and *aktionsart* classes—active vs stative, accomplishment vs achievement, are further candidates.

The linguistic symmetries of $G$ induce additional structure on $\mathrm{Aut}_G$ according as they permute whole $\mathrm{PH}(C)$ or just expressions within each $\mathrm{PH}(C)$.

## 13.8  Invariants of Type (2) and Higher

### 13.8.1  Universal Uniform Invariants ($\mathrm{INV}_2$)

The $F \in \mathrm{Rule}_G$ are trivially invariant as automorphisms by definition fix them.

Moreover, several of the syntactic conditions investigated in generative grammar over the last two generations ("island constraints", such as Coordinate Structure, Subjacency, etc.) can be stated as invariant properties of $F \in \mathrm{Rule}_G$. For example

a. If $F \in \mathrm{Rule}_G$ is a movement rule then $F$ satisfies island constraints.

b. If $F \in \mathrm{Rule}_G$ is a copy rule (Kandybowicz, 2008, Kobele, 2008) $F$ does not iterate. (For example, usually reduplication rules do not iterate; but see Blust, 2001).

Note that these last two conditions concern the action of the structure building functions—obviously a critical domain to investigate, but not one we have discussed until now.

$\mathrm{INV}_2$, the set of *invariant binary relations*, includes $\emptyset$ and $\mathcal{L}(G) \times \mathcal{L}(G)$, and like $\mathrm{INV}_1$ is a complete atomic boolean algebra—in fact it is a proper *relation algebra* as it is closed under composition, converse, and contains the identity relation.

If $A, B \in \mathrm{INV}_1$ then $A \times B$ and $[A \to B]$, the set of functions: $A \to B$, are in $\mathrm{INV}_2$.

Structural equivalence, $\simeq$, and logical equivalence, $\equiv$, are independent, where we say that sentences $\varphi$ and $\psi$ are *logically equivalent* iff they have the same truth value in all situations (models), a notion we explore in more detail in Chapter 8.

*Proof.* In one direction consider that $s$ and $t$ below are logically equivalent.

$$s \;=\; (\text{Exactly half of American males are overweight, S})$$
$$t \;=\; (\text{Exactly half of American males are not overweight, S})$$

But $t$ is not structurally equivalent to $s$; its predicate is the negation of that of $s$.

Going the other way, consider $s$ and $t$ below:

$$s \;=\; (\text{Seven boys sang eight songs each, S})$$
$$t \;=\; (\text{Eight boys sang seven songs each, S})$$

As there seem to be no grammatical differences between *seven* and *eight* it is reasonable that an automorphism of English could interchange these sentences, so they are structurally equivalent. But obviously they are not logically equivalent. □

But there are other uniformly definable relations of major linguistic interest that are not prominent in the more general algebraic setting. Fundamental here are constituency relations. We define *immediate constituent* (ICON), *proper constituent* (PCON), and *constituent* (CON) below:

**Definition 13.14.**

a. $s$ICON$t$ iff for some $F \in \text{Rule}_G$, some $u \in \mathcal{L}(G)^* \cap \text{Dom}(F)$, $t = F(u)$ and $s = u_i$, for some $1 \leq i \leq |u|$.

b. $s$PCON$t$ iff for some $n > 1$, there is a $u \in \mathcal{L}(G)^n$ with $s = u_1$, $t = u_n$ and each $u_i$ICON$u_{i+1}$ for $1 \leq i < n$.

c. $s$CON$t$ iff $s = t$ or $s$PCON$t$.

d. These relations are invariant in all $G$, as are ones defined in terms of them, such as *sister of* and *c-command*: $s$ *sister* $t$ in $u$ iff for some constituent $v$ of $u$, $s$ICON$v$, $t$ICON$v$ and $s \neq t$. $s$ *c-commands* $t$ in $u$ iff $t$ is a constituent of a sister of $s$ in $u$.

## 13.8.2 Remarks on Constituency Relations

Firstly, we do not define them in terms of trees. The use of standard trees in generative grammar only depicts derivations for a very restricted class of concatenative functions. They cannot represent substitution functions, such as Montague's "Quantifying in" which derived

*Every student likes some teacher* from ((*some teacher*), (*every student likes v*)) by substituting *some teacher* for *v* (see Montague, 1970a). We do expect however that our constituency analysis would coincide with usual ones in a grammar whose rules just concatenate arguments, inserting fixed lexical items if needed.

Second, we can now see how our grammars—algebras of partial functions—differ massively from ordinary numerical algebras. Consider for example the set $\mathbb{Z}$ of integers (positive, negative and zero) under the binary function $+$. Since any two integers can be added, every pair of integers $(n, m)$ is in the domain of $+$. That is, $+$ is a total function. Now, let $n$ be an arbitrary integer. We claim that any integer $m$ is a "constituent" of $n$. That is, there is an integer $x$ such that $+(m, x) = n$. Just choose $x = (n-m)$. But a derived expression in a natural language never has all expressions in the language as constituents.

Third, CON as defined is reflexive and transitive but may fail to be antisymmetric, contrary to the ordinary usage of *is a constituent of*. That is, it may be that $s$CON$t$ and $t$CON$s$ but that $s \neq t$. To see this in the general algebraic setting consider the squaring function $^2$ (on the positive real numbers) and the positive square root function $\sqrt{\phantom{x}}$. 3CON9 since $3^2 = 9$, and 9CON3 since $\sqrt{9} = 3$. But $9 \neq 3$. As an artificial linguistic case let $f, g \in$ Rule with $g(x, A) = (xb, A)$ and $f(yb, A) = (y, A)$, all $x, y \in V^*$. So $g$ suffixes a $b$ and $f$ erases string final $b$'s. So $(x, A)$CON$(xb, A)$ by $g$, and $(xb, A)$CON$(x, A)$ by $f$, but $(x, A) \neq (xb, A)$. Note that in this case, $(x, A)$PCON$(x, A)$.

In practice we find no convincing cases in NL where an expression, especially a lexical item, is a *proper* constituent of itself (see the earlier discussion of Pullum's Duke of York derivations). We suggest *Foundation* below as an axiom of natural language grammars:

**Axiom 13.1.** For all natural languages $G$:

a. **Full Foundation**: for all $s, t \in \mathcal{L}(G)$, $s$PCON$t \to s \neq t$.

b. **Lexical Foundation**: for all $s \in$ Lex$_G$, all $t \in \mathcal{L}(G)$, $s$PCON$t \to s \neq t$.

Lexical Foundation is weaker than Full Foundation (and properly entailed by it). But it suffices for our later purposes, as automorphisms are decided by their behavior on the lexical items. We note further:

**Theorem 13.18.**

a. *G satisfies Full Foundation $\to$ CON is antisymmetric.*

b. *Lexical Foundation $\to$ Eliminability of derived lexical items.*

*Proof.*

a. Lemma: PCON is transitive. Let $s$PCON$t$ and $t$PCON$u$. Then the derivation of $t$ from $s$ followed by that of $u$ from $t$ is a derivation of $u$ from $s$ in $n > 1$ steps, so $s$PCON$u$.

Now, let $s$CON$t$ & $t$CON$s$. Assume for contradiction that $s \neq t$. Then $s$PCON$t$ and $t$PCON$s$, so by the lemma, $s$PCON$s$. By Full Foundation $s \neq s$, a contradiction. So $s = t$.

b. Let $G$ satisfy Lexical Foundation with $s \in$ Lex$_G$ derived, so $s = F(u)$, for some $u \in \mathcal{L}(G)^*$. Let $G \backslash s$ be that grammar like $G$ except Lex$_{G \backslash s}$ = Lex$_G$ − $\{s\}$. Then $\mathcal{L}(G \backslash s) = \mathcal{L}(G)$ and Aut$_G$ = Aut$_{G \backslash s}$. Suppose for some $i$, $s$CON$u_i$. Then $s$PCON$s$ since $s = F(u)$, so by Lexical Foundation $s \neq s$, a contradiction. So $\neg s$CON$u_i$ any $i$. So any derivation of $F(u)$ in $\mathcal{L}(G)$ consists entirely of expressions in $\mathcal{L}(G \backslash s)$, so $s \in \mathcal{L}(G \backslash s)$ whence $\mathcal{L}(G \backslash s) = \mathcal{L}(G)$ and trivially Aut$_G$ = Aut$_{G \backslash s}$.

$\square$

**Corollary 13.19.** *Since Lex$_G$ is finite, induction using Theorem 13.18b allows us to remove all derived lexical items without changing $\mathcal{L}(G)$ or Aut$_G$. So a $G$ with Lexical Foundation behaves like a $G$ with no derived lexical items (whence Lex$_G$ and thus all Lex$_n$ are invariant).*

Lexical Foundation also implies a deeper property, *Bounded Structure* (Keenan and Stabler, 2003). The idea is that the structural complexity of a natural language is determined by a finite initial fragment. Beyond a certain complexity level more complex expressions iterate structure already known. We can state this intuition explicitly. We begin by treating each Lex$_n$ as a language in its own right:

**Definition 13.15.** For each $n$, a *local automorphism* of Lex$_n$ is a map $h :$ Lex$_n \rightarrow$ Lex$_n$ satisfying:

a. $h$ is bijective,

b. for each $F \in$ Rule$_G$, $h$ fixes Dom($F_n$), where $F_n =_{df} (F|$Lex$_n)$, and

c. if $n > 0$ then $h(F_n(t)) = F_n(h(t))$, all $t \in Lex_{n-1}^* \cap$ Dom($F$)

For $h \in$ Aut$_G$, $h|$Lex$_n$ is a local automorphism of Lex$_n$. But there may be other local automorphisms of Lex$_n$ that do not extend to $h'$ in Aut$_G$. In our model of Korean Lex$_0$ has DPs, case markers, and P$_{1n}$'s. DPs and case markers combine to form KPn's and KPa's, nominative (and accusative) Kase Phrases, in $Lex_1$. Then in $Lex_2$ KPns but not KPas combine with $P_1$ to form $P_0$. So local automorphisms of $Lex_0$ can interchange the *-nom* and *-acc* case markers but they don't extend to automorphisms in general, not even to automorphisms of $Lex_2$. And Bounded Structure (below) says that for some $n$, the automorphisms of $Lex_n$ are just the restrictions of the $h \in Aut_G$ to $Lex_n$. So in this sense the structures of expressions in $\mathcal{L}(G)$ is expressed by a finite subset of $\mathcal{L}(G)$.

**Theorem 13.20** (Bounded Structure). *If G satisfies Lexical Foundation then there is an n such that the automorphisms of $Lex_n$ are exactly the automorphisms of G restricted to $Lex_n$.*

### 13.8.3   The Role of Categories in Recursion

A last approach to the types of recursion in natural language is built on the notion of a *derivational cycle*. Let us say that a *cycle* is a sequence $C \in Cat^n$, for some $n > 1$ with $C_1 = C_n$, such that for every positive integer $k$ there is a $t \in \mathcal{L}(G)$ which embeds $k{\cdot}C = (C_1, \ldots, C_{n-1})^{k-1}, C$. That is, there is a sequence of $n + (n-1)(k-1)$ expressions with each $s_i$ of category $C_i$ an immediate constituent of $s_{i+1}$, and the last expression in the sequence is an immediate constituent of $t$.

For example, a grammar of English might have $C = \langle DP, Det, DP \rangle$ as a cycle. Then an expression of English which embeds $1 \cdot C$ would be *John's teacher*, where *John* has category DP, *John's* has category Det, and *John's teacher* has category DP. (39a) below embeds $2 \cdot C$, and (39b) embeds $3 \cdot C$.

(39)    a. John's teacher's doctor

       b. John's teacher's doctor's father

**Axiom 13.2.** Cyclicity: All $G$ for natural languages have a cycle.

Cyclicity guarantees that $\mathcal{L}(G)$ is infinite as long as the last expression instantiating a cycle $(C_m, \ldots, C_{m+n-1})$ is longer than the first. Full Foundation has the same effect.

### 13.8.4   Universal Empirical Invariants?

Plausible cases, assuming language independent definitions of the relevant notions, are:

a. Category Uniformity (sameness of grammatical category)

b. The Anaphor-Antecedent relation

c. Agreement relations (gender, number, case, definiteness)[6]

---

[6]See Corbett (1991) and Barlow and Ferguson (1988) for some of the possibilities.

Lastly, we also hypothesize that *Theta Role assignment* is invariant. Theta roles (Agent, Recipient, Patient, ...) are relations between individuals and the properties and relations expressed by predicates. Somewhat more precisely:

(40) For $s, t$ constituents of $u$: $\theta(s, t)$ iff $s$PCON$t$ and $s$ is assigned $\theta$ in $t$ but not in any proper constituent of $t$.

(41)   a. John praised the teacher
          Agent(John, John praised the teacher)
          Theme (the teacher, praised the teacher)

       b. The teacher was criticized by John
          Agent(John, was criticized by John)
          Theme (the teacher, the teacher was criticized by John)

       c. The teacher's criticism of John
          Agent(the teacher, the teacher's criticism of John)
          Theme (John, criticism of John)

We claim that the $\theta$ relations are invariant: $\theta(s, t)$ iff $\theta(hs, ht)$, for all automorphisms $h$. So if expressions are isomorphic their corresponding constituent pairs stand in the same theta relations. So if the theta roles of corresponding constituent pairs in (42a,a′) are different then (42a,a′) are not isomorphic. Similarly for (42b,b′):

(42)   a. John produced the play
       a′. John enjoyed the play
       b. John danced
       b′. John vanished

In contrast, theta equivalence does not imply structural equivalence. Each of (41a,b,c) is *theta equivalent* to the others in the sense of presenting the same number of pairs with the same theta roles but none is isomorphic to any of the others. And of course we would like a more rigorous definition of theta role assignment.

## 13.9   Structure Preserving Operations on Grammars

Such operations are ones which do not change $\mathcal{L}(G)$ or $\text{Aut}_G$ but they may change derivations. The most important is *generalized composition*.

**Definition 13.16.** For $F, H \in \text{Rule}_G$, $F \circ_i H$ is defined by:

$$F(s_1, \ldots, s_{i-1}, H(t_1, \ldots, t_m), s_{i+1}, \ldots, s_n),$$

for each
$$(t_1, \ldots, t_m) \in \mathrm{Dom}(H) \text{ and each}$$
$$(s_1, \ldots, s_{i-1}, H(t_1, \ldots, t_m), s_{i+1}, \ldots, s_n) \in \mathrm{Dom}(F).$$
Here $F \circ_i H$ is the $i$th *composition* of $F$ with $H$.

**Theorem 13.21.** *Closing $\mathrm{Rule}_G$ under* generalized composition *preserves structure.*

Compare now the two derivations for (Sam praised Dan, $P_0$) in ENG'
closed under $i$th compositions:

(43)  a.  Merge: (Sam praised Dan, $P_0$)

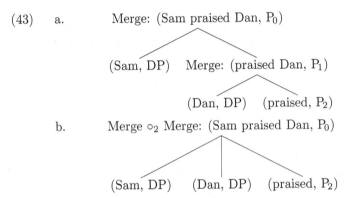

b.  Merge $\circ_2$ Merge: (Sam praised Dan, $P_0$)

Each non-terminal node in (43a) is binary branching, the only non-terminal node in (43b) is ternary branching. Adding compositions of rules to $\mathrm{Rule}_G$ does not lose derivations, it just adds new ones. Given $G$, write $G^\circ$ for the grammar that results from closing $\mathrm{Rule}_G$ under generalized composition ($i$th compositions, all $i$).

**Corollary 13.22.** *If $\mathcal{L}(G)$ is infinite and $\mathrm{Rule}_G$ finite (our typical case) then*

a. *Every derived $s \in \mathcal{L}(G^\circ)$ has a derivation tree of depth 1 (and usually many others of greater depth). Every non-derived $s \in \mathcal{L}(G^\circ)$ has a derivation tree of depth 0.*

b. *For every $n$ there is an $m \geq n$ such that some expression of $\mathcal{L}(G)$ has a derivation tree of depth 1 whose root node is $m$-ary branching.*

c. *$\mathrm{Rule}_{G^\circ}$ is infinite.*

Corollary 13.22 suggests rethinking the significance of the binary branching requirement (Kayne, 1984) on derivations. If $G$ is binary branching and $\text{Rule}_G$ is finite then just adding in (not closing) some $\{F \circ_i H \mid F, H \in \text{Rule}_G\}$ results in a $G$ still with just finitely many rules, but often some derivations with ternary branching nodes, as with (Sam praised Dan,$P_0$) above. So given a binary branching derivational system we can construct an extensionally (same expressions) and structurally (same automorphisms) equivalent one which fails to be binary branching.

But Corollary 13.22 is just one datum influencing the form of rules, learnability is another, more important one. Plus, too many cases in nature seem to opt for just one among two or more symmetric (automorphic) alternatives: Life forms are built only from right spiraling DNA, its left spiraling counterpart can be created in the lab and is stable, and so does not violate any basic law of nature. Why are there not two types of life forms—right spiraling and left spiraling ones? The physicist Feynman can wonder "Why is nature so nearly symmetric?" (Bunch, 1989, p. 189).

# List of Symbols

## The Greek Alphabet

| name | | | | name | | |
|---|---|---|---|---|---|---|
| alpha | $\alpha$ | | | nu | $\nu$ | |
| beta | $\beta$ | | | xi | $\xi$ | $\Xi$ |
| gamma | $\gamma$ | $\Gamma$ | | omicron | $o$ | |
| delta | $\delta$ | $\Delta$ | | pi | $\pi$ | $\Pi$ |
| epsilon | $\epsilon$ | | | rho | $\rho$ | |
| zeta | $\zeta$ | | | sigma | $\sigma$ | $\Sigma$ |
| eta | $\eta$ | | | tau | $\tau$ | |
| theta | $\theta$ | $\Theta$ | | upsilon | $\upsilon$ | $\Upsilon$ |
| iota | $\iota$ | | | phi | $\varphi$ | $\Phi$ |
| kappa | $\kappa$ | | | chi | $\chi$ | |
| lambda | $\lambda$ | $\Lambda$ | | psi | $\psi$ | $\Psi$ |
| mu | $\mu$ | | | omega | $\omega$ | $\Omega$ |

# Bibliography

Abiteboul, Serge, Richard Hull, and Victor Vianu. 1995. *Foundations of Databases*. Addison-Wesley.

Abney, Steven and Mark Johnson. 1991. Memory requirements and local ambiguities for parsing strategies. *Journal of Psycholinguistic Research* 20(3):233–250.

Aboh, Enoch and Marina Dyakonova. 2009. Predicate doubling and parallel chains. *Lingua* 119(7):1035–1065.

Aissen, Judith L. 1987. *Tzotzil Clause Structure*. Dordrecht: D. Reidel.

Artstein, Ron. 2005. Quantificational arguments in temporal adjunct clauses. *Linguistics and Philosophy* 28:541–597.

Büring, Daniel. 2005. *Binding Theory*. Cambridge: Cambridge University Press.

Babyonyshev, Maria and Edward Gibson. 1999. The Complexity of Nested Structures in Japanese. *Language* 75(3):423–50.

Bach, Emmon, Eloise Jelinek, Angelika Kratzer, and Barbara Partee, eds. 1995. *Quantification in Natural Language*. Dordrecht: Kluwer.

Baker, Mark C. 2001. *The Atoms of Language*. New York: Basic Books.

Baker-Shenk, Charlotte and Dennis Cokely. 1991. *American Sign Language*. Washington, DC: Clare Books / Gallaudet University Press.

Barker, Chris and Pauline Jacobson. 2007. *Direct Compositionality*. Oxford: Oxford University Press.

Barlow, M. and C.A. Ferguson. 1988. *Agreement in Natural Language*. Stanford: CSLI.

Barwise, Jon. 1979. On branching quantifiers in English. *Journal of Philosophical Logic* 8:47–80.

Barwise, Jon and Robin Cooper. 1981. Generalized quantifiers and natural language. *Linguistics and Philosophy* 4:159–219.

Beaver, David and Bart Geurts. 2014. Presupposition. In E. N. Zalta, ed., *The Stanford Encyclopedia of Philosophy (Winter 2014 Edition)*. URL: http://plato.stanford.edu/archives/win2014/entries/presupposition/.

Beesley, Kenneth R. and Lauri Karttunen. 2003. *Finite State Morphology*. Palo Alto, CA: CSLI Publications.

Beghelli, Filippo. 1992. Comparative quantifiers. In P. Dekker and M. Stokhof, eds., *Proceedings of the Eighth Amsterdam Colloquium*, pages 37–56. Amsterdam: ILLC, University of Amsterdam.

Beghelli, Filippo. 1994. Structured quantifiers. In Kanazawa and Piñón (1994), pages 119–145.

Ben-Shalom, Dorit. 2001. One connection between standard invariance conditions on modal formulas and generalized quantifiers. *Journal of Logic, Language, and Information* 10:1–6.

Bittner, Maria. 1995. Quantification in Eskimo: A challenge for compositional semantics. In Bach et al. (1995), pages 59–80.

Bittner, Maria and Kenneth Hale. 1995. Remarks on definiteness in Warlpiri. In Bach et al. (1995), pages 81–107.

Blank, Glenn D. 1989. A finite and real time processor for natural language. *Communications of the ACM* 32:1174–1189.

Blevins, James. 1994. Derived constituent order in unbounded dependency constructions. *Journal of Linguistics* 30:349–409.

Blust, R. 2001. Thao triplication. *Oceanic Linguistics* 40(2):324–335.

Boole, George. 1854. *The Laws of Thought*. Macmillan. Reprinted with corrections, Dover Publications, New York NY, 1958.

Boolos, George. 1981. For every A there is a B. *Linguistic Inquiry* 12:465–466.

Boolos, George and Richard Jeffrey. 1980. *Computability and Logic.* Cambridge: Cambridge University Press, 2nd edn.

Bresnan, Joan. 2001. *Lexical-Functional Syntax.* Oxford: Blackwell.

Bresnan, Joan, R.M. Kaplan, Stanley Peters, and A. Zaenen. 1982. Cross-serial dependencies in Dutch. *Linguistic Inquiry* 13:613–635.

Büchi, Richard J. 1989. *Finite Automota, Their Algebras and Grammars.* Springer-Verlag.

Bunch, B. 1989. *Reality's Mirror.* John Wiley & Sons.

Bybee, J., R. Perkins, and W. Pagliuca. 1994. *The Evolution of Grammar.* Chicago: University of Chicago Press.

Carpenter, Bob. 1997. *Type-logical semantics.* Cambridge, MA: MIT Press.

Chierchia, Gennaro. 1992. Anaphora and dynamic binding. *Linguistics and Philosophy* 15:111–183.

Chierchia, Gennaro. 2004. Scalar Implicatures, Polarity Phenomena and the Syntax/Pragmatics Interface. In A. Belletti, ed., *Structures and Beyond*, vol. 3, pages 39–104. Oxford: Oxford University Press.

Chomsky, Noam. 1956. Three models for the description of language. *IRE Transactions on Information Theory* 2(3):113–124.

Chomsky, Noam. 1959. On certain formal properties of grammars. *Information and Control* 2(2):137–167.

Chomsky, Noam. 1996. *The Minimalist Program.* Cambridge, MA: MIT Press.

Chomsky, Noam and Morris Halle. 1968/1995. *The sound pattern of English.* Harper and Row. First printing 1968, third printing 1995.

Chomsky, Noam and Howard Lasnik. 1977. Filters and control. *Linguistic Inquiry* 8:425–504.

Chomsky, Noam and George A. Miller. 1963. Introduction to the formal analysis of natural languages. In R. Luce, R. Bush, and E. Galanter, eds., *The Handbook of Mathematical Psychology*, vol. II, pages 269–321. New York: Wiley.

Church, Alonzo. 1936. A note on the Entscheidungsproblem. *Journal of Symbolic Logic* 1(1):40–41.

Church, Kenneth W. 1980. *On Memory Limitations in Natural Language Processing*. Master's thesis, MIT.

Cole, P. and G. Hermon. 2008. VP raising in a VOS language. *Syntax* 11(2):144–197.

Comrie, Bernard. 1985. Derivational Morphology. In T. Shopen, ed., *Language Typology and Syntactic Description*, vol. 3, pages 309–349. Cambridge: Cambridge University Press.

Comrie, Bernard. 2000. Valency-changing derivations in Tsez. In R. Dixon and A. Aikhenvald, eds., *Changing Valency: Case Studies in Transitivity*, pages 360–375. Cambridge: Cambridge University Press.

Cook, Theodore A. 1914. *The Curves of Life*. Dover. Dover reprint, 1979.

Cooper, Robin. 1979. The interpretation of pronouns. In F. Heny and H. Schnelle, eds., *Syntax and Semantics*, vol. 10, pages 61–92. Academic Press.

Cooper, Robin. 1982. Binding in Wholewheat Syntax (unenriched with inaudibilia). In P. Jacobson and G. Pullum, eds., *The Nature of Syntactic Representation*, pages 59–77. Dordrecht: Reidel.

Corbett, Greville. 1991. *Gender*. Cambridge: Cambridge University Press.

Corbett, Greville. 2000. *Number*. Cambridge: Cambridge University Press.

Cotton, F. Albert. 1990. *Chemical Applications of Group Theory*. John Wiley & Sons.

Craig, William. 1957. Three uses of the Herbrand-Gentzen theorem in relating model theory and proof theory. *Journal of Symbolic Logic* 22(3):269–285.

Creider, Chet, Jorge Hankamer, and Derek Wood. 1995. Preset two-head automata and natural language morphology. *International Journal of Computer Mathematics* 56:3–4.

Culy, Christopher. 1985. The complexity of the vocabulary of Bambara. *Linguistics and Philosophy* 8:345–351.

D'Arcy Thompson, W. 1942. *On Growth and Form.* Dover reprint, 1992.

Davis, Martin, ed. 1965. *The Undecidable. Basic Papers on Undecidable Propositions, Unsolvable Problems and Computable Functions.* Hewlitt, NY: Raven Press.

Dawkins, Richard. 2006. *The Selfish Gene.* Oxford University Press. 30th anniversary edition (orig, 1976).

de Roeck, Anne, Roderick Johnson, Margaret King, Michael Rosner, Geoffrey Sampson, and Nino Varile. 1982. A Myth about Centre-Embedding. *Lingua* 58:327–340.

de Swart, Henriëtte. 1994. (In)definites and genericity. In Kanazawa and Piñón (1994), pages 171–195.

de Swart, Henriëtte. 1996. Quantification Over Time. In van der Does and van Eijck (1996), pages 311–337.

de Swart, Henriëtte. 1998. Licensing of negative polarity items under inverse scope. *Lingua* 105(3–4):175–200.

Dez, Jacques. 1990. *Cheminements linguistiques malgaches au-dela des grammaires usuelles.* Paris: Peeters / Selaf.

Doetjes, Jenny and Martin Honcoop. 1997. The semantics of event-related readings: a case for pair quantification. In Szabolcsi (1997), pages 263–297.

Dowty, David. 1982. Derivational Morphology. *Linguistics and Philosophy* 5:23–58.

Dresher, Elan. 2009. *The Contrastive Hierarchy in Phonology.* Cambridge: Cambridge University Press.

Dryer, Matthew. 2007. Word Order. In T. Shopen, ed., *Language Typology and Syntactic Description*, pages 61–131. Cambridge: Cambridge University Press, 2nd edn.

Emmorey, K. 1984. The intonation system of Toba Batak. In P. Schachter, ed., *Studies in the Structure of Toba Batak*, no. 5 in UCLA Occasional Papers in Linguistics, pages 37–58. UCLA.

Enderton, Herbert B. 1972. *A Mathematical Introduction to Logic.* New York: Academic Press.

Enderton, Herbert B. 1977. *Elements of set theory.* New York-London: Academic Press.

Enderton, Herbert B. 1985. Elements of recursion theory. In J. Barwise, ed., *The Handbook of Mathematical Logic*, pages 527–567. Elsevier.

Evans, Gareth. 1977. Pronouns, quantifiers, and relative clauses. *Canadian Journal of Philosophy* 7:467–536.

Evans, Nick. 1995. A-quantifiers and scope in Mayali. In Bach et al. (1995), pages 207–270.

Fauconnier, Gilles. 1975. Do quantifiers branch? *Linguistic Inquiry* 6:555–578.

Flum, J. 1975. Characterizing logics. In J. Barwise and S. Feferman, eds., *Model-Theoretic Logics*, chap. 3, pages 77–121. Springer-Verlag.

Freidin, Robert, ed. 1992. *Principles and Parameters in Comparative Grammar.* Cambridge, MA: MIT Press.

Gärdenfors, Peter, ed. 1987. *Generalized Quantifiers: Linguistic and Logical Approaches.* Dordrecht: Reidel.

Gabbay, Dov and Julius Moravcsik. 1974. Branching quantifiers, English, and Montague grammar. *Theoretical Linguistics* 1:141–157.

Gardner, M. 2005. *The New Ambidextrous Universe.* Dover, 3rd edn.

Geach, Peter. 1962. *Reference and Generality.* Cornell University Press.

Giannakidou, Anastasia. 2011. Negative and positive polarity items. In K. von Heusinger, C. Maienborn, and P. Portner, eds., *Semantics. An International Handbook of Natural Language Meaning*, pages 1660–1712. Berlin: Mouton de Gruyter.

Giegerich, Heinz. 1992. *English Phonology.* Cambridge: Cambridge University Press.

Gil, David. 1993. Nominal and verbal quantification. *Sprachtypologie und Universalienforschung* 46(4):275–317.

Ginsburg, Seymour. 1966. *The Mathematical Theory of Context Free Languages.* New York: McGraw-Hill Book Co.

Givon, T. 1971. Historical syntax and synchronic morphology: an archaeologist's field trip. *CLS* 7:394–415.

Goldsmith, John. 1976. *Autosegmental Phonology*. Ph.D. thesis, MIT.

Grädel, Erich, Phokion Kolaitis, and Moshe Vardi. 1997. On the decision problem for two-variable first-order logic. *Bulletin of Symbolic Logic* 3(1):53–69.

Groenendijk, Jeroen and Martin Stokhof. 1991. Dynamic predicate logic. *Linguistics and Philosophy* 14:39–100.

Groenendijk, Jeroen and Martin Stokhof. 2011. Questions. In van Benthem and ter Meulen (2011), pages 1059–1132.

Guenthner, Franz and J. Hoepelmann. 1974. A note on the representation of "branching quantifiers". *Theoretical Linguistics* 1:285–291.

Gutierrez-Rexach, Javier. 1997. Questions and Generalized Quantifers. In Szabolcsi (1997), pages 409–453.

Halmos, Paul. 1974. *Naive set theory*. Undergraduate Texts in Mathematics. New York-Heidelberg: Academic Press.

Hankamer, Jorge. 1986. Finite state morphology and left to right phonology. In M. Dalrymple, J. Goldberg, K. Hanson, M. Inman, C. Piñon, and S. Wechsler, eds., *Proceedings of the West Coast Conference on Formal Linguistics, vol. 5*, pages 41–52. Stanford: CSLI.

Harary, Frank. 1972. *Graph Theory*. Addison-Wesley. Third printing.

Harel, David. 1987. *Algorithmics: The spirit of computing*. UK: Addison-Wesley.

Harris, Zellig. 1991. *A Theory of Language and Information*. Oxford: Clarendon Press.

Hayes, Bruce. 2009. *Introductory Phonology*. Wiley-Blackwell.

Heim, Irene. 1982. *The Semantics of Definite and Indefinite Noun Phrases*. Ph.D. thesis, UMass Amherst.

Heim, Irene. 1990. E-type pronouns and donkey anaphora. *Linguistics and Philosophy* 13:137–177.

Heim, Irene and Angelika Kratzer. 1998. *Semantics in Generative Grammar*. Oxford: Blackwell.

Heine, B. and T. Kuteva. 2002. *World Lexicon of Grammaticalization*. Cambridge: Cambridge University Press.

Heine, B. and M. Reh. 1984. *Grammatical Categories in African Languages*. Hamburg: Helmut Buske.

Hewitt, B. G. 1979. *Abkhaz*. Lingua Descriptive Studies. North-Holland. In collaboration with Z.K. Khiba.

Higginbotham, James. 1994. Mass and count quantifiers. *Linguistics and Philosophy* 17(5):447–480.

Higginbotham, James and Robert May. 1981. Questions, quantifiers, and crossing. *Linguistic Review* 1:41–79.

Hindley, J. Roger and J. P. Seldin. 1986. *Introduction to Combinators and the λ-Calculus*. Cambridge: Cambridge University Press. London Mathematical Society Student Texts.

Hintikka, Jaako. 1974. Quantifiers vs. quantification theory. *Linguistic Inquiry* 5:153–177.

Homer, Vincent. 2012. Domains of polarity items. Ms., UCLA.

Hopcroft, John E., Rajeev Motwani, and Jeffrey D. Ullman. 2001. *Introduction to Automata Theory, Languages, and Computation*. Addison-Wesley. Second Edition.

Hopcroft, John E. and Jeffrey D. Ullman. 1979. *Introduction to automata theory, languages, and computation*. Reading, MA: Addison-Wesley. Addison-Wesley Series in Computer Science.

Hopper, P.J. 1991. On some principles of grammaticalization. In E. Traugott and B. Heine, eds., *Grammaticalization Vol. 1*, pages 17–36. Amsterdam: John Benjamins.

Hopper, P.J. and E.C. Traugott. 1993. *Grammaticalization*. Cambridge: Cambridge University Press.

Horn, Laurence R. 1989. *Natural History of Negation*. Chicago: University of Chicago Press.

Huck, Geoffrey and Almerindo Ojeda. 1987. *Discontinuous Constituency: Syntax and Semantics*. New York: Academic Press.

Hyman, Larry. 1975. *Phonology: Theory and Analysis*. Holt, Rinehart and Winston.

Jacobson, Pauline. 1999. Towards a variable-free semantics. *Linguistics and Philosophy* 22:117–184.

Jacobson, Pauline. 2008. Direct compositionality and variable-free semantics: the case of antecedent-contained deletion. In K. Johnson, ed., *Topics in Ellipsis*, pages 60–68. Cambridge: Cambridge University Press.

Jaeggli, Osvaldo and Kenneth J. Safir, eds. 1989. *The Null Subject Parameter*. Dordrecht: Kluwer.

Jakobson, Roman, C. Gunnar, M. Fant, and Morris Halle. 1952. *Preliminaries to Speech Analysis*. Cambridge, MA: MIT Press.

Johnson, C.D. 1970. *Formal aspects of phonological representation*. Ph.D. thesis, University of California, Berkeley.

Joshi, Aravind K. and Philip Hopely. 1999. A parser from antiquity: An early application of finite state transducers to natural language parsing. In A. Kornai, ed., *Extended finite state models of language*, pages 6–15. Cambridge, UK: Cambridge University Press.

Kahr, A. S., Edward F. Moore, and Hao Wang. 1962. Entscheidungsproblem reduced to the $\forall\exists\forall$ case. *Proceedings of the National Academy of Sciences* 48:365–377.

Kamp, Hans. 1981. A theory of truth and semantic representation. In J. Groenendijk, T. Janssen, and M. Stokhof, eds., *Formal Methods in the Study of Language*, pages 277–322. Amsterdam: Mathematisch Centrum.

Kanazawa, Makoto. 1994. Weak vs. strong readings of donkey sentences and monotonicity inferences in a dynamic setting. *Linguistics and Philosophy* 17(2):109–159.

Kanazawa, Makoto and Chris Piñón, eds. 1994. *Dynamics, Polarity, and Quantification*. Lecture Notes 48. Stanford: CSLI.

Kandybowicz, J. 2008. *The Grammar of Repetition*. Amsterdam: John Benjamins.

Kaplan, Ronald M. and Martin Kay. 1994. Regular models of phonological rule systems. *Computational Linguistics* 20:331378.

Kaye, Richard. 2007. *The Mathematics of Logic*. Cambridge: Cambridge University Press.

Kayne, R. 1984. *Connectedness and Binary Branching*. Dordrecht: Foris.

Keenan, Edward L. 1979. On surface form and logical form. *Studies in Linguistic Science* 8(2):163–203.

Keenan, Edward L. 1981. A boolean approach to semantics. In J. Groenendijk, T. Janssen, and M. Stokhof, eds., *Formal Methods in the Study of Language*, pages 343–379. Amsterdam: Math. Centre, University of Amsterdam.

Keenan, Edward L. 1987. Multiply-headed NPs. *Linguistic Inquiry* 18(3):481–490.

Keenan, Edward L. 1988a. Complex Anaphors and Bind Alpha. In I. Macleod, G. Larson, and D. Brentani, eds., *Papers from the 24$^{th}$ Annual Regional Meeting of the Chicago Linguistic Society*, pages 216–232. Chicago: CLS.

Keenan, Edward L. 1988b. On semantics and the binding theory. In J. Hawkins, ed., *Explaining Language Universals*, pages 105–144. Basis Blackwell.

Keenan, Edward L. 1989. Semantic Case Theory. In R. Bartsch, J. van Benthem, and P. van Emde Boas, eds., *Semantics and Contextual Expression*, pages 33–57. Dordrecht: Foris.

Keenan, Edward L. 1992. Beyond the Frege Boundary. *Linguistics and Philosophy* 15:199–221.

Keenan, Edward L. 1993. Natural Language, Sortal Reducibility and Generalized Quantifiers. *Journal of Symbolic Logic* 58(1):314–325.

Keenan, Edward L. 1995. Predicate-argument structure in Malagasy. In C. Burgess, K. Dziwirek, and D. Gerdts, eds., *Grammatical Relations: Theoretical Approaches to Empirical Questions*, pages 171–217. Stanford: CSLI.

Keenan, Edward L. 1996. The semantics of determiners. In S. Lappin, ed., *The Handbook of Contemporary Semantic Theory*, pages 41–63. Oxford: Blackwell.

Keenan, Edward L. 2003. The definiteness effect: semantics or pragmatics? *Natural Language Semantics* 11(2):187–216.

Keenan, Edward L. 2007. On the denotations of anaphors. *Research on Language and Computation* 5(1):5–17.

Keenan, Edward L. 2008. Quantifiers. In K. von Heusinger, C. Maienborn, and P. Portner, eds., *The Handbook of Semantics*, pages 1058–1087. Mouton de Gruyter, 2nd edn.

Keenan, Edward L. 2009. Voice determines co-argument anaphora in West Austronesian. In S. Chung, D. Finer, I. Paul, and E. Potsdam, eds., *Proceedings of the XVIth Annual Meetings of the Austronesian Formal Linguistics Association (AFLA XVI)*, pages 77–91. London, ON: University of Western Ontario.

Keenan, Edward L. 2016. *In Situ* Interpretation without Type Mismatches. *Journal of Semantics* 33(1):87–106.

Keenan, Edward L. and Bernard Comrie. 1977. Noun Phrase Accessibility and Universal Grammar. *Linguistic Inquiry* 8(1):63–99.

Keenan, Edward L. and Matthew Dryer. 2007. Passive in the world's languages. In T. Shopen, ed., *Language Typology and Syntactic Description*, vol. 1, pages 325–362. Cambridge: Cambridge University Press.

Keenan, Edward L. and Leonard Faltz. 1985. *Boolean Semantics for Natural Language*. Dordrecht: Reidel.

Keenan, Edward L. and Lawrence S. Moss. 1985. Generalized Quantifiers and the Expressive Power of Natural Language. In van Benthem and ter Meulen (1985), pages 73–126.

Keenan, Edward L. and Denis Paperno, eds. 2012. *Handbook of Quantifiers in Natural Language*. Springer.

Keenan, Edward L. and Denis Paperno, eds. to appear. *Handbook of Quantifiers in Natural Language. Vol 2*. Springer.

Keenan, Edward L. and Edward P. Stabler. 2003. *Bare Grammar*. Stanford: CSLI.

Keenan, Edward L. and Jonathan Stavi. 1986. A semantic characterization of natural Language determiners. *Linguistics and Philosophy* 9:253–326.

Keenan, Edward L. and Alan Timberlake. 1988. Natural Language Motivations for Extending Categorial Grammar. In R. T. Oehrle, E. Bach, and D. Wheeler, eds., *Categorial Grammars and Natural Language Structures*, pages 265–295. Dordrecht: Kluwer.

Keenan, Edward L. and Dag Westerståhl. 2011. Generalized Quantifiers in Linguistics and Logic. In van Benthem and ter Meulen (2011), pages 859–910.

Kelley, Dean. 1995. *Automata and Formal Languages*. Prentice-Hall.

Kimenyi, A. 1980. *A Relational Grammar of Kinyarwanda*. UC Press.

Kleene, Stephen. 1956. Representation of events in nerve nets and finite automata. In *Automata Studies*. Princeton, NJ: Princeton University Press.

Klima, Edward. 1964. Negation in English. In J. Groenendijk and J. Katz, eds., *The Structure of Language*, pages 245–323. Englewood Cliffs, NJ: Prentice-Hall.

Kobele, G. 2008. *Generating Copies: An investigation into Structural Identity in Language and Grammar*. Ph.D. thesis, UCLA.

Kolaitis, Phokion. 2006. On the expressive power of logics on finite models. In E. Grädel, P. Kolaitis, L. Libkin, M. Marx, M. Vardi, and S. Weinstein, eds., *Finite model theory and its applications*, pages 27–123. Springer.

Kolaitis, Phokion and J. Väänänen. 1995. Generalized quantifiers and pebble games on finite structures. *Annals of Pure and Applied Logic* 74:23–75.

Kornai, András, ed. 1999. *Extended finite state models of language*. Cambridge: Cambridge University Press.

Koskenniemi, K. K. 1983. *Two-level morphology: A general computational model for wordform recognition and production*. Ph.D. thesis, University of Helsinki.

Kratzer, Angelika. 1995. Stage-level and individual level predicates. In G. Carlson and F. J. Pelletier, eds., *The Generic Book*, pages 125–175. Chicago: University of Chicago Press.

Krauwer, Steven and Louis des Tombe. 1981. Transducers and grammars as theories of language. *Theoretical Linguistics* 8:173–202.

Krifka, Manfred. 1989. Nominal reference, temporal constitution and quantification in event semantics. In R. Bartsch, J. van Benthem, and P. van Emde Boas, eds., *Semantics and Contextual Expression*, pages 75–117. Dordrecht: Foris.

Krifka, Manfred. 1990. Four thousand ships passed through the lock. *Linguistics and Philosophy* 15(5):487–520.

Krynicki, Michał, Marcin Mostowski, and Lesław Szczerba, eds. 1995. *Quantifiers: Logics, Models and Computation*. Dordrecht: Kluwer.

Ladefoged, Peter and Ian Maddiesson. 1996. *The Sounds of the World's Languages*. Oxford: Blackwell.

Ladusaw, William. 1983. Logical form and conditions on grammaticality. *Linguistics and Philosophy* 6:389–422.

Langendoen, D. Terence. 1981. The generative capacity of word-formation components. *Linguistic Inquiry* 12:320–322.

Langendoen, D. Terence. 2003. Finite state languages. In W. J. Frawley, ed., *Oxford International Encyclopedia of Linguistics*, vol. 3, pages 26–28. Oxford University Press, 2nd edn.

Lappin, Shalom. 1996. Generalized quantifiers, exception phrases, and logicality. *Journal of Semantics* 13:197–220.

Lasnik, Howard and Juan Uriagereka. 1988. *A Course in GB Syntax*. Cambridge, MA: MIT Press.

Lasnik, Howard, Juan Uriagereka, and Cedric Boeckx. 2003. *A Course in Minimalist Syntax*. Oxford: Blackwell.

Lassaigne, Richard and Michel de Rougement. 1993. *Logique et Fondements de L'Informatique*. Paris: Hermes.

Laughren, Mary. 2002. Syntactic constraints in a free word order language. In M. Amberger and P. Collins, eds., *Language Universals and Variation*, pages 83–130. Westport, CT: Praeger.

Lewis, David. 1970. General semantics. *Synthese* 22:18–67.

Lewis, David. 1975. Adverbs of quantification. In E. L. Keenan, ed., *Formal Semantics of Natural Language*, pages 3–15. Cambridge: Cambridge University Press.

Lewis, Paul M., ed. 2009. *Ethnologue Languages of the World*. Dallas: SIL.

Li, Charles and Sandra Thompson. 1981. *Mandarin Chinese: a functional reference Grammar*. UC Press.

Lindström, Per. 1966. First order predicate logics with generalized quantifiers. *Theoria* 32(3):186–195.

Lindström, Per. 1969. On extensions of elementary logic. *Theoria* 35(1):1–11.

Linebarger, Maria. 1987. Negative polarity and grammatical representation. *Linguistics and Philosophy* 10:325–387.

Lønning, Jan Tore. 1996. Plurals and collectivity. In van Benthem and ter Meulen (2011), pages 1011–1059.

Loveland, Donald W., Richard E. Hodel, and S.G. Sterrett. 2014. *Three Views of Logic: Mathematics, Philosophy, and Computer Science*. Princeton University Press.

Manaster-Ramer, Alexis. 1987. Dutch as a formal language. *Linguistics and Philosophy* 10:221–246.

Mates, Benson. 1972. *Elementary Logic*. Oxford: Oxford University Press, 2nd edn.

Matthews, Peter H. 1981. *Syntax*. Cambridge: Cambridge University Press.

Matthewson, Lisa. 2008. *Quantification: a Cross-Linguistic Persepctive*. Bingley.

McCarthy, J. 2003. Sympathy, cumulativity, and the Duke-of-York gambit. In C. Féry and R. van de Vijver, eds., *The Syllable in Optimality Theory*, pages 23–76. Cambridge: Cambridge University Press.

McCawley, James D. 1982. Parentheticals and Discontinuous Constituent Structure. *Linguistic Inquiry* 13:99–107.

McCawley, James D. 1988. *The Syntactic Phenomena of English*, vol. 1. Chicago: University of Chicago Press.

Mendelson, Elliott. 1970. *Boolean Algebra and Switching Circuits*. McGraw-Hill Book Co.

Miller, George A. and S. Isard. 1964. Free recall of self-embedded English sentences. *Information and Control* 7:292–303.

Milsark, Gary. 1977. Toward an explanation of certain peculiarities in the existential construction in English. *Linguistic Analysis* 3:1–30.

Moltmann, Friedericke. 1996. Resumptive quantification in exception sentences. In M. Kanazawa, C. Piñón, and H. de Swart, eds., *Quantifiers, Deduction, and Context*, pages 139–170. Stanford: CSLI.

Monk, Donald J. 1976. *Mathematical Logic*. Springer-Verlag.

Montague, Richard. 1970a. English as a Formal Language. In R. Thomason, ed., *Formal Philosophy: Selected Papers of Richard Montague*, pages 188–221. New Haven, CT: Yale University Press.

Montague, Richard. 1970b. Universal Grammar. In R. Thomason, ed., *Formal Philosophy: Selected Papers of Richard Montague*, pages 222–247. New Haven, CT: Yale University Press.

Moortgat, Michael. 2011. Categorial type logics. In van Benthem and ter Meulen (2011), pages 95–180.

Morrill, Glyn V. 2011. *Categorial Grammar*. Oxford: Oxford University Press.

Mortimer, Michael. 1975. On languages with two variables. *Mathematical Logic Quarterly* 21(1):135–140.

Mundy, J. L. and A. Zisserman. 1992. *Geometric Invariance in Computer Vision*. Cambridge, MA: MIT Press.

Nam, Seungho. 1994. Another type of negative polarity item. In Kanazawa and Piñón (1994), pages 3–16.

Nederhof, Mark-Jan. 2000. Practical Experiments with Regular Approximation of Context-free Languages. *Comput. Linguist.* 26(1):17–44.

Ojeda, Almerindo. 1987. Discontinuity and Phrase Structure Grammar. In A. Manaster-Ramer, ed., *Mathematics of Language*, pages 257–277. Amsterdam: John Benjamins.

Özkaragöz, Inci. 1986. Mono-clausal double passives in Turkish. In D. Slobin and K. Zimmer, eds., *Studies in Turkish Linguistics*, pages 77–93. Amsterdam: John Benjamins.

Partee, Barbara. 1985. Noun Phrase interpretation and type-shifting principles. In J. Groenendijk, D. de Jongh, and M. Stokhof, eds., *Studies in Discourse Representation Theory and the Theory of Generalized Quantifiers*, vol. 8 of *GRASS*, pages 115–143. Dordrecht: Foris.

Partee, Barbara. 1995. Quantificational structures and compositionality. In Bach et al. (1995), pages 541–601.

Partee, Barbara, Alice ter Meulen, and Robert Wall. 1990. *Mathematical Methods in Linguistics*. Dordrecht: Kluwer.

Paul, Ileana. 2005. Disjunction in free choice and polarity in Malagasy. In C. Gurski, ed., *Proceedings of the 2005 Conference of the Canadian Linguistic Association*. CLA.

Payne, John. 1985. Negation. In T. Shopen, ed., *Language Typology and Syntactic Description*, vol. 1, pages 197–242. Cambridge: Cambridge University Press.

Pederson, E. 1993. Zero negation in South Dravidian. In L. Dobrin, L. Nichols, and R. Rodriguez, eds., *CLS 27, papers from the $27^{th}$ regional meeting of the Chicago Linguistics Society 1991, part two: Parasession on Negation*, pages 233–245. Chicago: CLS.

Pelletier, Francis J. and Lenhart K. Schubert. 1989. Generically speaking. In G. Chierchia, B. H. Partee, and R. Turner, eds., *Properties, Types, and Meaning*, vol. 2, pages 193–268. Dordrecht: Kluwer.

Perlmutter, David and Paul Postal. 1983a. Some Proposed Laws of Basic Clause Structure. In D. M. Perlmutter, ed., *Studies in Relational Grammar*, vol. 1, pages 81–128. Chicago: University of Chicago Press.

Perlmutter, David and Paul Postal. 1983b. The Relational Succession Law. In D. M. Perlmutter, ed., *Studies in Relational Grammar*, vol. 1, pages 30–80. Chicago: University of Chicago Press.

Perlmutter, David and Paul Postal. 1983c. Towards a universal characterization of passivization. In D. M. Perlmutter, ed., *Studies in Relational Grammar*, vol. 1, pages 3–29. Chicago: University of Chicago Press.

Peters, Stanley and Dag Westerståhl. 2006. *Quantifiers in Language and Logic*. Oxford: Oxford University Press.

Pollard, Carl and Ivan A. Sag. 1994. *Head-Driven Phrase Structure Grammar*. CSLI and the University of Chicago Press.

Pratt, Ian and Nissim Francez. 2001. Temporal prepositions and temporal generalized quantifiers. *Linguistics and Philosophy* 24(2):187–222.

Pullum, G. 1976. The Duke of York gambit. *Journal of Linguistics* 12:83–102.

Radford, Andrew. 2004. *Minimalist Syntax*. Cambridge: Cambridge University Press.

Radzinski, Daniel. 1990. Unbounded syntactic copying in Mandarin Chinese. *Linguistics and Philosophy* 13:277–299.

Rajemisa-Raolison, Régis. 1971. *Grammaire malgache*. Fianarantsoa: Librairie Ambozontany.

Resnik, Philip. 1992. Left-corner Parsing and Psychological Plausibility. In *Proceedings of the Fourteenth International Conference on Computational Linguistics (COLING '92)*, pages 191–197. Nantes, France.

Reuland, Eric J. and Alice ter Meulen. 1987. *The Representation of (In)definiteness*. Cambridge, MA: MIT Press.

Roach, Peter. 2009. *English Phonetics and Phonology: A Practical Course*. Cambridge: Cambridge University Press, 4th edn.

Roberts, John R. 1987. *Amele*. Croom Helm.

Roca, Iggy. 1994. *Generative Phonology*. Routledge.

Roche, Emmanuel and Yves Schabes, eds. 1997. *Finite-state devices for natural language processing*. Cambridge, Mass.: MIT Press.

Rooth, Mats. 1987. Noun phrase interpretation in Montague grammar, file change semantics, and situation semantics. In Gärdenfors (1987), pages 237–268.

Rothstein, Susan. 1988. Conservativity and the syntax of determiners. *Linguistics and Philosophy* 26(6):999–1021.

Russell, Bertrand and Alfred North Whitehead. 1910. *Principia Mathematica*. Cambridge: Cambridge University Press.

Sag, Ivan A., Thomas Wasow, and Emily M. Bender. 2003. *Syntactic Theory*. Stanford: CSLI.

Schachter, P. 1984. *Studies in the Structure of Toba Batak*, vol. 5 of *Occasional Papers in Linguistics*. UCLA.

Shieber, S. 1985. Evidence against the Context-Freeness of Natural Language. *Linguistics and Philosophy* 8:333–343.

Sipser, Michael. 2012. *Introduction to the Theory of Computation*. Boston, MA: Cengage Learning, 3rd edn.

Smessaert, Hans. 1996. Monotonicity properties of comparative determiners. *Linguistics and Philosophy* 19(3):295–336.

Spencer, Andrew. 1991. *Morphology*. Oxford: Blackwell.

Spencer, Andrew. 1996. *Phonology*. Oxford: Blackwell.

Stabler, Edward P. 1997. Derivational minimalism. In C. Retoré, ed., *Logical Aspects of Computational Linguistics*, pages 68–95. Springer.

Steedman, Mark. 2012. *Taking Scope*. Cambridge, MA: MIT Press.

Steedman, Mark and Jason Baldridge. 2007. Combinatory categorical grammar. In R. Borsley and K. Börjars, eds., *Non-Transformational Syntax*, pages 181–224. Oxford: Blackwell.

Szabolcsi, Anna. 1997. Strategies for scope taking. In A. Szabolcsi, ed., *Ways of Scope Taking*, pages 109–155. Dordrecht: Kluwer.

Thomason, Richmon H., ed. 1974. *Formal Philosophy*. New Haven, CT: Yale University Press.

Thysse, Elias. 1983. *Laws of Language*. Master's thesis, Filosofisch Instituut, Rijksuniversiteit, Groningen.

Torrence, Harold and Khady Tamba. 2014. Factive relative clauses in Wolof. Ms., Dept. of Linguistics, UCLA.

Trakhtenbrot, Boris. 1950. The impossibility of an algorithm for the decision problem for finite domains (Russian). *Doklady Akademii Nauk SSSR* 70:569–572. English translation in AMS Transl. Ser. 2 vol 23, 1963:1–6.

Turing, Alan M. 1936. On computable numbers, with an application to the Entscheidungsproblem. *Proc. London Math. Soc.* 42:230–265. Reprinted in Davis (1965), pages 115–153.

van Benthem, Johan. 1984a. Questions about quantifiers. *Journal of Symbolic Logic* 49:443–466.

van Benthem, Johan. 1984b. Tense logic and time. *Notre Dame Journal of Formal Logic* 25(1):1–16.

van Benthem, Johan. 1986. *Essays in Logical Semantics*. Dordrecht: D. Reidel.

van Benthem, Johan and Alice ter Meulen, eds. 1985. *Generalized Quantifiers in Natural Language*. Dordrecht: Foris.

van Benthem, Johan and Alice ter Meulen, eds. 2011. *Handbook of Logic and Language*. London: Kluwer Academic Publishers, 2nd edn.

van Dalen, Dirk. 2004. *Logic and Structure*. Berlin: Springer, 4th edn.

van der Does, Jaap and Jan van Eijck, eds. 1996. *Quantifiers, Logic, and Language*. Lecture Notes 54. Stanford: CSLI.

Vendler, Zeno. 1957. Verbs and times. *The Philosophical Review* 66:143–160.

Verkuyl, Henk and Jaap van der Does. 1996. The semantics of plural noun phrases. In van der Does and van Eijck (1996), pages 337–413.

von Fintel, Kai. 1993. Exceptive constructions. *Natural Language Semantics* 1(2):123–148.

von Fintel, Kai. 1995. The formal semantics of grammaticalization. In J. N. Beckman, ed., *NELS 25 Proceedings*, vol. 2: Papers from the Workshops on Language Acquisition and Language Change, pages 175–189. Amherst, MA: GLSA.

Weber, David John. 1989. *A Grammar of Huallaga (Huánuco) Quechua*. Berkeley and Los Angeles: University of California Press.

Westerståhl, Dag. 1985. Logical constants in quantifier languages. *Linguistics and Philosophy* 8:387–413.

Westerståhl, Dag. 1989. Quantifiers in formal and natural languages. In D. Gabbay and F. Guentner, eds., *The Handbook of Philosophical Logic*, vol. IV, pages 1–131. Dordrecht: Reidel.

Weyl, H. 1952. *Symmetry*. Princeton: Princeton University Press.

Wilson, Robin. 1979. *Introduction to Graph Theory*. Academic Press. Third edition.

Wilson, Robin. 2002. *Four Colors Suffice*. Princeton: Princeton University Press.

Winter, Yoad. 1998. *Flexible Boolean Semantics: coordination, plurality and scope in natural language*. Ph.D. thesis, Utrecht University.

Winter, Yoad. 2001. *Flexibility Principles in Boolean Semantics*. Cambridge, MA: MIT Press.

Zuber, Richard. 2008. A semantic constraint on binary determiners. Paper presented to the Semantics Reseach Group meeting, Tokyo, Japan.

Zwarts, Frans. 1981. Negatief polaire Uitdrukkingen. *Glot* 4:35–132.

Zwarts, Frans. 1996. Facets of Negation. In van der Does and van Eijck (1996), pages 385–421.

# Author Index

# Language Index

# Subject Index